Lecture Notes in Computer Science 5371

Commenced Publication in 1973
Founding and Former Series Editors:
Gerhard Goos, Juris Hartmanis, and Jan van Leeuwen

W0235153

Benoit Huet   Alan Smeaton
Ketan Mayer-Patel   Yannis Avrithis (Eds.)

Advances in Multimedia Modeling

15th International Multimedia Modeling
Conference, MMM 2009
Sophia-Antipolis, France, January 7-9, 2009
Proceedings

 Springer

Volume Editors

Benoit Huet
Eurecom
Sophia-Antipolis, France
E-mail: benoit.huet@eurecom.fr

Alan Smeaton
School of Computing
Dublin City University
Dublin, Ireland
E-mail: alan.smeaton@dcu.ie

Ketan Mayer-Patel
Department of Computer Science
University of North Carolina
Chapel Hill, NC, USA
E-mail: kmp@cs.unc.edu

Yannis Avrithis
Image, Video and Multimedia Systems Laboratory
School of Electrical and Computer Engineering
National Technical University of Athens, Greece
E-mail: iavr@image.ntua.gr

Library of Congress Control Number: Applied for

CR Subject Classification (1998): H.5.1, H.5, I.4, H.2.4, I.3, H.3-4, E.4

LNCS Sublibrary: SL 3 – Information Systems and Application, incl. Internet/Web and HCI

ISSN   0302-9743
ISBN-10   3-540-92891-X Springer Berlin Heidelberg New York
ISBN-13   978-3-540-92891-1 Springer Berlin Heidelberg New York

springer.com

© Springer-Verlag Berlin Heidelberg 2009

Typesetting: Camera-ready by author, data conversion by Scientific Publishing Services, Chennai, India
Printed on acid-free paper   SPIN: 12596034   06/3180   5 4 3 2 1 0

Preface

Welcome to the 15th International Multimedia Modeling Conference (MMM 2009), held January 7–9, 2009 at EURECOM, Sophia-Antipolis, France. MMM is a leading international conference for researchers and industry practitioners to share their new ideas, original research results and practical development experiences from all multimedia-related areas. MMM 2009 was held in co-operation with the ACM Special Interest Group on MultiMedia (ACM SIGMM).

It was a great honor to host MMM 2009, one of the most long-standing multimedia conferences, at EURECOM in Sophia-Antipolis, France. The 15th edition of MMM marked the return of the conference to Europe after numerous years of activity in Asia, and we are proud to have organized such a prestigious conference on the French Riviera. EURECOM is an engineering school in the domain of information and communication technology and a research center in communication systems. Since its creation in 1991 by TELECOM ParisTech and EPFL, it has developed strong international links with both academic and industrial partners. The heart of EURECOM is its internationally renowned research activities which focus on three areas: networking and security, mobile communications, and multimedia.

MMM 2009 featured a comprehensive program including two keynote talks, six oral presentation sessions, three poster sessions and one demo session. The 135 submissions included a large number of high-quality papers in multimedia content analysis, indexing, coding, as well as applications and services. We thank our 153 Technical Program Committee members and reviewers who spent many hours reviewing papers and providing valuable feedback to the authors. Based on the 3 or 4 (sometimes 5) reviews per paper, the Program Chairs decided to accept only 22 as oral papers and 20 as poster papers. The acceptance rate of 32% follows the MMM tradition of accepting only the papers of the highest technical quality. Additionally, one award for the Best Paper was chosen.

The technical program is an important aspect but only has full impact if surrounded by challenging keynotes. We are pleased with and thankful to our keynote speakers, Steffen Staab and Marcel Worring, for having accepted to present their work at MMM 2009.

We are also heavily indebted to many individuals for their significant contribution. We thank the MMM Steering Committee for their invaluable input and guidance on crucial decisions. We wish to acknowledge and express our deepest appreciation to the Local Organizing Co-chairs, Jean-Luc Dugelay and Bernard Merialdo, the Demo Chair, Ana Cristina Andres Del Valle, the Finance Chair, Marc Antonini, the Publicity and Sponsorship Chair, Nick Evans, the Submission Chair, Hyowon Lee, the Webmaster, Marco Paleari and the Local Arrangements Committee. Without their efforts and enthusiasm, MMM 2009 would not have been made a reality.

We gratefully thank the "Région Provence-Alpes-Cote d'Azur", the "Conseil Général des Alpes Maritimes", Orange Labs - France Telecom, l'Institut TELECOM and EURECOM for their generous support of MMM 2009, which made several key aspects of the conference possible.

Finally, we wish to thank all committee members, reviewers, session Chairs, student volunteers and supporter. Their contribution is much appreciated.

January 2009

Benoit Huet
Alan Smeaton
Ketan Mayer-Patel
Yannis Avrithis

Conference Organization

General Chair

Benoit Huet   EURECOM, France

Program Co-chairs

Alan Smeaton   Dublin City University, Ireland
Ketan Mayer-Patel   UNC-Chapel Hill, USA
Yannis Avrithis   National Technical University of Athens,
                                 Greece

Local Organizing Co-chairs

Jean-Luc Dugelay   EURECOM, France
Bernard Merialdo   EURECOM, France

Demo Chair

Ana Cristina
     Andres Del Valle   Accenture Technology Labs

Finance Chair

Marc Antonini   University of Nice Sophia-Antipolis, France

Publicity and Sponsorship Chair

Nick Evans   EURECOM, France

Submission Chair

Hyowon Lee   Dublin City University, Ireland

US Liaison

Ketan Mayer-Patel   UNC-Chapel Hill, USA

Asian Liaison

Liang Tien Chia   Nanyang Technological University, Singapore

European Liaison

Suzanne Boll   University of Oldenburg, Germany

Webmaster

Marco Paleari   EURECOM, France

Steering Committee

Yi-Ping Phoebe Chen   Deakin University, Australia
Tat-Seng Chua   National University of Singapore, Singapore
Tosiyasu L. Kunii   The University of Tokyo, Japan
Wei-Ying Ma   Microsoft Research Asia, Beijing, China
Nadia
   Magnenat-Thalmann   University of Geneva, Switzerland
Patrick Senac   Ensica, France

Program Committee

Laurent Amsaleg   CNRS-IRISA, France
Yasuo Ariki   Kobe University, Japan
Lora Aroyo   Vrije Universiteit Amsterdam,
                           The Netherlands
Werner Bailer   Joanneum Research, Austria
Selim Balcisoy   Sabanci University, Turkey
Sid-Ahmed Berrani   Orange Labs - France Télécom, France
Catherine Berrut   Université Joseph Fourier, France
Marco Bertini   University of Florence, Italy
Jesus Bescos   UAM, Spain
Stefano Bocconi   Università degli studi di Torino, Italy
Susanne Boll   University of Oldenburg, Germany
Nozha Boujemaa   INRIA, France
Nouha Bouteldja   CNAM, France
Patrick Bouthemy   IRISA / INRIA Rennes, France
Herve Bredin   Dublin City University, Ireland
Paul Buitelaar   DFKI, Germany
Pablo Castells   UAM, Spain
Pablo Cesar Garcia   CWI, The Netherlands
Lekha Chaisorn   Institute for Infocomm Research, Singapore

Dan Jurca   KTH, Sweden
Mohan Kankanhalli   National University of Singapore, Singapore
Jiro Katto   Waseda University, Japan
Philip Kelly   Dublin City University, Ireland
Andruid Kerne   Texas A&M University, USA
Seon Ho Kim   University of Denver, USA
Yiannis Kompatsiaris   CERTH, Greece
Markus Koskela   Helsinki University of Technology, Finland
Duy-Dinh Le   National Institute of Informatics, Japan
Riccardo Leonardi   University of Brescia, Italy
Clement Leung   Victoria University, Australia
Michael Lew   Leiden University, The Netherlands
Paul Lewis   University of Southampton, UK
Mingjing Li   University of Science and Technology of
                                  China, China

Te Li   Institute for Infocomm Research, Singapore
Rainer Lienhart   University of Augsburg, Germany
Joo Hwee Lim   Institute for Infocomm Research, Singapore
Chia-Wen Lin   National Tsing Hua University, China
Weisi Lin   Nanyang Technological University, Singapore
Craig Lindley   University of Gotland, Sweden
Zhu Liu   AT & T Laboratories, USA
Guojun Lu   Monash University, Australia
Jiebo Luo   Kodak Research, USA
Nadia
   Magnenat-Thalmann   Miralab, Switzerland
Stephane
   Marchand-Maillet   University of Geneva, Switzerland
Ferran Marques   Technical University of Catalonia, Spain
Jean Martinet   University of Lille, France
Jose Martinez   UAM, Spain
Tao Mei   Microsoft Research Asia
Bernard Merialdo   EURECOM, France
Hisashi Miyamori   NICT, Japan
Simon Moncrieff   Curtin University, Australia
Jan Nesvadba   Phillips Research, The Netherlands
Eamonn Newman   Dublin City University, Ireland
Chong-Wah Ngo   City University of Hong Kong, Hong Kong
Lyndon Nixon   Free University of Berlin, Germany
Ciaran O'Conaire   Dublin City University, Ireland
Noel O'Connor   Dublin City University, Ireland
Neil O'Hare   Dublin City University, Ireland
Nuria Oliver Ramirez   Telefonica R&D, Spain
Wei Tsang Ooi   National University of Singapore, Singapore
Vincent Oria   NJIT, USA

Kazuhiro Otsuka	NTT, Japan
Marco Paleari	EURECOM, France
Eric Pauwels	CWI, The Netherlands
Fernando Pereira	Instituto Superior Técnico, Portugal
Beatrice	
Pesquet-Popescu	GET / Telecom Paris, France
Yannick Pri	LIRIS, France
Guo-Jun Qi	University of Science and Technology of China, China
Georges Quenot	LIG/IMAG, France
Matthias Rauterberg	Eindhoven University of Technology, The Netherlands
Gael Richard	GET-ENST, France
David Sadlier	Dublin City University, Ireland
Andrew Salway	Burton Bradstock Research Labs, UK
Shin'ichi Satoh	National Institute of Informatics, Japan
Nicu Sebe	University of Amsterdam, The Netherlands
Ishwar Sethi	Oakland University, USA
Koichi Shinoda	Tokyo Institute of Technology, Japan
Francisco Jose	
Silva Mata	Centro de Aplicaciones de Tecnologias de Avanzada, Cuba
Cees Snoek	University of Amsterdam, The Netherlands
Ola Stockfelt	Göteborg University, Sweden
Hari Sundaram	Arizona State Univeristy, USA
Audrey Tam	RMIT University, Australia
Wai-tian Tan	Hewlett-Packard, USA
Kiyoshi Tanaka	Shinshu University, Japan
Jinhui Tang	National University of Singapore
Cuneyt Taskiran	Motorola, USA
Taro Tezuka	Ritsumeikan University, Japan
Georg Thallinger	Joanneum Research, Austria
Daniel Thalmann	EPFL, Switzerland
Jo-Yew Tham	Institute for Infocomm Research, A*STAR, Singapore
Christian Timmerer	University of Klagenfurt, Germany
Ivana Tosic	EPFL, Switzerland
Raphael Troncy	CWI, The Netherlands
Georg Turban	Darmstadt University of Technology, Germany
George Tzanetakis	University of Victoria, Australia
Shingo Uchihashi	Fuji Xerox Co., Ltd., Japan
Nuno Vasconcelos	University of California, San Diego, USA
Benjamin Wah	University of Illinois Urbana-Champaign, USA
Jinjun Wang	NEC Laboratories America, Inc., USA

Meng Wang   University of Science and Technology of
                          China, China
Gerhard Widmer   Johannes Kepler University Linz, Austria
Marcel Worring   University of Amsterdam, The Netherlands
Feng Wu   Microsoft Research Asia
Shiqian Wu   Institute for Infocomm Research, Singapore
Nobuyuki Yagi   NHK Science and Technical Research
                          Laboratories, Japan
Weiqi Yan   Queen's University Belfast, UK
Keiji Yanai   University of Electro-Communications, Japan
Susu Yao   Institute for Infocomm Research, Singapore
Rongshan Yu   Dolby Laboratories, USA
Eric Zavesky   Columbia University, USA
Zhongfei Zhang   State University of New York at Binghamton,
                          USA
Haifeng Zheng   Fuzhou University, China
Yan-Tao Zheng   National University of Singapore, Singapore
Yongwei Zhu   Institute for Infocomm Research, Singapore
Roger Zimmermann   National University of Singapore, Singapore

External Reviewers

Yue Feng   Jie Ouyang
Hanlin Goh   Reede Ren
Michael Hausenblas   Ansgar Scherp
Akisato Kimura   Klaus Seyerlehner
Shiro Kumano   Mohammad-Reza Siadat
Haojie Li   Vassilios Stathopolous
Yiqun Li   Vijayaraghavan Thirumalai
Zhong Li   Thierry Urrutty
Craig Lindley   Sandra Witt
Dong Liu   Kok Sheik Wong
Corey Manders   Chunlei Yang
Dan Mikami   Jie Yu
Bernhard Niedermayer   Zheng-Jun Zha

Table of Contents

Searching and Finding in Large Video Collections

Marcel Worring

Intelligent Sensory Information Systems
Computer Science Institute
Faculty of Science, University of Amsterdam
Kruislaan 403, 1098 SJ Amsterdam, The Netherlands
m.worring@uva.nl

1 Bio

Marcel Worring received the MSc degree (honors) and PhD degree, both in computer science, from the Vrije Universiteit, Amsterdam, The Netherlands, in 1988 and the University of Amsterdam in 1993, respectively. He is currently an associate professor at the University of Amsterdam. His interests are in multimedia search and systems. He is leading the MediaMill team which has been succesful in the last years in the TRECVID benchmark. Methods are applied to visual search in broadcast archives as well as in the field of Forensic Intelligence . He has published over 100 scientific papers and serves on the program committee of several international conferences. He is the chair of the IAPR TC12 on Multimedia and Visual Information Systems, associate editor of the IEEE Transactions on Multimedia and of Pattern Analysis and Applications journal, general chair of the 2007 ACM International Conference on Image and Video Retrieval in Amsterdam and co-organizer of the first and second VideOlympics.

2 Abstract

Finding information in a large video collection is a daunting task. To help the user in their quest, we start off by analyzing the content of the collection at three levels. Automatically computed semantic indexes describe the visual content of individual shots. Dissimilarity spaces describe the relations between different shots. Various content based threads through the set of shots describe the collection as a whole. These additional metadata and structures added to the data provide the basis for a number of innovative interactive video browsers each geared towards different steps in the video search process. In this talk we will highlight the underlying methodologies, show how we have analyzed the characteristics of the tools based on simulated users and show their evaluation in the context of the TRECVID interactive search benchmark.

B. Huet et al. (Eds.): MMM 2009, LNCS 5371, p. 1, 2009.

Structuring and Accessing Semantic Multimedia Data

Steffen Staab

Uni. Koblenz
Koblenz, Germany
staab@uni-koblenz.de

1 Bio

Steffen Staab is professor for databases and information systems at the University of Koblenz-Landau, leading the research group on Information Systems and Semantic Web (ISWeb). His interests lie in researching core technology for ontologies and semantic web as well as in applied research for exploiting these technologies for knowledge management, multimedia and software technology. He has participated in numerous national, European and intercontinental research projects on these different subjects and his research has led to more than 100 refereed contributions in journals and conferences. Dr. Staab held positions as researcher, project leader and lecturer at the University of Freiburg, the University of Stuttgart/Fraunhofer Institute IAO, and the University of Karlsruhe and he is a co-founder of Ontoprise GmbH. He is on several journal editorial boards and is incoming Editor-in-Chief of Elsevier's Journal of Web Semantics. For more information see: http://isweb.uni-koblenz.de/ and http://www.uni-koblenz.de/ staab/

2 Abstract

Navigating large heterogeneous media repositories is difficult because of the heterogeneity of possible data representations and because it requires frequent search for the 'right' keywords, as traditional searching and browsing do not consider the semantics of multimedia data. To resolve these issues we use ontologies and semantic data in two core areas of multimedia storage and access. First, we represent multimedia data in our Core Ontology for MultiMedia - COMM. COMM is an ontology content design pattern able to accomodate heterogeneous representations of low- and high-level multimedia data in a homogeneous manner. Second, we allow for searching and browsing by exploiting semantic background knowledge at a large scale using our Networked Graphs reasoning infrastructure. The methods are integrated into the SemaPlorer prototype allowing for the easy usage of Flickr data based on semantic sources such as DBpedia, GeoNames, WordNet and personal FOAF files. The computational demands are met by federating data access on Amazon's Elastic Computing Cloud (EC2) and Simple Storage Service. Thus, SemaPlorer remains scalable with respect to the amount of distributed components working together as well as the number of triples managed overall.

B. Huet et al. (Eds.): MMM 2009, LNCS 5371, p. 2, 2009.

Adaptive Model for Integrating Different Types of Associated Texts for Automated Annotation of Web Images

Hongtao Xu[1], Xiangdong Zhou[1,2], Lan Lin[3], Mei Wang[2], and Tat-Seng Chua[2]

[1] School of Computer Science, Fudan University, Shanghai, China
{061021054,xdzhou}@fudan.edu.cn
[2] National University of Singapore, Singapore
{wangmei,chuats}@comp.nus.edu.sg
[3] Tongji University, Shanghai, China
linlan@mail.tongji.edu.cn

Abstract. A lot of texts are associated with Web images, such as image file name, ALT texts, surrounding texts etc on the corresponding Web pages. It is well known that the semantics of Web images are well correlated with these associated texts, and thus they can be used to infer the semantics of Web images. However, different types of associated texts may play different roles in deriving the semantics of Web contents. Most previous work either regard the associated texts as a whole, or assign fixed weights to different types of associated texts according to some prior knowledge or heuristics. In this paper, we propose a novel linear basic expansion-based approach to automatically annotate Web images based on their associated texts. In particular, we adaptively model the semantic contributions of different types of associated texts by using a piecewise penalty weighted regression model. We also demonstrate that we can leverage the social tagging data of Web images, such as the Flickr's Related Tags, to enhance the performance of Web image annotation. Experiments conducted on a real Web image data set demonstrate that our approach can significantly improve the performance of Web image annotation.

Keywords: Image annotation, adaptive model, image content analysis.

1 Introduction

Automatic Image Annotation (AIA) is the key issue in keyword-based image retrieval and other semantic-aware image management applications, such as Web image searching and browsing. Since manually annotating images is a tedious and expensive task, AIA has attracted a great deal of research interests in recent years[12,10,9,4,18,15]. It involves the automated labeling of semantic content of images using a predefined set of concepts(keywords). Various machine learning techniques have been exploited to deal with this problem. However, due to the intrinsic problems, such as the semantic gap and multi-label propagation, the effectiveness of AIA is still unsatisfactory.

B. Huet et al. (Eds.): MMM 2009, LNCS 5371, pp. 3–14, 2009.

Previous work of AIA can be divided into two main categories, probabilistic-based methods and classification-based methods. The first category focuses on inferring the correlations or joint probabilities between images and annotation keywords. The representative work include Co-occurrence Model[13], Translation Model(TM)[7], Latent Dirichlet Allocation Model(LDA)[3], Cross-Media Relevance Model(CMRM)[10], Multiple Bernoulli Relevance Model(MBRM)[9], graphical model[18], etc. The classification-based methods try to associate keywords(concepts) with images by learning classifiers. Methods like linguistic indexing[11], SVM-based methods[5], Bayes point machine[3], and Multi-instanced learning[20] fall into this category. However, differing from general images, plentiful of texts are ubiquitously associated with Web images. Examples of associated texts of Web images include image file name, ALT texts, captions, surrounding texts and page title, etc. A common view is that the semantics of Web images are well correlated with their associated texts. Because of this, many popular search engines offer Web image search based only on the associated texts. Fig.1(a) shows an example of the relationships between different types of associated texts and the corresponding Web image. However, in many cases, the associated texts are verbose and varied, and their effectiveness of Web image search is not guaranteed.

In order to improve the effectiveness of Web image annotation based on textual evidences, researchers employed text mining techniques to process the associated texts. For instance, significant words or proper noun phrases are extracted and assigned to the corresponding Web images[15,17]. Furthermore, as shown in Fig.1(a), the associated texts of Web images usually consist of different types of texts located in various parts of the HTML layout. It is well known that different types of associated texts play different roles in deriving the semantics of Web contents. However, most previous work either regard associated texts as a whole, or assigned fixed weights to different types of associated texts according

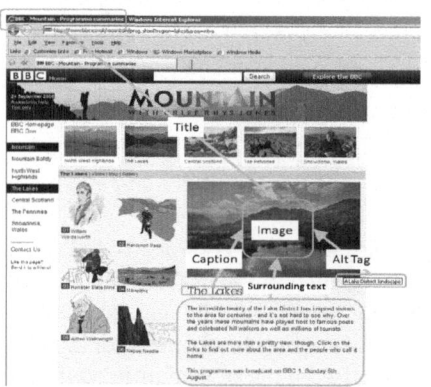

Type	Keywords Distribution	Keywords Distribution
FileName	**beach**20. jpg	siam **ocean**.jpg
ALT	Virginia **Beach** **ocean** front at dawn	siam **ocean** world
Caption	Virginia **Beach**	siam **ocean** world
Text	...Virginia **Beach**... Atlantic **Ocean**...	Siam **ocean** ... Paragon ... **fishes** ...
PageTitle	Virginia **Beach**: Virginia is for lover	Preview of siam **ocean** world

(a) The relationships between the Web image and the types of associated texts

(b) Web images and the corresponding associated texts

Fig. 1. Examples of Web images

to some prior knowledge or heuristics[16,12,19]. It is observed that the correlation of semantics of Web images and their associated texts varies with the types of images or semantic concepts. As shown in Fig.1(b), the distributions of the keyword "ocean" on different types of associated texts in two different pages are not the same; and even in the same Web page, different keywords, such as "beach" and "ocean" of the left image, have various distributions. Therefore, in such cases, the assignment of fixed weights to specific types is ineffective in predicting the correct annotations of the corresponding Web images.

In this paper, we present a novel automated supervised learning approach based on associated texts to perform the annotation of Web images by leveraging on the auto-generated training set. The auto-generation of training set is valuable and important to Web-scale learning. In the auto-generation of training set, the semantic keywords of training images are derived from their associated texts and enhanced by a Web-scale image concept space built from the popular Web Photo Community site Flickr[2]. In particular, our system obtains the initial set of semantic keywords of Web images heuristically from associated texts; then it submits these keywords to Flickr to obtain the Related Tag(RT)[1] set in order to expand the semantic keyword set to deal with the problem of inconsistency and incompleteness of the annotation keywords. Next, based on the generated training set, we propose a linear basic expansion-based approach to annotate Web images. We model the semantic contributions of different types of associated texts via a piecewise penalty weighted regression model. We conduct experiments on about 4,000 images downloaded from the Web. The results demonstrate the effectiveness of the proposed Web AIA approach.

The main contribution of this paper are that we propose a new method to automatically generate training set by combining the associated texts and the Web-scale image concept space; and a novel piecewise penalty weighted regression model to adaptively model the distributions of semantic labels of Web images on their associated text types.

The rest of the paper is organized as follows: Section 2 describes the proposed method. Section 3 presents our experimental settings and results, and Section 4 concludes the paper.

2   The Proposed Method

To improve the effectiveness of mining the associated texts for Web AIA, many machine learning approaches, such as semi-supervised learning[8], have been applied. However, most existing approaches employ only simply heuristics, such as keyword frequency and fixed weight assignment. Although such heuristic approaches can indeed solve part of the problems of Web AIA, the effectiveness of such methods is limited, unreliable, and highly dependent on image collection. This prompts us to explore automated unsupervised approach to collect training

---

[1] RT can be obtained by using Flickr's APIs: flickr.tags.getRelated. It returns "a list of tags 'related' to the given tag based on clustered usage analysis "–refer to: http://www.flickr.net/services/api/flickr.tags.getRelated.html

set from Web, and apply supervised learning to derive semantic labels for the image collection. Specifically, for those images that cannot be labeled with simply heuristics, we adaptively model the semantic distribution on their associated text types according to an auto-generated training set.

2.1 The Overview of the Linear Basic Expansion-Based Web AIA

For a given training set L_{train}, each labeled image $J \in L_{train}$ can be represented by $J = \{W, B, T\}$, where the annotation keywords W is a binary annotation keyword vector indicating whether a keyword is the annotation of J; B is a set of region-based visual features of J; and $T = \{T_1, T_2, \ldots, T_n\}$ is a set of the types of associated texts (see Figure 1).

We adopt the linear basic expansion model for estimating the semantic labels of the unlabeled image I distributed on its associated texts T and their higher order interaction structures to be described in Section 2.3. Let $H(T)$ denotes the set of expansion functions, which represents the associated texts T and their interaction structures; $\omega = \{\omega_1, \ldots, \omega_N\}$ represents the weights of semantic contributions of $H(T)$ to I; and $X_i = p(\cdot|h_i(T))$ denotes the semantic contributions of $h_i(T) \in H(T)$ to I, which is measured by the probability of keywords being generated from $h_i(T)$. Then the probability of the keyword w_i being the semantic annotation of image I can be estimated by a linear model as follows:

$$P(w_i, I) = \sum_{j=1}^{N} \omega_j(w_i) X_j(w_i) \tag{1}$$

The semantic annotation $Anno(I)$ of I is defined as the top-k keywords as:

$$Anno(I) = \{w_i | P(w_i, I) > P_{k+1}(w, I)\} \tag{2}$$

where $P_l(w, I)$ is the lth permutation of the value of $P(w, I)$ and $P_k(w_i, I) \geq P_{k+1}(w_j, I), i \neq j, k = 1, 2, \ldots, (|W| - 1)$.

2.2 Auto-Generation of Training Set

As the basis of supervised Web-scale AIA, we automatically generate training set as follows. First, we use a simple heuristic method to obtain the basic semantic keyword set $BA(I)$ for image I by mining the corresponding associated texts. Second, we use Web-scale image concept space learning to expand and enhance the quality of $BA(I)$ to generate the final semantic keyword set $An(I)$.

The idea of generating the basic annotation is similar to tf/idf heuristic[14]. Here we consider two kinds of term frequency, that is, the frequency of keyword w appears in one type of the associated texts, and the frequency that accounts for the number of the associated texts types that w appears in. The basic idea is that keywords with higher frequency are more important to the semantic of the corresponding Web image. Here we denote the $i^{th}(i = 1, \ldots, m)$ type of associated texts as T_i. After filtering the stop words, the keyword set of the associated texts of image I is denoted as WS_I. For each keyword $w \in WS_I$, the confidence of w being the semantic annotation of image I is defined as follows:

$$Conf(w, I) = \frac{df(w)}{m} \times \sum_{i=1}^{m} \alpha_i * \frac{tf(w, T_i)}{|T_i|} \qquad (3)$$

where $df(w)$ refers to the number of T_i that w appears in; $tf(w, T_i)$ refers to the frequency of w in T_i; $|T_i|$ denotes the total number of keywords appeared in T_i; and $\alpha_i (\sum \alpha_i = 1)$ denotes the weight of T_i.

Given the confidence threshold η, the basic annotation keyword set $BA(I)$ of image I is defined as follows:

$$BA(I) = \{w | w \in WS_I \& Conf(w, I) \geq \eta\} \qquad (4)$$

Similar to the traditional model of Web image analysis, the method of generating the basic annotation is a kind of one directional approach, that is, the semantic of Web images is inferred from just the associated textual data. However, such approach is insufficient and incomplete. To enhance the quality of the auto-generated training set, we exploit the Web social knowledge, such as tagging concept correlation available in public Web-based image(photo) tagging resource. More specifically, we use the popular Web Photo Community site Flickr as a Web-Scale Image Concept Space (ICS), and submit each basic annotation keyword w in BA to Flickr to obtain the Image Concept Neighbor (ICN) of w in ICS. The ICN of w is equivalent to the Related Tag (RT) of w in Flickr terminology. Defining the common ICN (CICN) of image I as the intersection of the ICN of all keywords in $BA(I)$. We expect the CICN of image I to closely reflect the semantic of image I correctly. In order to alleviate the verbose and spamming problems in the Web tagging resources, we employ stop word pruning and noun word extraction tools from WordNet[6] to filter the related tags obtained from Flickr.

We denote the ICN of w as $ICN(w)$. We add the keyword w to the final annotation set $An(I)$ if and only if w appears in $BA(I)$ or $CICN$ of image I:

$$An(I) = BA(I) \cup \{w | w \in \cap_{w_i \in BA(I)} ICN(w_i)\} \qquad (5)$$

By denoting the original data set as L, the training set L_{train} is defined as those images I that $An(I)$ is not empty, and the test set $L_{test} = L \setminus L_{train}$.

2.3   The Probability Estimation and the Use of Higher-Order Associated Text Structures

Since it is difficult to infer the semantics of Web images from individual type of associated texts on their own, we consider the semantic contributions of the higher-order interaction structures among the types. For the n types of associated texts, we can define the kth order structural combinations as $ST^k = \{(T_1 T_2 \ldots T_k), \ldots, (T_{n-k+1} \ldots T_n)\}$. The simplest higher order structure is the 2nd order that can be defined as $ST^2 = \{(T_1 T_2), (T_1 T_3), \ldots, (T_{n-1} T_n)\}$. Figure.2

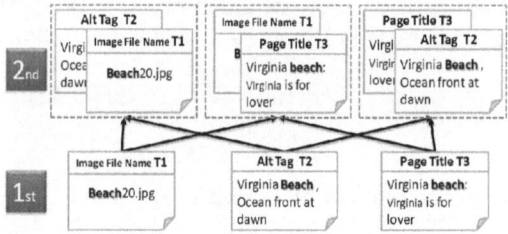

Fig. 2. The 1st and 2nd order interaction structures of different types of the associated texts of the Web image appeared on the left of Fig.1(b)

illustrates the 1st and 2nd order combinational structures of the associated texts of the left-hand Web image shown in Fig.1(b). The Figure also shows the distributions of keyword "beach" on different types of associated texts.

Basic expansion approach is usually applied to extend or add some nonlinear flavors to linear model. Here we define expansion function set $H(T)$ to represent the associated texts and their higher-order interaction structures identically. For simplicity, we just consider the semantic contributions of T and their 2nd order interaction structures. The transformation function $h_j(T) \in H(T)$ is defined as:

$$h_j(T) = \begin{cases} T_j & j = 1, \ldots, n \\ T_i T_l \ (i \neq l) \leq n, n < j \leq N, T_i T_l = T_l T_i \end{cases} \tag{6}$$

where $N = \frac{n(n+1)}{2}$ is the expanded dimension of the transformation space. Noticed that other transformation functions, such as the higher order interaction structures or other nonlinear transformations, can also be applied.

Without loss of generality, it is assumed that T_i and $T_j (i \neq j)$ are independent on condition of keyword w, then we have $p(w|T_i T_j) = \frac{p(w|T_i)p(w|T_j)}{p(w)}$. Let $p(w)$ be uniformly distributed, then the probability $p(w|h_j(T))$ can be estimated as:

$$\hat{p}(w|h_j(T)) = \begin{cases} p(w|T_j) & j = 1, \ldots, n \\ p(w|T_i)p(w|T_l) \ (i \neq l) \leq n, n < j \leq N \end{cases} \tag{7}$$

where $p(w|T_i)$ denotes the probability that w is generated from T_i, which can be estimated by maximum likelihood estimation on multinomial distribution[21].

To further improve the accuracy of the probability estimation, we explore the correlations between keywords to help "smooth" the model sparsity. In particular, we employ the semantic correlation $Similar(w, T_i)$ between keyword w and text T_i to smooth the probability $p(w|T_i)$ as:

$$\hat{p}(w|T_i) = \lambda \frac{tf(w)}{|T_i|} + (1 - \lambda)Similar(w, T_i) \tag{8}$$

where λ is the smoothing parameter.

In this paper, we measure the semantic correlation between w and text $T = \{w_1, w_2, \ldots, w_{|T|}\}$ based on the keywords correlation $Sim(w, w_i)$[14,21].

2.4   The Piecewise Penalty Weighted Regressive Estimation of the Weights of Different Types of Associated Texts

The key issue of the proposed adaptive model is to adaptively determine the weights $\omega(w)$ of associated text types of Eq.1. We expect that semantic distributions of Web images on their associated texts to follow some statistical distributions. Therefore, we can assume that those images with similar visual features and associated texts may obey similar semantic distributions. We apply supervised learning approach to estimate the weights of semantic contributions of associated texts $H(T)$ to the corresponding image. We first determine a neighborhood of I in the training set, and then employ a regression model to learn the weights of associated text types based on the corresponding neighborhood.

The generation probability estimation approach is applied to measure Web image similarity, which is the basis of determining the neighborhood of image I. We first assume that the visual and textual features of images are orthogonal, then the probability of images I being generated from J is defined as:

$$p(I|J) = p(B_i, T_i|J) = p(B_i|J)p(T_i|J) = p(B_i|B_j)p(T_i|T_j) \qquad (9)$$

where $p(B_i|B_j)$ equals to the product of the regional generation probabilities which can be estimated by non-parameter kernel-based density estimation. $p(T_i|T_j)$ denotes the probability of T_i being generated from T_j, which can be estimated by maximum likelihood estimation.

For a given unlabeled image I and the candidate annotation keyword w, let $neighbor(I, w)$ denote the set of neighbor images whose labels contain the keyword w. Thus we can estimate the weights $\omega(w)$ for image I based on $neighbor(I, w)$. To reduce the prediction error of the full model, we shrinkage the model coefficients by imposing a penalty on their size. In order to differentiate the contribution of textual data and their interaction structures, we propose a piecewise penalty method which impose different penalties to different subsets of the model coefficients. The set of $s^{th}(s = 1, \ldots, k)$ order structure's model coefficients is denoted by D_s. The piecewise penalty weighted regression coefficients minimize a piecewise penalty weighted residual sum of squares as follows:

$$\hat{\omega}(w) = arg \min_{\omega(w)}\{\sum_{i=1}^{K} \mu_i(y_i - \omega_0 - \sum_{j=1}^{N} X_{ij}\omega_j(w))^2 + \sum_{s=1}^{k} \gamma_s \sum_{\omega_j \in D_s} \omega_j(w)^2\} \quad (10)$$

where K is the number of images in $neighbor(I, w)$. We estimate ω_0 by $\bar{y} = \sum_1^K y_i/K$, and the remaining coefficients by a regression model without intercept by centering X_{ij}. Let $\omega'_s(w) = \omega_j$ when $\omega_j \in D_s$ and otherwise 0, we have:

$$RSS(\lambda) = \mu(y - X\omega(w))^T(y - X\omega(w)) + \sum_{s=1}^{k} \gamma_s \omega'_s(w)^T \omega'_s(w) \qquad (11)$$

Then the regression solution can be easily seen as:

$$\hat{\omega}(w) = (\mu X^T X + \sum_{s=1}^{k} \gamma_s I_s)^{-1} X^T y \qquad (12)$$

where I_s is $N \times N$ matrix, and the components are 0 except for the components of the diagonal line, and $I_s[j][j] = 1$ when $\omega_j \in D_s$ and otherwise 0.

The inputs of the regression model is the probability that w is generated from $H(T)$, that is $X_{ij} = p(w|h_j(T))$. The predicted value y_i is the probability that w being the annotation of image. Since we have known that w is the annotation of training image J_i, we have $y_i = p(w|J_i) = 1$. The weight μ_i of training image J_i is the similarity of J_i and I. Due to our expansion process, we expect that the contribution of T and their i^{th} order interaction structures to image semantic to be different, thus we partition the weight coefficients into k subsets corresponding to T and their $i^{th}(i = 2, \ldots, k)$ order interaction structures. Our aim is to shrinkage the regression coefficients by imposing a L_2 penalty to each part, where the penalty parameters are $\gamma = \{\gamma_1, \ldots, \gamma_k\}(\gamma_1 \geq \ldots \geq \gamma_k)$.

Analogy to ridge regression, we use quadratic regularization to penalize the regression coefficients. The larger the penalty parameter, the greater the amount of shrinkage. We use the following method to help choose the penalty parameters γ, that is, for two adjacent order structures of T, such as the text T_i and $T_i \times T_j$, the ratio $\frac{T_i T_j}{T_i}$ is $p(w|T_i)$. Therefore we can estimate the ratio $\rho(0 \leq \rho \leq 1)$ between the significance of the two different adjacent order structures by the average of the contributions of the lower order structure, that is $\rho = \frac{1}{n}\sum_{i=1}^{n} p(w|T_i)$. Then we choose the regularization parameter γ_1 by using validation data set, and others $\gamma_j = \rho * \gamma_{j-1}, j = (2, \ldots, k)$.

3   Experiments

3.1   The Experiments Data and Setup

We downloaded images and the accompanying Web pages by feeding the query keywords into Yahoo search engine, and employed a "lightweight" tool *HTML-Parser*[1] to parse the html documents into DOM tree before extracting the embedded images and their corresponding associated texts to form the data set L. The set of concepts or query keywords used in our experiment is: *beach, bear, birds, bridge, building, car, Egypt pyramid, flower, great wall, tree, tiger, whale*, etc. We classified the associated texts into 5 categories: image file name, ALT text (ALT tag), caption text (Heading tag), surrounding text and page title. After parsing the pages and filtering the noisy images (such as the small logo images, the images with non-proper length/width ratio, etc.), we obtained the final set L with about 4,000 images, which are used as control set in our experiments.

We use the proposed training set auto-generation method to automatically selects a subset of 640 images from L as training set L_{train} using the proposed training set auto-generation method. The rest of control set of images is then used as test set L_{test}. From the training set, the system derives an initial set BA of 180 keywords from associated texts using Eq.4. It then submits these keywords to Flickr to obtain the Related Tags, and returns about 2,467 keywords. After lexical filtering of invalid keywords, and performing the concept space learning

(Eq.5), The system obtains 87 keywords for incorporation into BA to obtain the final semantic keyword set.

Next, the system randomly partitions half of the training set. The validation set is used to determine the model parameters, such as smoothing parameter λ and regularization parameter γ_1, which are respectively set as 0.6 and 0.6. In the auto-generation of training set, m is set as 4(surrounding text is not included), $\alpha_i = 0.25(i = 1, \ldots, 4)$, and confidence threshold η is set as 0.2.

In order to provide ground truth for testing, we manually label the L_{test} by 3 students(two of them are not familiar with this filed), and each image is labeled with 1-7 keywords. The vocabulary of manual annotations consists of about 137 keywords. Each image of L is segmented into 36 blobs based on fixed size grid, and 528 dimensional visual feature for each blob is extracted according to $MPEG7$ standard. We adopt the *recall, precision* and *F1* measures are adopted to evaluate the performance in our experiments. That is, given a keyword w, let $|W_G|$ denotes the number of human annotated images with label w in the test set, $|W_M|$ denotes the number of images annotated with the same label by our algorithm. The *recall, precision* and *F1* are defined as: $Recall = \frac{|W_M \cap W_G|}{|W_G|}$, $Precision = \frac{|W_M \cap W_G|}{|W_M|}$, $F1 = \frac{2(Precision \times Recall)}{Precision + Recall}$. The size of annotation is set to 4, and the average *recall, precision* and *F1* over all the keywords are calculated as the evaluation of the overall performance.

3.2   The Experimental Results

In our experiments, two baseline methods are used for comparison: (1) AIAW: the baseline approach that regards all the associated texts as a whole; and (2) AIAFIX: the baseline method that treats different associated text types as separate but assigns only fixed weights and does not consider higher order structures.

The evaluation aims to demonstrate the effectiveness of each component technology and their contributions to the overall system. The component technologies tested are: (a) the use of adaptive model for adaptively learning of the weights of the associated text types, denoted as "Adap"; (b) the use of basic expansion method that incorporates higher-order associated text structures, denoted as "Exp"; and (c) the use of Flickr in the process of auto-generation of training set (Trg+Flickr). The following sub-Sections present the results.

The Effectiveness of the Adaptively Learning of the Weights of the Associated Text Types: To test the effectiveness of "Adap" approach, we compare it with the two baseline approaches. For "AIAFIX", we use Ridge Regression (RR) to learn the weights of the associated text types. All approaches use the training image set "Trg+Flickr". Figure 3(a) presents the comparison results.

The experiment results in Figure 3(a) demonstrate the importance of considering the types of associated texts, as Baseline 2 (AIAFIX+RR) that treats each associated type as separate though with fixed weights, performs much better than Baseline 1 (AIAW) that regards all associated texts as a whole. The results also show that the "Adap+RR" approach which adaptively learns the

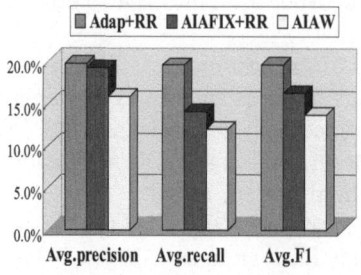

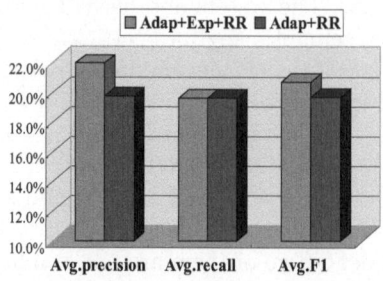

(a) The effectiveness of adaptively learning of the weights of associated text types

(b) The effectiveness of employing higher order associated text structures

Fig. 3. Experimental results

weights of associated text types is superior to the baseline approaches which use fixed weights assignment or regard all associated texts as a whole.

The Effectiveness of Employing Higher-Order Associated Text Structures in Probability Estimations: To test the effectiveness of "Exp" approach, we compare the performance of "Adap" approach that considers only the contributions of 5 basic associated text types, against the "Adap+Exp" approach that also takes advantage of the higher order structures. Similar to Experiment 1, we use Ridge Regression (RR) to learn the associated text weights and "Trg+Flickr" as training. Figure 3(b) gives the comparison results.

The results in Figure 3(b) show that the use of higher order interaction structures (Adap+Exp+RR) is superior to that without taking advantage of the interaction structures among the basic associated text types (Adap+RR). The reason for the improvement in performance is that we can estimate the likelihood of keywords being the semantic annotation of Web images more accurately by further considering the semantic contributions of the higher order interaction structures.

The Overall Performance of the proposed Annotation Approach: Fig.5 summarizes the overall performance of the proposed Web image annotation approach (Adap+Exp). We compare the effectiveness of using our proposed Piecewise Penalty Weighted Regression (PPWR) method against Ridge Regression (RR) in learning the weights of the associated text types. Furthermore, we test the effectiveness of using Flickr in the process of auto-generation of training set. Thus we generated two training sets: the one without using Flickr (Trg) and the one enhanced by Flickr social tagging data (Trg+Flickr).

The results in Figure 4 show that: (a) The "Adap+Exp+PPWR+Trg+Flickr" is superior to "Adap+Exp+RR+Trg+Flickr" approach. It demonstrates that "PPWR" is more effective than ridge regression in learning the weight distribution of the associated text types and their higher order structures when annotating Web images. (b) The results derived from the training set enhanced

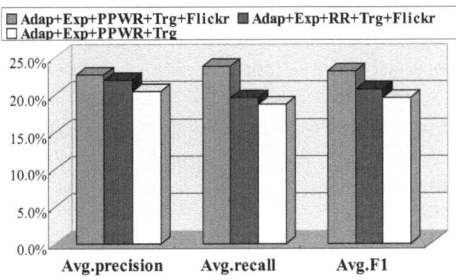

Fig. 4. The overall performance of the proposed annotation approach

by Flickr (Adap+Exp+PPWR+Trg+Flickr) are superior to that without using Flickr (Adap+Exp+PPWR+Trg). It demonstrates that we can improve the quality of training set by exploiting the knowledge within the Web-scale image concept space, and hence the overall performance of Web AIA. Through observation, we found that the annotation set obtained by only mining associated texts is partial and incomplete, and the use of Web image social tagging data from Flickr helps to improve the completeness of the training set significantly.

4 Conclusions

Ubiquitous image resources on the Web have long been attractive to research community. Web-based AIA is a promising way to manage and retrieve the fast growing number of Web images. However, its effectiveness still needs to be improved. In this paper, we developed and evaluated a linear basic expansion-based Web image annotation algorithm. In particular, we adaptively modeled the distribution of semantic labels of Web images on their associated texts via the proposed piecewise penalty weighted regression model. We also demonstrated that the social tagging data of Web image (Flickr) can be utilized effectively to improve the quality of the automatically acquired training data set, and hence the Web AIA performance significantly.

Acknowledgment

This work was partially supported by the NRF of Singapore Grant R-252-000-325-279, NSF of China Grant 60403018 and 60773077.

References

1. http://htmlparser.sourceforge.net
2. http://www.flickr.com
3. Blei, D., Jordan, M.: Modeling annotated data. SIGIR, 127–134 (2003)
4. Carneiro, G., Chan, A., Moreno, P., Vasconcelos, N.: Supervised learning of semantic classes for image annotation and retrieval. PAMI (2007)

5. Chang, E., et al.: Cbsa: Content-based soft annotation for multimodal image retrieval using bayes point machines. CirSysVideo 13(1), 26–38 (2003)
6. Christiane, F.: Wordnet: An electronic lexical database. MIT Press, Cambridge (1998)
7. Duygulu, P., Barnard, K., de Freitas, J., Forsyth, D.: Object recognition as machine translation: Learning a lexicon for a fixed image vocabulary. In: Heyden, A., Sparr, G., Nielsen, M., Johansen, P. (eds.) ECCV 2002. LNCS, vol. 2353, pp. 97–112. Springer, Heidelberg (2002)
8. Feng, H., Shi, R., Chua, T.-S.: A bootstrapping framework for annotating and retrieving www images. ACM Multimedia, 960–967 (2004)
9. Feng, S., Manmatha, R., Lavrenko, V.: Multiple bernoulli relevance models for image and video annotation. In: CVPR, pp. 1002–1009 (2004)
10. Jeon, J., Lavrenko, V., Manmatha, R.: Automatic image annotation and retrieval using cross-media relevance models. SIGIR, 119–126 (2003)
11. Li, J., Wang, J.: Automatic linguistic indexing of pictures by a statistical modeling approach. IEEE Trans. on Pattern Analysis and Machine Intelligence 25(19), 1075–1088 (2003)
12. Li, X., Chen, L., Zhang, L., Lin, F., Ma, W.-Y.: Image annotation by large-scale content-based image retrieval. ACM Multimedia, 607–610 (2006)
13. Mori, Y., Takahashi, H., Oka, R.: Image-to-word transformation based on dividing and vector quantizing images with words. MISRM (1999)
14. Ricardo, B., Berthier, R.: Modern information retrieval. ACM Press, New York (1999)
15. Rui, X., Li, M., Li, Z., Ma, W.-Y., Yu, N.: Bipartite graph reinforcement model for web image annotation. ACM Multimedia, 585–594 (2007)
16. Sanderson, H., Dunlop, M.: Image retrieval by hypertext links. SIGIR, 296–303 (1997)
17. Shen, H., Qoi, B., Tan, K.: Giving meaning to web images. ACM Multimedia, 39–47 (2000)
18. Tang, J., Hua, X.-S., Qi, G.-J., Wang, M., Mei, T., Wu, X.: Structure-sensitive manifold ranking for video concept detection. ACM MM, 23–29 (2007)
19. Tseng, V., Su, J., Wang, B., Lin, Y.: Web image annotation by fusing visual features and textual information. In: SAC, pp. 1056–1060 (2007)
20. Yang, C., Dong, M.: Region-based image annotation using asymmetrical support vector machine-based multiple-instance learning. In: CVPR, pp. 2057–2063 (2006)
21. Zhou, X., Wang, M., Zhang, Q., Zhang, J., Shi, B.: Automatic image annotation by an iterative approach:incorporating keyword correlations and region matching. In: CIVR, pp. 25–32 (2007)

SenseCam Image Localisation
Using Hierarchical SURF Trees

Ciarán Ó Conaire, Michael Blighe, and Noel E. O'Connor

Centre for Digital Video Processing, Dublin City University, Ireland
oconaire@eeng.dcu.ie,
http://www.cdvp.dcu.ie

Abstract. The SenseCam is a wearable camera that automatically takes photos of the wearer's activities, generating thousands of images per day. Automatically organising these images for efficient search and retrieval is a challenging task, but can be simplified by providing semantic information with each photo, such as the wearer's location during capture time. We propose a method for automatically determining the wearer's location using an annotated image database, described using SURF interest point descriptors. We show that SURF out-performs SIFT in matching SenseCam images and that matching can be done efficiently using hierarchical trees of SURF descriptors. Additionally, by re-ranking the top images using bi-directional SURF matches, location matching performance is improved further.

Keywords: Image matching, SenseCam, localisation, SURF.

1 Introduction

The SenseCam is a wearable camera that automatically captures images of a user's activities (figure 1). In order to organise the thousands of images generated per day, the physical location of the user for each image captured could potentially be very useful as additional metadata. For example, if you had lost your briefcase, your SenseCam could help you automatically retrace your steps. Similarly, at a conference it could be used to establish what posters you had visited, providing the basis for determining where you spent your time (and thus by implication what you found most interesting).

Of course, a number of technological solutions are available for localisation, such as GPS [1], GSM [2] and RF-based localisation using base-station signal strength [3]. It is not always desirable or even possible to use these technologies. For example, GPS localisation is unreliable indoors; GSM or RF-based localisation may not support localisation to a fine granularity, required for some applications. The SenseCam could, for example, replace the traditional audio-guide used in many museums [4]. This would require no additional overhead in terms of infrastructure and would allow wearers to follow a more natural path through the museum, rather than obeying the predefined audio-guide route. In

B. Huet et al. (Eds.): MMM 2009, LNCS 5371, pp. 15–26, 2009.

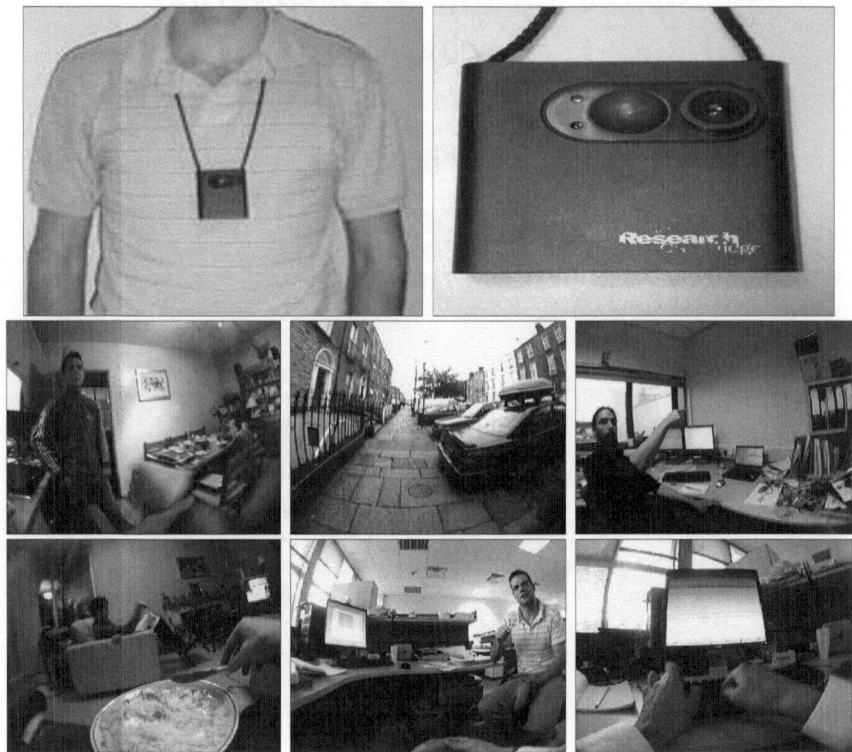

Fig. 1. The SenseCam: a prototype wearable camera. The bottom two rows show some typical SenseCam images.

applications, such as the monitoring of people with age-dementia [5], a wearable visual monitor is a useful diagnostic tool, and knowledge of the wearer's location could facilitate more efficient browsing of a large repository of captured images or video.

In this paper, we address the problem of estimating a person's trajectory through a space, using only their SenseCam images. In our proposed approach, we begin by creating an image database of known positions. SURF image features [6] are extracted from the database images and clustered into a hierarchical-tree. This data structure allows fast matching of a query image with its most similar database images. Finally, since SenseCam images have a temporal order, we can use this to impose some constraints on the user's path through the space. Three strategies for path optimisation are evaluated.

This paper is organised as follows: In section 2, we provide a brief background literature review to contextualise our work. The recently proposed SURF descriptor is compared to the standard SIFT method in section 3. Section 4 describes our experimental setup. We present results in section 5, demonstrating the localisation accuracy of the proposed approach and give our conclusions and directions for future work in section 6.

2   Related Work

Many different approaches to automatic user localisation have been proposed in the literature. In [3], Bahl and Padmanabhan present an RF-based system for location estimation that uses signal-strength information from wireless network base-stations at known locations. Using a similar approach, GSM has also shown potential for providing good localisation [2]. Additionally, GPS has been used in many systems, but it does not work indoors and recent studies have shown that GPS coverage is only available for 4.5% of the time a user carries a device over a typical day [1]. Image based localisation provides an alternative and complementary approach to these technologies.

A great deal of work has been done in the autonomous vehicle community on Simultaneous Localisation and Mapping (SLAM), whereby a mobile robot builds a map of its environment and at the same time uses this map to compute its own location [7]. In this paper, we tackle a different problem whereby we cannot control the movements of the camera wearer and the image capture rate is significantly lower than for video.

Kosecka and Yang [8] use SIFT features [9] for user localisation by creating an image database of known locations and matching query images to their database. The SIFT descriptor is a gradient orientation histogram robust to illumination and viewpoint changes. In a similar vein to SIFT and other interest point descriptors (many of which are evaluated in [10]), the recently proposed SURF method [6] locates interest points and extracts an invariant descriptor for each point. However, SURF achieves greater computational efficiency by using integral images. In order to efficiently locate relevant images in a large database, Nistér and Stewnius [11] propose the use of a *vocabulary tree* of SIFT descriptors.

Our previous work on the SenseCam includes [12] and [13], where we have focused on developing SenseCam-image clustering techniques to assist user browsing by grouping the thousands of images generated by the device into *events*. We have also examined matching events in a person's life [14]. We believe that knowledge of the user's location will be a valuable additional aid to efficient organisation of SenseCam images.

3   Feature Comparison

3.1   Data Capture

In order to perform a straight-forward comparison between the SIFT and SURF descriptors, SenseCam images of static scenes are captured by fixing the camera in place and taking one image every 5-10 minutes. The interest-point descriptors found in each image of a single static scene should have unique corresponding points in other images of the scene. SenseCam images have high noise, due to the lack of a flash, and a high number of compression artifacts, since a JPEG compression quality of 60% is used. These static scene comparisons test each method's robustness to these distortions. We also test the more difficult scenario of a severe lighting change. This is simulated by turning on another set of lights

Fig. 2. Some of the images use to compare SURF and SIFT. The first two columns differ only by ambient lighting, camera noise and compression effects. The third column shows images that contain a severe change in lighting.

in the room. Previous works, notably [10] and [6], have more thoroughly tested other interesting distortions not considered in this work, such as camera rotation, scaling and blur. In total, 7 static scenes and 2 lighting-change scenes were captured, with approximately 9 images each. In each scene, all pairs of images are compared.

Table 1. Static scene comparison of SIFT and SURF. Rows show figures for Stability and Average Precision. Columns show SIFT and 4 SURF variants. the SIFT descriptor is a 128-dimensional vector. The number beside each SURF descriptor indicates the size of the descriptor and USURF is a non-rotationally-invariant version of SURF. Since all SURF variants use the same detector, their stability scores are equal. $USURF_{64}$ performs best in these tests overall.

	$SIFT$	$SURF_{64}$	$SURF_{128}$	$USURF_{64}$	$USURF_{128}$
Stability	0.7190	**0.8094**	**0.8094**	**0.8094**	**0.8094**
Average Precision	0.9965	0.9960	0.9952	**0.9974**	0.9970

Table 2. Severe lighting changes: Comparison of SIFT and SURF for feature matching. See table 1 for details of table abbreviations. $USURF_{128}$ performs marginally better than $USURF_{64}$ in these tests.

	$SIFT$	$SURF_{64}$	$SURF_{128}$	$USURF_{64}$	$USURF_{128}$
Stability	0.3081	**0.4706**	**0.4706**	**0.4706**	**0.4706**
Average Precision	0.6600	0.8099	0.8054	0.8379	**0.8392**

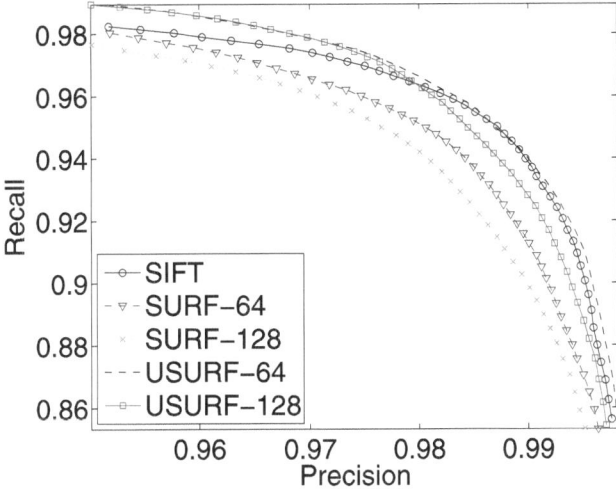

Fig. 3. Robustness to camera noise, JPEG compression and ambient lighting changes: Precision-Recall curve for the evaluated descriptors

3.2   Evaluation: SIFT vs. SURF

In our tests, the implementation used for SIFT was the original version by Lowe [9]. Similarly, the code provided online for SURF by Bay et al. was used [6]. Due to the camera noise, SIFT returned many interest points at small scales. These were found to be very unstable. Therefore, to improve SIFT performance, points with scales less than 2 were removed. The standard SURF descriptor is rotationally invariant, but since the images captured with a SenseCam are almost always upright, the non-rotationally invariant USURF is appropriate for our application. We compared these two variants, as well as there *extended* versions that are twice as long but increase matching accuracy. In total, the four variants of SURF we tested were: $SURF_{64}$, $SURF_{128}$, $USURF_{64}$ and $USURF_{128}$.

To measure the stability (or repeatability) of the interest point detectors of the methods, we computed (for a pair of images) the fraction of interest points in the 1st image that had a match in the 2nd image. Since each point is described by a (circular) region, a match was declared if for two regions, the intersection area divided by the union area was greater than 0.5, as proposed in [10]. The stability value shown in the tables is an average of all image comparisons.

To measure the performance of the descriptors, we used the distance ratio test [9]. To examine whether a point from the 1st image has a match in the 2nd, its two most similar descriptors in the 2nd image are found. If the ratio of the nearest distance to the second nearest distance is less than α, a match is declared. By varying this α parameter, the precision-recall curves in figures 3 and 4 were generated. For each descriptor, the average precision was computed as the area under the curve.

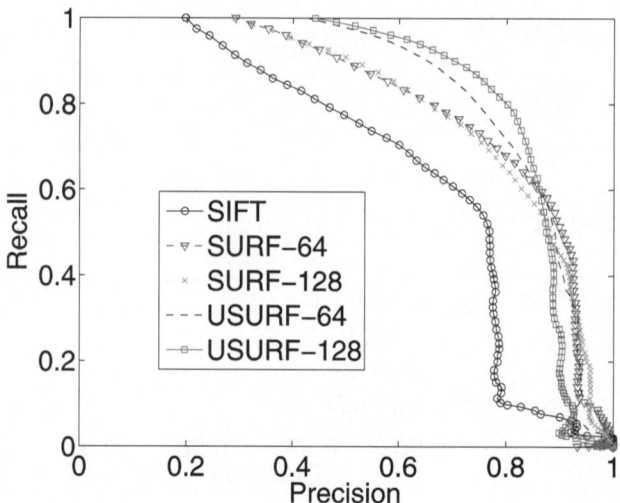

Fig. 4. Robustness to severe lighting changes (as well as camera noise, JPEG compression and ambient lighting changes): Precision-Recall curve for the evaluated descriptors. The SIFT descriptor fares quite poorly here compared to the SURF descriptors.

Table 1 shows the results when the testing images only differ by slight changes in ambient lighting, camera noise and compression effects. Examples are shown in the first two columns of figure 2. To examine more drastic changes, table 2 shows the results when the testing images suffer a severe lighting change (as well as camera noise and compression effects). For example, compare the image in the first two columns of figure 2 to the images in the third column.

Both sets of results indicated that the USURF$_{64}$ descriptor provided high stability and matching performance and therefore this was adopted for our experiments in image matching. USURF$_{128}$ is marginally better for severe lighting changes, but the trade-off is that the descriptor is twice as large, so we retained the smaller descriptor. SIFT was adversely affected by the severe lighting change, as can be seen in figure 4.

In terms of choosing a threshold for matching, Lowe suggests using a value of $\alpha = 0.6$ [9]. We found that by optimising various performance measures (such as the F_1 measure), larger values of α were preferred for SenseCam image matching, due to the higher noise. In the rest of this work we use $\alpha = 0.7$.

4   Experimental Setup

In our experiments, we wished to trace the path of an individual through our labs, comprising of two large office spaces and a corridor (see map in figure 10). A database of 156 images was created by capturing SenseCam images uniformly over the area. The median distance from a point in the space to the position of

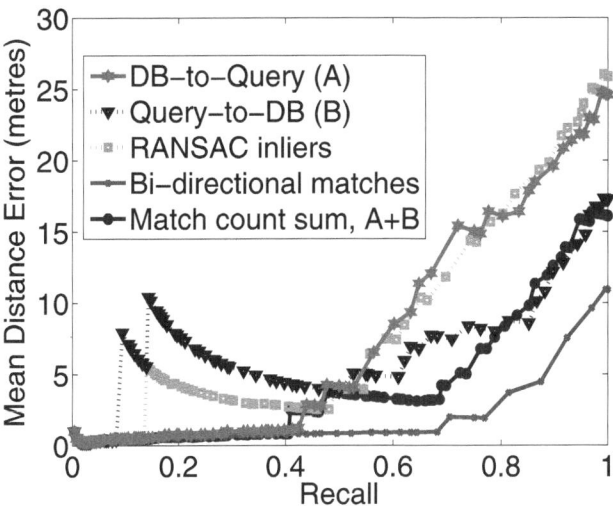

Fig. 5. Evaluating the methods of evaluating if two images are a location *match*: using the 9 training sequences (273 images). Bi-directional matches clearly out-perform the other matching measures.

the nearest database image is 1.19m. The position of each image was manually annotated using an interactive map-based tool. Testing sequences were similarly annotated to act as a ground truth for our experiments. Image distortion due to the fish-eye lens was removed using the Camera Calibration Toolbox for Matlab [15]. Examples of out database and testing images are shown in figures 7 and 8.

To measure how likely it is that 2 images are of the same location, Kosecka and Yang [8] simply counted the number of SIFT feature matches between the query and database (DB) image. We experimented with this measure and various others, such as reverse matching (number of matches from DB-to-query), summing both counts (sum of query-to-DB and DB-to-query) and RANSAC inliers (estimating the fundamental matrix using all matches, and counting the inliers). We found the best strategy was to perform matching in both directions (query-to-DB and DB-to-query) and to count the number of correspondences that were found in both directions (e.g. point A matches to B in query-to-DB matching, and point B matches to point A in DB-to-query matching). We refer to these as *bi-directional matches*. To compare the 5 strategies, we used all 273 images in 9 training sequences and compared each one to all 156 database images. Figure 5 illustrates the robustness of each measure in image matching. By varying a threshold on the measure, we can trade-off the recall of the correct location with the average position error. Bi-directional matches significantly out-perform the other measures in this regard.

Ideally, we would rank database images by their bi-directional matches with the query image, but this is computationally expensive, so inspired by [11], a fast voting method was developed to narrow the search to a small subset

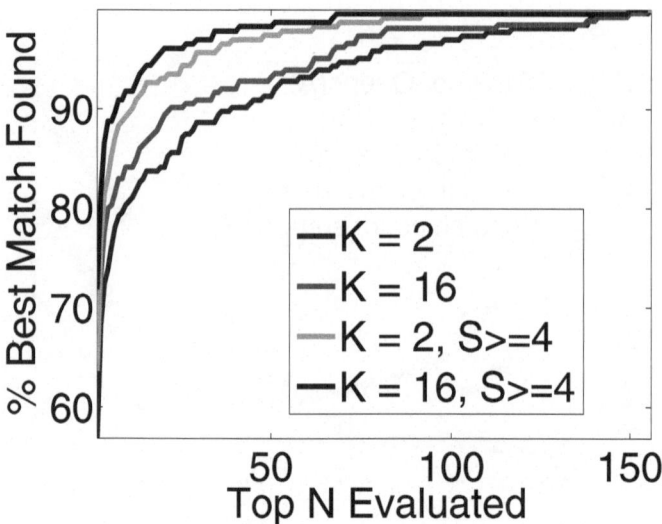

Fig. 6. Evaluating the voting performance: This graphs shows how well the voting performs in quickly finding the best matching image. K is the branching factor and S is the number of bi-directional matches.

of the database. All $42,595$ SURF descriptors were extracted from the 156 database images. They were split into two groups $(+1/-1)$ based on the sign of the Laplacian (which is included in the SURF descriptor). For each group, we then applied the K-means clustering algorithm recursively. First, clustering the data-points into K clusters, then clustering the points in each cluster into K sub-clusters and continuing recursively until a cluster contains less than K data-points. This created two hierarchical-SURF-trees which allowed rapid descriptor matching. Given a SURF descriptor, it can be compared to the K root nodes of the tree matching its Laplacian sign. The closest node can then be chosen and its subtree traversed recursively. The matched leaf node is then the approximate nearest-neighbour of the query descriptor. Unlike [11] where inverse files are used, we label each leaf-node with the DB image from which it is derived. We adopt a simple voting strategy to find potential DB images. Each SURF point in the query image is matched to its approximate-NN by the SURF-tree, and then casts one vote for the corresponding DB image. Our MATLAB code for K-means-hierarchical-tree generation and matching is available online at: http://elm.eeng.dcu.ie/~oconaire/source/

In order to estimate how well this voting strategy approximates bi-directional match ranking, we measured how frequently the best database match (highest *score* according to bi-directional matching) appeared in the top N results. Figure 6 shows the results of this test, and also examines the effects of the branching factor K. As in [11], we found that larger values of K perform better, though decreasing speed slightly. In this work, we used $K = 16$, making the feature matching more than 600 times faster than an exhaustive search. Query

Fig. 7. Examples of annotated database images of the environment

Fig. 8. Examples of testing images

images with a low score probably do not have a good match in the database. When we ignore images that have less than 4 bi-directional-matches, then the performance can be seen to be even better.

The task of image matching in our chosen environment was quite challenging. Both the database and testing data contain distracting objects, such as people. The database images were taken 3 months before the testing images, so objects had been moved, Christmas decorations introduced, etc. Additionally, both offices spaces are structurally almost identical.

Our user localisation approach works as follows. For a query image Q_i, we extract SURF descriptors and use the hierarchical-SURF-trees to vote for DB images. The 7 highest scoring DB images are then processed to find bi-directional matches. The DB image with the most bi-directional matches is determined to be the best match. Let B_i denote the (x, y) ground position of the best match to query image Q_i, obtaining S_i bi-directional matches. Let W_i denote the estimated (x, y) position of the user when image Q_i was captured.

We evaluated 3 strategies in determining a user's motion through the space. Method 1 is simply to use the best match: $W_i = B_i$. Method 2 is to set a confidence threshold, T, and use it to determine if we should use the best match. If $S_i \geq T$ then a reliable match is declared and $W_i = B_i$, otherwise it's position would be interpolated linearly using other reliable matches. Using 9 training sequences, we found the minimum average distance error occurred at $T = 5$. Method 3 is the same as method 2, but the interpolation is performed using the geodesic distance, which takes into account the positions of walls and doors. Additionally, if the distance between the estimated positions of two consecutive images was greater than 10m, the position of the image with the lower score was interpolated.

5   Experimental Results

Figure 9 shows some examples of the matching. In column 1, the images are matched despite occlusion and one image captured during the day, the other at

Fig. 9. (top row) query images, (2nd row) their best matching database images

night. Similarly, columns 2, 3 and 4 indicate the robustness of the matching to the introduction of new objects and scale changes. An example of an estimated trajectory, along with the ground truth is shown in figure 10. Table 3 shows the overall localisation accuracy of the three methods over 9 training and 9 testing sequences. From the improvement of method 2 over method 1, it is clear that the use of the image temporal ordering is important for accurate path estimation. The use of the geodesic distance and outlier elimination reduces the error further by over 12%.

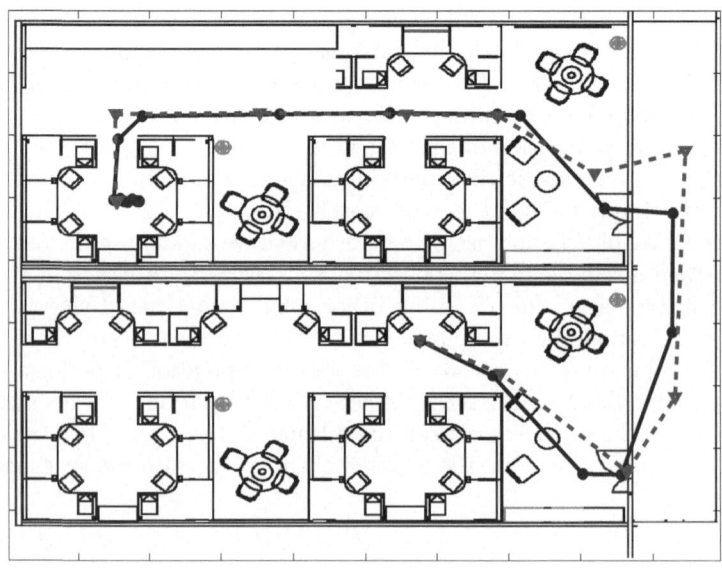

Fig. 10. Example trajectory: ground truth (solid blue line) and estimated trajectory (dashed red line)

Table 3. Average distance error in metres

Sequence	*Method 1*	*Method 2*	*Method 3*
Training Data	2.26m	1.34m	1.10m
Testing Data	3.11m	1.77m	1.55m

6   Conclusion and Future Work

In this paper we presented our approach to user localisation using SenseCam images. Firstly, the newer SURF descriptor was compared to the commonly used SIFT descriptor and was found to have superior stability and matching performance in SenseCam imagery. Secondly, inspired by [11], we developed a fast method of finding potential query matches in our annotated location database. Thirdly, we demonstrated that SURF *bi-directional matching* out-performs other measures for image matching. Finally, we evaluated three strategies for estimating the path a user walked through the space and showed that accurate user localisation is possible, despite challenging image data. Future work will investigate fusing image information with complementary RF-based localisation using multiple wireless network base-stations.

References

1. LaMarca, A., et al.: Place lab: Device positioning using radio beacons in the wild. In: Proceedings of the Third International Conference on Pervasive Computing (May 2005)
2. Varshavsky, A., et al.: Are gsm phones the solution for localization? In: 7th IEEE Workshop on Mobile Computing Systems and Applications (2006)
3. Bahl, P., Padmanabhan, V.N.: Radar: An in-building rf-based user location and tracking system. In: Proceedings of the IEEE Infocom (March 2000)
4. Fasel, B., Gool, L.V.: Interactive museum guide: Accurate retrieval of object descriptions. In: Marchand-Maillet, S., Bruno, E., Nürnberger, A., Detyniecki, M. (eds.) AMR 2006. LNCS, vol. 4398, pp. 179–191. Springer, Heidelberg (2007)
5. Megret, R., Szolgay, D., Benois-Pineau, J., Joly, P., Pinquier, J., Dartigues, J.F., Helmer, C.: Wearable video monitoring of people with age dementia: Video indexing at the service of healthcare. In: International Workshop on Content-Based Multimedia Indexing (CBMI) (2008)
6. Bay, H., Tuytelaars, T., Gool, L.V.: Surf: Speeded up robust features. In: Leonardis, A., Bischof, H., Pinz, A. (eds.) ECCV 2006. LNCS, vol. 3951, pp. 404–417. Springer, Heidelberg (2006)
7. Durrant-whyte, H., Bailey, T.: Simultaneous localisation and mapping (slam): Part 1, the essential algorithms. Robotics and Automation Magazine (2006)
8. Kosecka, J., Yang, X.: Global localization and relative positioning based on scale-invariant keypoints. In: 17th International Conference on Pattern Recognition, vol. 4, pp. 319–322 (August 2004)
9. Lowe, D.G.: Distinctive image features from scale-invariant keypoints. International Journal of Computer Vision 60(2), 91–110 (2004)

10. Mikolajczyk, K., Schmid, C.: A performance evaluation of local descriptors. IEEE Transactions on Pattern Analysis and Machine Intelligence 27(10), 1615–1630 (2005)
11. Nistér, D., Stewénius, H.: Scalable recognition with a vocabulary tree. In: IEEE Conference on Computer Vision and Pattern Recognition, pp. 2161–2168 (June 2006)
12. Ó Conaire, C., O'Connor, N.E., Smeaton, A., Jones, G.J.F.: Organising a daily visual diary using multi-feature clustering. In: Proc. of 19th annual Symposium on Electronic Imaging (2007)
13. Blighe, M., Borgne, H.L., O'Connor, N., Smeaton, A.F., Jones, G.: Exploiting context information to aid landmark detection in sensecam images. In: International Workshop on Exploiting Context Histories in Smart Environments (ECHISE 2006) - Infrastructures and Design, 8th International Conference of Ubiquitous Computing (Ubicomp 2006) (September 2006)
14. Doherty, A.R., Ó Conaire, C., Blighe, M., Smeaton, A.F., O'Connor, N.E.: Combining image descriptors to effectively retrieve events from visual lifelogs (under review). Multimedia Information Retrieval, MIR (2008)
15. Bouguet, J.Y.: Camera calibration toolbox for matlab, http://www.vision.caltech.edu/bouguetj/calib_doc/index.html

General Highlight Detection in Sport Videos

Reede Ren and Joemon M. Jose

Department of Computing Science
University of Glasgow
17 Lilybank Gardens, Glasgow, UK
{reede,jj}@dcs.gla.ac.uk

Abstract. *Attention* is a psychological measurement of human reflection against stimulus. We propose a general framework of highlight detection by comparing *attention* intensity during the watching of sports videos. Three steps are involved: adaptive selection on salient features, unified *attention* estimation and highlight identification. Adaptive selection computes feature correlation to decide an optimal set of salient features. Unified estimation combines these features by the technique of multi-resolution auto-regressive (MAR) and thus creates a temporal curve of *attention* intensity. We rank the intensity of *attention* to discriminate boundaries of highlights. Such a framework alleviates semantic uncertainty around sport highlights and leads to an efficient and effective highlight detection. The advantages are as follows: (1) the capability of using data at coarse temporal resolutions; (2) the robustness against noise caused by modality asynchronism, perception uncertainty and feature mismatch; (3) the employment of Markovian constrains on content presentation, and (4) multi-resolution estimation on *attention* intensity, which enables the precise allocation of event boundaries.

Keywords: highlight detection, attention computation, sports video analysis.

1 Introduction

As one of the most popular video genres in the video-on-demand service, sports video has shown its commercial value in the media industry [11]. Many value-add services, *e.g.* adaptive video skimming and content sensitive video encoding, are proposed to improve service quality. Therefore, sports highlight detection attracts great interests from both industry and academics [6], as a key function to above services.

A highlight is "something (as an event or detail) that is of major significance or special interest" (Merriam-Webster Online Dictionary 2008). This linguistic definition shows that highlights are contingent on sports contents as well as video context. A predefined collection of video events could hardly cover all possible highlights. On the other hand, a highlight may be an interesting detail rather than an event. Therefore, event-based approaches are ineffective for the identification of sports highlights. Given that all highlights incur strong reflections

B. Huet et al. (Eds.): MMM 2009, LNCS 5371, pp. 27–38, 2009.

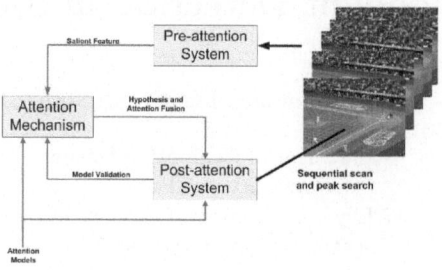

Fig. 1. Attention Perception System

among viewers, *i.e.* happiness or surprise, *attention*, the psychological measurement of human reflection, is proposed in [3] [10] as an efficient method to identify general highlights. Moreover, the estimation of *attention* intensity concerns few sports semantics. This indicates that attention-based approaches avoid semantic uncertainty caused by various video contents.

An *attention* perception system [13] consists of three components (Figure 1): pre-attentive, attention combination and post-attentive system. The pre-attentive system is also called as feature-attention modelling [10], which calculates stimulus strength as well as extracts salient features. However, such an extraction of salient features is usually incomplete [8]. These features may be ineffective for the discrimination of actual attention peaks [13], because of strong perceptual noise and variant stimulus types. *Attention* combination simulates the mechanism of *attention* perception in human minds, which fuses stimuli from vision, auditory and text understanding to create a unified *attention*. The post-attentive system justifies conclusions got in the prior steps by domain knowledge.

In our mind, an *attention*-based system should answer the following research questions: (1) how to identify a set of effective salient features in a given sports video; (2) how to combine noisy salient features robustly; (3) how to estimate an unified *attention* to reflect interesting contents; and (4) how to analyse the unified attention to allocate highlights. We here take video segments which incur the strongest reflections, as highlights [10] [12]. This provides a post-attentive explanation to question 4.

In this paper, we model the perception process of sports video watching to estimate the intensity of viewer reflection. This leads to two improvements in comparison with prior works [10][3][12]: adaptive selection on salient features and the framework of attention fusion, *i.e.* multi-resolution autoregressive (MAR). Adaptive selection extends the pre-attentive system, which identifies the most effective salient features to improve the robustness of *attention* estimation. The technique of MAR is equivalent to a Markovian process on graph [15], the general temporal model of video content presentation [16]. Such a combination framework therefore imposes the Markovian constraint on video presentation to *attention* perception. This is a significant improvement on *attention* based video analysis. Moreover, a video contains multiple modalities, *i.e.* audio and visual streams. These modalities are independent representation of video contents at different temporal resolutions. By sampling and matching these modalities gradually, the MAR alleviates the problem of modality over-sampling and media asynchronism. This results in a precise and robust estimation of *attention* intensity.

The paper is structured as follows. Section 2 provides a brief overview on sports highlight detection, especially *attention*-based approaches. A twofold model of *attention* perception is proposed in Section 3 to simulate the process of sports video watching. Based on this model, Section 4 presents the selection algorithm on salient features. Section 5 describes the MAR framework for *attention* fusion. The experiments on real football game videos are stated in Section 6. Conclusion is found in Section 7.

2 Related Work

The literature of highlight detection could be roughly categorised into two groups, event-based and attention-based. Event-based approaches regard some specific events as so-called highlights, although such an event collection can hardly cover all possible aspects. The detection of sports highlights is therefore specified into a sequence of event discrimination, *e.g.* goal, corner and free-kick [2]. Various Markov models have been proposed to identify these events. Lenardi *et al.* [7] model shot transmissions around game events with a controlled Markov chain. The authors take embedded audio energy as the controlling token and rank highlight candidates by the loudness. Their experimental results are evaluated by the coverage of goal events among the top 5 of candidate lists. Kang *et al.* [5] propose a bidirectional Markov model to alleviate the problem of modality asynchronism. The authors identify excited speech whilst search video objects such as goalposts in nearby shots. Xu *et al.* [17] create a group of middle-level content modalities by coupling low-level features, such as dominant colour and caption text. By these content modality, the authors build a hierarchical hidden Markov model for event detection.

Attention-based approach is an exploration from computing psychology to content analysis [10]. This methodology is relatively new in sports video analysis [3]. Ma *et al.* [10] employ a series of psychological models on pre-attention, *i.e.* motion attention model, static attention model and audio salient model, to describe the process of video watching. A set of temporal curves are created to display feature related *attention* such as motion attention, and are linearly combined to estimate the joint intensity of *"viewer attention"*. However, this massive feature extraction introduces too much noise and challenges the later attention combination. With the increase of feature number, noise overwhelms actual attention peaks and thus fails highlight detection. Hanjalic *et al.* [3] carefully choose three features to estimate the intensity of viewer reflection, including block motion vector, shot cut density and audio energy. The authors furthermore employ a 1-minute long low-pass Kaiser window filter to smooth these features as well as enhance the signal noise rate (SNR) of feature related *attention* [4]. A robust method of attention combination is also developed. A sliding window is introduced to limit the range of observation and the authors count *attention* peaks inside to guess the appearance probability of a highlight. However, the sliding window makes constant the temporal resolution of event detection. It is difficult to allocate event boundaries precisely as well as segment video events. Such an ability is essential in many applications, *e.g.* adaptive video encoding.

3   Temporal Attention Perception Modelling

In this section, we address the temporal modelling of *attention* perception and show how to develop a MAR framework to simulate such a process.

Attention perception is a discreet temporal process in psychology: "*people notice something at this moment and other things later*". A general stimulus-attention model is proposed in [8], which consists of two differential equations to quantify the relationship among *interest*, *attention* and *reflection* of a human being in an unknown environment. Some complex issues are considered in this model, *i.e.* cultural background, personal experience and possible activity. However, the context of sports video watching indicates a predictable viewer behaviour and leads to a direct model of *attention* perception.

A sports video records a combination of reflections. There are three major reaction roles, spectators, commentators and video directors. These observers watch the game at the same time. They understand game content and keep video context. In psychological terminology, these observers are ready to accept stimulus. Their reflection therefore follows the stimulus-reflection model [8] (Equation 1).

$$A(t) = pX(t - \tau) + \alpha + w(t) \tag{1}$$

where $A(t)$ denotes attention intensity at the moment t; $X(t - \tau)$ refers to stimulus strength with a reflection delay τ; α stands for the threshold triggering a response; p is a reflection parameter and $w(t)$ is perceptual noise. τ is a constant related to the modality, *e.g.* 0.384 sec for vision [14]. Individual understandings from these observers affect video viewer's feeling. Directors watch camera videos, decide shot styles such as field view and close-up, and insert video editing effects, *i.e.* replay, to present the story. Spectators and commentators dominate audio tracks. As a group, stadium audience cheer at exciting moments and remain relatively silent in the rest of a game. They attract video viewers by loud plaudits. Commentator's behaviour is a little complex. On one hand, commentators reiterate game contents and their professional jargons are detected for events annotation. On the other hand, commentators are ad-hoc spectators. Hence, the *attention* model for a viewer to watch a sports video is a combination of above observer reflections (Equation 4).

$$A_{viewer}(t) = A_{director} + aA_{spectator} + bA_{commentator} \tag{2}$$

$$= \sum_{x \in X} ((1 + a + b)p_x x(t - \tau_x) + \alpha_x + w_x(t)) \tag{3}$$

$$= \sum_{x \in X} (kx(t - \tau_x) + \alpha_x + w_x(t)) \tag{4}$$

where a,b are combination parameter for spectator and commentator reflections, respectively; x denotes a stimulus from the collection of salient features X; α refers to the response threshold; w(t) is perceptual noise and $k = (1 + a + b)p_x$.

Furthermore, a sports video is a smooth Markovian process on both time and content presentation [17]. Game contents can be described by a directed semantic graph $G = (\nu, \epsilon)$, in which vertices set ν denotes game semantics and edge set ϵ links pairs of vertices $(s,t), s, t \in \nu$, a possible event sequence. A game is therefore presented by a discrete-time Markov process $x(.)$ on G with finite states. Such a process on graph can always be extended to a state chain without loops by intuitive labelling and dynamic programming. Moreover, Hammersly-Clifford theorem [1] proves the equality between a Markov chain and an auto-regressive (AR) by comparing clique potential. In addition, a video is always with a definite start point (the root of a graph). Such a Markov process can be expressed by a first order AR model,

$$x[n] = a[n-1]x[n-1] + w[n] \tag{5}$$

where $w[n]$ is a set of independent Gaussian noise, $x[0]$ is the root and $x[1 \ldots n]$ are a sequence of Markov states. Given that *attention* intensity reflects the importance of a game content, Equation 5 is transformed as follows.

$$A[n] = k[n-1]A[n-1] + w[n] \tag{6}$$

where $A[n]$ is *attention* intensity of a viewer at an event n, $k(n-1)$ is the parameter for reflection combination, which is also regarded as the impact of a past event $n-1$. This indicates that some efficient methods of signal processing, such as moving average, can be used for the analysis of *attention* perception.

In summary, we build a twofold model of *attention* perception for sports video watching: Equation 4 describes the transient *attention* reflection against a stimulus; and Equation 6 denotes an accumulation of *attention* in a long period.

4   Adaptive Salient Feature Selection

Here we propose an adaptive selection on possible salient features to improve system robustness. A large collection of salient features are listed in Section 4.1 for *attention* estimation in sports videos. Section 4.2 presents the algorithm for feature selection, which decides a subset of salient features for later *attention* combination, according to given video data. In another words, the set of salient features for *attention* estimation is adaptive to videos.

4.1   Salient Feature

As the theory of psycho-biology asserts, temporal variation, stimuli strength and spatial contrast are major facts in visual attention [9]. Video directors mainly rely on fast shot variation to excite viewers, such as replay and quick switching camera viewpoints [18]. Loud and greatly varying noise from spectators always catches

Table 1. Attention Related Salient Feature, + stands for the positive qualitative relation between feature strength and *attention*, where the feature induces an increase of *attention* intensity. − denotes negative qualitative relation, which decreases *attention* intensity, and ∗ for unsure.

Salient Feature	Psychological Facts	Qualitative Affection on Attention
football size	zoom depth	+
uniform size	zoom depth	+
face area	zoom depth	+
domain color ratio	zoom depth	−
edge distribution	rect of interest	∗
goalpost	rect of interest	∗
penalty box	rect of interest	∗
shot cut frequency	temporal variance	+
motion vector	temporal variance	∗
zoom-in sequence	temporal variance	+
visual excitement	motion	+
lighting	spatial variance	∗
colour energy	stimuli strength	∗
replay	temporal contrast	∗
off-field shot	temporal contrast	∗
base band energy	loudness	+
cross zero ratio	sound variation	+
speech band energy	sound variation	+
keyword	semantic	∗
MFCC and delta	sound variation	∗
spectral roll-off	sound variation	+
spectral centroid	loudness	+
spectral flux	loudness	+
octave energy	loudness	+
music scale	sound variation	∗
audio type proportion	valance classification	∗
scene affect vector	valance classification	∗

notice. Moreover, the watching of sports videos requires rich domain knowledge. The semantics of video objects and audio key words plays an important role in *attention* computation. For example, a goalpost attracts great interest as the forecast of a goal [2].

Table.1 lists most salient features reported in literature [18][10][2][3]. Psychological explanations and possible affection on *attention* intensity are also annotated. In addition, related algorithms for feature extraction are found in [12].

4.2   Feature Selection

Equation 6 shows that effective salient features should reach local extremes at important game events. Signal correlation (Equation 7) therefore becomes an effectiveness measurement for salient features in *attention* estimation, if perceptual noise is a Gaussian white noise with zero mean.

$$r_{XY} = \| \frac{\sum_{i=1}^{n} x_i y_i - n\bar{X}\bar{Y}}{(n-1)s_X s_Y} \| \tag{7}$$

where X,Y are two salient features with n samples; $\bar{X}, \bar{Y}$ denote the average and s_X, s_Y refer to standard deviations of X and Y, respectively. $r_{XY} \in (0, 1]$ and $r_{XY} = 1$ iff the strength of X and Y are of the same linear direction. However, this measurement is not so robust in computation. This is because: (1) salient signals, e.g. shot frequency and audio energy, are of various sequence length due to the difference in sampling rate[1], (2) random perceptual delay mismatches salient signals (Equation 4).

There are two facts in video watching which can alleviate the above problem: (1) the duration of most events is less than 5 minutes [2]; (2) the average reflection delay is less than 15 sec for ready viewers [18]. We therefore use a 5-minute moving average to smooth salient signals. This could reduce perceptual noise effectively. We collect maximum and minimum every five minutes and compute the correlation between respective maximum/minimum sequences. We assume the correlation distribution is a Gaussian with the mean of one (Equation 7). Therefore, a score which suggests feature effectiveness, is decided as the probability of a correlation value belonging to the given Gaussian distribution. Salient signals with the largest N scores are kept for *attention* combination.

5   Multi-resolution Auto-Regressive Fusion

In this section, we address the problem of *attention* combination. Equation 6 shows that attention perception can be described by an autoregressive (AR) process. Given that salient features are sampled at different temporal resolutions, it is reasonable to employ a MAR for *attention* combination.

A MAR is a scale-recursive linear dynamic model, which simulates a random process by a set of AR models on multiple scales. A general two-pass parameter estimation algorithm is proposed in [15], which includes a fine-to-coarse filtering followed by a coarse-to-fine smoothing. The fine-to-coarse step is a three-step recursion of measurement updating, fine-to-coarse prediction and information fusion when moving to a coarse resolution. The coarse-to-fine step combines smoothed estimations and covariances at coarse resolutions with the statistics computed in the first fine-to-coarse sweep. We extend this general algorithm for *attention* combination. Different from the prior work [12], we start from the salient signal with the finest temporal resolution, e.g. zoom depth and game pitch ratio; and gradually impose other salient features as an updated measurement in the merge step. The details of our algorithm are presented as follows.

---

[1] We compute shot frequency every 50 sec and audio energy every 0.3 sec.

5.1   Fine-to-Coarse Filtering

Let $\hat{x}(s|s)$ be the optimal estimation of attention intensity $x(s)$ at a node s, together with $P(s|s)$, the error covariance.

Initialisation. Start with salient features at the finest temporal resolution. For each leaf s, the estimation of $\hat{x}(s|s-)$ and the covariance $P(s|s-)$ from the sub-tree are as follows.

$$\hat{x}(s|s-) = 0 \tag{8}$$
$$P(s|s-) = P_x(s) \tag{9}$$

Measure Updating is identical to the analogous step in a Kalman filter, although only estimations are changed here. If there is no measure available, go to sub-tree fusion directly.

$$\hat{x}(s|s) = \hat{x}(s|s-) + K(s)v(s) \tag{10}$$

where $v(s)$ is the measurement innovations,

$$v(s) = y(s) - H\hat{x}(s|s-) \tag{11}$$

which is zero-mean with covariance,

$$V(s) = HP(s|s-)H^T \tag{12}$$

and where the gain $K(s)$ and the updated error covariance $P(s|s)$ are given by,

$$K(s) = P(s|s-)H^T V^{-1}(s) \tag{13}$$
$$P(s|s) = [I - K(s)H]P(s|s-) \tag{14}$$

Repeat the above steps until $\|P(s|s)\|$ is smaller than a given threshold.

Sub-Tree Fusion merges estimations from immediate children at s. Let $\hat{x}(s|sa_i)$ be the optimal estimate at one of children sa_i of node s and v_{sa_i}, the sub-tree rooted at sa_i, and $P(s|sa_i)$ for the corresponding error covariance.

$$\hat{x}(s|s-) = P(s|s-) \sum_{i=1}^{K_s} P^{-1}(s|sa_i)\hat{x}(s|sa_i) \tag{15}$$

$$P^{-1}(s|s-) = P_x^{-1}(s) + \sum_{i=1}^{K_s} [P^{-1}(s|sa_i) - P_x^{-1}(s)] \tag{16}$$

Error covariance matrix $P(s|sa_i)$ indicates the distribution of *attention* weight on salient features at the given resolution. This matrix is kept for the later coarse-to-fine smoothing. To avoid noise incurred by signal interpolation [12], we regard every layer in the MAR tree as an individual Markov process and limit the scope of recursive smoothing.

Fine-to-Coarse Prediction estimates $\hat{x}(s|sa_i)$ and error covariance matrix $P(s|sa_i)$ of the parent s from its children sa_i.

$$\hat{x}(s|sa_i) = F(sa_i)\hat{x}(sa_i|sa_i) \tag{17}$$

$$P(s|sa_i) = F(sa_i)P(sa_i|sa_i)F^T(sa_i) + U(sa_i) \tag{18}$$

where

$$F(s) = P_x(s\bar{r})A^T(s)P_x^{-1}(s) \tag{19}$$

$$U(s) = P_x(s\bar{r}) - F(s)A(s)P_x(s\bar{r}) \tag{20}$$

5.2 Coarse-to-Fine Smoothing

When the fine-to-coarse filtering reaches a predefined coarse resolution or the root, the MAR has experienced all possible reflection delays and completed parameter estimation. The error covariance and optimised estimations are calculated at all nodes. Then the coarse-to-fine smoothing spreads optimal estimations and covariance from parents $s\bar{r}$ and improves the estimation at finer resolutions s.

$$\hat{x}_s(s) = x(\hat{s}|s) + J(s)[\hat{x}_s(s\bar{r}) - \hat{x}(s\bar{r}|s)] \tag{21}$$

$$\hat{P}_e(s) = P(s|s) + J(s)[P_e(s\bar{r}) - P(s\bar{r}|s)] \tag{22}$$

where

$$J(s) = P(s|s)F^T(s)P^{-1}(s\bar{r}|s) \tag{23}$$

6 Experiment

The evaluation collection includes six entire game videos in MPEG-1 format from FIFA World Cup 2002, World Cup 2006, and UEFA Champions League 2006: three from World Cup 2002, Brazil vs Germany (final), Brazil vs Turkey (semi final), and Germany vs Korea (semi final); one from World Cup 2006, Italy vs France (final); and two from Champions League 2006, Arsenal vs Barcelona and AC Milan vs Barcelona. We gathered game records from the FIFA and BBC Sports website as the ground truth of video event list. All videos are divided into halves, *e.g.* Brazil-Germany I for the first half of the final game in World Cup 2002. The middle break is removed but we keep other broadcasting aspects such as player entering, triumph, and coach information board.

We use the ratio of *attention* intensity on events and other general video clips (Equation 24) to evaluate system robustness. A high ratio is preferred.

$$R_{attention} = \frac{E(A_{events})}{E(A)} \sim \frac{E(A_{goal})}{E(A)} \tag{24}$$

where E is the expectation function, and A_{events}, A_{goal}, A denote estimated attention intensity on events, goals and the entire game, respectively. Table 2

Table 2. Attention intensity under different resolution in the $2^{n}d$ half in Brazil vs Germany, World Cup 2002

Temporal Resolution (sec)	1.2	38	76	152	304	600
Event Mean	6.628	6.628	**6.807**	6.743	6.671	6.563
Average	4.020	3.974	4.122	3.532	3.432	**3.342**
Delta	2.608	2.654	2.685	3.211	**3.239**	3.221

Table 3. Attention ratio(goals vs. general contents) under different combination algorithms

	Linear I	Linear II	MAR I	MAR II	Linear III	MAR III
Ger-Bra II	1.522	1.874	1.802	1.997	1.333	**2.141**
Bra-Tur II	1.671	1.944	1.972	2.187	1.461	**2.245**
Ger-Kor II	1.142	1.326	1.411	1.563	1.274	**1.665**
Mil-Bar II	1.377	1.700	1.741	2.043	1.276	**2.226**
Ars-Bar I	1.274	1.427	1.419	1.778	1.143	**1.912**
Ars-Bar II	1.192	1.325	1.422	**1.760**	1.151	1.732
Ita-Fra I	1.302	1.377	1.420	**1.723**	1.044	1.658

compares the average of attention intensity over different temporal resolutions. Many interesting conclusions are reached: (1) the maximum of average attention appears at the temporal resolution of 76 sec; (2) the delta maximum is at the resolution of about 5 min (304sec). The observation window with 5-minute width is the best choice for event detection whilst 1-minute for event segmentation.

Feature set {average block motion, shot cut density, base band audio energy}[4] is used to evaluate approaches of attention combination. We take linear combination [10] as baseline. Table 3 presents six approaches: Linear I directly adds up normalised salient features [10]; Linear II linearly combines normalised salient features but with the weight from the fine-to-coarse filtering; MAR I uses the self-information [12]; MAR II works on 1-minute resolution; Linear III and MAR III are similar to Linear I and MAR II respectively, but employ a set of seven salient features from adaptive feature selection. The MAR outperforms linear combination in most cases. Adaptive selection is effective to improve the ratio of average attention intensity (Equation 24). The performance of Linear III is worse than Linear I, because linear combination cannot afford perceptual noise.

Table 4. Game highlights and attention Rank in France vs Italy (I,II game halve)

FIFA	BBC Sports	Rank
Players enter the field	-	3(I)
Penalty	Zidane Penalty	1(I)
Goal	Goal	2,4(I)
-	Zidane expulsion	3(II)
Italian Triumph	-	1(II)

The MAR based approach achieved 100% precision in the detection of goal events. As an interesting case study, we compare professionally marked highlight lists from BBC Sports and FIFA website in Table 4 for Italy vs. France, World Cup 2006. *Attention*-based detection covers most of manually selected highlights.

7   Conclusion

Attention-based approach is an application of computing psychology in video analysis. Such an approach is efficient in the identification of sports highlights. We propose an abstract model of *attention* perception to simulate the process of video watching, which leads to an adaptive selection on salient features and a combination framework of multi-resolution autoregressive. Adaptive selection exploits the characters of temporal accumulation on *attention* perception. A measurement of signal correlation is therefore suggested at a coarse temporal resolution to evaluate feature effectiveness. The MAR framework is based on the multi-resolution nature of *attention* perception. The advantages of the MAR framework are as follows: (1) the employment of data at coarse temporal resolutions, which can hardly be used before in content-based video analysis; (2) the multi-resolution framework of data sampling and matching, which alleviates media asynchronism; (3) the extensibility and robustness on a large feature space.

Acknowledgement

The research leading to this paper was supported by European Commission under contracts FP6-045032 (Semedia).

References

1. Besag, J.: Spatial interaction and statistical analysis of lattice system. Journal of Royal Statistical Society 36(2), 192–236 (1974)
2. Ekin, A., Tekalp, A., Mehrotra, R.: Automatic soccer video analysis and summarization. IEEE Trans. on Image Processing 12(7), 796–807 (2003)
3. Hanjalic, A.: Adaptive extraction of highlights from a sport video based on excitement modeling. IEEE Trans. on Multimedia 7(6), 1114–1122 (2005)
4. Hanjalic, A., Xu, L.Q.: Affective video content repression and model. IEEE Trans on Multimedia 7(1), 143–155 (2005)
5. Kang, Y., Lim, J., Kankanhalli, M., Xu, C.-S., Tian, Q.: Goal detection in soccer video using audio/visual keywords. In: ICIP 2004, vol. 3, pp. 1629–1632 (2004)
6. Kokaram, A., Rea, N., Dahyot, R., Tekalp, M., Bouthemy, P., Gros, P., Sezan, I.: Browsing sports video: trends in sports-related indexing and retrieval work. Signal Processing Magazine 23(2), 47–58 (2006)
7. Lenardi, R., Migliorati, P., Prandini, M.: Semantic indexing of soccer audio-visual sequence: A multimodal approach based on controlled markov chains. IEEE Trans. on Circuits and System for Video Technology 14, 634–643 (2004)

8. Lesser, M.J., Murray, D.K.C.: Mind as a dynamical system: Implications for autism. In: Durham conference Psychobiology of autism: current research and practice (1998)
9. Lew, M.S.: Principles of Visual Information Retrieval. Springer, Heidelberg (1996)
10. Ma, Y., Lu, L., Zhang, H., Li, M.: A user attention model for video summarization. In: ACM Multimedia 2002 (2002)
11. News, G.: 3g football best mobile service (January 2005)
12. Ren, R., Jose, J.M., He, Y.: Affective sports highlight detection. In: The 15th European Signal Processing Conference, Poznan, Poland, September 2007, pp. 728–732 (2007)
13. Tagare, H.D., Toyama, K., Wang, J.G.: A maximum-likelihood strategy for directing attention during visual search. IEEE Trans. on Pattern Analysis and Machine Intelligence 23(5), 490–500 (2001)
14. Treisman, A.M., Kanwisher, N.G.: Perceiving visually presented objects: recognition, awareness, and modularity. Current Opinion in Neurobiology 8, 218–226 (1988)
15. Willsky, A.: Multiresolution markov models for signal and image processing. Proceedings of the IEEE 90(8), 1396–1458 (2002)
16. Xu, C., Wang, J., Wan, K., Li, Y., Duan, L.: Live sports event detection based on broadcast video and web-casting text. In: ACM Multimedia 2006 (2006)
17. Xu, G., Ma, Y., Zhang, H., Yang, S.: An hmm-based framework for video semantic analysis. IEEE Trans. on Circuits and System for Video Technology 15, 1422–1433 (2005)
18. Zettl, H.: Sight, Sound, Motion: Applied Media Aesthetics. Wadsworth, Belmont CA (1990)

Probabilistic Integration of Tracking and Recognition of Soccer Players

Toshie Misu, Atsushi Matsui, Simon Clippingdale,
Mahito Fujii, and Nobuyuki Yagi

Science & Technical Research Laboratories, NHK (Japan Broadcasting Corporation)
1-10-11, Kinuta, Setagaya-ku, Tokyo 157-8510, Japan
{misu.t-ey, matsui.a-hk, simon.c-fe, fujii.m-ii, yagi.n-iy}@nhk.or.jp

Abstract. This paper proposes a method for integrating player trajectories tracked in wide-angle images and identities by face and back-
number recognition from images by a motion-controlled camera. In order
to recover from tracking failures efficiently, the motion-controlled camera scans and follows players who are judged likely to undergo heavy
occlusions several seconds in the future. The candidates of identities for
each tracked trajectory are probabilistically modeled and updated at
every identification. The degradation due to the passage of time and occlusions are also modeled. Experiments showed the system's feasibility
for automatic real-time formation estimation which will be applied to
metadata production with semantic and dynamic information on sports
scenes.

Keywords: soccer formation, probabilistic integration, tracking, face
recognition, back-number recognition.

1 Introduction

In large-scale video archives, we often encounter difficulties in finding video resources that meet our requirements for genre, title, actor, director, place, video
format, etc. The difficulty would reach the level of impossibility if we were to access scenes or shots of specific semantic situations without temporally segmented
video indices (segment metadata). Depending on the temporal and semantic
granularity, the production of manually-indexed segment metadata usually requires a vast amount of time, manpower, and concentration, especially in the
case of sports video, where prompt editing operations are required despite the
unavailability of a priori scenarios.

To support metadata production, automatic event detection and scene analysis have been widely studied[1] for audio and speech[2][3], video[4][5][6], and
their combination[7]. Since the player formations play important roles in tactics
in team sports, we developed a set-play classifier for soccer that classifies the
player positions, velocities, and team memberships, which are observed in fixed
wide-angle images, into twelve event classes (kick-off, free kick, etc.)[8]. Since
the classifier did not consider any individual identities, however, no information
on the subjects (i.e. the kickers) were available in the output metadata.

B. Huet et al. (Eds.): MMM 2009, LNCS 5371, pp. 39–50, 2009.

However, trajectories with identities (IDs) throughout the game are indispensable if we are to produce sufficient metadata to meet queries for tactical conditions related to specific players. To obtain them, we require a robust tracking algorithm that can handle frequent occlusions. Although multiple hypothesis tracking[9] might be a solution for this, the algorithm has a drawback of difficulty in modeling/implementing graph operations.

In this paper, we propose a versatile scheme for decomposing the trajectory identification process into inidividual phenomena asscociated with disambiguation and ambiguation due to object recognition and tracking errors. To handle merge-and-split of IDs, the accumulating ambiguities are modeled by probabilistic transitions of spatial mixing-up and temporal oblivion. The algorithm also incorporates ID measurements (e.g. the recognized face IDs with motion-controlled camera) that infrequently but strongly narrow down the ID candidates.

2   System Framework

Figure 1 depicts the framework for integrating tracking and recognition processes to acquire identified trajectories. Two types of cameras are employed in the system: (1) a fixed wide-angle camera (WA-cam) for player tracking, and (2) a motion-controlled camera (MC-cam) with zoom lens for player recognition.

The player tracking process detects and tracks all the players and estimates their positions on the pitch using the WA-cam by back-projecting the image coordinates of detected players using precalibrated camera parameters and Kalman filtering. We employed a simple tracking algorithm that pursues the silhouette closest to the predicted centroid. Let $\ell \in \{1, 2, \ldots, L\}$ and $\boldsymbol{x}_t^{(\ell)}$ respectively be the index and the position (at the time-step t) of the ℓ-th tracked trajectory, the identity $n_t^{(\ell)} \in \{1, 2, \ldots, N\}$ of which may experience tracking failures, and is not necessarily consistent throughout the game. Actually, due to the simplicity of the tracker, the indices are frequently assigned, mixed up, and deleted, and the index numbers tend to inflate as $\ell = 3468$–3607 in Fig. 7.

Then, the MC-cam examines and follows a player whose trajectory suggests that s/he will imminently undergo significant occlusion by other players, and

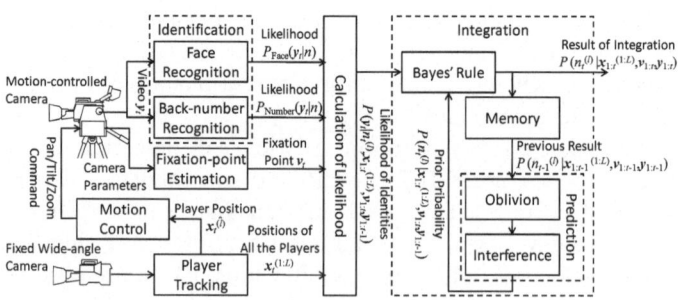

Fig. 1. System Framework

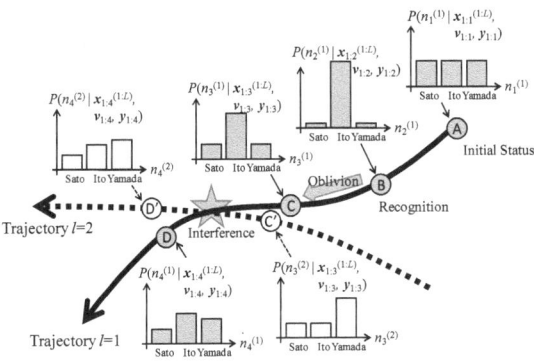

Fig. 2. Update of Probability

attempts to identify the player before and after a possible confusion of tracks due to the occlusion. Using the MC-cam parameters measured by rotary encoders, the fixation point v_t in the world coordinates can also be calculated by backprojecting the intersection of the MC-cam's optical axis and the waist-level plane (0.9 [m]) above the ground.

The player recognition process estimates the identity of the player followed by the MC-cam. Based upon the results of above mentioned processes, the system calculates the likelihood of identities of the player of fixation. The posterior probabilities of players' identities are updated sequentially by applying Bayes' rule based on the prior probability and the likelihood.

Figure 2 illustrates the way of updating probability $P(n_t^{(\ell)} \mid \boldsymbol{x}_{1:t}^{(1:L)}, \boldsymbol{v}_{1:t}, \boldsymbol{y}_{1:t})$ of identity n_t^ℓ given all the trajectories $\boldsymbol{x}_{1:t}^{(1:L)}$, fixation points $\boldsymbol{v}_{1:t}$ and WA-cam's image sequence $\boldsymbol{y}_{1:t}$, where the subscript $1:t$ denotes the temporal sequence between the instants 1 and t, and the superscript $(1:L)$ denotes the set of the trajectories 1 through L (i.e. all the trajectories in the game).

At an initial instant A in Fig. 2, no information on identity is available and a uniform probability distribution is assigned. At B, if the trajectory is identified to be the player "Ito" by the recognition process, for example, the distribution is updated to increase his probability and diminish the others' probabilities. As time elapses without further evidence of identity, the distribution flattens (from B through C in Fig. 2). This behavior of oblivion is also implemented in the system. When the player come closer to another player, during the instants C upto D, the distribution is updated by mixing that of interfering player.

3   Formulation

The system tags names (identities) to trajectories tracked in the WA-cam images by individually updating the probabilistic distribution of identities of a specific player who is followed by the MC-cam. A method for updating probabilities of identities is formulated in this section.

3.1   Posterior Probability

Bayes' rule gives the probability that the ℓ-th trajectory is of the player with the identity $n_t^{(\ell)}$ given all the trajectories $\boldsymbol{x}_{1:t}^{(1:L)}$, the fixation point $\boldsymbol{v}_{1:t}$, and images $\boldsymbol{y}_{1:t}$ by the MC-cam:

$$
\begin{aligned}
P(n_t^{(\ell)} \mid \boldsymbol{x}_{1:t}^{(1:L)}, &\boldsymbol{v}_{1:t}, \boldsymbol{y}_{1:t}) \\
&\propto P(\boldsymbol{y}_t \mid n_t^{(\ell)}, \boldsymbol{x}_{1:t}^{(1:L)}, \boldsymbol{v}_{1:t}, \boldsymbol{y}_{1:t-1}) \times P(n_t^{(\ell)} \mid \boldsymbol{x}_{1:t}^{(1:L)}, \boldsymbol{v}_{1:t}, \boldsymbol{y}_{1:t-1}) \\
&\overset{\text{def}}{=} \text{Likelihood} \times \text{Prior} ,
\end{aligned}
\tag{1}
$$

where the factor "likelihood" is that of player identity $n_t^{(\ell)}$ given the recognition result $\boldsymbol{y}_t$ of the player tracked by the MC-cam.

3.2   Update by Image Recognition

The system returns the likelihood of recognition result for the trajectory $\hat{\ell}$ whose position locates nearest to the fixation point $\boldsymbol{v}_t$. For other trajectories, the system returns a uniform distribution. The position of the fixation point is calculated by backprojecting the center of the image onto the plane whose height is 90cm (the average height of the centroids of players) above the pitch plane.

$$
\text{Likelihood} \overset{\text{def}}{=} P(\boldsymbol{y}_t \mid n_t^{(\ell)}, \boldsymbol{x}_t^{(1:L)}, \boldsymbol{v}_t) \overset{\text{def}}{\propto}
\begin{cases}
P(\boldsymbol{y}_t \mid n_t^{(\hat{\ell})}, \boldsymbol{x}_t^{(\hat{\ell})}, \boldsymbol{v}_t) & (\text{if } \ell = \hat{\ell}) \\
1 & (\text{otherwise})
\end{cases}
\tag{2}
$$

$$
\hat{\ell} = \operatorname*{argmin}_{\ell \in \{1,\dots,L\}} \| \boldsymbol{x}_t^{(\ell)} - \boldsymbol{v}_t \| .
\tag{3}
$$

3.3   Prediction

The "prior" defined in Eq. (1) can be expanded as follows by belief propagation:

$$
\begin{aligned}
\text{Prior} &= \sum_{\ell'=1}^{L} \sum_{n_t^{(\ell')}=1}^{N} \{ P(n_t^{(\ell)} \mid n_{t-1}^{(\ell')}, \boldsymbol{x}_{1:t}^{(1:L)}, \boldsymbol{v}_{1:t}, \boldsymbol{y}_{1:t-1}) \times P(n_{t-1}^{(\ell')} \mid \boldsymbol{x}_{1:t}^{(1:L)}, \boldsymbol{v}_{1:t}, \boldsymbol{y}_{1:t-1}) \} \\
&\overset{\text{def}}{=} \sum_{\ell'=1}^{L} \sum_{n_t^{(\ell')}=1}^{N} \{ \text{Predict} \times \text{Previous} \} .
\end{aligned}
\tag{4}
$$

The factors "predict" and "previous" in Eq. (4) are the prediction from the instant $t-1$ to the instant t, and the integrated result at the instant $t-1$, respectively.

The prediction formula models increasing errors and ambiguities due to tracking failures and interference among players.

In "predict" of Eq. (4), the fixation points $v_{1:t}$ and observed images $y_{1:t-1}$ can be omitted since they are independent of the prediction process, and we get:

$$\text{Predict} \stackrel{\text{def}}{=} P(n_t^{(\ell)} \mid n_{t-1}^{(\ell')}, x_t^{(1:L)})$$

$$= \sum_{n_{t-1}^{(\ell)}=1}^{N} \left\{ P(n_t^{(\ell)} \mid n_{t-1}^{(\ell)}, x_t^{(1:L)}) \times P(n_{t-1}^{(\ell)} \mid n_{t-1}^{(\ell')}, x_t^{(1:L)}) \right\}$$

$$\stackrel{\text{def}}{=} \sum_{n_{t-1}^{(\ell)}=1}^{N} \left\{ \text{Oblivion} \times \text{Mix} \right\} , \tag{5}$$

where belief propagation is employed in the second line.

3.4 Oblivion

As the risk of tracking failures increases with time, we modeled the process of ambiguation by asymptotically converging the probabilities to a predefined distribution (e.g. typically a uniform distribution).

The factor "Oblivion" in Eq. (5) models the increase of ambiguity of identities between the time indices $t-1$ and t as follows:

$$\text{Oblivion} \stackrel{\text{def}}{=} \exp\left(-\frac{\Delta T_t}{T}\right) \delta_{n_t^{(\ell)}, n_{t-1}^{(\ell)}} + \left\{ 1 - \exp\left(-\frac{\Delta T_t}{T}\right) \right\} P(n_t^{(\ell)} \mid x_t^{(1:L)}) , \tag{6}$$

where ΔT_t and T are the time interval between the indices $t-1$ and t, and the time constant of oblivion, and $\delta_{\bullet,\bullet}$ denotes the Kronecker delta. The previous belief (the first term) fades out and is replaced by an a priori ID distribution (the second term) as time elapses.

3.5 Mixing-Up

In case of occlusions, the trajectories may mix up the players to be tracked. This error is modeled by mixing the trajectory's probability distribution with those of other trajectories in the vicinity. The mixing weight is determined based on the distance between the trajectories (exponentially decreasing weight to the distance):

$$\text{Mix} \stackrel{\text{def}}{\propto} \delta_{n_{t-1}^{(\ell)}, n_{t-1}^{(\ell')}} \exp\left(-\frac{\|x_{t-1}^{(\ell')} - x_{t-1}^{(\ell)}\|}{R}\right) . \tag{7}$$

3.6 Previous Result

By ignoring dependency on the current formation (player positions) $x_t^{(1:L)}$ and the current fixation point v_t in the factor "Previous" in Eq. (4);

$$\text{Previous} \stackrel{\text{def}}{=} P(n_{t-1}^{(\ell')} \mid x_{1:t-1}^{(1:L)}, v_{1:t-1}, y_{1:t-1}) , \tag{8}$$

Eqs. (1)–(8) form a recurrence formula that updates probabilities of identities based on the recognition result.

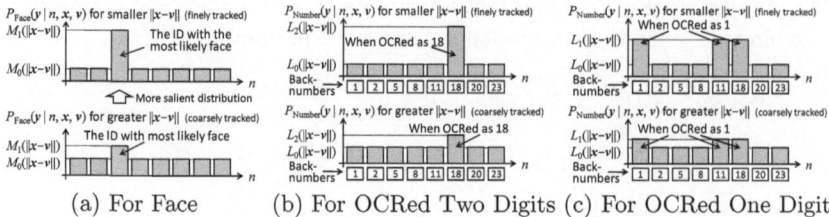

(a) For Face   (b) For OCRed Two Digits (c) For OCRed One Digit

Fig. 3. An Example of Likelihood for Identity Recognition

3.7 Implementation

We implemented face recognition and back-number recognition methods for identifying a player who is followed by the MC-cam. $P_{\mathrm{Face}}(\boldsymbol{y}_t \mid n_t, \boldsymbol{x}_t, \boldsymbol{v}_t)$ and $P_{\mathrm{Number}}(\boldsymbol{y}_t \mid n_t, \boldsymbol{x}_t, \boldsymbol{v}_t)$ denote the likelihoods given by each. The overall likelihood $P(\boldsymbol{y}_t \mid n_t, \boldsymbol{x}_t, \boldsymbol{v}_t)$ is defined by the following factorization:

$$P(\boldsymbol{y}_t \mid n_t, \boldsymbol{x}_t, \boldsymbol{v}_t) \stackrel{\mathrm{def}}{=} P_{\mathrm{Face}}(\boldsymbol{y}_t \mid n_t, \boldsymbol{x}_t, \boldsymbol{v}_t) \times P_{\mathrm{Number}}(\boldsymbol{y}_t \mid n_t, \boldsymbol{x}_t, \boldsymbol{v}_t) \ . \tag{9}$$

We adopted the distribution shown in Fig. 3(a) for face recognition:

$$P_{\mathrm{Face}}(\boldsymbol{y}_t \mid n_t, \boldsymbol{x}_t, \boldsymbol{v}_t) = \begin{cases} M_1(\|\boldsymbol{x}_t - \boldsymbol{v}_t\|) & (n_t \text{ is the most likely candidate.}) \\ M_0(\|\boldsymbol{x}_t - \boldsymbol{v}_t\|) & (\text{otherwise}) \end{cases}, \tag{10}$$

and the distributions shown in Figs. 3(b) and (c) for back-number recognition:

$$P_{\mathrm{Number}}(\boldsymbol{y}_t \mid n_t, \boldsymbol{x}_t, \boldsymbol{v}_t) = \begin{cases} L_2(\|\boldsymbol{x}_t - \boldsymbol{v}_t\|) & \begin{pmatrix} 2 \text{ digits are detected, and they} \\ \text{are the ID } n_t\text{'s back-number.} \end{pmatrix} \\ L_1(\|\boldsymbol{x}_t - \boldsymbol{v}_t\|) & \begin{pmatrix} 1 \text{ digit is detected, and it is part} \\ \text{of the ID } n_t\text{'s back-number.} \end{pmatrix}, \\ L_0(\|\boldsymbol{x}_t - \boldsymbol{v}_t\|) & (\text{otherwise}) \end{cases} \tag{11}$$

where $M_\bullet$ and $L_\bullet$ can be tuned by considering the MC-cam's tracking precision (i.e. a small $\|\boldsymbol{x}_t - \boldsymbol{v}_t\|$ means that the target player is imaged in the center).

As the back-numbers are sometimes partially occluded by the player or by others, the recognition may give one of the two digits of the player's back-number. The function with multiple peaks in Fig.3(c) is intended to deal with these partial occlusions. Note that the likelihood function should have a uniform distribution $P_\bullet(\boldsymbol{y}_t \mid n_t, \boldsymbol{x}_t, \boldsymbol{v}_t) = 1$ when no recognition results are available in order not to influence the posterior.

4   Components

The functions of peripherals other than the integration component are described in this section.

(a) Original Wide-angle Camera Image   (b) Extracted Silhouettes

(c) Tracked and Classified Players

Fig. 4. Player Tracking

4.1 Player Tracking

Based on a background subtraction method, this component firstly extracts the player silhouettes (Fig. 4(b)) from the images (Fig. 4(a)) shot by the WA-cam. The image coordinates of silhouettes are tracked simply by searching the blob nearest to the predicted centroid. Player-wise extended Kalman filters with pinhole projection and constant velocity models back-project observed centroids onto the pitch-fixed world coordinates (Fig. 4(c)).

Then, the colors of players' shirts are classified into the categories of left/right goalkeepers, left/right field players, and referees by comparing color statistics (mean, covariance, and histogram) with preregistered color samples. The component has three criteria for measuring color distance: Mahalanobis distance, and L_1 or Bhattacharyya distances between histograms.

4.2 Motion Control

The MC-cam follows and attempts to identify a player who, from the WA-cam tracking, appears likely to undergo significant occlusion several seconds hence. By doing so, the system may correct erroneous trajectories based on the recognitions of identities before and after the occlusions.

In the first stage, the component linearly predicts the formation five seconds in the future based on the current estimated positions and the velocities of the players. The system virtually places rectangular parallelepipeds at the predicted

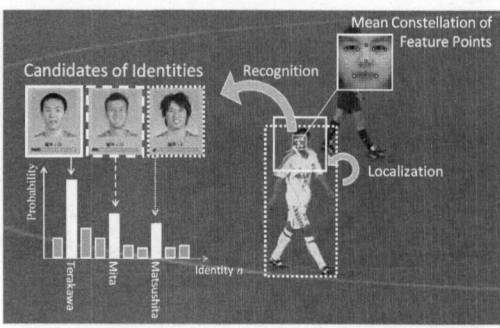

Fig. 5. Face Recognition

positions, and they are projected onto the image coordinates of the WA-cam. The system determines "the player to be followed" by selecting a player (trajectory) $\tilde{\ell}$ who maximizes the following "congestion factor" $C^{(\ell)}$:

$$C^{(\ell)} = \frac{\displaystyle\sum_{k \in \{1,2,\ldots,L\} \setminus \{\ell\}} \exp \left\{ -\frac{1}{2} \left(\frac{c_x^{(\ell)} - c_x^{(k)}}{r_x^{(\ell)}} \right)^2 - \frac{1}{2} \left(\frac{c_y^{(\ell)} - c_y^{(k)}}{r_y^{(\ell)}} \right)^2 \right\}}{2\pi r_x^{(\ell)} r_y^{(\ell)}} \quad (12)$$

$$\tilde{\ell} = \underset{\ell \in \{1,2,\ldots,L\}}{\operatorname{argmax}} \ C^{(\ell)} \ , \quad (13)$$

where $(c_x^{(\ell)}, c_y^{(\ell)})$ and $(r_x^{(\ell)}, r_y^{(\ell)})$ are the center and the dimensions of the bounding box of projected parallelepiped around the player ℓ. The $C^{(\ell)}$ in Eq.(12) places a bounding-box-sized Gaussian weight function around the target ℓ's centroid, and sums up the weight values at interfering players' centroids.

The pan, tilt, and zoom of the camera is controlled by ARW-PID (anti-reset windup proportional, integral and differential) logic to shoot the target player $\tilde{\ell}$ in the center of image at a predefined size.

4.3 Face Recognition

Firstly, the face position of the target player is roughly localized based on the camera parameters of MC-cam and WA-cam, tracked image coordinates and the

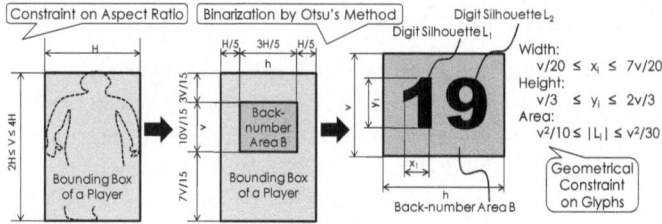

Fig. 6. Extraction of Back-number

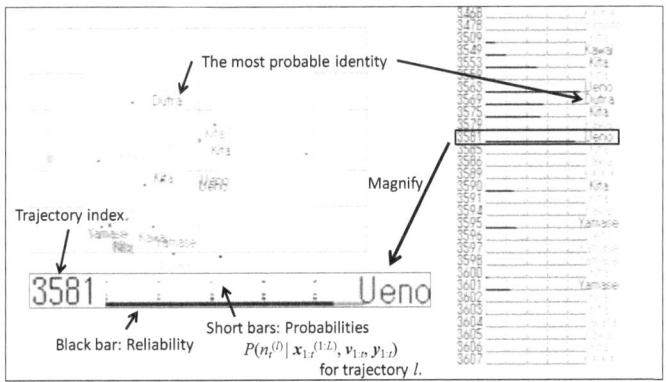

Fig. 7. An Example of Formation Aqcuired by the System

silhouette of the target player in the WA-cam image (the dotted bounding box in Fig. 5). The position is refined by our proposed sequential importance search[10] for Bayesian face detection with the Haar-cascade face detector[11]. The sequential search efficiently decimates less probable face candidates in a sequential Monte-Carlo framework making use of the visual continuity of the input image sequence.

The face recognition processes the image around detected faces to recognize their identities. It estimates the probabilities of identities of a target player in a Bayesian manner by evaluating similarities of Gabor-wavelet coefficients around nine feature points (including eye corners, nose tip, and mouth corners) on the face and deformation of the constellation of features[12].

4.4   Back-Number Recognition

The back-number of the player, who is tracked by the MC-cam, is extracted in the manner illustrated in Fig. 6. The player silhouette is extracted by "chroma-keying," which classifies each pixel by judging whether it belongs to the preregistered turf color or not.

A smaller region around the player's back is mechanically cropped, and the luminance is binarized based on Otsu's method[13]. Non-digit-like silhouettes are filtered out by evaluating their aspect ratios and sizes to get one or two digit-like silhouettes.

Finally, a commercially available OCR[1] processes the obtained glyphs to recognize the back-number.

5   Experiments

We placed a WA-cam and an MC-cam on the stand of a soccer stadium, and took videos of a soccer game played by Japanese professional soccer teams. The

---

[1] The OCR function of the system is provided by "YondeKoko typed document OCR library." YondeKoko is a registered trademark of EPSON SALES JAPAN CORPORATION.

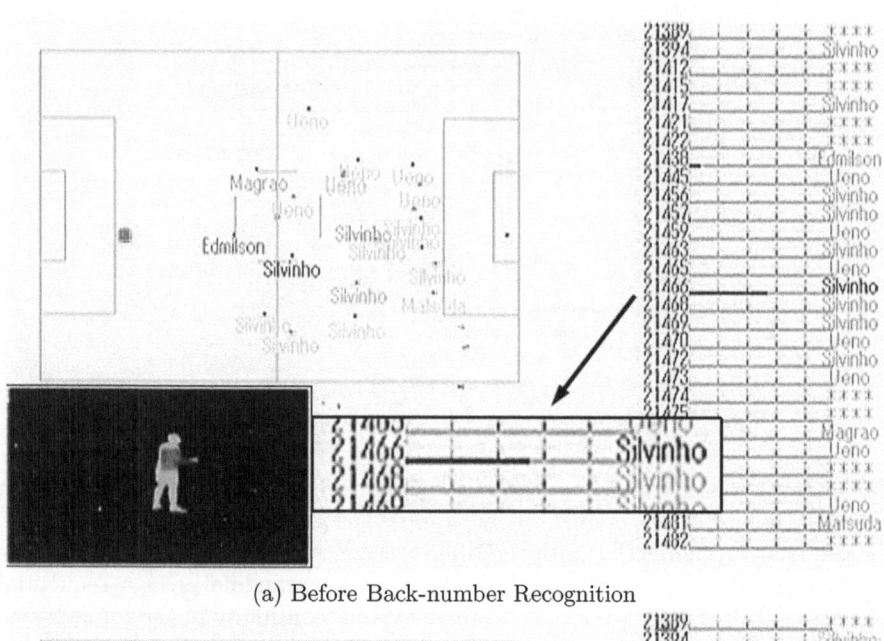

(a) Before Back-number Recognition

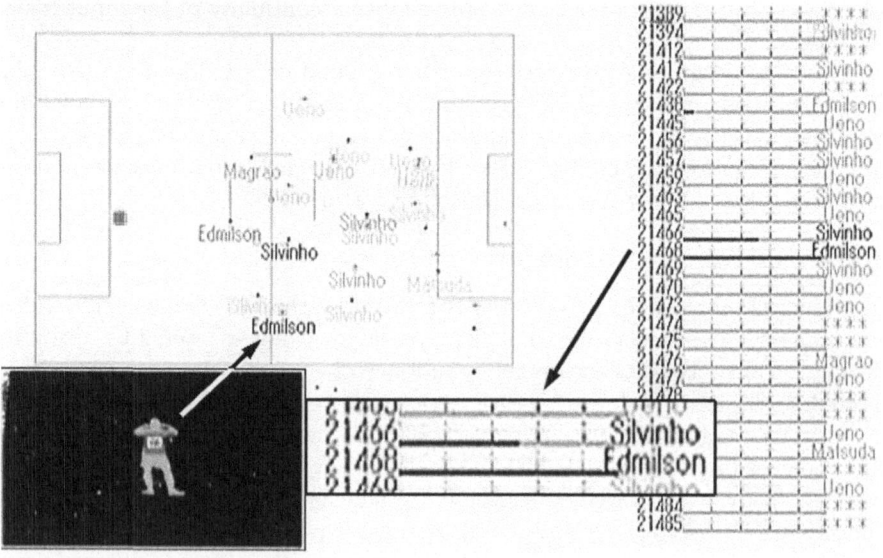

(b) After Back-number Recognition

Fig. 8. Probabilistic Update after Back-number Recognition

MC-cam was actually automatically operated on site based on the tracking of prospective occludees in WA-cam images. The two video streams and the MC-cam's camera parameters (pan, tilt, and zoom) are recorded synchronously by means of SMPTE time-codes.

Using the recorded data, we performed experiments on recognition, tracking, and their integration later in our laboratory. Although the total process is divided into those two stages in the experiments, they can theoretically be merged and be assumed to work online except for the face recogntion which has not been implemented as a real-time module yet.

Figure 7 is an example of identities estimated by integration of player tracking, back-number recognition, and face recognition. The dots in the upper-left soccer pitch area visualize the positions of the players. The string under each dot denotes the most probable identity (name) n_1:

$$n_1 = \operatorname*{argmax}_{n \in \{1,2,\dots,N\}} P(n_t^{(\ell)} \mid \boldsymbol{x}_{1:t}^{(1:L)}, \boldsymbol{v}_{1:t}, \boldsymbol{y}_{1:t}) \tag{14}$$

$$n_2 = \operatorname*{argmax}_{n \in \{1,2,\dots,N\} \setminus \{n_1\}} P(n_t^{(\ell)} \mid \boldsymbol{x}_{1:t}^{(1:L)}, \boldsymbol{v}_{1:t}, \boldsymbol{y}_{1:t}), \tag{15}$$

where n_2 is the second most probable identity.

The probabilities of identities for a specific trajectory distributes as shown by the short bars in the bottom-left closeup of the trajectory $\ell = 3581$. The reliability ρ of each identity is visualized by the brightness of the name string and by the long bar under the short bar-graph. The reliability is defined by a normalized difference between the probabilities of the first and the second candidates n_1 and n_2:

$$\rho = \{P(n_1 | \boldsymbol{x}_{1:t}^{(1:L)}, \boldsymbol{v}_{1:t}, \boldsymbol{y}_{1:t}) - P(n_2 | \boldsymbol{x}_{1:t}^{(1:L)}, \boldsymbol{v}_{1:t}, \boldsymbol{y}_{1:t})\} / P(n_1 | \boldsymbol{x}_{1:t}^{(1:L)}, \boldsymbol{v}_{1:t}, \boldsymbol{y}_{1:t}). \tag{16}$$

The behavior of the probabilistic update is exemplified in Fig. 8. The system recognized the back-number 10 for a trajectory $\ell = 21468$ in (b), and updated the probabilistic distribution. The system weakly assumed the trajectory to be Silvinho's at first as in Fig. 8(a), but it revised the estimate in (b) to have a firm conviction that it was Edmilson's.

6   Conclusion

We proposed a framework for acquiring player-identified formations from passively and actively sensed soccer videos. The processes of identification, degradation, and confusion are probabilistically modeled in a Bayesian manner.

We integrated a system with techniques of active sensing, back-number recognition, and face recognition in this framework, and performed field experiments on active sensing and laboratory investigations on data fusion. We observed the system's reasonable behavior regarding probabilistic transitions on recognition, with the passage of time, and due to interference among the players.

As the experiments above gave just a preliminary indication of the system capabilities, however, we need to collect more video and other data to evaluate system performance (robustness, error rate) quantitatively.

We are planning to extend the probabilistic formulations to utilize a priori knowledge on formations, to divert broadcasting cameras, to perform simultaneous estimation of IDs and tracks, etc. Applications to content production should also be developed to verify the usability of metadata acquired with the system.

References

1. Beetz, M., Kirchlechner, B., Lames, M.: Computerized Real-Time Analysis of Football Games. IEEE Pervasive Computing 4(3), 33–39 (2005)
2. Nitanda, N., Haseyama, M., Kitajima, H.: Audio Signal Segmentation and Classification Using Fuzzy Clustering. IEICE Trans. D-II J88-D-II(2), 302–312 (2005)
3. Sano, M., Yamada, I., Sumiyoshi, H., Yagi, N.: Automatic Real-Time Selection and Annotation of Highlight Scenes in Televised Soccer. IEICE Trans. Information and Systems E90-D(1), 224–232 (2007)
4. Ekin, A., Tekalp, A.M., Mehrotra, R.: Automatic Soccer Video Analysis and Summarization. IEEE Trans. Image Process. 12(7), 796–807 (2003)
5. Matsumoto, K., Sudo, S., Saito, H., Ozawa, S.: Optimized Camera Viewpoint Determination System for Soccer Game Broadcasting. In: Proc. MVA 2000, pp. 115–118 (2000)
6. Figueroa, P.J., Leite, N.J., Barros, R.M.L.: Tracking Soccer Players Aiming their Kinematical Motion Analysis. Computer Vision and Image Understanding 101(2), 122–135 (2006)
7. Snoek, C.G.M., Worring, M.: A Review on Multimodal Video Indexing. In: Proc. ICME 2002, vol. 2, pp. 21–24 (2002)
8. Misu, T., Takahashi, M., Tadenuma, M., Yagi, N.: Real-Time Event Detection Based on Formation Analysis of Soccer Scenes. Information Technology Letters (FIT 2005) 4 LI-003, 141–144 (2005) (in Japanese)
9. Chia, A.Y.S., Huang, W., Li, L.: Multiple Objects Tracking with Multiple Hypotheses Graph Representation. In: Proc. ICPR 2006, vol. 1, pp. 638–641 (2006)
10. Matsui, A., Clippingdale, S., Matsumoto, T.: Bayesian Sequential Face Detection with Automatic Re-initialization. In: Proc. ICPR 2008 (to appear, 2008)
11. Viola, P., Jones, M.: Rapid Object Detection Using a Boosted Cascade of Simple Features. In: Proc. CVPR 2001, vol. 1, pp. 511–518 (2001)
12. Clippingdale, S., Ito, T.: A Unified Approach to Video Face Detection, Tracking and Reognition. In: Proc. ICIP 1999, p. 232 (1999)
13. Otsu, N.: A Threshold Selection Method from Gray-level Histograms. IEEE Trans. Syst. Man Cybern. 9(1), 62–66 (1979)

A Fast and Fully Format Compliant Protection of JPEG2000 Code-Streams[*]

Yang Ou[1], Chul Sur[2], and Kyung Hyune Rhee[3],[**]

[1] Department of Information Security, Pukyong National University,
599-1, Daeyeon3-Dong, Nam-Gu, Busan 608-737, Republic of Korea
ouyang@pknu.ac.kr
[2] Department of Computer Science, Pukyong National University
kahlil@pknu.ac.kr
[3] Division of Electronic, Computer and Telecommunication Engineering,
Pukyong National University
khrhee@pknu.ac.kr

Abstract. Direct encryption for the JPEG2000 code-streams by using a conventional block cipher needs an additional processing time, whereas the joint compression and encryption schemes increase the coding efficiency but with some sacrifices in security. In this paper, a Dually Randomized MQ coder (DRMQ) is presented to support both compression and encryption functionalities, and to achieve tradeoff between security and efficiency. The proposed DRMQ coder avoids the permutations of input/output bits to enhance security. It makes use of a dual randomization to provide more protected results. Furthermore, we show that the DRMQ coder can be combined with a format compliant header encryption algorithm to achieve a fast and full protection of JPEG2000 code-streams. The experimental results confirm the efficiency and encryption performance of our scheme.

Keywords: JPEG2000, Joint Compression and Encryption, Arithmetic Coding, Packet Header Encryption.

1 Introduction

With the spreading use of multimedia applications, securing multimedia data has become an important research field. The problem of efficient multimedia data encryption, in particular, has recently gained more attention in both academia and industry. Due to the large volumes of multimedia data, most multimedia data encryption algorithms are applied during or after compression.

In the area of still image compression, JPEG2000 [10] is the newest scalable image coding standard, where a number of encryption algorithms has been made concerning the security of JPEG2000 images. A straightforward approach

---

[*] This work was supported by the Korea Science and Engineering Foundation(KOSEF) grant funded by the Korea government(MOST) (No. R01-2006-00-10260-0).
[**] Corresponding author.

B. Huet et al. (Eds.): MMM 2009, LNCS 5371, pp. 51–62, 2009.

is to encrypt entire code-streams by using conventional cryptographic algorithms, such as DES and AES. However, the computational cost associated with encrypting the entire content is often high. In order to increase the encryption efficiency, several selective encryption schemes have been proposed [7,8], where only a fraction of compressed bitstream is selectively encrypted. Nevertheless, this kind of encryption may degrade the security level since the information contained in the non-encrypted data can be used to find out the visual information of encrypted version [9]. In addition, direct encryption on compressed data should be avoided destroying the format syntax so that the encrypted bitstream can be compatible with standard format decoder [12].

The recent trend in JPEG2000 encryption research has more attention on joint compression and encryption schemes, which aim to improve the efficiency by doing both compression and encryption in a single step. Especially, introducing randomness into entropy coder for joint schemes is becoming more attractive. JPEG2000 uses binary arithmetic coder, called MQ coder, for entropy coding. There are several encryption algorithms designed based on arithmetic coder recently, where the representative ones include Arithmetic Coding with Key-based interval Splitting (KSAC) [11] and Randomized Arithmetic Coding (RAC) [3]. KSAC uses keys to specify how the intervals will be partitioned in each iteration of the arithmetic encoding. However, the interval splitting doubles the amount of memory and an additional multiplication is needed for renormalization. In contrast with KSAC, RAC is implemented by randomly swapping the order of two intervals in a binary arithmetic coder, where the interval swap is controlled by a pseudo-random bit sequence. It achieves almost similar coding efficiency as original arithmetic coder and can be utilized to encrypt JPEG2000 images. On the other hand, the security of several joint algorithms is discussed in [5], which shows that KSAC is vulnerable to the known plaintext attack. Accordingly, a secure arithmetic coder (SAC) [6] adding permutations on both inputs and outputs of KSAC is proposed to improve the security level. The enhancing algorithm, however, only focuses on scrambling of input/output symbols but not actually strengthening the coding conventions of entropy coder. In addition, it is claimed that a cryptographic secure pseudorandom number generator should be used in RAC in order to ensure the security of this encryption algorithm.

More recently, Engel et al. [1,2] discuss that only encryption of the packet body data cannot provide complete confidentiality, because the packet header data in JPEG2000 code-streams also leaks image visual information which can be utilized to reconstruct a rough thumbnail image. Consequently, they proposed a set of transformations that allows protection of the JPEG2000 packet header data in a fully format-compliant way. Furthermore, it is demonstrated that the protection of packet headers can be combined with partial packet body encryption for a decrease in computational demands.

Our Contributions. In this paper, aiming to achieve tradeoff between efficiency and security, we propose a Dually Randomized MQ coder (DRMQ) which carries out the encryption and compression simultaneously in a secure and fast

manner. Our approach is motivated by an efficient error detecting MQF coder
[4] and we simply transform it into a fast joint encryption algorithm. The DRMQ
coder is more efficient than SAC since it avoids permutations in input/output
bits, and also there is no need to double the amount of memory and additional
multiplications. Our DRMQ coder provides a higher security level than RAC by
means of the dual randomization as well as key composition and space. Moreover,
we show that a format compliant header encryption algorithm [2] can be combined with our DRMQ coder to achieve a fast and full protection of JPEG2000
code-streams, rather than combining with a conventional encryption scheme of
packet bodies using additional block cipher. The experimental results confirm
the efficiency and encryption performance of our approach.

The remainder of the paper is organized as follows. In Section 2, we review
the MQ coder and code-stream structure in JPEG2000. Section 3 presents our
proposed scheme. We give the efficiency and security evaluations of the proposed
scheme in Section 4. Finally, we conclude the paper in Section 5.

2 Preliminaries

In JPEG2000, each code-block in wavelet sub-bands is independently entropy
coded by a context-based adaptive arithmetic coder, e.g. MQ coder. The compressed bitstreams of each code-block are truncated and embedded into the final
JPEG2000 code-stream. In the following, we review the coding algorithm of MQ
coder and the code-stream structure of JPEG2000.

2.1 The MQ Coder

The multiplication free arithmetic coder, known as MQ coder, is a binary and
adaptive arithmetic coder used to encode the decision bits d_i corresponding to
a bit-plane of a code-block in a JPEG2000 image. The encoding task is based
on the recursive probability interval partition. At each iteration, the interval
is split into two subintervals. In the partition of probability interval, the MQ
coder decides in advance whether the interval related either to the least probable
symbol (LPS) or to the most probable symbol (MPS) comes first.

The code string $\mathbf{C}$ is adjusted as to point to the base of the subinterval that
corresponds to the input symbol d_i. The probability model is adapted to the
source statistics by updating the probability Q_e of LPS for the next iteration.
Moreover, MQ partitions the interval without using multiplications. In fact, the
probability interval A is guaranteed to be in the range $0.75 \leq A < 1.5$, so as that
the approximations are assumed: (a) If the LPS occurs, the interval is reduced to
$Q_e \simeq A \cdot Q_e$; (b) If the MPS occurs, the interval is updated to $A - Q_e \simeq A - A \cdot Q_e$.
In the latter case Q_e is added to the code string $\mathbf{C}$, in order to make it point to
the base of the MPS subinterval. The MQ decoder performs the dual operation
and, given the code string $\mathbf{C}$ and the context labels, outputs the corresponding
binary decision bits d_i. The decoding process should be synchronized in order to
decode the image correctly.

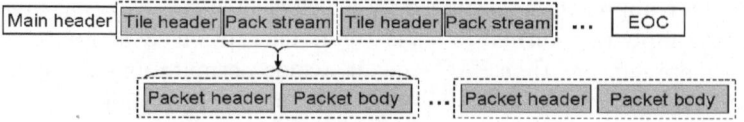

Fig. 1. The Code-stream Structure of JPEG2000

2.2   The Code-Stream Structure of JPEG2000

The JPEG2000 code-stream consists of headers (main headers, tile headers) and packets that include packet headers and packet bodies as shown in Fig.1. The output of MQ coder, i.e. the compressed bitstream, is contained in the packet bodies. The packet header contains four main types information as follows:

- *Code-block inclusion.* The inclusion information for a certain quality layer for all code-blocks in the precinct associated with the packet.
- *Zero bit-plane information.* The number of leading zero bit-planes (LZB) from the most significant bit-plane.
- *Number of coding passes.* The number of coding passes (NCP) that are contained in the packet for each code-block.
- *Code-block Contribution.* The length of the contribution of each code-block to the packet (CCP).

3   Fast and Full Protection of JPEG2000 Code-Streams

3.1   Naive Approach

Our approach exploits the fact that the arithmetic decoding is very sensitive to errors, where a single erroneous decoding step is able to cause an irreversible drift, thus it makes the decoded data completely useless. If we can force decoding errors in an arithmetic coder using a decoding key, then the compressed data will not be properly decoded without knowing the key. Consequently, we are motivated by a modified MQ coder, called MQF coder [4], which is originally used for error detection. The MQF coder is a ternary arithmetic coder where there is a Forbidden region with probability Q_f added at the base of the probability interval to provide some redundancy, while a synchronized decoder can detect error occurring and conceal wrong decision bits (Fig.2). The main merit of MQF is that the encoder complexity is almost the same as standard MQ coder since only one supplementary addition is needed.

On the other hand, referring to the coding details of MQ coder introduced in Section 2.1, we notice that in decoding side, there is a vital parameter which determine the value of next decision bit, i.e. the code string **C**. Without knowing the code string **C** at the decoder, the decision bits cannot be correctly decoded. Thus, we can utilize the addition of Q_f to secretly alter the code string **C**. The Q_f should be secretly kept in a small interval range to reduce the coding redundancy.

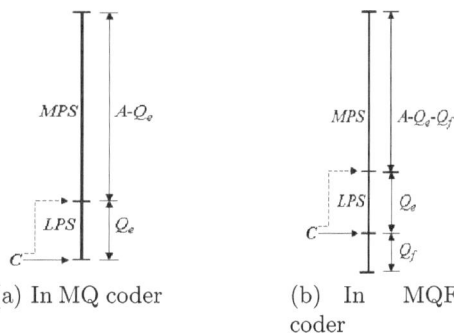

(a) In MQ coder   (b) In MQF coder

Fig. 2. Interval splitting

Direct encryption to the codes string $\mathbf{C}$ will cause a totally different value. So we randomly add a subinterval, since $\mathbf{C}$ should be kept as much as possible in order to avoid the destruction of compression efficiency. It is worth noting that, the goal of our algorithm is to design a secure arithmetic coder, but not to target on increasing the error control capability. Nevertheless, our scheme saves all the error resilience tools in JPEG2000 baseline.

The value of Q_f should be kept secretly, while the coding redundancy carried by it amounts to $R_f = -log_2(1 - Q_f)$ bits per input symbol [4]. In JPEG2000 the rate-distortion optimization may disturb this added redundancy. The total data rate-increasing ratio, however, could expose the subinterval Q_f. Therefore, adding a fixed Q_f to the code string $\mathbf{C}$ for each input symbol would cause that the encryption is vulnerable to the known plaintext attack.

3.2 Dually Randomized MQ Coder

To ensure the security of compressed/encrypted bitstream, we propose a dually randomized MQ coder to make the output bits more protected. In our proposed DRMQ coder, the code string $\mathbf{C}$ is not always changed at every iteration, but is selected randomly. It also happens when we use random Q_f instead of fixed Q_f. The details of coding procedures are shown in Fig.3. There are two Pseudo-Random Number Sequences (PRNG) driven to carry out the dual randomization:

- PRNG$_1$: randomly generate a controlling bit to control whether the code string C is modified or not.
- PRNG$_2$: randomly generate the subinterval Q_f within a predefined range M_{Q_f}.

where two seed values S_1 and S_2 are needed to initialize the PRNGs. Here we assume that the two PRNGs are cryptographically secure.

In practice, the pseudo-random bit sequence is taken on value 0 and 1 with probability 0.5. This invariant probability would also reveal information of Q_f. Moreover, since the arithmetic coder is very sensitive to errors, a small probability can cause a decoding drift that makes the decoded data completely useless.

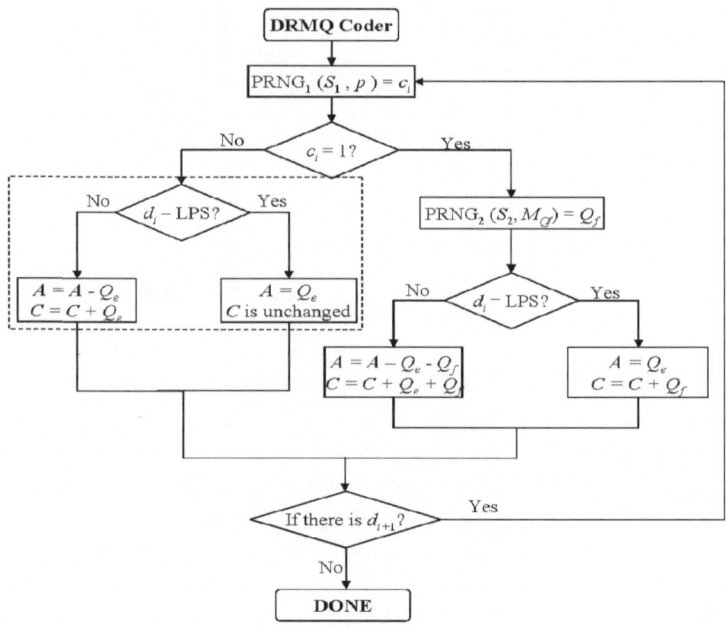

Fig. 3. The coding pipeline of DRMQ coder

Therefore, the subinterval addition can be triggered with a predefined probability p which should also be kept secretly. In particular, at each encoding step, a controlling bit c_i is drawn to decide whether adding Q_f or not with probability p or $1 - p$, respectively.

The subinterval Q_f is randomly generated by the second PRNG. Q_f can be flexibly adjusted to a proper precision in an acceptable range depending on the requirement of different applications, where the range should be no more than the interval of LPS in order to guarantee that MQ coder works without any crash. Due to the compression redundancy brought by Q_f, it is suggested to randomly generate Q_f in the small range M_{Q_f}. In particular, for each decision bit d_i, when $c_i = 0$, d_i is encoded as normal as original MQ coder. Otherwise, a random subinterval Q_f is added to conceal the original intervals.

Our DRMQ coder works with a fourfold key $\mathbf{K} = (S_1, S_2, p, M_{Q_f})$ since the two parameters p and M_{Q_f} controlling PRNGs should also be kept secretly like seed values. Given the same $\mathbf{K}$, both encoder and decoder generate the same controlling bit sequence. The subinterval Q_f is also generated for decision bits d_i and is added to the corresponding code string $\mathbf{C}$ in order to synchronize with each other. Moreover, four key components are cooperated closely with each other. As long as one of them is unknown or incorrectly given, the decoder cannot decode the compressed data properly, and the decompressed data is almost meaningless. It is worth noticing that, in JPEG2000 each code block in wavelet sub-bands is arithmetically encoded independently. A code block can be taken as the basic encryption cell in DRMQ coder and integrated with different $\mathbf{K}$.

Selection of Two Secret Parameters: p **and** M_{Q_f}. The probability p can be arbitrarily chosen on $(0, 1]$. When $p = 0$, it means no additive operation of Q_f and no code string $\mathbf{C}$ is modified. Hence the DRMQ coder is performed exactly the same as original MQ coder (The dotted lines in Fig.3). With the increasing of p, more values of Q_f are randomly generated and added to the corresponding code string $\mathbf{C}$. It seems that larger p may results in an incremental compression redundancy, whereas small p may not achieve an expected security level. However, due to the sensitivity of arithmetic coder, a very small p can induce the decoded data meaningless. In the following Section, we will show that a satisfactory encryption performance can be achieved when $p > 0.002$.

The selection of M_{Q_f} should be restricted in a small range in order to confine the compression redundancy increases. However, the upper limit of this overhead is a little ambiguous. Sometimes, during JPEG2000 compression, the usage of segmentation markers has also a certain negative influence on compression performance, e.g. in [1] it is pointed that inserting SOP and EPH markers results in a moderate overhead of 1.68%. Therefore, we may consider a proper threshold depending on the application requirements. For example, the increasing of final bitstream size due to encryption should not be higher than 3% of the original coded bitstream, with an approximated $M_{Q_f} = 0.06$.

Both p and M_{Q_f} are binary represented and normalized with an available precision. For example, if 16-bit is used, the precision will be 2^{-16} which is approximately equal to 10^{-6}. More details and discussion about the selection of p and M_{Q_f} will be presented in Section 4.

3.3   Combination with Packet Header Protection

Since the encrypted/compressed bitstream by DRMQ coder is contained in packet bodies, the packet headers are still left in plaintext. Here we present how to employ an efficient packet header encryption algorithm to protect header information.

The packet header protection is firstly presented in [2]. A set of transformations of four classes information are proposed to protect packet header. However, from the similarity test of header information in [2], we find that the similarity of inclusion information for 175 test images is above 0.8. That means the inclusion information may not serve as a clear discriminating feature. Moreover, the permutation of inclusion information should be restricted to a rigorously transition between two packets belonging to two neighboring layers in order to preserve format syntax. For the sake of simplicity and efficiency, we only employ the transformations of LZB, NCP and CCP in packet header, and do not touch the inclusion information. To combine DRMQ coder with header protection, firstly, an image is fed into JPEG2000 compression engine with our DRMQ coder, then after forming the final code-stream, the LZB, NCP and CCP in each packet header are collected and encrypted. More details of packet header encryption can be referred to [1,2].

4   Evaluations

In this section, we evaluate our proposed scheme in terms of three different aspects: compression efficiency, encryption performance and security.

The proposed scheme has been implemented based on the publicly available JPEG2000 implementation JJ2000 (Version 4.1) [14]. The encryption is simulated on gray level images with 8 bit per pixel (bpp). In our experiments, we use the JPEG2000 default parameter settings. For the sake of simplicity, p and M_{Q_f} are set with precision of 10^{-3} and 10^{-6}, respectively. It is worth noting that this precision is not fixed and can be flexibly adjusted depending on the requirement of the target application.

4.1   Evaluation of Compression Efficiency

The fundamental goal of multimedia compression is to reduce the bitstream length to minimize the possible extent. The multimedia encryption schemes should ensure that there is little or no destruction on compression ratio. The subinterval Q_f in our DRMQ coder seems to be a threat to compression efficiency. However, in Fig.4 we show that the increase of redundancy caused by Q_f is so small that it can be neglected. We demonstrate the overheads caused by fixed and random Q_f in three different probabilities. Obviously, use of the fixed Q_f introduces a faster increase of redundancy. This increment in Fig.4(a) may reveal a rough range of Q_f which can be utilized to attack the exactly Q_f on condition that the attacker knows exact p. However, use of the random value of Q_f can introduce more confusions, since even though one may find the range of Q_f, he cannot exactly know what random value is added at which position. Moreover, we find that in some cases, the increase redundancy ratios are lower than 0. This means that the compression efficiency in DRMQ coder is higher than original one.

4.2   Evaluation of Encryption Performance

The probability p is an interesting secret parameter which controls the number of encryption bits. One may consider that small p cannot guarantee the complete

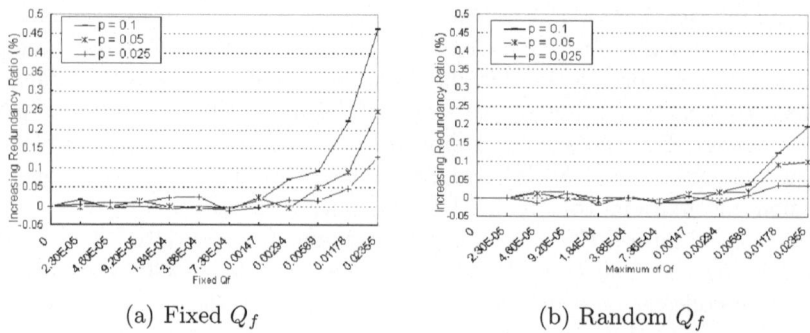

(a) Fixed Q_f (b) Random Q_f

Fig. 4. The increasing redundancy ratio with random/fixed Q_f

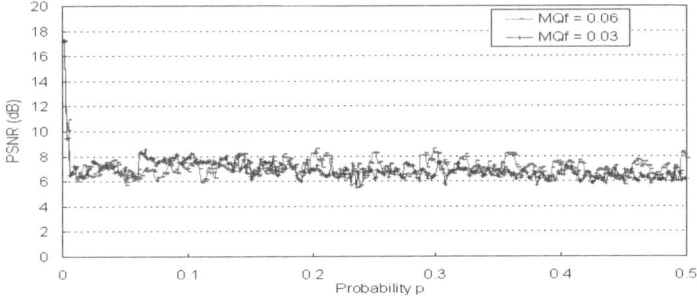

Fig. 5. PSNR performance with increasing probability p

visual destruction of an image. Nevertheless, this viewpoint is denied in Fig.5. We demonstrate the PSNR performance with a probability in $(0, 0.5]$. It is observed that only the first two PSNR values exceed 10dB but less than 18dB. The other PSNR values are stably fluctuating in $5 \sim 9$dB. Generally, an image with a PSNR less than 15 dB cannot be recognized totally. This means that by using DRMQ coder, as long as $p > 0.002$, the encrypted image is fully meaningless. One example of visual performance after encryption is shown in Fig.6. On the other hand, we find that the PSNR values from two different M_{Q_f} are overlapping each other. This result is very satisfactory and reflects that different M_{Q_f} can also generate stable encryption performance. Therefore, there is no need to worry about the encryption effectiveness of small M_{Q_f}.

(a) Original image   (b) $p=0.001$,PSNR=17.1dB   (c) $p=0.005$,PSNR=9.5dB

Fig. 6. The visual performance of encrypted Goldhill with $\mathbf{K} = (1024, 1024, p, 0.06)$

Table 1. Comparisons of encryption time costs between DRMQ and AES (time: ms; PSNR: dB)

Image	AES PBE+PHE		DRMQ+PHE		Reducing
	Time	PSNR	Time	PSNR	ratio (time)
Lena	1718	9.36	734	9.83	57.3 %
Baboon	1765	10.13	796	10.76	54.9 %
Grave	1712	5.66	781	5.86	54.4 %

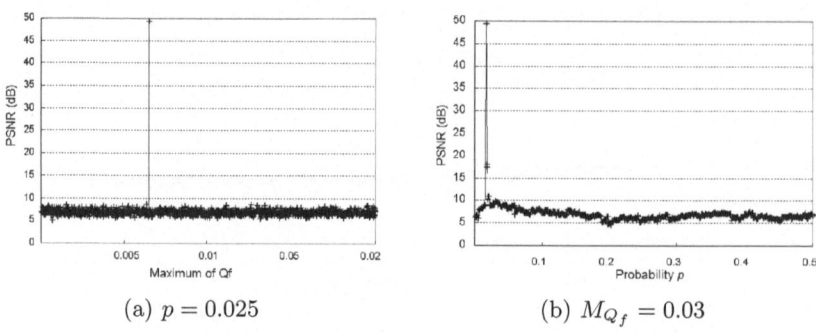

(a) $p = 0.025$ (b) $M_{Q_f} = 0.03$

Fig. 7. Heuristic attempts of M_{Q_f} and p

The encryption time cost of combining DRMQ coder (using **K**=1024,1024, 0.05,0.03) with packet header encryption (PHE) is shown in Table 1. We also demonstrate the time cost of the header encryption combining with packet body encryption (PBE) using AES. Due to the unstable processes in computer system, we take 20 trials and select the most frequently occurred result as the final time cost value. Obviously, Table.1 reflects that in order to fully protect JPEG2000 code-streams, joint schemes combining with packet header encryption achieve a much faster performance than conventional cryptographic algorithms.

4.3 Evaluation of Security

The fourfold **K** used in our DRMQ coder is very attractive since four key parameters must cooperate closely with each other for decryption. At the first sight, there seems that close values of M_{Q_f} lead to similar offset of code string **C** which in turn lead to similar PSNR performance. Of course, this might be a threat to the security of the system since an attacker does not need to know the parameter M_{Q_f} exactly to get a "decrypted" image with sufficient quality. However, Fig.7 obviously depicts that our scheme is adequately secure against this heuristic attack. Suppose that the attacker knows every key parameters but except M_{Q_f}, and tries possible values of M_{Q_f} in $(0, 0.02]$. As can be seen in Fig.7(a), the decoder achieves very low PSNR (below 9 dB) nearly everywhere except the position of the correct M_{Q_f} where this is an isolated single quality peak of PSNR. In addition, the situation of probability p is not as optimistic as M_{Q_f} but still acceptable as shown in Fig.7(b). Moreover, due to the robustness of M_{Q_f}, p cannot be easily snatched. On the other hand, the two seed values (S_1, S_2) are not intended to be discussed in detail since different seeds can generate totally different outputs of PRNG which are surely satisfied for our DRMQ coder.

In the following, we discuss the advantages of our DRMQ coder by comparing with other schemes. The main difference between our DRMQ coder and other arithmetic coder-based encryption schemes is that in encoder side we never touch the added subinterval Q_f. Nevertheless, KSAC and RAC divide or swap the probability intervals in each iterations, while all modified subintervals are used for encoding input symbols. Since the final output of arithmetic coder depends on the last subinterval at the last iteration step, known-planintext attack is vulnerable for both KSAC and RAC by making use this coding convention [5]. Moreover, the fact that, in KSAC there are some restrictions for selecting the splitting positions, is also favorable for attackers. In contrast with these two schemes, our DRMQ coder preserves a similar size of subinterval in each iteration step, where a decoding error (encryption) is brought by the cumulation of adding Q_f. Therefore, the output of DRMQ coder is not explicitly related with Q_f. From this merit we can deduce that the known-plaintext attack is difficult for our DRMQ coder, at least, the cryptanalysis algorithm in [5] could not work well with DRMQ coder.

On the other hand, since all schemes based on arithmetic coder are relied on the modification of the interval ranges at each coding iteration in order to mess up the outputs, here we consider about the randomization in only one encoding iteration in DRMQ coder and other coders. Concerning KSAC, note that the number of splitting intervals in KSAC should be small in order to save the computational cost. It is suggested that two bits should be used to specify the interval splitting [5], thus there will be four available choices for one symbol. Hence, one can simply try $4! = 24$ trials to find the correct splitting position. Moreover, it is more easily observed that in RAC there are only two possible choices in one iteration: swap and no swap. However, in our DRMQ coder, if Q_f is assumed only to 16-bit, one should try $2^{16} = 65536$ trials in one iteration which is larger than KSAC and RAC. Therefore, depending on the above discussion, our DRMQ coder provides a higher security level than as in both previous schemes.

5   Conclusion

In this paper, we have proposed a joint compression and encryption scheme called DRMQ coder, based on a modified arithmetic coder to encrypt JPEG2000 images. The proposed DRMQ coder can be efficiently implemented since it avoids permutations and there is no additional multiplications. We have demonstrated that DRMQ coder has negligible overhead on compression efficiency, also the encryption performance is satisfactory. Moreover, we showed how to combine packet header encryption with our DRMQ coder to achieve a fast and full protection of JPEG2000 code-streams. Finally, we have compared the DRMQ coder with other two previous schemes and analyzed that our DRMQ coder has a comparable, even higher security level than other schemes.

Acknowledgments. We are grateful to Dominik Engel for providing JPEG2000 packet header encryption source code. And we thank the anonymous reviewers for their valuable comments.

References

1. Engel, D., Stütz, T., Uhl, A.: Format-compliant JPEG2000 Encryption in JPSEC: Security, Applicability and the Impact of Compression Parameters. EURASIP Journal on Information Security, Article ID 94565 (2007)

2. Engel, D., Stütz, T., Uhl, A.: Format-Compliant JPEG2000 Encryption with Combined Packet Header and Packet Body Protection. In: Multimedia and Security Workshop, ACM Multimedia, pp. 87–95 (2007)
3. Grangetto, M., Magli, E., Olmo, G.: Multimedia Selective Encryption by Means of Randomized Arithmetic Coding. IEEE Transactions on Multimedia 8(5), 905–917 (2006)
4. Grangetto, M., Magli, E., Olmo, G.: A Syntax-preserving Error Resilience Tool for JPEG2000 Based on Error Correcting Arithmetic Coding. IEEE Transactions on Image processing 15(4), 807–818 (2006)
5. Jakimoski, G., Subbalakshmi, K.P.: Cryptanalysis of Some Multimedia Encryption Schemes. IEEE Transactions on Multimedia 10(3), 330–338 (2008)
6. Kim, H., Wen, J., Villasenor, J.D.: Secure Arithmetic Coding. IEEE Transactions on Signal processing 55(5), 2263–2272 (2007)
7. Lian, S., Sun, J., Zhang, D., Wang, Z.: A Selective Image Encryption Scheme Based on JPEG2000 Codec. In: Aizawa, K., Nakamura, Y., Satoh, S. (eds.) PCM 2004. LNCS, vol. 3332, pp. 65–72. Springer, Heidelberg (2004)
8. Norcen, R., Uhl, A.: Selective Encryption of the JPEG2000 Bitstream. In: Lioy, A., Mazzocchi, D. (eds.) CMS 2003. LNCS, vol. 2828, pp. 194–204. Springer, Heidelberg (2003)
9. Said, A.: Measuring the Strength of Partial Encryption Schemes. In: IEEE International Conference on Image Processing (ICIP), pp. 1126–1129 (2005)
10. Taubman, D., Marcellin, M.: JPEG2000 Image Compression Fundamentals, Standards and Practice. Kluwer Academic Publishers, Boston (2002)
11. Wen, J., Kim, H., Villasenor, J.D.: Binary Arithmetic Coding with Key-based Interval Splitting. IEEE Signal Processing Letters 13(2), 69–72 (2006)
12. Wu, Y., Deng, R.H.: Compliant Encryption of JPEG2000 Codestreams. In: IEEE International Conference on Image Processing, pp. 3439–3442 (2004)
13. Wu, C.P., Kuo, C.C.J.: Design of Integrated Multimedia Compression and Encryption Systems. IEEE Transactions on Multimedia 7(5), 828–839 (2005)
14. JJ2000-Java Implementation of JPEG2000, http://jpeg2000.epfl.ch/

Towards a New Image-Based Spectrogram Segmentation Speech Coder Optimised for Intelligibility

K.A. Jellyman[1], N.W.D. Evans[1,2], W.M. Liu[1], and J.S.D. Mason[1]

[1] School of Engineering, Swansea University, UK
174869@swan.ac.uk, 199997@swan.ac.uk, j.s.d.mason@swan.ac.uk
[2] EURECOM, Sophia Antipolis, France
nicholas.evans@eurecom.fr

Abstract. Speech intelligibility is the very essence of communications. When high noise can degrade a speech signal to the threshold of intelligibility, for example in mobile and military applications, introducing further degradation by a speech coder could prove critical. This paper investigates concepts towards a new speech coder that draws upon the field of image processing in a new multimedia approach. The coder is based on a spectrogram segmentation image processing procedure. The design criterion is for minimal intelligibility loss in high noise, as opposed to the conventional quality criterion, and the bit rate must be reasonable. First phase intelligibility listening test results assessing its potential alongside six standard coders are reported. Experimental results show the robustness of the LD-CELP coder, and the potential of the new coder with particularly good results in car noise conditions below -4.0dB.

1 Introduction

Speech communications has been revolutionised by mobile communications allowing phone calls to be made almost "anywhere and at anytime" [1]. One consequence of this expectation is the increased potential for background noise that can be sufficiently strong so that it threatens intelligibility.

Intelligibility is the very essence without which communication does not exist. Originally high levels of noise would have been more common place with military and security applications. Now though, phone usage is no longer restricted to the typical relatively quiet home and office environments. It is therefore perhaps surprising that despite the potential for high levels of background noise relatively little attention has been given to the topic of intelligibility assessment, certainly when compared with the more general overarching speech quality assessment [2]. It is perhaps even more surprising that this is the case even in military and security applications [3, 4, 5, 6].

Quality is all encompassing and includes intelligibility along with many other attributes including naturalness, ease of listening, and loudness. Unfortunately predicting intelligibility from overall quality tends not to be straightforward. A number of authors have observed this including [3, 2, 7, 8].

B. Huet et al. (Eds.): MMM 2009, LNCS 5371, pp. 63–73, 2009.

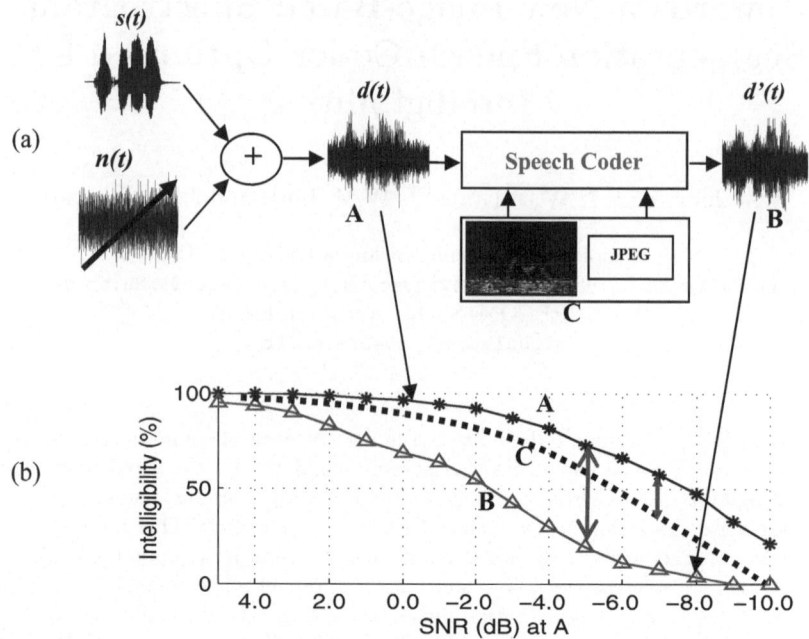

Fig. 1. Figure (a) shows clean speech degraded by an increasing level of additive noise, (A), followed by encoding and de-coding, to give speech further degraded by the coding (B) with the corresponding intelligibility profile (B) in Figure (b); the coder profile (B) is a standard MELP coder. The goal is to reduce this additional degradation by using an alternative coder, to give enhanced (here hypothetical) profile, example (C). A new image-based spectrogram segmentation coder that uses JPEG compression is investigated for this role.

The situation considered is illustrated in Figure 1(a). A clean speech signal $s(t)$ is combined with high levels of additive noise $n(t)$. As the SNR decreases the intelligibility of the signal combination $d(t)$ falls, as shown in Figure 1(b), profile A. Profiles A and B in Figure 1(b) come from intelligibility tests performed by a small group of listeners. Following the coding and transmission operations it is likely that the resultant signal $d'(t)$ suffers further degradation and consequently now exhibits lower intelligibility; this is shown in the lowest profile in Figure 1(b), profile B. This profile comes from a second set of tests performed by the same small group of listeners. The contribution to the additional fall in intelligibility (profile A to profile B) is due to the encoder and decoder operations, in this case a standard low bit rate MELP coder [9]. It can be seen that the level of intelligibility loss due to the coder increases and is particularly severe when the SNR is in the region of -2 to -8dB. The goal of the work presented here is to design a speech coder which minimises this additional coder degradation, while maintaining a reasonable bit rate. For illustrative purposes this is indicated by the hypothetical coder profile, labelled C in Figure 1(a).

The major contribution of this paper is in the investigation of concepts towards a new image-based spectrogram segmentation speech coder designed for intelligibility preservation in high noise conditions. The segmentation procedure, originally proposed by Hory and Martin [10], identifies potentially useful speech dominant information in time and frequency. The coder fuses both speech and image processing techniques in a new multimedia approach applied to the well researched problem of speech coding.

In the reported experiments we consider utterances comprising of connected, four-digit strings. The utterances span typically 1.5 to 2.0s. The coder is therefore not suitable for normal telephony usage because of the inherent delay from using spectrograms. For conversational communications the delay must typically not exceed 0.3s [11]. Thus this coder is targeted towards one way communication applications, such as military and security recording systems, where delay can be readily tolerated.

The structure of this paper is as follows: Section 2 presents an assessment of 6 standard coders, with bit rates ranging from 2.4kb/s up to 32kb/s, for their contributions to intelligibility in high noise. The assessment is presented in a manner similar to that used to derive profile B in Figure 1(b). The results from the standard coders form benchmarks for the new coder. This assessment is believed to be a first comparing a range of coders under otherwise identical noise conditions using intelligibility as the cost function; Section 3 describes the experimental image-based spectrogram segmentation coder; and Section 4 presents an intelligibility assessment of the spectrogram segmentation coder in comparison to the results from Section 2.

2   Assessment of Standard Coders

Six coders are assessed here. They are: (i) the G.721 adaptive differential pulse code modulation coder [12]; (ii) the adaptive multi-rate (AMR) coder [13]; (iii) the low delay-code excited linear predictive coder [14] (iv) the Groupe Special Mobile-full rate (GSM-FR) coder [15]; (v) the mixed excitation linear predictive (MELP) coder [9]; and (vi) the linear predictive coder (LPC-10) [16]. All six coders are used widely, are reported to have reasonable speech quality performances and have bandwidths of 32.0kb/s, 12.2kb/s, 16.0kb/s, 13kb/s, 2.4kb/s and 2.4kb/s respectively. Software implementations of all six coders are freely available at [17, 18, 19, 20, 21, 22].

2.1   Intelligibility Assessment

Reliable intelligibility assessment is an extremely difficult task. Human opinion is costly, and scores can vary across vocabulary, language, context, listeners and many such practical factors. To help circumvent some of the difficulties we restrict our assessment to digit strings, following a procedure which we proposed in [23]. Digits provide for a straightforward scoring process with minimal dependence on listeners' language abilities. Whilst it is acknowledged that digits have a limited phonetic range the use of wider vocabularies would possibly lead

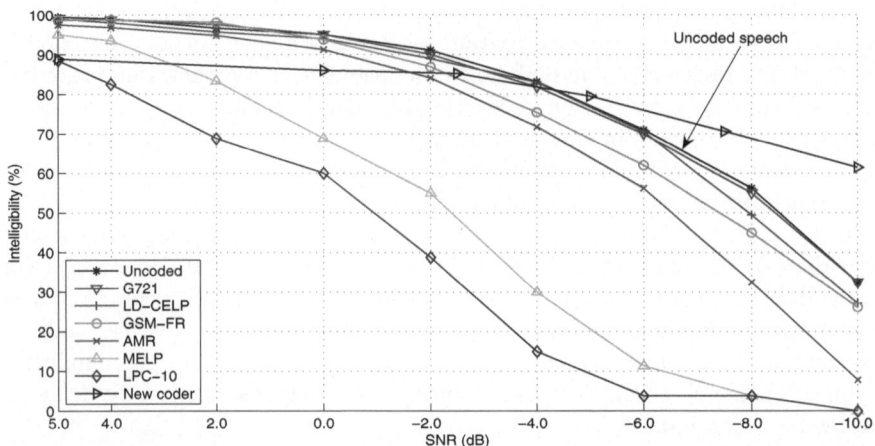

Fig. 2. Subjective intelligibility scores in car noise conditions with uncoded, with the 6 standard coders, and with the new coder. The profile for the new coder begins at 89% and crosses the uncoded profile -4.0dB. This implies that below this SNR the coder actually enhances intelligibility; however these results pertain to a fixed segmentation mask derived at 5dB SNR. Work with masks derived from the lower SNRs continues. The SNRs considered for the new coder are at 5, 0, -2.5, -5.0, -7.5 and -10.0dB.

to decreased scores across the board, with the ranking remaining largely unchanged. Thus the use of digits is seen as an acceptable compromise especially where system ranking is required rather than absolute scores.

Here we assess the intelligibility in high levels of car noise, a challenging application environment. Using standard noise addition software, from ITU-T Rec. P.56 [24], car noise was added to clean speech from 5.0dB down to -10.0dB. The speech utterances were 556 four-digit utterances sampled at 8kHz selected from the ETSI-AURORA2 digit string corpus [25].

Each SNR dataset was then processed with each of the six coders giving a total of seven conditions: 1 uncoded speech + 6 coded speech sets. Listener responses were obtained by combining previous collected responses in [26] with some newly collected responses. To maximise the potential for recruitment listeners performed tests using an on-line graphical user interface which may be viewed at *http://eeceltic.swan.ac.uk/subj*. During the tests listeners keyed in the digits they heard with intelligibility indicated by the total number of digits correctly identified.

2.2 Results

Averaged intelligibility scores for the six standard coder conditions and uncoded condition are presented in Figure 2. Included in Figure 2 is the profile for the new coder described in Section 3. The graph shows decreasing intelligibility as the SNR falls from 5.0dB to -10.0dB. For uncoded speech an intelligibility score of 100% at 5dB falls to a little over 30% at -10dB. For any given SNR four out of the six standard coder profiles, namely excluding G721 and LD-CELP, show the additional intelligibility degradation over that from the uncoded noise alone condition. The differences between the uncoded and lower four standard coder profiles is most prominent at lower SNRs. At -4.0dB, for example, MELP and LPC-10 have intelligibility scores of approximately 30% and 15% respectively. Compared with the uncoded speech at 83%, the coders introduce additional losses of 53% and 68% respectively. However the additional loss introduced by G721 and LD-CELP is negligable compared with the uncoded speech. Other than in SNR levels lower than -6.0dB, where for example LD-CELP introduces a loss of approximately 6% at -8.0dB compared with the uncoded speech, there is no meaningful difference between the two speech coders. The performance of the G721 coder is perhaps not un-expected given the high bit rate of 32kb/s. The robustness of the LD-CELP is though somewhat surprising considering that is half the bit rate of the G721 coder at 16kb/s. The results shown in Figure 2 provide a benchmark against which the performance of the experimental coder, described in the following section, may be compared.

3   Spectrogram Segmentation Coder

In this section we present an experimental image-based spectrogram segmentation speech coder designed to preserve intelligibility in high noise conditions. The overall speech quality is not of concern; however, a reasonable bit rate.

The inspiration behind the coder comes from our previous work which applied the image-based spectrogram segmentation procedure, proposed by Hory and Martin [10], to noise robust speech recognition [27]. The coder thus combines image processing techniques with speech in a multimedia-type scenario. The coding process can be considered in 3 stages, each of which are illustrated in Figure 3. They are spectrogram segmentation, phase coding and image compression. Each of the 3 coding stages and the re-synthesis stage are now presented in turn.

3.1   Spectrogram Segmentation

The result of the procedure with one spectrogram are illustrated in Figures 3(b) and 3(c). The example speech recording corresponds to a male person speaking the digit string '1390'. Figure 3(a) illustrates the time waveform of the speech signal with added car noise at a SNR of 0dB. Immediately below, in 3(b), is the corresponding spectrogram. Regions of the spectrogram that are dominated by speech are characterised by high energy pitch harmonic lines. The spectrogram segmentation procedure can be used to extract these regions to produce a segmented magnitude spectrogram as illustrated in Figure 3(c). Thus noise dominant regions can be suppressed and removed from the encoding process which now functions only on speech dominated regions, hence the potential for preserving intelligibility. Of secondary benefit is the potential for bit rate reduction achieved through noise suppression; that should incur minimal encoding costs for noise dominated regions.

The spectrogram segmentation procedure is effectively an image processing technique. Conceptually the magnitude spectrogram is considered as a whole

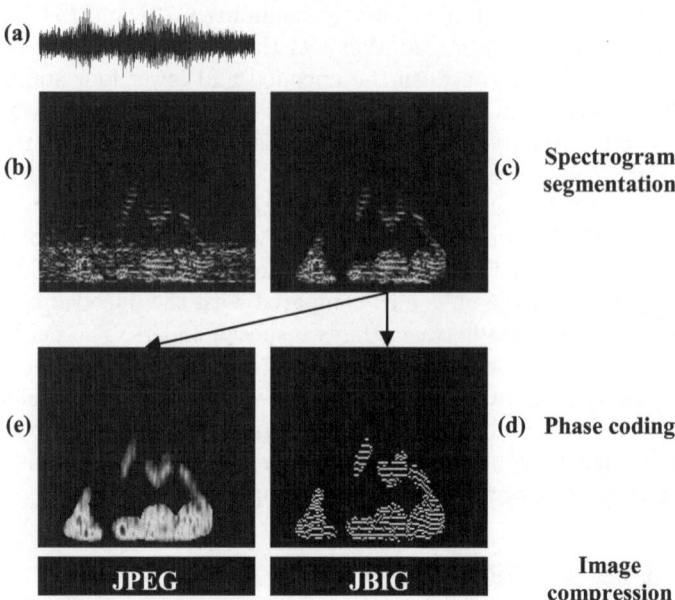

Fig. 3. Figure illustrating a 4 digit speech signal degraded by car noise to 0dB undergoing spectrogram segmentation coding

image. Features are then derived from sub-images across the whole spectrogram image. Here a sub-image size of 3 by 7 spectrograms coefficients is used that was empirically determined in [28]. The frame size is 32ms and the overlap is 8ms. The underlying principle assumed by Hory and Martin [10] is that speech and noise dominated regions are statistically different and thus identifiable. Mean and standard deviation scores for the sub-images are used as features from which a two dimensional feature space is formed. Regions dominated by either speech or noise cluster within the feature space enabling segmentation. Inherently, regions will exist in the spectrogram that essentially fall between the speech and noise dominant classes. These regions correspond to the boundaries of the dominant speech regions and thus represent regions of uncertainty.

The spectrogram segmentation procedure identifies speech dominated regions in a morphological growth process. Growth seed points in the magnitude spectrogram are selected using the feature space. The selected speech regions are then iteratively grown from the seed points. This morphological growth process continues until only noise dominant regions are deemed to remain. Hory and Martin define the end point according to the convergence of a normalised maximum likelihood [10]. A full description of the segmentation procedure is presented by Hory and Martin in [10] and also by Rodriguez *et al* in [27].

3.2 Phase Coding

Phase information as well as magnitude information is usually needed to reconstruct the time domain signal. Exploiting redundancies within the phase spectrogram image for efficient transmission proves to be extremely difficult. The phase spectrogram appears almost entirely random with no obvious pattern. Thus in an alternate strategy we estimate the phase spectrum using the magnitude spectrogram by generating a binary peak map image. An example is shown in Figure 3(d). Peaks in the binary peak map can be seen to correspond to pitch harmonics in the segmented magnitude spectrogram in Figure 3(c). The binary peak map is generated using the principles of sinusoidal transform coding (STC) proposed by McAulay and Quatieri [29].

STC exploits the quasi-periodic nature of speech by representing speech signals as a sum of sinusoids. Each sinusoid contains three parameters that are necessary for re-synthesis, namely amplitude, frequency and phase.

$$\tilde{s}(n) = \sum_{l=1}^{L(k)} \hat{A}_l^k cos[n\hat{\omega}_l^k + \hat{\theta}_l^k] \tag{1}$$

Equation 1, taken from [29], illustrates this concept where a discretely sampled speech signal $s(n)$ estimated over a short frame k is represented by $\hat{A}_l^k$, $\hat{\omega}_l^k$ and $\hat{\theta}_l^k$ which each represent the estimated amplitude, frequency and phase for the lth sinusoid. Compression in STC is obtained by reducing the number of sinusoids needed for re-synthesis and exploiting redundancy in the 3 parameters. The relationship between magnitude and phase is highly complex. The sinusoid summation model proposed in Equation 1 effectively simplifies this problem approximating the relationship to a linear system.

The sinusoidal selection process proposed by McAulay and Quatieri [29] is a frame based peak selection process of the magnitude spectrum. In the approach adopted all the peaks over the entire frequency bandwidth in the magnitude spectrum of a frame are first selected. The peaks are then kept dependent on whether they exist in the next frame in a nearest neighbour procedure. This peak selection process leads to the "birth" and "death" concept where sinusoids start in 1 frame and end in a later frame when no continuing peaks exist in subsequent frames. An example binary peak map is shown in Figure 3(d). During voiced speech the selected sinusoids can be seen to correlate with the pitch harmonics in the original magnitude spectrogram, shown in Figure 3(b). During unvoiced speech periods McAulay and Quatieri [29] state that provided the frame increment is not more than 20ms, the sinusoidal representation is successful. Here a frame duration of 32ms and increment of 8ms is used i.e., well within the proposed limit.

The binary peak map image effectively acts as a substitute image for the phase spectrogram. Its characteristics make it far more efficient for image compression. During the re-synthesis process a random set of phase values is assigned for the first frame of a given spectrogram. The phase values are then incremented for subsequent time frames, producing the phase approximation.

To avoid redundancy and increase efficiency the pitch lines in the segmented magnitude spectrogram are removed using low pass cepstral domain filtering. The resultant smoothed spectrogram is shown in Figure 3(e).

3.3   Image Compression

The speech signal is considered as two images: a smoothed magnitude spectrogram and a binary peak map. Both must be encoded for transmission. Given that both are images we investigate the use of standard image compression techniques. Here, JPEG [30] is used to encode the smoothed magnitude and JBIG [31], a binary image encoder, for the binary peak map.

The level of image compression is variable and will influence the trade off between intelligibility and bit rate. Here bit rate is of secondary importance; the primary cost function is the maintaining of intelligibility. We have therefore chosen to set the level of JPEG compression to 20%, following initial informal intelligibility experiments to identify a knee point in the profile of intelligibility against bit rate. For the binary peak map JBIG is used in lossless mode. The corresponding combined bit rate is in the region of 17kb/s and was calculated by dividing the image file sizes for each of the 566 four digit utterances under test by their corresponding time periods. The maximum bit rate is 26kb/s and the lowest is 10kb/s.

3.4   Time Domain Re-synthesis

The re-synthesis process is in essence simply an inverse process of the image compression and spectrogram generation. The smoothed magnitude spectrogram and binary peak map are first de-compressed by reverse JPEG and JBIG coding respectively. Upon decompression the 2 images are then combined by multiplication to form 1 magnitude spectrogram image.

To reconstruct the time domain signal phase information is also needed. Following the procedure described in Section 3.2, a random set of phase values is generated for the first time frame and then advanced incrementally for subsequent frames. The inverse-discrete Fourier transform (I-DFT) is then computed for each frame to revert back to the time domain. To complete the time domain re-synthesis the framing process is then reversed by retaining only the initial frame increment period for each frame.

The time domain re-synthesis process used here represents an initial strategy which likely can be further optimised. For example, attempting to ensure smoothness at frame transition boundaries using overlap and add or interpolation procedures [29] may help to maintain intelligibility. These ideas warrant future investigation.

4   Experiments

The objective of the experiments reported here is to assess the potential of the spectrogram segmentation coder and, specifically, how well intelligibility is preserved in high noise conditions. We replace the conventional, standard speech coder, illustrated in Figure 1, with the spectrogram segmentation coder and repeat similar experiments to those described in Section 2. For the coder to be of benefit in the current context it should operate in high noise conditions, minimising any further intelligibility loss whilst delivering a reasonable bit rate.

To assess the potential of the coder a fixed segmentation mask was used for each SNR. In each case the mask was that obtained from the same speech signal degraded at 5dB with additive white Gaussian noise (AWGN). The coder is assessed under essentially the same experimental conditions as those used for the standard coder assessment as reported in Section 2. Here, a total of 17 different listeners were used. Each SNR condition was assessed by between 7 and 10 listeners. Each listener scored a minimum of four utterances per SNR condition. An average of 43 responses were collected for each SNR condition and the listening tests were performed over a period of approximately 2 weeks.

The subjective intelligibility scores for the spectrogram segmentation coder are shown in Figure 2, combined with the earlier results from Section 2. These results show an intelligibility score of 89% at an SNR of 5.0dB, similar to the worst of the standard coders, LPC-10. However, the profile remains relatively flat down to -4.0dB at which point the coder profile coincides approximately with the no-coder condition with an intelligibility level of 82%. Below -4.0dB the coder outperforms all of the standard coders. Furthermore intelligibility scores obtained with the experimental coder exceed performance without coding. This suggests that the coder can potentially enhanced speech intelligibility provided a good segmentation mask is used.

5   Conclusion

Two contributions are made in this paper. The first is the somewhat surprising robustness found for the LD-CELP [14] coder with preserving intelligibility in high noise. The second is the investigation of concepts towards a new image based speech coder. This coder is optimised against an intelligibility criterion rather than the more common and embracing criterion of overall quality.

The coder is motivated by an image processing spectrogram segmentation procedure proposed by Hory and Martin [10]. Image processing techniques are thus fused with speech processing techniques in a new multimedia approach to speech coding. Experimental subjective intelligibility listening tests show that the coder is potentially able to enhance intelligibility in car noise levels below -4.0dB, albeit with a spectrogram segmentation mask obtained from corresponding 5dB SNR conditions. The bit rate for this coder is in the region of 17kb/s.

Work is currently on-going into developing reliable segmentation masks that are successful at lower SNRs. The segmentation procedure was developed for chirp signals degraded by AWGN [10]. A dominant characteristic of speech that is not taken advantage of in the original procedure is pitch. Two common characteristics of pitch harmonics in the magnitude spectrogram image are long lines and wide spacing between harmonics. Thus the idea being investigated is to restrict the image based segmentation procedure to narrow frequency bands. This work is on going with some early promising results.

Acknowledgements

The authors wish to thank Her Majesty's Government Communications Centre (HMGCC) for sponsoring this work.

References

1. Martin, R.: Speech enhancement using MMSE short time spectral estimation with gamma distributed speech priors. In: Proc. IEEE ICASSP, vol. 1, pp. 253–256 (2002)
2. Beerends, J.G.: Extending p.862 PESQ for assessing speech intelligibility. White contribution COM 12-C2 to ITU-T Study, Group 12 (October 2004)
3. Chong-White, N.R., Cox, R.V.: An intelligibility enhancement for the mixed excitation linear prediction speech coder. IEEE Signal Processing Letters 10(9), 263–266 (2003)
4. Martin, R., Malah, D., Cox, R.V., Accardi, A.J.: A noise reduction preprocessor for mobile voice communication. EURASIP Journal on Applied Signal Processing, 1046–1058 (2004)
5. Demiroglu, C., Anderson, D.V.: A soft decision MMSE amplitude estimator as a noise preprocessor to speech coders using a glottal sensor. In: Proc. ICSLP, pp. 857–860 (2004)
6. Quatieri, T.F., Brady, K., Messing, D., Campbell, J.P., Campbell, W.M., Brandstein, M.S., Clifford, C.J., Tardelli, J.D., Gatewood, P.D.: Exploiting nonacoustic sensors for speech encoding. IEEE Trans. on ASLP 14(2), 533–544 (2006)
7. Hu, Y., Loizou, P.C.: A comparative intelligibility study of speech enhancement algorithms. ICASSP 4(4), 561–564 (2007)
8. Liu, W.M.: Objective assessment of comparative intelligibility. PhD Thesis, University of Wales Swansea University (2008)
9. Supplee, L.N., Cohn, R.P., Collura, J.S., McCree, A.V.: MELP: The new federal standard at 2400 bps. In: Proc. ICASSP, vol. 2, pp. 1591–1594 (1997)
10. Hory, C., Martin, N.: Spectrogram segmentation by means of statistical features for non-stationary signal interpretation. IEEE Trans. on Signal Processing 50, 2915–2925 (2002)
11. Cox, R.V.: Three new speech coders from the ITU cover a range of applications. IEEE Communications Magazine, 40–47 (1997)
12. Gibson, J.D.: Adaptive prediction in speech differential encoding system. Proc. IEEE 68, 488–525 (1980)
13. Ekudden, E., Hagen, R., Johansson, I., Svedberg, J.: The adaptive multi-rate speech coder. In: Proc. IEEE Workshop on Speech Coding, pp. 117–119 (1999)
14. Chen, J.-H., Cox, R.V., Lin, Y.-C., Jayant, N., Melchner, M.J.: A low-delay CELP coder for the CCITT 16 kb/s speech coding standard. IEEE Selected Areas in Communications 10(5), 830–849 (1992)
15. Vary, P., Hellwig, K., Hofmann, R., Sluyter, R.J., Galand, C., Rosso, M.: Speech codec for the european mobile radio system. In: Proc. ICASSP, pp. 227–230 (1988)
16. Tremain, T.E.: The government standard linear predictive coding algorithm: LPC-10. In: Speech Technology, pp. 40–49 (1982)
17. Sun Microsystems. CCITT ADPCM encoder G.711, G.721, G.723, encode (14/04/2008), ftp://ftp.cwi.nl/pub/audio/ccitt-adpcm.tar.gz

18. 3GPP. European digital cellular telecommunication system 4750.. 12200 bits/s speech CODEC for adaptive multi-rate speech traffic channels, encoder, v6.0.0 (29/06/2008), http://www.3gpp.org/ftp/Specs/html-info/26073.htm
19. Zatsman, A., Concannon, M.: 16 kb/s low-delay CELP algorithm, ccelp, v2.0 (14/04/2008),
    ftp://svr-ftp.eng.cam.ac.uk/comp.speech/coding/ldcelp-2.0.tar.gz
20. Jutta. ETSI 06.10 GSM-FR, toast, v1.8 (14/04/2008),
    http://kbs.cs.tu-berlin.de/~jutta/toast.html
21. Texas Instruments, Inc. 2.4 kb/s proposed federal standard MELP speech coder, melp, v1.2 (14/04/2008)
22. Fingerhut, A.: U.S. department of defence LPC-10 2400bps voice coder, nuke, v1.5 (14/04/2008), http://www.arl.wustl.edu/~jaf/lpc/
23. Liu, W.M., Jellyman, K.A., Mason, J.S., Evans, N.W.D.: Assessment of objective quality measures for speech intelligibility estimation. In: Proc. ICASSP (2006)
24. ITU recommendation P.56. Objective measurement of active speech level. ITU (1993)
25. Hirsch, H.G., Pearce, D.: The aurora experimental framework for the performance evaluation of speech recognition systems under noisy conditions. ISCA ITRW ASR2000 Automatic Speech Recognition: Challenges for the next Millenium (2000)
26. Liu, W.M., Jellyman, K.A., Evans, N.W.D., Mason, J.S.D.: Assessment of objective quality measures for speech intelligibility. Publication in ICSLP (accepted, 2008)
27. Romero Rodriguez, F., Liu, W.M., Evans, N.W.D., Mason, J.S.D.: Morphological filtering of speech spectrograms in the context of additive noise. In: Proc. Eurospeech (2003)
28. Evans, N.W.D.: Spectral subtraction for speech enhancement and automatic speech recognition. PhD Thesis, University of Wales Swansea (2003)
29. McAulay, R.J., Quatieri, T.F.: Speech analysis/synthesis based on a sinusoidal representation. IEEE Trans. ASSP 34(4), 744–754 (1986)
30. ImageMagick Studio LLC. Imagemagick, v6.3.0, http://www.imagemagick.org
31. Kuhn, M.: JBIG-KIT package, v1.6, http://www.cl.cam.ac.uk/~mgk25/jbigkit/

Robust 3D Face Tracking on Unknown Users with Dynamical Active Models

Dianle Zhou and Patrick Horain

Institut Telecom, Telecom & Management SudParis
9 rue Charles Fourier, 91011 Évry Cedex France
{Dianle.Zhou,Patrick.Horain}@IT-SudParis.eu

Abstract. The Active Appearance Models [1] and the derived Active Models (AM) [4] allow to robustly track the face of a single user that was previously learnt, but works poorly with multiple or unknown users. Our research aims at improving the tracking robustness by learning from video databases. In this paper, we study the relation between the face texture and the parameter gradient matrix, and propose a statistical approach to dynamically fit the AM to unknown users by estimating the gradient and update matrices from the face texture. We have implemented this algorithm for real time face tracking and experimentally demonstrate its robustness when tracking multiple or unknown users' faces.

Keywords: Face Tracking, Active Appearance Models, Face Animation, Virtual Reality.

1   Introduction

Head pose and facial gesture estimation is a crucial task in computer vision applications such as human-computer interaction, biometrics, etc. It is a challenge because of the variability of facial appearance within a video sequence. This variability is due to changes in head pose (particularly out-of-plane head rotations), facial expression, lighting, or occlusions, or a combination of all of them.

Classical active appearance models (AAM) [1], [2] work by globally registering a face model onto images. They require initially learning off-line a statistical model from example images of a user. This model describes appearance variations, *i.e.* image variation, with respect to model parameters variations as a matrix of gradients. Parameter variations can then be retrieved from residual appearance variations using an update matrix computed as a pseudo-inverse of the gradients matrix. Face tracking then consists in optimally registering the face model that was learnt onto input images using a gradient descent.

Feature-based approach such as elastic bunch graph matching (EBGM) [3] is robust to homogeneous illumination changes and affine deformations of the face image. The AAM approach was found to be more precise than the feature based approach [1], but unfortunately AAM tracking highly depends on learning the user to be tracked, so it fails with unknown users.

B. Huet et al. (Eds.): MMM 2009, LNCS 5371, pp. 74–84, 2009.
© Springer-Verlag Berlin Heidelberg 2009

Following Dornaika and Ahlberg [4], we consider an Active Model (AM) that is simplified version of AAM, *i.e.* we learn the shape variations and grab face texture online while we do not learn texture variations.

In this paper we address tracking unknown users by enhancing the AM approach. We show there is a relation between the face model texture and the gradient matrix that we model by using a combined principal component analysis (PCA) [5] on the texture and the gradient matrix. So, we can generate an update matrix for each user, no matter if that user was learnt or not. We demonstrate this with a real-time application to capture head pose and facial gesture using a commodity web camera, which works even on unknown users with controlled lighting conditions and camera.

The rest of the paper is organized as follows. In Section 2, we analyze the AM and point out its short-coming, and propose the new algorithm and framework. Then we give the implement detail in Section 3. Experimental result and conclusion are presented in Sections 4 and 5.

2 Tracking Framework

We divided the framework of our tracking application into two parts: offline learning and online tracking. For the offline learning part, we will describe how to get the statistic information from training data. Then we will introduce how to use those information in Active Model search.

2.1 Offline Learning

Offline learning consists in estimating:

(1) Face Shape
(2) Face Texture
(3) Update matrix
(4) Relation between the update matrix and the face texture.

Steps (1) to (3) are classical in AM learning [4]. We introduce (4) for handling unknown users

(1) Face Shape
Face shape consists in face morphology and current face expressions. These should be captured by registering the 3D face model. To obtain this "shaped 3D face model", we displace the vertices of a generic 3D-face model such as CANDIDE-3 [6]. Fig. 1 shows the CANDIDE-3 wireframe.

The 3D shape of this deformable 3D model is described as vertices coordinates. The 3D face model is given by the 3D coordinates of the vertices P_i, $i = 1, 2, 3 \ldots m$ where m is the number of vertices. Thus, the shape up to a global scale can be fully described by the 3m-vector g that is the concatenation of the 3D coordinates of all the vertices. The shape with its variations is approximated by a linear relation:

$$\mathbf{g} = \overline{\mathbf{g}} + \mathbf{S\sigma} + \mathbf{A\alpha} , \tag{1}$$

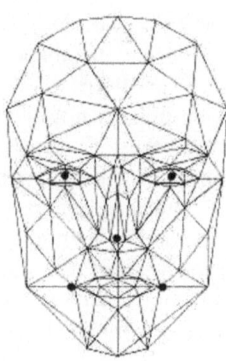

Fig. 1. The CANDIDE-3 wireframe [6]

where **g** is the standard shape of the model, and the columns of matrices **S** and **A** are Shape and Animation Units. A Shape Unit provides a way to deform the 3D wireframe, such as to adapt the eye width, the head width, the eye separation distance, etc. σ and α are coordinate vectors in the shape and animation spaces. Thus, **S**σ accounts for shape variability (inter-person variability) while **A**α accounts for the facial animation (intra-person variability). We assume that the two kinds of variability are independent.

The generic 3D face model is meant to describe various persons with various face expressions [5]. This avoids the need for a statistical model for face shape as originally introduced by Cootes [1]. This is similar to the Direct Appearance Models by Hou [7] where the relationship between the texture and the shape is many to one that is one shape can correspond to many textures, but no texture is associated with more than one shape. They claim that one can thus predict the shape directly from the texture, which leads to a faster and more reliable search algorithm.

(2) Face Texture
A face texture is a geometrically normalized image of a face that is independent from shape, so appearance variations resulting from shape variations are removed. It is created by first interactively adjusting the face model to an image captured, and then mapping that image onto the model, and finally reshaping the face model to the mean shape in the front view. Normalized face textures all have the same size, 64 by 64 in our experiments.

Given the vector **b** of the model pose and animation parameters and an input image **y**, the face texture **T(b)** is the result of a warping function W:

$$\mathbf{T(b)} = \mathbf{W(y,b)}, \tag{2}$$

W is an affine transform with respect to each model mesh triangle. It requires two costly computations for each pixel: its mesh triangle, and the three barycentric coordinates in that triangle. Fortunately, these time-consuming operations can be pre-computed offline [8].

In this step, face textures from various users with various poses and expressions are obtained. They are used to build a statistical model of the face textures with a PCA which outputs eigenfaces, so describing the texture variation around the mean texture [5]. This can be done either on a single user or dedicated to multiple users. The former is a *person specific model*, while the later is a *generic model* [9].

(3) Update Matrix

Tracking consists in registering the 3D model onto a sequence of input images $\mathbf{y}$ so that it minimizes their difference with the projected model texture. Equivalently, but faster because the reference texture is smaller than input images, we rather minimize the residue image $\mathbf{r}(\mathbf{b})$ between the warped input image $W(\mathbf{y},\mathbf{b})$ and the reference face texture $\mathbf{T}_{model}$:

$$\mathbf{r}(\mathbf{b}) = W(\mathbf{y},\mathbf{b}) - \mathbf{T}_{model} . \tag{3}$$

$\|\mathbf{r}(\mathbf{b})\|^2$ is to be minimized with respect to $\mathbf{b}$, the vector of the pose and animation parameters, that is composed of the global model rotation θ, translation $\mathbf{t}$ and the animation vector α.

$$\mathbf{b} = [\theta_x, \theta_y, \theta_z, t_x, t_y, t_z, \alpha] . \tag{4}$$

This is classically achieved by gradient descent. A first order Taylor expansion gives:

$$\mathbf{r}(\mathbf{b} + \Delta\mathbf{b}) = \mathbf{r}(\mathbf{b}) + \frac{\partial \mathbf{r}(\mathbf{b})}{\partial \mathbf{b}} \Delta\mathbf{b} . \tag{5}$$

Iterations consist in updating the value of $\mathbf{b}$ with $\Delta\mathbf{b}$ such that:

$$\Delta\mathbf{b} = \mathbf{U}\mathbf{r}(\mathbf{b}) , \tag{6}$$

where:

$$\mathbf{U} = -(\mathbf{G}^T\mathbf{G})^{-1}\mathbf{G}^T , \tag{7}$$

$$\mathbf{G} = \frac{\partial \mathbf{r}(\mathbf{b})}{\partial \mathbf{b}} . \tag{8}$$

The update $\mathbf{U}$ matrix can be computed offline before tracking. It is known as the negative pseudo-inverse of the gradient matrix $\mathbf{G}$. It is computed by numerical differentiation, so the jth column of $\mathbf{G}$ is computed with:

$$\mathbf{G}_j = \frac{\mathbf{r}(\mathbf{b} + h\mathbf{q}_j) - \mathbf{r}(\mathbf{b} - h\mathbf{q}_j)}{2h} . \tag{9}$$

where h is a step value and $\mathbf{q}_j$ is a vector with all elements zero except the jth element that equals to one.

(4) Relation between the Update Matrix and the Face Texture

In thesis [10], Ahlberg builds a training database from $N = 330$ images of 6 persons. He also builds the update matrix for various head poses and facial expressions. The estimated gradient is simply estimated as an average of the N images gradient matrices.

$$\overline{\mathbf{G}}_j = \frac{1}{N} \sum_{n=1}^{N} \frac{\mathbf{r}(\mathbf{b} + h\mathbf{q}_j) - \mathbf{r}(\mathbf{b} - h\mathbf{q}_j)}{2h}. \tag{10}$$

Here $n = 1, \ldots, N$, is the images number in the training set with various head poses and facial expressions. Ahlberg assumes that the gradient matrix is similar for the different users, which we find is not a valid assumption.

Let's look at the gradient matrix and the update matrix $\mathbf{U}$. It is the negative pseudo-inverse of the gradient matrix $\mathbf{G}$. In fact, the matrix $\mathbf{G}$ is a 3D matrix with the size $K{\times}L{\times}M$, where K is the number of parameters, L is the width of the texture and M is the height of the texture. To make it easy to analyze matrix $\mathbf{G}$, we will separate it into K channels, so each of the matrix $\mathbf{G}$ can be described by K images. These are named Steepest Descent Images (SDIs) [12] because they provide the direction in which the descent toward the optimum is steepest. By looking into the SDIs from different persons, Fig. 2, we can see that the gradient matrix is extremely different from user to user. So averaging user gradient matrices into a single gradient matrix is not suitable. In our experiments, we found that while tracking a user that was learnt works good, averaging multiple users' gradient matrices gives poor tracking results (see Fig. 4, first row), because the gradient matrix is highly related to the user.

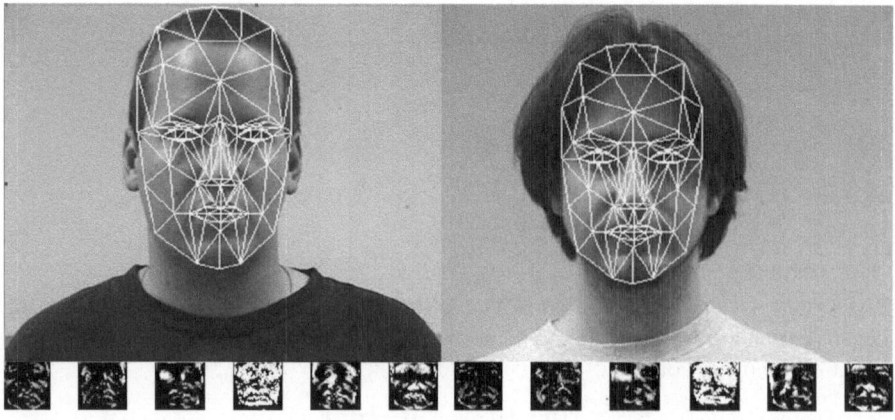

Fig. 2. Example of Steepest Descent Images from two users in the training database [16]. The left image is the training image with the model registered manually. Each set of 6 images on the bottom is the steepest descent images for the 6 head pose.

Since the gradient matrix is user specific, it must be adjusted for each user. This is usually achieved with tedious training with the user to be tracked. Even worse, this prevents tracking unknown users. Tracking multiple or unknown users requires adjusting the gradient matrix to each user. Such an approach is supported by the intuitive evidence that the gradient matrix is related to the face texture, because the texture can be directly used to predict the shape [7].

Matthews and Baker [12] have pointed out that there is linear relationship between $\mathbf{G}$ and $\nabla_x \mathbf{T}$. Since the user specific texture $\mathbf{T}_{model}$ does not vary during tracking, so equations (8) can be rewritten:

$$\mathbf{G} = \frac{\partial \mathbf{T(b)}}{\partial \mathbf{b}} = \nabla_x \mathbf{T} \cdot \nabla_b \mathbf{x} . \qquad (11)$$

where $\mathbf{x}$ is the pixel coordinate in the texture, so $\nabla_x \mathbf{T}$ is the image gradient of the face texture. $\nabla_x \mathbf{T}$ holds all the information related to "color" in the gradient matrix $\mathbf{G}$, for example user face color, illumination condition and so on. The second part $\nabla_b \mathbf{x}$ is only related to the geometrical transform that is the "shape" part of $\mathbf{G}$. So the relationship between $\mathbf{G}$ and $\nabla_x \mathbf{T}$ appears to be independent from either illumination conditions or the user being tracked.

We propose to model statistically the dependency (11) of $\mathbf{G}$ on $\nabla_x \mathbf{T}$ so that a gradient matrix can be estimated from any user face texture that is readily available while tracking. Learning is achieved on some database of face images. For each image n in the training database, we manually set the position, rotation and the animation parameters. With those parameters, we extract texture $\mathbf{T}_n$, and compute the correspondinggradient matrix $\mathbf{G}_n$ for image n using expression (8). We use PCA on both the texture gradient and the gradient matrices:

$$\begin{aligned}
\nabla_x \mathbf{T} &= \overline{\nabla_x \mathbf{T}} + \mathbf{E}_T \mathbf{p}_T \\
\mathbf{G} &= \overline{\mathbf{G}} + \mathbf{E}_G \mathbf{p}_G
\end{aligned} . \qquad (12)$$

where $\mathbf{E}_T$ and $\mathbf{E}_G$ are the eigenvectors of texture gradient space and gradient matrix space and $\mathbf{p}_T$ and $\mathbf{p}_G$ are eigenvalue vectors.

For each example we generate the concatenated vector:

$$\mathbf{p} = \begin{pmatrix} \mathbf{p}_T \\ \mathbf{p}_G \end{pmatrix} . \qquad (13)$$

Because $\mathbf{p}$ has a zero average value, a further PCA gives:

$$\mathbf{p} = \mathbf{E}_c \mathbf{c} , \qquad (14)$$

where:

$$\mathbf{E}_c = \begin{pmatrix} \mathbf{E}_{cT} \\ \mathbf{E}_{cG} \end{pmatrix} . \qquad (15)$$

By substituting $\mathbf{p}_T$ and $\mathbf{p}_G$ back in (12) we get:

$$\nabla_x T = \overline{\nabla_x T} + E_T E_{cT} c = \overline{\nabla_x T} + Q_T c$$
$$G = \overline{G} + E_G E_{cG} c = \overline{G} + Q_G c$$

(16)

where:

$$Q_T = E_T E_{cT}$$
$$Q_G = E_G E_{cG}$$

(17)

So we model $\nabla_x T$ and the G with a single coordinates vector c. With this function we can predict the user specific gradient matrix from the current texture that was captured from the input video sequence.

2.2 Online Tracking: Active Model Search

(1) Initialization
The fitting algorithm of AM may get trapped in some local minima so it requires coarse initialization. Thanks to the robustness of the AM, in most cases a face detection algorithm can meet the conditions. A survey on face detection can be found in [11]. We used the AdaBoost approach proposed by Viola and Jones [13], the implementation is freely available from the OpenCV library [14].

(2) On line Tracking Flow
For each iteration, the parameter update Δb is computed using expression (6). Notice that the update matrix U is now dynamically calculated form input texture. Given a texture T, function (16) provides the combined texture and gradient coordinates in the PCA space:

$$c = Q_T (\nabla T - \overline{\nabla T}),$$

(18)

The predicted gradient matrix can be calculated using function (16). Notice that the gradient matrix is updated dynamically during tracking, so we call it dynamical AM while the classical AM relies on a constant gradient matrix.

3 Implementation

The algorithm has been implemented on a low-end PC with an Intel 1.8 GHz Pentium IV processor and 512 MB memory. We use a consumer web camera to grab the video sequences. OpenGL is used for texture mapping and OpenCV for video capture and processing. We retained the following six animation parameters of the Candide model for tracking the facial gestures described in [4]:

(1) upper lip raiser,   (4) lip corner depressor,
(2) jaw drop,   (5) eyebrow lowerer,
(3) mouth stretch,   (6) outer eyebrow raiser.

Based on the algorithm described above, six head position parameters and six animation parameters are separately trained and tracked. For comparison purposes, both the original and the dynamical AM have been implemented. They run at 25 and 20 frames / second, respectively. The dynamical AM still can work in near real time since

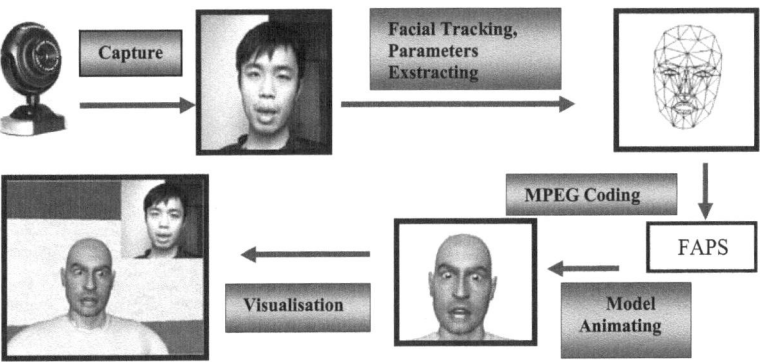

Fig. 3. Render GRETA using dynamical AM face tracking (video available from the website: https://picoforge.int-evry.fr/projects/svn/myblog3d/video/Gretafaceanimation.avi)

dynamically predicting the gradient matrix only requires a further PCA in a low dimensional space.

The captured face animation can be converted to MPEG-4 facial animation parameters (FAPs) [4] for rendering with an avatar e.g. the free MPEG-4 player named GRETA [15].

4   Experimental Results

In our experiments we use the Head Pose Image Database [16] for training the global parameter face position, rotation and scale, and the BIOMET database [17] for training the animation parameters.

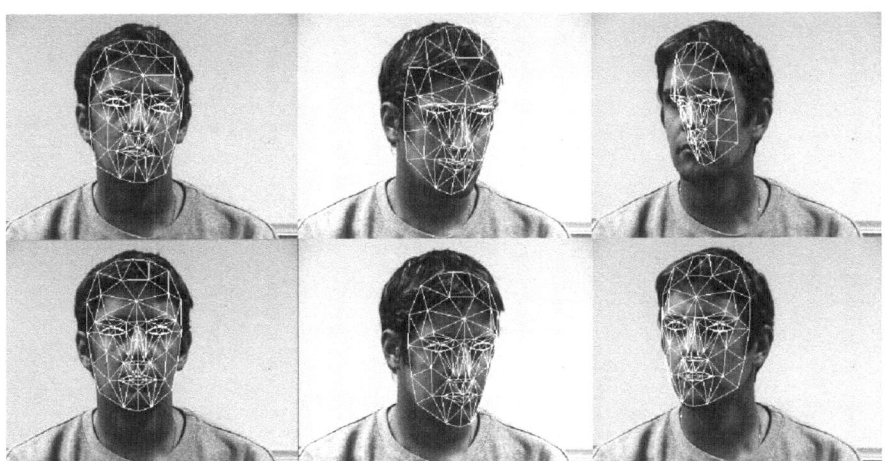

Fig. 4. Example for the tracking result using the DAM algorithm from top to bottom: tracking using averaging multiple users' gradient matrices and tracking with dynamically predict the gradient matrix (images from the Head Pose Image Database [16])

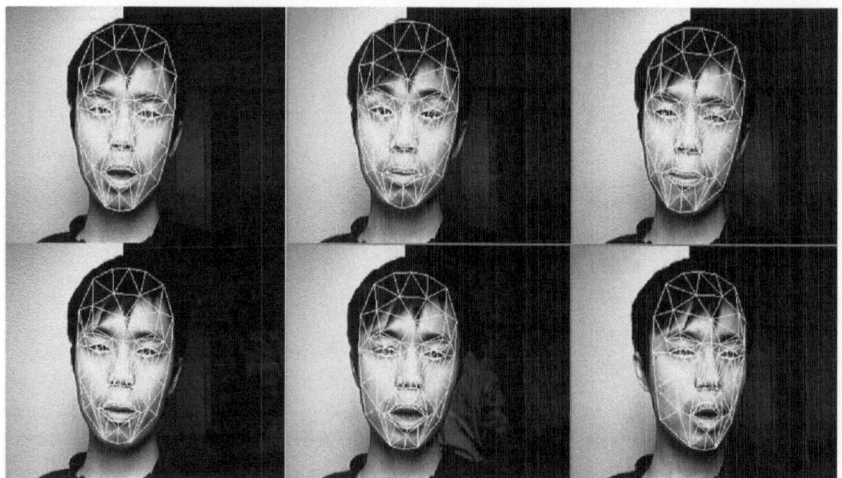

Fig. 5. Dynamically tracking on video sequence (video available at: https://picoforge. int-evry.fr/projects/svn/myblog3d/video/Facetracking.avi)

Experiments on head pose tracking were first achieved with training with ten persons with varying skin color and 7 images per person. Fig. 4 presents some tracking results. We find that the dynamical AM algorithm gives better result than the algorithm averaging multiple users' gradient matrices.

In our second experiments (Fig. 5), a person is speaking with lots of facial expressions and head motions. We can observe that even if the background is complex, the facial expressions and the head pose are well recovered. Note that those results are obtained without any previous camera calibration or manual initialization. The AdaBoost-based initialization is done only on the first frame of the sequence, without any interactive operation.

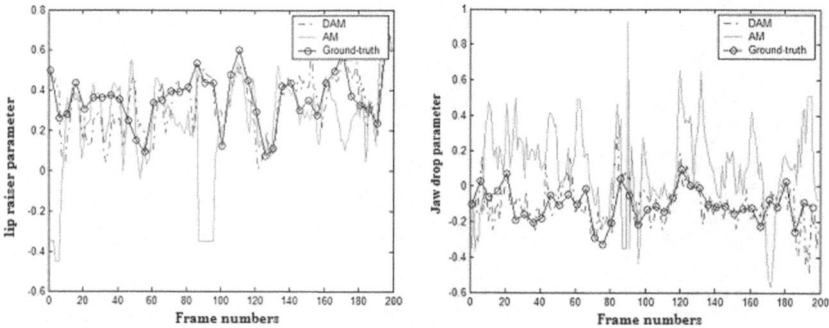

Fig. 6. Tracking result of upper lip raiser animation parameter (left) and jaw drop parameter (right)

In order to accurately evaluate the accuracy of tracking system, we mutually set the parameter for the test sequence and as ground-truth. Both the trackers of AM and dynamical AM have been applied to the video, and we compare all the twelve head position parameters and animation parameters to the true values. The result of two parameters: upper lip raiser and jaw drop are plotted in (Fig. 6), and the root mean square error (RMSE) between the tracking result and the ground-truth is given by Table 1. From the result we can see the dynamical AM algorithm gives better result. Note in the fig. 6 the tracking is lost for the original AM algorithm form the 60th to the 140th frame.

Table 1. The root mean square error (RMSE) between animation parameter (AP) tracking result with the ground-truth. The AP(1~6) is noted for (1) upper lip raiser, (2) jaw drop, (3) mouth stretch, (4) lip corner depressor, (5) eyebrow lowerer, (6) outer eyebrow raiser separately.

Algorithm	RMSE AP(1)	RMSE AP(2)	RMSE AP(3)	RMSE AP(4)	RMSE AP(5)	RMSE AP(6)
AM	0.0534	0.0967	0.0586	0.0394	0.0250	0.0211
DAM	0.0166	0.0206	0.0112	0.0310	0.0093	0.0091

From these experiments, the dynamical AM algorithm is more robust and accurate than AAM for unseen users. Actually, the illumination and camera parameters are "embedded" in the update matrix. This makes the algorithm work robustly when training and tracking the faces in the same acquisition conditions, but it achieves poor results in case of uncontrolled lighting or variation of the camera parameters. Ideally the illumination could be corrected with eigenlight-fields and Bayesian face sub-regions [18] and the camera parameters could be calculated as optimization problem. But both of those processes are not compatible with real-time processing.

5   Conclusion and Future Work

In this paper, we propose an enhancement to the active model approach for real-time tracking the face of unknown users. The main aim of the work is to exploit the existent video database to improve the tracking robustness. The whole flow of the system: initialization, training and tracking is introduced. Our experimental result demonstrate the improvement of the dynamically AM compare to the classical AM. The tracking algorithm has been applied for animating avatar by using MPEG-4 as a common communication and animation standard. The future research work will be focus on facial expressions analysis and emotion recognition from dynamic images by using our face tracking system.

Acknowledgment

We wish to thank Professor Catherine Pelachaud for providing GRETA and her assistance in using it. And also Dr. Jörgen Ahlberg gives us the CANDIDE-3 face model. At last I would like to thank Dr. Dijana Petrovska who give me suggestion in my whole work period and kindly proved the BIOMET Database.

References

1. Cootes, T., Edwards, G., Taylor, C.: Active appearance models. IEEE Transactions on Pattern Analysis and Machine Intelligence 23(6), 681–685 (2001)
2. Xiao, J., Baker, S., Matthews, I., Kanade, T.: Real-time combined 2d+3d active appearance models. In: Proceedings of the IEEE Conference on Computer Vision and Pattern Recognition, vol. 25, pp. 535–542 (2004)
3. Wiskott, L., Fellous, J.M., Kruger, N., Malsburg, C.: Face recognition by elastic bunch graph matching, Tech. Rep. IR-INI 96–08 (1996)
4. Dornaika, F., Ahlberg, J.: Fast and Reliable Active Appearance Model Search for 3D Face Tracking. IEEE Transactions on Systems, Man, and Cybernetics–Part 34, 1838–1853 (2004)
5. Turk, M., Pentland, A.: Eigenfaces for Recognition. Journal of Cognitive Neuroscience 3(1), 71–86 (1991)
6. Ahlberg, J.: Candide-3 – an updated parameterized face. Technical Report LiTH-ISY-R-2326, Linkoping University, Sweden (2001)
7. Hou, X.W., Li, S.Z., Zhang, H.J.: Direct appearance models. In: Proceedings of IEEE Computer Society Conference on Computer Vision and Pattern Recognition, pp. 828–833 (2002)
8. Ahlberg, J.: Real-Time Facial Feature Tracking Using an Active Model With Fast Image Warping. In: International Workshop on Very Low Bitrates Video, pp. 39–43 (2001)
9. Gross, R., Matthews, I., Baker, S.: Generic vs. person specific active appearance models. Image and Vision Computing 23(11), 1080–1093 (2005)
10. Ahlberg, J.: Model-based Coding - Extraction, Coding, and Evaluation of Face Model Parameters, PhD Thesis (2002)
11. Yang, M.H., Kriegman, D., Ahuja, N.: Detecting Faces in Images: A Survey. IEEE Transactions on Pattern Analysis and Machine Intelligence 24, 34–58 (2002)
12. Matthews, I., Baker, S.: Active appearance models revisited. International Journal of Computer Vision 60(2), 135–164 (2004)
13. Viola, P., Jones, M.J.: Robust real-time object detection. Cambridge Research Laboratory, Technical Report Series (2001)
14. Bradski, G., Kaehler, A.: Pisarevsky: Learningbased computer vision with intel's open source computer vision library. Intel Technology Journal 9(2), 1 (2005)
15. Poggi, I., Pelachaud, C., Derosis, F., Carofiglio, V., Decarolis, B.: GRETA. A Believable Embodied Conversational Agent. In: Stock, O., Zancarano, M. (eds.) Multimodal Intelligent Information Presentation. Kluwer, Dordrecht (2005)
16. Gourier, N., Hall, D., Crowley, J.L.: Estimating Face Orientation from Robust Detection of Salient Facial Features. In: International Workshop on Visual Observation of Deictic Gestures (2004)
17. Salicetti, S., Beumier, C., Chollet, G., Dorizzi, B., Jardins, J.L.l., Lunter, J., Ni, Y., Petrowska Delacretaz, D.: BIOMET: A multimodal person authentication database including face, voice, fingerprint, hand and signature modalities. In: Kittler, J., Nixon, M.S. (eds.) AVBPA 2003. LNCS, vol. 2688, pp. 845–853. Springer, Heidelberg (2003)
18. Gross, R., Baker, S., Matthews, I., Kanade, T.: Face Recognition Across Pose and Illumination. In: Li, S.Z., Jain, A.K. (eds.) Handbook of Face Recognition, Springer, Heidelberg (2004)

A Fast Hybrid Decision Algorithm for H.264/AVC Intra Prediction Based on Entropy Theory*

Guifen Tian, Tianruo Zhang, Takeshi Ikenaga, and Satoshi Goto

Graduate School of Information, Production and Systems, Waseda University, Japan
tianguifen@fuji.waseda.jp

Abstract. Rate Distortion Optimization based spatial intra coding is a new feature of H.264/AVC standard. It efficiently improves the video coding performance by brutally utilizing variable block sizes and multiple prediction modes. Thus, extremely high computation complexity is required. This paper proposes a hybrid decision algorithm which can reduce unimportant block sizes and prediction modes. Entropy feature of each MB is extracted to decide the optimal block size. Then Prewitt operators based edge direction extraction module is designed to select only promising prediction modes. In addition, above two decision modules can function together to form a fast hybrid decision algorithm for intra prediction. Sufficient experiments prove that this hybrid algorithm is able to achieve 63% time reduction with PSNR loss limited to 0.07dB, bit rate increase at most 2.02%. It is expected to be utilized as a favorable accelerator for a real-time H.264 encoder for HDTV.

Keywords: H.264/AVC, Intra Prediction, Entropy Theory, Block Size Decision, Mode Decision.

1 Introduction

H.264/AVC is known as the newest international coding standard jointly developed by the ITU-T video coding experts group and ISO/IEC Moving Picture Experts Group (MPEG) [1]. Compared with earlier existed standards, H.264/AVC has shown significantly higher coding efficiency, for it introduces many new techniques, such as variable block size motion estimation, quarter pixel motion compensation and multiple reference frame in inter coding. In intra coding, variable block sizes (16x16,8x8,4x4) and multiple prediction modes (9 for 4x4 and 8x8 blocks, 4 for 16x16 blocks and 4 for 8x8 chroma blocks) for the first time are utilized. In addition, a process called Rate Distortion Optimization (RDO) for selecting the optimal block size and prediction mode is employed to achieve the highest coding performance. RDO based intra prediction is a new topic in

---

* This work was supported by fund from MEXT via Kitakyushu innovative cluster projects and CREST, JST.

B. Huet et al. (Eds.): MMM 2009, LNCS 5371, pp. 85–95, 2009.

H.264/AVC coding standard. It exhaustively examines all block sizes and prediction modes to get the best compression performance. However, terribly high computational complexity is required. Therefore, fast but video quality keeping intra prediction algorithms are desirable. Also tt is believed that fast intra prediction algorithms are very important in reducing the overall complexity of H.264/AVC considering following two reasons: the cost of computing RD cost of intra mode is about five times higher than for the case of inter modes [2]; intra modes are also exhaustively examined in P and B slice.

In the research history of intra coding, Pan's algorithm [5] is the most representative work and also a milestone in intra mode decision. In his work, edge direction histogram for each mode firstly is calculated. Then the maximum one and its' two neighbors plus DC mode are selected as candidate modes. Similar work and improvements can be found in [7]-[13]. However, these algorithms still needs 4 candidate modes for 4x4 blocks. Consequently, processing cycles in hardware and computational complexity in software are still high.

The concept behind block size decision is that the optimal block size highly correlates to the smoothness of macroblock [3][4]. Lin [3] utilizes AC/DC ratio of DCT transform to extract the smoothness of macroblock. Based on AC/DC ratio and two variable thresholds, promising block size can be decided. One problem with his work is that the bit-rate increase is a little high compared with similar work[4]. Zhang [4] uses amplitude and SATD(sum of absolute Hadamard transform differences) value of macroblock to select the best block size. However, this method can only gain about 10%~18% computation reduction.

This paper concentrates on both decision problems and organize them together to form a hybrid decision algorithm to achieve better performance. On the one hand, entropy feature is employed to get the smoothness of each macroblock. Since smooth macroblock has lower entropy value than that with detailed or complex information, entropy feature can be utilized to distinguish macroblock and select the optimal block size. On the other hand, Prewitt operators are used to get the edge directions for decided block, further to select only efficient modes instead of full search.

The rest of the paper is organized as follows. Section 2 reviews fast algorithms in intra prediction in H.264/AVC. Section 3 introduces proposed entropy theory based block size decision and mode decision algorithms in detail. Experimental results will be given in Section 4. Conclusion will be drawn in Section 5.

2   Intra Prediction in H.264/AVC

Different from previous coding standards, intra prediction in H.264 is always conducted in spatial domain. In baseline and main profile, for luma samples, the prediction block may be formed for each 4x4 block (denoted as I4MB) or for an entire MB (denoted as I16MB). The 4x4 prediction is suitable for images with significant details. It supports 8 directional modes plus one DC mode. The I16MB prediction, which is well suited for smooth image areas, supports four prediction modes. For the chroma 8x8 block of an macroblock (denoted as C8MB), it is always predicted using a similar prediction technique as for I16MB.

Since variable block sizes and multiple prediction modes are supported in the standard, there are two ways to speed up intra prediction: reduce inefficient modes(known as mode decision, MD for short) or reduce inefficient block sizes(known as block size decision,BSD for short). Fast MD algorithm aims to predict the direction of pixel changes within one MB, to reduce unpromising mode candidates. One problem with fast mode decision algorithm [5] [6]-[12] is that PSNR loss is significant and not so suitable for applications which require very high quality videos. Fast BSD algorithm aims to select the best block size based on the smoothness of MBs. The intuitive behind block size decision is that the intra coding block size is highly dependent on the smoothness of MB. Previously, researchers utilize AC/DC ratio [3] and amplitude of edge vector[4] to extract smoothness of MB. In this paper, we take entropy feature to measure the smoothness of MBs. The entropy value of one MB can be minimized only when all the 256 pixels in one MB have the same intensity. Based on this observation, it is obvious that if one MB is smooth/homogenuous, it has very high potential to be encoded in 16x16; otherwise if it contains complex or detailed information, it tends to be separated into 16 4x4 blocks to ensure encoding performance.

3   Hybrid of Block Size Decision and Mode Decision Algorithm

3.1   BSD Algorithm Based on Entropy Theory

Entropy Extraction. A key measure of information that comes up in the theory known as information entropy is usually expressed by the average number of bits needed for storage or communication. Intuitively, entropy quantifies the uncertainty involved in a random variable. The entropy H of a discrete random variable X is a measurement of the amount of uncertainty associated with the value of X. If X is the set of all messages x that X could be, then the entropy of X can be defined as:

$$H(X) = - \sum_{x \in X} p(x) \log p(x) \tag{1}$$

also

$$\sum_{x \in X} p(x) = 1 \tag{2}$$

Here, $P(X)$ is the probability that Xequals to x. An important property of entropy is that it is minimized only when all the messages in the message space are equiprobable. Intuitively, if we take the intensities of all the 256 pixels of one MB to represent set X, we can extract the entropy feature of this MB as:

$$H = - \sum_{i=0}^{255} p(Y(i)) \log p(Y(i)) \tag{3}$$

$Y(i)$denotes the intensity of pixel i. $p(Y(i))$ denotes the probability that X equals to$Y(i)$. From the property of entropy feature, we can get conclusion as:

- If $Y(i)$tends to be equiprobable, entropy H tends to be low and we can judge the macroblock to be smooth/homogenous. This MB tends to be encoded as a entire 16x16 block;
- Otherwise, H tends to be high and the MB contains complex or detailed information. This MB will be partitioned into 16 4x4 blocks.

Figure 1(a) shows the entropy distribution of 16x16 and 4x4 blocks of the sequence "foreman.cif", respectively. Qp in this paper stands for quantization parameter. The red-dash line shows the entropy value distribution of I4MBs; the blue-solid line shows the entropy value distribution of I16MBs. This figure verifies the property of entropy that smooth blocks have lower entropy value and complex blocks have relatively much higher entropy value. This observation functions as a solid theory base for proposed BSD method.

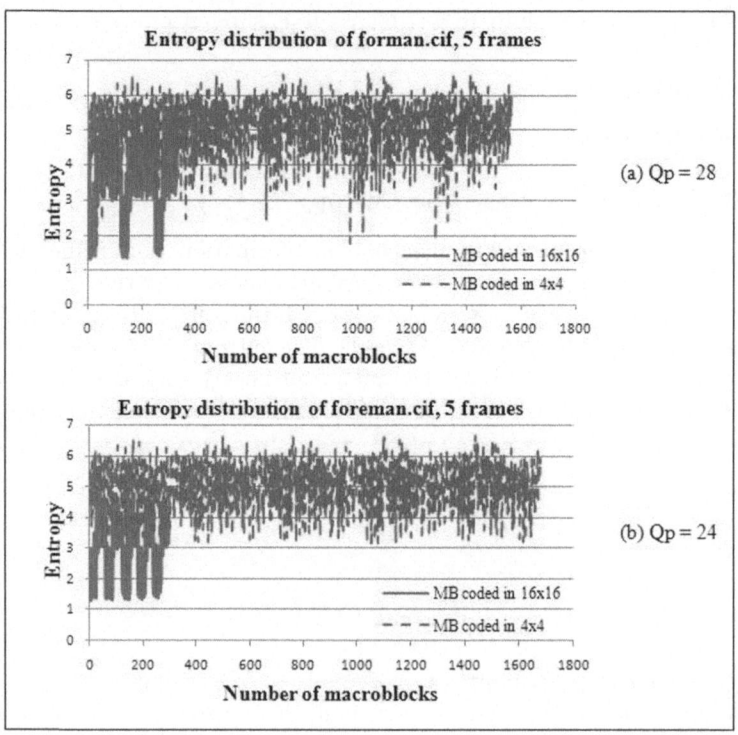

Fig. 1. (a)Entropy distribution of 16x16 blocks and 4x4 blocks of forman.cif, Qp=28. (b)Entropy distribution of 16x16 blocks and 4x4 blocks of forman.cif, Qp=24.

Block Size Decision. Since the entropy feature of smooth and complex blocks are separable, we can use two thresholds, denoted as α and β, to distinguish I4MBs and I16MBs. The decision rule becomes as:

- If the entropy feature H of one macroblock is smaller than α, only 16x16 block size is used for intra coding;
- If the entropy H of one macroblock is larger than β, only 4x4 block size is used for intra coding;
- Otherwise both block sizes are used, to gurantee video quality.

Upper part of Figure 2 shows the encoding flow of BSD process. One issue for block size decision is how to set thresholds. Work [3] uses a linearly-simulated equation to update thresholds, for it uses AC/DC ratio got by discrete cosine transform to represents smoothness of MB. In our work, since the entropy feature of each MB is pre-extracted directly from image pixels before intra coding, it will not change with any coding parameters. So it is reasonable to use fixed thresholds to do block size decision. Different Qp values (from 20 to 40) have been tested on different video sequences to get entropy distributions. Results show that the critical entropy value at the intersection part formed by 4x4 and 16x16 entropy distributions remain to be the same. Figure 1(b) shows the entropy value distribution for foreman.cif when Qp is set to 24. It is almost the same with that of Qp set to 28 in Figure 1(a). Compared with the linearly-simulated thresholds in work [3], proposed decision procedure is simpler but efficient.

Furthermore, when α is set to 3.2 and β is set to 4.6, we get the decision accuracy of proposed BSD algorithm for various CIF sequences, shown in

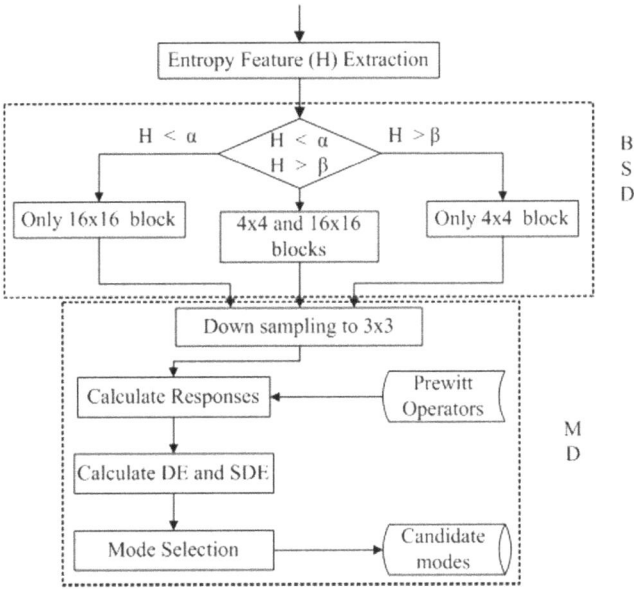

Fig. 2. Encoding flow of hybrid decision algorithms

Table 1. Block Size Decision Accuracy of CIF Sequences, 5 Frames

Sequence	Number of I6MB		Number of I4MB		Accuracy
	JM	Propose	JM	Propose	
Foreman	411	388	1569	1592	94.65%
News	620	646	1360	1334	96.06%
Mobile	68	76	1912	1904	98.33%
Akiyo	880	771	1100	1209	90.20%
Container	796	775	1184	1205	92.98%
Coast	65	27	1915	1953	97.58%
Mother	748	772	1232	1208	94.39%
Average	**512**	**494**	**1478**	**1486**	**94.88%**

Table 1. We can see that the decision accuracy is always higher than 90% and averagely equals to 94.88%. Similar work [3] can only distinguish 4x4 blocks from 16x16 and 8x8 blocks. As frame size becomes larger, work [3] will suffer higher erroneous decisions, for the percentage of I4MB becomes lower in larger frame sizes. Experimental results for proposed BSD algorithm can be found in Tables 3-6, as target application is from QCIF to HDTV(1080), respectively.

3.2 Mode Decision

Since multiple directional prediction modes (8 for 4x4 and 8x8 blocks, 2 for 16x16 blocks and 8x8 chroma channels) are strongly co-related to the edge direction of target blocks, it is straightforward to extract edge direction to predict potential good modes [7]-[12].Proposed MD algorithm uses Prewitt operators to extract the two most dominant edge directions of each block. These two directions are utilized to reduce unpromising modes. Proposed algorithm is able to reduce the 9 modes in I4MB to 3 modes and reduce the 4 modes in I16MB and Chroma MB to 2 modes, in high speed and with little loss of visual quality. The encoding flow of MD is shown in Figure 2. Totally there are 3 steps to do:

Step 1: Down sample all blocks into 3x3 size. Each coefficient of the down-sampled block is the average value of original pixels.For 16x16 block, one coefficient is the average of 64 pixels; for 4x4 block, it is the average of 4 pixels.

Step 2: 4 Prewitt operators, specified in Figure 3, are used to extract edge directions in vertical, horizontal, diagonal 45° and diagonal 135° , respectively. These four directions are defined as mode 0, mode 1, mode 3 and mode 4 in intra coding of H.264/AVC standard. For each direction, calculate the edge response of the 3x3 block to corresponding operator. Select the maximum and second maximum, denoted as dominant edge (DE) and second dominant edge (SDE).

Step 3: This step does the mode decision:

(1) The mode corresponding to DE will be chosen as candidate 1;

(2) The mode closely adjacent to DE, locating between candidate 1 and $SDE,$ will be chosen as candidate 2;

(3) DC mode is always chosen as candidate 3.

Horizontal

-1	-1	-1
0	0	0
1	1	1

Vertical

-1	0	1
-1	0	1
-1	0	1

Diagonal 45

-1	-1	0
-1	0	1
0	1	1

Diagonal 135

0	1	1
-1	0	1
-1	-1	0

Fig. 3. 4 Prewitt operators used for mode decision

Most edge detection based mode decision algorithms not only use *DE* but also use its two adjacent modes as candidates directly. However, if the two adjacent modes were candidates [5] [9] [12], it is obvious that mode between *DE* and *SDE* has higher possibility to be a better predictor than the other adjacent mode does. Thus, proposed algorithm is able to save mode and can further reduce computation. Coding performance for MD only is shown in Table 2.

4   Experiments and Results

Proposed BSD and MD methods have been tested individually and together on JM software 12.4 on a PC with 2.4G Hz CPU and 1 GB memory. Rate distortion optimization is enabled, rate control is off. Three measurement parameters, ΔPSNR, Δ Bitrate and Δ Time defined in [6], are used to evaluate encoding performance.

Table 2 shows the experimental results of MD method for all-I and IPPPP CIF sequences. It can be seen that proposed MD method outperforms Pan's

Table 2. Experimental results for MD algorithm on all-I QIF sequences, 300 I and IPPPP frames, Qp=28

I Frames						
Sequence	Pan's Algorithm[5]			Proposed MD Algorithm		
	ΔPSNR (dB)	ΔBitrate (%)	ΔTime (%)	ΔPSNR (dB)	ΔBitrate (%)	ΔTime (%)
Paris	-0.230	3.21	-57.779	-0.074	2.661	77.134
Mobile	-0.255	3.168	-59.086	-0.091	2.893	76.514
Tempete	-0.299	3.514	-57.697	-0.080	2.504	76.564
Bus	-0.218	3.849	-58.118	-0.086	3. 174	77.029
Stefan	-0.242	3.717	-57.972	-0.102	2.351	75.538
Average	**-0.236**	**3.492**	**-58.130**	**-0.087**	**2.712**	**-76.556**
IPPPP Frames						
Sequence	Pan's Algorithm[5]			Proposed MD Algorithm		
	PSNR(dB)	BR (%)	Time (%)	PSNR(dB)	BR (%)	Time (%)
Paris	-0.023	0.504	-26.901	-0.013	0.425	-29.610
Mobile	-0.018	0.451	-27.665	-0.009	0. 340	-32.360
Tempete	-0.029	0.812	-26.732	-0.019	0.672	-33.825
Bus	-0.013	0.325	-26.048	-0.008	0.259	-34.085
Stefan	-0.017	0.406	-26.224	-0.06	0.301	-34.304
Average	**-0.02**	**0.500**	**-26.714**	**-0.011**	**0.398**	**-32.837**

Table 3. Experimental results of BSD algorithm for all-I CIF and HDTV (1080p) sequences, Qp=28

CIF				HDTV			
sequences	Compare with [4]			Sequence	Compare with JM		
	ΔPSNR (dB)	ΔBitrate (%)	ΔTime (%)		ΔPSNR (dB)	ΔBitrate (%)	ΔTime (%)
Foreman	+0.0018	+0.178	-20.472	Blue_sky	-0.0085	+0.3553	-33.476
News	+0.002	+0.095	-16.403	Station2	-0.00083	+0.2479	-18.32
Mobile	+0.002	-0.011	-20.984	Riverbed	+0.00133	+0.1115	-10.523
Coastguard	+0.0036	+0.038	-20.926	Rush_hour	-0.00733	+0.961	-26.981
Average	**+0.00235**	**+0.075**	**-19.69**	**Average**	**-0.0038**	**+0.418**	**-22.33**

algorithm. In all-I case, proposed MD algorithm is able to save about 76%coding time with average bitrate increase at about 2.7% and PSNR drop is 0.087dB. In IPPPP case, MD is able to save about 33% computation complexity with acceptable performance decrease.

Table 3 and part of Tables 4-6 aim to evaluate the performance of BSD algorithm. From QCIF to HDTV cases, PSNR performance is the same as original video signals with computational complexity reduced by 22%~30% at the cost that bitrate is increased less than 0.5%. Comparison results with [4] on BSD can be seen in Table 3. Proposed BSD outperforms [4] in time reduction but keeping the same video quality. As a conclusion, the proposed BSD algorithm can achieve nearly 95% decision accuracy, with PSNR loss less than 0.004dB; bitrate increase is negligible and time reduction at about 22%~30%. It is expected to be a video-quality-keeping accelerator for H.264 encoder.

Tables 4-6 aims to show the comparison experimental results for BSD and HD algorithms, as target frame changing from QCIF to SDTV(720). On the one hand, PSNR and bitrate performance of BSD is almost no change compared with original videos, with 27.1%~29.2% complexity reduction. Especially, PSNR of BSD is even increased by 0.0009dB when complexity is reduced by nearly 30% in Table 4. Take notice that the time reductions of BSD on "Stefan" and

Table 4. Experimental results for BSD and HD on all-I QCIF sequences, 300 frames, Qp=28

Sequences	BSD Algorithm Only			Proposed HD Algorithm		
	ΔPSNR (dB)	ΔBitrate (%)	ΔTime (%)	ΔPSNR (dB)	ΔBitrate (%)	ΔTime (%)
foreman	0.0000	+0.1767	-30.43	-0.098	+1.591	-62.84
news	-0.00067	+0.2459	-30.54	-0.0523	+0.361	-62.86
mobile	+0.0022	+0.0435	-31.20	-0.0335	+0.704	-61.58
tempete	+0.0013	+0.0292	-30.77	+0.0355	+0.692	-62.99
coast	+0.002	+0.0863	-22.57	-0.0585	+1.19	-62.62
silent	+0.0006	+0.0396	-30.24	-0.0411	+1.603	-64.49
Average	**+0.0009**	**+0.1035**	**-29.29**	**-0.0413**	**+1.023**	**-62.89**

Table 5. Experimental results for BSD and HD on all-I CIF sequences, 300 frames, Qp=28

Sequences	BSD Algorithm Only			Proposed HD Algorithm		
	ΔPSNR (dB)	ΔBitrate (%)	ΔTime (%)	ΔPSNR (dB)	ΔBitrate (%)	ΔTime (%)
foreman	0.0008	+0.3682	-31.67	-0.084	+1.722	-63.46
news	+0.001	+0.554	-34.07	+0.05667	+3.341	-64.36
mobile	+0.0013	+0.0498	-34.17	-0.039	+0.481	-58.43
akiyo	-0.125	+1.351	-37.88	-0.07	+3.402	-65.14
container	+0.0035	+0.593	-31.06	-0.02466	+1.345	-61.09
football	+0.0012	+0.099	-6.183	-0.06516	+1.542	-60.94
mother	+0.00283	+1.5113	-33.85	-0.0936	+1.721	-63.64
stefan	0	+0.0904	-6.329	-0.0645	+0.958	-63.65
coast	+0.002	+0.0815	-28.58	-0.0526	+1.294	-62.42
Average	**-0.0131**	**+0.5221**	**-27.09**	**-0.0485**	**+1.756**	**-62.57**

Table 6. Experimental results for BSD and HD on all-I SDTV (720p) sequences, 300 frames, Qp=28

Sequences	BSD Algorithm Only			Proposed HD Algorithm		
	ΔPSNR (dB)	ΔBitrate (%)	ΔTime (%)	ΔPSNR (dB)	ΔBitrate (%)	ΔTime (%)
city	+0.003	+0.1479	-26.45	-0.009	+0.928	-62.79
crew	-0.0013	+0.5021	-29.14	+0.06883	+4.875	-67.63
harbour	+0.0006	+0.1223	-26.64	-0.02	+0.679	-63.49
knight	+0.001	+0.1847	-26.39	-0.0026	+1.29	-64.76
parkunner	+0.0021	+0.1062	-27.01	-0.037	+0.404	-62.94
Average	**+0.0011**	**+0.2127**	**-27.13**	**0**	**+1.617**	**-64.33**

"football" are relatively low, for there are many high level of motions and details contained. On the other hand, PSNR drop of HD for QCIF/CIF/SDTV is less than 0.049dB with bitrate increase limited to 2%. However, computational complexity reduction of HD is up to 63% in almost every video, for BSD functions together with MD.

Tables 7-8 are designed to show the experimental results for HD algorithm compared with 2 similar works [3][4]. Proposed HD algorithm greatly outperformances [3] in computational complexity reduction by about 50%, at the cost that performances on PSNR and bitrate is acceptably decreased. Compared with [3], 7% complexity and 1.1% bitrate is saved, at the cost that PSNR is slightly dropped by 0.03dB, However, the overall PSNR drop of proposed HD is limted to 0.007dB.

One thing worth mentioning and also revealed by experimental results is that HD algorithm is a trade-off on video quality and complexity reduction. Experimental results in this paper and in [3][4] show that HD algorithm achieves acceptable good performance on PSNR and Bitrate, but time reduction is little lower than MD does even when it functions together with MD. Because the

Table 7. Comparison results with reference [4] for All-I CIF sequences, Qp=28, 300 frames

Sequences	Reference [4]			Proposed HD Algorithm		
	ΔPSNR (dB)	ΔBitrate (%)	ΔTime (%)	ΔPSNR (dB)	ΔBitrate (%)	ΔTime (%)
akiyo	-0.001	0.30	-22.34	-0.07	3.402	-65.14
coast	+0.000	-0.01	-6.15	-0.0526	+1.294	-62.42
container	+0.006	+0.18	-9.39	-0.024	+1.345	-61.09
mobile	0.000	+0.01	-9.50	-0.039	0.481	-58.43
mother	-0.002	+0.13	-20.36	-0.093	+1.721	-63.64
news	-0.01	+0.15	-19.27	-0.056	+3.341	-64.36
foreman	0.010	+0.02	-10.60	-0.084	+1.722	-63.46
Average	**+0.0004**	**+0.111**	**-13.94**	**-0.05**	**+1.9**	**-62.46**

Table 8. Comparison results with reference [3] for All-I sequences, Qp=28, 300 frames

Sequences	Reference [3]			Proposed HD Algorithm		
	ΔPSNR (dB)	ΔBitrate (%)	ΔTime (%)	ΔPSNR (dB)	ΔBitrate (%)	ΔTime (%)
mother	-0.05	+2.49	-54.5	-0.093	+1.721	-63.64
foreman	-0.06	+1.5	-57.8	-0.084	+1.722	-63.46
stefan	-0.01	+4.27	-52.1	-0.0645	+0.958	-63.65
parkrunner	0	+0.94	-59.5	-0.037	+ 0.404	-62.94
Average	**-0.03**	**+2.3**	**-55.9**	**-0.069**	**+1.201**	**-63.42**

calculation spent on BSD is partially wasted when entropy feature is not accurate enough to separate 4x4 and 16x16 blocks.

5   Conclusion

This paper proposes a fast hybrid decision algorithm for H.264 intra prediction. Entropy feature is pre-extracted directly from image pixels to decide the smoothness of MB. Based on smoothness judgment, the best block size for each MB can be selected, avoiding exhaustively examining all possible block sizes. In addition, Prewitt operators are used to get the edge directions to select only efficient modes instead of full search. Experimental results show that about 95% BSD accuracy with less than 0.007dB PSNR loss and acceptable bit rate increase has been be achieved, complexity reduction is up to 63%.

References

1. Joint Video Team: Draft ITU-T Recommendation and Final Draft International Standard of Joint Video Specification (2003)
2. Jeon, B., Lee, J.: Fast Mode Decision for H.264 ITU-T Q.6/16, Doc.JVT-J033 (2003)

3. Lin, Y., Chang, Y.: Fast Block Type Decision Algorithm for Intra Prediction in H.264/FRext. In: ICIP 2005, vol. 1, pp. I-585–1-588. IEEE Press, Los Alamitos (2005)
4. Kun, Z., Chun, Y., Qiang, L., Yuzhou, Z.: A Fast Block Type Decision Method for H.264/AVC Intra Prediction. In: The 9th International Conference on Advanced Communication Technology, vol. 1, pp. 673–676. IEEE Press, Los Alamitos (2007)
5. Pan, F., Lin, X.: Fast Mode Decision Algorithm for Intra Prediction in H.264/AVC Video Coding. IEEE Transactions on Circuits and System for Video Technology, 813–822 (2005)
6. Bjontegarrd, G.: Calculation of Average PSNR Differences between RD-curve. In: 13th VCEG-M33 Meeting, Austin, TX (April 2001)
7. Huang, Y., Hsieh, B., Chen, U.: Analysis, Fast Algorithm and VLSI Architecture Design for H.264/AVC Intra Frame Coder. IEEE Transactions on Circuits and System for Video Technology 15, 378–401 (2005)
8. Wei, Z., Li, H., Ngi Ngan, K.: An efficient Intra Mode Selection Algorithm for H.264 Based on Fast Edge Classification. In: IEEE International Symposium on Circuits and Systems, ISCAS 2007, pp. 3630–3633. IEEE Press, Los Alamitos (2007)
9. Li, S., Wei, X., Ikenaga, T., Goto, S.: A VLSI Architecture Design of an Edge Based Fast Intra Prediction Mode Decision Algorithm for H.264/AVC. GLSVLSI, Italy (2007)
10. Wei, Z., Li, H., Ngi Ngan, K.: An efficient Intra Mode Selection Algorithm for H.264 Based on Fast Edge Classification. In: IEEE International Symposium on Circuits and Systems, ISCAS 2007, pp. 3630–3633 (2007)
11. Tseng, C.-H., Wang, H.-M., Yang, J.-F.: Enhanced Intra 4x4 Mode Decision for H.264/AVC coders. IEEE Transactions on Circuits and System for Video Technology 16, 1027–1032 (2006)
12. Wang, J., Yang, J., Chen, J.: A Fast Mode Decision Algorithm and Its VLSI Design for H.264. IEEE Transactions on Circuits and System for Video Technology, 1414–1422 (October 2007)
13. Li, H., Ngan, K.N.: Fast and efficient method for block edge classification. In: Proceeding of ACM IWCMC 2006 Multimedia over Wireless, pp. 67–72 (July 2006)

Low Complexity Video Compression Using Moving Edge Detection Based on DCT Coefficients

Chanyul Kim and Noel E. O'Connor

CLARITY: Centre for Sensor Web Technologies, Dublin City University, Glasnevin,
Dublin, Ireland
Chanyul.kim,oconnorn@eeng.dcu.ie

Abstract. In this paper, we propose a new low complexity video compression method based on detecting blocks containing moving edges using only DCT coefficients. The detection, whilst being very efficient, also allows efficient motion estimation by constraining the search process to moving macro-blocks only. The encoders PSNR is degraded by 2dB compared to H.264/AVC inter for such scenarios, whilst requiring only 5% of the execution time. The computational complexity of our approach is comparable to that of the DISCOVER codec which is the state of the art low complexity distributed video coding. The proposed method finds blocks with moving edge blocks and processes only selected blocks. The approach is particularly suited to surveillance type scenarios with a static camera.

Keywords: Low complexity video compression, Moving edge, DCT.

1 Introduction

New digital video applications have recently emerged such as private internet broadcasting and wireless multimedia sensor networks. These kinds of applications fundamentally need a low power and low complexity encoder in order to operate on power limited devices such as wireless video phones, personal digital assistants (PDA) and sensor platforms. Of course, apart from coding computational complexity, the coding gain of a compression algorithm plays a vital role in determining its practical usefulness. Therefore, much research has targeted *reasonable* coding gains whilst keeping complexity low. However, the challenge comes in finding the optimum trade-off as the dual requirements of coding gains and low complexity are not comfortable bed-fellows.

H.264/AVC has been standardized with a target for coding gains regardless of complexity [1]. Although the power of digital devices has increased steadily, it is still hard to realize real-time operation on power limited devices. Recently, much research for achieving low complexity with reasonable coding gains has been performed using H.264/AVC [2,3,4]. In hybrid coding, such as the standardization efforts of ITU-T and MPEG, two main coding tools are used to

B. Huet et al. (Eds.): MMM 2009, LNCS 5371, pp. 96–107, 2009.
© Springer-Verlag Berlin Heidelberg 2009

obtain reasonable coding gains: transform and prediction. The most time consuming functions of H.264/AVC are motion estimation, compensation and prediction. Therefore low complexity algorithms based on H.264/AVC typically attempt to reduce the complexity of these three functions. In [2,3], the authors' approaches focus on reducing the complexity needed to find motion vectors and make mode decisions as required by the variable block size feature of H.264/AVC. Many fast algorithms are reviewed in [4]. As an example of other approaches investigated to obtain low complexity, Hiratsuka *et al.* proposed adaptive tree based video coding where their approach has similarity to 3D DCT based coding [5]. However, its drawback is low coding gains even though low complexity is achieved compared to standard codecs. Perhaps the most popular approach to obtain coding gains is region of interest (ROI) based coding. However this approach needs an additional step of object or region segmentation that requires significant computational overhead. In the case of low motion video such as surveillance, low complex algorithms are possible such as that proposed in [6]. Sriram S *et al.* proposed foveation based low complexity video coding [7]. Their approach uses human visual system (HVS) modeling to obtain coding gains whereby a DCT based foveation filter is used to reduce complexity for detecting foveation regions.

For implementing low complexity encoders, a coding paradigm named distributed video coded (DVC) based on Wyner-Ziv [8] and Slepian-Wolf [9] information theory has recently emerged. The basic concept is that the complexity shifts from the encoder to the decoder by using error correction codes (ECC). The distributed probability between the current frame and the previous frame is defined similar to a channel in communication theory and only parity bits of ECC are sent to the decoder. The decoder decodes the current frame with parity bits and a reference frame sent as side information. In this approach, the encoder only performs the matrix multiplications between the parity matrix and data bits, whilst the decoder requires more complexity to decode the ECC. Puri and Ramchandran proposed the PRISM codec for multimedia transmissions on wireless networks using syndromes [10]. Aaron and Girod proposed a video coding framework using intraframe encoding as side information with turbo codes named Stanford DVC and transform based coding [11,12]. Recently, X.Artigas *et al.* proposed the DISCOVER codec including more advanced tools to obtain coding gains such as a rate-distortion module and virtual channel modeling. Despite their efforts, however, coding quality still suffers degradation compared to H.264/AVC [13].

We propose very low complexity video compression in a similar vein to ROI based coding. The proposed method does not perform object or region segmentation which can introduce computational complexity but rather detects moving edges using only DCT coefficients. The approach can be adapted from low motion to high motion sequences. The motivation for the research is presented in the next section. The proposed approach is explained in Section 3. The performance of the proposed method is compared to H.264/AVC and the DISCOVER codec in Section 4. Finally, concluding remarks are made in Section 5.

2 Motivation

The computational complexity of video coding comes from the motion estimation, compensation and prediction block. As mentioned in Section 1, many researchers focus on reducing motion estimation time to obtain low complexity in hybrid coding. A motion search algorithm has the role of finding matched blocks without any prior knowledge of the image. If prior knowledge of image contents was available, this would enable us to perform better motion estimation, but focusing on the regions that really need it, thereby satisfying the requirements of high coding gains and low complexity at the same time. A ROI-based encoder effectively attempts to predict the content of the scene to achieve coding gains. However, it usually requires an additional segmentation block and pre-/post-processing of the video which means significant computational cost [14]. We propose a ROI-based scheme that detects only moving edges and not complete moving objects. This facilitates low complexity encoding, particularly as this detection can be done using the DCT directly. Static edges give a hint for the boundary of object and moving edges give information of on which area has motion. Using this knowledge of moving regions then allows us to perform low complexity motion estimation. Moving edges are detected through classification of edges using DCT coefficients in a 4×4 sub block. An algorithm for reducing falsely detected moving edges is also suggested in this paper. Block based moving edge classification is more adaptable for video compression than a frame based approach since a frame based approach needs to find the block position and edge types which requires additional computational complexity.

3 Proposed Approach

The proposed video compression approach can use a modified standard H.264/AVC encoder to generate the necessary information corresponding to the edge direction number (ED) and the standard deviation of the AC DCT coefficients (SD) as well as to generate the required intra coded frame. However, in this paper, our previously proposed intra coding method is used as the intra encoder [15]. The encoder proposed in this paper consists of the moving edge detection and video compression functional blocks as shown in Fig. 1. The moving edge detection function block detects not only moving edges but also removes false moving edges via a reduction function block (RFME). Both processes are performed using 4×4 DCT coefficients.

After moving edge detection, video compression in our method is performed with a similar approach to a standard H.264/AVC codec. However, in order to obtain low complexity, our video compression method does not use variable block size (only 4×4 blocks are used in this paper), $\frac{1}{4}$ pel motion estimation/compensation or rate distortion optimization as used in H.264/AVC. Of course, this causes degradation of video quality, however, since our ROIs correspond to only moving edge blocks the slight degradation of video quality is offset by the bit savings obtained. Therefore, the overall rate-distortion performance is not severely degraded compared to H.264/AVC (see Fig. 6 and the discussion

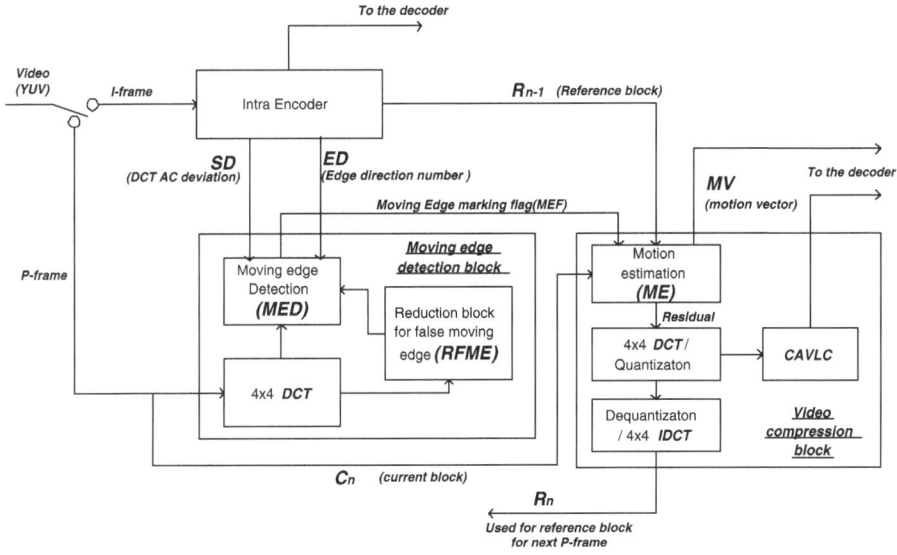

Fig. 1. The proposed video compression functional blocks, bold italics indicate abbreviations used in the paper

in the results section). The detailed functionalities of the proposed method are explained in the following.

3.1 Moving Edge Detection

Moving edge detection. If the current 4×4 block has a specific edge feature (such as horizontal, vertical, diagonal or texture as shown in Fig. 2(a)), the standard deviation (SD) of AC coefficients as calculated in equation (1) indicates whether edge or non-edge information is present [16]. As an object moves in the scene it covers and uncovers background around its borders. Also, the object may deform, changing its shape. Both of these phenomena result in a change of the edge characteristics within blocks on the object's boundary. This can be used to detect moving edge blocks from frame to frame. There are 3 possibilities:

- An edge block changes to a non-edge block;
- A non-edge block changes to an edge block;
- The edge direction within the block changes to another one of directions depicted in Fig. 2(b).

$$\sigma_{ac} = \frac{\sum_{i=1}^{15} C_i^2}{15} - (\frac{\sum_{i=1}^{15} C_i}{15})^2 \qquad (1)$$

Where σ_{ac} is a standard deviation of all AC coefficients in a 4x4 block, C_i is the ith DCT coefficient as depicted in Fig. 2(a). If the current block is a non-edge block, we set the edge strength measure to a pre-defined threshold value(TH).

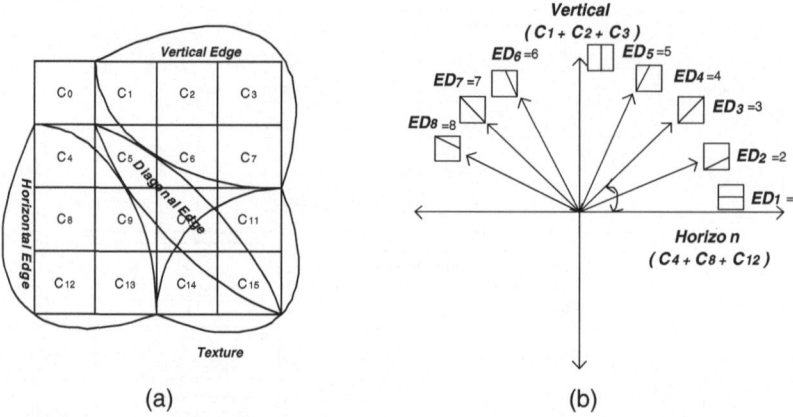

Fig. 2. (a) Edges related to DCT coefficients; (b) Edge direction classification as numbers from 1 to 8

Then the edge strength value of a non-edge block at the same spatial position in the previous frame is examined. If the difference of edge strength value is zero between two blocks, this means that there is no change between blocks, so this block is not a candidate for a moving edge. If the difference of edge strength value is more than zero, there is a transition from an edge to a non-edge or a non-edge to an edge. We consider both cases as moving edges. Algorithm 1 shows a simple procedure for obtaining a moving edge. Whilst straightforward to implement, this algorithm means that moving edges are easily affected by the threshold value so that many false edges are introduced as shown in Fig. 3(b). Thus, we need to reduce these false moving edges. This algorithm, based on edge direction modeling, is explained in the next section.

Algorithm 1. Moving edge detection

1: **if** $\sigma_{sd} < TH$ **then**
2:     set non-edge, SD = TH,   save SD value to SD_n
3: **else**
4:     edge, save SD value to SD_n
5: **end if**
6: **if** *current frame* $\neq$ *intra frame* **then**
7:     **if** $| SD_n - SD_{n-1} | > 0$ **then**
8:        moving edge
9:     **else**
10:        static edge
11:     **end if**
12: **end if**

Reducing false moving edges. A false moving edge arises from image noise and an incorrect threshold value for deciding moving edges with the SD of DCT coefficients. The image noise could be eliminated by a pre-processing filter; however, this inevitably generates more computational complexity. We cannot simply

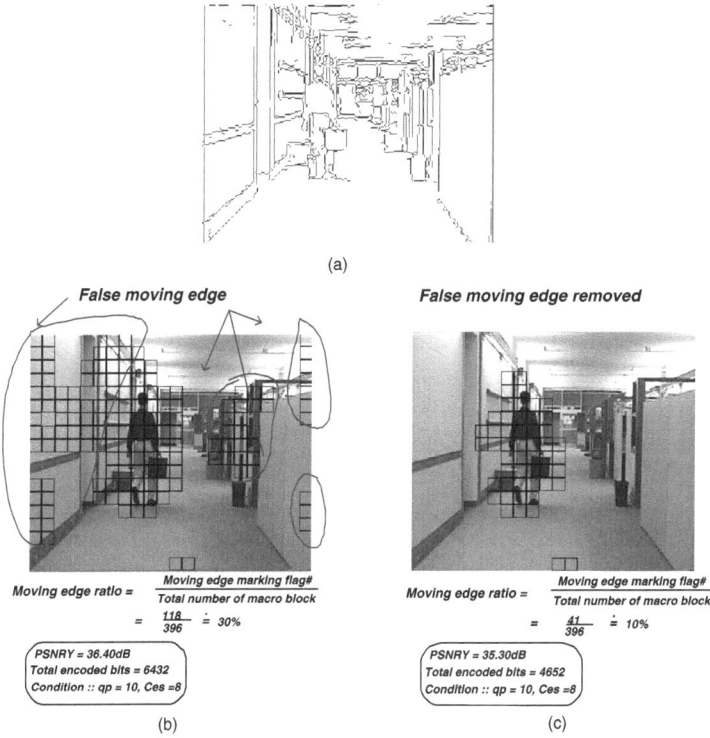

Fig. 3. (a) An edge image for 50th frame of Hall Monitor, qp =10, C_{es} = 8: (a) an edge frame considering edge directions; (b) After moving edge detection, with false moving edges indicated; (c) After false moving edge reduction – moving macro blocks decrease by 20%, PSNR = -1.1dB, required bits = -28% compared to (a)

increase the threshold used, since real moving edges are also removed when a strong threshold value is applied. Therefore we should select real moving edges out of the total suggested moving edges whilst keeping a reasonable threshold value by observing critical variation of the edge direction (more than 45°) between the current block and the reference block. Our reduction block for false moving edges (RFME) can select real moving edges by defining edge directions and measuring the edge direction difference. Edge directions can be obtained as following:

$$\theta = \arctan\langle \frac{\sum_{i=1}^{3} C_i}{\sum_{i=1}^{3} C_{4i}} \rangle \qquad (2)$$

Where C_i is the ith DCT coefficient of a 4×4 sub-block. We consider edge directions , $0°, \pm 45°, 90°, \pm 26.5°, \pm 63.4°$ shown in Fig. 2(b), which are used in H.264/AVC intra prediction. The obtained edge map by classifying edge directions is depicted in Fig. 3(a). We allocated numbers from one to eight each of these directions by equation (2). The difference of an edge direction number

(ED) between the current block and the reference block is defined as a distance (D) as in equation (3).

$$D = |[(M + shift)\%8)] - 4| \quad \text{if}[(N + shift)\%8] == 4 \qquad (3)$$

Where $[n]$ is a near integer number n, $\%$ is a remainder, M and N are EDs of the reference block and the current block respectively. When D is greater than a pre-defined threshold value, usually set to two, we consider this block as a moving block since the edge direction has changed more than $45°$. The maximum difference value of ED occurs between ED_1 and ED_8 as shown in Fig. 2(b). However, the difference edge direction between ED_1 and ED_8 is only $26.5°$ even though the difference between them is generated as the maximum value (7). Therefore a compensation routine should be applied. If the ED of the current block and the reference block are N, M respectively, the edge difference is not calculated as $|N - M|$ but as in equation (3). First, the shift value is found as a pre-condition of equation (3). The ED of the current block shifts to the centre number (which is 4 since eight numbers are allocated for all directions), therefore the total difference between them is calculated as a shifted value of ED of the current block. For instance, let the current ED is one (horizontal direction) and a reference ED is eight($-26.5°$), the shift value is three and the distance (D) is not seven but one. This case is then not a candidate for a moving edge by setting the threshold to two($45°$). Fig. 3(b)(c) shows the result of a moving edge detection and false moving edge reduction blocks. Although PSNR is ultimately degraded 1.1dB compared to considering all moving edges, the required encoder bits are also reduced by 28%. Also the number of macro blocks required to process is decreased dramatically, significantly reducing the processing time. In the example shown in Fig. 3(c), Only 41 macro blocks are considered for further processing out of all 118 macro blocks if false moving edges are not removed.

3.2 Video Compression Block

The video compression block consists of four blocks: motion estimation and compensation (ME), DCT/Quantization, IDCT/Dequantization and content adaptive variable length coding (CAVLC). The ME block is performed only for macro blocks which have the moving edge flag (MEF) from the MED block as shown in Fig. 1. The flag is set for each macroblock by considering neighboring blocks near moving edges as shown in Fig. 4. For example, if a 4×4 moving block is located in the 6th sub-block of a macro block in the raster scan order, we select the search area so that the moving edge sub-block is located in the centre. The resulting overlapping areas with neighboring macro blocks are depicted in grey in Fig. 4. The moving edge flag (MEF) is also set for these macro blocks.

After deciding the macro blocks that require processing, ME is then performed with full search with a 16×16 search range, no variable size blocks (i.e. one motion vector per a 4×4 sub block), no sub-pel compensation and no motion prediction to guarantee low complexity. The IDCT/Dequantization is performed for reconstructing the current image. After ME, content adaptive variable length

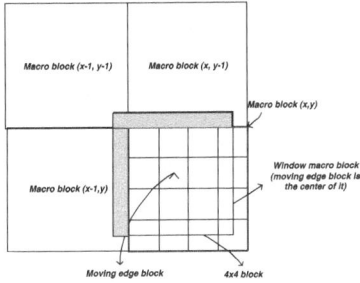

Fig. 4. Additional needed macro blocks to maximize the motion search range of a moving edge 4×4 sub block

coding (CAVLC) is performed in the same way as in H.264/AVC. The in-loop-filter (de-blocking filter) is not used in the proposed method.

4   Implementation and Experimental Results

This section verifies the performance of the proposed low complex video compression framework. The performance is compared to H.264/AVC reference software KTA 1.6 based on JM 11.0 with baseline profile released in Jan. 2008[1], H.263+ based on TMN code[2] and the DISCOVER codec [13]. The KTA reference has more advanced features than H.264/AVC such as an adaptive quantization matrix selection, a $\frac{1}{8}$ pel motion compensated prediction, an adaptive prediction error etc. H.263+ is designed as a low bitrate compression by adding several annexes which can substantially improve coding efficiency. The DISCOVER codec is the state of the art in distributed video coding, focusing on low complexity encoder[3]. Only luminance coefficients are considered in this paper, so U and V coefficients and the de-blocking filter are disabled in the reference software.

Hall monitor with QCIF and CIF resolution, Camera and Foreman sequences at QCIF resolution, down-sampled to 15Hz are selected as test sequences. The Hall Monitor and Camera sequence have no global motion and they are representative of surveillance applications. Foreman has significant global motion, leading PSNR saturation explained in Chapter 4.1. All tests are performed with GOP size 8 and one I-frame per every seven P-frames (IPPPPPPPI). Our low complex video compression framework is written in ANSI C++ and a Intel Integrated Performance Primitive 5.3 library. All tests are performed on an Intel Core(TM)2 Duo 3.6GHz with 2GB RAM using Window XP version 2002 with service pack 2.

---

[1] The source code is available at http://iphome.hhi.de/suehring/tml/download/KTA
[2] The source code is available at http://whkong.myrice.com/download/src/vcomp
[3] The executable DISCOVER codec is available at http://www.discoverdvc.org/

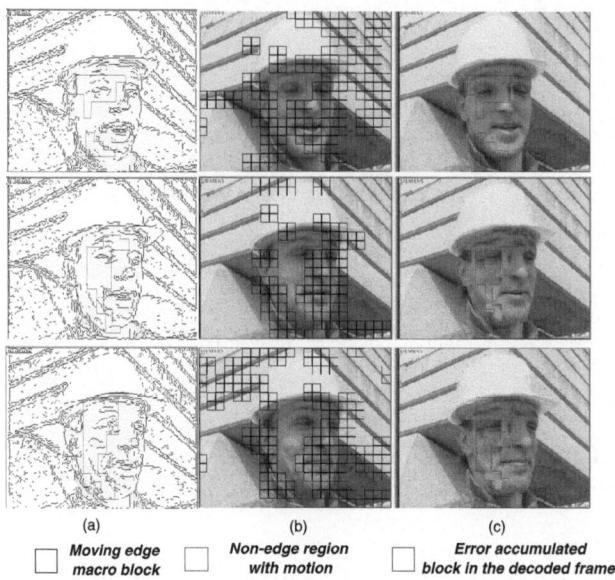

(a)   (b)   (c)

☐ Moving edge   ☐ Non-edge region   ☐ Error accumulated
  macro block   with motion   block in the decoded frame

Fig. 5. (a) Edge images (b) Moving edge macro blocks: regions classified as non-edges but that have motion are not detected properly as shown by the area within the blue line (c) Decoded frames: accumulated errors are displayed within the red line

4.1 Rate-Distortion performance

Fig. 6 depicts the compression results compared to the H.264/AVC, H.263+ and the DISCOVER codecs. The proposed method shows good compression, albeit degraded by 2dB compared to H.264/AVC. However, this constitutes an increase of almost 4dB and 1.5dB compared to the DISCOVER codec and H.263+ for the Hall Monitor and Camera sequence as shown in Fig. 6(a),(b)&(c). However, PSNR saturation occurred for the Foreman sequence as shown in Fig. 6(d). This problem arises from detecting non-edge blocks that actually exhibit motion. For example, when the camera is constantly moving, this generates moving edges near the object boundary. If there are non-edge regions with motion inside the object, this is not detected by our approach. Fig. 5 shows the block artifacts in the decoded frame. Regions classified as non-edges but that have motion are not detected properly as shown by the area within the blue line. This generates block artifacts due to the difference in DC values of the current and reference sub blocks. This error is accumulated (red lines) until an intra frame is encountered. Therefore, our application is particularly suited to surveillance-type applications without global motion or non-edge regions with motion.

4.2 Execution Time

Fig. 7(a) shows execution time for 30 frames at hall monitor and foreman sequence according to coding methods. Our approach is almost the same or better

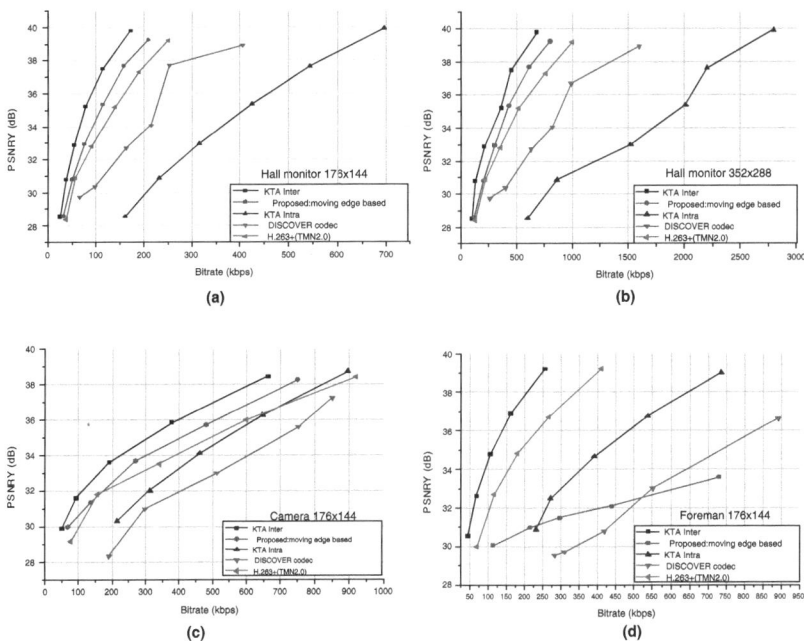

Fig. 6. Rate-Distortion – (a)(c) QCIF (b) CIF resolution: These sequences have no-edge regions without motion; (d) This sequence has no-edge regions with motion. For (a)(b)(c) the PSNR of the proposed method is degraded by maximum 2dB compared to H.264, for (d) PSNR saturation has occurred.

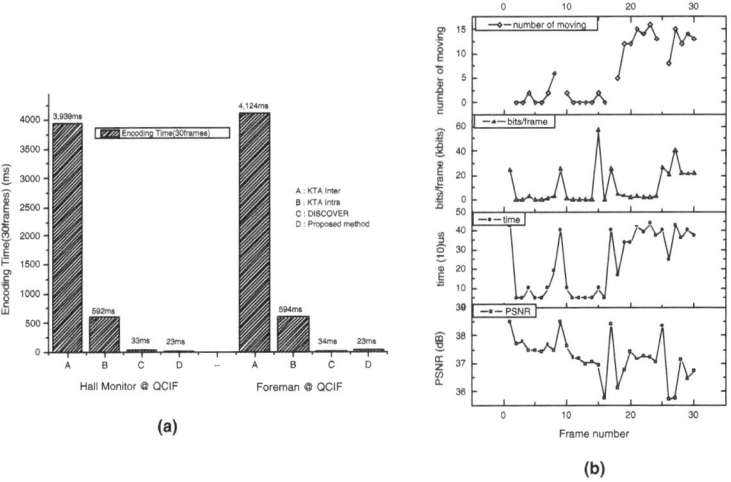

Fig. 7. (a) Average complexity comparison between encoder (30frames) (b) PSNR, encoding time, the number of encoded bits, the number of moving edge macro block verse frame number (hall monitor with QCIF)

than DISCOVER codec well known as a very low complexity encoder. Additional DCT is introduced to obtain moving edges, but it does not generate severe computational complexity due to its integer transform that occupies less than 3% of whole complexity in H.264 [17]. Moving edges give which macro blocks should be treated as motion estimation block. Typically, the moving edges are less than one of tenth of the whole macro blocks, sometimes the number of moving edges goes to zero (no needed any processing) as shown in Fig. 7(b). The execution time is less than 5% compared to H.264/AVC intra coding since our approach does not use advanced coding tools introduced in H.264 and whole macro blocks.

5   Conclusion and Future Considerations

In this paper, a low complexity video compression algorithm based on detecting moving edges in the compressed domain is suggested. In terms of coding gains, PSNR is degraded by 2dB and enhanced by 1.5dB and 4dB compared to H.264/AVC, H263+ and the DISCOVER codec respectively. In terms of computational complexity, it shows almost the same complexity as the DISCOVER codec which is the state of the art in low complexity distributed video coding. However, error accumulation occurs in non-edge areas with motion. Clearly, in the future we need to consider not only moving edges but also the entire moving object in order to overcome this drawback. We would also like to investigate integrating our approach into a DVC framework.

Acknowledgements

Authors would like to acknowledge the support of Samsung Electronics and Science Foundation Ireland under grant 07/CE/I1147.

References

1. 14496-10, H.: Advanced video coding. Technical report, ITU-T (2003)
2. Tourapis, H.-Y.C., Tourapis, A.M.: Fast motion estimation within the h.264 codec. In: Proceedings of International Conference on Multimedia and Expo, 2003. ICME 2003, vol. 3, pp. 517–520 (July 2003)
3. gon Kim, D., jung Yoo, C., bae Chang, O., mi Kim, E., Choi, J.R.: Improved fast mode decision algorithm for variable macro block motion compensation in h.264. In: International Symposium on Information Technology Convergence, 2007. ISITC 2007, Joenju, pp. 184–187 (November 2007)
4. Wong, H.M., Au, O.C., Chang, A., Yip, S.K., Ho, C.W.: Fast mode decision and motion estimation for h.264 (FMDME). In: IEEE Proceedings of International Symposium on Circuits and Systems, 2006. ISCAS 2006 (May 2006)
5. Hiratsuka, S., Goto, S., Baba, T., Ikenaga, T.: Video coding algorithm based on adaptive tree for low electricity consumption. In: Proceedings of the 2004 IEEE Asia-Pacific Conference on Circuits and Systems, 2004, vol. 1, pp. 5–8 (December 2004)

6. Magli, E., Mancin, M., Merello, L.: Low-complexity video compression for wireless sensor networks. In: Proceedings of 2003 International Conference on Multimedia and Expo, 2003. ICME 2003, vol. 3, pp. 585–588 (July 2003)
7. Sriram Sankaran, R.A., Khokhar, A.A.: Adaptive multifoveation for low-complexity video compression with a stationary camera perspective. In: Proc. SPIE, vol. 5685, p. 1007 (2005)
8. Wyner, A., Ziv, J.: The rate-distortion function for source coding with side information at the decoder. IEEE Transactions on Information Theory 22, 1–11 (1976)
9. Slepian, D., Wolf, J.: Noiseless coding of correlated information sources. IEEE Transactions on Information Theory 19, 471–480 (1973)
10. Puri, R., Ramchandran, K.: Prism: A new robust video coding architecture based on distributed compression principles. In: Proc. Allerton Conf. (October 2002)
11. Aaron, A., Rane, S., Zhang, R., Girod, B.: Wyner-ziv coding for video: applications to compression and error resilience. In: Proceedings of Data Compression Conference, 2003. DCC 2003, pp. 93–102 (March 2003)
12. Aaron, A., Rane, S., Setton, E., Girod, B.: Transform-domain wyner-ziv codec for video. In: Proceedings of SPIE Visual Communications and Image Processing Conference, San Jose, USA (January 2004)
13. Artigas, X., Ascenso, J., Dalai, M., Klomp, S., Kubasov, D., Ouaret, M.: The discover codec: Architecture, techniques and evaluation. In: Picture Coding Symposium, Lisbon, Portugal (2007)
14. Chi, M.C., Chen, M.J., Yeh, C.H., Jhu, J.A.: Region-of-interest video coding based on rate and distortion variations for h.263+. Image Commun. 23(2), 127–142 (2008)
15. Kim, C., O'Connor, N.E.: Low complexity intra video coding using transform domain prediction. In: International Conference on Visualization, Imaging, and Image Processing, Palma de Mallorca, Spain (2008)
16. Labit, C., Marescq, J.P.: Temporal adaptive vector quantization for image sequence coding. In: SPIE, Advances in Image Processing, Hague, Netherlands, vol. 804 (April 1989)
17. Kim, C., O'Connor, N.E.: Reducing complexity and memory accesses in motion compensation interpolation in video codecs. In: China-Ireland International Conference on Information and Communications (2007)

Converting H.264-Derived Motion Information into Depth Map

Mahsa T. Pourazad, Panos Nasiopoulos, and Rabab K. Ward

Electrical and Computer Engineering Department, University of British Columbia
Vancouver, BC, V6T 1Z4, Canada
{pourazad,panos,rababw}@ece.ubc.ca

Abstract. An efficient method that estimates the depth map of a 3D scene using the motion information of its H.264-encoded 2D video is presented. Our proposed method employs a revised version of the motion information. This is obtained based on the characteristics of the 3D human visual perception. The low complexity of our approach and its compatibility with future broadcasting networks allow its real-time implementation at the receiver, i.e. the 3D signal is delivered at no additional burden to the network. Performance evaluations show that our approach outperforms the other existing H.264-based technique by up to 1.5 dB PSNR i.e. it provides more realistic depth information of the scene. Moreover the subjective comparison of results (obtained by viewers watching the generated stereo video sequences on 3D display system) confirms the higher efficiency of our method.

Keywords: 2D to 3D conversion, Depth map estimation, 3D TV, Stereoscopic TV.

1 Introduction

The commercialization of three-dimensional television (3D TV) applications will bring another revolution in TV's history (the last one being the introduction of color TV). 3D TV generates a compelling sense of physical real space for the viewers by allowing on-screen scenes to emerge and penetrate into the viewers' space. Viewers thus feel they are part of the scene they are watching.

The successful introduction of 3D TV to the consumer market relies not only on technological advances but also on the availability of a wide variety of 3D content. Thus the creation of new 3D video content will be important. Equally important is the ability to convert existing 2D material to 3D format. This will allow the existing popular movies and documentaries to be watched on 3D screens. Converting 2D content to 3D video streams is possible if the depth information could be estimated from the original 2D video sequence. Using the depth information, two temporally synchronized video streams (for right and left eyes) can be rendered from the 2D video stream, via a process known as depth image based rendering (DIBR) [1].

Depth map estimation techniques generally fall into one of the following categories: manual, semi automatic and automatic. For the manual methods, an operator would manually draw the outlines of objects that are associated with an artistically

B. Huet et al. (Eds.): MMM 2009, LNCS 5371, pp. 108–118, 2009.
© Springer-Verlag Berlin Heidelberg 2009

chosen depth value. As expected, these methods are extremely time consuming and expensive. For this reason, semi automatic and automatic techniques are preferred for the depth map estimation.

A machine learning approach for estimating the depth map for 2D video sequences is proposed in [2]. Although the results of this approach are promising, it requires an operator to input the local depth information of some selected frames. Extraction of depth from blur has also been explored by researchers [3]. The problem in this case is that depth is not the only cause of the blur in a picture. Other reasons include motion, climate conditions and fuzziness of objects within a scene. The estimation of depth based on the edge information has also been studied [4, 5].

The existing relationship between the distance of moving objects from camera and the registered motion for them has also been utilized for estimating the depth map [6, 7]. Based on this relationship, the closer is the object to the camera the faster is its registered motion by camera.

The study in [7] uses motion information estimated by color segmentation and KLT feature tracker to approximate the depth map. In this approach, factors like camera movement, scene complexity and the magnitude are used for converting motion information into the depth map. In [6] however, this conversion is obtained using a constant factor. The motion estimation is derived via H.264 encoder using fixed block-size matching technique. In other words, the use of constant conversion factor is justified by the assumption that the motion of every object is directly proportional to its distance from the camera. Unfortunately, this is only true for a relatively small part of real life footage (for example, when there is camera panning across a stationary scene). There would be depth ambiguity when the objects' motion is independent of camera motion.

In this paper, an effective scheme that finds approximate values of the depth map using the motion information embedded in H.264-encoded video is presented. The relative motion between two consecutive frames is derived at quarter pixel accuracy via matching different block sizes that dynamically adjust to video content (H.264/AVC motion estimation process). Our proposed scheme provides a solution to resolve the depth ambiguity problem, when the motion of an object is independent of camera motion.

Estimation of the motion vectors in H.264/AVC estimated are defined by optimizing the performance related to compression purposes and might not resemble the scene depth. To resolve this issue, we propose an algorithm that examines motion vectors and properly revise them if necessary. Since H.264 uses block-based matching technique motion estimation, depth ambiguity exists between foreground and background in object boundaries. Thus our algorithm re-evaluates and revises the estimated motion vectors of each pixel on the boundaries of objects. Later, the absolute horizontal value of the motion vectors are converted to depth map information based on the relationship between the depth and the viewing distance of the moving objects.

The rest of this paper is organized as follows. Section 2 elaborates on our scheme, followed by Section 3 which presents the performance evaluation of our scheme and discusses the results in detail. Section 4 presents the conclusions.

2 Proposed Scheme

The displacement between the left and right camera images of a 3D sequence is directly related to the depth of an object (or the distance from the viewer). This displacement is known as disparity [8].

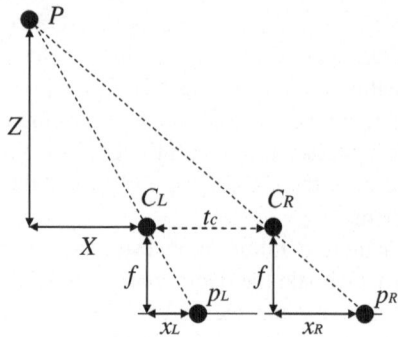

Fig. 1. Stereo geometry for two identical parallel cameras

Figure 1 illustrates how the disparity is related to depth for two identical parallel cameras. P is a scene point whereas p_L and p_R are its images captured by the left (C_L) and right (C_R) cameras, respectively.

For this case, the disparity, d, is expressed as:

$$d = x_R - x_L = \frac{ft_c}{Z},\qquad(1)$$

where x_R and x_L are the coordinates of p_L and p_R, respectively. Z is the distance of point P from the cameras (depth), t_c is the distance between the two cameras (baseline), and f is the focal length of the cameras.

In our approach, the displacement of an object over two consecutive frames (due to its motion) in the single camera case is approximated as the disparity between the right and left images of a stereo camera set-up. Disparity is thus considered to be equivalent to motion in a 2D scenario, when the two frames are consecutive in time rather than space. In other words, the pair of stereo images is considered as consecutive frames in time. Our proposed scheme utilizes this relationship to estimate the depth map from a 2D video sequence. The following sub-sections elaborate on our proposed algorithm.

2.1 Motion Vector Estimation

The H.264/AVC motion vectors are basically the inputs to our algorithm. H.264 Motion vectors (MVs) are estimated using variable block sizes of 16x16, 16x8, 8x16, 8x4, 4x8 and 4x4 pixels, and quarter-pixel matching accuracy [9]. These two H.264 features (variable block size and quarter-pixel matching accuracy) have been shown to yield motion vector precision that is far superior to those of any previous standards [9]. An additional advantage of using the H.264/AVC standard is the fact that H.264 has been chosen as the platform for 3D TV applications [10]. This means that the proposed scheme will be compatible with future 3D networks and players, and also could be implemented at the receiver-end where motion vectors will be readily available at no additional computational cost. The existing approach in [6] forces the encoder to use only 4x4 block sizes. Thus when implemented at the transmitter side, it would result in a large increase in the bit rate and when implemented on the receiver end, it would significantly increase the computational complexity (due to the need for MV estimation based on 4x4 block sizes) [6].

The use of small block sizes results in many wrong matches due to ambiguities and noise, however it preserves object shapes in relatively fine details. In contrast, the use of large block sizes cuts down on the wrong matches, but also may blur the objects boundaries [8]. Thus we use variable block size to deal with the basic trade-off involved in selecting the best window size.

2.2 Camera Motion Correction

One of the potential problems that may arise in motion-based depth estimation is depth ambiguity when both the objects and the camera have motion. In this case the object with greater amount of captured motion is not necessarily closer to camera, since camera might have moved the same direction as the object. To resolve this issue camera motion needs to be approximated and the captured motion information by camera is corrected accordingly.

In the case of camera panning, the estimated motion vector for stationary areas of the scene is approximated as camera motion. These areas are often flagged as 'Skip Mode' by H.264/AVC motion estimation process. The 'Skip Mode' is used for 16x16 blocks, if the motion characteristics of the block can be effectively predicted from the motion of its neighboring blocks, and the quantized transform coefficients of the block are all zeros. Note that, when a block is skipped, the transformed coefficients and the motion data are not transmitted, since the motion of the block is equivalent to the median of motion vectors of surrounding blocks, known as predicted motion vector (MV_p).

When camera panning is present in the scene, the MV_p for the skip-mode blocks contain stationary background areas is not zero. Thus in our proposed scheme, the predicted motion vector with the maximum occurrence is used as the camera motion. To find such a vector the histogram of non-zero MV_ps of skipped blocks for each frame is computed. To extract the net object motion, the camera motion is subtracted from the MV of all blocks within the frame. This procedure is not an option in [6] since only 4x4 blocks are used. The following code summarizes the above-mentioned procedure:

```
for each frame:
1. find skipped-mode blocks with MV_p~=0.
2. calculate the histogram of the MV_ps of blocks found
in 1.
3. assign the MV_p with maximum occurrence to camera pan-
ning motion.
```

```
4. subtract camera panning motion from all the MVs
within the frame.
```

Besides panning, camera zoom-in/out can also cause depth ambiguity. To address this issue, we apply the algorithm proposed in [7], which checks the tendency of MVs in four corners of the frame to detect zoom in/out. The estimated MVs are scaled accordingly. Note that, zoom-in/out may cause reverse depth or eye fatigue if not corrected in the depth estimation.

2.3 Matching Block Correction

The MVs obtained by H.264/AVC coding are derived so as to optimize the coding performance. Thus the matching blocks determined by a motion vector do not necessarily relate the same part of an object in the scene. In the case that the matching blocks do not represent the same part of an object then they do not form the corresponding left and right areas as defined by the disparity in a stereoscopic scenario (Fig. 1).

To make sure a motion vector points to the same area in the consecutive frame, our proposed scheme compares the estimated MV with the predicted MV, i.e., MV_p. If the difference is more than a pre-defined threshold, it means there is a difference between the motion of the block and the motion of its neighboring blocks (MV_p is calculated based on the estimated MV of neighbouring blocks). MV correction is necessary unless the block includes the boundary pixels of a moving object. To resolve this ambiguity the "residue frame" is computed as of difference between the luma of the current frame (which includes the block) and that of the previous frame. The edge of objects that have motion appears thicker and with higher density compared to static objects and background. If the variance of the corresponding block in residue frame is less than a predefined threshold, the estimated motion vector needs correction since it is not part of a moving object's border. For correction, the median of MVs of adjacent blocks is assigned as the estimated MV of the block. The following code summarizes the procedure of matching block correction:

```
for each frame:
1. calculate MVdiff=abs(MV-MVₚ)for each block.
2. compute residue frame as:
   resFrame= abs(luma_current frame-luma_previous frame)
3. calculate the variance of each block within residue
frame (resVAR).
4. for the blocks which MVdiff>Th1 & resVar<Th2, new
MVs are calculated as of median MV of their instant
neighboring blocks. Without loss of generality assume
Th1=1 & Th2=1000.
```

2.4 Object Border Correction

Since disparity is the horizontal displacement between the two camera images (Fig. 1), we propose to only use the absolute value of the horizontal component of the motion vectors (i.e., $abs(MV_x)$) for estimating the depth map. Since all the pixels within each matching block are assumed to have the same amount of motion, $abs(MV_x)$ is assigned to each pixel within a block. This assumption is not valid for blocks that partially include stationary background pixels and partially include the moving object pixels. If correction is not performed the objects borders are blurred and small detail or even objects are removed in a stereoscopic image that is rendered based on the estimated depth map.

One computationally expensive solution is to perform pixel-based motion vector estimation for object-border pixels. Our proposed alternative solution detects the blocks with non-zero motion vector, then, classifies each pixel within each of these blocks as background pixel or object pixel. To do this classification, the average luma intensity of the corresponding block in the residue frame is calculated. Then those pixels within the block (in the current frame) whose corresponding pixels in the residue frame have lower luma intensities than the calculated average, are marked as background pixels and the rest are marked as object pixels. The estimated $abs(MV_x)$ is assigned to object pixels, and for the background pixels the median of $abs(MV_x)$ of the surrounding pixels that are not object pixels is assigned. Here, for motion correction of background pixels, we start from the corner pixels within the block to employ non-object pixels of the surrounding blocks in the process. The background pixels within the block might be utilized in the motion estimation process only if the updated $abs(MV_x)$ has been assigned to them. The following code summarizes object-border correction process:

```
for each frame:
1. find blocks which MVₓ~=0.
2. find corresponding blocks of the ones found in 1 in
the resFrame.
3. compute average luma intensity of blocks found in 2
(resAVR)
4. find pixels within each block found in 2 (in the
resFrame), that have lower luma intensity than resAVR
(starting from corner pixels)and mark them as
background pixels and the rest as object pixels
5. label the corresponding pixels within the blocks
found in 1 (in the current frame) according to the ones
in 4.
6. for background pixels within the blocks found in 1
recalculate motion as of median of abs(MVₓ) of instant-
neighboring background-pixels. For the object pixels
assign the estimated abs(MVₓ) for the block.
```

In the single camera case, since the horizontal motion values between two consecutive frames are approximated as the disparity between right and left images in the stereoscopic set-up; the relationship between the depth and horizontal motion values can be approximated as the relationship between disparity and the depth. However as described in the previous subsections, the motion vectors need to be refined before they can resemble depth information. Then the depth map is approximated as follows:

$$D(x,y) = C \times abs(\tilde{MV}_x(x,y)) \tag{2}$$

where D is the depth value of the pixel with x and y coordinates, $\tilde{MV}_x$ is the modified motion vector and C is a constant factor. Using the approximated depth map and the

2D video sequence, the stereoscopic pair images can be rendered via the depth-image-based rendering algorithm proposed in [1]. This algorithm includes a depth map smoothing process (using asymmetric Gaussian filter) to resolve the occlusion problem in depth-image-based rendering. Here, only the right-eye stream is rendered based on the estimated depth map and the 2D video sequence, and the original 2D video is used as the left-eye stream [5].

3   Performance Evaluation and Discussion

The performance of our proposed method for depth map estimation is tested using 2D video sequences known as "Interview" and "Orbi". The depth maps of the test streams have been captured by a 3D-depth range camera (Zcam) [11]. The 2D stream of Interview and Orbi are 10 second and 5 second long respectively, with 720×576 pixels resolution and 4:2:2 YUV format. The depth consists of luma information only.

In our experiments, the motion between two consecutive frames is estimated using the JM 12.2 version of the H.264/AVC standard.

We compare our method with that presented in [6]. Since the recorded depth per each pixel is an integer number between 0 and 255, (where 255 represent the shortest distance from the camera), the estimated depth maps of our method and of [6] are normalized accordingly.

Figure 2 shows a snap-shot of the original 2D stream, the original depth map, and the estimated depth maps generated by [6] and our approach. We observe that our approach estimates more realistic depth compared to [6]. However both techniques fail to estimate depth maps for static objects (e.g., the table in Fig. 2).

The visual quality of the resulting 3D video streams using our method and the one presented in [6] are subjectively tested against the original depth map based on ITU-R Recommendation BT.500-11 [12]. Fifteen people graded the videos from 1 to 10 in terms of 3D visual perception and visual quality. The evaluation is performed using SeeReal, C_n 3D display. Table 1 illustrates the subjective test scores.

The original stereoscopic video had the highest scores in terms of visual quality and our method yielded highest scores in terms of 3D visual perception. These tests show that the approximated depth map obtained by our method provides the best 3D visual perception and the visual quality of the results by our technique is higher than the ones by the existing method.

Since our technique and the one in [6] are both capable of approximating the depth information only for areas with moving objects, watching the resultant stereoscopic video streams create visual discomfort for viewers. On the other hand, since the depth values are prominent in moving-object boundaries, the 3D visual perception is enhanced. Figure 3 demonstrates this effect clearly. As can be observed the fingers of moving hand are longer in the right image rendered based on the estimated depth by our technique compare to the ones based on the real depth map and the estimated depth map by [6], which will increase the 3D perception when it is watched on 3D display.

Fig. 2. 2D video sequence (a & b), recorder depth map (c & d) estimated depth map by [6] (e & f), and estimated depth map by our approach (g & h)

Table 1. Subjective test scores for test streams

	Visual 3D Perception			Visual Quality		
	Actual Depth	Our Method	Existing Method	Actual Depth	Our Method	Existing Method
Interview	5.5	6.4	5.5	7.9	6.6	6.0
Orbi	7.1	7.4	7.3	6.9	6.0	4.9

For the quantitative analysis, we chose to compare the quality of the stereoscopic videos synthesized using our technique with those of the technique proposed in [6] and the stereoscopic videos rendered from the actual (recorded) depth map.

Fig. 4 illustrates the five different PSNR comparisons that we chose for our analysis. In one scenario we compare the right view generated by our method and the one

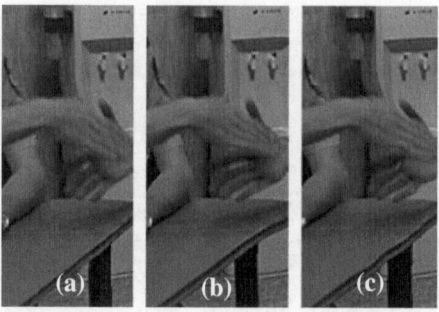

Fig. 3. Rendered right image based on real depth map (a), estimated depth map by our approach (b), estimated depth map by [6] (c)

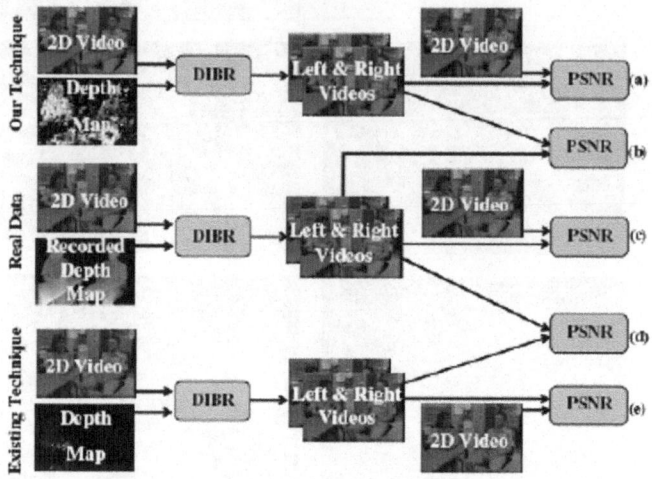

Fig. 4. Quantitative analysis of the results

by technique in [6] with the right view rendered based on recorded depth map (b & d in Fig. 4). These comparisons show how close the average quality of the estimated 3D views is to the actual ones. In this case, the higher PSNR values indicate better visual quality. Table 2 shows the average PSNR values obtained for this case. We observe that our method outperforms the proposed method in [6] by 1.3dB to 1.5 dB.

In addition to the above, we also compare the generated right views with the actual 2D video stream (a, c & e in Fig. 4). These comparisons show how effectively the two different techniques generate depth perception. In this case, since there is no depth present in the 2D video stream, large PSNR values indicate failure in adding significant depth perception to the stream. Table 3 shows the average PSNR values obtained for this case. As expected we observe that the actual 3D views have the least similarity with the 2D video (no depth perception). More importantly, our method yields a PSNR value very similar to the actual 3D views while the PSNR value obtained by the [6] is higher than the original recorded depth. This conveys the fact that the depth map estimated by [6] creates the least 3D perception.

Table 2. Average PSNR comparison case B & D in Fig. 4

Comparing Average PSNR (dB)	Interview	Orbi
3D views based on our method vs actual 3D views	35.97	31.4
3D views based on existing method vs actual 3D views	34.47	30.1

Table 3. Average PSNR comparison case A, C & E in Fig. 4

Comparing Average PSNR (dB)	Interview	Orbi
Right view rendered based on the actual depth map vs actual 2D view	32.27	27.85
Right view rendered based on our estimated depth map vs actual 2D view	32.52	28.71
Right view rendered based on the estimated depth map by existing method vs actual 2D view	36.99	33.34

Also the percentage of the badly matched pixels for the estimated depth by our scheme and [6] was computed as:

$$B = \frac{1}{N} \sum_{(x,y)} (|D(x,y) - D_r(x,y)| \triangleright Th) \qquad (3)$$

where N is the number of all pixels within the depth map, D is the estimated depth map, D_r is the recorded depth map and Th is the error tolerance. In our experiment we use Th=1 [13]. The results show the percentage of correctly matched pixels is 48% (Interview) and 44% (Orbi) for our method. For [6], the percentage of correctly matched pixels is 34% (Interview) and 27% (Orbi). The comparison confirms our method outperforms the existing method by 14% to 17%.

4 Conclusion

We present a new and efficient method that approximates the depth map of a 2D video sequence using its H.264/AVC estimated motion information. This method exploits the existing relationship between the motion of objects and the distance of them from the camera, to estimate the depth map of the scene. Our proposed method revises the motion information based on the characteristics of the 3D visual perception. In this study, the 2D horizontal motion is approximated to be the displacement between the right and left frames of a 3D set up. Our proposed method provides solutions for issues regarding camera motion, border of objects and wrong match selection. The proposed approach can be implemented in real-time at the receiver-end, without increasing the transmission bandwidth requirements. Performance evaluations show that our approach outperforms the other existing H.264 motion-based depth map estimation technique by up to 1.5 dB PSNR, i.e., our method provide better approximation for the scene's depth map.

The visual quality of our created 3D stream was also tested subjectively, by having viewers watch the generated 3D streams on a stereoscopic display. The subjective tests show that the 3D streams created based on our approach provide viewers with superior 3D experience. Moreover in terms of visual quality, our approach outperforms the other existing H.264-based depth estimation method.

Acknowledgements

This work is supported by British Columbia Innovation Council, Canada.

References

1. Zhang, L.: Stereoscopic image generation based on depth images for 3D TV. IEEE Trans. Broadcasting 51(2), 191–199 (2005)
2. Harman, P., Flack, J., Fox, S., Dowley, M.: Rapid 2D to 3D Conversion. In: Proceedings of SPIE, vol. 4660, pp. 78–86 (2002)
3. Lai, S.H., Fu, C.W., Chang, S.: A generalized depth estimation algorithm with a single image. PAMI 14(4), 405–411 (1992)
4. Tam, W.J., Soung Yee, A., Ferreira, J., Tariq, S., Speranza, F.: Stereoscopic image rendering based on depth maps created from blur and edge information. In: Proceedings of Stereoscopic Displays and Applications XII, vol. 5664, pp. 104–115 (2005)
5. Tam, W.J., Speranza, F., Zhang, L., Renaud, R., Chan, J., Vazquez, C.: Depth image based rendering for multiview stereoscopic displays: Role of information at object boundaries. In: Three-Dimensional TV, Video, and Display IV, vol. 6016, pp. 75–85 (2005)
6. Ideses, I., Yaroslavsky, L.P., Fishbain, B.: Real-time 2D to 3D video conversion. Journal of Real-Time Image Processing 2(1), 3–9 (2007)
7. Kim, D., Min, D., Sohn, K.: Stereoscopic video generation method using motion analysis. In: Proceedings of 3DTV Conf., pp. 1–4 (2007)
8. Scharstein, D.: View Synthesis Using Stereo Vision. LNCS. Springer, Heidelberg (1999)
9. Richardson, I.E.G.: H.264 and MPEG-4 Video Compression: Video Coding for Next generation Multimedia. John Wiley & Sons, Inc., England (2003)
10. Vetro, A., Pandit, P., Kimata, H., Smolic, A.: Joint Multiview Video Model (JMVM) 5.0, ISO/IEC JTC1/SC29/WG11/N9214, Lausanne, Switzerland (July 2007)
11. Fehn, C.: A 3D-TV system based on video plus depth information. Signals, Systems and Computers 2, 1529–1533 (2003)
12. Methodology for the subjective assessment of the quality of television pictures, ITU-R Recommendation BT.500-11
13. Scharstain, D.: A Taxonomy and Evaluation of Dense Two-Frame Stereo Correspondence Algorithms. International Journal of Computer Vision 47, 7–42 (2004)

A Novel Approach for Fast and Accurate Commercial Detection in H.264/AVC Bit Streams Based on Logo Identification

Klaus Schöffmann, Mathias Lux, and Laszlo Böszörmenyi

Institute of Information Technology (ITEC), University of Klagenfurt
Universitätsstr. 65-67, 9020 Klagenfurt, Austria
{ks,mlux,laszlo}@itec.uni-klu.ac.at

Abstract. Commercial blocks provide no extra value for video indexing, retrieval, archiving, or summarization of TV broadcasts. Therefore,
automatic detection of commercial blocks is an important topic in the
domain of multimedia information systems. We present a commercial detection approach which is based on logo detection performed in the compressed domain. The novelty of our approach is that by taking advantage
of advanced features of the H.264/AVC coding, it is both significantly
faster and more exact than existing approaches working directly on compressed data. Our approach enables removal of commercials in a fraction
of real-time while achieving an average recall of 97.33% with an average
precision of 99.31%. Moreover, due to its run-time performance, our approach can also be employed on low performance devices, for instance
DVB recorders.

1 Introduction

Many free to air TV broadcast stations define advertisements as one of their
main revenues. Therefore news, series, movies, etc. are interrupted by groups
of advertisements. While commercial detection is certainly appealing for home
users to skip unwanted content, also many professional applications in the domain of video indexing, retrieval, archiving, or summarization require removal
of commercial breaks in order to focus on the actual content.

Although a lot of work has already been done in the area of commercial
detection (see Section 2), most exact approaches work in the uncompressed domain (i.e. pixel data). Since practically every video is stored in compressed form,
such approaches require to decode the video before commercial detection can be
applied. However, as state-of-the-art encoding standards introduced increased
complexity not only for encoding but also for decoding, working on pixel data
has a serious drawback when run-time is an important criterion. Moreover, high
resolution content as currently *HD* increases not only the requirement on decoding performance but also on required memory. In Digital Video Broadcasting
(DVB) systems content is typically encoded with MPEG-2 or in case of HD
with H.264/AVC[8]. Therefore, a commercial detection approach directly working on compressed data has a significant run-time advantage. However, existing

B. Huet et al. (Eds.): MMM 2009, LNCS 5371, pp. 119–127, 2009.
© Springer-Verlag Berlin Heidelberg 2009

approaches working in the compressed domain usually neither provide sufficiently exact results, nor do they support state-of-the art decoding standards (such as H.264/AVC). To the best of our knowledge, no approach has been presented until now, which can directly operate on H.264/AVC bit streams and achieves results comparable to techniques used in the uncompressed domain.

In this paper we present an approach, which is able to detect commercials in H.264/AVC bit streams in only a fraction of the time required for actual decoding. Our approach is based on the assumption that the broadcasting stations display a logo when sending real content while hiding the logo when sending commercials (or showing a different logo when sending self-advertisements[1]). Even though this assumption is not true for all broadcasting stations, it applies to many of them (it applies to the majority in Europe; in particular, to all popular German speaking channels). We emphasize that if our basic assumption is not fulfilled then - obviously - it cannot be applied. The novel idea of our approach is utilizing intra-prediction modes of macroblock partitions in order to detect whether a logo within a particular region is visible. This allows extremely fast processing since only a minimal part of decoding (namely the entropy decoding) has to be performed.

The paper is structured as follows. First we give a short overview on related work and state our research question. Then we describe our approach following by an evaluation on a recently recorded and annotated test data set. Finally we summarize the paper and present our conclusions.

2   Related Work

Research in the area of commercial detection can be classified in different ways. First, it can be based on visual or audio information or a combination of both. Some research projects (e.g. [6]) employ textual information acquired from text streams, optical character recognition (OCR) or speech recognition for classification. The authors of [3], for instance, employ common characteristics of advertisement blocks, like black frames and silence between commercials, to detect cuts and classify commercials based on OCR. Two different use cases can be identified for commercial detection: (i) recognize broadcasts of known commercials with high accuracy (e.g. with the help of fingerprinting or hashing) and (ii) detect previously unknown commercials. A further classification is to distinguish between approaches focusing on online (real-time) and offline processing. Some approaches need to analyze the video as a whole to determine thresholds and to compute features with temporal dependencies (e.g. windowed shot length average or shot boundary variance), while others focus on on-the-fly detection of commercials. There are also differences between commercial detection in compressed and uncompressed domain. While detection in compressed domain is faster, in general it is also a more challenging task and recognition rates are lower than in uncompressed domain. Some research groups focus on specific domains like for instance in [10], where commercial detection is applied to news broadcasts and anchorman detection is employed as a domain specific feature.

[1] Like program preview and broadcaster's merchandise.

In [11] important features for detection of commercial broadcasts in Germany in the uncompressed domain are described. The authors focus on groups of monochrome or black frames in between commercials and an increased number of hard cuts in commercial blocks. Increased visual activity in commercials is reflected by the features *edge change ratio* and the *motion vector length*. They further increase the accuracy of their approach based on rules for maximum commercial length and other heuristics derived from German laws. Their evaluation based on German broadcasts showed that the approach resulted in a detection rate of 96.14% of the commercial block frames and 0.09% misclassifications.

In [5] classification of MPEG-2 video segments (based on a fixed number of I-frames) in compressed domain is presented. The authors employ logo recognition, black frame detection and color variance between I frames. They achieved a detection rate of 93% in terms of number of advertisements roughly in real-time (e.g. 1 min of processing for 1 minute of video content).

In [13] a system for real-time recognition of commercials within the first half second of broadcast in uncompressed domain based on color features is presented. The authors evaluate different hash functions to compute similarity of arbitrary video frames to already known commercials and achieve a recall of 96% with precision of 100%.

In [1] discriminative features for commercial detection that can be extracted within an MPEG encoding process in real-time are investigated as means for commercial detection by applying genetic algorithms. The authors focus on the selection of a set of features optimal for the task and chose *key frame distance*, *luminance* and *letterboxing*. Their best result is recall of 82% with precision of 97%. They furthermore present an approach for determining necessary thresholds for commercial detection by employing genetic algorithms. This approach outperforms thresholds set manually by experts in precision and recall as well as time needed to find the threshold. From the same research group another approach in compressed domain based on monochrome frames in between commercials is presented in [2]. While the approach allows real-time processing, classification of a commercial is done at the end of the commercials, which means that a commercial can only be identified after its last frame. The authors also use rather restrictive heuristics like a maximum commercial block length based on their test data set.

Evaluation results indicate in general precision levels beyond 90% and recall levels of 80% and more. Results of different research groups, however, cannot be compared directly as they use different test data sets from different broadcasting stations, different times and different regions. Evaluations also differ regarding the boundaries of the shots. Some groups use the second nearest to the recognized start and end frame of a commercial block for evaluation, others the exact frame number for determining what portion of the video has been classified correctly. Others use the number of correctly classified commercials for determining accuracy. Furthermore approaches are optimized in a different way. While for some application high recall (not missing a single commercial) is important other require a high precision (no real content frames get cut out).

3   Commercial Detection in H.264/AVC

In Europe, a trend towards digital TV, especially DVB-S and DVB-T can be observed. Also consumer products capable of receiving and displaying high definition video content are getting more and more common. As already mentioned, high definition content broadcasted in DVB is encoded in the H.264/AVC format. Compared to MPEG-2, H.264/AVC offers in general better visual quality at lower bitrates at the cost of higher computational effort for both the encoder and the decoder [12]. Concepts employed for encoding H.264/AVC are more sophisticated than the ones used in MPEG-2. For commercial detection in compressed domain we interpret particular compression concepts as features for logo detection. The idea of taking advantage of features already extracted by the encoder is not new; it has been discussed in the context of MPEG-2 DC coefficients and motion vectors (see e.g. [1], [2] or [5]). In the following we describe the selection of the appropriate H.264/AVC features and a distance function.

In contrast to earlier standards, H.264/AVC[8] allows partitioning of macroblocks to partitions of the size 16x16, 16x8, 8x16, 8x8, 8x4, 4x8, and 4x4 pixels. The possible partitions of intra coded macroblocks are limited to 16x16 and 4x4 pixels. Intra prediction is used for every partition of an intra coded macroblock. Four possible intra prediction modes for 16x16 partitions and nine possible intra prediction modes for 4x4 partitions are defined by the standard, as shown in Table 1 and Fig. 1.

As mentioned earlier, our commercial detection approach is based on the observation that many broadcasters hide their logo while broadcasting commercials. For the suggested algorithm we assume that commercial content has no logo, while regular program content shows a logo of the broadcaster on a fixed position. In our experience the location of a logo and its (structural) design changes

Table 1. Intra prediction modes in H.264/AVC

16x16 Partitions		4x4 Partitions			
Mode	Name	Mode	Name	Mode	Name
0	Vertical	0	Vertical	5	Vertical Right
1	Horizontal	1	Horizontal	6	Horizontal Down
2	DC	2	DC	7	Vertical Left
3	Plane	3	Diagonal Down Left	8	Horizontal Up
		4	Diagonal Down Right		

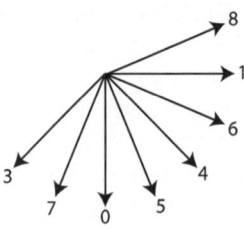

Fig. 1. Intra prediction modes of 4x4 partitions

rarely. So we further assume that position and size of the logo are known for each broadcaster. For a particular use case this constraint can be tackled by providing this information to be retrieved from a server, which is updated every time the position or structure of the logo changes for a particular broadcaster. Another approach is to let the user paint a boundary box around the logo. Obviously, if the position of the logo is not fixed (e.g. move around or rotate), the performance (i.e. recall) of our algorithm will degrade.

For detection of frames containing no broadcaster logo we employ intra prediction modes used for intra coded macroblocks in the area of the logo. We extract the intra prediction modes of the macroblocks - the so called *Intra Prediction Layout* (IPL) - within the logo region. According to the prediction modes introduced in Fig. 1, Fig. 2 shows a visualization of how the nine 4x4 intra prediction modes are applied to a particular logo. Note that it is not necessarily required to use all 4x4 partitions the logo is contained in. In some cases it might be sufficient to use only some relevant partitions within the logo area.

We further focus on intra coded frames (I frames) only and leave aside predicted (P) and bidirectional predicted (B) frames. Motivated by a high definition DVB use case, where HD content is broadcasted according to the DVB standard [4], we can assume that 2 seconds is the maximum distance between two consecutive I frames. In other words for a 25 fps video every 50-th frame is an I frame. Restricting the approach to I frames assures that macroblocks in the area of the logo use intra coding and we can obtain an IPL for each frame investigated. As the H.264/AVC standard [8] allows an intra coded macroblock to be encoded either as one 16x16 partition or as 16 4x4 partitions, we transform intra prediction modes of 16x16 partitions to 4x4 intra prediction in order to ease the comparison of the respective IPLs (and simply use 4x4 partitions as the basis). The transformation is quite simple as three out of four intra prediction modes for 16x16 partitions (namely Vertical, Horizontal, and DC) are also used for 4x4 partitions. There is one intra prediction mode (Plane) which is not used for 4x4 partitions. In our transformation rules we use the 4x4 DC mode for that one as it seems to be the most similar mode. Therefore, our transformation rules are:

- 16x16 Vertical → 4x4 Vertical
- 16x16 Horizontal → 4x4 Horizontal

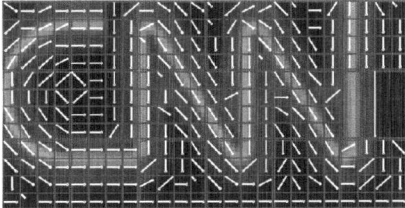

Fig. 2. Prediction modes (white) of intra-coded partitions (red) in the area of the CNN logo

4x4 IP	0	1	2	3	4	5	6	7	8
0	0	90	D	45	45	26.6	63.4	26.6	111
1	90	0	D	135	45	63.4	26.6	111	26.6
2	D	D	0	D	D	D	D	D	D
3	45	135	D	0	90	71.6	108	18.4	162
4	45	45	D	90	0	18.4	18.4	71.6	71.6
5	26.6	63.4	D	71.6	18.4	0	36.8	53.2	90
6	63.4	26.6	D	108	18.4	36.8	0	90	53.2
7	26.6	111	D	18.4	71.6	53.2	90	0	143
8	111	26.6	D	162	71.6	90	53.2	143	0

Fig. 3. Distance matrix M for comparing IPL

- 16x16 DC → 4x4 DC
- 16x16 Plane → 4x4 DC

On every I frame we extract the IPL from the area of the broadcaster's logo, and compare it with the a-priori known prototype IPL [2] for the selected broadcaster. For comparison we use a distance function based on angle differences between each possible pair of 4x4 intra prediction modes given by a matrix $M = (m_{i,j})$ with $i, j \in \{0, 1, \ldots 8\}$ shown in Fig. 3. In M, every column and every row represents one 4x4 intra prediction mode, as defined in Table 1 / Fig. 1, and D represents the difference from or to 4x4 DC intra prediction mode. For the IPL of the n-th I frame l_n, we calculate the normalized distance to the prototype IPL l_S denoted as $d(l_n, l_S)$. Both IPLs l_n and l_S have by definition the same number of 4x4 partitions k. The prediction mode of the i-th partition, $i \leq k$, of an IPL is l_n^i for the n-th frame and l_S^i for the prototype IPL respectively.

$$d(l_n, l_S) = \frac{\sum_{i=0}^{k} m_{l_n^i, l_S^i}}{k} \quad (1)$$

To tackle the problem of single I frames containing visual content in the same color as the logo in the logo region we compute the average $d_n^{avg}(l_n, l_S)$ over r I frames. This process flattens single peaks but retains sequences of high values that occur in commercial blocks.

$$d_n^{avg}(l_n, l_S) = \frac{\sum_{i=-\lfloor \frac{r}{2} \rfloor}^{\lfloor \frac{r}{2} \rfloor} d(l_{n+i}, l_S)}{r} \quad (2)$$

Based on the averaged distance for each I frame n we classify all I frames with $d_n^{avg}(l_n, l_S) > t$, where t is a predefined threshold, as I frames containing commercial content. We further employ a heuristics to extend the quality of classification. Therefore, we only assume sequences of 15 and more I frames as commercials.

---

[2] This a-priori known prototype IPL could also be stored on a server and be updated when the structure of a logo changes.

This is implicitly based on the heuristics that a commercial block has a minimum length of 30 seconds.

4   Evaluation

We have investigated 19 different channels [3] popular in German speaking countries. All of them suppress their logo while broadcasting commercials. Our evaluation is based on roughly 10 hours of DVB-S recordings from nine of those channels with different genres (see Table 2). The proportion of commercial material in the recorded content of 10 hours (i.e. 594 minutes) is 20.98% (i.e. 124.66 minutes) in average.

We manually classified every second of content into *Commercial* or *Real Content* and used that classification as ground truth. Self advertisement (e.g. commercials intros, teasers, and program preview) was also classified as *Commercial*. We run our commercial detection approach on the test data and evaluated *Recall* and *Precision*. As test setting we used $D = max(m_{i,j})$, $r = 5$ and $t = 0.28$. All videos have been encoded with the x264 [9] encoder with a bit rate of 4096 Kb/s. As the DVB specification [4] suggests using 2 seconds as a maximum time interval between two random access points in the bit stream, we have encoded our 25fps videos with a *Group-of-Picture* (GOP) size of 50 frames. Thus, the evaluation of our test data reflects the performance of our approach if used in an on-the-fly manner for content received via DVB.

Table 2. Evaluation results

Genre	Channel	Minutes	Commercial proportion	Recall	Precision
Documentary	N24	53	21%	97.67%	100.00%
Documentary	ZDF	30	9%	99.39%	99.51%
Feature film	SuperRTL	110	18%	99.76%	99.56%
Feature film	Pro7	39	20%	99.23%	96.23%
News show	CNN Int.	58	19%	99.00%	100.00%
Sports	DSF	106	24%	98.82%	99.65%
Thriller	SAT 1	25	28%	100.00%	99.39%
Reality show	ATV	98	25%	98.10%	99.47%
Live show	RTL	75	20%	84.03%	100.00%

Our approach achieves an average recall of 97.33% with an average precision of 99.31% in total. As shown in Table 2, for almost all recordings we achieved results near to 100% for both precision and recall. However, for one channel in our evaluation recall decreased to about 84%. The reason is that this channel uses the same logo while showing self advertisement as while showing real content.

---

[3] 3sat, ARD, ATV, BR, CNN, Das Vierte, DSF, Eurosport, Kabel-1, N24, n-tv, ORF 1, ORF 2, Pro 7, RTL, RTL II, Sat 1, Super RTL, VOX, WDR, ZDF.

In that case self advertisement is not detected as "commercial" (which was our requirement) and, thus, recall decreases.

Regarding run-time, our approach performs very well due to several reasons. First, as only I Frames are considered, the number of frames to process is strongly reduced. Moreover, as our approach solely requires information already available after entropy decoding (no DCT/Integer transform, no motion compensation, no pixel interpolation, no deblocking), the run-time is further reduced to roughly one quarter (refer to [7] for a workload characterization of H.264/AVC). In addition, if the logo is used in the upper part of the image, we can simply skip entropy-decoding for all macroblocks after the logo. If the logo is in the bottom part of the image, preceding macroblocks need to be entropy-decoded due to the variable length of macroblocks (i.e. encoded with CAVLC or CABAC). Depending on the position of the broadcaster's logo, commercial detection required between 4.46 % and 6.97% of the full decoding time for our test data. In other words, if a decoder would be able to decode a 60 minutes sequence in 50 minutes (i.e. in real-time), a commercial detection tool using our approach would require less than 3.5 minutes to detect all commercials.

5   Summary and Conclusion

We have presented a method for commercial detection in compressed domain utilizing encoding concepts of H.264/AVC. Experiments show that the method has very high precision and reasonable recall: While we minimize the number of false positives we miss in certain cases intros, teasers, and self advertisement of broadcasters. Beside the high precision and reasonable recall the contribution of this approach lies in the run-time performance and efficiency. Less than 7% of the decoding process has to be done to reach the accuracy documented in this paper. Therefore the proposed method can also be applied to HD content, where real-time or even faster analysis in the uncompressed domain is still a challenging problem. Also the implementation is rather easy to reproduce. In comparison to other approaches we use a minimum number of heuristics. We assume that the size of a commercial block is greater than 30 seconds and that the broadcasting logo is suppressed as long as commercials are broadcasted. Although not implemented in our current version, the accuracy of our approach could be improved if P or B frames containing intra coded macroblocks in the area of the logo are considered too. However for utilizing P and B frames we need higher decompressing effort.

References

1. Agnihotri, L., Dimitrova, N., Mcgee, T., Jeannin, S., Schaffer, D., Nesvadba, J.: Envolvable visual commercial detector. In: IEEE Conference on Computer Vision and Pattern Recognition (CVPR 2003), vol. 02, p. 79. IEEE Computer Society Press, Los Alamitos (2003)

2. Dimitrova, N., Jeannin, S., Nesvadba, J., McGee, T., Agnihotri, L., Mekenkamp, G.: Real-time commercial detection using mpeg features. In: 9th Int. Conf. On Information Processing and Management of Uncertainty in knowledge-based systems (IPMU 2002), Annecy, France (2002)
3. Duan, L.-Y., Wang, J., Zheng, Y., Jin, J.S., Lu, H., Xu, C.: Segmentation, categorization, and identification of commercial clips from tv streams using multimodal analysis. In: Proceedings of the 14th annual ACM international conference on Multimedia (ACM Multimedia 2006), pp. 201–210. ACM, New York (2006)
4. dvb.org (ETSI). ETSI TS 101 154 v1.7.1, Specification for the use of Video and Audio Coding in Broadcasting Applications based on the MPEG-2 Transport Stream (February 2007)
5. Glasberg, R., Tas, C., Sikora, T.: Recognizing commercials in real-time using three visual descriptors and a decision-tree. In: IEEE International Conference on Multimedia and Expo 2006 (ICME 2006), Toronto, July 2006. IEEE Computer Society Press, Los Alamitos (2006)
6. Hauptmann, A.G., Witbrock, M.J.: Story segmentation and detection of commercials in broadcast news video. In: ADL 1998: Proceedings of the Advances in Digital Libraries Conference, Washington, DC, USA, p. 168. IEEE Computer Society, Los Alamitos (1998)
7. Holliman, M., Chen, Y.: MPEG Decoding Workload Characterization. In: Proc. of Workshop on Computer Architecture Evaluation using Commercial Workloads, pp. 23–34 (2003)
8. ISO/IEC JTC 1/SC 29/WG 11. ISO/IEC FDIS 14496-10: Information Technology - Coding of audio-visual objects - Part 10: Advanced Video Coding (March 2003)
9. Aimar, L., Merritt, L., Petit, E., Chen, M., Clay, J., Rullgard, M., Czyz, R., Heine, C., Izvorski, A., Wright, A.: x264 - a free h264/avc encoder
10. Li, S., Li, H., Wang, Z.: A novel approach to commercial detection in news video. In: Eighth ACIS International Conference on Software Engineering, Artificial Intelligence, Networking, and Parallel/Distributed Computing 2007 (SNPD 2007), vol. 2, pp. 86–90. IEEE Computer Society Press, Los Alamitos (2007)
11. Lienhart, R., Kuhmunch, C., Effelsberg, W.: On the detection and recognition of television commercials. In: International Conference on Multimedia Computing and Systems (ICMCS 1997), p. 509. IEEE Computer Society Press, Los Alamitos (1997)
12. Ostermann, J., Bormans, J., List, P., Marpe, D., Narroschke, M., Pereira, F., Stockhammer, T., Wedi, T.: Video coding with H. 264/AVC: tools, performance, and complexity. Circuits and Systems Magazine 4(1), 7–28 (2004)
13. Shivadas, A., Gauch, J.: Real-time commercial recognition using color moments and hashing. In: Fourth Canadian Conference on Computer and Robot Vision (CRV 2007), pp. 465–472. IEEE Computer Society Press, Los Alamitos (2007)

Bit Allocation for Spatio-temporal Wavelet Coding of Animated Semi-regular Meshes

Aymen Kammoun, Frédéric Payan, and Marc Antonini

Laboratoire I3S (UMR 6070 CNRS-Université de Nice - Sophia Antipolis)
2000, Route des Lucioles - 06903 Sophia Antipolis - France
{kammoun,fpayan,am}@i3S.unice.fr
www.i3s.unice.fr/~creative/

Abstract. In this paper, we propose a compression scheme for animated semi-regular meshes. This scheme includes a spatio-temporal wavelet filtering to exploit the coherence both in time and space. In order to optimize the quantization of both spatial and temporal wavelet coefficients, the proposed compression scheme also includes a model-based bit allocation. The experimental results show that this approach significantly improves the compression performances, when comparing with previous similar approaches.

Keywords: Spatio-temporal decomposition, Wavelet filtering, Animation, Semi-regular meshes, Bit Allocation, Coding.

1 Introduction

Typically, an animation is represented by a sequence of triangular meshes sharing the same connectivity at any frame. Even if the static triangulation has the advantage to strongly reduce the amount of information needed to represent such data, compression is useful when the number of vertices increases, because of the amount of geometric information.

During the last decade, most of works focused on the compression for sequences of irregular meshes. When observing the state of the art for such data, we can note techniques using spatial and/or temporal prediction [1,2]; principal component analysis (PCA) [3,4,5]; motion-based segmentation [6,7]; wavelet-based analysis tool [8,9,10,11].

Among the wavelet-based methods, the pioneering coder for sequences of irregular meshes was based only on temporal wavelet filtering [8]. The reason is that the geometry of an animation has a regular temporal sampling (same connectivity at any frame), while having an irregular "spatial" sampling (the frames are irregular meshes). And it is well-known that wavelets are more efficient on regular grids than irregular ones (in image coding for instance). Recently, another coder using temporal wavelet filtering but implemented in lifting scheme was proposed [10]. In parallel, a motion-compensated temporal wavelet filtering has been also developed in [6]. The main idea of all these coders is to apply a one-dimensional wavelet filtering on the successive positions of each vertex.

B. Huet et al. (Eds.): MMM 2009, LNCS 5371, pp. 128–139, 2009.

Despite the challenge of applying wavelets on irregular grids, some coders using irregular spatial wavelet were proposed. For instance, Guskov and Khodakovsky have developed in [9] a coder for parametrically coherent mesh sequences, using an irregular wavelet-based decomposition. Unfortunately, from an analysis point-of-view, this method tends to be suboptimal since wavelets are not fully exploited both in spatial and temporal dimension. With this outlook, Cho et al. recently proposed in [11] to expand the wavelet-based coder for static irregular meshes of [12] to the time-varying surfaces.

In geometry compression, it has been shown that combining remesher and wavelets based on semi-regular sampling leads to efficient techniques for compressing static shapes [13,14,15]. The semi-regular meshes have the advantage to present a multiresolution structure which facilitates wavelet filtering (to exploit the spatial coherence), and also visualization, levels of details, progressive transmission and so on. In order to have the same properties for animations, similar approaches have been lately proposed for animations defined by sequences of meshes with static or independent connectivity [16,17]. The resulting semi-regular animations finally have the same relevant properties as the static meshes and also a temporal coherence which can be exploited to perform efficient compression.

We propose in this paper a spatio-temporal wavelet-based coding scheme for sequences of semi-regular meshes sharing the same connectivity. The proposed coder includes an improved version of the bit allocation process presented in [16], which optimizes the quantization of the temporal wavelet coefficients but also the spatial ones (contrary to [16]). The key contribution of this paper is a formulation of the distortion criterion which takes into account the quantization errors of all the data (temporal wavelet coefficients, spatial wavelet coefficients and low frequency signal).

The rest of this paper is organized as follows. Section 2 gives an overview of the proposed method. Section 3 shows the principle of a spatio-temporal wavelet filtering. Section 4 shows the bit allocation for a spatio-temporal decomposition. Section 5 shows some results for several animations, and we conclude in section 6.

2   Overview of the Proposed Approach

Let us consider an animated semi-regular mesh $\mathcal{F}$, represented by a sequence of T meshes sharing the same connectivity: $\mathcal{F} = \{f_1, f_2, ..., f_t, ...f_T\}$. Each mesh f_i corresponds to one *frame* of the animation. Semi-regular animations can be obtained by using a remeshing technique such as [16,17]. Here is the outline of our method, illustrated by figure 1.

– **Spatio-temporal Analysis:** The animation $\mathcal{F}$ has a regular sampling in time but also a semi-regular one in "space". So, a temporal wavelet-based filtering is first applied, followed by the spatial butterfly-based lifting scheme [13]. Hence, we obtain a spatio-temporal decomposition of the input animation (see figure 2): several sets of temporal and spatial high-frequency details (or *wavelet coefficients*), and a short sequence of coarse meshes (*low*

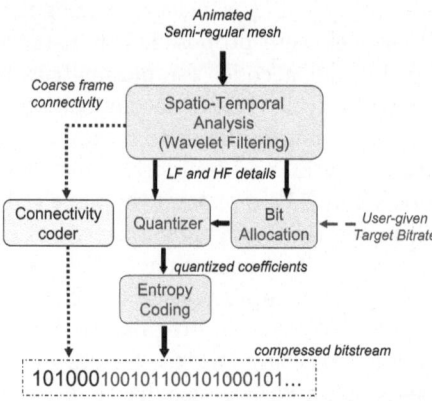

Fig. 1. Overview of the complete proposed coding scheme

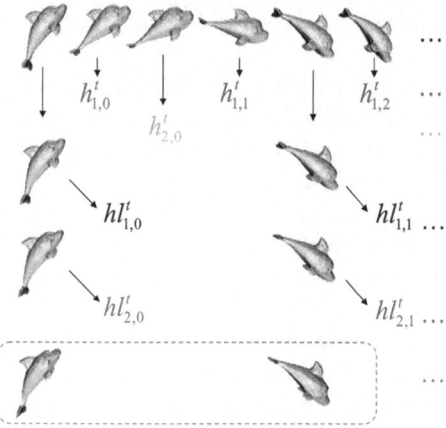

Fig. 2. Spatio-temporal decomposition based on wavelet filtering: 2 levels of temporal decomposition giving the temporal wavelet coefficients (in red and orange), and 2 levels of spatial decomposition giving the spatial ones (in blue). The meshes in the dotted rounded box (in green) represent the coarse sequence (spatio-temporal low frequency signal).

frequency signal). The list of triangles of one sole coarse mesh represents the whole connectivity information.

- **Bit Allocation:** this process optimizes the rate-distortion trade-off relative to the data quantization. The objective is to efficiently dispatch the bits across the subbands of wavelet coefficients, according to their influence on the quality of the reconstructed mesh sequence. With this outlook, this process will compute the optimal quantization step for each subband, for one user-given total bitrate.

- **Entropy coding:** once quantized, the coefficients are entropy coded with the context-based arithmetic coder of [10].
- **Connectivity coder:** to reconstruct the compressed data after storage and/or transmission, the connectivity information must be preserved. For this purpose, the list of triangles is encoded in parallel with [18] and included in the compressed bitstream.

3   Spatio-temporal Decomposition

To create a spatio-temporal decomposition of a semi-regular animation, we choose to apply successively a temporal wavelet filtering and a spatial one. These two filterings are based on lifting scheme implementations [19].

Temporal Wavelet Filtering

The principle of our temporal wavelet filtering is to consider each vertex trajectory as a one-dimensional (1D) signal [10]. Therefore, a classical 1D lifting scheme is applied on the successive positions of each vertex in parallel. After this step, we obtain two subsets: a high frequency subband H_1^t defined by $T/2$ detail frames (*temporal wavelet coefficients*): $H_1^t = \{h_{1,0}^t, h_{1,1}^t, ..., h_{1,T/2}^t\}$ and a low frequency subband L_1^t defined by $T/2$ approximation frames (*temporal low frequency signal*): $L_1^t = \{l_{1,0}^t, l_{1,1}^t, ..., l_{1,T/2}^t\}$. One can obtain a multiresolution decomposition by subsequent filterings of the low frequency subbands. This decomposition finally consists in N_t subbands of detail frames $H_{r^t}^t$ (where r^t represents the temporal resolution), and the low frequency sequence $L_{N_t}^t$.

Spatial Wavelet Filtering

After applying the temporal wavelet filtering, we apply the spatial wavelet filtering based on the butterfly lifting scheme [13] on all the frames of the low frequency sequence $L_{N_t}^t$. For each frame $l_{N_t,k}^t$ of this sequence, this step gives N_s subbands of spatial wavelet coefficients $h^s l_{r^s,k}^t$ (where r^s represents the spatial resolution level) and a coarse version $l^s l_{N_s,k}^t$ of the given frame.

The principle of this decomposition is illustrated by figure 2. In this figure, we apply 2 levels of temporal decomposition, and 2 levels of spatial decomposition on the animated DOLPHIN.

Given the resulting output multiresolution structure of this analysis stage, we now have to deal with the necessary bit allocation process which will optimize the quantization of the different subbands.

4   Bit Allocation

Given a multiresolution structure, we can not use the same quantizer for all the subbands since the energy is not uniformly dispatched between them. We recall that once transformed, the relevant data (from a coding point of view) is most of times concentrated in the lower frequency subbands, while having the fine and perhaps negligible details in the highest frequency subbands. Therefore we generally use a bit allocation process, to compute the best quantizer for each subband, in order to obtain the best trade-off between rate (compressed file size) and quality of the reconstructed data (distortion).

In our case, the general purpose of the bit allocation process is precisely to determine the best set of quantization steps $\{q_{i,j}^s, q_{i,j}^t\}$ -where $q_{i,j}^s$ and $q_{i,j}^t$ are respectively the quantization steps for the spatial subbands and for the temporal subbands- that minimizes the reconstruction error $D_T(\{q_{i,j}^s, q_{i,j}^t\})$ for a given rate R_{target}. This can be formulated by the following problem:

$$(\mathcal{P}) \begin{cases} \text{minimize} & D_T\left(\{q_{i,j}^s, q_{i,j}^t\}\right) \\ \text{with constraint } R_T\left(\{q_{i,j}^s, q_{i,j}^t\}\right) = R_{target}. \end{cases} \tag{1}$$

Before solving this problem, we first must formulate the reconstruction error D_T.

Note: To know how solving such an optimization problem and have more details, please refer to [15].

4.1   Distortion Criterion

Temporal decomposition. Let us consider a temporal wavelet coder, using one level of decomposition (see figure 3). In this case, the reconstruction error D_T can be written as the weighted sum of the MSE $(\sigma_{01}^t)^2$ and $(\sigma_{11}^t)^2$ relative to the quantization of the low frequency signal and of the wavelet coefficients [20]:

$$D_T = \frac{1}{2}w_{01}^t(\sigma_{01}^t)^2 + \frac{1}{2}w_{11}^t(\sigma_{11}^t)^2, \tag{2}$$

where w_{ij}^t are the weights due to the non-orthogonality of the temporal wavelet filters ($i = 0$ gives a low frequency subband, $i = 1$ a high frequency subband and j is the resolution level). Those weights are given by:

$$w_{01}^t = \frac{2}{N}tr\left((G_{01}^t)^T G_{01}^t\right) \tag{3}$$

and

$$w_{11}^t = \frac{2}{N}tr\left((G_{11}^t)^T G_{11}^t\right), \tag{4}$$

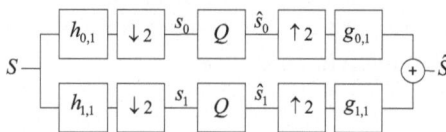

Fig. 3. Model of a temporal wavelet coder used to link the quantization effects with the reconstruction error after decoding. $(h_{0,1}, g_{0,1})$ and $(h_{1,1}, g_{1,1})$ are respectively the low-pass analysis/synthesis filters and the high-pass ones. Q represents the quantization process. $\downarrow 2$ and $\uparrow 2$ are respectively the downsampling and upsampling stages.

where N is the number of vertices and G_{ij}^t is the matrix of reconstruction relative to the synthesis filter g_{ij}^t.

Let us consider now a temporal wavelet coder with N_t levels of decomposition. By using (2), we find that the reconstruction error at any level of decomposition $(n-1)$ $(2 \leq n \leq N_t)$ can be given by:

$$(\sigma_{0(n-1)}^t)^2 = \frac{1}{2} w_{0n}^t (\sigma_{0n}^t)^2 + \frac{1}{2} w_{1n}^t (\sigma_{1n}^t)^2. \tag{5}$$

Since we use the same synthesis filter for each level of decomposition,

$$g_{0i} = g_{01} \ and \ g_{1i} = g_{11} \ \forall i \in [2, N_t], \tag{6}$$

and consequently, the weights are also similar whatever the level:

$$w_{0i}^t = w_{01}^t = w_{lf}^t \ and \ w_{1i}^t = w_{11}^t = w_{hf}^t \ \forall i \in [2, N_t]. \tag{7}$$

By combining the new weights of (7), (2) and (5), we finally obtain:

$$D_T = \frac{1}{2^{N_t}} (w_{lf}^t)^{N_t} (\sigma_{0N_t}^t)^2 + \sum_{j=1}^{j=N_t} \left(\frac{1}{2^j} (w_{lf}^t)^{j-1} w_{hf}^t (\sigma_{1j}^t)^2 \right). \tag{8}$$

Spatial decomposition. The distortion for N_s levels of spatial decomposition of a given triangular mesh can be estimated by [15]:

$$(\sigma_S)^2 = (w_{lf}^s)^{N_s} (\sigma_{0N_s}^s)^2 + \sum_{j=1}^{j=N_s} \left((w_{lf}^s)^{j-1} w_{hf}^s (\sigma_{1j}^s)^2 \right), \tag{9}$$

where w_{lf}^s and w_{hf}^s are the weights due to the non-orthogonality of the spatial wavelet transform for the low and high frequency subbands, respectively.

Spatio-temporal decomposition. Now, we can generalize the distortion criterion for a spatio-temporal decomposition with N_t levels of temporal decomposition and N_s levels of spatial decomposition. For each frame of the temporal low frequency subband, we obtain N_s spatial subbands. So, the number of spatial subbands is $N_{LF} N_s$, where N_{LF} is the number of frames in the temporal low frequency subband. By replacing $(\sigma_{0N_t}^t)^2$ by (9) in (8), we finally obtain:

$$D_T = \frac{1}{2^{N_t}} (w_{lf}^t)^{N_t} \frac{1}{N_{LF}} \sum_{f=1}^{f=N_{LF}} \left((w_{lf}^s)^{N_s} (\sigma_{0N_s}^s)^2 \sum_{j=1}^{j=N_s} \left((w_{lf}^s)^{j-1} w_{11}^s (\sigma_{1j}^s)^2 \right) \right)$$
$$+ \sum_{j=1}^{j=N_t} \left(\frac{1}{2^j} (w_{lf}^t)^{j-1} w_{11}^t (\sigma_{1j}^t)^2 \right) \tag{10}$$

4.2   Model Based Bit Allocation

As explained in [15], a bit allocation is generally processed with an iterative algorithm. At each iteration, we need to evaluate the distortion (and the associated bitrate) of each subband for one given set of quantization steps to check the convergence of the algorithm. In this way, one can achieve a real pre-quantization and then compute real distortion and bitrate for each subband. But such a method is time-consuming, particularly when dealing with large animations. One relevant method to overcome this problem is using statistical models to estimate distortion and bitrate of each subband without quantizing data. To perform such a model-based process, we must study the distribution of the processed wavelet coefficients. Figure 4 shows some results for the animated VENUS. We observe that the data follow a Gaussian distribution whatever the level of decomposition, and consequently we can use the model-based bit allocation proposed in [15].

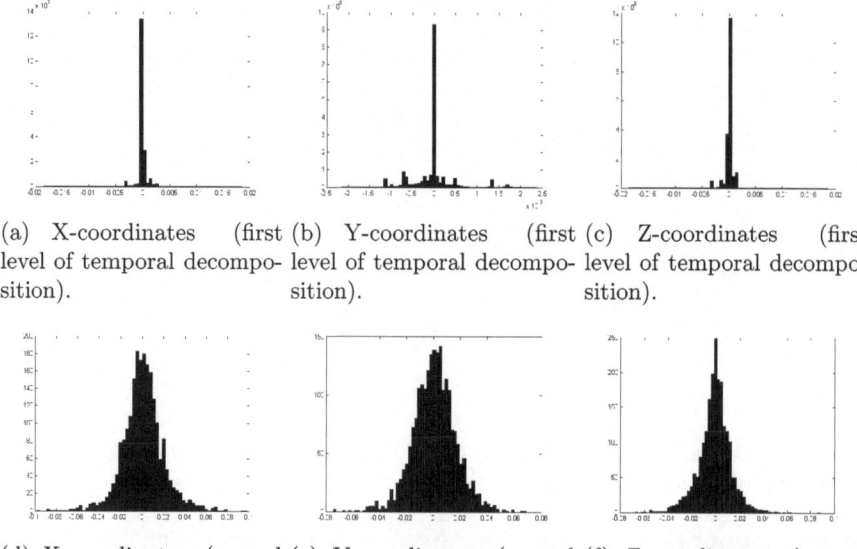

(a) X-coordinates (first level of temporal decomposition).

(b) Y-coordinates (first level of temporal decomposition).

(c) Z-coordinates (first level of temporal decomposition).

(d) X-coordinates (second level of spatial decomposition).

(e) Y-coordinates (second level of spatial decomposition).

(f) Z-coordinates (second level of spatial decomposition).

Fig. 4. Typical distribution of the wavelet coefficients of the animated semi-regular VENUS with the spatio-temporal decomposition used

5   Results

In this section we compare the proposed compression scheme to the following coders:

- The temporal wavelet coder proposed in [10] applied to the original irregular animations;

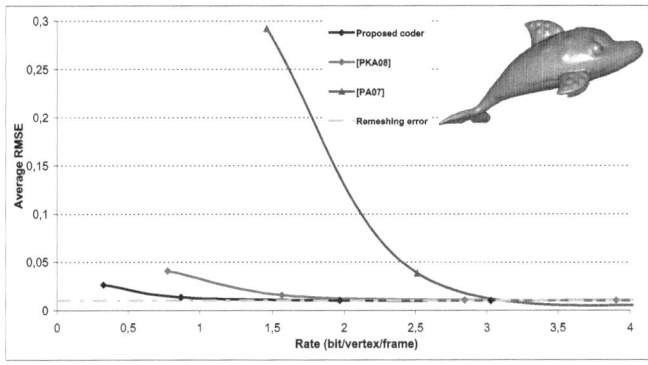

Fig. 5. Rate-Distortion curve for the animated DOLPHIN

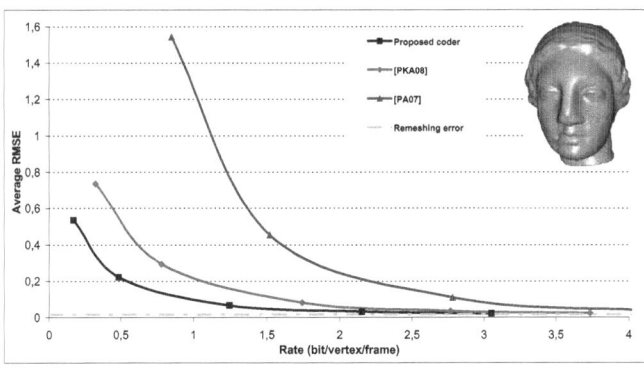

Fig. 6. Rate-Distortion curve for the animated VENUS

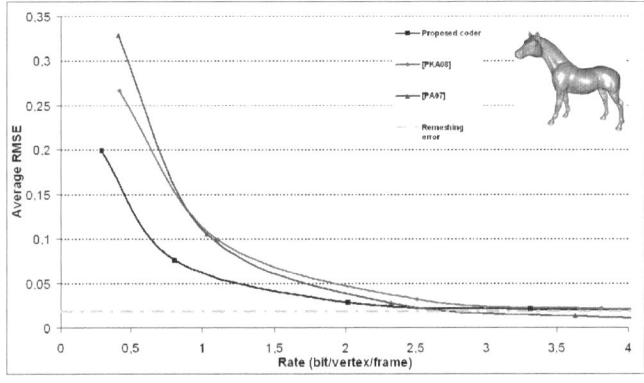

Fig. 7. Rate-Distortion curve for the animated HORSE

– The previous spatio-temporal wavelet coder without an optimal bit allocation proposed in [16].

To evaluate the quality of compressed animations, we use the RMSE metric based on Hausdorff distance given in [21]. First, figures 5, 6, and 7 show the average reconstruction error (computed on all the frames) of these coders in function of different bitrates, for the animated DOLPHIN, VENUS and HORSE. We observe that the proposed compression scheme based on a spatio-temporal decomposition and an optimal model-based bit allocation gives the best results. It clearly proves the interest of using a spatio-temporal decomposition and an optimal bit allocation process for such data instead of the previous allocation process proposed in [16].

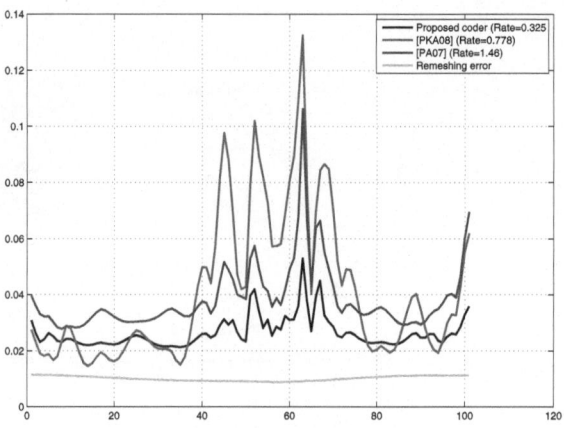

Fig. 8. RMSE-frame curve for the animated DOLPHIN

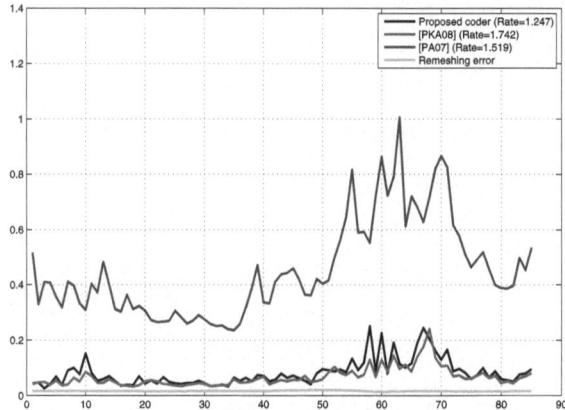

Fig. 9. RMSE-frame curve for the animated VENUS

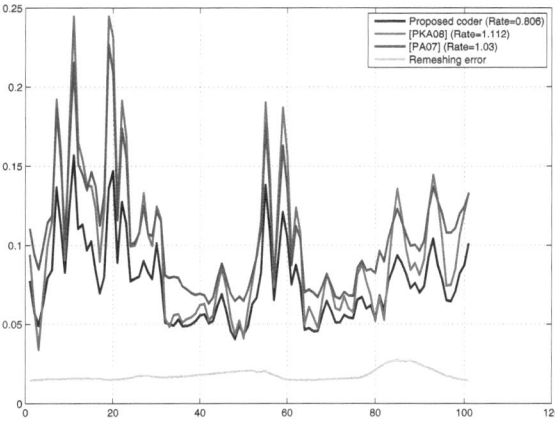

Fig. 10. RMSE-frame curve for the animated HORSE

In addition, figures 8, 9 and 10 show the evolution of the RMSE frame after frame when using the different coders, at given bitrates. We can observe that the proposed coder significantly improves the coding performances. With a smaller bitrate, the proposed coder gives a smaller reconstruction error for the majority of frames. Furthermore, it tends to produce a more regular quality over the frames (no peak of distortion, unlike the two other coders).

6   Conclusion and Future Works

In this paper, we have presented a new framework for compressing animations sharing the same connectivity at any frame. Inspired by works in geometry processing for static meshes, we have developed a spatio-temporal wavelet-based coding scheme for animated semi-regular meshes. Semi-regular animations offers the advantage of making the spatial wavelet-based analysis easier, since wavelets are more efficient on (semi-)regular grids than on irregular ones. The key contribution of this paper is the bit allocation process which optimizes the quantization of all the subbands of temporal and spatial wavelet coefficients created by the analysis tool. Furthermore, the statistics of the wavelet coefficients allows us to use a model-based algorithm, which makes the allocation process very fast. Experimentally, we show that the proposed method improves significantly the compression performances of the previous coders [10] and [16], which makes our new coder particularly interesting. For future works we plan to improve the spatio-temporal filtering and add a motion estimation/compensation technique to further improve the performances of our coder.

Acknowledgements

Original VENUS HEAD and HORSE models is courtesy of Cyberware. We are particularly grateful to J-H. Yang for providing us the original DOLPHIN model.

The animated models DOLPHIN, VENUS and HORSE can be found at: http://www.i3s.unice.fr/~fpayan/

References

1. Ibarria, L., Rossignac, J.: Dynapack: space-time compression of the 3D animations of triangle meshes with fixed connectivity. In: ACM Symp. Computer Animation, pp. 126–135 (2003)
2. Yang, J., Kim, C., Lee, S.U.: Compression of 3D triangle mesh sequences based on vertex-wise motion vector prediction. IEEE Transactions on Circuits and Systems for Video Technology 12(12), 1178–1184 (2002)
3. Alexa, M., Muller, W.: Representing animations by principal components. Computer Graphics Forum 19, 3 (2000)
4. Karni, Z., Gotsman, C.: Compression of soft-body animation sequences. Computers and Graphics 28, 25–34 (2004)
5. Vasa, L., Skala, V.: Coddyac: Connectivity driven dynamic mesh compression. In: 3DTV Conference 2007 (2007)
6. Boulfani, Y., Antonini, M., Payan, F.: Motion-based mesh clustering for mcdwt compression of 3d animated meshes. In: Proceedings of EUSIPCO 2007, Poland (September 2007)
7. Mamou, K., Zaharia, T., Prêteux, F., Kamoun, A., Payan, F., Antonini, M.: Two optimizations of the mpeg-4 famc standard for enhanced compression of animated 3d meshes. In: Proceedings of IEEE International Conference in Image Processing (September 2008)
8. Lopes, A., Gamito, M.: Wavelet compression and transmission of deformable surfaces over networks. In: Proceedings of the 10th Portuguese Computer Graphics Meeting, pp. 107–114 (2001)
9. Guskov, I., Khodakovsky, A.: Wavelet compression of parametrically coherent mesh sequences. In: Eurographics/ACM SIGGRAPH Symposium on Computer Animation (August 2004)
10. Payan, F., Antonini, M.: Temporal wavelet-based geometry coder for 3d animations. Computer & Graphics 31, 77–88 (2007)
11. Cho, J., Kim, M., Valette, S., Jung, H., Prost, R.: 3d dynamic mesh compression using wavelet-based multiresolution analysis. In: IEEE International Conference on Image Processing (ICIP 2006) (October 2006)
12. Valette, S., Prost, R.: A wavelet-based progressive compression scheme for triangle meshes: Wavemesh. IEEE Transactions on Visualization and Computer Graphics 10(2) (mars/avril 2004)
13. Khodakovsky, A., Schröder, P., Sweldens, W.: Progressive geometry compression. In: Akeley, K. (ed.) Siggraph 2000, Computer Graphics Proceedings, pp. 271–278. ACM Press / ACM SIGGRAPH / Addison Wesley Longman (2000)
14. Khodakovsky, A., Guskov, I.: Normal mesh compression. In: Geometric Modeling for Scientific Visualization. Springer, Heidelberg (2002)
15. Payan, F., Antonini, M.: An efficient bit allocation for compressing normal meshes with an error-driven quantization. Computer Aided Geometric Design, Special Issue on Geometric Mesh Processing 22, 466–486 (2005)
16. Payan, F., Kamoun, A., Antonini, M.: Remeshing and spatio-temporal wavelet filtering for 3d animations. In: Proceedings of IEEE International Conference on Acoustics, Speech, and Signal Processing (ICASSP), Las Vegas, US (March-April 2008)

17. Yang, J., Kim, C., Lee, S.: Semi-regular representation and progressive compression of 3d dynamic mesh sequences. IEEE Transactions on Image Processing 15(9), 2531–2544 (2006)
18. Touma, C., Gotsman, C.: Triangle mesh compression. In: Graphics Interface 1998, pp. 26–34 (1998)
19. Sweldens, W.: The lifting scheme: A custom-design construction of biorthogonal wavelets. Applied and Computational Harmonic Analysis 3(2), 186–200 (1996)
20. Usevitch, B.: Optimal bit allocation for biorthogonal wavelet coding. In: DCC 1996: Proceedings of the Conference on Data Compression, Washington, DC, USA, p. 387. IEEE Computer Society, Los Alamitos (1996)
21. Aspert, N., Santa-Cruz, D., Ebrahimi, T.: Mesh: Measuring errors between surfaces using the hausdorff distance. In: IEEE International Conference in Multimedia and Expo (ICME) (2002)

Modeling the Quantizer Behavior of Subbands for Data Rate Limitations in JPEG2000

Christian Günter and Albrecht Rothermel

Institute of Microelectronics
University of Ulm, Germany
{christian.guenter,albrecht.rothermel}@uni-ulm.de
http://www.uni-ulm.de/in/mikro

Abstract. In the JPEG2000 standard the very cost intensive EBCOT encoder based on an arithmetic encoder with an embedded quantization is said to be the optimum. Embedded systems with limited processing power have difficulties to encode images into this JPEG2000 image format due to its high processing load. A rekursive optimization of the quantization is not possible. This paper proposes a new method based on a model for subband quantization behavior of two-dimensional wavelet transformations to estimate a good quantizer stepsize for data rate limitations. With an additional, simple optimization algorithm an average variation in the resulting data length of $< 1.6\%$ is achieved.

Keywords: image encoding, jpeg2000, quantization, rate control.

1 Introduction

The control as well as the reduction of the resulting data size in image processing systems are very important aspects due to the more and more increasing high definition of still images taken by digital cameras. State of the art compression techniques are used in typical compression standards like JPEG or other well known image formats. Due to high redundancies of neighboring image samples (pixels) a lossless reduction of nearly a factor of two can be achieved using a typical entropy encoder combined with a transformation like a discrete cosine transformation (DCT) or a discrete wavelet transformation (DWT) for data decorrelation. Further reduction is achieved by a lossy compression using a kind of quantization or truncation. In this paper we propose a method of modeling the quantizer behavior for the JPEG2000 image compression format [1], [2].

The JPEG2000 standard defines two different DWTs and a very special entropy encoding engine called Embedded Block Code with Optimum Truncation (EBCOT) [3]. The outputs of the two-dimensional DWT (2D-DWT) are four subbands containing horizontal and vertical filtered high- (H) and low-pass (L) fractions of the image data where the 2D-DWT is recursivly applied on the resulting LL subband (horizontal and vertical low-pass filtering) in each level. Fig. 1(a) depicts this subband decomposition for a maximum level depth of $l_{max} = 3$. The

B. Huet et al. (Eds.): MMM 2009, LNCS 5371, pp. 140–149, 2009.
© Springer-Verlag Berlin Heidelberg 2009

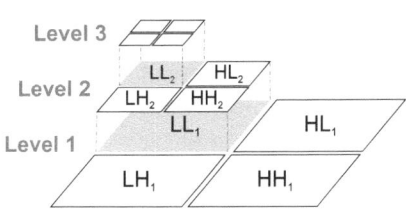

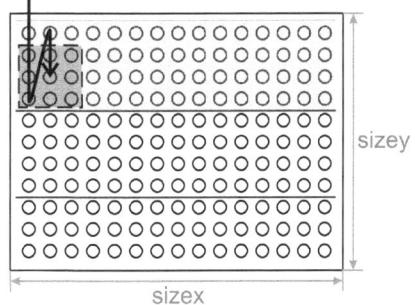

(a) Three-dimensional wavelet subband decomposition representation. Each LL_x subband is divided into four subbands HL_{x+1}, LH_{x+1}, HH_{x+1} and LL_{x+1}. Each 2D-DWT is applied recursively on the next LL_{x+1} subband until the maximum userdefined level is reached (here $l_{max} = 3$).

(b) Introducing bitplane scanning of one codeblock and one bitplane. The circles are the representation of single bits and the dashed box depicts the eight nearest neighbors for the current encoded bit. For each scanning pass each bitplane is split into stripes with a height of four Pixels.

Fig. 1. Basic principles of the JPEG2000 encoder

next step is a quantizer module focused on in section 2. For an embedded codestream we need to split each subband into codeblocks where the block sizes are user defined but fix for all subbands. As an entropy encoder, a combination of a context modeling mechanism and the IBM's binary MQ coder [4], [5] from the arithmetic encoding family is used, where each bitplane of each codeblock is handled separately starting at the most significant bitplane as shown in Fig. 1(b) to generate so called context information. Context is generated taking the eight surrounding bits into account and using the lookup tables defined in the JPEG2000 standard. Each context along with its data bit is sent to the arithmetic encoder and produces a binary codestream for each codeblock. This binary scan algorithm is very cost intensive and accounts for nearly 60-70% (depending on the implementation) of the complete processing performance as determined in [6] and [7].

Assuming the post compression rate distortion (PCRD) model proposed in [1], first all encoding is done prior to the rate control mechanism is applied. Due to this fact many research is done reducing the complexity of this entropy encoding part as well as of the rate control. Using high compression factors $F \gg 2$ the codestream after the entropy encoder is truncated searching for optimum truncation points of each codeblock. The prefixed quantizer is normaly unused and has quantizer stepsizes of $\Delta q = 1$ or predefined stepsizes $\Delta q \simeq 1$. The idea of defining a quantizer stepsize, applying the entropy encoder, checking for the output data size of the binary codestream and readjust the quantizer stepsize until the correct length is reached is very cost intensive. In contrast this article shows an analysis of the subband coding and proposes a model for an adaptive quantization scheme which is also aplicable on other wavelet-based image encoders (e.g. SPHIT [8]). In our research the JPEG2000 encoder is used because it can be shown, that the proposed method is applicable in complex image encoding systems and does not affect its high flexibilities.

In the following section 2 we present an analysis of the subband quantization behavior. Derived from this analysis we propose a new model for quantizer step-size estimation used for data rate limitation in wavelet-based image compression algorithms. Section 3 gives an evaluation of the proposed model for different data rates and this research work is summarized in section 4.

2   Subband Analysis

In previous works [6], [7] the authors analyzed the entropy behavior of the sub-bands. After each DWT level the entropy of each subband was calculated and the values were normalized due to their size decimation. The simulation results are shown in Fig. 2 for the test image 'lena' of size 512×512 Pixels and its luminance component. The original image has the maximum resolution of 8 Bits per Pixel for each of the three components. It can be detected that a very high reduction of the overall entropy is achieved in the first two levels ($l = 1, 2$). Further entropy reduction in the following DWT levels may be neglected. The processing costs for each level scales linear with the size of the subbands and the total costs for DWT processing are proportional to $\mathcal{C}_{DWT}$ which can be expressed as

$$\mathcal{C}_{DWT} = \sum_{n=1}^{l_{max}-1} \frac{1}{4^{(n-1)}} \,. \tag{1}$$

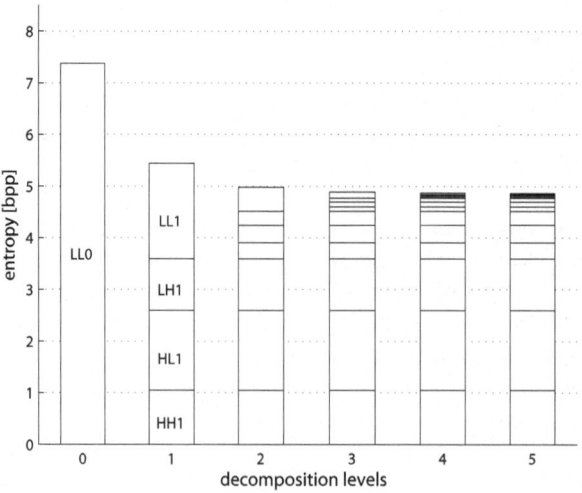

Fig. 2. Entropy bahavior of the luminance subbands of test image 'lena'

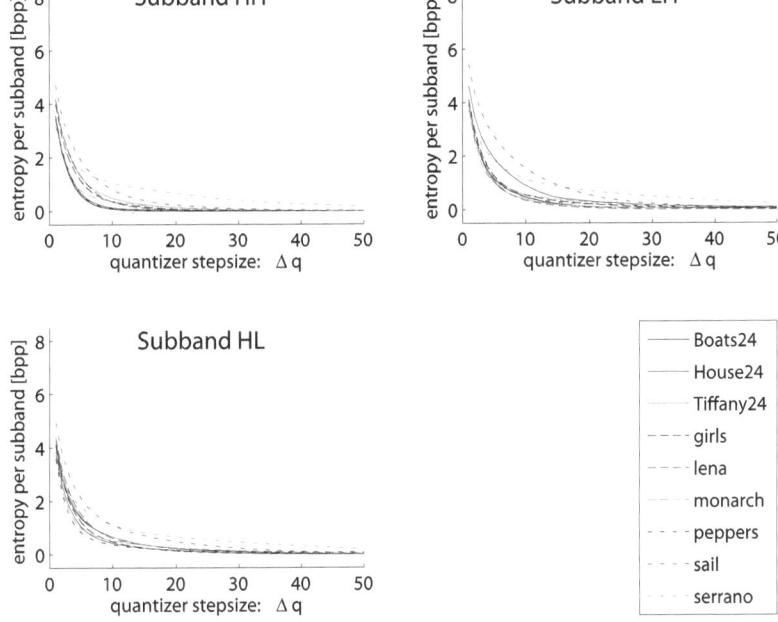

Fig. 3. Simulation results for different quantization stepsize parameters Δq in level 1 of the luminance subbands HH_1, LH_1 and HL_1

If we assume to neglect the level $l = 5$ and $l = 6$, the processing cost reduction is given as

$$\mathcal{C}_{red.} = \sum_{n=1}^{5} \frac{1}{4^{(n-1)}} - \sum_{n=1}^{3} \frac{1}{4^{(n-1)}} = \frac{1}{4^4} + \frac{1}{4^5} = 0.0048828125 \approx 0.49\% . \quad (2)$$

Reducing the processing costs by reducing the number of DWT decomposition levels gives only a minimum complexity reduction as shown in equation (2) but the concept is still of interest for embedded systems. For higher cost savings new concepts need to be evaluated as proposed in this paper.

The next step is to analyze the quantization behavior of the subbands. In the JPEG2000 standard a dead-zone quantization is specified which can be applied on each subband separately. Normaly, fix quantizer stepsizes are defined at design time for a maximum data rate limitation. Due to the fact that a wide range of compression values may be used (from $F = 1...200$) which are user defined at run time, there is no possibility at the moment to adjust these stepsizes. In our research we first simulated different stepsizes on different test images and the results are shown in Fig. 3 for the three subbands HH, LH and HL of level 1. Different entropy values at $\Delta q = 1$ and different slopes are because of the varying image characteristics and its random content.

Knowing the behavior of the subbands will help to calculate a desired quantizer stepsize for a given data rate. To evaluate a model which is applicable, all curves of all subbands are shifted to a common point. We have chosen to use the maximum possible entropy $E_{max} = 8$ bpp (bits per pixel) as the common point because it can be guaranteed that all values are positive. Shifting all values to E_{max} results in Fig. 4. Doing this we should know the difference ΔE between the original unquantized entropy values $E_{(\Delta q=1),s}$ for the current subband s and E_{max} before. For the proposed model we have observed that a function for the lower bound of these curves is necessary to calculate a quantization stepsize for a desired data rate. The file length can be calculated using the average entropy of the image multiplied with the number of pixels and the number of color components. Is this average entropy the newly estimated entropy we know the resulting length L of the encoded data stream. From the user defined data rate we are able to calculate the target length L_{max}. An additional constraint for the model is that the resulting data length L should be $L \geq L_{max}$ and therefore we propose a model for the lower bound of the curves in Fig. 4 and Fig. 5 as well as the curves of all the other subbands. From the same figures we can observe that we have to expect only a sub-optimum model because of the big variation of the curves. The estimated entropy is for some images from our test set nearly the half of the original entropy value. Further improvements are discussed in section 3.

The lower bound of the entropy, which is the dot-and-dashed curve named 'estimation' in Fig. 4 and is chosen to be identical for all subbands, follows

$$E_{est} = E_{max} \cdot \Delta q^{\alpha} + \Delta E \quad \text{with} \quad \Delta E = E_{(\Delta q=1),s} - E_{max} \qquad (3)$$

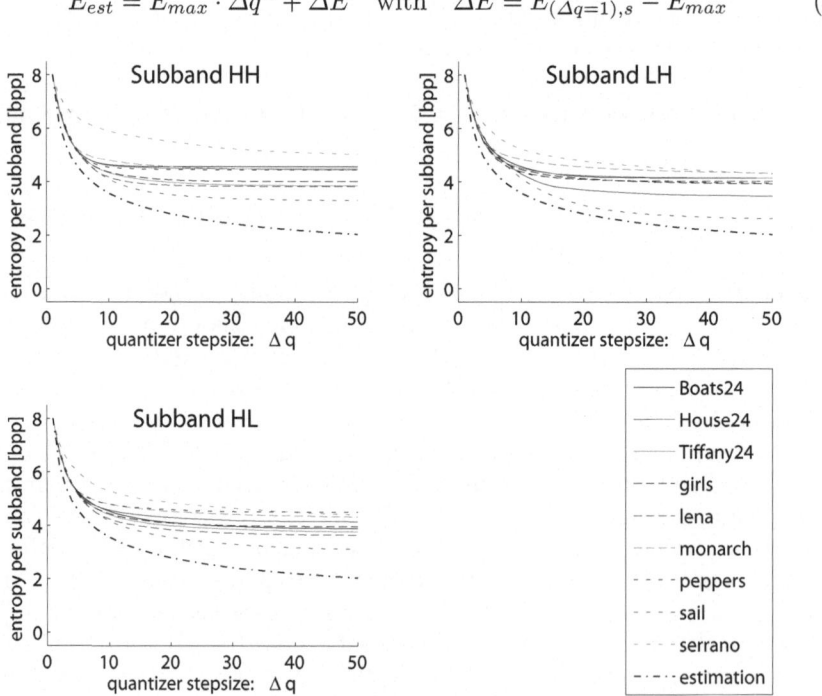

Fig. 4. Simulation results for different quantization stepsize parameters in Level 1 of the luminance subbands LH_1, HL_1 and HH_1 with a shift to $E_{max} = 8$ bpp

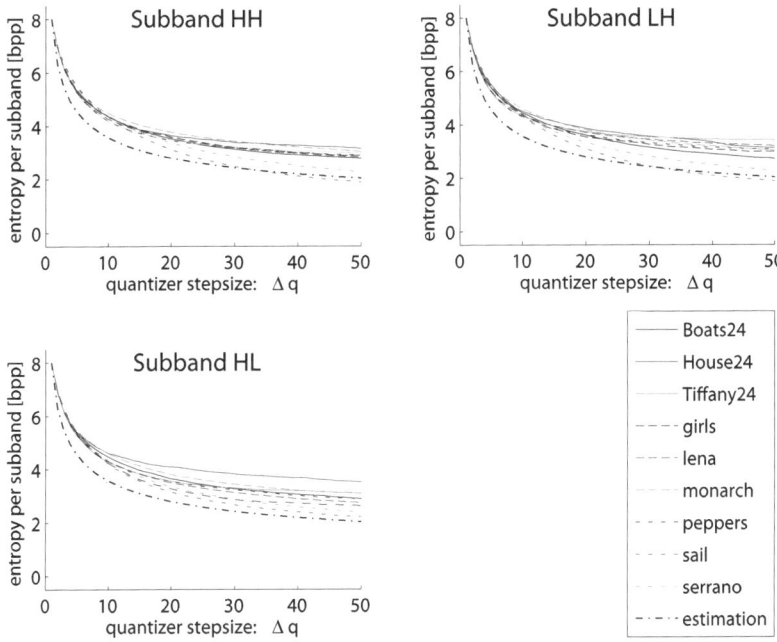

Fig. 5. Simulation results for different quantization stepsize parameters in Level 3 of the luminance subbands LH_3, HL_3 and HH_3 with a shift to $E_{max} = 8$ bpp

where in our case the maximum entropy value is set to $E_{max} = 8$ bpp and the exponent value is set to $\alpha = -0.35$. The value Δq represents the quantizer stepsize for the simulation and ΔE is the difference between the original entropy value $E_{(\Delta q=1),s}$ of the unquantized subband s and E_{max}. Out of this model we can calculate the desired quantization stepsize Δq with

$$\Delta q = \left[\frac{(E_{desired} - \Delta E)}{E_{max}} \right]^{\frac{1}{\alpha}} \tag{4}$$

for the desired entropy $E_{desired}$. $E_{desired}$ can be calculated directly from the desired data length of the encoded bitstream depending on the rate control strategy listed below. Specially in the current Fig. 4 we see a big variance and a saturation of some of the curves between 4 and 5 bpp. Comparing Fig. 3, we can see that exactly those curves have nearly zero entropy for higher quantizer stepsizes and have therefore a saturation behavior due to the shifting operation. If the proposed model is applied to any image the starting point of the model is the average entropy of this image and we have to care about the saturation with $E_{desired} \geq 0$ bpp.

With this approach we have the benefit to apply afterwards additional rate control techniques as suggested in the PCRD method with the lambda-optimization strategy for a Lagrange Multiplier [9] or other control methods found in the literature. Knowing the behavior of the system with this model, we have the advantage to apply different strategies to the image:

1. We can use the same quantizer stepsize for all subbands and all components.
2. We can change the accuracy of the chroma components independent to the luma component in the YUV color space.
3. We can select a special subband or a complete DWT level to change its behavior.
4. We can support chroma subsampling (e.g. YUV422) also for decoders which do not support it by removing chroma subbands in the first level.
5. We can give different loads for each subband (e.g. fine granularity in quantization on the smallest $LL_{l_{max}}$ subband and coarse granularity at the first high frequency subbands HL_1, LH_1 and HH_1)

In all this cases we are able to know the estimated data length of the encoded bitstream. The limited accuracy of such a rate control can be improved using again an entropy calculation to have the possibility to readjust the quantizer stepsize. The main goal of this work is to evaluate a new, low processing time consuming rate control. An additional quality measurement may be adopted at this stage but does not work as optimal as done in the EBCOT part. Other strategies as discussed in [10] or [11] can also be applied.

3   Simulation Results

The simulation assumes that all subbands are equaly handled. This means that we do not discuss different rate control strategies at this moment as described in the enumeration at the end of section 2. Only the same quantization stepsize is applied to all subbands except the smallest subband LL which contains unchanged data. We use our own JPEG2000 encoder implementation which is standard conform in respect to the reference implementation [12]. Due to our goal of data reduction the irreversible 9/7 DWT is used on the three YUV components. The simulation with the test set of images described in Table 1 is done

Table 1. Image metadata about the test set used in the simulation environment

Filename:	Dimensions:	Format:
Boats24	787×576	RGB, 24 Bits
House24	256×256	RGB, 24 Bits
Tiffany24	512×512	RGB, 24 Bits
girls	256×256	RGB, 24 Bits
lena	512×512	RGB, 24 Bits
monarch	768×512	RGB, 24 Bits
peppers	512×512	RGB, 24 Bits
sail	768×512	RGB, 24 Bits
serrano	629×794	RGB, 24 Bits

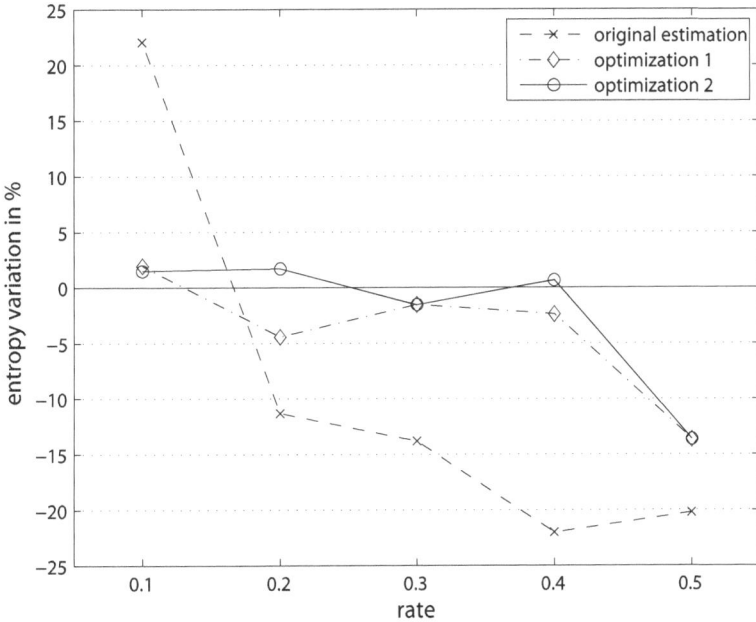

Fig. 6. Average variation of the estimated entropy for the set of all test images

for different allowed file lengths where the quantizer stepsizes are estimated. Fig. 6 shows the simulation results for the rates $r = 0.1, 0.2, 0.3, 0.4$ and 0.5.

The first set of data labeled as 'original estimation' are exported directly out of the proposed model with an average difference to the desired entropy of $\pm 23\%$ which is not acceptable for a rate control mechanism. Calculating again the entropies after quantization returns the difference of the real entropy and the expected one. Simple optimization strategies are applied here to show additional improvements. The variation is used to recalculate a new quantization stepsize for a maximum of five loops. Optimization 1 takes only the last stepsize at loop count five while optimization 2 selects the minimum variation of this set of five elements. Further optimization strategies are not part of this paper.

One big problem can be observed at the data rate of $r = 0.5$ where also the other optimization techniques do not achieve acceptable entropy values. For this problem there is an simple explanation. Taking again Fig. 2 into account, we can see that for test image 'lena' the maximum entropy is around 4.9 bpp. Other images have an maximum entropy less than 4 bpp and therefore the desired rate of $r = 0.5$ can not be achieved and we get therefore a high variation. Simulations are therefore done for rates $r \leq 0.5$. Optimization 1 and 2 show that only a variation $< 5\%$ for optimization 1 and a variation $< 1.6\%$ for optimization 2 is achieved for the other remaining data rates $r < 0.5$. The proposed model is used to estimate a first quantizer stepsize for a 2D-DWT based transformation and gives a starting point for further optimization without using cost intensive entropy encoders. Using the JPEG2000 standard we have additional data for header information and file format and counts nearly 2% of the data length. As long as a lazy length computation for the amount of header data is used inside a JPEG2000 implementation we have to deal with an additional variation of nearly 2% which may be added or subtracted to the results shown in Fig. 6. The target application of this model is a 2D-DWT encoder implementation with limited processing performance where higher variations are acceptable.

4   Summary

In this paper we showed an analysis of the subband behavior in respect to the variation of the quantizer stepsizes. We observed that there is a high variation between different images also if these curves are shifted to a common point. Out of this observation a model is proposed for the lower bound to estimate a quantizer stepsize to limit the encoded data to a maximum allowed data rate with the same variation. An additional, minimum cost intensive optimization strategy for the quantizer stepsize is used to lower the variation. This adaptive model for quantizer helps to find a good quantizer stepsize without using the cost intensive arithmetic encoder in JPEG2000.

References

1. ISO/IEC 15444-1: Information technology - JPEG 2000 image coding system: Core coding system. 2004(e) edn. (September 2004)
2. Skodras, A., Christopoulos, C., Ebrahimi, T.: The jpeg 2000 still image compression standard. IEEE Signal Processing Magazine 18(5), 36–58 (2001)
3. Taubman, D., Marcellin, M.: JPEG2000: Image Compression Fundamentals, Standards and Practice. Kluwer Academic Publishers, Dordrecht (2002)
4. Pennebaker, W., Mitchell, J., Langdon, G., Arps, R.: An overview of the basic principles of the q-coder adaptive binary arithmetic coder. IBM Journal of Research and Development 32(6), 717–726 (1988)
5. Rissanen, J., Langdon, G.: Arithmetic coding. IBM Journal of Research and Development 23(2), 149–162 (1979)
6. Günter, C., Rothermel, A.: Quantizer effects on ebcot based compression. Proc. Digest of Technical Papers. International Conference on Consumer Electronics ICCE 2007 (January 2007)
7. Günter, C., Rothermel, A.: Quantizer and entropy effects on ebcot based compression. IEEE Transactions on Consumer Electronics 53(2), 661–666 (2007)
8. Said, A., Pearlman, W.: A new, fast, and efficient image codec based on set partitioning in hierarchical trees. IEEE Transactions on Circuits and Systems for Video Technology 6(3), 243–250 (1996)
9. Everett, H.: Generalized lagrange multiplier method for solving problems of optimum allocation of resources. Operations Research 11, 399–417 (1963)

10. Battiato, S., Buemi, A., Impoco, G., Mancuso, M.: Jpeg2000 coded images optimization using a content-dependent approach. IEEE Transactions on Consumer Electronics 3(3), 400–408 (2002)
11. Llinas, F.A.: Model-Based JPEG2000 Rate Control Methods. PhD thesis, Universitat Autonoma de Barcelona, Departament d'Enginyeria de la Informacio i de les Comunicaciones (October 2006) ISBN 978-84-690-4006-5
12. ISO/IEC 15444-5: Information technology - JPEG 2000 image coding system: Reference software. 2003 edn. (software implementation in use: JASPER, Version 1.900.1) (June 2008)

Performance and Waiting-Time Predictability Analysis of Design Options in Cost-Based Scheduling for Scalable Media Streaming*

Mohammad A. Alsmirat and Nabil J. Sarhan

Department of Electrical and Computer Engineering, Wayne State University
5050 Anthony Wayne Drive, Detroit, MI 48202, USA

Abstract. Motivated by the impressive performance of cost-based scheduling for media streaming, we investigate its effectiveness in detail and analyze opportunities for further tunings and enhancements. Guided by this analysis, we propose a highly efficient enhancement technique that optimizes the scheduling decisions to increase the number of requests serviced concurrently and enhance user-perceived quality-of-service. We also analyze the waiting-time predictability achieved by the new technique. The simulation results show that it can achieve significant performance improvements while providing users with highly accurate expected waiting times.

Keywords: Scheduling, stream merging, video streaming, waiting-time prediction.

1   Introduction

Media streaming applications have grown dramatically in popularity. This paper considers video streaming of pre-recorded content. Unfortunately, the number of video streams that can be supported concurrently is highly constrained by the stringent requirements of multimedia data, which require high transfer rates and must be presented continuously in time. Stream merging techniques [1,2,3,4,5,6,7,8] address this challenge by aggregating clients into successively larger groups that share the same multicast streams. These techniques include *Patching* [4], *Transition Patching* [1,5], and *Earliest Reachable Merge Target*(ERMT) [2,3]. Periodic broadcasting techniques [9,10] (and references within) also address this challenge but can be used for only popular videos and require the requests to wait until the next broadcast time of the first corresponding segment. This paper considers the stream merging approach.

The degrees of resource sharing achieved by stream merging depend greatly on how the waiting requests are scheduled for service. Despite the many proposed stream merging techniques and the numerous possible variations, there has been only little work on the issue of scheduling in the context of these scalable techniques. We stress that the choice of a scheduling policy can be as important as or even more important than the choice of a stream merging technique, especially when the server is loaded. *Minimum*

---

* This work is supported in part by NSF grant CNS-0626861.

B. Huet et al. (Eds.): MMM 2009, LNCS 5371, pp. 150–162, 2009.

Cost First (MCF) [11] is a cost-based scheduling policy that has recently been proposed for use with stream merging. MCF captures the significant variation in stream lengths caused by stream merging through selecting the requests requiring the least cost. *Predictive Cost-based Scheduling* (PCS) [12] is another cost-based scheduling policy that has been proposed to enhance the server bandwidth utilization. PCS predicts future system state and uses the prediction results to potentially alter the scheduling decisions. It delays servicing requests at the current scheduling time (even when resources are available) if it is expected that shorter stream will be required at the next scheduling time. Cost-based scheduling policies perform significantly better than all other scheduling policies.

Motivated by the excellent performance of cost-based scheduling, we investigate here its effectiveness in great detail and discuss opportunities for further tunings and enhancements. In particular, we seek to answer the following two important questions. First, is it better to consider the stream cost only at the current scheduling time or consider the expected overall cost over a future period of time? Second, should the cost computation consider future stream extensions done by ERMT to satisfy the needs of new requests? Based on our detailed analysis, we propose a highly efficient technique, called *Adaptive Regular Stream Triggering* (ART), and analyze its effectiveness when it is used with other scheduling policies. Moreover, we analyze the waiting-time predictability of MCF when ART is applied. Motivated by the rapidly growing interest in human-centered multimedia, the ability to inform users about how long they need to wait for service has become of great importance [13]. Today, even for short videos with medium quality, users of online video websites may experience significant delays. Providing users with waiting-time feedback enhances their perceived QoS and encourages them to wait, thereby increasing throughput.

We study the effectiveness of different cost-computation alternatives and ART through extensive simulation. The analyzed performance metrics include customer defection (i.e. turn-away) probability, average waiting time, unfairness against unpopular videos, average cost per request, waiting-time prediction accuracy, and percentage of clients receiving expected waiting times. The waiting-time prediction accuracy is determined by the average deviation between the expected and actual waiting times. Moreover, we consider the impacts of customer waiting tolerance, server capacity, request arrival rate, number of videos, and video length. The results demonstrate that the proposed ART technique significantly enhances system throughput and reduces the average waiting time for service. Additionally, it can provide accurate expected waiting time to a larger number of clients. The rest of the paper is organized as follows. Section 2 provides background information. Section 3 analyzes cost-based scheduling, explores alternative ways to compute the cost, and presents the proposed ART technique. Section 4 discusses the performance evaluation methodology and Section 5 presents and analyzes the main results.

2   Background Information and Preliminary Analysis

2.1   Stream Merging

Stream merging techniques aggregate clients into larger groups that share the same multicast streams. In this subsection, we discuss three main stream merging techniques:

Patching [4], Transition Patching [1], and *Earliest Reachable Merge Target* (ERMT) [2]. With Patching, a new request joins immediately the latest multicast stream for the object and receives the missing portion as a *patch* using a unicast stream. When the playback of the patch is completed, the client continues the playback of the remaining portion using the data received from the multicast stream and already buffered locally. Since patch streams are not sharable with later requests and their cost increases with the temporal skew to the latest multicast stream, it is more cost-effective to start new full multicast stream (also called *regular stream*) after some time. Thus, when the patch stream length exceeds a certain value called *regular window* (Wr), a new regular stream is initiated instead. Transition Patching allows some patch streams to be sharable by extending their lengths. It introduces another multicast stream, called *transition patch*. The threshold to start a regular stream is Wr as in Patching, and the threshold to start a transition patch is called the *transition window* (Wt). A transition patch is shared by all subsequent patches until the next transition patch. ERMT is a near optimal hierarchical stream merging technique. Basically, a new client or a newly merged group of clients snoops on the closest stream that it can merge with if no later arrivals preemptively catch them [2]. ERMT performs better than other hierarchical stream merging alternatives and close to the optimal solution.

2.2   Request Scheduling

A scheduling policy selects an appropriate video for service whenever it has an available *channel*. A channel is a set of resources (network bandwidth, disk I/O bandwidth, etc.) needed to deliver a multimedia stream. All waiting requests for the selected video can be serviced using only one channel. The number of channels is referred to as *server capacity*. All scheduling policies are guided by one or more of the following primary objectives:(i) minimize the overall customer defection (turn-away) probability, (ii) minimize the average request waiting time, and (iii) minimize unfairness. The defection probability is the probability that a user leaves the system without being serviced because of a waiting time exceeding the user's tolerance. It is the most important metric because it translates directly to the number of customers that can be serviced concurrently and to server throughput. The second and the third objectives are indicators of customer-perceived QoS. It is usually desirable that the servers treat equally the requests for all videos. Unfairness measures the bias of a policy against unpopular videos.

The main scheduling policies include *First Come First Serve* (FCFS) [14], *Maximum Queue Length* (MQL) [14], *Minimum Cost First* (MCF) [11], and *Predictive Cost-Based Scheduling* (PCS) [12]. FCFS selects the video with the oldest waiting request, whereas MQL selects the video with the largest number of waiting requests. MCF policy has been recently proposed to exploit the variations in stream lengths caused by stream merging techniques. *MCF-P* (P for "Per"), the preferred implementation of MCF, selects the video with the least cost per request. The objective function here is $F(i) = \frac{L_i \times R_i}{N_i}$, where L_i is the required stream length for the requests in queue i, R_i is the (average) data rate for the requested video, and N_i is the number of waiting requests for video i. To reduce the bias against videos with higher data rates, R_i can be removed from the objective function (as done in this paper). MCF-P has two variants: *Regular as Full* (RAF) and *Regular as Patch* (RAP). RAP treats regular and transition streams as if they where patches, whereas RAF uses their normal costs. MCF-P performs significantly better than all other scheduling policies when stream merging techniques are used. PCS is based on MCF, but it predicts future system state and uses this prediction to possibly alter the scheduling decisions. When a channel becomes available, PCS determines using the MCF-P objective function the video V_{Now} which is to be serviced tentatively at the current scheduling time (T_{Now}) and its associated delivery cost. Before actually servicing that video, it predicts the system state at the next scheduling time (T_{Next}) and estimates the delivery cost at that time assuming that video V_{Now} is not serviced at time T_{Now}. PCS does not service any request at time T_{Now} and thus postpone the service of video V_{Now} if the delivery cost at time T_{Next} is lower than that at time T_{Now}. Otherwise, video V_{Now} is serviced immediately. To reduce possible channel underutilization, PCS delays the service of streams only if the number of available server channels is smaller than a certain threshold. PCS has two alternative implementations: *PCS-V* and *PCS-L*, which differ in how to compute the delivery cost or required stream length at the next scheduling time. They perform nearly the same and thus we consider only PCS-V because of its simplicity.

3 Alternative Cost Computations

3.1 Analysis of Cost-Based Scheduling

We seek to understand the behavior of cost-based scheduling and its interaction with stream merging. Understanding this behavior helps in developing solutions that optimize the overall performance. One of the issues that we explore in this study is determining the duration during which the cost should be computed. In particular, we seek to determine whether the cost should be computed only at the current scheduling time (T_{sched}) or over a future duration of time, called *prediction window* (W_p). In other words, should the system select the video with the least cost per request at time T_{sched} or the least cost per request during W_p. The latter requires prediction of the future system state.

We devise and explore two ways to analyze the effectiveness of computing the cost over a period of time: *Lookahead* and *Combinational*. In Lookahead, the service rate (which is the rate at which a video gets serviced) is computed dynamically for each video that has waiting requests. The total cost for servicing each one of these videos is computed during W_p. Lookahead Scheduling selects the video j that minimizes the expected cost per request. Thus, the objective function to minimize is $F(j) = \frac{\sum_{i=1}^{n} C_i}{\sum_{i=1}^{n} N_i}$, where n is the number of expected service times for video j during W_p, C_i is the cost required to service the requests for video j at service time i, and N_i is the number of requests expected to be serviced at service time i. The number of requests at future service times is predicted by dynamically computing the arrival rate for each video. As discussed earlier, ERMT may extend streams to satisfy the needs of new requests. MCF-P, however, does not consider later extensions in computing the cost. In analyzing cost-based scheduling, we also need to consider whether it is worthwhile to predict and consider these later extensions. Hence, we consider a variant of Lookahead Scheduling that considers these extensions.

In contrast with Lookahead Scheduling, Combinational scheduling predicts the best sequence in which various videos should be serviced and performs scheduling based on this sequence. Thus, it considers any correlations on the cost among successive video selections. The best sequence is found by generating all possible sequences for the next n stream completion times during W_p, for only the n-best videos according to the MCF-P objective function. The objective function of each sequence is then calculated. Consider the sequence $S_j = \{V_1, V_2, V_3, ..., V_n\}$, where V_i is the video selected to be serviced at the next i^{th} stream completion time. The objective function for this sequence is $F(S_j) = \frac{\sum_{i=1}^{n} C_{V_i}}{\sum_{i=1}^{n} N_{V_i}}$, where C_{V_i} is the cost required to service V_i, and N_{V_i} is the number of waiting requests for that video. C_{V_i} is determined based on the used MCF-P variant. Combinational Scheduling chooses the sequence that is expected to lead to the least overall cost. Although many optimizations are possible to reduce the implementation complexity, we focus primarily on whether exploiting the correlations between successive video selections is indeed important in practical situations.

3.2 Proposed Adaptive Regular Stream Triggering (ART)

As will be shown later, our extensive analysis reveals a significant interaction between stream merging and scheduling decisions. One of the pertaining issues is how to best handle regular (i.e., full) streams. MCF-P (RAP) considers the cost of a regular stream as a patch and thus treats it in a differentiated manner. The question arises as to whether it is worthwhile, however, to delay regular streams in certain situations. Guided by extensive analysis, we propose a highly efficient technique, called *Adaptive Regular Stream Triggering* (ART). A possible implementation is shown in Figure 1. The basic idea here is to delay regular streams as long as the number of free channels is below a certain threshold, which is to be computed dynamically based on the current workload and system state.

Figure 2 shows an algorithm to dynamically find the best value of $freeChannelThresh$. As in [12], the algorithm changes the value of the threshold and observes its impact on customer defection (i.e., turn-away) probability over a certain time interval. The value of the threshold is then updated based on the trend in defection

```
V_Now = find the video that will be serviced at T_Now;
if (freeChannels ≥ freeChannelThresh)
    Service the requests for V_Now;
else {
    currStreamLen =
        find the required stream length to serve V_Now at T_Now;
    if (currStreamLen < movieLen) // not a full stream
        Service the requests for V_Now;
    else //full stream
        Postpone the requests for V_Now;
}
```

Fig. 1. Simplified Implementation of ART

```
// This algorithm executed periodically
currDefectionRate = defectedCustomers/servedCustomers;
if (currDefectionRate < lastDefectionRate) {
    if (last action was decrement
        and freeChannelThresh > 2)
        freeChannelThresh − −;
    else if (last action was increment)
        freeChannelThresh + +;
} else if (currDefectionRate > lastDefectionRate){
    if (last action was increment
        and freeChannelThresh > 2)
        freeChannelThresh − −;
    else if (last action was decrement)
        freeChannelThresh + +;
}
lastDefectionRate = currDefectionRate;
```

Fig. 2. Simplified Algorithm for Computing *freeChannelThresh* Dynamically [12]

probability (increase or decrease) and the last action (increase or decrease) performed on the threshold. The algorithm is to be executed periodically but not frequently to ensure stable system behavior.

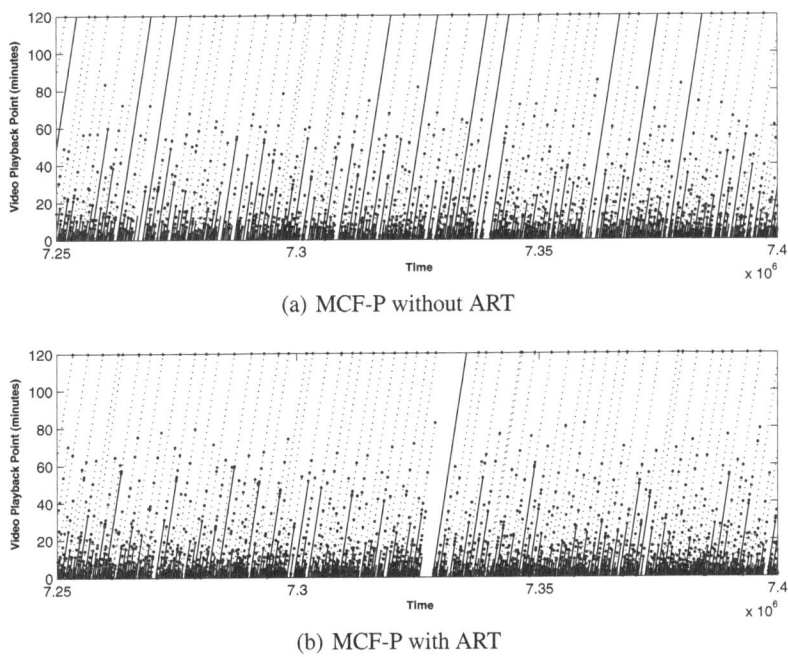

(a) MCF-P without ART

(b) MCF-P with ART

Fig. 3. Impact of ART on ERMT Stream Merge Tree [*Video 11, MCF-P, Server Capacity = 450*]

To further demonstrate the main idea of ART, Figure 3 plots the ERMT merge tree without and with ART, respectively. The solid lines show the initial stream lengths and the dotted lines show later extensions. The circles identify successive extensions. With ART, we can see a gap before the initiation of a regular stream because of the postponement. We can also observe that the number of initial regular streams in the merge tree (called *I Streams* in this paper) is relatively much smaller with ART. For example, there is only one *I Stream* in the merge tree with ART while there are many more *I Streams* in the merge tree without ART.

4   Evaluation Methodology

We study the effectiveness of the proposed policy through simulation. The simulation stops after a steady state analysis with 95% confidence interval is reached. Table 1 summarizes the workload characteristics used.

Table 1. Summary of Workload Characteristics

Parameter	Model/Value(s)
Request Arrival	Poisson Process
Request Arrival Rate	Variable, Default is 40 Req./min
Server Capacity	300 to 750 channels
Video Access	Zipf-Like with $\theta = 0.271$
Number of Videos	120
Video Length	120 min
Waiting Tolerance Model	A, B, C, Default is A
Waiting Tolerance Mean (μ_{tol})	Variable, Default is 30 sec

We characterize the waiting tolerance of customers by three models: A, B, and C. In *Model A*, the waiting tolerance follows an exponential distribution with mean μ_{tol}. In *Model B*, users with expected waiting times less than μ_{tol} will wait and the others will have the same waiting tolerance as Model A. We use *Model C* to capture situations in which users either wait or defect immediately depending on the expected waiting times. The user waits if the expected waiting time is less than μ_{tol} and defects immediately if the waiting time is greater than $2\mu_{tol}$. Otherwise, the defection probability decreases linearly from 1 to 0 for the expected waiting times between μ_{tol} and $2\mu_{tol}$.

The analyzed performance metrics include customer defection probability, average waiting time, and unfairness against unpopular videos. The waiting-time predictability is analyzed by two metrics: waiting-time prediction accuracy and the percentage of clients receiving expected waiting times. The waiting-time prediction accuracy is determined by the average deviation between the expected and actual waiting times. For waiting-time prediction, we use the algorithm in [13]. Note that this algorithm may not provide an expected waiting time to each client because the prediction may not always be performed accurately.

5   Result Presentation and Analysis

5.1   Comparing Different Alternatives for Computing the Cost

Let us start by studying the effectiveness of Lookahead and Combinational Scheduling. Interestingly, there is no clear benefit for computing the cost over a future period of time. In some cases, as shown in Figures 4 and 5, the performance in term of customers defection and average waiting time may be worse than when computing the cost at the current scheduling time. Although computing the cost over a time interval seems intuitively to be an excellent choice, it interferes negatively with stream merging.

Next, we discuss how the interaction between stream merging and scheduling can be utilized by using the proposed ART technique, which can be used with any scheduling policy. Based on the prior results, we only consider next computing the cost at the current scheduling time.

5.2   Effectiveness of ART

Figure 6 shows the effectiveness of the proposed ART technique when ERMT is used. With MCF-P, ART reduces the defection probability and average waiting time by up

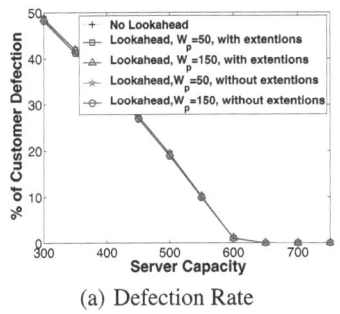
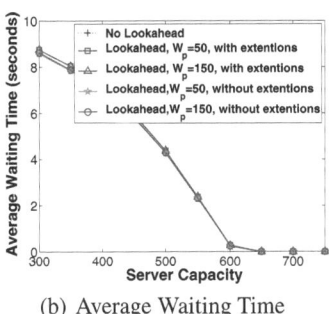

(a) Defection Rate   (b) Average Waiting Time

Fig. 4. Effectiveness of Lookahead Scheduling, with and without Future Extensions [*ERMT*]

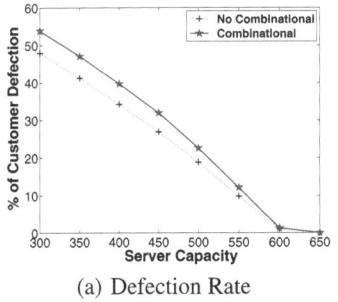
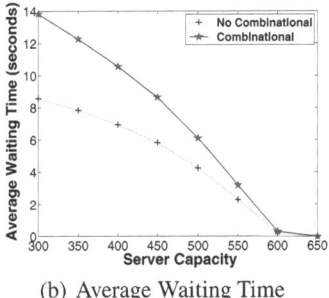

(a) Defection Rate   (b) Average Waiting Time

Fig. 5. Effectiveness of Combinational Scheduling [*ERMT, W_p = 4 next stream completion times*]

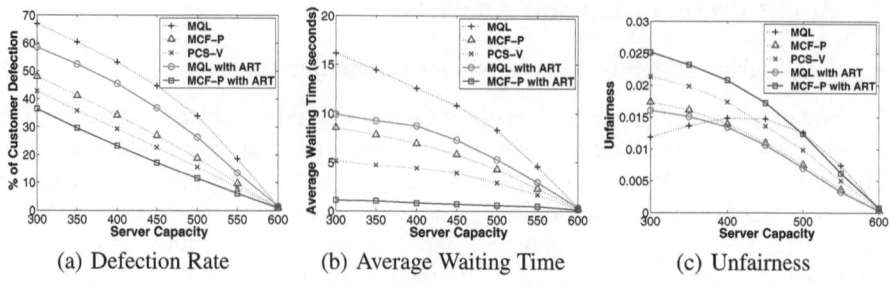

(a) Defection Rate   (b) Average Waiting Time   (c) Unfairness

Fig. 6. Effectiveness of ART [*ERMT*]

to 25% and 80%, respectively. It also yields significant improvements when used with MQL. Moreover, MCF-P when combined with ART performs better than PCS-V in terms of the defection probability and average waiting time. Unfairness, the least important metric, is a little larger with ART because of its nature in favoring videos with shorter streams, but it is still acceptable compared with MQL and PCS-V. These results indicate that MCF-P when combined with ART is the best overall performer.

Figure 7 depicts the impact of ART on regular streams in ERMT. We observe that when ART postpones regular streams, it forces ERMT to make more merges, which in turn, increases system utilization. We can also observe that the number of regular streams does not decrease significantly despite of postponing these streams. In contrast, Figure 7(a) indicates that the average time between two successive regular streams for popular videos is even smaller with ART than that without it. ERMT keeps extending streams, which eventually become regular streams. Figures 7(b) and 7(c) compare the percentage of initial regular streams (I Streams) and extended regular streams (E Streams) without and with ART, respectively. We can see that the percentage of extended regular streams with ART is much higher. This supports the fact that the number of regular streams is not reduced by postponing. In summary, we can say that ART improves ERMT by replacing many *I Streams* with *E Streams*. To further support the fact that more customers are served with only one stream when using ART, Figure 8 demonstrates the impact of ART on the cost per request. We can see that the cost per request with ART is lower for different server capacities.

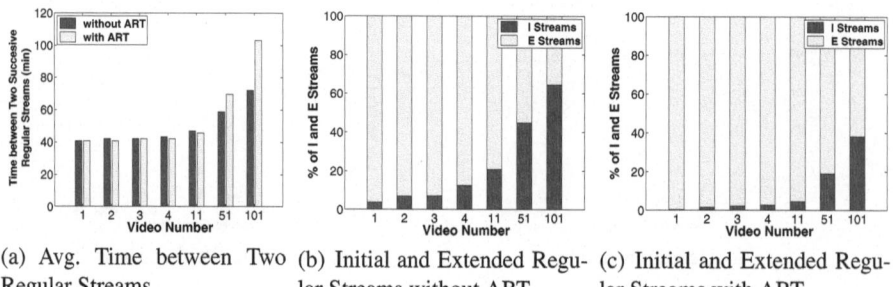

(a) Avg. Time between Two Regular Streams   (b) Initial and Extended Regular Streams without ART   (c) Initial and Extended Regular Streams with ART

Fig. 7. Impact of ART on Regular Streams [*ERMT, MCF-P, Server Capacity = 450*]

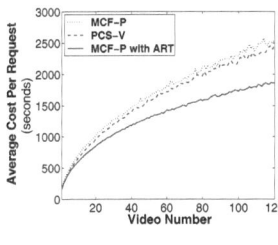
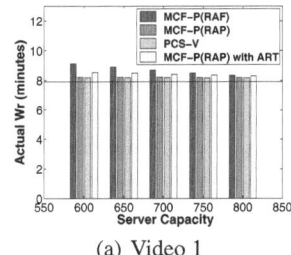
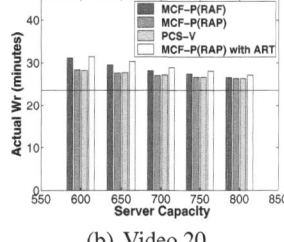

(a) Video 1   (b) Video 20

Fig. 8. Comparing the Impact of PCS and ART on Cost per Request [*ERMT, MCF-P, Server Capacity = 300*]

Fig. 9. Comparing Actual *Wr* in MCF-P (RAF), MCF-P (RAP), PCS-V and MCF-P (RAP) with ART [*Patching*]

The results for Transition Patching and Patching have the same behavior as ERMT and thus are not shown for space limitation. Patching results can be found partially in Figures 10 and 11. As with ERMT, ART reduces significantly the customer defection

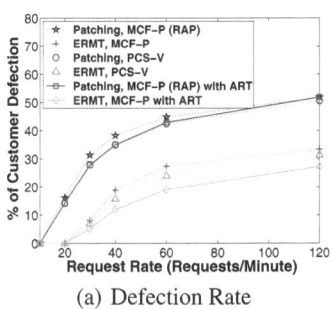
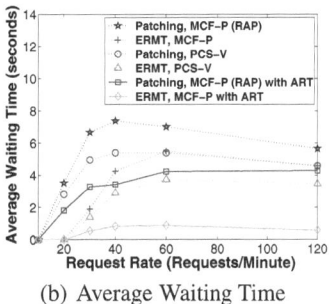

(a) Defection Rate   (b) Average Waiting Time

Fig. 10. Impact of Request Arrival Rate [*Server Capacity = 500*]

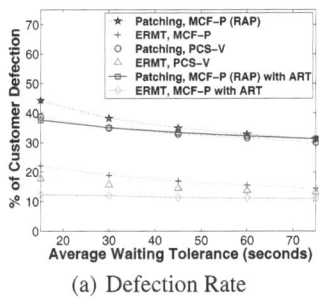
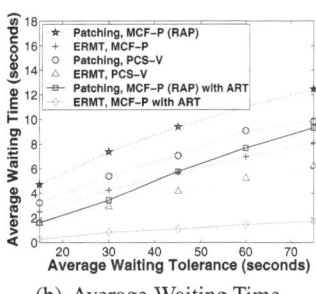

(a) Defection Rate   (b) Average Waiting Time

Fig. 11. Impact of Customer Waiting Tolerance [*Server Capacity = 500*]

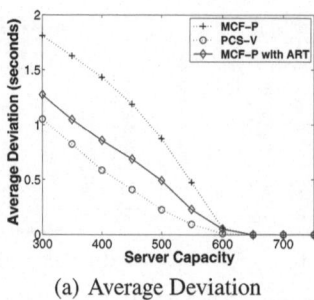

(a) Average Deviation

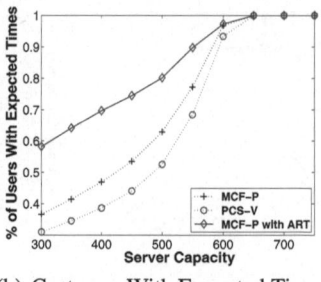

(b) Customer With Expected Time

Fig. 12. Waiting-Time Predictability of MCF-P, MCF-P with ART, and PCS-V [*ERMT*, $W_p = 0.5\mu_{tol}$, *Model B*]

rate and the average waiting time when it is combined with MCF-P (RAP) and MQL. MCF-P (RAP) combined with ART gives almost the same results as PCS-V in terms of customer defection probability, but it reduces the average waiting time significantly. Unfairness with ART is a little larger but still acceptable compared with that of MQL for medium and high server capacities and remains less than that of PCS-V.

Interestingly, ART improves Transition Patching and Patching despite that their best scheduling policy, MCF-P (RAP), depends on a conflicting principle. As discussed earlier, MCF-P (RAP) gives preference to regular streams while ART postpones them in certain situations. As illustrated in Figure 9, the main impact of ART is dynamically optimizing Wr, which is larger than that of MCF-P (RAP) and smaller than that of MCF-P (RAF) for popular videos, and even greater than that of MCF-P (RAF) for unpopular videos. With PCS-V, Wr values are very close to that of MCF-P (RAP). The horizontal line in the figure marks the equation-based value of Wr [15]. (Note that the equation does not yield optimum values because it is based on important simplifying assumptions.)

5.3 Impact of Workload Parameters on the Effectiveness of ART

Figures 10 and 11 illustrate the impact of the request arrival rate and customer waiting tolerance on the effectiveness of ART. The results for both Patching and ERMT are shown. We have also studied the impacts of the number of videos and video length, but the figures are not shown to save space. The results demonstrate that ART always yields significant performance improvements under all studied workload parameters. In addition, ART always achieves smaller customer defection probability and average waiting time than PCS-V in the case of ERMT. In Patching, the same trend is observed for the average waiting time, but PCS-V and "MCF-P combined with ART" perform nearly the same in terms of customer defection probability, especially when the server is highly loaded.

5.4 Waiting-Time Predictability with ART

Figure 12 compares the predictability of MCF-P, MCF-P combined with ART, and PCS-V in terms of the average deviation and percentage of clients receiving expected time of service (PCRE) under waiting tolerance Model B. The results with Model C are similar and thus are not shown to save space. The results demonstrate that ART significantly improves the predictability of MCF-P. In particular, ART reduces the average deviation by up to 30% and 75% for models B and C, respectively. It also increases the number of clients receiving expected times by up to 35%. Moreover, MCF-P combined with ART gives more customers expected times than PCS-V with a relatively less significant increase in the average deviation.

6   Conclusions

We have analyzed cost-based scheduling for scalable video streaming. The results indicate that there is no clear advantage of computing the cost over a future time window, compared with computing the cost only at the next scheduling time. The results also show that the proposed ART technique substantially improves the customer defection probability and the average waiting time. With ART, significantly more clients can receive expected waiting time for service, but at a somewhat lower waiting time accuracy.

References

1. Cai, Y., Hua, K.A.: An efficient bandwidth-sharing technique for true video on demand systems. In: Proc. of ACM Multimedia, pp. 211–214 (October 1999)
2. Eager, D.L., Vernon, M.K., Zahorjan, J.: Optimal and efficient merging schedules for Video-on-Demand servers. In: Proc. of ACM Multimedia, pp. 199–202 (October 1999)
3. Eager, D.L., Vernon, M.K., Zahorjan, J.: Bandwidth skimming: A technique for cost-effective Video-on-Demand. In: Proc. of Multimedia Computing and Networking Conf (MMCN), pp. 206–215 (January 2000)
4. Cai, Y., Hua, K.A.: Sharing multicast videos using patching streams. Multimedia Tools and Applications journal 21(2), 125–146 (2003)
5. Cai, Y., Tavanapong, W., Hua, K.A.: Enhancing patching performance through double patching. In: Proc. of 9th Intl. Conf. on Distributed Multimedia Systems, September 2003, pp. 72–77 (2003)
6. Rocha, M., Maia, M., Cunha, I., Almeida, J., Campos, S.: Scalable media streaming to interactive users. In: Proc. of ACM Multimedia, pp. 966–975 (November 2005)
7. Ma, H., Shin, G.K., Wu, W.: Best-effort patching for multicast true VoD service. Multimedia Tools Appl. 26(1), 101–122 (2005)
8. Qudah, B., Sarhan, N.J.: Towards scalable delivery of video streams to heterogeneous receivers. In: Proc. of ACM Multimedia, pp. 347–356 (October 2006)
9. Huang, C., Janakiraman, R., Xu, L.: Loss-resilient on-demand media streaming using priority encoding. In: Proc. of ACM Multimedia, pp. 152–159 (October 2004)
10. Shi, L., Sessini, P., Mahanti, A., Li, Z., Eager, D.L.: Scalable streaming for heterogeneous clients. In: Proc. of ACM Multimedia, pp. 337–346 (October 2006)
11. Sarhan, N.J., Qudah, B.: Efficient cost-based scheduling for scalable media streaming. In: Proc. of Multimedia Computing and Networking Conf. (MMCN) (January 2007)
12. Alsmirat, M., Sarhan, N.J.: Predictive cost-based scheduling for scalable media streaming. In: Proc. of IEEE International Conference on Multimedia and Expo (June 2008)

13. Alsmirat, M., Al-Hadrusi, M., Sarhan, N.J.: Analysis of waiting-time predictability in scalable media streaming. In: Proc. of ACM Multimedia (September 2007)
14. Dan, A., Sitaram, D., Shahabuddin, P.: Scheduling policies for an on-demand video server with batching. In: Proc. of ACM Multimedia, pp. 391–398 (October 1994)
15. Qudah, B., Sarhan, N.J.: Analysis of resource sharing and cache management techniques in scalable video-on-demand. In: Proc. of the 14th IEEE International Symposium on Modeling, Analysis, and Simulation of Computer and Telecommunication Systems (MASCOTS), pp. 327–334 (September 2006)

Evaluating Streaming Rate Controllers: A Support Tool

Cristian Koliver[1], Jean-Marie Farines[2], Barbara Busse[3],
and Hermann De Meer[3]

[1] University of Caxias do Sul, CP 1352, Caxias do Sul, Brazil
`ckoliver@ucs.br`
[2] Federal University of Santa Catarina, CP 476, Florianopolis, Brazil
`farines@das.ufsc.br`
[3] University of Passau, Innstrae 43, 94032 Passau, Germany
`demeer@fmi.uni-passau.de`

Abstract. The Internet has been experiencing a large growth of the multimedia traffic of applications performing over an RTP stack implemented on top of UDP/IP. Since UDP does not offer a congestion control mechanism (unlikely TCP), studies on the rate control schemes have been increasingly done. Usually, new proposes are evaluated, by simulation, in terms of criteria such as fairness towards competing TCP connections and packet losses. However, results related to other performance aspects − quality achieved, overhead introduced by the control, and actual throughput after stream adaptation − are difficult to obtain by simulation. In order to provide actual results about these criteria, we developed a comprehensive rate controlled video delivery tool for testing RTP-based controllers. The tool allows to easily incorporate new control schemes. In this paper, we describe the tool and the results achieved by using a LDA+ based controller.

Keywords: rate control, MPEG, RTP, evaluation.

1 Introduction and Motivation

Many end-to-end rate control strategies for real-time multimedia applications have been proposed in the last years. Most of them are driven to UDP applications running over the best effort Internet. They are control systems-like, on which the server adapts its throughput based on feedback messages from the clients. The messages are sent in short intervals. The goals of the rate control strategies include to avoid network congestion and to provide TCP-friendliness [1]. Since the RTP (Real-time Transport Protocol) was designed by the IETF (Internet Engineering Tasking Force) for multimedia communication in the Internet and offers support for collecting information about network load, packet losses and end-to-end delays, the strategies are usually based upon this protocol (see, for example, [5,6]). By simulation, the authors show the performance of their strategies with regard to network utilization, reduction of the possibility of

B. Huet et al. (Eds.): MMM 2009, LNCS 5371, pp. 163–174, 2009.

network congestion, packet losses, fairness towards competing TCP connections, and scalability.

However, simulations do not provide results about performance criteria such as the quality oscillation and the overhead introduced by the controller and the actuator. In this paper, we describe a modular rate-controlled video delivery tool designed for testing RTP-based rate controllers. The tool allows to easily incorporate new rate control schemes. We also show the results obtained by using a controller based on the Enhanced Loss-Delay Algorithm, proposed by Sisalem and Wolisz [11,12].

The paper is organized as follows. The architecture of the tool is presented in Sect. 2. In Sect. 3, we provide implementation details of the tool. We investigate the performance of our tool and the LDA+ controller in Sect. 4. In Sect. 5, we discuss the results and further work to improve the tool.

2   Architecture

Figure 1 depicts the architecture of our video delivery tool. At the server-side, the tool is formed of four separated modules: the MPEG-2 encoder, the packetizer, the controller, and the actuator.

The encoder compresses the raw video stream on the fly and has N QoS parameters ρ_k ($k = 1, 2, 3, ..., N$) to be set. They have influence on the stream bit rate (by affecting the compression rate) and quality. A combination of QoS parameters settings is a QoS level. The ith QoS level L_i is a N-tuple

$$L_i = < \rho_{1_i}, \rho_{2_i}, ..., \rho_{N_i} > \tag{1}$$

where $i = 1, 2, ..., I$ (I is the module of the Cartesian product of the QoS parameters domains). When the encoder is set as L_i, the *expected* stream bit rate is rn_i (the *nominal rate*) and the quality is qn_i (the *nominal quality*). This latter metric should reflect the stream quality according to the user perspective. In our tool, it is used to rank QoS levels (see details in Sec. 3.1).

The packetizer assembles the MPEG-2 video stream provided by the encoder in RTP packets and delivers them over the network. At the client-side, there are two modules: the depacketizer and the MPEG-2 decoder. The depacketizer converts RTP packets into MPEG-2 elementary streams and feedbacks the packetizer through receive report (RR) packets. The packetizer computes and provides the controller with losses (l) and round trip delay (τ). In the adaptation instant t, the controller computes the *target rate* $rt(t)$ providing it to the actuator.

The actuator uses the function QoS to find a QoS level L_k whose rn_k matches $rt(t)$. The function is

$$QoS : rt(t) \mapsto < L_k, rn_k, qn_k >, rn_k \leq rt(t). \tag{2}$$

Then, the actuator adjusts the encoder parameters

$$\rho_1, \rho_2, ..., \rho_N$$

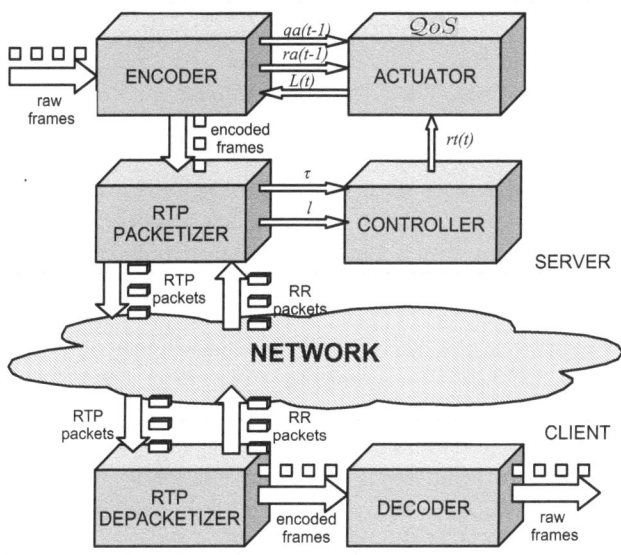

Fig. 1. Video delivery tool architecture

to $< \rho_{1_k}, \rho_{2_k}, ..., \rho_{N_k} >$. The configuration of the encoder after adapting is $L(t) = L_k$. Each adaptation instant $t + 1$, the actuator measures the encoder throughput between $t - 1$ and t (the *actual rate* achieved after adaption instant $t - 1$ or $ra(t - 1)$) as well as $qa(t - 1)$ (the quality actually achieved after adapting). These values are provided to the actuator to tune $\mathcal{Q}oS$. Note that it is expected that $ra(t - 1) \approx rt(t - 1) \approx rn_j$ and $qa(t - 1) \approx qn_j$ $(L_j = L(t - 1))$.

Figure 1 shows a single client but the server may multicast the video stream to m clients.

3   Implementation

In this section, we provide the main implementation details of each module, since some of the achieved results are closely related to the tool design aspects. Furthermore, some ideas used here may be useful for other rate controllers implementations.

3.1   The Controller

The controller can be viewed as a black box whose inputs are the round trip delay and the loss rate and the output is the target throughput. It is implemented as a periodic task whose period is P. Period P is the feedback period defined by the RTP. In the current implementation, the controller follows the Enhanced Loss-Delay Algorithm (LDA+), proposed by Sisalem and Wolisz [11]. However, we designed and implemented the modules interfaces in such way that the controller can easily be replaced by any RTP-based rate controller.

The LDA+ Controller. The LDA+ controller regulates the server throughput based on end-to-end feedback information about losses, delays and the bandwidth capacity measured by the m clients. This information is sent by the clients to the server in the RR packets of RTCP protocol. The LDA+ controller uses additive increase and multiplicative decrease factors determined dynamically at the server-side to compute $rt(t)$. The factors come from an estimative of the current network status from the above information (see [11] for more details about $rt(t)$ computation).

The LDA+ controller may generate $rt(t)$ values slightly different from $rt(t-1)$ values (less than 50 Kbps). Thus, a LDA+ controller (and other similar ones) may generate highly granular target bit rates. Since LDA+ was designed focusing on multimedia transmission, its use requires a strategy to configure the application in order to achieve a throughput similar to the target throughput $rt(t)$ computed by the LDA+ controller. In our tool, the strategy is implemented by the actuator, described in the next section.

The Actuator. The actuator is responsible for configuring the encoder parameters as L_k in time t, such that rn_k is close (but not greater) to the target throughput $rt(t)$ provided by the controller.

Since the controller can generate values of the target bit rates differing by few Kbps, our main concern in the actuator design was to define a strategy for providing fine granularity in terms of rn_i and qn_i values. Common strategies of actuation focusing on a single quality dimension (e.g., strategies based on frame dropping or quantizer adjustment) are unsuitable, since they provide a very discrete set of bit rates values. The application user perceives such limitation as sudden changes of quality; under the network point of view, the mapping from $rt(t)$ into a QoS level L_k possibly leads to the bandwidth underutilization. Thus, we opted to use N dimensional QoS levels composed by the following parameters: alternate scan (als), prediction type (mtc), quantization factor or quantizer (qtz), intra-inter matrix combination (mqt), DC precision (dcp), and matrix of coefficients[1] (mcf). We run several tests using different set of parameters. The above one was chosen by providing a fine quality/rate granularity.

The actuator selects the QoS level L_i from a table called TQoS. TQoS is a table whose entries are tuples as

$$<< als_i, mtc_i, mqt_i, qtz_i, dcp_i, mcf_i >, rn_i, qn_i > \qquad (3)$$

where als_i is the value of parameter als in the i-th table entry, mtc_i is the value of parameter mtc, and so on; rn_i is the nominal throughput of the encoded video stream configured as L_i; and qn_i is the nominal quality of this stream given by

---

[1] See http://www.mpeg.org/MSSG/tm5/index.html for more details about purpose and influence of these parameters on the compression process.

          (a)   (b)

Fig. 2. Same frame of the reference video when the stream QoS levels are: (a) $<<$ $1, 4, 62, 2, 8, 2 >, 1047.86, 8.96 >$ and (b) $<< 6, 6, 10, 4, 8, 2 >, 1045.09, 21.80 >$

the average SNR[2]. Indeed, TQoS represents QoS and it is an extension of the degradation path strategy[2,3,4][3].

Construction of TQoS. TQoS is automatically built once for a given server prior the transmission (note that different power processing servers may generate different values of rn_i). The TQoS construction is an iterative process, where the same short raw clip (the reference video) is compressed again and again setting the encoder parameters, in each iteration i, as L_i. For each iteration i, the variables rn_i and qn_i are computed and stored as a TQoS entry the tuple given by (3). Figure 2 shows a same frame of the reference video, used to build TQoS for our tests, compressed with two QoS levels L_i (Fig. 2 (a)) and L_j (Fig. 2 (b)). Note that whereas $rn_i \approx rn_j$, qn_i and qn_j are very different.

The TQoS magnitude may introduce a non-trivial overhead when seeking a QoS level L_i such that $rn_i \approx rt(t)$. In order to reduce this delay, TQoS is represented internally like a multilist whose first level nodes represent throughput subranges. Thus, the complexity of seeking is reduced to the number of subranges rather than the number of QoS levels. We defined the actuator granularity as 25 Kbps steps and 10,000 Kbps as the maximum nominal throughput. The granularity is a constant easily changeable. However, we believe that lower values improve

---

[2] We are aware that SNR does not reflect well the quality, as perceived by the users. On the one hand, SNR does not effectively predict subjective responses for MPEG video systems. In tests performed by Nemethova et al. [9], SNR captured only about 21% of the subjective information that could be captured considering the level of measurement error present in the subjective and objective data. On the other hand, results based on the difference between the degraded sequence and the reference used for subjective quality evaluation can differ significantly in some cases according to the test method, thus also providing limited means for the appropriate quality estimation.

[3] The degradation path is an ordered list of available QoS levels and encodings and their resource requirements (particularly, bandwidth). The list is limited by user's choices and by hardware constraints. The degradation path varies according to what the users trade offs are.

granularity but, on the other hand, they degrade accuracy. Therefore, node 0 represents the throughput subrange $[0; 25[$ Kbps; node 1 represents $[25; 50[$; node k represents the throughput subrange $[k \times 25; (k+1) \times 25[$; the 401st node represents the subrange $[10000; \infty[$. Each first level node k has associated a second level list (sublist) whose nodes contain tuples $<< als_i, mtc_i, mqt_i, qtz_i, dcp_i, mcf_i >, qn_i >$. The value rn_i is not stored but it follows the property

$$rn_i \in [k \times 25; (k+1) \times 25[. \tag{4}$$

Sublists are sorted in descendant order by qn. Fig. 3 shows the multilist structure. Some first level list nodes may contain an empty sublist; most of the sublists contain thousands of nodes. During transmission, TQoS adjusts itself to the video which is currently transmitted: at the adaptation instant t, the quality qn_i and the throughput rn_i of the current QoS level $L_i = L(t-1)$ are recomputed ($qn_i \leftarrow qa(t-1)$ and $rn_i \leftarrow ra(t-1)$). As a result, a head node of a sublist can change its position within its sublist or even move to another sublist. Then, the sublist heads are not static (the reason for keeping the sublists rather than only the heads).

Actuation Steps. Let L_i be the current QoS level at instant $t-1$ (i.e., $L(t-1) = L_i$). In adaptation instant t, the actuator receives the estimated $rt(t)$ value from the LDA+ controller and performs the following steps:

1. seeks a node k such that $rt(t) \geq (k+1) \times 25$ and whose sublist head is the QoS level L_j of highest qn_j;
2. sets the encoder as L_j (now, L_j is the current QoS level);
3. updates the nominal throughput and quality values of L_i ($rn_i \leftarrow ra(t-1)$ and $qn_i \leftarrow qa(t-1)$).

For example, let $L(t-1) = L_i = < 0, 6, 2, 4, 0, 0 >$ be the current QoS level of the stream (see Fig. 3 (a)); the current nominal throughput $rn(t-1)$ is a value between $[8525; 8550[$ Kbps and the current nominal quality $qn(t-1) = qn_i$ is 30.2154. Let us suppose that at the adaptation instant t, the controller computes $rt(t) = 8612.80$. In this case, the actuator:

1. seeks, among the first level nodes, that one whose upper limit of subrange is less or equal to 8612.80 (then, the search goes until the subrange $[8600; 8625[$). The selected QoS level is that one with the highest nominal quality whose node is the sublist head of the subrange $[8600; 8625[$ ($L_j = < 0, 3, 2, 3, 8, 1 >$ and $qn_j = 30.9252$; Fig. 3 (b));
2. sets the encoder as L_j (Fig. 3 (c));
3. letting 7851.4567 Kbps and 30.2001 dB respectively the throughput and the quality measured by the actuator between $t-1$ and t (we mean, $ra(t-1)$ and $qa(t-1)$), then it updates rn_i to 7851.4567 and qn_i to 30.2001. This implies in relocating L_i to the subrange $[7850; 7875[$.

3.2   Encoder

The encoder is a modified version of University of Berkeley's encoder, which follows the test model 5 (TM5). Since its source code is freely distributed and

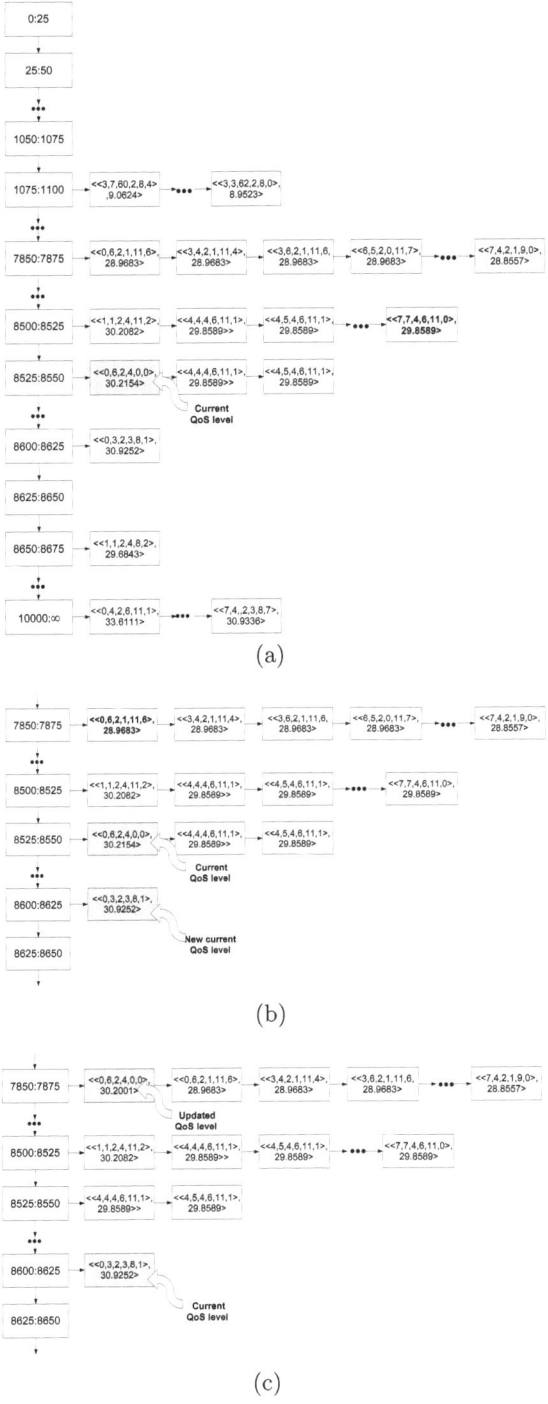

Fig. 3. Self-adjustment mechanism of the multilist representing $\mathcal{Q}oS$

reasonably well documented, this encoder has been used for educational purposes and as reference for other implementations[4]. Originally, the encoder input
is a parameter configuration (*par*) file with the encoder configuration (resolution, frame rate, quantization matrices, and so on) and the raw video file name
to be compressed; the output is a file containing a MPEG-1/2 stream. We modified the Berkeley's encoder so that it supports: **(1) variable bit rate (VBR)
stream generation:** originally, the encoder generates CBR streams whose target throughput is specified in the *par* file. This throughput is achieved adjusting, during the compression process, the quantizer value. Our version generates a
VBR stream, since the target throughput generated by the controller is variable;
(2) stream transmission: the original encoder/decoder are independent programs whose inputs and outputs are files. Our version follows the client-server
model. The server begins the transmission to a host (the client) or to a multicast
address; **(3) command line configuration:** the *par* file is not used anymore;
the encoder configuration can be done by command line. This modification is
needed to generate automatically the table TQoS (afterward, the configuration
is not necessary anymore since the encoder settings change dynamically during
video compression/transmission); **(4) mean signal–to–noise ratio computation:** originally, Berkeley encoder computes SNR for each component Y, U
and V of each frame[5]. Now, it computes the mean SNR ($\overline{SNR}$) between frames
i and $i + k$ ($k \in \mathbb{N}^*$) according to the following equation:

$$\overline{SNR} = \frac{\displaystyle\sum_{j=i}^{i+k} SNR_Y(j) + SNR_U(j) + SNR_V(j)}{k+1} \tag{5}$$

where j is the j-th sample (frame), and $SNR_Y(j)$, $SNR_U(j)$ and $SNR_V(j)$ are
the SNR values of the frame components Y, U, and V ($\overline{SNR}(L_i) = qn_i$); and **(5)
mean throughput computation:** the encoder now computes the throughput
between frames j and $j + k$. This computation is needed to the creation and to
the self-adjustment mechanism of TQoS.

4   Results

In order to evaluate the capabilities of the proposed tool, we conducted a set of
transmissions to investigate the performance of the LDA+ controller. We analyzed
several aspects such as: reduction of losses, smoothness of throughput change, fairness with TCP flows, adaptation overhead, frame rate at the client-side, and so
on. Due to the lack of space, we only present here the LDA+ controller results

---

[4] We chose an encoder that generates MPEG-1/2 streams rather than H.264 (more
suitable for compression on the fly) due to the simplicity of the Berkeley's encoder
code, what makes it easily modifiable. However, the other modules of the tool are
reasonably (but not totally) independent from the encoder.

[5] Y represents the luminance or luma component of a pixel, and U and V the color
difference components or chroma.

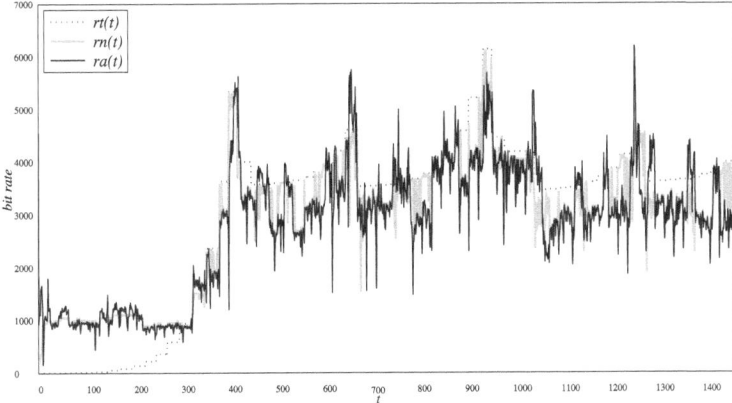

Fig. 4. Behavior of $rt(t)$, $rn(t)$ and $ra(t)$ during the transmission

in terms of loss rate and throughput/quality changes. We chose the first one to compare with Sisalem and Wolisz's results achieved by simulation and described in [11]; the latter is specially interesting because our motivation in developing the tool is mainly to provide to the rate controllers designers a way for obtaining such results, hard to get by simulation.

The tests were performed using a server host connected to a client host via a router host configured with the RED algorithm to drop packets whenever congestion arises in the network. The physically available bandwidth among the hosts was 100 Mbps, but the server-client link bandwidth was restricted to 6 Mbps, in order to represent a network bottleneck. The reference video used to construct TQoS was a "talking heads"–type slow motion clip (The News clip, see Fig. 2 (a) and (b)). The test video was the Salesman clip[6]. The feedback period is 5 seconds (the same RTCP sending interval used by Sisalem and Woliz); the actuation is performed only after the end of a GOP (then, the period varies according to the GOP time processing[7]).

Figure 4 shows the behavior of $rt(t)$, $rn(t)$ and $ra(t)$. Note that the behavior of the curve rn is close to the behavior of the curve rt. Indeed, these variables are strongly correlated: the correlation coefficient obtained was 0.949 and the p-value is 0.0. The relationship between rn and ra is also strong, since the correlation coefficient is 0.911 and the p-value is also 0.0 (the curve rn practically overlaps the curve ra). The difference between rn and ra decreases during the transmission, due to the TQoS self adjustment mechanism. The curves $rt(t)$ and $ra(t)$ are pretty similar, indicating a trivial control/actuation overhead.

---

[6] Both videos are YUV QCIF format raw video sequences available for downloading at http://trace.eas.asu.edu/yuv

[7] The change of some parameters during a GOP processing may cause side-effects (e.g., runtime errors due to absence of enough structures to store macroblocks, since the number of structures allocated depends on the GOP pattern and they are allocated in the beginning of the GOP processing).

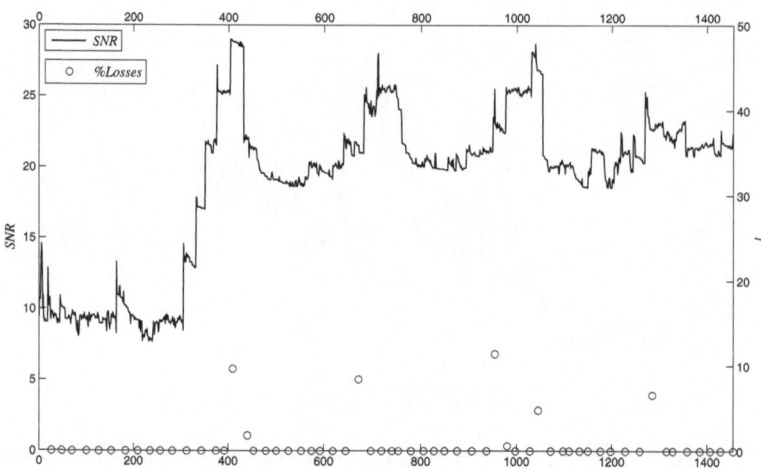

Fig. 5. Percentage of packets lost between two RR packets and SNR behavior during the transmission for the LDA+ controller

Figure 5 shows the percentage of packets lost between two RR packets. The losses are kept between 0% and 16%. This upper limit is too high: according to D. Miras [7], the user expectation of data loss for video streaming applications is that it should be lower than 3%. A faster controller reaction to the network status may decrease the values. This is possible reducing the feedback period. However, in a multicast transmission to many clients, a short feedback period may lead to a feedback implosion. In addition, according to Lee and Chung [6], frequently applying TCP-friendly throughput change to the video stream would seriously degrade the video quality. It is widely accepted the limit of 20db as a minimum of SNR for a picture to be viewable (the resultant clip is available for the reader to draw own conclusions).

Figure 5 also shows the quality (SNR) dynamics during the transmission. Comparing it to Fig. 4, we can see that the relationship between quality and throughput is very alike. This behavior shows that the actuator generally selects the QoS level that better fulfills the estimated available bandwidth.

5   Conclusions and Future Work

In this paper, we described a video delivery tool that can be used to test RTP-based rate controllers providing complementary results to those ones achieved by simulation. Particularly, it is useful to provide results related to actual achieved quality, overhead introduced by the control, and actual throughput. The tool may aid rate controller designers to test their strategies regarding performance aspects hard to evaluate by simulation (e.g., control overhead, frame rate at the clients, quality achieved, quality oscillation, etc.). Since it is highly modular, the tool can use any controller structured as black box whose inputs are round trip delay and loss rate and the output is the target throughput. Here, we described the results achieved by using the LDA+ controller.

Our results indicate that: (1) the actuator often finds a nominal throughput *close to* the target throughput; (2) the self adjustment mechanism of TQoS satisfactorily corrects the throughput and quality nominal values of the QoS levels used for rate adapting during the video transmission (note that these values are strongly related to the reference video in the beginning of the transmission); and (3) the encoding/control overhead is not critical in the end-to-end delay when the server answers a single video requisition.

Even though our tool has been projected and implemented to be a tool for RTP-based controller test support, its actuation strategy can be exploited as part of a rate control mechanism of real-time video delivery tools. Note that it was not our intent to build a fully functional video streaming application since there are many libraries supporting the development of applications and even fully functional open source applications. However, to provide support for different encoders, many of them have a large and complex source code. In addition, some of them generate only CBR streams. Therefore, our tool can be used to test and compare different control approaches prior the construction of a real-time video delivery application with rate control.

Some limitations of the current version of our tool include: use of pre-stored raw video rather than real-time captured video, absence of client-side buffering for smoothing jitter, and MPEG-2 encoding rather than MPEG-4, which delivers with similar quality at lower data rates. However, a future work includes to replace the MPEG-2 encoder by the finer grain scalable (FGS) MPEG-4 in order to incorporate to the QoS level the resolution layers dimension or new forms of scalability [8] and to test more recent TCP-friendly rate control mechanisms, oriented to MPEG-4 streams such as proposed in [10]. The use of a VBR MPEG-4 encoder performing transmission over an RTP stack rather than the current MPEG-2 would request minor modifications. More precisely, it would be necessary: (1) to identify in the source code the variables used for the encoder settings and select those ones to compound QoS levels; (2) to allocate them as shared memory assuring mutual exclusion (since the actuator runs concurrently with the encoder); and (3) to identify the relationship of these variables with others and the encoder data structures, specially for variables related to the temporal compression (this is the hardest part!).

The source code, the documentation and a clip demonstrating the quality variation are available for downloading at `http://ccet.ucs.br/dein/ckoliver/creval`.

References

1. Boudec, J.-Y.L.: Rate Adaptation, Congestion Control and Fairness: a Tutorial (2006)
2. Fischer, S., Hafid, A., Bochmann, G.V., Meer, H.: Cooperative QoS Management in Multimedia Applications. In: IEEE 4th Int. Conf. on Multimedia Computing and Systems (ICMCS 1997), pp. 303–310. IEEE Press, New York (1997)

3. Fry, M., Seneviratne, A., Witana, V.: Delivering QoS Ccontrolled Media on the World Wide Web. In: IFIP 4th International Workshop on Quality of Service (IWQoS 1996), Paris (1996)
4. Ghinea, G., Thomas, J.P.: Improving Perceptual Multimedia Quality with an Adaptable Communication Protocol. Journal of Computing and Information Technology (CIT) 13(2), 149–161 (2005)
5. Koliver, C., Nahrstedt, K.O., Farines, J.-M., Fraga, J.S., Sandri, S.: Specification, Mapping and Control for QoS Adaptation. The Journal of Real-Time Systems 23(1-2), 143–174 (2002)
6. Lee, S., Chung, K.: TCP-friendly Rate Control Scheme based on RTP. In: Chong, I., Kawahara, K. (eds.) ICOIN 2006. LNCS, vol. 3961, pp. 660–669. Springer, Heidelberg (2006)
7. Miras, D.: A Survey on Network QoS Needs of Advanced Internet Applications - Working Document. Technical report, University College London, London, England (2002)
8. Mys, L.S., Neve, P.W., Verhoeve, P., Walle, R.: SNR scalability in H.264/AVC using Data Partitioning. In: Zhuang, Y.-t., Yang, S.-Q., Rui, Y., He, Q. (eds.) PCM 2006. LNCS, vol. 4261, pp. 329–338. Springer, Heidelberg (2006)
9. Nemethova, O., Ries, M., Siffel, E., Rupp, M.: Quality Assessment for H.264 Coded Low-rate and Low-resolution Video Sequences. In: Proceedings of 3rd Conference on Communications, Internet, and Information Technology (CIIT 2004), pp. 136–140. St. Thomas (2004)
10. Shih, C.H., Shieh, C.K., Wang, J.Y., Hwang, W.S.: An Integrated Rate Control Scheme for TCP-friendly MPEG-4 Video Transmission. Image Commun. 23(2), 101–115 (2008)
11. Sisalem, D., Wolisz, A.: LDA+: A TCP-friendly Adaptation Scheme for Multimedia Communication. In: IEEE International Conference on Multimedia and Expo (III), pp. 1619–1622. IEEE Press, New York (2000)
12. Sisalem, D., Wolisz, A.: Constrained TCP-friendly congestion control for multimedia communication. In: Smirnov, M., Crowcroft, J., Roberts, J., Boavida, F. (eds.) QofIS 2001. LNCS, vol. 2156, p. 17. Springer, Heidelberg (2001)

Graph-Based Pairwise Learning to Rank for Video Search⋆

Yuan Liu[1], Tao Mei[2], Jinhui Tang[3], Xiuqing Wu[1], and Xian-Sheng Hua[2]

[1] University of Science and Technology of China, Hefei, 230027, P.R. China
yuanliu.ustc@gmail.com, wuxq@ustc.edu.cn
[2] Microsoft Research Asia, Beijing, 100190, P.R. China
{tmei,xshua}@microsoft.com
[3] National University of Singapore, Computing 1, Law Link, 117590, Singapore
jhtang@gmail.com

Abstract. Learning-based ranking is a promising approach to a variety of search tasks, which is aimed at automatically creating the ranking model based on training samples and machine learning techniques. However, the problem of lacking training samples labeled with relevancy degree or ranking orders is frequently encountered. To address this problem, we propose a novel *graph-based learning to rank* (GLRank) for video search by leveraging the vast amount of unlabeled samples. A relation graph is constructed by using sample (i.e., video shot) pairs rather than individual samples as vertices. Each vertex in this graph represents the "relevancy relation" between two samples in a pair (i.e., which sample is more relevant to the given query). Such relevancy relation is discovered through a set of pre-trained concept detectors and then propagated among the pairs. When all the pairs, constructed with the samples to be searched, receive the propagated relevancy relation, a round robin criterion is proposed to obtain the final ranking list. We have conducted comprehensive experiments on automatic video search task over TRECVID 2005-2007 benchmarks and shown significant and consistent improvements over the other state-of-the-art ranking approaches.

Keywords: video search, graph-based learning, semi-supervised learning, learning to rank, relation propagation.

1 Introduction

Learning to rank is the task to learn the ranking model from the ranking orders of the documents. It is mostly studied in the setting of supervised learning, which typically includes a learning stage followed by a ranking (search) stage [1][2]. In learning stage, a ranking function is built using the training samples with relevancy degrees or ranking orders, while in ranking stage, the documents are ranked according to the relevance obtained by the ranking function. When

---

⋆ This work was performed when Yuan Liu was visiting Microsoft Research Asia as a research intern.

B. Huet et al. (Eds.): MMM 2009, LNCS 5371, pp. 175–184, 2009.

applied to video search, the ranking order represents the relevance degree of the documents (i.e., video shots) with respect to the given query.

Existing methods for learning to rank can be categorized into the following three dimensions: *pointwise*, *pairwise*, and *listwise*. In pointwise learning, each sample and its rank is used as an independent sample. For example, Prank [3] aims to find a rank-prediction rule that assigns each sample a rank which is as close as possible to the sample's true rank. In pairwise learning, each sample pair is used as a training sample and the goal of learning is to find the differences between the ranking orders of sample pairs. For example, Ranking SVM [4] is such a method which reduces ranking to classification on document pairs. The recently developed listwise learning [1] directly uses the list of relevance scores associated to the retrieved documents as training samples.

It is observed that most of the above methods for learning to rank are based on the assumption that a large collection of "labeled" data (training samples) is available in learning stage. However, the labeled data are usually too expensive to obtain. Especially in video search, users are reluctant to provide enough query examples (i.e., video shots which can be regarded as "labeled" data) while searching. To alleviate the problem of lacking labeled data, it is desired to leverage the vast amount of "unlabeled" data (i.e., all the video shot documents to be searched). In this paper, we propose a novel *graph-based learning to rank* (GLRank) for video search.

In general, users rank samples by comparing one with each other [8]. Motivated by this observation, we propose to investigate the ranking order of samples pairwisely and introduce *relevancy relation* to represent which sample is more relevant to the given query in a sample pair. We first combine the query examples with the randomly selected samples (i.e., video shots) to form the labeled pairs, and then form the unlabeled pairs with all the samples to be searched. Second, we construct a *relation graph*, in which sample pairs, instead of the individual samples, are used as vertices. Each vertex represents the relevancy relation of a pair in a semantic space, which is defined by the vector of confidence scores of concept detectors [5][6][7]. Then, we propagate the relevancy relation from the labeled pairs to the unlabeled pairs based on Linear Neighborhood Propagation (LNP) [9] [10], in which the weights of edges can be effectively solved in a closed form. When all the unlabeled pairs receive the propagated relevancy relation, a round robin criterion is proposed to obtain the final ranking list. Clearly, GLRank belongs to *pairwise* learning.

2   GLRank

In this section, we present the overview of the proposed GLRank, as demonstrated in Figure 1. We first construct the labeled pairs using query examples. For the general case in which only relevant examples are provided without any other relevant degrees or irrelevant examples, we randomly select samples in the video shots corpus and combine them with the relevant examples to construct the labeled pair set $L = \{t_1, t_2, \cdots t_l\}$, where l denotes the number of labeled pairs $t_i (1 \leq i \leq l)$.

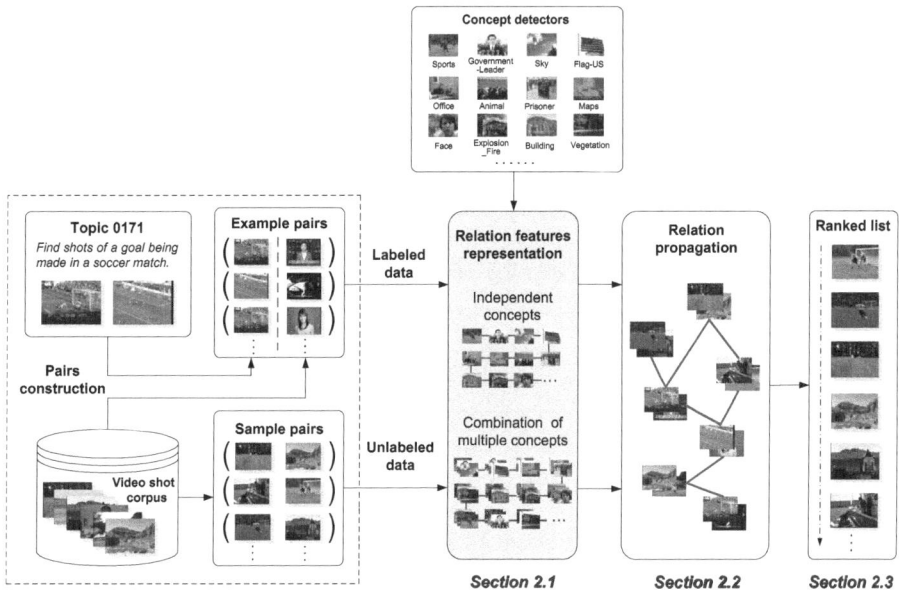

Fig. 1. Framework of the proposed GLRank

On the other hand, we convert the individual samples in the video corpus to be another pair set $U = \{t_{(l+1)}, t_{(l+2)}, \cdots t_{(l+u)}\}$, where u denotes the number of unlabeled pairs $t_i(l + 1 \leq i \leq l + u)$. To make the processing more efficient, all the shots are pre-clustered based on the semantic features vectors. Then, each shot is only combined with the centroids of the other clusters to form pairs rather than combined with all the other samples. Let P denotes the number of samples and Q denotes the number of clusters, there are $P \times (Q - 1)$ possible pairs in total. The pairs in labeled pair set L are labeled as $y_i = 1.0(1 \leq i \leq l)$, while pairs in unlabeled pair set U are assigned to 0.5 as the initial labels.

A relation graph G is then constructed with pairs in whole pair set $T = L \cup U$. The relation features of the vertices are represented in Section 2.1. The relevancy relation is then propagated using the LNP approach [9][10], which will be presented in Section 2.2. When the relation propagation is finished, the round robin criterion to obtain the final ranking list will be described in Section 2.3.

2.1 Relation Features Representation

The vertices in the relation graph G should represent the relevancy relation between the two samples in a pair, and it is the key problem in the GLRank. We propose the relation features by using a set of pre-defined concept detectors $D = \{d_1, d_2, \cdots d_c\}$, where $d_i(1 \leq i \leq c)$ are the concept detectors in the lexicon with the size of c. The corresponding scores are denoted by $S^j = \{s_1^j, s_2^j, \cdots s_c^j\}$ for sample x_j.

Algorithm 1. Relation propagation

Input: labeled pair set $L = \{t_1, t_2, \cdots, t_l\}$ with the fixed labels $y_i = 1.0(1 \leq i \leq l)$, unlabeled pair set $U = \{t_{(l+1)}, t_{(l+2)}, \cdots, t_{(l+u)}\}$ with the initial labels $y_i = 0.5(l+1 \leq i \leq l+u)$. The number of the nearest neighbors k.

Output: Relation labels of all pairs.

1: Construct the neighborhood graph by solving Eq. (3) for the reconstruction weights of each pair from its k-nearest neighbors;
2: Construct the relation label propagation coefficients matrix **S** according to Eq. (5);
3: Iterate Eq. (10) until convergence, then the unlabeled pairs' real-value relation labels can be obtained.

Similar to the term frequency in the text domain, the concept detector scores of a shot indicate the importance of concepts to the shot [6][7]. Thus it is reasonable to leverage the concepts detector scores of the two shots for comparing them semantically. We define the posterior probabilities of the concepts using a logistic function and use them to construct the semantic feature vector, in which the kth dimension is given by:

$$p(d_k|t^{(i,j)}) = 1/(1 + e^{-(s_k^i - s_k^j)}) \tag{1}$$

where $t^{(i,j)}$ denotes the pair constructed by the sample x_i and x_j, corresponding to a vertex in the graph G. We can see that $p(d_k|t^{(i,j)})$ is approaching to 1 when s_k^i is much larger than s_k^j, while it is approaching to 0 when s_k^i is much lower than s_k^j. When s_k^i is equal to s_k^j, $p(d_k|t^{(i,j)}) = 0.5$, it denotes that s_k^i and s_k^j is vague to determine which sample, x_i or x_j, is more relevant to the given query according to the concept detector d_k.

In general, most of the search queries contain multiple concepts simultaneously. Taking the TRECVID 2007 query "*Topic 0210: Find shots with one or more people walking with one or more dogs.*" [11] for example, it contains concepts "people," "walking," and "animal" at least. Shots in the corpus are irrelevant if any concept misses. Motivated by the observation, the combination of multiple concepts plays an important role in video search. Considering the relationship between the concepts, we use $p(d_1, d_2, \cdots, d_N|t^{(i,j)})$ to denote the probability of the concurrence of N concepts $d_1, d_2, \cdots, d_N$ for the given pair $t^{(i,j)}$. It indicates the co-operation of multiple concepts to determine the relevancy difference between the two samples in a pair. Typically, it can be estimated by "MIN" [12] as follows.

$$p(d_1, d_2, \cdots, d_N|t^{(i,j)}) = \min_k \{p(d_k|t^{(i,j)})\} \tag{2}$$

Obviously, Eq. (1) is a special case of Eq. (2) when $N = 1$.

2.2   Relation Propagation

In ranking learning systems, we often face a lack of sufficient labeled data, as labeling ranking order often requires expensive human labor. Consequently, semi-supervised learning (SSL), which aims to learn from both labeled and unlabeled data, is well suited for learning to rank.

As a major family of SSL, graph-based methods have attracted more and more recent research. Graph-based SSL define a graph where the vertices are labeled and unlabeled samples in the dataset, and edges which is often weighted, reflect the similarity of samples. After the graph construction, the labels of the unlabeled vertices are predicted according to a label propagation scheme.

In the proposed GLRank, we use the label propagation scheme based on the LNP [9][10]. Specifically, the vertices are pair samples and the edges reflect the similarity of pair samples for relation propagation. Unlike the other traditional graph-based SSL methods, the edge weights of the graph constructed by LNP can be solved automatically in closed form, rather than calculated based on a Gaussian function, in which the variance σ is a free parameter[9].

First, the pairs are linearly reconstructed from their neighborhoods and the objective is to minimize the following reconstruction error:

$$\varepsilon = \sum_i \left\| t_i - \sum_{i_j : t_{i_j} \in N(t_i)} \omega_{ii_j} t_{i_j} \right\|^2 \tag{3}$$
$$s.t. \ \ \sum_{i_j \in N(t_i)} \omega_{ii_j} = 1, \omega_{ii_j} \geq 0$$

where $N(t_i)$ represents the neighborhood of t_i, t_{i_j} is the jth neighbor of t_i, and ω_{ii_j} is the contribution of t_{i_j} to t_i.

Second, the optimal prediction function f is obtained by minimizing the following cost function:

$$C(f) = \frac{1}{2} \sum_i \sum_{i_j : t_{i_j} \in N(t_i)} \omega_{ii_j} \left(f_i - f_{i_j} \right)^2 + \infty \sum_{i \in L} (f_i - y_i)^2 \tag{4}$$

where f_i is the label of pair t_i. Then, we define a sparse matrix $\mathbf{S}$ with the entry in the ith row and j^{th} column as:

$$s_{ij} = \begin{cases} \omega_{ii_j}, t_{i_j} \in N(t_i) \\ 0, \quad others \end{cases} \tag{5}$$

Thus the optimization objective is represented formally as:

$$f^* = \arg\min_f \tfrac{1}{2} \sum_{i,j} s_{ij} (f_i - f_j)^2 \tag{6}$$
$$s.t. \ \ f_i = y_i (1 \leq i \leq l)$$

This is a standard graph-based SSL problem [13]. Notice that $\sum_j s_{ij} = 1$ and split the matrix $\mathbf{S}$ after the lth row and column:

$$\mathbf{S} = \begin{bmatrix} \mathbf{S}_{LL} & \mathbf{S}_{LU} \\ \mathbf{S}_{UL} & \mathbf{S}_{UU} \end{bmatrix} \tag{7}$$

Let f_L and f_U denotes the predicted labels of labeled and unlabeled data, respectively. The optimization problem can be rewriten in a matrix manner:

$$\mathbf{f}^* = \arg\min_{\mathbf{f}} \mathbf{f}^T (\mathbf{I} - \mathbf{S}) \mathbf{f} \tag{8}$$
$$s.t. \ \ \mathbf{f}_L = \mathbf{y}$$

Similar to [13], the optimal solution can be obtained as:

$$\mathbf{f}_U^* = (\mathbf{I} - \mathbf{S}_{UU})^{-1} \mathbf{S}_{UL} \mathbf{y} \tag{9}$$

Table 1. Experimental results for three ranking strategies on TRECVID 2005-2007 test sets and query topics

Method	CMap [15]	RSVM [4]		GLRank	
Evaluation	MAP	MAP	Gain	MAP	Gain
2005	0.0399	0.0691	+73.2%	0.0863	+116.3%
2006	0.0247	0.0286	+15.8%	0.0289	+17.0%
2007	0.0378	0.0379	+0.3%	0.0402	+6.3%
Average	0.0341	0.0452	+32.6%	0.0518	+51.9%

We can accomplish this form of results in an iterative manner as follows, which is the relation propagation process.

$$\mathbf{f}_U^{(new)} = \mathbf{S}_{UL}\mathbf{f}_L^{(old)} + \mathbf{S}_{UU}\mathbf{f}_U^{(old)}$$
$$s.t. \quad \mathbf{f}_L^{(old)} \equiv \mathbf{y} \tag{10}$$

Except for the number of nearest neighbors k, the whole optimization process has no free parameters, which is suitable for the practical search systems. The main procedure of the relation propagation is summarized in Algorithm 1.

2.3   Round Robin Ranking

To obtain the final ranking list of individual samples, a ranking method, called round robin ranking, is proposed based on the relation labels.

As aforementioned, all the samples in the corpus are pre-clustered. Obviously, each sample composes the same number of pairs, i.e., $(Q - 1)$, where Q is the cluster number. The round robin ranking first assigns the real-value relation label to the first sample of each pair, while the second sample of each pair is assigned to 0. Then add all the labels assigned to the same sample. The samples are finally ranked in descending order of the sum of the labels they are assigned.

The above method is very straightforward and it can be viewed as a *soft* voting with real-value votes, while hard voting only has integer votes [14].

3   Experiments

To evaluate the performance of the proposed GLRank, we conduct several experiments on automatic search task over the benchmark TRECVID 2005-2007[11]. All the videos are segmented into shots provided by NIST, and then the three collections contain 45765, 79484 and 18142 shots, respectively. In each year, 24 query topics with several image/video examples are provided with the ground truth of relevance. For each query, video search systems are required to return a ranked list of up to 1,000 shots. The system performance is measured via non-interpolated average precision (AP) and mean average precision (MAP) which are widely accepted in information retrieval and search [11].

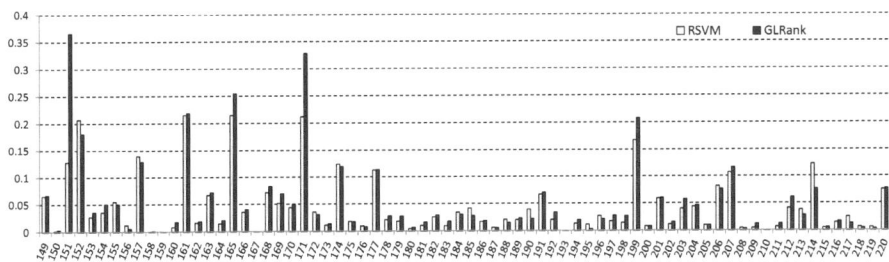

Fig. 2. Comparison between GLRank and RSVM measured by AP for each query topic over TRECVID 2005-2007 test sets

Table 2. MAP of three feature spaces for GLRank on TRECVID 2005-2007 test sets and query topics

Method	GLRank.Color	GLRank.OneCon	GLRank.TwoCon
2005	0.0398	0.0668	0.0863
2006	0.0236	0.0273	0.0289
2007	0.0278	0.0394	0.0402
Average	0.0304	0.0445	0.0518

In our experiments, we select the concept mapping (CMap) [15] as the baseline method, which is widely used in the current search systems [15][16]. In order to improve the efficiency of the ranking algorithm, we first use the CMap to filter the shots with the low confidence scores and select the top 1,600 shots to conduct the experiments, that is, $P = 1,600$. The number of the examples for each query is about 5~30, and the cluster number is set by $Q = max(P/25, 6)$. The semantic space is constructed by a series of concept detectors. Specifically, we used the lexicon of 39 concepts defined in LSCOM-Lite [17]. The detectors were trained by SVMs over three visual features [15]: color moments on a 5-by-5 grid, edge distribution histogram and wavelet textures. The scores of the three SVM models over the video shots are then averaged to be the final concept detection confidence scores. The more details of the feature extraction and concept detection can be found in [15].

3.1 Evaluation on Ranking Strategies

In this section, we will compare the proposed GLRank with the baseline method (CMap) [15] and Ranking SVM (RSVM) [4], which can be viewed as a representative of unsupervised and supervised learning to rank, respectively. In GLRank, we adopt k-NN here to find the neighboring points (k is empirically set to 30 [10]) in relation propagation and combine two concepts, i.e., $N = 2$ in Eq.(2) . In RSVM runs, we use RBF kernels and select globally kernel parameters. The same training set is used in both GLRank and RSVM. The comparisons of

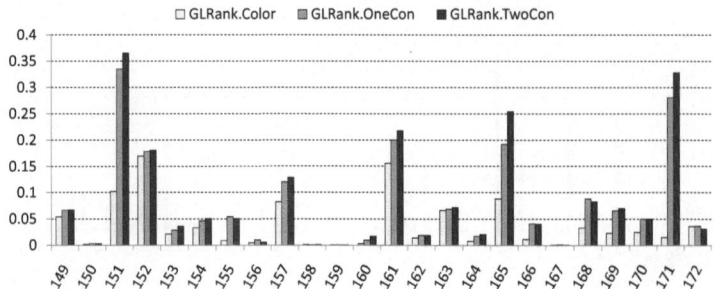

Fig. 3. AP of each query topic over TRECVID 2005 test set for GLRank in three feature spaces: Color, OneCon and TwoCon

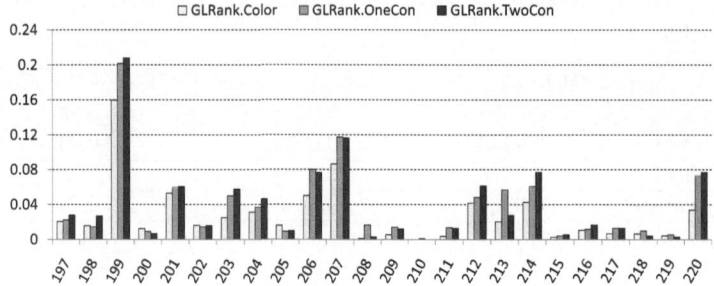

Fig. 4. AP of each query topic over TRECVID 2006 test set for GLRank in three feature spaces: Color, OneCon and TwoCon

these methods are shown in Table 1. From Table 1, we see that the proposed GLRank outperforms the other two methods in all the collections. Specifically, the MAP of GLRank is 0.0518, which has an improvement of 51.9% over the baseline method in average. Figure 2 illustrates the comparison of the GLRank and RSVM on all the 72 search topics in TRECVID 2005-2007. We can easily find that most of query topics (more than 70%) have the better performance in GLRank. Specially, some topics with few but very related concepts has much better performance in GLRank, such as *Topic 0151* (Omar Karami) and *Topic 0171* (Soccer goal).

3.2   Evaluation on Feature Spaces

This section analyzes the effect of the different feature spaces on GLRank, including low-level color feature space (Color), semantic space considering independent concepts (OneCon) and combination of multiple concepts (TwoCon), which corresponds to $N = 1$ and $N = 2$ in Eq.(2) , respectively. The color features we used here are 225-D block-wise color moments in LAB color space [10], which are extracted over 5×5 fixed grid partitions, each block is described by a 9-D feature. The performance comparisons of the three feature spaces for GLRank are

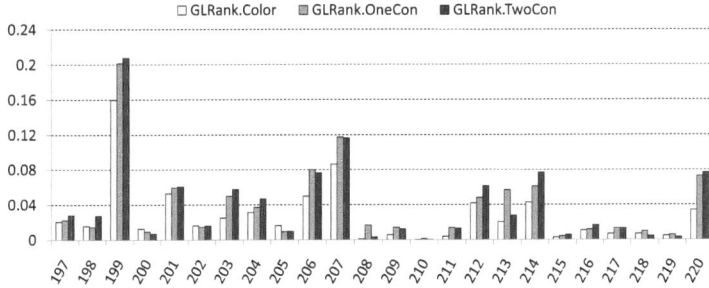

Fig. 5. AP of each query topic over TRECVID 2007 test set for GLRank in three feature spaces: Color, OneCon and TwoCon

shown in Table 2 and Figure 3~5. We can easily find that GLRank in semantic space work much better than in low-level color feature space. It proves that the different relevancy degrees of the two samples in a pair mostly consist in which concepts they contain, rather than which color they are or what they are like. On the other hand, TwoCon has consistent improvements over OneCon in the three collections. From the results, we can see that the video search can highly benefit from the cooperation of the multiple concepts, considering the semantic linkage within a query.

4   Conclusions

In this paper, we have proposed a novel and effective graph-based semi-supervised learning to rank (GLRank) for video search in semantic space. GLRank can deal with limited labeled data, as well as large-scale unlabeled data by treating each pair as a sample. Experiments on the widely used benchmark TRECVID data set demonstrated that GLRank is superior to the other traditional ranking approaches. The future work includes the following two aspects: (1) studying how the performance will change with the increasing of visual concepts; (2) investigating the relationship between samples listwisely.

References

1. Zhe, C., Qin, T., Liu, T.-Y., Tsai, M.-F., Li, H.: Learning to rank: From pairwise approach to listwise approach. In: Proceedings of International Conference on Machine Learning (2007)
2. Yan, R., Hauptmann, A.G.: Efficient Margin-Based Rank Learning Algorithms for Information Retrieval. In: Sundaram, H., Naphade, M., Smith, J.R., Rui, Y. (eds.) CIVR 2006. LNCS, vol. 4071, pp. 113–122. Springer, Heidelberg (2006)
3. Crammer, K., Singer, Y.: Pranking with ranking. In: Advances in Neural Information Processing Systems (2002)
4. Herbrich, R., Graepel, T., Obermayer, K.: Large margin rank boundaries for ordinal regression. In: Advances in Large Margin Classifiers (2000)

5. J. Tešić, A. Natsev, and J.-R. Smith. Cluster-based Data modeling for Semantic Video Searach. In: Proceedings of International Conference on Image and Video Retrieval (2007)
6. Li, X., Wang, D., Li, J., Zhang, B.: Video Search in Concept Subspace: A Text-Like Paradigm. In: Proceedings ofInternational Conference on Image and Video Retrieval (2007)
7. Liu, Y., Mei, T., Qi, G.-J., Wu, X., Hua, X.-S.: Query-independent learning for video search. In: Proceedings of IEEE International Conference on Multimedia and Expo (2008)
8. Liu, Y., Mei, T., Hua, X.-S., Tang, J., Wu, X., Li, S.: Learning to video search rerank via pseudo preference feedback. In: Proceedings of IEEE International Conference on Multimedia and Expo (2008)
9. Wang, F., Zhang, C.: Label propagation through linear neighborhoods. In: Proceedings of International Conference on Machine Learning (2006)
10. Tang, J., Hua, X.-S., Qi, G.-J., Song, Y., Wu, X.: Video Annotation Based on Kernel Linear Neighborhood Propagation. IEEE Transactions on Multimedia (2008)
11. TRECVID, http://www-nlpir.nist.gov/projects/trecvid/
12. Yager, R.: On a general class of fuzzy connectives. Fuzzy Sets and Systems (1980)
13. Zhu, X., Ghahramani, Z., Lafferty, J.: Semi-supervised learning using gaussian fields and harmonic function. In: Proceedings of International Conference on Machine Learning (2003)
14. Duong, D., Goertzel, B., Venuto, J., Richardson, R., Bohner, S., Fox, E.: Support vector machines to weight voters in a voting system of entity extractors. In: Proceedings of IEEE International Joint Conference on Neural Networks (2006)
15. Mei, T., Hua, X.-S., Lai, W., Yang, L., Zha, Z., Liu, Y., Gu, Z., Qi, G.-J., Wang, M., Tang, J., Lu, Z., Liu, J.: MSRA-USTC-SJTU at TRECVID 2007: High-Level Feature Extraction and Search. In: Online Proceedings of NIST TRECVID Workshops (2007)
16. Chang, S.-F., Hsu, W., Jiang, W., Kennedy, L., Xu, D., Yanagawa, A., Zavesky, E.: Columbia University TRECVID-2006 Video Search and High-Level Feature Extraction. In: Online Proceedings of NIST TRECVID Workshops (2006)
17. Naphade, M.R., Kennedy, L., Kender, J.R., Chang, S.-F., Smith, J.R.: A Light Scale Concept Ontology for Multimedia Understanding for TRECVID 2005. IBM Research Technical Report (2005)

Comparison of Feature Construction Methods
for Video Relevance Prediction

Pablo Bermejo[1], Hideo Joho[2], Joemon M. Jose[2], and Robert Villa[2]

[1] Computing Systems Dept., Universidad de Castilla-La Mancha, Albacete, Spain
pbermejo@dsi.uclm.es
[2] Department of Computing Science, University of Glasgow, UK
{hideo,jj,villar}@dcs.gla.ac.uk

Abstract. Low level features of multimedia content often have limited
power to discriminate a document's relevance to a query. This motivated
researchers to investigate other types of features. In this paper, we investigated four groups of features: low-level object features, behavioural
features, vocabulary features, and window-based vocabulary features, to
predict the relevance of shots in video retrieval. Search logs from two
user studies formed the basis of our evaluation. The experimental results show that the window-based vocabulary features performed best.
The behavioural features also showed a promising result, which is useful
when the vocabulary features are not available. We also discuss the performance of classifiers.

Keywords: video retrieval, relevance prediction, feature construction.

1 Introduction

Multimedia databases have become a reality and as such, the need has arisen
for effective multimedia information retrieval systems that work as accurately
and fast as possible. Much research has been carried out on this problem from
different points of views: ranking algorithms, feature construction, collaborative
retrieval, etc., but unfortunately the performance of MIR systems is still far
from that of text Information Retrieval (IR) due to the semantic gap: there
is a discontinuity between low level visual features and the semantics of the
query. Multimedia information retrieval systems usually use algorithms to create a ranking [14,19] of results relevant to the text or image query submitted
by the user. Some of these rankings have the problem of supporting just a very
small number of features, such as those based on Term Frequency (TF) and
Inverse Document Frequency (IDF) values. In the literature we can find several
studies to select ([6]) or construct ([1]) features in order to improve the performance of ranking algorithms. However, there is limited work on the comparison
of different groups of features to predict the relevance in Multimedia Information Retrieval (MIR), which is the main contribution of this paper. To do this,
we project the retrieval problem into a classification problem and we work with
databases constructed from logs created during two users studies. We consider

B. Huet et al. (Eds.): MMM 2009, LNCS 5371, pp. 185–196, 2009.

the information retrieval task as a supervised classification problem with a binary class attribute ("Relevant" and "Non Relevant"), where the documents which will be classified are a set of instances, each one representing a video shot described by a set of features. Formally the problem can be defined as a set of instances $C_{train} = \{(s_1, l_1), \ldots, (s_{|S|}, l_n)\}$, such that $s_i \in S$ is the instance which corresponds to the ith shot of the set of shots S, l_j corresponds to the value of the class attribute that contains it and $L = \{Relevant, NonRelevant\}$ is the set of possible values for the class attribute. The goal is to build a classifier $c : S \rightarrow L$ to solve the prediction of a shots relevance; that is, the value of the class attribute for each instance. We will construct four kinds of features to find out which performs best and feature selection will be used to find which features (for each type of feature) are the most important.

We expect that our conclusions, found when performing classification, can also be used for the ranking process in a retrieval system, where classifiers can be mixed with ranking algorithms to improve the performance of retrieval systems. The structure of this paper is as follows: Section 2 summarizes some work found in the literature related to feature construction and feature selection applied to information retrieval and classification. Section 3 presents our approach to creating different kinds of features, our selection method and how we perform the evaluation. The results for our experiments are shown in Section 4 and finally we present our main conclusions.

2   Related Work

The quality of the used set of features is of great importance for the classifier to achieve good performance [2]. This performance will depend on the individual relevance of each feature with respect to the class, relationship among features and the existence of features which influence negatively on the classifier.

It is possible to improve the quality of the available features by performing: (1) **Feature Subset Selection**, a widely studied task [10,7] in data mining, which consists of reducing the set of available features by selecting the most relevant ones using filter metrics (statistical, distances, etc.) or wrappers (goodness of the classifier); and (2) **Feature Construction**: sometimes it is also possible to obtain new features with a higher quality from the original ones by computing some relation or statistic [9].

2.1   Feature Subset Selection

Feature Subset Selection (FSS) is the process of identifying the input variables which are relevant to a particular learning (or data mining) problem.

Though FSS is of interest in both supervised and unsupervised data mining, in this work we focus on supervised learning, and in particular in the classification task. Classification oriented FSS carries out the task of removing most irrelevant and redundant features from the data with respect to the class. This process helps to improve the performance of the learnt models by alleviating the effect of the curse of dimensionality, increasing the generalization power, speeding up the learning and inference process and improving model interpretability.

In supervised learning FSS algorithms can be (roughly) classified in three categories: (1) embedded methods; (2) filter methods; and, (3) wrapper methods. By embedded methods we refer to those algorithms, e.g. C4.5, that implicitly use the subset of variables they need. Filter techniques are those that evaluate the goodness of an attribute or set of attributes by using only intrinsic properties of the data. Filter techniques have the advantage of being fast and general. On the other hand wrapper algorithms are those that use a classifier in order to asses the quality of a given attribute subset. Wrapper algorithms have the advantage of achieving a greater accuracy than filters but with the disadvantage of being more time consuming and obtaining an attribute subset that is biased toward the used classifier, although in the literature we can find some attempts to alleviate this problem [4].

In [6] some limitations of feature selection methods are stated when applied to ranking, which they consider as an optimization problem.

2.2   Feature Construction

Several techniques [9] have been developed for the construction of new attributes through the application of operations over the available attributes. Attribute construction is most important when working with real world databases, which have not been created with thought to their application to data mining, and thus it is possible they do not contain attributes meaningful enough for beneficial use [5]. In attribute construction the main goal is to get a new attribute which represents the regularities of our database in a simpler way and thus makes the classification task easier [12]. Related to MIR, [1] created attributes which could represent the user behavior while searching data and thus be able to predict relevance for the user. Shots can also be represented by the visual features (texture, color layout, etc.) extracted from their keyframes. A lot of effort is currently being made to cross the semantic gap between query semantics and low level visual features (such as work on textual features [8]). To extract visual features from shots, several tools can be used, the most currently used being the MPEG-7 Visual Standard for Content Description [16]. Text created from transcript speech is another common way of representing shots. As stated in [22], although it can be used to gain good performance, it cannot be applied to all videos in general due to the lack of speech in some videos, or the fact that the speech does not relate to the visual content of the video.

3   Methodology

In order to learn how different kinds of constructed features affect relevance prediction, we have used data logs from two users experiments (see Section 4) and, from these logs, we have constructed finaldatasets (with different kinds of features) used to evaluate classifiers. In this section we explain how our final datasets are constructed, the different kinds of features used, and how the classifiers are evaluated.

3.1 Datasets Creation from User Logs

We denote 'user study' to refer to an experiment in which several users tested a video retrieval system searching under different topics and conditions. A log file was created from each of the users studies [21] and [20] (see Section 4.2). Each log file contains verbose data explaining the actions each user performed (on which shots[1] actions were performed, the kind of action performed, timestamp, user condition, topic of search,...). For each query search, the user interacts with a set of shots. So, for each tuple ⟨search,user,condition,topic,shot⟩ a new instance is created from a log for the final dataset. Each instance in the final dataset consists of: tuple features (⟨search, user, condition, topic, shot⟩), features constructed to predict the class feature and which represent the shot, and the class feature itself. Class features are either Relevant or Non Relevant, and refers to the relevance of the shot in the corresponding tuple. For the same log, different final datasets have been constructed because different kind of features have been tested (see Section 3.2) to predict relevance and additionally, different kinds of relevance have been tested (see Section 4.1).

3.2 Kind of Features Used to Predict Relevance

As mentioned above, an instance in the final dataset will follow the pattern

Tuple Features, Relevance Prediction Features, Class Feature.

We have used four different kinds of *Relevance Prediction Features*: User Behavior Features, Object Features, Vocabulary Features and Windowed Vocabulary Features. Thus, for the logs from each user study four final datasets $DS1$, $DS2$, $DS3$ and $DS4$ are derived, where the four datasets contain the same values for *Tuple Features* and *Class Feature* but each one contains one of the four kind of features constructed.

Our User Behavior Features where designed similar to [1]. These features give information about how the user interacts with a document. In our case, the information is related to the actions the user performed through shots suggested by the information retrieval system after he/she ran a query under a concrete topic and condition. Behavior features used in this work are shown in Table 1 and they can be split into three groups: *Click-Through features*, which represent information about clicks the user performed on shots; *Browsing features*, which show different metrics about time spent on shots and *Query-Text features*, which count words in the current text query and make comparisons with other text queries. Note that the values for these features are computed for each tuple (⟨search,user,condition,topic,shot⟩) from the users studies logs.

---

[1] In Multimedia IR systems, retrieved documents are not the whole videos but shots, where a shot is one of the splits a video can be divided into.

Table 1. Behavior Features used to predict shots relevance

Feature name	Description
ClickFreq	Number of mouse clicks on shot
ClickProb	*ClickFreq* divided by total number of clicks
ClickDev	Deviation of *ClickProb*
TimeOnShot	Time the user has been performing any action on shot
CumulativeTimeOnShots	*TimeOnShot* added to time on previous shots
TimeOnAllShots	Sum of time on all shots
CumulativeTimeOnTopic	Time spent under current topic
MeanTimePerShotForThisQuery	Mean of all values for *TimeOnShot*
DevAvgTimePerShotForThisQuery	Deviation of *MeanTimePerShotForThisQuery*
DevAvgCumulativeTimeOnShots	Deviation of *CumulativeTimeOnShots*
DevAvgCumulativeTimeOnTopic	Deviation of *CumulativeTimeOnTopic*
QueryLength	Number of words in current text query
WordsSharedWithLastQuery	Number of equal words in current query and last query

Table 2. Object Features used to predict shots relevance

Feature name	Description
Color Layout	vector containing 10 values
Dominant Color	vector containing 15 values
Texture	vector containing 62 values
Edge Histogram	vector containing 80 values
Content Based Shape	vector containing 130 values
Length	Time length of shot
Words	#words in Automatic Speech Transcription from shot audio
DifferentWords	#Different words in ASR from shot audio
Entropy	Shannon entropy of ASR from shot audio

Object Features are not extracted from logs. They represent both *Low-Level Features* and *Metadata* and they are shown in Table 2. Using these features, the *Relevance Prediction Features* describe the shot appearing in *Tuple Features*. *Metadata* keeps information about length of shots and also information related to the Automatic Speech Recognition (ASR) from shots audio. Text transcripts from a shots' audio is filtered through a stop-words list and a Porter stemming filter ([13]), and then used to extract some statistics about the text.

Vocabulary Features are a bag of words created from the ASR. In this case the text is not used to compute statistics about the text, but to create a vocabulary of words to perform the task of text classification. The transcripted text is also filtered through a stop-word list and a Porter stemming filter. Then, the resulting text is transformed into Weka format using a tool based on Lucene [2]. For this kind of feature the video relevance classification becomes a problem of text classification.

It is expected that video relevance classification based on ASR works relatively well due to the fact that text has more descriptive power than, for example, low level visual features. However, in the literature some complaints about using ASR can be found, as in [22] where the authors state that some speeches might not have anything in common with their respective shots.

Finally, Windowed Vocabulary Features refer to a common technique in video retrieval systems which use ASR to create the results list. This uses the same procedure performed when using Vocabulary Features but in this case the text

---

[2] http://lucene.apache.org/who.html

used to construct the bag of words does not come only from the ASR of the corresponding shot but also from the n previous shots in time and the later n shots. This is call *n-Windowed ASR* and in our case we use a 6-Windowed Vocabulary. It is expected that 6-Windowed Vocabulary features perform better than creating a bag of words from only the ASR of a single shot.

When we use ASR to create a bag of words and evaluate using a bayesian classifier, we do not use Naive Bayes but the Naive Bayes Multinomial, which is recommended for text classification ([11]).

3.3   Evaluation Method

Evaluation is performed without using the *Tuple Features* so that the evaluation is totally free of context differentiation. In the case of using Behavior Features, which are continuous values and user dependent, it is difficult to construct a dataset with repeated instances. But, when using Object or Vocabulary Features, the same shot can appear in different tuples so the *Relevance Prediction Features* are repeated; then we would have several repeated instances in the dataset where the class feature is sometimes set as *Relevant* and other times as *NonRelevant*. This contradiction is solved by deleting all repeated instances and setting the class feature to the most frequent value.

Datasets are evaluated by performing ten times a 10 cross validation (10x10CV) using three different classifiers (two statistical and one vector space based classifier): Naive Bayes, SVM (polynomial kernel, since this was the best configuration found) and kNN (k=1). As happens in information retrieval systems, datasets are very skewed due to a larger number of non relevant documents than relevant. So training sets are balanced by randomly deleting as many non relevant documents as needed so that the classifier is trained with the same number of relevant and non relevant documents. Although not a sophisticated way to balance datasets, the subject of balancing training data is outside the scope of this paper. For each 10x10CV, two metrics have been computed:

- TPrate(R) True Positive Rate for relevant documents represents the *recall* of relevant documents. The higher this metric is, the more relevant documents an information retrieval system will return.

$$TPrate(R) = \frac{\#relevant\ documents\ classified\ as\ relevant}{\#relevant\ documents} \qquad (1)$$

- TPrate(NR) Although TPrate(R) is high, precision for relevant document could be low so TPrate(NR) would be low as well, what would make the system return many non relevant documents classified as relevant. Then, the main goal is to get both TPrate(R) y TPrate(NR) as high as it is possible.

$$TPrate(NR) = \frac{\#non\ relevant\ documents\ classified\ as\ non\ relevant}{\#relevant\ documents}$$

$$(2)$$

We have not used *Accuracy* to evaluate the classifiers because, although it is a standard metric used to evaluate the predictive power of classifiers, the tests sets are so unbalanced that computing Accuracy is roughly the same as computing TP_{NR}. Although training sets are balanced, test sets are not: if a classifier always marks documents as belonging to the majority class value, accuracy would be incredibly high but documents belonging to the minority class values would never be correctly predicted. For information retrieval systems, documents belonging to minority class value (relevant documents) are what we want to predict correctly and so accuracy on its own is not an appropriate metric.

Finally, we performed an incremental wrapper-based feature selection based on ([3]), using the best configuration found in that study for the selection process. The goal for this selection is to find out what constructed features are most important for each kind of *Relevance Prediction Feature*.

This selection consists of an incremental wrapper-based feature subset selection (IWSS). First, a filter ranking by Symmetrical Uncertainty with respect to the class is constructed to rank all the available features. Then, from the beginning of the ranking to the end, the inclusion of each feature in the final subset of selected features is evaluated to decide if it must be added or not. This is presented in [15], and we use the best configuration found in [3] for this algorithm.

4   Experiments

Experiments were carried out on datasets constructed from logs obtained in two user studies. For each constructed dataset, four new datasets are derived using either User Behavior, Object, Vocabulary or 6-Windowed Vocabulary Features (see Section 3.2) to predict each shots' relevance. For each dataset, a 10x10CV is performed (using three different classifiers). For each evaluation, $TPrate_R$ and $TPrate_{NR}$ metrics are computed to compare classifiers capacity to predict relevance using different kinds of constructed features.

4.1   Kinds of Relevance

We have used two sources of information to decide if a shot is relevant for a topic or not: Official Relevance and User Relevance. This means that for each final dataset, its evaluation is performed twice, once for each kind of relevance: (1) **Official Relevance**: Shots used in the users experiments belong to the TRECVid 2006 collection [17], which provides a list of the relevant shots for each topic based on the standard information retrieval pooling method of relevance assessment; and (2) **User Relevance**: In the user experiments, users could explicitly mark shots as relevant to the topic. In a dataset, a shot can be considered relevant if the user marks it as such.

One of the user studies this work is based on did not use the official TRECVid 2006 topics, so Official Relevance for that study cannot be used. Table 3 summarizes all the different evaluations performed for datasets obtained from each of the users studies (Collaborative and StoryBoard studies, introduced in Section 4.2).

Relevance predictions have a different meaning depending on the kind of features and relevance used. Predicting User Relevance using User Behavior Features can be

Table 3. User studies used under different combinations of kind of features and kind of relevance

	Official Relevance	User Relevance
User Behavior Features	Collaborative	Collaborative & StoryBoard
Object Features	Collaborative	Collaborative & StoryBoard

seen as predicting explicit user feedback because users marked videos (or not) after interacting with them. Predicting Official Relevance using User Behavior Features predicts the relevance of a shot decided by a third group by actions users performed on the shots influenced by their perceptions. If we use Official Relevance when feeding our classifier with Object or Vocabulary Features values, we are assuming that low level features (as Color Layout) are meaningful enough to cross the semantic gap[3] [18] to high level concepts. Similarly, when predicting User Relevance using Object Features, some influence between low level features and metadata in user perception is assumed. When using Vocabulary Features, relevance prediction is similar to when Object Features are used, but in this case there is not a semantic gap, the problem becoming a text classification task.

4.2   User Studies and Datasets Created

To create the datasets which will be evaluated, we have used logs coming from two users studies: the Collaborative study [21] and the StoryBoard study [20]:

- *Collaborative study.* In this study, users where grouped into pairs and searched for shots relevant to four Trecvid2006 topics under four different conditions: user A could see what user B was doing, user B could see user A, both users could see each other and, lastly, both users performed a search independently.
- *StoryBoard study.* In this study, users had to use two different interfaces (a common interface as baseline and a storyboard-style interface), to search for shots relevant to two different non-TRECVid topics.

As it can be seen in Table 3, 4 datasets were created from the Collaborative user study and 2 datasets from the StoryBoard user study. For each of these datasets, evaluation was performed using each of the four kinds of feature introduced in section 3.2.

4.3   Results

In this section we show the results obtained when performing classification with three different classifiers. Evaluation is performed over two databases created from 2 users studies. For each database, evaluation is performed using one of the four kinds of features, with the Collaborative users study represented twice, one for each kind of relevance.

Evaluations. We show the results of the performed evaluations in Tables 4, 5 and 6. If our aim is to get a TP_R as high as possible without worrying about

---

[3] Distance between low level features (which have no meaning) and high level concepts.

Table 4. Results for datasets constructed from Collaborative users study - Official Relevance

	Behavior		Object		Vocabulary		W6-Vocabulary	
	TP_R	TP_{NR}	TP_R	TP_{NR}	TP_R	TP_{NR}	TP_R	TP_{NR}
NBayes/NBM	0.42	0.87	0.76	0.49	0.61	0.47	0.80	0.52
SVM	0.52	0.71	0.65	0.64	0.47	0.62	0.68	0.72
kNN	0.68	0.69	0.79	0.51	0.44	0.65	0.53	0.92
mean	**0.54**	**0.75**	**0.73**	**0.55**	**0.51**	**0.58**	**0.67**	**0.72**

Table 5. Results for datasets constructed from Collaborative users study - User Relevance

	Behavior		Object		Vocabulary		W6-Vocabulary	
	TP_R	TP_{NR}	TP_R	TP_{NR}	TP_R	TP_{NR}	TP_R	TP_{NR}
NBayes/NBM	0.55	0.82	0.67	0.41	0.73	0.45	0.71	0.48
SVM	0.62	0.70	0.57	0.56	0.53	0.64	0.54	0.66
kNN	0.70	0.71	0.60	0.47	0.47	0.58	0.63	0.48
mean	**0.63**	**0.74**	**0.61**	**0.48**	**0.58**	**0.56**	**0.63**	**0.54**

TP_{NR}, on average both Object and W6-Vocabulary Features are the best choice. If we are seeking for high TP_{NR}, both Behavior Features and W6-Vocabulary Features perform best. Since we need a good balance in both TP rates we can conclude that using the text from ASR of current shot and nearby shots to create the vocabulary is the best option to perform shot categorization. However, there are many videos in multimedia databases which have no text at all, or their text is not related to the contents, so in those cases another kind of feature would be needed to be constructed. Additionally it should be noted that Vocabulary Features created from a single shot have less predictive power than any other kind of constructed features presented in this work. If we do not compare results on average but taking into consideration classifiers on their own, we find that NBM for Vocabulary Features (windowed and not windowed) perform well for TP_R, although they perform with a lot of noise, besides working much faster than kNN. SVM is known to usually be the best classifier when performing text document classification; however, in this case the regarded problem is not that of text categorization so it is not very surprising that SVM has performed the worst. If our databases do not contain speech in their videos, it can be seen that Behavior Features work better than Object Features to predict Non Relevant documents, when it is important in an information retrieval system to get rid of noisy results. This means that using Behavior Features would create a system with less noise, but one which would also return fewer relevant shots.

As mentioned in Section 4.1, prediction of relevance has a different meaning depending on the kind of feature and relevance used in evaluation. So, if our aim is to construct an information retrieval system to collect relevant documents, behavior features would only make sense if we construct a collaborative information retrieval system, where the interactions performed by previous users through retrieved documents are stored and used in future searches from other users. While object features could be used in a standard information retrieval system and would always retrieve the same documents for the same queries.

Table 6. Results for datasets constructed from StoryBoard users study - User Relevance

	Behavior		Object		Vocabulary		W6-Vocabulary	
	TP_R	TP_{NR}	TP_R	TP_{NR}	TP_R	TP_{NR}	TP_R	TP_{NR}
NBayes/NBM	0.42	0.87	0.71	0.39	0.67	0.48	0.75	0.73
SVM	0.52	0.71	0.57	0.55	0.56	0.57	0.75	0.72
kNN	0.68	0.69	0.64	0.48	0.36	0.71	0.74	0.72
mean	**0.54**	**0.75**	**0.64**	**0.47**	**0.53**	**0.59**	**0.75**	**0.73**

Table 7. Results after performing Incremental Wrapper-Based Selection

	Collaborative - Official R.				Collaborative - User R.				StoryBoard - User R.			
	Behavior		Object		Behavior		Object		Behavior		Object	
	TP_R	TP_{NR}	TP_R	TP_{NR}	TP_R	TP_{NR}	TP_R	TP_{NR}	TP_R	TP_{NR}	TP_R	TP_{NR}
NBayes	0.48	0.88	0.67	0.59	0.62	0.83	0.33	0.76	0.15	0.96	0.59	0.52
SVM	0.24	0.92	0.62	0.64	0.58	0.74	0.62	0.55	0.40	0.81	0.47	0.56
kNN	0.72	0.64	0.65	0.57	0.76	0.70	0.55	0.54	0.78	0.78	0.59	0.48
mean	**0.48**	**0.81**	**0.65**	**0.60**	**0.65**	**0.76**	**0.50**	**0.62**	**0.44**	**0.85**	**0.55**	**0.52**

Feature Selection. Feature Selection has been performed based on ([3]), using the best configuration found in that study for the selection process. Selection has only been run on Behavior and Object Features, since selection on Vocabulary features would only return a set of words with no generalization power. Besides the Object Features set have a cardinality much higher than the Behavior Features set, so the final number of selected features in both should not be an issue.

In Table 7 we show the results of evaluations using only the selected features for each dataset. We can observe that feature selection decreases a bit the true positive rate for relevant shots, but on the other hand it significatively increases true positive rate for non relevant shots. This means that an information retrieval system would generate less noisy results than the same system not using feature selection. Since the number of relevant shots is so small, a tiny change in TP_R is not significant, meanwhile these large increases in TP_{NR} would mean a great change in the global accuracy.

In Table 8 we show the constructed features chosen by the incremental selection. With respect to Behavior Features, we can see that features constructed to represent statistics about clicks performed are the most frequently selected. This makes sense and can be expected, since clicks can be regarded as explicit feedback about the interests of the user.

With respect to Object Features, we indicate with a number the quantity of indexes selected from visual features vectors. We can see that visual features are more frequently selected than metadata computed for shots. Although this result has been a surprise it can be explained as being the effect of the larger number of visual features (if we count each index for each vector) compared to the four metadata features.

5   Conclusions and Future Work

We have tested four different kinds of features in a classification domain (with three different classifiers) where the class attribute is binomial with values {Relevant, Non Relevant}. All features have been tested on their own, without mixing

Table 8. Selected features when performing Incremental Wrapper-Based Selection

Behavior	Official R.	User R.	User R.	Object	Official R.	User R.	User R.
ClickFreq	x	x	x	Color Layout[10]			
ClickProb	x	x		Dominant Color[15]	1		5
ClickDev	x	x	x	Texture[62]		1	
TimeOnShot			x	Edge Histogram[80]	10	2	5
CumulativeTimeOnShots			x	Content Based Shape[130]	1	1	
TimeOnAllShots	x			Length			x
CumulativeTimeOnTopic				Words			
MeanTimePerShotForThisQuery	x	x	x	DifferentWords			
DevAvgTimePerShotForThisQuery				Entropy		x	
DevAvgCumulativeTimeOnShots			x				
DevAvgCumulativeTimeOnTopic		x	x				
QueryLength	x		x				
WordsSharedWithLastQuery			x				

different types. In order to not overfit, we have tested these features with databases constructed using logs from two different users studies and two different kinds of relevance.

Our main conclusion is that Windowed Vocabulary Features perform, on average, better than the rest, where a good performance is regarded as the best possible balance between TP_R and TP_{NR}.

Feature selection helps to decrease noise while insignificantly losing a little performance for relevant documents. Additionally, the most relevant features have been identified for User Behavior Features and Object Features.

For future work, it would be interesting to study the effect on relevance prediction when mixing different kind of constructed features, and also testing how different contexts affect the classifier's performance. It would also be interesting to apply our techniques to re-ranking the output of an information retrieval system, to investigate potential improvements in performance.

Acknowledgments

This work has been partially supported by the JCCM under project (PCI08-0048-8577), MEC under project (TIN2007-67418-C03-01), FEDER funds, MI-AUCE project (FP6-033715), and SALERO Project (FP6-027122).

References

1. Agichtein, E., Brill, E., Dumais, S.: Improving web search ranking by incorporating user behavior information. In: SIGIR 2006: Proceedings of the 29th annual international ACM SIGIR conference on Research and development in information retrieval, pp. 19–26. ACM Press, New York (2006)
2. Bekkerman, R., McCallum, A., Huang, G.: Automatic categorization of email into folders: Bechmark experiments on enron and sri corpora. Technical report, Department of Computer Science. University of Massachusetts, Amherst (2005)
3. Bermejo, P., Gámez, J., Puerta, J.: On incremental wrapper-based attribute selection: experimental analysis of the relevance criteria. In: IPMU 2008: Proceedings of the 12th Intl. Conf. on Information Processing and Management of Uncertainty in Knowledge-Based Systems (2008)

4. Flores, M.J., Gámez, J., Mateo, J.L.: Mining the esrom: A study of breeding value classification in manchego sheep by means of attribute selection and construction. Computers and Electronics in Agriculture 60(2), 167–177 (2007)
5. Freitas, A.A.: Understanding the crucial role of attributeinteraction in data mining. Artif. Intell. Rev. 16, 177–199 (2001)
6. Geng, X., Liu, T.-Y., Qin, T., Li, H.: Feature selection for ranking. In: SIGIR 2007: Proceedings of the 30th annual international ACM SIGIR conference on Research and development in information retrieval, pp. 407–414. ACM, New York (2007)
7. Guyon, I., Elisseeff, A.: An introduction to variable and feature selection. Journal of Machine Learning Research 3, 1157–1182 (2003)
8. Howarth, P., Rüger, S.M.: Evaluation of texture features for content-based image retrieval. In: Enser, P.G.B., Kompatsiaris, Y., O'Connor, N.E., Smeaton, A.F., Smeulders, A.W.M. (eds.) CIVR 2004. LNCS, vol. 3115, pp. 326–334. Springer, Heidelberg (2004)
9. Hu, Y.-J.: Constructive induction: covering attribute spectrum In Feature Extraction, Construction and Selection: a data mining perspective. Kluwer, Dordrecht (1998)
10. Liu, H., Motoda, H.: Feature Extraction Construction and Selection: a data mining perspective. Kluwer Academic Publishers, Dordrecht (1998)
11. McCallum, A., Nigam, K.: A comparison of event models for naive bayes text classification. In: AAAI/ICML 1998 Workshop on Learning for Text Categorization, pp. 41–48 (1998)
12. Otero, F., Silva, M., Freitas, A., NIevola, J.: Genetic programming for attribute construction in data mining. In: Ryan, C., Soule, T., Keijzer, M., Tsang, E.P.K., Poli, R., Costa, E. (eds.) EuroGP 2003. LNCS, vol. 2610. Springer, Heidelberg (2003)
13. Porter, M.F.: An algorithm for suffix stripping, pp. 313–316 (1997)
14. Robertson, S.E., Walker, S., Jones, S., Hancock-Beaulieu, M., Gatford, M.: Okapi at TREC-3. In: Proceedings of the Third Text REtrieval Conference (TREC 1994), Gaithersburg, USA (1994)
15. Ruiz, R., Riquelme, J.C., Aguilar-Ruiz, J.S.: Incremental wrapper-based gene selection from microarray data for cancer classification. Pattern Recogn. 39, 2383–2392 (2006)
16. Sikora, T.: The mpeg-7 visual standard for content description-an overview. 11(6), 696–702 (June 2001)
17. Smeaton, A.F., Over, P., Kraaij, W.: Evaluation campaigns and trecvid. In: MIR 2006: Proceedings of the 8th ACM International Workshop on Multimedia Information Retrieval, pp. 321–330. ACM Press, New York (2006)
18. Smeulders, A.W.M., Worring, M., Santini, S., Gupta, A., Jain, R.: Content-based image retrieval at the end of the early years. IEEE Trans. Pattern Anal. Mach. Intell. 22(12), 1349–1380 (2000)
19. Sparck Jones, K.: A statistical interpretation of term specificity and its application in retrieval. Journal of Documentation 28(1), 11–21 (1972)
20. Villa, R., Gildea, N., Jose, J.M.: Facetbrowser: a user interface for complex search tasks. In: ACM Multimedia 2008 (in press, 2008)
21. Villa, R., Gildea, N., Jose, J.M.: Joint conference on digital libraries. In: A Study of Awareness in Multimedia Search, pp. 221–230 (June 2008)
22. Yan, R., Hauptmann, A.G.: Co-retrieval: A boosted reranking approach for video retrieval. In: Enser, P.G.B., Kompatsiaris, Y., O'Connor, N.E., Smeaton, A.F., Smeulders, A.W.M. (eds.) CIVR 2004. LNCS, vol. 3115, pp. 60–69. Springer, Heidelberg (2004)

Large Scale Concept Detection in Video Using a Region Thesaurus

Evaggelos Spyrou, Giorgos Tolias, and Yannis Avrithis

Image, Video and Multimedia Systems Laboratory,
School of Electrical and Computer Engineering
National Technical University of Athens
9 Iroon Polytechniou Str., 157 80 Athens, Greece
espyrou@image.ece.ntua.gr
http://www.image.ece.ntua.gr/~espyrou/

Abstract. This paper presents an approach on high-level feature detection within video documents, using a Region Thesaurus. A video shot is represented by a single keyframe and MPEG-7 features are extracted locally, from coarse segmented regions. Then a clustering algorithm is applied on those extracted regions and a region thesaurus is constructed to facilitate the description of each keyframe at a higher level than the low-level descriptors but at a lower than the high-level concepts. A model vector representation is formed and several high-level concept detectors are appropriately trained using a global keyframe annotation. The proposed approach is thoroughly evaluated on the TRECVID 2007 development data for the detection of nine high level concepts, demonstrating sufficient performance on large data sets.

1 Introduction

One of the most interesting problems in multimedia content analysis remains the detection of high-level concepts within multimedia documents. Due to the continuously growing volume of audiovisual content, this problem attracts a lot of interest within the multimedia research community. Many research efforts set focus on the extraction of various low-level features, such as audio, color, texture and shape properties of audiovisual content. Moreover, many techniques such as neural networks, fuzzy systems and Support Vector Machines (SVM) have been successfully applied in order to link the aforementioned features to high-level features. However, the well-known "semantic gap" often characterizes the differences between descriptions of a multimedia object by different representations and the linking from the low- to the high-level features.

An important step for narrowing this gap is to provide a description based on higher-level properties than the low-level descriptors. Many research efforts make use of a visual dictionary to describe a decomposed image derived after either clustering or segmentation or keypoint extraction. A mean-shift algorithm is used in [1], to cluster an image and extract local features. In [2] image regions are clustered and a codebook of region types occurs. Moreover, in [3] visual categorization is achieved using a bag-of-keypoints approach. Then, a bag-of-regions approach is used for scene detection. A hybrid thesaurus approach for object recognition within video news archives is

B. Huet et al. (Eds.): MMM 2009, LNCS 5371, pp. 197–207, 2009.
© Springer-Verlag Berlin Heidelberg 2009

presented in [4], while in [5] a a region-based approach that uses knowledge encoded in the form of an ontology is applied. Finally, a multi-modal machine learning technique is used in [6].

However, the growth of multimedia content has not been accompanied by a similar growth of the available annotated data sets. Very few are the databases that provide an annotation per region, such as LabelMe [7]. On the other hand, annotating an image globally, appears a much easier task. Such an annotation is provided from LSCOM workshop [8]. Therein, a very large number of shots of news bulletins are globally annotated for a large number of concepts. Moreover, during the last few years, TRECVID [9] evaluation continues to attract many researchers interested in comparing their work in various tasks and among them the high-level feature detection within video documents. Within this task, the goal is to globally annotate shots of video for certain concepts.

This work falls within the scope of TRECVID and tackles 9 concepts within the 2007 development data using a common detection approach for all concepts and not specialized algorithms. The concepts that have been selected are *Vegetation*, *Road*, *Explosion_fire*, *Sky*, *Snow*, *Office*, *Desert*, *Outdoor* and *Mountain* and as obvious, they cannot be described as "objects", but rather as "materials" or "scenes". These concepts have been selected since they are the only materials from the TRECVID's set of concepts. Thus, color and texture features are the only applicable MPEG-7 low-level features. For each concept a neural network-based detector is trained based on features extracted from keyframe regions, while keyframes are annotated globally. The presented framework is depicted in figure1, where the off-line steps, i.e. those that comprise the training part are marked as yellow.

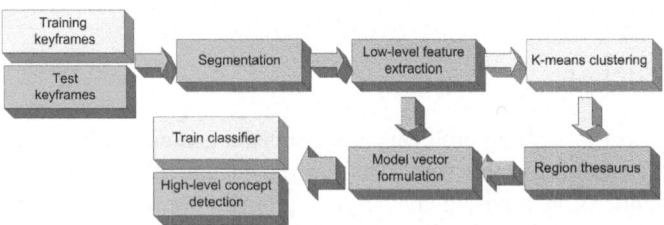

Fig. 1. High-level concept detection framework

This paper is organized as follows: Section 2 presents the method used for extracting color and texture features of a given keyframe. The construction of the region thesaurus is presented in section 3, followed by the formulation of the model vectors used to describe a keyframe in section 4. Then, training of the neural-network detectors is presented in section 5. Extensive experimental results data are presented in section 6 and finally, conclusions are drawn in section 7.

2   Low-Level Feature Extraction

At a preprocessing step, a video document, is first segmented into shots and from each shot a representative frame (keyframe) is extracted. Each keyframe k_i is then segmented into regions, using a (color) RSST segmentation algorithm [10], tuned to produce an under-segmented image. Let R denote the set of all regions and $R(k_i) \subset R$ the set of all regions of the keyframe k_i.

Several MPEG-7 descriptors [11] have been selected to capture the low-level features of each region $r_i \in R$. More specifically, *Dominant Color Descriptor* (DC), *Color Structure Descriptor* (CS), *Color Layout Descriptor* (CL) and *Scalable Color Descriptor* (SC) are extracted to capture the color properties and *Homogeneous Texture Descriptor* (HT) and *Edge Histogram Descriptor* (EH) the texture properties.

To obtain a single region description from all the extracted region descriptions, we choose to follow an "early fusion" method, thus merging them after their extraction [12]. The vector formed will be referred to as "feature vector". The feature vector that corresponds to a region $r_i \in R$ is thus depicted in equation (1):

$$f(r_i) = [CL_i, DC_i, CS_i, SC_i, HT_i, EH_i] \tag{1}$$

where $DC(r_i)$ is the Dominant Color Descriptor for region r_i, $CL(r_i)$ is the Color Layout Descriptor for region r_i etc. Each feature vector is denoted by f_i and F is the set of all feature vectors. In other words: $f_i \in F$, $i = 1 \dots N_F = N_R$. Herein, we should note that regarding the Dominant Color Descriptor, we choose to keep only the most dominant color and its percentage, since the length of the full descriptor is generally not fixed.

Since many of the MPEG-7 descriptors allow the user to select their level of detail, thus offer a large number of available extraction profiles, we follow a procedure similar to the one presented in [13], in order to select the one that best suits the needs of our approach. The dimensions of the extracted descriptors are depicted in table 1, while the final dimension of the merged feature vector is 286.

Table 1. Dimension of the extracted MPEG-7 color and texture descriptors

Descriptor	DC	SC	CL	CS	EH	HT
Number of Coefficients	4	64	12	64	80	62

3 Region Thesaurus

Given the entire training set of images and their extracted low-level features, it may be easily observed that regions belonging to similar semantic concepts, have similar low-level descriptions. Also, images containing the same high-level concepts are consisted of similar regions. For example, all regions that belong to the semantic concept *Sky* should be visually similar, i.e. the color of most of them should be some tone of blue. Moreover, images that contain *Sky*, often contain some similar regions. Finally, and in large problems, such as TRECVID discussed herein, common keyframe extraction algorithms sometimes extract visually similar keyframes, that belong to neighboring shots within the same video.

The aforementioned observations indicate that certain similar regions often co-exist with some high-level concepts. In other words, region co-existences should be able to characterize the concepts that exist within a keyframe. Thus, initially, regions derived from keyframes of the training set are organized in a structure, able to facilitate the description of a given keyframe with respect to a subset of them.

A K-means clustering algorithm is first applied on the feature vectors of the regions of the training set images. The number of clusters N_T is selected experimentally. The definition of the region thesaurus is the one depicted in Eq. (2).

$$T = \left\{ w_i, \quad i = 1 \ldots N_T \right\}, \quad w_i \subset R \tag{2}$$

where w_i is the i-th cluster, which is a set of regions that belong to R. Then, from each cluster, the region that lies closest to its centroid is selected. These regions will be referred to as "region types" and their corresponding feature vector is depicted in Eq. (3), where $z(w_i)$ is the centroid of the i-th cluster in the feature space.

$$f(w_i) = f\left(\arg \min_{r \in w_i} \left\{ d\big(f(r), z(w_i)\big) \right\} \right) \tag{3}$$

A region type does not contain conceptual semantic information, although appears a higher description than a low-level descriptor; i.e. one could intuitively describe a region type as "green region with a coarse texture", but would not be necessarily able to link it to a specific concept, which neither is necessary a straightforward process, nor falls within the scope of the presented approach.

In order to create the region thesaurus, a large number of regions is obviously necessary, in order for it to be able to describe effectively every image. When the training set is significantly small, then all available regions are used. On the other side, when the training set is significantly large, i.e. in the TRECVID case, regions derived from images containing the semantic concepts to be detected are selected, accompanied by an equal number of randomly selected regions among the remaining images.

4   Model Vectors

After forming the region thesaurus, described in section 3, a model vector is formed in order to represent the semantics of a keyframe, based on the set of region types. Let r_1, r_2, be two image regions, described by feature vectors f_1, f_2, respectively. The Euclidean distance is applied in order to calculate their distance $d(f_1, f_2)$.

Having calculated the distance between each region of the image and all region types, the "model vector" is then formed by keeping the smallest distance of all image regions to each region type. More specifically, the model vector m_i describing keyframe k_i is the one depicted in eq. (4).

$$m_i = \left[m_i(1), m_i(2), \ldots, m_i(j), \ldots, m_i(N_T) \right] \tag{4}$$

where

$$m_i(j) = \min_{r \in R(k_i)} \left\{ d\big(f(w_j), f(r) \big) \right\} \tag{5}$$

and $j = 1 \ldots N_T$.

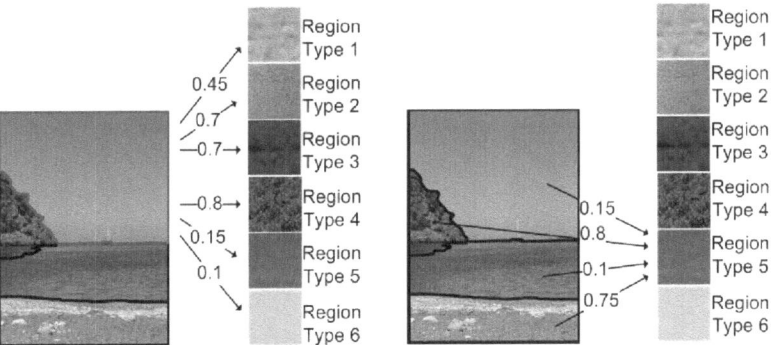

Fig. 2. Distances between regions and region types

In fig.2, an under-segmented image and a region thesaurus consisted of 6 regions are depicted. The distances between the upper image region (the one corresponding to *Sky*) and every region type are shown on the left, while those of every image region to a specific region type are shown on the right. As obvious, for the 5th region type the corresponding value of the model vector will be 0.1 as the minimum distance among this region type and all other regions of the given image.

5   High-Level Concept Detectors

After extracting model vectors from all images of the (annotated) training set, a neural network-based detector is trained separately for each high-level concept. The input of the detectors is a model vector m_i describing a keyframe in terms of the region thesaurus. The output of the network is the confidence that the keyframe contains the specific concept. It is important to clarify that the detectors are trained based on annotation per image and not per region. The same stands for their output, thus they provide the confidence that the specific concept exists somewhere within the keyframe in question. Several experiments, presented in 6 indicate that the threshold above which it is decided that a concept exists, also varies depending on the classifier and should be determined experimentally, in a separate process for each concept.

6   Experimental Results

This section presents the results of the aforementioned algorithm, applied on the TRECVID 2007 Development Data, a large dataset consisting of 110 videos, segmented into shots. A keyframe has been extracted from each shot, thus 18113 keyframes have been made available. The annotation used results from a joint effort among several TRECVID participants [14]. Table 2 summarizes the detected concepts and the number of positive examples within the development data and the constructed training/testing sets for each of them. After the under-segmentation, 345994 regions have been available.

Using the constructed training set, due to the large number of regions derived after segmentation, not all available regions are used. Rather, an adequate number of regions

Table 2. Number of positive examples within the development data and the constructed training/testing sets

concept	development data	training	testing
Desert	52	36	16
Road	923	646	277
Sky	2146	1502	644
Snow	112	78	34
Vegetation	1939	1357	582
Office	1419	993	426
Outdoor	5185	3000	1556
Explosion_Fire	29	20	9
Mountain	97	68	29

Table 3. Average Precision on a test set with $\lambda_{ts} = 1$, for several values of the ratio λ_{tr} within the training set

concept	$\lambda_{tr} = 1$	$\lambda_{tr} = 2$	$\lambda_{tr} = 3$	$\lambda_{tr} = 4$	$\lambda_{tr} = 5$
Desert	0.6593	**0.6994**	0.3653	0.4775	0.6634
Road	0.5944	0.6091	0.5954	0.6062	**0.6957**
Sky	0.6791	0.723	0.6883	0.7197	**0.7369**
Snow	0.9144	0.9054	0.9293	0.9174	**0.9504**
Vegetation	0.7175	0.7731	0.7649	0.7522	**0.7802**
Office	0.6337	0.7073	**0.7382**	0.7077	0.7235
Outdoor	0.6832	0.6842	**0.6978**	-	-
Expl._Fire	0.3879	0.3679	0.3485	**0.647**	0.3827
Mountain	0.6878	0.6119	0.5458	0.625	**0.7662**

derived from the training sets of all high-level concepts, in other words from keyframes that contain at least one of the high-level concepts, and an equal number of random regions derived from keyframes that do not contain any of the high-level concepts, are used to form the region thesaurus. K-means clustering is applied, with N_T set to 100 region types.

First of all, several experiments are performed by varying the ratio λ_{tr} of negative to positive examples within the training set. For a complex problem, such as TRECVID, it is very difficult to "model" positive examples of each concept. Of course, modeling the negative examples appears more difficult. Thus, a larger number of negative examples is needed, but should be selected appropriately, in order to avoid biasing the detectors towards the negative examples. To test the performance of the differently trained classifiers, a testing set with a ratio $\lambda_{ts} = 1$, i.e. consisting of an equal number of positive and negative values is used. Results are summarized in table 3. It may be easily observed that for almost every concept, a value of λ_{tr} between 4-5 is appropriate to achieve the highest possible average precision (AP) [15] by the classifiers. We should note that the number of the available examples is inadequate in order to investigate more values of λ for most of the concepts. Thus we choose to stop at the value of $\lambda_{tr} = 5$, in order to have comparable results for most of the examined high-level concepts.

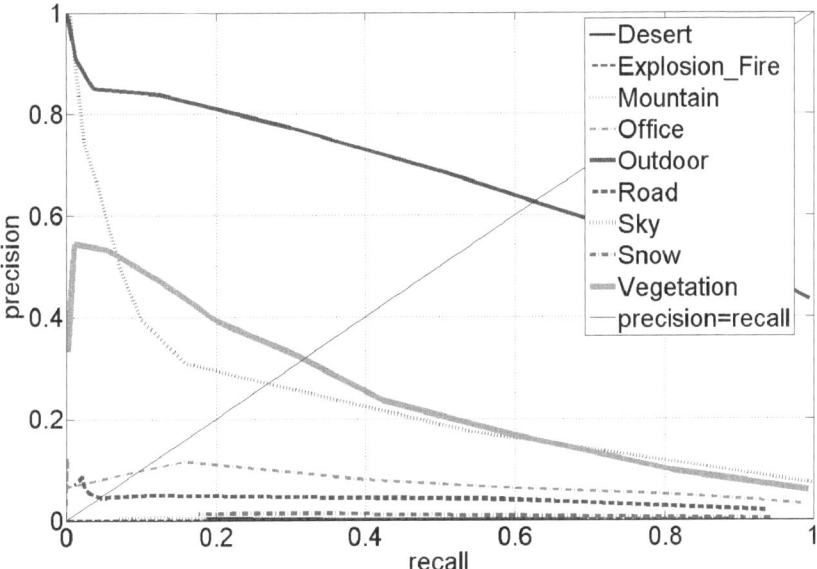

Fig. 3. Precision-Recall for increasing threshold values

Table 4. Thresholds for the high-level concept detectors

concept	threshold
Desert	0.8
Road	0.5
Sky	0.3
Snow	0.6
Vegetation	0.4
Office	0.5
Outdoor	0.3
Explosion_Fire	0.2
Mountain	0.8

Having selected the training set, experiments on the threshold confidence value for each classifier are performed. As testing set for each concept, the set of all remaining keyframes is used. Precision and recall measures are calculated for each high-level concept and for a range of threshold values, starting from 0 and increasing with a step of 0.1 until they reach 0.9. Then, the threshold value where precision is almost equal to recall is selected, as depicted in fig. 3. This way, both measures are kept in equally good values, as it is generally desirable. Table 4 summarizes the selected threshold values for all 9 concepts. As it may be observed, for those concepts that their positive examples do not vary a lot, in respect to their model vectors, such as *Desert* and *Mountain*, a high threshold value is selected.

In the last part of the experiments, the proposed approach is evaluated on the testing sets derived from the TRECVID 2007 development data. The testing set of each concept contains 30% of all positive examples and is complemented using part from negative examples, i.e. from all keyframes that do not contain the specific concept. The number

Table 5. Precision (P), Recall (R) and Average Precision (AP) for all concepts

concept	$\lambda_{ts} = 4$			$\lambda_{ts} = max$		
	P	**R**	**AP**	**P**	**R**	**AP**
Vegetation	0.643	0.312	0.560	0.322	0.313	0.232
Road	0.295	0.046	0.407	0.045	0.047	0.043
Explosion_Fire	0.291	0.777	0.252	0.000	0.000	0.001
Sky	0.571	0.304	0.603	0.258	0.304	0.214
Snow	0.777	0.411	0.610	0.013	0.412	0.008
Office	0.446	0.157	0.418	0.117	0.157	0.072
Desert	0.333	0.312	0.457	0.003	0.313	0.064
Outdoor	0.425	0.514	0.361	0.425	0.514	0.361
Mountain	0.444	0.137	0.401	0.003	0.379	0.037

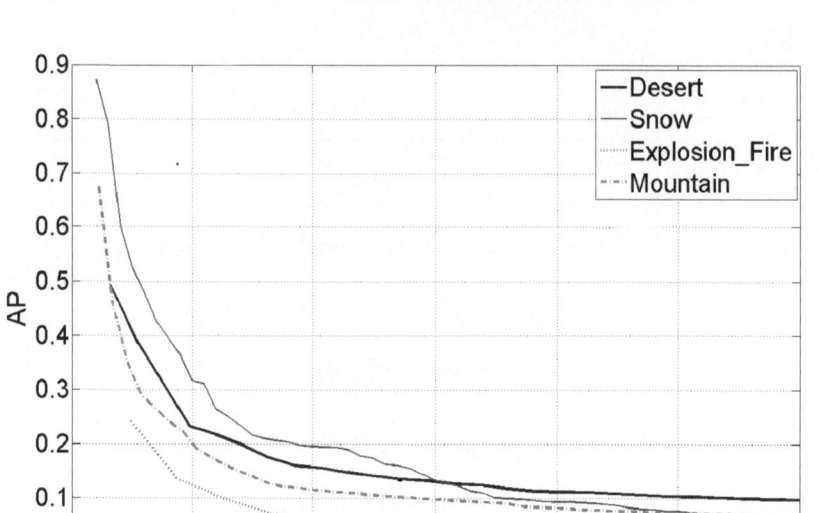

Fig. 4. AP vs. λ_{ts} for *Desert*, *Snow*, *Explosion_Fire* and *Mountain*

of negative keyframes increases gradually, until it reaches certain values of λ_{ts}. For each concept, the value of λ_{ts} is increased until it reaches its maximum possible value. Each time the AP is calculated, with a window equal to all the testing set.

Figures 4 and 5 show how AP changes with respect to λ_{ts}. The number of positive examples is kept fixed, while the number of negative increases. It may be observed that when the value of λ_{ts} is relatively small, i.e. $\lambda_{ts} = 4$, as in the case of typical test sets that are used for evaluation, the performances remain particularly high. When λ_{ts} increases, then the performances fall as expected.

Finally some comments regarding the detection results are presented, focusing on examples of true and false detections of high-level concepts. Examples are depicted for concepts *Sky* and *Vegetation* in figures 6, 7 and 8 for true positive, false negative and

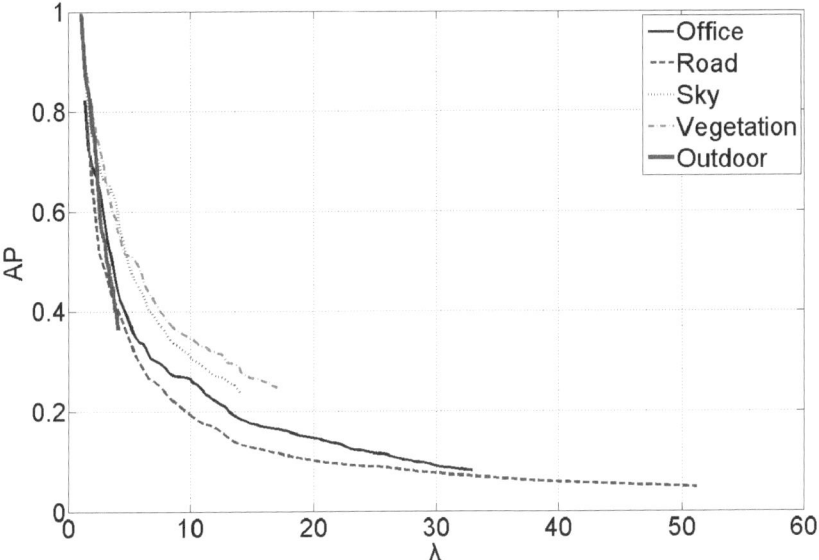

Fig. 5. AP vs. λ_{ts} for *Office*, *Outdoor*, *Road*, *Sky* and *Vegetation*

(a) concept *Sky*   (b) concept *Vegetation*

Fig. 6. True positive examples

(a) concept *Sky*   (b) concept *Vegetation*

Fig. 7. False negative examples

false positive examples, respectively. Typical regions of *Sky* and *Vegetation* detected successfully are depicted in figure 6. Figure 7 presents false negative keyframes, containing images in which the existing small regions of *Vegetation* and *Sky* are also merged with other regions as a result of the under-segmentation of the image. Thus visual features of the regions are degraded. Our approach was unable to detect an artificial region of sky, such as the one depicted in figure 7(a), because of the abnormal yellowish tone. Some false positive examples are depicted in figure 8. Images falsely detected as positive for the concept *Sky* (figure 8(a)) contain light blue regions which are similar to a

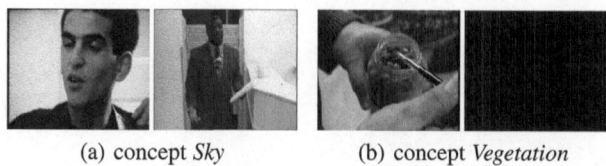

(a) concept *Sky*   (b) concept *Vegetation*

Fig. 8. False positive examples

typical region of *Sky* in both color and texture, while the right image in figure 8(b) has a dark green tone and texture too similar with the ones that a typical *Vegetation* region would have.

7   Conclusions and Discussion

In this paper we presented our current work towards efficient semantic multimedia analysis based on a region thesaurus and a methodology on working with large data sets, such as the TRECVID collections. Extensive experiments have been presented and the effect of the ratio λ_{tr} and λ_{ts} of negative to positive examples on training and testing data has been examined. The applied generic approach tackled successfully most of the selected high-level concepts. The proposed approach is difficult to be compared to other approaches on the TRECVID data set, since we use a test set derived from the 2007 development data collection and not the actual TRECVID 2007 test data. Moreover, there does not exist any annotation for this test set and in the evaluation of all submissions the ratio λ_{ts} is kept to the maximum value. Future work aims to compare the presented algorithm with other approaches, within the same data sets derived from the TRECVID collections and to exploit the model vector representation for other applications such as keyframe extraction from videos and content based image retrieval.

Acknowledgements

This research was partially supported by the European Commission under contracts FP6-027685 - MESH, FP6-027026 - K-Space and FP7-215453 - WeKnowIt. Evaggelos Spyrou is partially funded by PENED 2003 Project Ontomedia 03ED475.

References

1. Saux, B., Amato, G.: Image classifiers for scene analysis. In: International Conference on Computer Vision and Graphics (2004)
2. Gokalp, D., Aksoy, S.: Scene classification using bag-of-regions representations. In: IEEE Conference on Computer Vision and Pattern Recognition (2007)
3. Dance, C., Willamowski, J., Fan, L., Bray, C., Csurka, G.: Visual categorization with bags of keypoints. In: ECCV - International Workshop on Statistical Learning in Computer Vision (2004)

4. Boujemaa, N., Fleuret, F., Gouet, V., Sahbi, H.: Visual content extraction for automatic semantic annotation of video news. In: IS&T/SPIE Conf. on Storage and Retrieval Methods and Applications for Multimedia (2004)
5. Voisine, N., Dasiopoulou, S., Mezaris, V., Spyrou, E., Athanasiadis, T., Kompatsiaris, I., Avrithis, Y., Strintzis, M.G.: Knowledge-assisted video analysis using a genetic algorithm. In: 6th International Workshop on Image Analysis for Multimedia Interactive Services (WIAMIS (2005)
6. IBM: MARVEL Multimedia Analysis and Retrieval System. IBM Research White paper (2005)
7. Russell, B.C., Torralba, A., Murphy, K.P., Freeman, W.T.: Labelme: a database and web-based tool for image annotation. International Journal of Computer Vision (2008)
8. Naphade, M.R., Kennedy, L., Kender, J.R., Chang, S.F., Smith, J.R., Over, P., Hauptmann, A.: A Light Scale Concept Ontology for Multimedia understanding for trecvid (IBM Research Technical Report (2005)
9. Smeaton, A.F., Over, P., Kraaij, W.: Evaluation campaigns and trecvid. In: MIR 2006: Proceedings of the 8th ACM International Workshop on Multimedia Information Retrieval, pp. 321–330. ACM Press, New York (2006)
10. Avrithis, Y., Doulamis, A., Doulamis, N., Kollias, S.: A stochastic framework for optimal key frame extraction from mpeg video databases. Computer Vision and Image Understanding 75 (1/2), 3–24 (1999)
11. Manjunath, B., Ohm, J., Vasudevan, V., Yamada, A.: Color and texture descriptors. IEEE trans. on Circuits and Systems for Video Technology 11(6), 703–715 (2001)
12. Spyrou, E., LeBorgne, H., Mailis, T., Cooke, E., Avrithis, Y., O'Connor, N.: Fusing MPEG-7 visual descriptors for image classification. In: International Conference on Artificial Neural Networks (ICANN) (2005)
13. Molina, J., Spyrou, E., Sofou, N., Martinez, J.M.: On the selection of MPEG-7 visual descriptors and their level of detail for nature disaster video sequences classification. In: Falcidieno, B., Spagnuolo, M., Avrithis, Y., Kompatsiaris, I., Buitelaar, P. (eds.) SAMT 2007. LNCS, vol. 4816, pp. 70–73. Springer, Heidelberg (2007)
14. Ayache, S., Quenot, G.: TRECVID, collaborative annotation using active learning. In: TRECVID, Workshop, Gaithersburg (2007)
15. Kishida, K.: Property of average precision and its generalization: an examination of evaluation indicator for information retrieval. NII Technical Reports, NII-2005-014E (2005)

Multimedia Evidence Fusion for Video Concept Detection via OWA Operator

Ming Li[1,2,3], Yan-Tao Zheng[2], Shou-Xun Lin[1], Yong-Dong Zhang[1], and Tat-Seng Chua[2]

[1] Key Laboratory of Intelligent Information Processing, ICT, CAS, Beijing, China 100190
[2] Department of Computer Science, National University of Singapore, Singapore 117543
[3] Graduate School of the Chinese Academy of Sciences, Beijing, China 100039
{mli,sxlin,zhyd}@ict.ac.cn,
{yantaozheng,chuats}@comp.nus.edu.sg

Abstract. We present a novel multi-modal evidence fusion method for high-level feature (HLF) detection in videos. The uni-modal features, such as color histogram, transcript texts, etc, tend to capture different aspects of HLFs and hence share complementariness and redundancy in modeling the contents of such HLFs. We argue that such inter-relation are key to effective multi-modal fusion. Here, we formulate the fusion as a multi-criteria group decision making task, in which the uni-modal detectors are coordinated for a consensus final detection decision, based on their inter-relations. Specifically, we mine the complementariness and redundancy inter-relation of uni-modal detectors using the Ordered Weighted Average (OWA) operator. The 'or-ness' measure in OWA models the inter-relation of uni-modal detectors as combination of pure complementariness and pure redundancy. The resulting weights of OWA can then yield a consensus fusion, by optimally leveraging the decisions of uni-modal detectors. The experiments on TRECVID 07 dataset show that the proposed OWA aggregation operator can significantly outperform other fusion methods, by achieving a state-of-art MAP of 0.132.

Keywords: OWA, Fusion, Video Concept Detection.

1 Introduction

The multi-modal and multimedia nature of video demands the judicious use of all information channels, such as visual, textual, acoustic, etc, to analyze its semantic content [1] [2] [3] [13]. It is intuitive that the use of more information channels tends to deliver better performance than a single information channel. In the task of high-level feature (HLF) extraction in video, most state-of-arts systems [4] [5] adopt a multi-modal multi-feature framework to exploit multimedia evidences from different channels. The widely used multi-modal evidence fusion schemes can be generally classified into 2 types: early-fusion and late-fusion.

Early-fusion is the scheme that integrates uni-modal features before learning the video concepts. Though early-fusion is straightforward, it usually does not work well. This is so because the features of different modalities are not isomorphic. They tend

B. Huet et al. (Eds.): MMM 2009, LNCS 5371, pp. 208–216, 2009.
© Springer-Verlag Berlin Heidelberg 2009

to possess different dimensionality, representation form and measurement space. It is thus not reasonable to simply concatenate them into a common feature space. Moreover, the higher dimensionality caused by concatenation will worsen the scarceness of training data and curse of dimensionality. In fact, the early-fusion is more suitable for fusing raw data within single type of feature, such as to capture spatial information with different granularity, i.e. fusing grid-based visual features and image-based visual feature of same type.

In contrast to early-fusion, late-fusion first reduces uni-modal features to separately learned concept detection decisions and then integrates them to the final detection decision [6]. The late-fusion has been reported to outperform early fusions significantly [6]. The major criticism for late-fusion is its loss of linear correlation of multi-modal features. However, when the features come from completely different modalities or channels, their linear correlation becomes less critical. Instead, the complementariness and redundancy of individual uni-modal detectors are the key to effective fusion.

Hence, we need to develop a principled method to fuse the outputs of uni-modal detectors to form a final consensus detection decision. From this perspective, the multi-modal fusion can be regarded as a multi-criterion group decision making problem (GMD) [7], in which the group of uni-modal detectors should be consolidated synergically towards the common task. We therefore formulate the multi-modal fusion as an information aggregation task in the framework of group decision making (GMD) problem. Specifically, we employ the Ordered Weighted Average (OWA) operator to aggregate the group of decisions by uni-modal detectors, as it has been reported to be an effective solution for GMD problem [10]. Compared to existing fusion methods, the major advantage of OWA is that its 'or-ness' measure can explicitly reflect the complementariness and redundancy interrelation of uni-modal detectors, in between either a pure 'and-like' or a pure 'or-like' manner. Our main contributions are twofold: (a) we formulate the multi-modal fusion as a group decision making problem (GMD); (b) we employ the OWA operators to consolidate the uni-modal detections by mining their complementariness and redundancy interrelations. Experiments on TRECVID 07 dataset show that the proposed approach can significantly outperform other fusion methods.

2   Related Work

Our proposed fusion method belongs to late-fusion scheme, as it manipulates the outputs of uni-modal detectors. There are mainly two types of late-fusion schemes. The first views the late-fusion problem from the perspective of statistical machine learning. It regards the learned outputs of uni-modal detectors as input for another layer of statistical learning. For example, Snoek et al. [6] employed SVM to fuse the output of individual classifier on each set of uni-modal features. Though it has been reported to deliver outstanding performance [6], it has the following disadvantages: (a) it often requires extensive parameter tuning and model selection for the additional round of statistical machine learning; and (b) the possibility of over fitting in the supervised learning process limits its generalization ability.

The second type considers late-fusion as an information aggregation task, from the perspective of Information Theory. The fusion now aims to maximize the aggregated information by assigning proper weights to individual information channels. The examples include heuristic fusions like Weighted Average and Adaboost; and non-heuristic fusions like Maximum (Max), Minimum (Min) and Average [12] scheme. The major drawbacks of non-heuristic fusion methods are that they are not adaptive to different aggregation problems; and they may not converge well or the converged result may be local rather than global optimum.

Similar to the aforementioned fusion schemes, our proposed fusion belongs to the second type. However, different from the fusion methods above, our proposed OWA based fusion provides a general approach of parameterized decision aggregation, with an efficient global optimal weight vector searching strategy. To our best knowledge, this is also the first approach to investigate the inter-relations of uni-modal detectors, from the perspective of Information Theory.

3   OWA-Based Multi-model Fusion

For each shot, a set of uni-modal features $\{\mathbf{x}_i\}_{i=1}^n$ are first extracted from n different modalities $\{\mathbf{M}_i\}_{i=1}^n$, such as visual, auditory and text. The decision function T, such as Support Vector Machine, is then applied on each uni-modal to yield a separately learned concept score $a_i = T(\mathbf{x}_i)$, and $a_i \in [0,1]$. Our target now is to apply the OWA operator to learn the complementariness and redundancy of the group of uni-modal detection scores $\{a_i\}_{i=1}^n$ to yield a consensus final detection score.

The inter-relation of uni-modal detectors has two extreme cases: (a) complete redundancy; and (b) complete complementariness. In the case of complete redundancy, all uni-modal detectors contribute similarly on the given HLF detection task. This implies the final detection decision is positive, only if all the detectors deliver positive decisions. In this scenario, these detectors actually share an and-like inter-relation. In the case of complete complementariness, the uni-modal detectors perform differently on the given detection task. This means that the final decision can be positive, if one of the detectors yields positive decisions. In this case, the detectors share an or-like inter-relation. Our argument is that the inter-relation of detectors lies somewhere in between these two extremes. The OWA operator is exploited to discover.

3.1   OWA Aggregation Operator

An OWA operator is a mapping $F : \Re^n \to \Re$ from n uni-modal detection decisions to one final detection decision with a weight vector $W = (w_1, \cdots, w_n)^T$ subjects to

$$w_1 + \cdots + w_n = 1, 0 \le w_i \le 1, i = 1, \cdots, n \tag{1}$$

and such that

$$F(a_1, \ldots, a_n) = \sum_{i=1}^{n} w_i b_i \tag{2}$$

where a_i is the decision from uni-modal feature $\mathbf{x}_i$ and b_i is the ith largest element of the aggregated decision $\{a_1, \cdots, a_n\}$. Note that the re-ordering step is a critical aspect of

OWA operator, in which a_i is not associated with a particular weight w_i, but rather a weight w_i is associated with a particular ordered position b_i of a_i.

Yager [8] introduced two characterizing measures associated with the weight vector W of an OWA operator. The first one is the measure of 'or-ness' of the aggregation operator and is defined as:

$$orness(W) = \frac{1}{n-1} \sum_{i=1}^{n} (n-i)w_i \qquad (3)$$

The *orness* measures how much the aggregation associated with vector W is like "OR" aggregation operator. When $W = [1\,0\,0\,...\,]$, then $orness(W) = 1$ and the final decision $F(a_1,...,a_n) = \text{MAX}(a_i)$. This shows a complete redundancy inter-relation of uni-modal detectors, as the fusion only takes into account the decision of largest value. In contrast, when $W = [0\,0\,...\,1]$, $orness(W) = 0$ and the final decision $F(a_1,...,a_n) = \text{MIN}(a_i)$. This shows a complete redundancy inter-relation, as the fusion only takes into account the uni-modal decision of small value. Intuitively, Max is a pure "OR" operator and Min is a pure "AND", which are the two extreme conditions of information aggregation [8]. Obviously Max, Min and Average are special cases of OWA aggregation operator with certain weight vector.

The second measure in OWA is the 'dispersion' (entropy) of the aggregation operator. It is defined as:

$$dispersion(W) = -\sum_{i=1}^{n} w_i \ln w_i \qquad (4)$$

It measures how much information is taken into account in the aggregation. We can also derive the dispersions of Max, Min and Average aggregation operators; i.e. 0, 0 and $\ln n$, respectively. The dispersion is actually a Shannon entropy of weights. In a certain sense, the more disperse w is, the more information about the individual detection decision is being used in the aggregation of OWA operator [8].

4   Optimal OWA Weight Learning

4.1   Orness-Dispersion Space (OD-Space)

Intuitively, the optimal weights can be obtained by performing grid search in the n-dimension weight vector space, where n is the number of uni-modal concept detection decisions to aggregate. Such simple grid search is, however, proved to be computationally intractable, due to the high dimensionality of weight vector space [8].

Fortunately, it is found that the weight vectors with similar Orness and dispersion values are of similar aggregating performance [8]. Thus we can transform the search space from n-dimensional weight vector space into a 2 dimensional OWA OD-space. Given

$$orness(W) = \alpha, \ dispersion(W) = \beta \qquad (5)$$

To derive W subjects to Eqn (5) is equivalent to solving the following problem:

$$\frac{1}{n-1}\sum_{i=1}^{n}(n-i)w_i = \alpha, 0 \le \alpha \le 1$$

$$-\sum_{i=1}^{n}w_i \ln w_i = \beta, 0 < \beta < \ln n \qquad\qquad (6)$$

$$\sum_{i=1}^{n}w_i = 1, 0 \le w_i \le 1$$

4.2 Orness/ Dispersion Max-Space

As Eqn(6) cannot be solved analytically, we exploit some approximation to transform it into a optimization problem, which has many existing solutions, such as Lagrange multipliers. Here, we consider mainly two kinds of optimization formulation to solve for weights W.

First, we can optimize the variability by maximizing the dispersion or minimizing the variance of the weights while keeping the Orness at a fixed level [9].

$$\text{Maximize } \frac{1}{n-1}\sum_{i=1}^{n}(n-i)w_i$$

$$\text{(or Minimize } Var(W) = \frac{1}{n}\sum_{i=1}^{n}w_i^2 - \frac{1}{n^2}) \qquad\qquad (7)$$

$$\text{subject to } -\sum_{i=1}^{n}w_i \ln w_i = \beta, 0 < \beta < \ln n \ ; \ \sum_{i=1}^{n}w_i = 1, 0 \le w_i \le 1$$

The second solution is to maximize the Orness, while keeping the dispersion at a fixed level [10].

$$\text{Maximize } -\sum_{i=1}^{n}w_i \ln w_i$$

$$\text{subject to } \frac{1}{n-1}\sum_{i=1}^{n}(n-i)w_i = \alpha, 0 \le \alpha \le 1 \qquad\qquad (8)$$

$$\sum_{i=1}^{n}w_i = 1, 0 \le w_i \le 1$$

Both optimization formulations above are trying to transform the 2-dimension OD-space into 1-dimension maximum line space (Max-space). Although the mapping is not a full cover of the OD-space, Max-spaces are the most significant sub-spaces of it. In Orness Max-space modeled by Eqn (7), the weights of different dispersion are given with maximal Orness which means the operator is as disjunctive as possible using at least certain percentage of available information [9]. In Dispersion Max-space represented by Eqn (8), the weights of different Orness are given with maximal dispersion which means most individual criteria are being used in the aggregation that gives more robustness [10]. Both Eqn (7) and Eqn (8) are optimal problems which can be analytically solved using Lagrange multipliers. The results are optimal (maximal or minimal) Orness (or dispersion) weight vectors of different dispersions (or Orness). The weight vectors with different Orness and dispersion are evaluated in the cross-validation set and the one that gives the highest precision is chosen to be the OWA aggregation operator's weight vector.

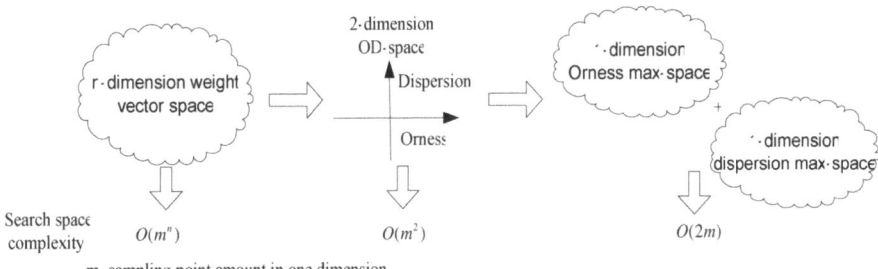

m sampling point amount in one dimension

Fig. 1. Search space complexity comparison among different spaces

4.3 Theoretic Analysis of OWA

Figure 1 compares the search space complexity among different weight vector search spaces. As shown, by transforming the search for optimal weights into an optimization task, the complexity of OWA learning is greatly reduced from n-dimension weight vector space $O(m^n)$ to Orness/dispersion max-space $O(2m)$ where m is the number of sampling points in one dimension. Besides, given a fixed Orness (dispersion), the first component of OWA weights vector can be calculated by solving an equation and others can be simply generated from the first component [10]. The complexity of OWA learning is linear to the training dataset, while SVM based fusion has a learning complexity of $O(N^3)$, due to the convex quadratic programming (QP) formulation of SVM. The Max, Min and Average are non-heuristic fusions that don't need training process. However, their performance is worse than that of the OWA fusion, which will be shown in next section.

5 Experiment and Results

5.1 Testing Dataset and Experimental Setup

We evaluate the proposed OWA-based fusion on TRECVID 07 dataset [11]. The TRECVID 2007 dataset comprises 100 hours of documentary video with ~40, 000 key frames. The dataset is equally divided into development and test sets, with each containing approximately 50 hours and around 20,000 key frames. In our experiments, we use the 20 semantic concepts listed in Figure 2 used in the TRECVID 07 valuation [11].

We further split the development set into 70% for training and 30% for validation. The training set is used to train the SVM detectors for individual uni-modal features; while the validation set is used to train the various fusion methods. For simplicity, we use a keyframe to represent a shot and extract 6 types of features from the keyframe of each shot. They are color correlogram (CC), color histogram (CH), color moment (CM), edge histogram (EH), texture co-occurrence (TC) and wavelet texture (WT). For CM, we compute the first 3 moments of RGB color channels over 5 ×5 grids to form a 225D feature vector. For WT, we divide a key frame into 4 × 3 grids and compute the variance in 9 Haar wavelet sub-bands for each grid. This gives rise to a 108D feature vector for a keyframe. The evaluation criteria is the mean average precision (MAP), which is the mean of average precision (AP) of each concept.

Table 1. MAPs of each uni-modal feature set

Feature	CC	CH	CM	EH	TC	WT
MAP	0.082	0.065	0.084	0.082	0.028	0.033

Table 2. MAP of various fusion models

Fusion	OWA	SVM	Adaboost	Max (OR)	Min (AND)	Average
MAP	0.132	0.122	0.064	0.088	0.075	0.12

5.2 Experiments and Discussion

We first perform SVM-based concept detection on each uni-modal feature. The cost and gamma parameters of SVM are set, based on cross validation. Table 1 shows the MAP of each feature set. Based on the individual concept scores of uni-modal detector, we apply the OWA operator to learn the optimal weights for ordered concept scores. As shown in Table 2, OWA achieves the best MAP of 0.132, which is substantially higher than that of all uni-modal detectors. This demonstrates that different features do complement each other and the proper fusion of decisions of all uni-modal concept detectors can yield a much more satisfactory detection performance.

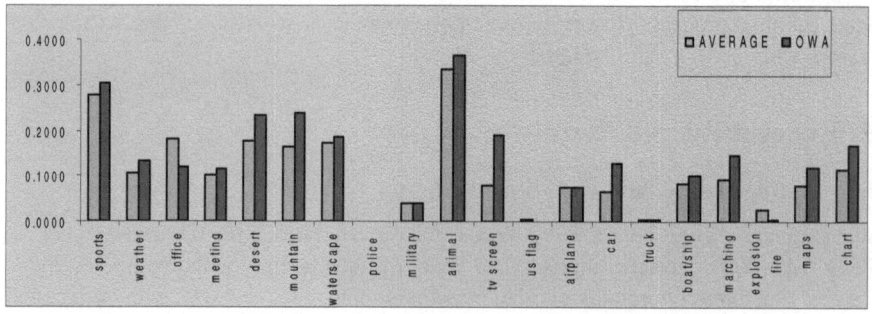

Fig. 2. MAP of each concepts by OWA and Average fusion respectively

Next, we compare OWA-based fusion with 5 commonly used late-fusion methods: SVM, Adaboost, Max, Min and Average. The SVM-based fusion is to take uni-modal detection score as input and yield a final detection decision in a supervised learning process. The Max fusion is a specialization of OWA fusion. It takes the maximum detection score of all uni-modal features as the final detection score, which is effectively a pure OR operator on the group of uni-modal detection decisions. The Min fusion is also a specialization of OWA fusion. It takes the minimum detection score of all uni-modal features as the final detection score, which is effectively a pure AND function. Average fusion is to take the mean of all uni-modal detection scores as the final detection score.

Table 2 lists the MAP of these 5 fusion methods. As shown, the Max and Min fusions do not yield good detection performance over uni-modal detectors. This is so because these two fusion schemes over-simplify the inter-relation among different features as either complete complementariness (pure OR inter-relation) or complete redundancy (pure AND inter-relation). On the other hand, the Average fusion gives a better MAP of 0.12, which demonstrates that the inter-relation between different features lies between the pure complementariness and pure redundancy. That the best MAP is achieved with OWA fusion, which demonstrates that OWA is effective to learn the inter-relations of different uni-modal features. We also observe that the SVM based fusion achieves an MAP of 0.122, which is much lower in performance than that of OWA but comparable to Average fusion. However, considering the expensive learning process of SVM with little improvement in performance over the simple Average fusion, the SVM based fusion is not cost-effective.

In order to capture a clearer view on the performance of OWA fusion, we examine the fusion performance on each concept. Figure 2, shows the MAP of Average and OWA fusion for each concept. We observe that OWA outperforms the Average fusion in 17 out of 20 concepts. Of the 3 concepts that Average fusion outperforming OWA fusion, we found that the number of positive training samples in these concept classes are too small. These 3 concepts have an average of 613 positive samples, while the average number of samples for all concepts is 1591. This is one reason why OWA, which is essentially a supervised learning process, might yield inaccurate results.

Table 3. MAP of various fusion models

	OWA	**[4]**	**[5]**	**[12]**
MAP	0.132	0.1311	0.099	0.098

Benchmark on TRECVID 07: We compare our system with other reported systems. Table 3 tabulates the MAPs of the top performing systems in TRECVID 2007. As shown, the proposed approach based on OWA outperforms most of the existing systems, and delivers a comparable result with the best reported system [4], which however exploited a computationally expensive Multi-Label Multi-Feature learning process [4].

6   Conclusion and Future Work

We have proposed a multi-modal fusion method for HLF detection in video. By exploiting the OWA operator, we mine the inter-relation of uni-modal detectors and then coordinate them with averaging weights to yield a final consensus detection decision. The experiments on TRECVID 07 showed that the OWA based fusion can outperform other fusion method, such as SVM, Adaboost, with statistically significant improvements.

Several issues remain open. First, we do not exploit other subspaces, such as Variance Min-space, for weight learning. Though this does not improve learning efficiency, it does give a different perspective to learn OWA weights. Second, the Bayesian formulation can be incorporated to learn the weights in a probabilistic manner.

Acknowledgments. This work was supported in part by the National Nature Science Foundation of China (60873165), the National Basic Research Program of China (973 Program, 2007CB311100), the National High Technology and Research Development Program of China (863 Program, 2007AA01Z416).

References

1. Chang, S.-F., Hsu, W., Kennedy, L., Xie, L., Yanagawa, A., Zavesky, E., Zhang., D.-Q.: Columbia university trecvid 2005 video search and high-level feature extraction. In: TREC Video Retrieval Evaluation Proceedings (March 2006)
2. Dorai, C., Venkatesh., S.: Bridging the semantic gap with computational media aesthetics. IEEE MultiMedia 10(2), 15–17 (2003)
3. Hauptmann, A.G., Chen, M.-Y., Christel, M., Lin, W.-H., Yan, R., Yang, J.: 2006. Multilingual broadcast news retrieval. In: Proceedings of TREC Video Retrieval Evaluation Proceedings (March 2006)
4. Mei, T., Hua, X., Lai, W., Yang, L., Zha, Z., Liu, Y., Gu, Z., Qi, G., Wang, M., Tang, J., Yuan, X., Lu, Z., Liu, J.: MSRA-USTC-SJTU at TRECVID 2007: High-level feature extraction and search (2007),
http://www-nlpir.nist.gov/projects/tvpubs/tv.pubs.org.html
5. Le, H. D., Satoh, S., Matsui, T.: NII-ISM, Japan at TRECVID 2007: High Level Feature Extraction (2007),
http://www-nlpir.nist.gov/projects/tvpubs/tv.pubs.org.html
6. Snoek, C., Worring, M., Gemert, J., Geusebroek, J.-M., Smeulders, A.: 2006. The challenge problem for automated detection of 101 semantic concepts in multimedia. In: Proceedings of ACM MM, pp. 421–430 (2006)
7. Kacprzyk, J., Fedrizzi, M., Nurmi, H.: OWA operators in group decision making and consensus reaching under fuzzy preferences and fuzzy majority. In: Yager, R.R., Kacprzyk, J. (eds.) The Ordered Weighted Averaging Operators: Theory and Applications, pp. 193–206. Kluwer Academic Publishers, Dordrecht (1997)
8. Yager, R.R.: Ordered weighted averaging aggregation operators in multi-criteria decision making. IEEE Tran. On Systems, Man and Cybernetics 18, 183–190 (1988)
9. Marchant, T.: Maximal orness weights with a fixed variability for OWA operators. International Journal of Uncertainty Fuzziness and Knowledge Based Systems 14, 271–276 (2006)
10. Fuller, R., Majlender, P.: An analytic approach for obtaining maximal entropy OWA operator weights. Fuzzy Sets and System 124, 53–57 (2001)
11. Smeaton, A.F., Over, P., Kraaij, W.: Evaluation campaigns and TRECVid. In: Proceedings of the 8th ACM International Workshop on Multimedia Information Retrieval MIR 2006, pp. 321–330. ACM Press, New York (2006)
12. Ngo, C., Jiang, Y., Wei, X., Wang, F., Zhao, W., Tan, H., Wu, X.: Experimenting vireo-374: Bag-of-visual-words and visual-based ontology for semantic video indexing and search. In: TREC Video Retrieval Evaluation Proceedings (November 2007)
13. Magalhães, J., Rüger, S.: Information-theoretic semantic multimedia indexing. In: Proceedings of the 6th ACM international conference on Image and video retrieval (CIVR 2007) (July 2007)

Personalized Image Recommendation

Yuli Gao, Hangzai Luo, and Jianping Fan

CS Department, UNC-Charlotte, USA
{jfan,ygao,hluo}@uncc.edu

Abstract. We have developed a novel system to support personalized image recommendation via exploratory search from large-scale collections of weakly-tagged Flickr images. First, topic network is automatically generated to index and summarize large-scale collections of Flickr images at a semantic level. Hyperbolic visualization is used to allow users to navigate and explore the topic network interactively, so that they can gain insights of large-scale Flickr image collections at the first glance, build up their mental query models quickly and specify their queries more precisely by selecting the visible image topics directly. Second, the most representative images are automatically recommended according to their representativeness for a given topic and they are visualized according to their inherent visual similarity contexts, so that users can assess the diverse visual similarity contexts between the images interactively and evaluate the relevance between the recommended images and their real query intentions effectively. Our experiments on large-scale weakly-tagged Flickr image collections have obtained very positive results.

Keywords: personalized image recommendation, exploratory search.

1 Introduction

Automatic image understanding is still imperfect and error-prone due to the difficulty in bridging the semantic gap, therefore, collaborative image tagging is becoming very popular for people to manage, share and annotate images. With the exponential growth of such weakly-tagged images, it has become increasingly important to have mechanisms that can support keyword-based image retrieval. Unfortunately, keyword-based image retrieval may seriously suffer from the problems of query formulation and information overload. To tackle these problems, we have developed a novel system to support personalized image recommendation via exporatory search [1-2].

2 Personalized Query Recommendation

We have developed two innovative techniques to support personalized query recommendation and assist users on communicating their image needs more effectively: (a) Topic network is automatically generated to summarize large-scale weakly-tagged Flickr image collections at a semantic level and provide a good global overview to users; (b) Hyperbolic visualization and interactive exploration are used to disclose such topic network (i.e., a good global overview of large-scale image collections) to users and allow them to navigate the topic network without losing the inter-topic contexts, so that they can make better query decisions as shown in Fig. 1.

B. Huet et al. (Eds.): MMM 2009, LNCS 5371, pp. 217–219, 2009.

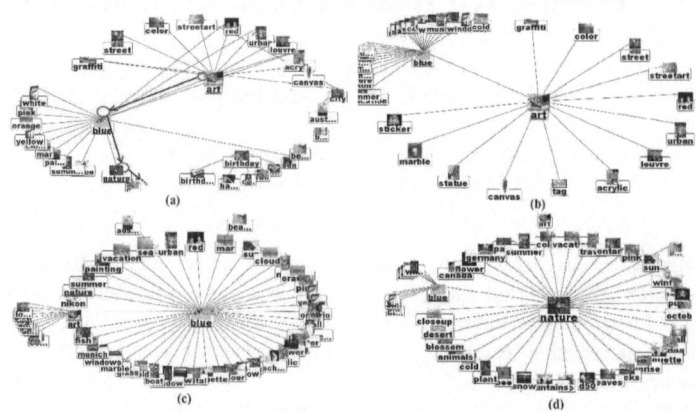

Fig. 1. (a) User's access path on a global context of the topic network; (b), (c) and (d) the local details of the semantic contexts for topic recommendation (what user can do next)

3   Personalized Image Recommendation

As shown in Fig. 2, we have developed a novel user-adaptive image recommendation algorithm and it consists of the following major components: (a) *Topic-Driven Image Recommendation*: The semantically-similar images under the same topic are first partitioned into multiple clusters according to their diverse visual similarity contexts, and a reasonable number of most representative images are automatically selected according to their representativeness for a given image topic. (b) *Intention-Driven Image Recommendation*: An interactive user-system interface is designed to capture the user's time-varying intentions for recommending the most relevant images according to the user's personal preferences.

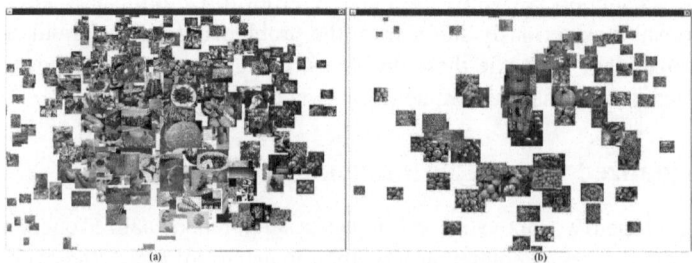

Fig. 2. Our system for personalized image recommendation: (a) The most representative images recommended for "vegetables"; (b) The most relevant images recommended according to the user's query intention of "tomato"

References

1. Marchionini, G.: Exploratory search: from finding to understanding. Commun. of ACM 49(4), 41–46 (2006)
2. Fan, J., Gao, Y., Luo, H.: Integrating concept ontology and multi-task learning to achieve more effective classifier training for multi-level image annotation. IEEE Trans. on Image Processing 17(3), 407–426 (2008)

Online Macro-segmentation of Television Streams

Gaël Manson, Xavier Naturel, and Sid-Ahmed Berrani

Orange Labs – France Telecom R&D
35510 Cesson-Sévigné, France
{gael.manson,xavier.naturel,sidahmed.berrani}@orange-ftgroup.com

Abstract. This demo presents a complete system that automatically structures TV streams on the fly. The objective is to precisely and automatically determine the start and the end of each broadcasted TV program. The extracted programs can then be stored in a database to be used in novel services such as TV-on-Demand. The system performs on-the-fly detection of inter-programs using a reference database of inter-programs, as well as an offline detection and classification of repeated sequences. This offline phase allows us to automatically detect inter-programs as repeated sequences. The macro-segmentation is performed using the online and the offline results of inter-program detection as well as metadata, when available, in order to label extracted programs. The demo shows results on large real TV streams.

1 Introduction

TV-on-Demand services aim at making TV content available to viewers without any constraint of location and/or time. Viewers get the possibility to access past TV programs from a large number of channels. Broadcasted metadata like Event Information Table (EIT) or Electronic Program Guide (EPG) provide information on the structure of TV streams. They are unfortunately imprecise, incomplete and not always available [1]. Moreover, TV channels cannot provide accurate metadata because of technical limitations (the complexity of the audio-visual chain) and because of organizational reasons (services making use of TV content can be developed by third parties) [2].

This demo is based on the techniques proposed in [2,3]. It shows how these techniques can be put together in order to perform accurate and fully automatic TV stream macro-segmentation.

2 System Overview

The system automatically extracts TV programs from live feed. The general architecture is presented in Figure 1. It is composed of three independent modules for the detection of inter-programs:

Commercial detection (online): detects unknown commercials using features like monochromatic frames, silence..., following classical methods [4].

Repetition Analysis (offline): performs a clustering-based identification of repeated sequences and a classification of detected repeated sequences in order to isolate inter-programs. This analysis is performed offline, periodically, or on demand [3].

B. Huet et al. (Eds.): MMM 2009, LNCS 5371, pp. 220–221, 2009.

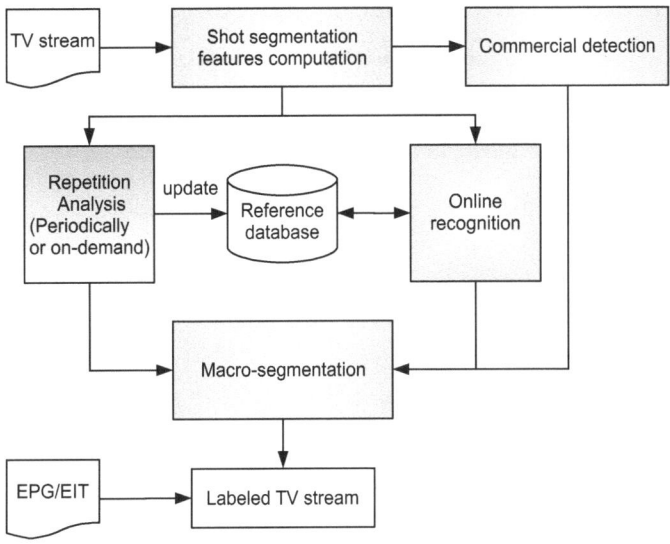

Fig. 1. Overview of the system. Online processing steps are in yellow, offline ones in blue.

Recognition (online): uses perceptual hashing to recognize online inter-programs in the stream from a reference database. This database is fed by the repetition analysis module. Hashing is performed using a method similar to [5].

The results of these three modules are then fused in order to identify the precise boundaries of the programs. The resulting program segments are then labeled using a straightforward matching procedure using the available metadata. Results show that the method is very accurate and outperforms the metadata-based macro-segmentation [3].

The demo presents results on real TV streams from two different channels: *France 2*, a French public TV channel, and *TF1*, a French private TV channel.

References

1. Berrani, S.A., Lechat, P., Manson, G.: TV broadcast macro-segmentation: Metadata-based vs. content-based approaches. In: Proc. of the ACM Int. Conf. on Image and Video Retrieval, Amsterdam, The Netherlands (July 2007)
2. Berrani, S.A., Manson, G., Lechat, P.: A non-supervised approach for repeated sequence detection in tv broadcast streams. Signal Processing: Image Communication, special issue on Semantic Analysis for Interactive Multimedia Services 23(7), 525–537 (2008)
3. Manson, G., Berrani, S.A.: An inductive logic programming-based approach for tv stream segment classification. In: Proc. of the IEEE Int. Symp. on Multimedia, Berkeley, CA, USA (December 2008)
4. Lienhart, R., Kuhmunch, C., Effelsberg, W.: On the detection and recognition of television commercials. In: Proc. of the IEEE Int. Conf. on Multimedia Computing and Systems, Ottawa, Canada (June 1997)
5. Naturel, X., Gros, P.: A fast shot matching strategy for detecting duplicate sequences in a television stream. In: Proc. of the 2nd Int. Workshop on Computer Vision meets Databases, Baltimore, MD, USA (June 2005)

A Real-Time Content Based Video Copy Detection System

Sid-Ahmed Berrani and Nicolas Gengembre

Orange Labs – Division R&D Technologies
4, rue du Clos Courtel
35510 Cesson Sévigné. France
{sidahmed.berrani,nicolas.gengembre}@orange-ftgroup.com

Abstract. This paper presents a content-based video copy detection system which achieves an optimal trade-off between effectiveness and efficiency. This is the most important feature for industrial applications such as copyright enforcement and duplicate detection in large databases.

1 Introduction

A content-based video copy detection system consists of two stages. The first is an off-line step during which *fingerprints* are computed from the referenced videos. Fingerprints are vectors that describe the visual/audio content of the video and are intended to be invariant to usual transformations. They are stored in an indexing structure that makes similarity search efficient (i.e. rapid). The second step is performed on-line and consists of analyzing the suspicious videos. Fingerprints are extracted from these videos and compared to those stored in the reference database. A content-based video copy detection system has to be therefore robust to transformations pirated videos may undergo (deliberately or not) through manipulations such as cropping, compression, color or contrast adjustments, etc. Efficiency is also essential for real world applications that manage large reference video databases.

2 System Description

Our system for video copy detection relies on extracting fingerprints from the visual content of the videos. It is based on a set of processing steps that are summarized as follows:

- *Keyframe extraction*: videos are composed of large sets of frames whose visual content is temporally highly correlated. Thus, computing fingerprints on keyframes allows the reduction of the computation cost without losing relevant information,
- *Fingerprint computation*: the fingerprints we propose to use rely on local visual descriptors. Each keyframe is not considered as a whole but as a set of regions of interest. Around each region, a visual feature vector is computed.

B. Huet et al. (Eds.): MMM 2009, LNCS 5371, pp. 222–223, 2009.

With this approach, our system is robust to transformations which discard parts of the frames (e.g. cropping). If parts of the frames are missing, the remaining part is sufficient to match the video with the original one,
- *Indexing structure*: during the off-line step, a fingerprint is computed around each region of interest and stored in an indexing structure derived from a hash table. The objective is to ensure an efficient similarity search. During the analysis step, fingerprints are computed on the query keyframes and their similar fingerprints from the reference database are rapidly found,
- *Voting*: a referenced keyframe is assumed similar to a query one if they share a minimum number of fingerprints. The minimum number of fingerprints is computed using the *a contrario* approach proposed in [1],
- *Spatial and temporal coherence verification*: once the matching between regions of interest of a referenced keyframe and those of a query keyframe is performed, spatial coherence of the matched regions are checked. This allows to remove false and random matches. Similarly, when different keyframes of a referenced video have been identified at different times within a query video, the temporal coherence of the keyframes is checked. This is done using a probabilistic procedure that has been proposed in [2].

3   Experiments

The system was successfully tested on two international benchmarks: CIVR'07 and TrecVid'08. Our approach has been validated and very good results have been obtained on these evaluation campaigns, both in terms of efficiency and effectiveness. In particular, on the CIVR'07 query set ST2 (60 hours of referenced videos and 45 minutes of queries), our system achieves a precision of 100% and a recall of 95% while the detection time is 4.7 times faster than real-time (i.e. it equals 0.21 the duration of the query video).

4   Applications

This system can be used for many applications. In particular, it can be applied to copyright enforcement in video platforms by filtering out pirated videos (for instance, in video web platforms such as Youtube or Dailymotion). It can also be used for the detection of near-duplicate videos in very large databases. It allows the structuration of the database by grouping videos sharing the same visual content. It also allows the clustering of the response list of video search engines.

References

1. Gengembre, N., Berrani, S.-A., Lechat, P.: Adaptive similarity search in large databases – application to video copy detection. In: Proc. of the 6th International Workshop on Content-Based Multimedia Indexing, London, UK (June 2008)
2. Gengembre, N., Berrani, S.-A.: A probabilistic framework for fusing frame-based searches within a video copy detection system. In: Proc. of the ACM International Conference on Image and Video Retrieval, Niagara Falls, Canada (July 2008)

Active Objects in Interactive Mobile TV

J. Deigmöller[1], G. Fernàndez[2], A. Kriechbaum[4], A. López[2], B. Mérialdo[3],
H. Neuschmied[4], F. Pinyol Margalef[2], R. Trichet[3], P. Wolf[5], R. Salgado[6],
and F. Milagaia[6]

[1] Institut für Rundfunktechnik, Munich, Germany
[2] GTAM - Enginyeria La Salle, Universitat Ramon Llull, Barcelona, Spain
[3] Institut Eurecom, Sophia Antipolis, France
[4] Institute of Information Systems, Joanneum Research, Graz, Austria
[5] Fraunhofer-Institute for Secure Information Technology, Darmstadt, Germany
[6] Portugal Telecom Inovação, Aveiro, Portugal

Abstract. The porTiVity project is developing a converged rich media iTV
system, which integrates broadcast and mobile broadband delivery to portables
and mobiles and which will enable the end-user to act on moving objects within
TV programmes. The developments of the project include the playout of
portable rich media iTV and the middleware, data and presentation engine in
the handheld receiver. In this demonstration, we will present, on the production
side, the Live Annotation Tool which allows the video editor to define and
include active objects in Live TV Programs, and on the user side, the interaction
with active objects on a mobile terminal.

1   porTiVity Live Authoring

The porTiVity project is developing a complete production chain to allow direct
interaction with video objects in content broadcast to mobile devices. In other words:
an object-based interactive mobile TV system [2]. Documentaries can be expanded
with further details, children programs can be augmented with games, live events
such as football matches may include online statistics, all extra information being at
the disposal and will of the user.

This demonstration will show how porTiVity enables the video editor to create
interactive programs from live broadcast with the Live Annotation Tool. Before the
program, the video editor prepares the list of interesting objects and defines
the relevant additional content. During the broadcast, the video editor will define the
objects using the authoring interface shown in Figure 1. The input video is displayed
in the top right window. At each new shot, a frozen view is automatically displayed in
the object selection window for a duration of 4 seconds. This leaves sufficient time
for the editor to draw a bounding box around the object, and identify the object in
the available list. The object is then automatically tracked in the remaining frames of
the shot, and the result is displayed in the bottom right window. Other event buttons
allow the video editor to dynamically include or suppress static objects in the
outgoing stream, or to stop the tracking in case of error.

B. Huet et al. (Eds.): MMM 2009, LNCS 5371, pp. 224–226, 2009.

Fig. 1. (1) Object selection window (2) Incoming video window (3) Outgoing video window (4) Progress bar (5) Moving objects (6) Event buttons

The resulting information is encoded in Laser scenes, and multiplexed with the video program, then broadcasted to the end-user terminal (we will not be able to demonstrate the complete broadcast chain, due to the extensive equipment required).

2 End-User Interaction

We will also demonstrate the interaction with a mobile terminal. The terminal receives a DVB-H stream (simulated for the demonstration), consisting of an audio, video and LASeR MPEG-4 Elementary Stream. The player for rendering the porTiVity service is based on the open source player Osmo4, which is integrated in the GPAC framework developed at ENST. The additional content, which is linked by interactive graphical elements in the LASeR DVB-H stream, can be accessed by an HTTP or Streaming Server via any broadband connection (here WiFi or UMTS). Examples of interaction can be seen on Figure.

Fig. 2. Children program scenario

Aknowledgements

This work was developed within porTiVity' (www.portivity.org), under the European Commission IST FP6 programme.

References

[1] Cardoso, B., et al.: Hyperlinked Video with Moving Objects in Digital Television. In: ICME 2005 (2005)
[2] Stoll, G., et al.: porTiVity: New Rich Media iTV Services for Handheld TV. In: Workshop on the Integration of Knowledge, Semantic and Digital Media Technologies. London (2005)
[3] Neuschmied, H., Trichet, R., Mérialdo, B.: Fast annotation of video objects for interactive TV. ACM Multimedia 2007, 158–159 (2007)
[4] Stockleben, B.: Approaches towards a Mobile Interactive Platform. In: Euro ITV Workshop on Interactive Applications for Mobile TV, Amsterdam, May 24-25 (2007)

Sparse Multiscale Patches (*SMP*) for Image Categorization

Paolo Piro, Sandrine Anthoine, Eric Debreuve, and Michel Barlaud

University of Nice-Sophia Antipolis / CNRS

Abstract. In this paper we address the task of image categorization using a new similarity measure on the space of Sparse Multiscale Patches (*SMP*). *SMP*s are based on a multiscale transform of the image and provide a global representation of its content. At each scale, the probability density function (*pdf*) of the *SMP*s is used as a description of the relevant information. The closeness between two images is defined as a combination of Kullback-Leibler divergences between the *pdfs* of their *SMP*s.

In the context of image categorization, we represent semantic categories by prototype images, which are defined as the centroids of the training clusters. Therefore any unlabeled image is classified by giving it the same label as the nearest prototype. Results obtained on ten categories from the Corel collection show the categorization accuracy of the *SMP* method.

1 Introduction

Image categorization is still one of the most challenging tasks in computer vision. It consists in labeling an image according to its semantic category. The main difficulty lies in using low-level information provided by digital images to retrieve semantic-level classes, which are generally characterized by high intra-variability.

Most approaches address the task of image categorization as a supervised learning problem. They use a set of annotated images to learn the categories and then assign to an unlabeled image one of these categories. These methods rely on extracting visual descriptors, which are to be highly specific, i.e. able to highlight visual patterns that characterize a category. Providing suitable sets of visual descriptors has been a topic of active research in the recent years and several approaches have been proposed.

1.1 Related Works

Visual descriptors for image categorization generally consist of either global or local features. The former ones represent global information of images and are based on global image statistics such as color histograms [1] or edge directions histograms [2]. Global feature-based methods were mostly designed to separate very general classes of images, such as indoor vs. outdoor scenes or city vs. landscape images. On the contrary, local descriptors extract information at specific

B. Huet et al. (Eds.): MMM 2009, LNCS 5371, pp. 227–238, 2009.

image locations that are relevant to characterize the visual content. Local approaches are more adapted to cope with the intra-class variability of real image categories. Indeed these techniques are able to emphasize local patterns, which images of the same category are expected to share.

Early approaches based on local features work on image blocks. In [3] color and texture features are extracted from image blocks to train a statistical model; this model takes into account spatial relations among blocks and across image resolutions. Then several region-based approaches have been proposed, which require segmentation of images into relevant regions. E.g. in [4], an algorithm for learning region prototypes is proposed as well as a classification of regions based on Support Vector Machines (SVMs). More recent techniques have successfully used bags-of-features, which collect local features into variable length vectors. In [5], the bags-of-features representing an image are spatial pyramid aggregating statistics of local features (e.g. "SIFT" descriptors); this approach takes into account approximate global geometric correspondences between local features. Other methods using bags-of-features are based on explicitly modeling the distribution of these vector sets. In fact, measuring the similarity between the bags-of-features' distributions is the main difficulty for this kind of categorization methods. For example, Gaussian Mixture Models (GMMs) have been used to model the distribution of bags of low-level features [6]. This approach requires both to estimate the model parameters and to compute a similarity measure to match the distributions.

Apart from what descriptors are used, computing a similarity measure between feature sets is crucial for most approaches. Measuring similarities is particularly adapted to categorization when one prototype of each category is defined in the feature space. In this context the similarity measure is used to find the prototype that best matches an unlabeled image. As pointed out in [7], this framework has provided the best results in image categorization. The main reason is that categorization based on similarity corresponds well to the way human beings recognize visual classes. Indeed human visual categories are mostly defined by similarity to prototype examples, as it results from research on cognitive psychology [8]. Taking advantage of these results, we propose a new categorization technique that is based on category prototypes and uses a similarity measure between feature set distributions.

1.2   Proposed Statistical Approach

The categorization method that we propose consists of two steps: the training step and the classification step. The training consists in selecting one prototype per category among a set of labeled images (training set). The classification step assigns to an unlabeled image (query image) the label of its closest prototype. Both training and query images are represented by their sets of Sparse Multiscale Patches (*SMP*s).

We have designed the *SMP* descriptors in order to exploit local multiscale properties of images, which generally convey relevant information about their category. Indeed *SMP*s describe local spatial structures of images at different scales by taking into account dependencies between multiscale coefficients across scale, space and color channels. An image is represented by the set of its *SMP*s at each scale and we measure the similarity between two images as the closeness between their *SMP* probability density functions (*pdf*). Namely we combine their Kullback-Leibler divergence, which has already shown good performances in the context of image retrieval [9].

We use this *SMP* similarity measure in both steps of the categorization, as depicted in the block diagram of Figure 1. During the training step we compute all pairwise *SMP*-based "distances" between images of the same training category C, thus obtaining a distance matrix for this category (see left column of Fig. 1). The entry $s_{i,j}$ of this matrix represents the distance between the image I_i (query image) and the image I_j (reference image); we denote this distance as $S(I_i|I_j)$. The distance matrix is used to select the prototype J_C, which we define as the image minimizing the distance to all other images of the same category:

$$J_C = \operatorname*{argmin}_{j|I_j \in C} \sum_{i|I_i \in C} s_{i,j} \tag{1}$$

Applying the same method to all training categories yields one prototype for each category in terms of *SMP* feature sets.[1]

In the second phase, which is the categorization, we compute the *SMP* similarity of an unlabeled image Q to all category prototypes (see right column of Fig. 1). The query image is given the same label as the nearest prototype.

1.3 Organization of the Paper

In the rest of this paper we explain in more details how the *SMP* similarity measure is defined and give some experimental results of categorization. The *SMP* similarity measure is described in two steps. Firstly we define the proposed feature set of Sparse Multiscale Patches in Section 2. Secondly we define the similarity between *SMP* probability densities in Section 3. We also propose a method for estimating this measure non-parametrically, thus avoiding to model the underlying *pdf*s. Finally, in Section 4, we present some results of performing our categorization method on a subset of the Corel database.

2 Feature Space: Sparse Multiscale Patches

Les us now define our feature space, which is based on a multiresolution decomposition of the images. Throughout the paper, we will denote by $w(I)_{j,k}$ the coefficient for image I at scale j and location in space k for a general multiresolution decomposition.

2.1 Multiscale Patches

The wavelet transform enjoys several properties that have made it quite successful in signal processing and it naturally yields good candidates for image

---

[1] Note that the proximity matrix is not symmetric here $s_{i,j} \neq s_{j,i}$.

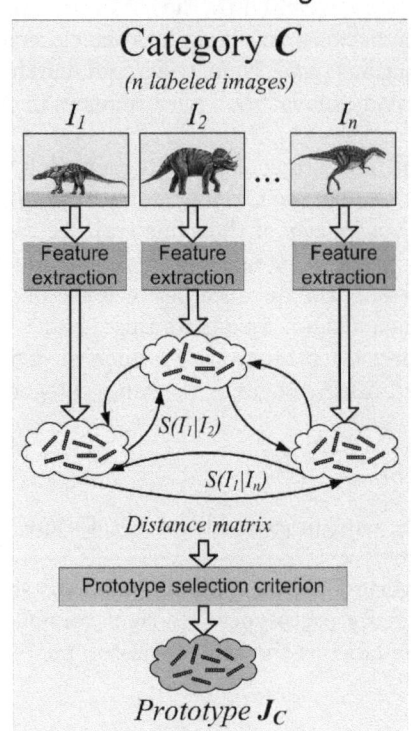
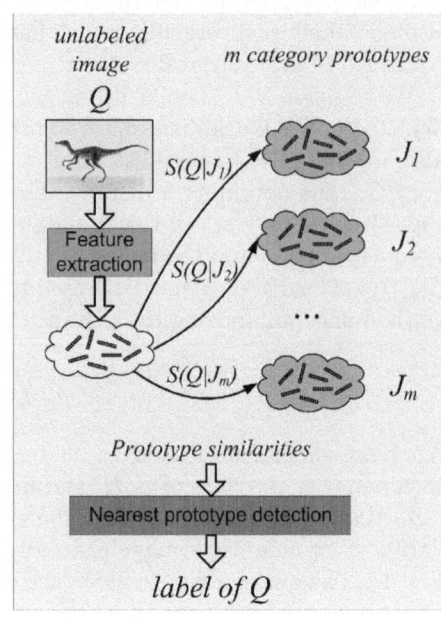

Fig. 1. Overview of the proposed method for image categorization

descriptors. Indeed, it provides a sparse representation of images, meaning that it concentrates the informational content of an image into few coefficients of large amplitude while the rest of the coefficients are small. Classical wavelet methods focus on these large coefficients and treat them separately, relying on their decorrelation, to efficiently process images. However, wavelet coefficients are not independent and these dependencies are the signature of structures present in the image. These dependencies have then been exploited in image enhancement (e.g [10,11]). In particular, the authors of [10] introduced the concept of patches of wavelet coefficients (called "neighborhoods of wavelet coefficients") to represent efficiently fine spatial structures in images.

Following these ideas, we define a feature space based on a sparse description of the image content by a multiresolution decomposition. More precisely, we group the Laplacian pyramid coefficients of the three color channels of image I into coherent sets called patches. Here the coherence is sought by grouping coefficients linked to a particular scale j and location k in the image.

In fact, the most significant dependencies are seen between a coefficient $w(I)_{j,k}$ and its closest neighbors in space: $w(I)_{j,k\pm(0,1)}$, $w(I)_{j,k\pm(1,0)}$ and in scale: $w(I)_{j-1,k}$, where scale $j-1$ is coarser than scale j. Grouping the closest neighbors

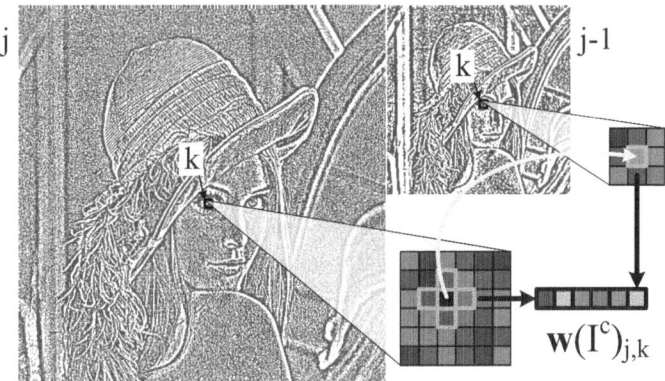

Fig. 2. Building a patch of multiscale coefficients, for a single color channel image

in scale and space of the coefficient $w(I)_{j,k}$ in a vector, we obtain the patch $\vec{w}(I)_{j,k}$ (see Fig. 2):

$$\vec{w}(I)_{j,k} = \left(w(I)_{j,k}, w(I)_{j,k\pm(1,0)}, w(I)_{j,k\pm(0,1)}, w(I)_{j-1,k}\right) \qquad (2)$$

which describes the structure of the grayscale image I at scale j and location k. The probability density functions of such patches at each scale j has proved to characterize fine spatial structures in grayscale images [10,12].

We consider color images in the luminance/chrominance space: $I=(I^Y, I^U, I^V)$. Since the coefficients are correlated through channels, we aggregate in the patch the coefficients of the three channels:

$$\mathbf{w}(I)_{j,k} = \left(\vec{w}(I^Y)_{j,k}, \vec{w}(I^U)_{j,k}, \vec{w}(I^V)_{j,k}\right) \qquad (3)$$

The low-frequency approximation that results from the Laplacian pyramid is also used to build additional feature vectors. The 3×3 pixel neighborhoods along the three channels are joined to form patches of dimension 27 (whereas patches from the higher-frequency subbands defined in Eq.(3) are of dimension 18). The union of the higher-frequency and low-frequency patches forms our feature space. For convenience, the patches of this augmented feature space will still be denoted by $\mathbf{w}(I)_{j,k}$.

2.2   Sparse Multiscale Patches

The coefficients are obtained by a Laplacian pyramid decomposition [13]. Indeed, critically sampled tensor wavelet transforms lack rotation and translation invariance and so would the patches made of such coefficients. Hence we prefer to use the Laplacian pyramid which shares the sparsity and inter/intrascale dependency properties with the wavelet transform while being more robust to rotations.

Multiscale coefficients provide a sparse representation of images and, similarly, patches of multiscale coefficients of large overall energy (sum of the square of all coefficients in a patch) also concentrate the information. Since the total number of patches in an image decomposition is 4/3N with N the number of pixels in the image, the number of samples we have in the feature space is quite large as far as measuring a similarity is concerned. The possibility of selecting a small number of patches which represent the whole set well is therefore highly desirable. In practice, we selected a fixed proportion of patches at each scale of the decomposition and proved that the resulting similarity measure (defined in Section 3) remains consistent (see [14] for details). This is exploited to speed up our computations. We now define a similarity on this feature space.

3   Similarity Measure

3.1   Definition

Our goal is to define a similarity measure between two images I_1 and I_2 from their feature space i.e. from their respective set of patches $\{\mathbf{w}(I_1)_{j,k}\}_{j,k}$ and $\{\mathbf{w}(I_2)_{j,k}\}_{j,k}$. When images are clearly similar (e.g. different views of the same scene, images containing similar objects...), their patches $\mathbf{w}(I_1)_{j_l,k_l}$ and $\mathbf{w}(I_2)_{j_l,k_l}$ do not necessarily correspond. Hence a measure comparing geometrically corresponding patches would not be robust to geometric transformations. Thus, we propose to compare the pdfs of these patches. Specifically, for an image I, we consider for each scale j the pdf $p_j(I)$ of the set of patches $\{\mathbf{w}(I)_{j,k}\}_k$.

To compare two pdfs, we use the Kullback-Leibler (KL) divergence which derives from the Shannon differential entropy (quantifies the amount of information in a random variable through its pdf). The KL divergence (D_{kl}) is the quantity [9]:

$$D_{kl}(p_1\|p_2) = \int p_1 \log(p_1/p_2). \tag{4}$$

This divergence has been successfully used for other applications in image processing in the pixel domain [15,16], as well as for evaluating the similarity between images using the marginal pdf of the wavelet coefficients [17,18]. We propose to measure the similarity $S(I_1|I_2)$ between two images I_1 and I_2 by summing over scales the divergences between the pdfs $p_j(I_1)$ and $p_j(I_2)$ (with weights α_j that may normalize the contribution of the different scales):

$$S(I_1|I_2) = \sum_j \alpha_j D_{kl}(p_j(I_1)\|p_j(I_2)) \tag{5}$$

3.2   Parametric Approach to the Estimation: Pros and Cons

The estimation of the similarity measure S consists of the evaluation of divergences between pdfs $p_j(I_i)$ of high dimension. This raises two problems. Firstly, estimating the KL divergence, even with a good estimate of the pdfs, is hard because this is an integral in high dimension involving unstable logarithm terms. Secondly, the accurate estimation of a pdf itself is difficult due to the lack of samples in high dimension (curse of dimensionality). The two problems should be embraced together to avoid cumulating both kinds of errors.

Parametrizing the shape of the pdf is not ideal. The KL divergence is easy to compute when it is an analytic function of the pdf parameters. This is the case for generalized Gaussians models, which fit well the marginal pdf of multiscale coefficients [17,18]. However, this model cannot be extended to account for the correlations we want to exploit in multiscale patches. Mixture of Gaussians on contrary are efficient multidimensional models accounting for these correlations [12] but the KL divergence is not an analytic function of the pdf parameters.

Thus, we propose to make no hypothesis on the pdf at hand. We therefore spare the cost of fitting model parameters but we have to estimate the divergences in this non-parametric context. Conceptually, we combine the Ahmad-Lin approximation of the entropies necessary to compute the divergences with "balloon estimate" of the pdfs using the kNN approach.

3.3   Proposed Non-parametric Estimation of the Similarity Measure

The KL divergence can be written as the difference between a cross-entropy H_x and an entropy H (see Eq.(4)):

$$H_x(p_1, p_2) = -\int p_1 \log p_2, \qquad H(p_1) = -\int p_1 \log p_1 \qquad (6)$$

Let us explain how to estimate these terms from i.i.d sample sets $\mathcal{W}^i = \{\mathbf{w}_1^i, \mathbf{w}_2^i, ..., \mathbf{w}_{N_i}^i\}$ of p_i for $i = 1$ or 2 (The samples are in $\mathbb{R}^d$.) Assuming we have estimates $\widehat{p_1}$, $\widehat{p_2}$ of the pdfs p_1, p_2, we use the Ahmad-Lin entropy estimators [19]:

$$H_x^{al}(\widehat{p_1}, \widehat{p_2}) = -\frac{1}{N_1} \sum_{n=1}^{N_1} \log[\widehat{p_2}(\mathbf{w}_n^1)], \qquad H^{al}(\widehat{p_1}) = -\frac{1}{N_1} \sum_{n=1}^{N_1} \log[\widehat{p_1}(\mathbf{w}_n^1)] \qquad (7)$$

to obtain a first estimator of the KL divergence:

$$D_{kl}^{al}(\widehat{p_1}, \widehat{p_2}) = \frac{1}{N_1} \sum_{n=1}^{N_1} \log[\widehat{p_1}(\mathbf{w}_n^1)] - \log[\widehat{p_2}(\mathbf{w}_n^1)]. \qquad (8)$$

General non-parametric pdf estimators from samples can be written as a sum of kernels K with possibly varying bandwidth h (see [20] for a review):

$$\widehat{p_1}(x) = \frac{1}{N_1} \sum_{n=1}^{N_1} K_{h(\mathcal{W}^1, x)}(x - \mathbf{w}_n^1) \qquad (9)$$

We use a balloon estimator i.e. the bandwidth $h(\mathcal{W}^1, x) = h_{\mathcal{W}^1}(x)$ adapts to the point of estimation x given the sample set $\mathcal{W}^1$. The kernel is binary and the bandwidth is computed in the k-th nearest neighbor (kNN) framework [20]:

$$K_{h(\mathcal{W}^1, x)}(x - \mathbf{w}_n^1) = \frac{1}{v_d \, \rho_{k,\mathcal{W}^1}^d(x)} \, \delta\left[||x - \mathbf{w}_n^1|| < \rho_{k,\mathcal{W}^1}(x)\right] \qquad (10)$$

with v_d the volume of the unit sphere in $\mathbb{R}^d$ and $\rho_{k,\mathcal{W}}(x)$ the distance of x to its k-th nearest neighbor in $\mathcal{W}$. This is a dual approach to the fixed size kernel methods and was firstly proposed in [21]: the bandwidth adapts to the local sample density by letting the kernel contain exactly k neighbors of x among a given sample set.

Although this is a biased pdf estimator (it does not integrate to one), it has proved to be efficient for high-dimensional data [20]. Plugging Eq.(10) in Eq.(8), we obtain the following estimator of the KL divergence, which is valid in any dimension d and robust to the choice of k: [2]

$$D_{kl}(p_1\|p_2) = \log\left[\frac{N_2}{N_1-1}\right] + \frac{d}{N_1}\sum_{n=1}^{N_1}\log[\rho_{k,\mathcal{W}^2}(\mathbf{w}_n^1)] - \frac{d}{N_1}\sum_{n=1}^{N_1}\log[\rho_{k,\mathcal{W}^1}(\mathbf{w}_n^1)] \quad (11)$$

4   Experiments

4.1   Database and Parameter Settings

An experimental evaluation of the *SMP* method has been made on a subset of the Corel database. It includes 1,000 images of size 384×256 or 256×384 which are classified in ten semantic categories (*Africa, Beach, Buildings, Buses, Dinosaurs, Flowers, Elephants, Horses, Food, Mountains*). This dataset is well known in the domain of content-based image retrieval and particularly it has been widely used to evaluate several methods of image categorization, like in [22], [23], [4] and [24].

The *SMP* descriptors of images were extracted as described in Section 2. In particular, to build the patches, the Laplacian pyramid was computed for each channel of the image (in the YUV color space) with a 5-point binomial filter $w5 = [1\ 4\ 6\ 4\ 1]/16$, which is a computationally efficient approximation of the Gaussian filter classically used to build Laplacian pyramids. Two high-frequency subbands and the low-frequency approximation were used. In the following experiments, 1/16 (resp. 1/8 and all) of the patches were selected in the first high-frequency (resp. second high-frequency and low-frequency) subband to describe an image (see Section 2.1). At each scale, the KL divergence was estimated in the kNN framework, with k = 10. The contributions to the similarity measure of the divergences in all subbands were equally weighted ($\alpha_j = 1$ in Eq. (5)).

Since the computation of KL divergences is a time-consuming task, we developed a parallel implementation of the kNN search on a Graphic Processing Unit (GPU) [25]. This implementation is based on a brute-force approach and was run on a NVIDIA GeForce 8800 GTX GPU (with 768 MB of internal memory). The computation of one similarity measure between two images required 0.1 s on average.

4.2   Categorization Results

In order to allow the prototype learning, we have randomly split the whole image set into a training set and a test set. We have tested our method for different

---

[2] Note that in the log term, N_1 has been replaced by $N_1 - 1$, which corresponds to ommitting the current sample $\mathbf{w}_i^1$ in the set $\mathcal{W}^1$ when estimating the entropy (Eq. (7) and (9)).

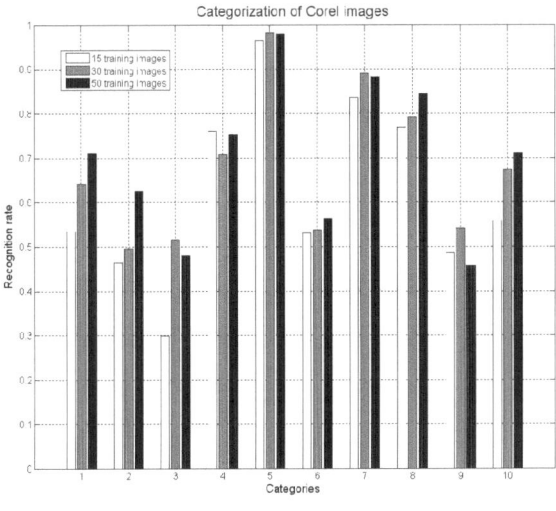

Cat. 1 *Africa*   Cat. 2 *Beach*   Cat. 3 *Buildings*   Cat. 4 *Buses*   Cat. 5 *Dinosaurs*

Cat. 6 *Elephants* Cat. 7 *Flowers*   Cat. 8 *Horses*   Cat. 9 *Mountains*   Cat. 10 *Food*

Fig. 3. Top: average recognition rate per category for 15, 30 and 50 training images per category. All results are averaged over 10 experiments with different randomly chosen training sets. Bottom: prototype images for one particular choice of the training sets.

sizes of the training set (15, 30 and 50 images per category), while using all the remaining images as a test set. For each value of the training set size we have repeated the same experiment ten times; hence all reported results are averaged over ten experiments with identical parameter values.

These results are shown in Fig. 3 in terms of the average recognition rate per category. This rate corresponds to the average proportion of correct classification as a function of the number of training images. We can see that the accuracy of categorization is quite stable with the size of the training set. In the same figure we can see an example of which images are selected as prototypes from the training set.

We have also measured the accuracy of our method by using a criterion for rejecting unreliable categorization results, so as to reduce the probability of mis-classifications. Namely we have empirically fixed a threshold value for the query-to-prototype distance. Hence, whenever the *SMP*-based "distance" between the

Table 1. The confusion matrix resulting from our image categorization experiments (over 10 randomly generated training sets containing 50 images per category). Entry on the row i and column j is the average percentage (over the 10 experiments) of images belonging to the category i which have been classified into the category j (see Fig. 3 for category names). The last column lists the percentage of non-classified images for each category.

	Cat. 1	Cat. 2	Cat. 3	Cat. 4	Cat. 5	Cat. 6	Cat. 7	Cat. 8	Cat. 9	Cat. 10	reject
Cat. 1	**74.8**	4.2	6.8	0.6	0.0	3.2	0.4	0	1.6	0.4	8.0
Cat. 2	2.0	**56.4**	5.4	0.4	0.0	4.4	0.0	0.0	21.4	0.0	10.0
Cat. 3	7.8	4.0	**74.0**	1.4	0.0	1.6	0.6	0.0	3.8	0.0	6.8
Cat. 4	0.6	1.4	9.4	**73.4**	0.0	0.0	0.0	0.0	1.2	0.2	13.8
Cat. 5	0.0	0.0	0.2	0.0	**88.8**	0.0	0.0	0.0	0.0	0.4	10.6
Cat. 6	4.2	0.6	0.4	0.0	0.0	**87.8**	0.0	0.8	1.8	0.6	3.8
Cat. 7	3.0	0.0	0.0	0.0	0.0	0.0	**89.0**	0.6	0.0	0.0	7.4
Cat. 8	1.2	0.4	0.0	0.0	0.0	1.2	0.4	**91.4**	0.6	0.0	4.8
Cat. 9	0.2	14.0	5.0	0.4	0.0	5.8	1.0	0.0	**62.0**	0.2	11.4
Cat. 10	12.8	1.8	8.2	1.2	0.4	2.4	0.0	0.0	1.2	**55.6**	16.4

query image and its nearest prototype is larger than the threshold, we reject the result, thus giving no label to the image. Table 1 contains the confusion matrix which summarizes the categorization results for the case of 50 training images per category. The generic element $a_{i,j}$ of this matrix represents the average percentage of the test images belonging to category i which have been classified into category j. Therefore, the entries on the main diagonal show the categorization accuracy for each category. On the contrary, off-diagonal entries show classification errors. Interestingly note that big values of some of these entries are related to a certain semantic "intersection" between two different categories. This is particularly clear for misclassifications between categories 2 (*Beaches*) and 9 (*Mountains*), since several images belonging to these categories share similar visual patterns (e.g. rocky seaside pictures are visually similar to mountain sceneries containing lakes or rivers).

Our method shows good overall categorization performances, typically of the same order of magnitude as those of state-of-the-art methods developed by Chen and colleagues [22,4], although not as accurate on some categories". This can be explained by the difficulty of choosing a representative prototype amongst the training images. Indeed, for diverse categories, the classification rate may vary a lot according to the randomly chosen training set which yields to choosing different prototypes. For example, in the category "Africa", some training sets lead to a prototype being a picture of a face (as displayed in Fig. 3) while others lead to village picture prototypes. Different methods are under study to tackle the problem of prototype selection, one of which being to create a poll of representative *SMP*s to define a *pdf* prototype. The patch selection strategy presented here is also basic: one retains a predefined percentage of the patches at each scale. The selection does not adapt to the specificity of the image considered and thus probably results in taking into account outliers of the underlying *pdf*s. Therefore we also study adaptive patch selection strategies. Considering the large prototype variations and the simplistic patch selection process used, the reasonably good performances obtained here show that the *SMP* similarity measure is promising regarding the classification step.

5 Conclusion

In this paper we tackled the task of image categorization by using a new image similarity framework. It is based on high-dimensional probability distributions of patches of multiscale coefficients which we call *Sparse Multiscale Patches or SMPs*. Image signatures are represented by sets of patches of subband coefficients, that take into account their intrascale, interscale and interchannel dependencies. The similarity between images is defined as the "closeness" between the distributions of their signatures, measured by the Kullback-Leibler divergence. The latter is estimated in a non-parametric framework, via a *k-th nearest neighbor* or kNN approach.

Our approach to image classification is to represent each category by an image prototype. The latter is defined as the image minimizing the *SMP*-based measure with all other images in the category's training set.

The experiments we made on a subset of the Corel collection show that the *SMP* similarity measure is a promising tool for the categorization problem. The prototype selection as well as the patch selection are to be improved and are among the subjects of ongoing work.

References

1. Szummer, M., Picard, R.W.: Indoor-outdoor image classification. In: CAIVD 1998: Proceedings of the 1998 International Workshop on Content-Based Access of Image and Video Databases (CAIVD 1998), Washington, DC, USA, p. 42. IEEE Computer Society, Los Alamitos (1998)
2. Vailaya, A., Figueiredo, M., Jain, A., Zhang, H.J.: Image classification for content-based indexing. IEEE Transactions on Image Processing 10, 117–130 (2001)
3. Li, J., Wang, J.Z.: Automatic linguistic indexing of pictures by a statistical modeling approach. IEEE Trans. Pattern Anal. Mach. Intell. 25, 1075–1088 (2003)
4. Bi, J., Chen, Y., Wang, J.Z.: A sparse support vector machine approach to region-based image categorization. In: CVPR 2005, pp. 1121–1128 (2005)
5. Lazebnik, S., Schmid, C., Ponce, J.: Beyond bags of features: Spatial pyramid matching for recognizing natural scene categories. In: CVPR, vol. (2), pp. 2169–2178 (2006)
6. Liu, Y., Perronnin, F.: A similarity measure between unordered vector sets with application to image categorization. In: CVPR (2008)
7. Zhang, H., Berg, A.C., Maire, M., Malik, J.: Svm-knn: Discriminative nearest neighbor classification for visual category recognition. In: CVPR, vol. (2), pp. 2126–2136 (2006)
8. Rosch, E., Mervis, C.B., Gray, W.D., Johnson, D.M., Braem, P.B.: Basic objects in natural categories. Cognitive Psychology 8, 382–439 (1976)

9. Puzicha, J., Rubner, Y., Tomasi, C., Buhmann, J.M.: Empirical evaluation of dissimilarity measures for color and texture. In: ICCV, pp. 1165–1172 (1999)
10. Portilla, J., Strela, V., Wainwright, M., Simoncelli, E.P.: Image denoising using a scale mixture of Gaussians in the wavelet domain. TIP 12, 1338–1351 (2003)
11. Romberg, J.K., Choi, H., Baraniuk, R.G.: Bayesian tree-structured image modeling using wavelet-domain hidden markov models. TIP 10, 1056–1068 (2001)
12. Pierpaoli, E., Anthoine, S., Huffenberger, K., Daubechies, I.: Reconstructing sunyaev-zeldovich clusters in future cmb experiments. Mon. Not. Roy. Astron. Soc. 359, 261–271 (2005)
13. Burt, P.J., Adelson, E.H.: The Laplacian pyramid as a compact image code. IEEE Trans. Communications 31, 532–540 (1983)
14. Piro, P., Anthoine, S., Debreuve, E., Barlaud, M.: Image retrieval via kullback-leibler divergence of patches of multiscale coefficients in the knn framework. In: CBMI, London, UK (2008)
15. Boltz, S., Debreuve, E., Barlaud, M.: High-dimensional kullback-leibler distance for region-of-interest tracking: Application to combining a soft geometric constraint with radiometry. In: CVPR, Minneapolis, USA (2007)
16. Angelino, C.V., Debreuve, E., Barlaud, M.: Image restoration using a knn-variant of the mean-shift. In: ICIP, San Diego, USA (2008)
17. Do, M., Vetterli, M.: Wavelet based texture retrieval using generalized Gaussian density and Kullback-Leibler distance. TIP 11, 146–158 (2002)
18. Wang, Z., Wu, G., Sheikh, H.R., Simoncelli, E.P., Yang, E.H., Bovik, A.C.: Quality-aware images. TIP 15, 1680–1689 (2006)
19. Ahmad, I., Lin, P.E.: A nonparametricestimationof the entropy absolutely continuousdistributions. IEEE Trans. Inform. Theory 22, 372–375 (1976)
20. Terrell, G.R., Scott, D.W.: Variable kernel density estimation. The Annals of Statistics 20, 1236–1265 (1992)
21. Loftsgaarden, D., Quesenberry, C.: A nonparametric estimate of a multivariate density function. AMS 36, 1049–1051 (1965)
22. Chen, Y., Wang, J.Z.: Image categorization by learning and reasoning with regions. J. Mach. Learn. Res. 5, 913–939 (2004)
23. Li, T., Kweon, I.S.: A semantic region descriptor for local feature based image categorization. In: ICASSP 2008, pp. 1333–1336 (2008)
24. Zhu, Y., Liu, X., Mio, W.: Content-based image categorization and retrieval using neural networks. In: ICME 2007, pp. 528–531 (2007)
25. Garcia, V., Debreuve, E., Barlaud, M.: Fast k nearest neighbor search using gpu. In: CVPR Workshop on Computer Vision on GPU (2008)

Multiple-Instance Active Learning for Image Categorization[*]

Dong Liu[1], Xian-Sheng Hua[2], Linjun Yang[2], and Hong-Jiang Zhang[3]

[1] School of Computer Science and Technology, Harbin Institute of Technology,
150001, Harbin, Heilongjiang, China
[2] Microsoft Research Asia, 100190, Beijing, China
[3] Microsoft Advanced Technology Center, 100190, Beijing, China
dongliu@hit.edu.cn, xshua@microsoft.com, linjuny@microsoft.com,
hjzhang@microsoft.com

Abstract. Both multiple-instance learning and active learning are widely employed in image categorization, but generally they are applied separately. This paper studies the integration of these two methods. Different from typical active learning approaches, the sample selection strategy in multiple-instance active learning needs to handle samples in different granularities, that is, instance/region and bag/image. Three types of sample selection strategies are evaluated: (1) selecting bags only; (2) selecting instances only; and (3) selecting both bags and instances. As there is no existing method for the third case, we propose a set kernel based classifier, based on which, a unified bag and/or instance selection criterion and an integrated learning algorithm are built. The experiments on *Corel* dataset show that selecting both bags and instances outperforms the other two strategies.

Keywords: Multiple-Instance Learning, Active Learning, Bag & Instance mixture selection, Image Categorization.

1 Introduction

There has been significant work on applying multiple-instance (MI) learning to image categorization [1,2]. Key assumptions of these works are that each image is represented as a bag which consists of segmented regions as instances and a bag receives a particular label if at least one of its constitutive instances possesses the label. In MI learning, it is difficult to predict the labels of instances given the bags' labels. This difficulty is so-called MI ambiguity. Active learning is also a widely applied method in image categorization as it can significantly reduce the human cost in labeling training images. In its setting, the learner has access to a large pool of unlabeled images and selects the most valuable images for manual annotation, such that the obtained training set is more effective. Although promising performance on image categorization has been reported using these two methods, they are generally applied separately.

---

[*] This work was performed when Dong Liu was visiting Microsoft Research Asia as an intern.

B. Huet et al. (Eds.): MMM 2009, LNCS 5371, pp. 239–249, 2009.

In this paper, we study the integration of multiple-instance learning and active learning in image categorization application. A first attempt on MI active learning [3] proposes a strategy that selectively labels certain portion of instances from positive training bags. It firstly trains a MI logistic regression classifier, then computes MI uncertainty of each instance in positive training bags using current classifier's prediction probability and selects the instance with the highest uncertainty as the next querying sample. After the corresponding instance label is provided by the oracle, it updates the training set by adding a new singleton bag containing only a copy of the queried instance. The MI classifier is retrained on the expanded training set with mixed-granularity labels and hence the MI classifier's performance can be improved.

We argue that whereas the above method works well for MIL by selecting only instances of labeled bags for labeling, MIL based image categorization can also benefit from selectively labeling some unlabeled bags. For MI learning, labeling instance and labeling bag provide different information to the classifier in different cases. For example, if the chosen bag is labeled positive, then it provides less information compared with labeling a positive instance in that bag, because in this case the label of the bag can be inferred from the label of the instance, but it is difficult to get the instance label through the bag label. On the other hand, if the chosen bag is labeled as negative, it provides more information then labeling any instance in that bag. Although labeling instance and labeling bag can benefit the MI classifier, it remains a problem which is the most effective labeling way for MI active learning, labeling bags, labeling instances, or labeling bags & instances simultaneously.

In this paper, we conduct a comparative study on three different MI active learning sample selection strategies for image categorization, including selecting bags only, selecting instances only, and selecting bags and instances simultaneously. As there is no existing method for the third case, we need to build a mixed bag and/or instance sample selection framework to perform MI active learning.

To develop such a unified MI active learning approach, two crucial problems need to be solved. One is a unified MI classifier which can classify instances as well as bags. The other is the sample selection criterion, which can maximally reduce the classification error by selecting the most valuable samples for labeling.

The unified MI classifier is realized using standard SVM with a MI normalized set kernel. By treating instances as singleton bags which comprise only one instance, the MI normalized kernel can be employed to estimate the similarity between bags and bags, instances and instances, bags and instances. To select the most informative samples, regardless of bags or instances, a MI informativeness measure that takes uncertainty, novelty and diversity into consideration is proposed to query unlabeled samples from the querying pool for labeling.

The experiments are conducted on *Corel* dataset. By comparing three different sample selection strategies: selecting instances, selecting bags, and selecting the mixture of bags & instances, we can conclude that: (1) selecting the mixture of bags & instances performs the best in most of the active learning querying rounds;

(2) selecting instances performs better than selecting bags when selected samples are few while selecting bags performs better when more samples are selected.

The rest of this paper is organized as follows. Section 2 presents a framework for MI active learning. Section 3 describes the experiments to evaluate three different sample selection strategies for MI active learning on benchmark CBIR dataset. Section 4 concludes the paper.

2   MI Active Learning

In this section, two critical problems in MI active learning, including the unified bag/instance classifier and the sample selection criterion, are addressed. In order to construct a MI classifier, which can classify bags (images) as well as instances (image regions) in a unified fashion, a MI set kernel is adopted, as described in section 2.1. With the MI set kernel, standard SVM is employed as the classifier for both bags and instances. In section 2.2, the MI sample selection criterion is proposed to maximize the performance of the classifier. The MI active learning framework is presented in section 2.3.

2.1   MI Set Kernel

To build a unified MI classifier which can classify instances as well as bags, we need to estimate the similarity between bags and bags, instances and instances, bags and instances. To this end, we adopt a particular MI kernel called normalized set kernel [4] in the learning of SVM. A kernel on sets can be derived from the definition of convolution kernels and can be formally represented as follows,

$$k_{set}(B, B^{'}) = \sum_{x \in B, x^{'} \in B^{'}} k(x, x^{'}) \tag{1}$$

where $k(., .)$ is any valid kernel function defined on instances, B and $B^{'}$ are two bags with x, $x^{'}$ are the corresponding instances. If the cardinalities of bags vary considerably, bag with large cardinalities will dominate the set kernel estimation. To overcome this problem, a natural normalization is given

$$k_{nset}(B, B^{'}) = \frac{k_{set}(B, B^{'})}{\sqrt{k_{set}(B, B)}\sqrt{k_{set}(B^{'}, B^{'})}} \tag{2}$$

To estimate the kernel between the bag B and the instance b, we can regard the instance as a singleton bag which consists of only one instance. Thus the kernel can be defined as follows,

$$k_{nset}(B, b) = k_{nset}(B, \{b\}) \tag{3}$$

where B is the bag and b is the instance.

Accordingly, the kernel between two instances can also be defined in the same way,

$$k_{nset}(b, b') = k_{nset}(\{b\}, \{b'\})$$
$$= \frac{k(b, b')}{\sqrt{k(b, b)}\sqrt{k(b', b')}} \qquad (4)$$

which is degenerated to be the usual normalized kernel.

Once the kernel between bags and bags, instances and instances, bags and instances, is defined, by employing standard SVM, a unified multiple-instance classifier, which can predict the label of bags as well as instances, is constructed.

2.2 MI Sample Selection Criterion

In active learning, the most "informative" samples to the classifier learning should be selected for labeling by oracles firstly, so as to maximally reduce the classification error. Some heuristic rules, such as uncertainty and diversity, are proposed to approximate the "informativeness" measure. In this paper, we approach the "informativeness" by taking multiple measures including uncertainty, novelty, and diversity, into consideration. As a result, a MI sample selection criterion is proposed by fusing the multiple measures.

Uncertainty. Tong [5,6] proposed a SVM active learning sample selection criterion from the perspective of version space, aiming at selecting the unlabeled samples which can provide most valuable information for the retraining of current SVM classifier. The basic idea is to find the unlabeled sample which results in the maximal reduction of the version space. An efficient implementation of this idea is to select the sample which is the closest to the SVM hyperplane in the kernel space. In other words, the samples with the largest $1 - |f(x)|$ are selected for labeling by oracles, where $f(x)$ is the prediction score of the sample x by the SVM classifier, as defined in the below from the dual view,

$$f(x) = \sum_{i=1}^{l} \alpha_i k_{nset}(x, x_i) + b \qquad (5)$$

where α_i is the coefficient and b is the offset.

The measure is called uncertainty in that the sample with larger $1 - |f(x)|$ is closer to the classification boundary $f(x) = 0$ and can be regarded the more uncertain to the prediction.

The uncertainty measure can be defined as follows

$$u(x) = 1 - |f(x)| \qquad (6)$$

Where x is a unlabeled sample and f is the decision function.

Novelty. One intuitive assumption in the sample selection is that the samples will be selected with less chance if they are similar to the existing training data. In other words, the samples which are more novel to the training data should be selected with higher probability. The novelty criterion aims to select the samples with minimum overlapping with the existing training samples and enforces that the redundancy in the training samples is minimized.

The novelty measure can be defined as follows,

$$d(x_j) = 1 - max_{1 \leq i \leq l} k_{nset}(x_i, x_j) \tag{7}$$

where x_j is the unlabeled sample and x_i is an existing training sample and l refers to the number of samples in the training set.

Diversity. In this paper, the MI active learning problem we would like to address is batch-mode active learning, i.e., we select multiple samples at one time and query for their labels before putting them into the training set. As shown in [7], the redundancy among the selected unlabeled samples at each query round needs to be reduced to maximally utilize the human labeler's labor. Thus the sample set, which comprises multiple unlabeled samples, with little inter similarity will be preferred to be selected together for labeling. The diversity among the sample set can be estimated by averaging similarities among the samples. Given a set of n selected unlabeled samples $U = \{x_1, x_2, \cdots, x_n\}$ that contains either bags or instances, the redundancy of the $(n+1)th$ sample x_{n+1} with them can be formulated as

$$r(x_{n+1}) = 1 - \sum_{i=1}^{n} k_{nset}(x_{n+1}, x_i)/n \tag{8}$$

MI Informativeness. Now we propose a MI sample selection criterion called MI informativeness based on the above three criteria. According to the theoretical analysis [8], it's more rational to use the diversity measure as a weight of the novelty measure than linearly combine them. Thus we weight the novelty with the diversity, and then linearly combine it with the uncertainty as

$$MI\_Informativeness(u_i) = \lambda \times u(u_i) + (1 - \lambda) \times d(u_i) \times r(u_i) \tag{9}$$

where λ is the trade-off parameter to adjust the individual importance of each criterion, u_i is the unlabeled sample. With the proposed MI informativeness sample selection criterion as defined in Equation (9), the most informative samples which are deemed to maximally benefit the classification learning are selected for labeling and then added to the training set.

2.3   A MI Active Learning Framework

Based on the MI set kernel and the MI informativeness sample selection criterion presented above, a MI active learning framework is proposed and summarized in algorithm 1. Three variant sample selection strategies can be applied in our MI active learning framework based on the type of query sample pool, including bags, instances, and bags & instances.

Algorithm 1. A MI Active Learning Framework

Require: L,initial training data;

$U = \{u_1, u_2, \cdots, u_N\}$,initial pool of samples to be selected for labeling;

n, the number of samples to be queried at each round;

m, the number of rounds.

Ensure: f,the trained classifier.

1. Initialization. Train the initial SVM classifier using the initial training data L, $f = SVM\_Train(L)$. The kernel is defined as Equation (2), (3), and (4).

2. Active Learning.

Repeat m rounds:

a. $S = \Phi$.

b. Repeat until $|S| = n$

- $x = argmax_{u_i \in U} MI\_Informative(u_i)$.
- $S = S \bigcup \{x\}$
- $U = U - \{x\}$

c. $L = L \bigcup S$

d. Retrain the SVM classifier using the new training set L. $f = SVM\_Train(L)$.

- Bags. Only the images in the test data set are selected for labeling, i.e. $u = \{B_i\}, i = 1, 2, \cdots, N$.
- Instances. Only regions in positive training images are selected for labeling, i.e. $u = \{b_i\}, i = 1, \cdots, N$ where b_i is a singleton bag that contains only a region in a positive training image.
- Bags & Instances. The pool u is composed of both testing images and regions of positive training images.

Our MI active learning framework mainly consists of two steps. The first step is to learn a MI normalized set kernel matrix using the initial training data L and train the initial SVM classifier. The second step is the active learning iterative procedure, in which we apply the proposed sample selection criterion to select the samples with maximum MI informativeness for labeling.

3   Experiments

In this section, we will evaluate three different sample selection strategies for MI active learning on *Corel* image data set. For convenience, we will name the bag and instance selecting strategy as mixed selecting strategy and the other two selecting strategies as bag only and instance only strategy, respectively. Firstly, we compare our active sample selection strategy with random sample selection strategy to confirm the effectiveness of MI active learning. Then we conduct experiments to evaluate the performances of three different sample selection strategies for MI active learning. We use *libSVM* [9] as kernel learner and RBF as basic kernel for normalized set kernel. The parameters γ and C for RBF

Fig. 1. Sample images from *Corel*

and SVM are determined through 10-fold cross validation. The parameter λ in Equation (9) is fixed to 0.7.

3.1 Experimental Testbed and Setup

We adopt the image data set with region labels in [10] as our test bed. This data set consists of 11 classes with 4002 natural scene images from *Corel*. These images are segmented using JSEG [11] into average 26 regions. Then 9-dimensional color moment in HSV color space and 20-dimensional Pyramid-structured wavelet texture are combined into a 29-dimensional region-level feature vector. The detail information of this data set is shown in Table 1. Some sample images form *Corel* are shown in Figure 1.

In the active learning experiments, the learner begins with 20 randomly drawn positive images and 20 random negative images as the initial training data while the remaining images are used as unlabeled test data. The samples are selected at each round from the unlabeled test images for labeling bag label, from the regions in the positive training images for labeling instance label, or both. The remaining samples in the test data are used for performance evaluation. The query batch size n is set to 10 and the query round m to 18 respectively.

The measure used to evaluate the performance of the active learning methods is AUROC [12], which is the area under the ROC curve. Five independent runs are conducted for each image class in the *Corel* data set and the results are averaged as the performance evaluation.

Following previous work on SVM active learning [13], we operate SVM using a kernel correction method which guarantees that the training set is linearly separable in kernel space [14]. This is done by modifying the kernel matrix K so that each diagonal element is added by a constant ξ and the all other elements remain the same. In all experiments in this paper, we fix $\xi = 4$ empirically.

3.2 Performance Evaluation

We firstly compare the average performance of MI active learning with that of random sample selection strategy on *Corel* dataset. From Figure 2, it can

Table 1. Detail Information For Corel Dataset

Concept	Image Num	Region Num	Concept	Image Num	Region Num
Water	1690	9257	Sky	3382	13540
Flower	251	1701	Mountain	1215	9809
Building	1852	19422	Rock	580	6573
Grass	1660	12820	Earth	953	7598
Animal	477	2699	Tree	2234	19454
Ground	553	1753	ALL	4002	104626

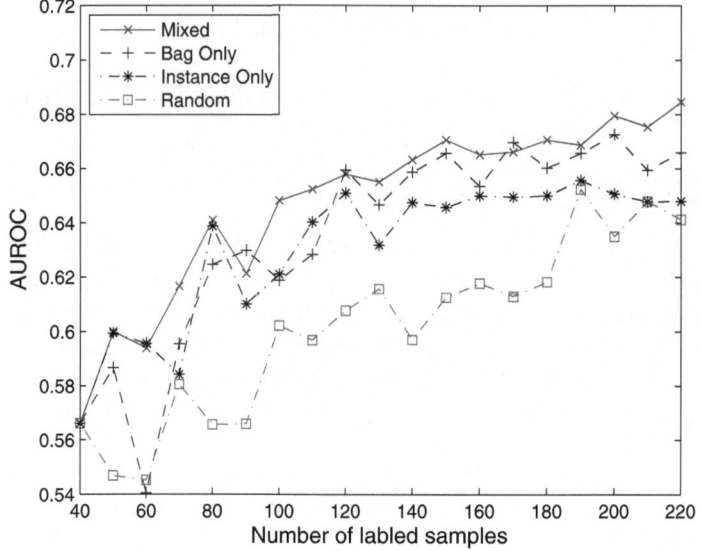

Fig. 2. The Performance of Different Querying Strategies

be observed that MI active learning methods perform significantly better than random sampling on all of the three sample selection strategies, including bags only, instances only, and the mixed bags & instances. This experimental result demonstrates that the proposed MI active learning framework is effective and helps to learn the classifier quickly.

We further conduct experiments to compare the bag & instance mixed selecting strategy with bag only and instance only selecting strategies. The average performances of the mixed selecting strategy, the bag only selecting strategy, and the instance only selecting strategy for MI active learning are shown in Figure 2. It's clear that the performance of the mixed selecting strategy is better than that of the bag only and instance only selecting strategies. We can also observe that instance selecting strategy performs better than bag selecting at the early query rounds. However, as the query rounds proceed as well as more and more samples are added into the training set, the bag selecting strategy shows better performance than instance selecting strategy.

Table 2. Average AUROC Improvement On *Corel*

Query Round	Random	Bag	Instance	Mixed
1	-0.019	+0.021	+0.033	*+0.034*
2	-0.021	-0.026	*+0.030*	+0.028
3	+0.015	+0.029	+0.018	*+0.050*
4	-0.001	+0.058	+0.072	*+0.075*
5	-0.001	*+0.064*	+0.044	+0.055
6	+0.036	+0.052	+0.055	*+0.082*
7	+0.031	+0.062	+0.074	*+0.086*
8	+0.042	*+0.093*	+0.085	+0.092
9	+0.050	+0.080	+0.066	*+0.089*
10	+0.031	+0.092	+0.081	*+0.097*
11	+0.046	+0.099	+0.080	*+0.104*
12	+0.052	+0.087	+0.084	*+0.099*
13	+0.047	*+0.103*	+0.083	+0.100
14	+0.052	+0.094	+0.084	*+0.104*
15	+0.086	+0.100	+0.090	*+0.103*
16	+0.069	+0.106	+0.085	*+0.113*
17	+0.082	+0.093	+0.082	*+0.109*
18	+0.075	+0.100	+0.082	*+0.119*

In Table 2 we summarize the learning curves in Figure 2 by reporting the average AUROC improvement over the initial MI classifier for each querying strategy. The values are averaged across all concepts in *Corel* dataset at each round. The winning strategy at each point is indicated with bold font. It's clear that the mixed selecting strategy improves leaner's performance mostly after a few query rounds, and the instance selecting strategy outperforms bag selecting at early rounds and then lose as query rounds increase.

3.3 Discussion

We can draw some conclusions from our experimental results.

- MI learner's performance can be improved if we select to label certain regions in positive training images. This may owe to the reduction of MI ambiguity in the training images when labels of some regions are provided to MI learner. However, the performance tends to improve gently as more and more regions are selected for labeling. This is reasonable since MI ambiguity cannot be further reduced with only limited training bags after MI learner reaches a certain performance. To further improve learner, more unlabeled bags are needed.
- Bag-only selecting strategy shows terrible performance at the early stage of active samples selection, which may imputes to the MI ambiguity in the training set. As MI ambiguity is solved at some extent after several querying rounds, adding more informative bags into the training set further helps to improve MI learner's generalization performance.

- Bag and instance mixed selecting strategy appears to be the most effective sample selection strategy. It integrates the advantages of both bag selecting and instance selecting strategies. At each query round, both informative instances and bags are selected for labeling. The selected instances help to reduce ambiguity and the selected bags help to improve learner's generalization ability.

4   Conclusion

In this paper, we study multiple-instance active learning with application to image categorization. A MI active learning framework that can query bags, instances or their combination is proposed. Within this framework, a comparative study is conducted on three MI active learning sample selection strategies for image categorization: selecting bags only, selecting instances only, selecting the mixture of bags and instances. Experimental results demonstrate that the mixed sample selection strategy outperforms the other two and appears to be the most effective sample selection strategy for MI active learning in image categorization.The main contribution of this work can be summarized as following:

- By proposing a set kernel based classifier, wc build a unified bag and/or instance instance sample selection strategy and an integrated learning algorithm,which make learning with mixed granularities operable.
- We conduct comparative study for MI active learning on image categorization task and prove that the bag and instance mixed sample selection strategy would be the best suitable strategy for MI active learning in image categorization applications.
- We explore the integration of two widely successful learning methods in image categorization,based on which, a reasonable strategy to improve the performance of MI based image categorization is built.

In the future, we plan to test our multiple-instance active learning strategy on other data collections with region labels and also conduct further research to reveal in principle why bag and instance mixture sample selection strategy benefits the multiple-instance classifier most.

References

1. Maron, O., Ratan, L.: Multiple-Instance learning for natural scene classification. In: Proceedings of the 15th International Conference on Machine Learning, pp. 341–349 (1998)
2. Bunescu, R.C., Mooney, R.J.: Multiple Instance Learning for Sparse Positive Bags. In: Proceedings of the 24th International Conference on Machine Learning, pp. 105–112 (2007)
3. Settles, B., Craven, M., Ray, S.: Multiple-Instance Active Learning. In: Advances in Neural Information Processing Systems (NIPS), vol. 20, pp. 1289–1296 (2007)
4. Gärtner, T., Flach, P., Kowalczyk, A., Smola, A.: Multi-Instance Kernels. In: Proceedings of 19th International Conference on Machine Learning, pp. 179–186 (2002)

5. Tong, S., Koller, D.: Support Vector Machine Active Learning with Applications to Text Classification. Journal of Machine Learning Research 2, 45–66 (2001)
6. Tong, S., Chang, E.: Support Vector Machine Active Learning for Image Retrieval. In: Proceedings of the ninth ACM international conference on Multimedia, pp. 107–118 (2004)
7. Brinker, K.: Incorporating Diversity in Active Learning with Support Vector Machines. In: Proceedings of the 20th International Conference on Machine Learning, pp. 59–66 (2003)
8. Cohn, D., Ghahramani, Z., Jordan, M.: Active Learning with Statistical Models. Journal of Artificial Intelligence Research 4, 129–145 (1996)
9. Chang, C., Lin, C.: LIBSVM: a library for support vector machines (2001), http://www.csie.ntu.edu.tw/~cjlin/libSVM
10. Yuan, J., Li, J., Zhang, B.: Exploiting Spatial Context Constraints for Automatic Image Region Annotation. In: Proceeding of ACM Multimedia, pp. 595–604 (2007)
11. Deng, Y., Manjunath, B.S.: Unsupervised Segmentation of Color-Texture Regions in Images and Video. IEEE Trans. Pattern Anal. Mach. Intell. 23(8), 800–810 (2001)
12. Fawcett, T.: An introduction to ROC Analysis. Pattern Recognition Letters 27(8), 861–874 (2006)
13. Baram, Y., Yaniv, R.E., Luz, K.: Online Choice of Active Learning Algorithms. Journal of Machine Learning Researh 5, 255–291 (2004)
14. Taylor, J.S., Christianini, N.: On the Generalization of Soft Margin Algorithms. IEEE Transaction on Information Theory 48(10), 2721–2735 (2002)

A New Multiple Kernel Approach for Visual Concept Learning

Jingjing Yang[1,2,3], Yuanning Li[1,2,3], Yonghong Tian[3], Lingyu Duan[3], and Wen Gao[1,2,3]

[1] Institute of Computing Technology, Chinese Academy of Sciences, Beijing, 100080, China
[2] Graduate School, Chinese Academy of Sciences, Beijing, 100039, China
[3] The Institute of Digital Media, School of EE & CS, Peking University, Beijing, 100871, China
{jjyang,ynli}@jdl.ac.cn, {yhtian,lingyu,wgao}@pku.edu.cn

Abstract. In this paper, we present a novel multiple kernel method to learn the optimal classification function for visual concept. Although many carefully designed kernels have been proposed in the literature to measure the visual similarity, few works have been done on how these kernels really affect the learning performance. We propose a Per-Sample Based Multiple Kernel Learning method (PS-MKL) to investigate the discriminative power of each training sample in different basic kernel spaces. The optimal, sample-specific kernel is learned as a linear combination of a set of basic kernels, which leads to a convex optimization problem with a unique global optimum. As illustrated in the experiments on the Caltech 101 and the Wikipedia MM dataset, the proposed PS-MKL outperforms the traditional Multiple Kernel Learning methods (MKL) and achieves comparable results with the state-of-the-art methods of learning visual concepts.

Keywords: Visual Concept Learning, Support Vector Machine, Multiple Kernel Learning.

1 Introduction

With the explosive growth of images, content-based image retrieval (CBIR), which searches images whose low-level visual features (e.g., color, texture, shape, etc.) are similar to those of the query image, has been an active research area in the last decade. However, retrieving images via low-level features has been proven to be unsatisfactory since low-level visual features cannot represent the high-level semantic content of images. To address this so-called semantic gap issue [1], a variety of machine learning techniques have been used to map the image features to semantic concepts, such as scenes (e.g. indoor/outdoor [2], and some specified natural scenes [3]) and object categories (e.g. airplane/motorbike/face) [4,5]. Most of these methods follow a supervised learning scheme, which learns visual concepts from a set of manually labeled images and classifies unseen images into one of learned concepts. However, these methods are application-specific and hard to be generalized from a relatively small data set to a much larger one.

B. Huet et al. (Eds.): MMM 2009, LNCS 5371, pp. 250–262, 2009.
© Springer-Verlag Berlin Heidelberg 2009

   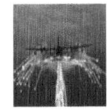

Fig. 1. Samples of "airplane" in Caltech101   **Fig. 2.** Samples of "military aircraft" in Wikipedia

Learning visual concept from numerous images is difficult: concept within the images has visual ambiguities. On one hand, images of different concepts can exhibit somewhat similarity on different attributes: scale, shape, color, texture, etc. For objects such as cars and buses, shape is an important clue to discriminate them while color is usually not. On the other hand, the same object can yield different visual appearance due to the variety of view point, illuminance, or shelter. Different instances of the same concept can also have diversity in appearance (see Fig.1, 2). In short, instances of visual concepts are usually of variation and redundancy in multiply image feature spaces. Learning visual concept requires making a trade-off between the invariant and discriminative power.

In this paper, we present a per-sample based multiple kernel learning (PS-MKL) method for visual concept, which aims at decoding the discriminative ability of every training sample in multiple basic kernel spaces and forms a unique and general classification function for each visual concept. In addition to learning an important weight for each training sample, we also determine a sample specific linear combination of basic kernels. We show that the learning of the sample weights and the per-sample based kernel weights can be formed as a Max-Min problem and solved in a global optimal manner.

We apply our technique on two dataset, the Caltech101 and the Wikipedia MM dataset [6]. Caltech101 is introduced in 2004 [7] with a numerous object categories. However, there is little variation in pose or scale within the object class (see Fig.1). To this end, we go on experiments on the Wikipedia image collection which contains approximately 150,000 images that are of diverse topics and more similar to those encountered on the Web (see Fig.2). We highlight the main contributions of our work as follow:

1. We introduce PS-MKL for visual concept. This technique provides a tractable solution to the combinational sample weighting and the sample-level kernel weighting, which is thinner than concept level in previous works [8,9].
2. Multiple kernels are automatically selected for each weighted training sample. New kernels can be utilized easily and systematically assess their performances in PS-MKL.

The remainder of this paper is organized as follows. Sec. 2 reviews the related work. In Sec.3, we propose the PS-MKL framework as a classifier for learning visual concept. Details of the learning procedure are described in Sec. 4. We depict the application of object recognition and image retrieval and present the experimental results in Sec. 5. The conclusions and future work are discussed in Sec. 6.

2 Related Works

Learning visual concept within the image is currently one of most interesting and difficult problems in computer vision. Much progress has been made in the past decades in investigating approaches that capture the visual and geometrical statistics of visual concepts. Three types of related approaches: generative approach, exemplar based approach, and kernel approach, will be surveyed in this section.

Generative Approach in Visual Concept Learning

In the past few years, generative approaches have become prevalent in visual concept learning. They learn concept from a share of low level features, and introduce a set of latent variables to fuse various cues. For example, part-based method (e.g. constellation mode [9,10]) and bag of words method [5,11] learn object categories via shape invariance. In recognition stage, a generative approach estimates the joint probability density function with Bayes' rule. Ng and Jordan [12] demonstrated both analytically and experimentally that in a 2-class setting the generative approach often has better performance for small numbers of training examples. However, recognition requires intermediate results based on the pre-computed and shared low level features. The performance declines sharply with the scale of the learning concepts.

Exemplar Based Method for Visual Concept Learning

Some researchers solve visual concepts learning problem in a manner of data association, which uses the image nearest neighbor to infer its own identity. Works in [13] learn separate distance function for each exemplar to improve recognition. Recently, several systems show that k-nearest-neighbor (KNN) search based on appearance archive surprising results [14].

Exemplars in these methods are assumed to be independent with each other and treated equally. Although exemplar based method are efficient in training stage, recognition is time consuming to match test image with every training exemplar. Another requirement is a very large data set to obtain all possible configurations of the visual concept within the image.

Kernel Based Method for Visual Concept Learning

While generative approach and exemplar based approach have archived some success, kernel based discriminative methods are known to efficiently find decision boundaries in kernel space and generalize well on unseen data [15].

(a). Single Kernel Method for Visual Concept Learning: So far, various kernels, carefully designed to capture different types of clues for visual concept learning, have been employed in Support Vector Machine (SVM) to find the optimal separating hyper-plane between the positive and negative classes. Kernels based on multi-resolution histogram, which compute image global histogram, are proposed in [16] to measure the image similarity at different granularity. Pyramid matching kernel which matches images with local spatial coordinates is proposed in [17] to enforce loose spatial information. Kernels for local feature distribution are presented in [18] to capture the image local context. However, these methods are designed to operate on one fixed input of feature vector, where each vector or vector entry corresponds to a particular aspect of image. These methods are not directly applicable to large scale concept learning since different attributes of the image or visual concepts are treated equally so that attributes can be easily overwhelmed by the major one. As mentioned in Sec. 1, weighting of multiple aspects is needed to be conducted to improve the discriminative power for visual ambiguity.

(b). Multiple Kernel Method for Visual Concept Learning: Recently, much progress has been made in the field of multiple kernel learning [19,20]. These methods follow a same framework as a linear combination of basic kernels but differ in the cost function to optimize. The combination of basic kernels shows two benefits. First, there is no need to work on a combined high dimensional feature space. Second, different types of feature, such as shape, color, texture can be formulated effectively in a uniform formula to avoid the over-fitting problem. However, weights of basic kernels in these works are learned at concepts level, where personalities of different concept instances are ignored.

Considering the approaches and the corresponding problems mentioned above, we propose a new multiple kernels learning method PS-MKL for visual concept to achieve a balance between the invariant and discriminative power throughout the training samples. In PS-MKL, sample selection is combined with a kernel weighting at sample level which is a thinner granularity over previous methods. Both the sample weights and the kernel weights are optimized in a unified convex problem.

3 A New Multiple Kernel Learning Framework

Given a labeled image dataset as $D_l = \{x_i, y_i\}_{i=1}^{N}$, where x_i is the i_{th} labeled training examples and $y_i = \{\pm 1\}$ is the corresponding binary label for a given visual concept, our goal is to train a classifier $f(x)$ from the training samples, which can accurately classify the unlabeled image dataset D_u.

The flowcharts of identifying visual concept of an unseen image by three binary classifiers are shown in Fig.3. All of the three strategies adopt a similar kernel based framework but different kernel structures. These top-down flowcharts have three layers including input layer, middle layer and decision layer. In the input layer on the top, x represents a test sample which needs to be identified with the relevant visual concept. In the middle layer, similarities between test sample x and training samples $\{x_i\}_{i=1}^{N}$ are measured respectively via different kernel structures. In the last layer, the sign of decision function including linear combination of weighted kernels determines the result whether the test sample x contain the given concept.

The leftmost flowchart of Fig.3 depicts the first paradigm: standard SVM method, which employs a single kernel to measure the sample similarity. The center flowchart of Fig.3 shows the second paradigm: multiple kernel method, which compares the similarity of each basic kernel is related with the corresponding feature sub-space and the adoptive kernel function. The rightmost flowchart of Fig.3 displays the third paradigm: our proposed per-sample based multiple kernel method, which also utilizes multiple basic kernels to measure similarity. The difference is that combined modality for basic kernels is distinguishable among different training sample. The visual characteristics of each training sample make an impact on the weight of each basic

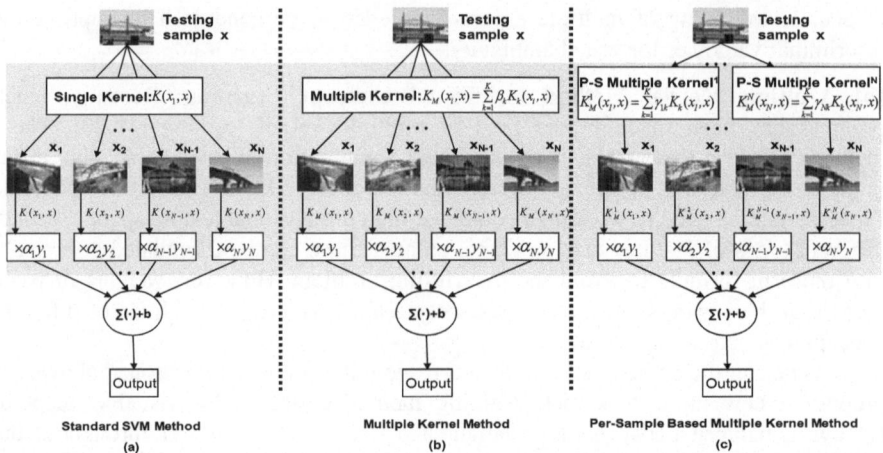

Fig. 3. Three paradigms of learning image concepts using (a) Standard SVM Method; (b) Multiple Kernel Method; (c) Per-Sample Based Multiple Kernel Method

kernel, which results in more learning parameters in such classifier compared with the former two strategies.

In this section, we first briefly review the standard SVMs and the traditional multiple kernel method in sec.3.1 and sec.3.2 respectively. Inspired by these methods, our proposed per-sample based multiple kernel method for visual concept learning is introduced in Sec.3.3.

3.1 Standard SVM

SVM uses a feature map ϕ to project the original data in input space to a higher dimensional feature space where SVM can set up a separating hyper plane and linearly classify samples. Via the "kernel trick", it does not need to represent the feature space explicitly, simply by defining a kernel function $K(x_i, x_j) = \langle \phi(x_i), \phi(x_j) \rangle$, which substitutes of the dot product in the feature space.

The decision function of SVM based on the single kernel for binary classification is an α weighted linear combination of kernels with a bias b as follows:

$$f(x) = \text{sign}(\sum_{i=1}^{N} \alpha_i \, y_i K(x_i, x) + b) \tag{1}$$

3.2 The Traditional Multiple Kernel Method

Multiple kernel methods extend the single kernel further to a convex linear combination of K basic kernels:

$$K(x_i, x) = \sum_{k=1}^{K} \beta_k K_k(x_i, x) \quad \text{with} \quad \sum_{k=1}^{K} \beta_k = 1 \text{ and } \forall k : \beta_k \geq 0 \, .$$

Correspondingly, the decision function of the multiple kernels learning (MKL) problem can be formulated as [20]:

$$f(x) = \text{sign}(\sum_{i=1}^{N} \alpha_i y_i \sum_{k=1}^{K} \beta_k K_k(x_i, x) + b) \tag{2}$$

where the optimized coefficients α can be used to stand for the importance of every training sample, and the kernel weight β measures the importance of different basic kernels for the discrimination.

3.3 Per-Sample Based Multiple Kernel Method

In classical multiple kernel method, all training samples share the same kernel weight β within the same concept, only considering the importance of the corresponding basic kernel for learning such concept. However, treating training samples in a uniform manner neglects the personality of instance. In fact, the importance of different basic kernels relates to the training sample. Hence, we reformulate the problem formulated in Eqn.(2) by replace the basic kernel weight β_k of γ_{ik}:

$$f(x) = \text{sign}(\sum_{i=1}^{N} \alpha_i y_i \sum_{k=1}^{K} \gamma_{ik} K_k(x_i, x) + b) \tag{3}$$

where γ_{ik} measures how the i-th training sample affects the discrimination in different basic kernel space. Compared with β_k in traditional multiple kernel method, γ_{ik} is no longer independent with the training sample. Accordingly, the number of the basic kernel weight rises from K to N×K.

Our goal is to optimize the coefficients α and the kernel weight γ for constructing the decision function $f(x)$ that can capture both the commonness of visual concept and diversity of the concept instance.

It is essential to note that, each basic kernel $K_k(x_i, x_j)$ could uses a distinct set of features of x_i and x_j, representing the similarity of the two images on a certain aspect. Furthermore, different basic kernels can use different kernel forms, which can simply be classical kernels (such as Gaussian or polynomial kernels) with different parameters, or defined specially considering the specialty associated with image. Details on the basic kernel forms utilized in this paper will be introduced in Sec. 5.1.

4 Learning the Classifier

We present in this section the mathematical formulation of our per-sample multiple kernel learning (PS-MKL) problem and the algorithm we proposed for optimizing the parameters in PS-MKL.

The PS-MKL Primal Problem

In the PS-MKL problem, the sample x_i is translated via a mapping $\{\phi_k(x) \mapsto \square^{D_k}\}_{k=1}^{K}$ from the input space into K feature spaces $(\phi_1(x_i), \cdots, \phi_K(x_i))$ where

D_k denotes the dimensionality of the k-th feature space. For each feature map there will be a separate weight vector $\mathbf{w_k}$. Here we consider linear combinations of the corresponding output functions:

$$f(x) = \sum_{k=1}^{K} \gamma_k' \langle \mathbf{w_k}, \phi_k(x) \rangle + b \tag{4}$$

The mixing coefficients γ_k' should reflect the utility of the respective feature map for the classification task. Inspired by SVM learning process, training can be implemented as the following optimization problem which involves maximizing the margin between training examples of two classes and minimizing the classification error:

$$\min_{\beta, w, b, \xi} \frac{1}{2} \sum_{k=1}^{K} \gamma_k' \|\mathbf{w}_k\|^2 + C \sum_{i=1}^{N} \xi_i$$

$$\text{s.t. } y_i(\sum_{k=1}^{K} \gamma_k' \langle \mathbf{w_k}, \phi_k(x_i) \rangle + b) \geq 1 - \xi_i \quad \xi_i \geq 0 \ \forall i; \quad \gamma_k' \geq 0 \ \sum_{k=1}^{K} \gamma_k' = 1 \ \forall k \tag{5}$$

where $\|\mathbf{w}_k\|^2$ is a regularization term which is inversely related to margin, $\sum_{i=1}^{N} \xi_i$ measures the total classification error.

The PS-MKL Dual Problem

Via introducing Lagrange multipliers $\{\alpha_i\}_{i=1}^{N}$ into the above inequalities constraint, formulating the Lagrangian dual function which satisfies the Karush-Kuhn-Tucker(KKT) conditions, and the addition of the kernel weights substitution, the former optimization problem further reduces to a convex program problem as follows:

$$\max_{\gamma} \min_{\alpha} \ J(\cdot)$$

$$J(\cdot) = \frac{1}{2} \sum_{i=1}^{N} \sum_{j=1}^{N} \alpha_i \alpha_j y_i y_j (\sum_{k=1}^{K} \gamma_{ik} K_k(x_i, x_j)) - \sum_{i=1}^{N} \alpha_i \tag{6}$$

$$\text{s.t.} \sum_{i=1}^{N} \alpha_i y_i = 0 \quad 0 \leq \alpha_i \leq C \ \forall i; \quad \gamma_{ik} \geq 0 \ \sum_{k=1}^{K} \gamma_{ik} = 1 \ \forall i \ \forall k$$

This max-min problem is the PS-MKL dual problem which relative to the primal problem as Eqn.(5). $J(\cdot)$ is a multi-object function for α and γ. For fixed parameters γ, minimization of $J(\cdot)$ over the sample weights α, which equals to minimize the global classification error and maximize the inter-class interval. When α is fixed, maximizing $J(\cdot)$ over kernel weight γ means to maximize the global intra-class similarity and minimize the inter-class similarity simultaneously.

Solving this Max-Min problem is a typical saddle point problem. Details of the solving procedure will be presented in the next part.

An Efficient Learning Algorithm

We adopt a two-stage alternant optimization approach, which is the traditional MKL route for parameter learning. Optimizing the sample coefficients α is to estimate which training samples are representative for learning this visual concept and the corresponding weightiness for discrimination. Fixing the kernel weights γ, the sample weight α can be estimated by minimizing $J(\cdot)$ under the constraint $\sum_{i=1}^{N} \alpha_i y_i = 0$ and $\forall i : 0 \le \alpha_i \le C$. It can be reduced to the SVM dual quadratic program (QP) problem with a mixed kernel $K(x_i, x_j) = \sum_{k=1}^{K} \gamma_{ik} K_k(x_i, x_j)$. Consequently, minimizing $J(\cdot)$ over α can be easily implemented as there already exists several efficient solvers for the corresponding QP.

Optimize the basic kernel coefficient γ_{ik} is in the interest of understanding which regulation on α promotes the sparsity of kernel weights. Hence if one would be able to obtain an accurate classification by a sparse kernel weights, then one can quite easily interpret the resulting decision function.

To conveniently optimize the model parameters γ_{ik}, the objective function concerning γ_{ik} can be rewritten as:

$$J(\cdot) = \sum_{i=1}^{N} \sum_{k=1}^{K} \gamma_{ik} S_{ik}(\alpha) - \sum_{i=1}^{N} \alpha_i ,$$

(7)

where

$$S_{ik}(\alpha) = \frac{1}{2} \sum_{j=1}^{N} \alpha_i \alpha_j y_i y_j K_k(\mathbf{x}_i, \mathbf{x}_j)$$

Then the optimization of $J(\cdot)$ over γ_{ik} turns to:

$$\max \ \theta$$
$$\text{s.t. } \sum_{i=1}^{N} \sum_{k=1}^{K} \gamma_{ik} S_{ik}(\alpha) - \sum_{i=1}^{N} \alpha_i \ge \theta; \gamma_{ik} \ge 0 \ \ \sum_{k=1}^{K} \gamma_{ik} = 1 \ \ \forall i \ \ \forall k$$

(9)

$$\text{for all } \alpha \text{ with } \sum_{i=1}^{N} \alpha_i y_i = 0 \ \ 0 \le \alpha_i \le C$$

For the fixed optimal α, the optimization of $J(\cdot)$ over γ is a linear program (LP) because θ and γ are only linearly constrained. Nevertheless, the constraint on θ has to hold for every compatible α resulting in infinite constraints. In order to solve this so-called semi-infinite linear program (SILP) problem, a column generation strategy is employed as follows: Solving the former QP from a fixed γ produces a special α, which then increase a constraint on θ. We add the new constraints iteratively in this way and solve the LP with all gained constraints. This procedure has been proven to be converged in [20].

5 Experiments

In this section, we show the studies on Caltech 101 and Wikipedia MM data set. Compared with Caltech101, Wikipedia MM dataset is more close to the web images where instants of concept have more variation in appearances. Our primary goal is to investigate the effectiveness of the proposed multiple kernels method on open data set and practical retrieval data set and how does the performance change with the difficulty of the problem.

For Caltech 101, we select N images from each class for 1-vs-all training, e.g. N = 10, 20, 30. The remaining images are used for testing. In Wikipedia image data set, about 150,000 images are clawed from Wikipedia with diverse topics. These images are associated with unstructured and noisy textual annotations in English. Fifteen teams engaged in Image CLEF 2008 Wikipedia MM task [6] are required to submit at most 1000 related image in the dataset for each of the 75 predefined topics. Among these 75 topics, 10 topics, which have more than 100 positive samples over the results submitted by all fifteen participants, are picked out for our experiments. About 100 samples including positive and negative image are used for each topic's one-vs-all training. The remaining images in each topic are used for testing. It is worthy to note that images submitted by fifteen participants are searched via visual or text retrieval and highly related with the topics.

5.1 Features and Kernels

SIFT and Dense Color-SIFT are employed to characterize the local region of the image. For SIFT, SIFT descriptor is computed over the interest regions extracted by Different-of Gaussian (DoG) detector, forming a 72(3×3×8) dimensional feature for each interest region. For Dense Color-SIFT, SIFT descriptor is computed on RGB 3-channels over 16×16 pixel patch with spacing of 8 pixels, forming a 3×72 dimensional feature for each patch. SIFT normalization is skipped when the gradient magnitude of the patch is too weak. We use k-means algorithm to quantize the extracted descriptors from the training images to obtain codebooks with the size of k(400) for SIFT and Dense Color-SIFT respectively.

We use our own implementation of two types of latest kernels for object recognition, Spatial Pyramid Kernels (SPK) [18] and Proximity Distribution Kernels (PDK) [19] as basic kernels. For SPK, image is divided into $2^l \times 2^l$ cells and features from the spatially corresponding cells are matched across any two images. The resulting kernel is a weighted combination of histogram intersections from the coarse cells to the fine cells. Four levels pyramid is used with grid sizes 8×8, 4×4, 2×2 and 1×1 respectively. For PDK, local feature distributions of the r-nearest neighbors are matched across two images. The resulting kernel is a combination of multiple scale of the local distribution, e.g. r = 1,…, k. k is set to (8, 16, 32, 64) from finest to coarsest neighborhood in our implementation.

5.2 Experiment Results

Caltech 101: Our first experiment is carried on the Caltech101dataset. As mentioned above, 4 Spatial Pyramid Kernels (SPK) and 4 Proximity Distribution Kernels (PDK) over two types of local features are utilized as basic kernels, forming totally 16 basic kernels. In Fig. 4(a), we show the mean recognition rate of the MKL and PS-MKL over two types of basic kernels. Generally, PDK based methods achieve better results than the SPK based methods. Notice that PS-MKL outperforms MKL in any types of basic kernels.

In Fig.4 (b), the performances of MKL and PS-MKL over all basic kernels are compared with other works in [8,21,22]. When training sample is less than 20, performance of MKL is slightly lower than that in [8], which adopt a similar multiple kernels methods. One possible reason is different implementation for feature quantization.

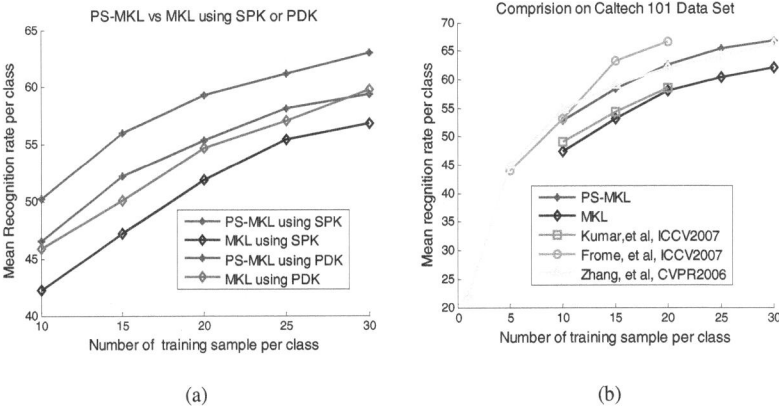

(a)   (b)

Fig. 4. Recognition results on Caltech 101 dataset

When MKL is fed with more training samples, disparity trends to be smaller. Overall, PS-MKL outperforms other traditional MKL methods. When the number of training samples for each object class reaches 30, PS-MKL obtains a performance of 66.7%, which is competitive with the latest reported results.

To summarize, PS-MKL has outperformed the existing MKL methods on the Caltech 101 dataset. More significantly, our approach can easily adopt and automatically weight the new basic kernels at sample level.

Wikipedia MM: For the Wikipedia MM dataset, we report the results using MKL and PS-MKL over the all basic kernels of SPK and PDK as before. With the regard of topic detection over thousands of image, we use F-score to measure the accuracy and effectiveness of concept learning. F-measure of each topic and its corresponding precision and recall are list in table 1 for MKL and PS-MKL.

Table 1. Recognition results on Wikipedia MM dataset

Topic	MKL			PS-MKL		
	Precision	**Record**	**F-score.**	**Precision**	**Record**	**F-score.**
Bridges	56.47%	76.42%	64.95%	54.88%	82.93%	**66.05%**
Cities by night	81.53%	80.56%	**81.04%**	79.75%	80.56%	80.15%
Football stadium	68.74%	62.51%	65.47%	69.81%	62.50%	**65.94%**
Historic castle	79.49%	82.35%	80.90%	72.72%	91.44%	**81.91%**
House architecture	68.94%	77.81%	73.11%	74.05%	76.80%	**75.39%**
Hunting dog	69.52%	60.71%	64.82%	59.66%	79.46%	**68.15%**
Mountains & sky	80.7%	84.4%	82.51%	80.80%	85.48%	**83.07%**
Military Aircraft	75.72%	58.82%	66.21%	72.52%	70.58%	**71.54%**
Race car	59.58%	86.67%	70.61%	64.62%	80.00%	**71.49%**
Star galaxy	84.99%	79.17%	**81.97%**	79.21%	79.16%	79.19%

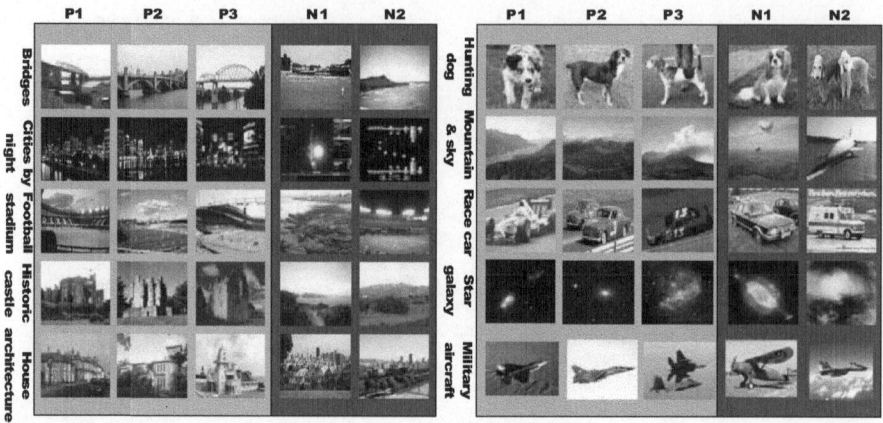

Fig. 5. Top three of the positive samples and top two of the negative samples in the recognized results on Wikipedia MM dataset

As shown in table1, comparable results are obtained in topics of "cities by night" and "star galaxy". With our sample based kernel weighting algorithm, PS-MKL archives different levels of improvement over MKL on the other eight topics. An interest observation is that three topics, "bridges", "house architecture" and "hunting dog", with bigger intra-class variation receive obvious improvement. One explanation is that PS-MKL outperforms MKL in seizing the characteristics of the training samples without losing generally discriminative ability.

To illustrate the affects of the concept learning, we show in Fig. 5, for each topic the top related positive and negative images. Note that some negative and positive images not only share the similar appearances, but also have correlations on semantic level, e.g. hunting dog with pet dog, and race car with vehicle.

6   Conclusion and Future Works

In this paper, we propose a novel multiple kernels approach called PS-MKL method for visual concept learning. Different from the traditional MKL methods, where kernels are weighted uniformly on concept level, PS-MKL aims to capture the distinct discriminative capability for each training sample in different basic kernel spaces. The proposed approach simultaneously optimizes the weights of the basic kernels for each training sample and the associated classifier in a supervised learning manner. The optimal parameters can be solved alternatively with off-the-shelf SVM solvers and simplex LPs. As shown in the experimental results on Caltech101 and Wikipedia MM dataset, PS-MKL archives significant improvement over the traditional MKL methods and competitive results with the state-of-the-art approaches for visual concept learning. PS-MKL provides a scalable solution for both combining large numbers of kernels and learning visual concept from a small training set.

We will continue our future works in two directions. First, we will add more elaborately designed basic kernels not only on visual feature, but also other types such as text feature, to improve the performance. Second, we will explore the faster learning algorithm to optimize the increasing number of model parameters.

Acknowledgments

This work is supported by grants from Chinese NSF under contract No. 60605020, National Basic Research Program (973) of China under contract No. 2009CB320906, and National Hi-Tech R&D Program (863) of China under contract No. 2006AA010105.

References

1. Smeulders, A.W.M., Worring, M., Santini, S., Gupta, A., Jain, R.: Content-based image retrieval at the end of the early years. IEEE Trans. PAMI 22(12), 1349–1380 (2000)
2. Szummer, M., Picard, R.W.: Indoor-outdoor image classification. In: ICCV Workshop on Content-based Access of Image and Video Databases, Bombay, India, pp. 42–50 (1998)
3. Vogel, J., Schiele, B.: Natural Scene Retrieval Based on a Semantic Modeling Step. In: Proc. Int'l. Conf. Image and Video Retrieval (July 2004)
4. Sivic, J., Russell, B., Efros, A., Zisserman, A.: Discovering Objects and Their Location in Images. In: Proceedings of the IEEE ICCV 2005, pp. 370–377 (2005)
5. Fergus, R., Fei-Fei, L., Perona, P., Zisserman, A.: Learning Object Categories from Google's Image Search. In: Proceedings of the Tenth ICCV 2005, vol. 2, pp. 1816–1823 (2005)
6. http://www.imageclef.org/2008/wikipedia
7. Fei-Fei, L., Fergus, R., Perona, P.: Learning Generative Visual Models from Few Training Examples: An Incremental Bayesian Approach Tested on 101 Object Categories. In: Conference on Computer Vision and Pattern Recognition Workshop (2004)
8. Kumar, A., Sminc, C.: Support Kernel Machines for Object Recognition. In: IEEE 11th International Conference on Computer Vision, 2007. ICCV 2007, October 14-21, 2007, pp. 1–8 (2007)
9. Crandall, D., Felzenszwalb, P., Huttenlocher, D.: Spatial priors for part-based recognition using statistical models. In: Proc. Computer Vision and Pattern Recognition (2005)
10. Fei-Fei, L., Fergus, R., Perona, P.: One-Shot learning of object categories. IEEE Trans. PAMI 28(4), 594–611 (2006)
11. Jia, L., Fei-Fei, L.: What, where and who? Classifying event by scene and object recognition. In: ICCV (2007)
12. Ng, A., Jordan, M.: On discriminative vs. generative classifiers: A comparison of logistic regression and naive bayes. In: Advances in NIPS, vol. 12 (2002)
13. Malisiewicz, T., Efros, A.A.: Recognition by Association via Learning Per-exemplar Distances. In: CVPR (June 2008)
14. Torralba, A., Fergus, R., Freeman, W.T.: Tiny images.Technical Report MIT-CSAIL-TR-2007-024, MIT CSAIL (2007)
15. Shawe-Taylor, J., Cristianini, N.: Kernel Methods for Pattern Analysis. Cambridge University Press, Cambridge (2004)
16. Grauman, K., Darrell, T.: The pyramid match kernel: discriminative classification with sets of image features. In: ICCV, October 17-21, 2005, vol. 2, pp. 1458–1465 (2005)

17. Lazebnik, S., Schmid, C., Ponce, J.: Beyond Bags of Features: Spatial Pyramid Matching for Recognizing Natural Scene Categories. In: 2006 IEEE Computer Society Conference on Computer Vision and Pattern Recognition, vol. 2, pp. 2169–2178 (2006)
18. Ling, H., Soatto, S.: Proximity Distribution Kernels for Geometric Context in Category Recognition. In: ICCV, October 14-21, 2007, pp. 1–8 (2007)
19. Bach, F.R., Lanckriet, G.R.G., Jordan, M.I.: Multiple kernel learning, conic duality, and the SMO algorithm. In: NIPS (2004)
20. Sonnenburg, S., Raetsch, G., Schaefer, C., Scholkopf, B.: Large scale multiple kernel learning. Journal of Machine Learning Research, 1531–1565 (2006)
21. Frome, A., Singer, Y., Sha, F., Malik, J.: Learning Globally-Consistent Local Distance Functions for Shape-Based Image Retrieval and Classification. In: ICCV 2007, pp. 1–8 (2007)
22. Zhang, H., Berg, A.C., Maire, M., Malik, J.: SVM-KNN: Discriminative Nearest Neighbor Classification for Visual Category Recognition. In: CVPR. pp. 2126–2136 (2006)

Integrating Image Segmentation and Classification for Fuzzy Knowledge-Based Multimedia Indexing*

Thanos Athanasiadis[1], Nikolaos Simou[1], Georgios Papadopoulos[2],
Rachid Benmokhtar[3], Krishna Chandramouli[4], Vassilis Tzouvaras[1],
Vasileios Mezaris[2], Marios Phiniketos[1], Yannis Avrithis[1],
Yiannis Kompatsiaris[2], Benoit Huet[3], and Ebroul Izquierdo[4]

[1] Image, Video and Multimedia Systems Laboratory,
National Technical University of Athens, Greece
(thanos,nsimou,tzouvaras,finik,iavr)@image.ntua.gr
[2] Informatics and Telematics Institute,
Centre for Research and Technology Hellas (CERTH), Greece
(papad,bmezaris,ikom)@iti.gr
[3] Institut Eurécom, Département Multimédia, France
(rachid.benmokhtar,benoit.huet)@eurecom.fr
[4] Department of Electronic Engineering, Queen Mary University of London, UK
(krishna.chandramouli,ebroul.izquierdo)@elec.qmul.ac.uk

Abstract. In this paper we propose a methodology for semantic indexing of images, based on techniques of image segmentation, classification and fuzzy reasoning. The proposed knowledge-assisted analysis architecture integrates algorithms applied on three overlapping levels of semantic information: i) no semantics, i.e. segmentation based on low-level features such as color and shape, ii) mid-level semantics, such as concurrent image segmentation and object detection, region-based classification and, iii) rich semantics, i.e. fuzzy reasoning for extraction of implicit knowledge. In that way, we extract semantic description of raw multimedia content and use it for indexing and retrieval purposes, backed up by a fuzzy knowledge repository. We conducted several experiments to evaluate each technique, as well as the whole methodology in overall and, results show the potential of our approach.

1 Introduction

Production of digital content has become daily routine for almost every person, leading to an immense size of accessible multimedia data. Consequently, public and research interest has partly shifted from the production of multimedia content to its efficient management, making apparent the need of mechanisms for automatic indexing and retrieval, thematic categorization and content-based

---

* This research was supported by the European Commission under contract FP6-027026 K-SPACE.

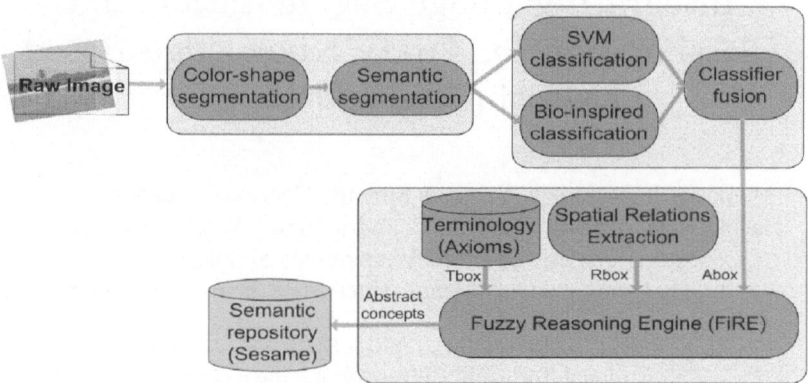

Fig. 1. Overview of the proposed architecture

search (among many others). Efficient multimedia content management and usability requires focus on the semantic information level, with which most users desire to interact; other than that would render any results ineffective.

The importance of semantic indexing and retrieval of multimedia has brought out several benchmarking activities, such as TRECVID [11] with increasing participation every year. Most approaches in semantic-based analysis and indexing are grounded on multimedia segmentation and object recognition techniques. The majority of classification techniques employ statistical modeling, associating low-level visual features with mid-level concepts [8]. There have been proposed techniques for region-based classification using machine learning techniques such as Self Organizing Maps (SOMs) [5], Genetic Algorithms [10], Support Vector Machines (SVMs) [16,10] and biologically inspired optimization techniques. To achieve better recognition rates, it has been found that, it is better to fuse multiple simple classifiers than to build a single sophisticated classifier [4].

During the late years, various attempts were made in order to extract complicated concepts using multimedia analysis results combined with taxonomies and ontologies. In [12] WordNet is used to include lexical relationships between abstract and detected mid-level concepts. Ontologies based on Description Logics (DLs) [3] are a family of knowledge representation languages; however, despite the rich expressiveness of DLs, they lack the ability to deal with vague and uncertain information which is commonly found in multimedia content. This was the reason that a variety of DLs capable of handling imprecise information, like probabilistic and fuzzy [14,13] have been proposed.

Within this context, our paper presents a knowledge assisted image analysis and semantic annotation methodology consisting of several novel and state-of-the-art techniques. As depicted in Figure 1, we discuss methods for semantic-aware segmentation, object detection and recognition, as well as detection of abstract concepts that cannot be detected directly, but can only be inferred using higher level knowledge. We follow a bottom-up approach and therefore we initially segment the image based on color and shape criteria, followed by a novel semantic region growing methodology which incorporates object detection simultaneously with region merging that improves extraction of semantic objects.

Next, two different classification approaches are employed and used for recognition of several concepts: i) Support Vector Machines and ii) a biologically inspired classifier. Combination of multiple classifier decisions is a powerful method for increasing classification rates in recognition problems. We fuse the two sets of classification results, using a neural network based on evidence theory method, obtaining a single list of concepts with degrees of confidence for all regions.

So far a list of concepts (together with degrees of confidence for each one) have been linked to the image. Our goal lies beyond this and we want to extract additional, implicit knowledge, improve region-based classification by incorporating spatial relations and neighborhood information and finally infer abstract concepts on a global image basis. Towards this aim, a fuzzy reasoning engine is employed. The final results are stored in an online semantic repository, in a strictly structured format, allowing query mechanisms for semantic retrieval.

The manuscript is structured as follows: Section 2 details the mechanism of each algorithm used towards a bottom-up image classification. Section 3 presents the role of fuzzy multimedia reasoning and its application in fuzzy semantic indexing, storing in appropriate knowledge bases and querying mechanisms for retrieval purposes. We provide extended experimental results of the overall approach in section 4 and we draw our conclusions in section 5.

2   Bottom-Up Image Classification

In this section we describe a series of image analysis techniques, whose integration leads to the detection and recognition of a set of concepts used as the basis for the semantic handling of the content. As a bottom-up technique, it starts from the pixel level jumping to the region level using a color and shape image segmentation, further refined with a semantic region growing technique (subsection 2.1). Two classifiers are used in parallel, described in subsection 2.2, which assign concepts in a fuzzy manner (i.e. with a degree of confidence) for each region of the image. The last subsection presents a fusion mechanism, based on a neural network, which fuses the results of the two classifiers and produces a single set of concepts detected in the image. This set of concepts provides the initial vocabulary for the semantic description of the image.

2.1   Semantic Image Segmentation

Initially, a segmentation algorithm, based on low-level features such as color and shape [1], is applied in order to divide the given image into a set of non overlapping regions. In previous work ([2]) we have shown how extracted visual descriptors can be matched to visual models of concepts resulting to an initial fuzzy labeling of the regions with concepts from the knowledge base, i.e. for region a we have the fuzzy set (following the sum notation [7]) $L_a = \sum_k C_k/w_k$, where $k = 1, \ldots, K$, K is the cardinality of the crisp set of all concepts $\mathbf{C} = \{C_k\}$

in the knowledge base and $w_k = \mu_a(C_k)$ is the degree of membership of element C_k in the fuzzy set L_a.

Segmentation based only on syntactic features usually creates more regions than the actual number of objects. We examine how a variation of a traditional segmentation technique, the Recursive Shortest Spanning Tree (RSST) can be used to create more semantically coherent regions in an image. The idea is that neighbor regions, sharing the same concepts, as expressed by the labels assigned to them, should be merged, since they define a single object. To this aim, we modify the RSST algorithm to operate on the fuzzy sets of labels $\mathcal{L}$ of the volumes in a similar way as if it worked on low-level features (such as color, texture) [2]. The modification of the traditional algorithm to its semantic equivalent lies on the re-definition of the two criteria: (i) The dissimilarity between two neighbor regions a and b (vertices v_a and v_b in the graph), based on which graph's edges are sorted and (ii) the termination criterion. For the calculation of the similarity between two regions we defined a metric between two fuzzy sets, those that correspond to the candidate concepts of the two regions. This dissimilarity value is computed according to the following formula and is assigned as the weight of the respective graph's edge e_{ab}:

$$w(e_{ab}) = 1 - \sup_{C_k \in \mathbf{C}} (\top(\mu_a(C_k), \mu_b(C_k))) \tag{1}$$

where $\top$ is a t-norm, a and b are two neighbor regions and $\mu_a(C_k)$ is the degree of membership of concept $C_k \in \mathbf{C}$ in the fuzzy set L_a.

Let us now examine one iteration of the S-RSST algorithm. Firstly, the edge e_{ab} with the least weight is selected, then regions a and b are merged. Vertex v_b is removed completely from the ARG, whereas v_a is updated appropriately. This update procedure consists of the following two actions:

1. Re-evaluation of the degrees of membership of the labels fuzzy set in a weighted average (w.r.t. the regions' size) fashion.
2. Re-adjustment of the ARG edges by removing edge e_{ab} and re-evaluating the weight of the affected edges.

This procedure continues until the edge e^* with the least weight in the ARG is bigger than a threshold: $w(e^*) > T_w$. This threshold is calculated in the beginning of the algorithm, based on the histogram of all weights of the set of all edges.

2.2   Region Classification

SVM-Based Classification. SVMs have been widely used in semantic image analysis tasks due to their reported generalization ability and their efficiency in solving high-dimensionality pattern recognition problems [15]. Under the proposed approach, SVMs are employed for performing the association of the computed image regions to one of the defined high-level semantic concepts based on the estimated region feature vector. In particular, a SVM structure is utilized, where an individual SVM is introduced for every defined concept $C_k \in \mathbf{C}$, to detect the corresponding instances. Every SVM is trained under the 'one-against-all' approach. The region feature vector, consisting of seven MPEG-7 visual descriptors, constitutes the input to each SVM, which at the evaluation stage returns for every image segment a numerical value in the range $[0, 1]$. This value denotes the degree of confidence, $\mu_a(C_k)$, to which the corresponding region is assigned to the concept associated with the particular SVM [10]. For each region, the maximum of the K calculated degrees of confidence, $argmax(\mu_a(C_k))$, indicates its concept assignment, whereas the pairs of all supported concepts and their respective degree of confidence $\mu_a(C_k)$ computed for segment a comprise the region's concept hypothesis set $H_a^C = \{\mu_a(C_k)\}$.

Bio-Inspired Classifier. Neural network based clustering and classification has been dominated by Self Organizing Maps (SOMs) and Adaptive Resonance Theory (ART). In competitive neural networks, active neurons reinforce their neighbourhood within certain regions, while suppressing the activities of other neurons. This is called on-center/off-surround competition. The objective of SOM is to represent high-dimensional input patterns with prototype vectors that can be visualized in a usually two-dimensional lattice structure. Input patterns are fully connected to all neurons via adaptable weights. During the training process, neighbouring input patterns are projected into the lattice, corresponding to adjacent neurons. An individual SOM network is employed to detect instances of the defined high-level semantic concepts. Each SOM is trained under the one against all approach. In the basic training algorithm are the prototype vectors trained according to $m_d(t+1) = m_d(t) + g_{cd}(t)[x - m_d(t)]$ where m_d is the weight of the neurons in the SOM network, $g_{cd}(t)$ is the neighbourhood function and d is the dimension of the input feature vector. Each SOM network corresponding to defined high-level concept returns for every segment a numerical value in the range of $[0, 1]$, denoting the degree of confidence to which the corresponding region is assigned to the concept associated with the particular SOM.

2.3 Classifier Fusion

In this section, we describe how the evidence theory can be applied to fusion problems and outline our recently proposed neural network based on evidence theory (NNET) to address classifier fusion [4]. The objective is to associate for each object x (image region), one class from the set of classes $\Omega = \{w_1, .., w_K\}$. In our case, the set of classes is equivalent to the set of concepts $\mathbf{C}$, defined previously. This association is given via a training set of N samples, where each sample can be considered as a part of belief for one class of Ω. This belief degree can be assimilated to evidence function m^i, with 2 focal elements: The class of x^i noted w_q, and Ω. So, if we consider that the object x^i is near to x, then a part of belief can be affected to w_q and the rest to Ω. The mass function is obtained by decreasing function of distance as follows:

$$\begin{cases} m^i(\{w_q\}) = \alpha^i \phi_q(d^i) \\ m^i(\Omega) = 1 - \alpha^i \phi_q(d^i) \end{cases} \tag{2}$$

Where $\phi(.)$ is a monotonically decreasing function such as an exponential function $\phi_q(d^i) = \exp\left(-\gamma_q(d^i)^2\right)$, and d^i is an Euclidean distance between the vector x and the ith vector of training base. $0 < \alpha < 1$ is a constant which prevents a total affectation of mass to the class w_q when x and i^{th} samples are equal. γ_q is a positive parameter defining the decreasing speed of mass function. A method for optimizing parameters (α, γ_q) has been described in [6]. We obtain N mass functions, which can be combined into a single one using (3):

$$m(A) = (m^1 \oplus ... \oplus m^N) = \sum_{(B_1 \cap ... \cap B_N)=A} \prod_{i=1}^{N} m^i(B_i) \tag{3}$$

We propose to resume work already made with the evidence theory in the connectionist implementation [4,6], and to adapt it to classifier fusion. For this aim, an improved version of RBF neural network based on evidence theory which we call NNET, with one input layer L_{input}, two hidden layers L_2 and L_3 and one output layer L_{output} has been devised.

Layer L_{input}. It contains N units and is identical to an RBF network input layer with an exponential activation function ϕ. d is a distance computed using training data and dictionary created (clustering method). K-means is applied on the training data in order to create a "visual" dictionary of the regions.

Layer L_2. Computes the belief masses m^i (2) associated to each prototype. It is composed of N modules of $K + 1$ units each $m^i = (m^i(\{w_1\}), ..., m^i(\{w_{K+1}\})) = (u_1^i s^i, ..., u_K^i s^i, 1 - s^i)$ where u_q^i is the membership degree to each class w_q, q class index $q = \{1, ..., K\}$. The units of module i are connected to neuron i of the previous layer. Note that each region in the image can belong to only one class.

Layer L_3. The Dempster-Shafer combination rule combines N different mass functions in one single mass, given by the conjunctive combination (3). For this aim, the activation vector $\overrightarrow{\mu^i}$ can be recursively computed by $\mu^1 = m^1$, $\mu_j^i = \mu_j^{i-1} m_j^i + \mu_j^{i-1} m_{K+1}^i + \mu_{K+1}^{i-1} m_j^i$ and $\mu_{K+1}^i = \mu_{K+1}^{i-1} m_{K+1}^i$.

Layer L_{output}. In [6], the output is directly obtained by $O_j = \mu_j^N$. The experiments show that this output is very sensitive to the number of prototype, where for each iteration, the output is purely an addition of ignorance. Also, we notice that a small change in the number of prototype can change the classifier fusion behavior. To resolve this problem, we use normalized output: $O_j = \frac{\sum_{i=1}^{N} \mu_j^i}{\sum_{i=1}^{N} \sum_{j=1}^{K+1} \mu_j^i}$. Here, the output is computed taking into account the activation vectors of all prototypes to decrease the effect of an eventual bad behavior of prototype in the mass computation.

The different parameters $(\Delta u, \Delta \gamma, \Delta \alpha, \Delta P, \Delta s)$ can be determined by gradient descent of output error for an input pattern x. Finally, the maximum of plausibility P_q of each class w_q is computed: $P_q = O_q + O_{K+1}$.

3   Fuzzy Reasoning and Indexing

Image classification algorithms can provide reliable results on the recognition of specific concepts, however, it is very difficult to recognize higher-level concepts that do not have specific low-level features. That kind of concepts can be effectively represented by an ontology capable of handling the imprecise information provided by image segmentation and classification algorithms. A DL that fullfills these requirements is f-SHIN [13]. Using fuzzy reasoning engine FiRE[1], which supports f-$\mathcal{SHIN}$ and its reasoning services, we improve region-based classification results and extract additional implicit concepts that categorize an image. The extracted information is stored in a semantic repository permitting fuzzy conjunctive queries for semantic image and region retrieval.

3.1   Fuzzy Reasoning Services and Querying

A f-$\mathcal{SHIN}$ knowledge base Σ is a triple $\langle \mathcal{T}, \mathcal{R}, \mathcal{A} \rangle$, where $\mathcal{T}$ is a fuzzy $TBox$, $\mathcal{R}$ is a fuzzy $RBox$ and $\mathcal{A}$ is a fuzzy $ABox$. $TBox$ is a finite set of fuzzy concept axioms which are of the form $C \equiv D$ called fuzzy concept inclusion axioms and $C \sqsubseteq D$ called fuzzy concept equivalence axioms, where C, D are concepts, saying that C is equivalent or C is a sub-concept of D, respectively. Similarly, $RBox$ is a finite set of fuzzy role axioms of the form $\mathsf{Trans}(R)$ called fuzzy transitive role axioms and $R \sqsubseteq S$ called fuzzy role inclusion axioms saying that R is transitive and R is a sub-role of S respectively. Ending, $ABox$ is as finite set of fuzzy assertions of the form $\langle a : C \bowtie n \rangle$, $\langle (a, b) : R \bowtie n \rangle$, where $\bowtie$ stands for $\geq, >, \leq$ or $<$ or $a \neq b$. Intuitively, a fuzzy assertion of the form $\langle a : C \geq n \rangle$ means that the membership degree of a to the concept C is at least equal to n. Finally, assertions defined by $\geq, >$ are called *positive* assertions, while those defined by $\leq, <$ *negative* assertions.

The main reasoning services of crisp reasoners are deciding satisfiability, subsumption and entailment of concepts and axioms w.r.t. an Σ. In other words, these tools are capable of answering queries like "Can the concept C have any instances in models of the ontology T?" (satisfiability of C), "Is the concept D more general than the concept C in models of the ontology T ?" (subsumption $C \sqsubseteq D$) of does axiom Ψ logically follows from the ontology (entailment of Ψ). These reasoning services are also available by FiRE together with *greatest lower bound queries* which are specific to fuzzy assertions. Since in fuzzy DLs individuals participate in concepts and are connected with a degree, satisfiability queries are of the form "Can the concept C have any instances with degree of participation $\bowtie n$ in models of the ontology T ?". Furthermore, it is in our interest to compute the best lower and upper truth-value bounds of a fuzzy assertion. The term of *greatest lower bound* of a fuzzy assertion w.r.t. Σ was defined in [14]. Greatest lower bound are queries like "What is the greatest degree n that our ontology entails an individual a to participate in a concept C?".

In order to store the fuzzy knowledge base produced by FiRE in a Sesame RDF Repository we serialize it into RDF triples. For this purpose, we use blank nodes in order to represent fuzzy information by defining three new entities: `frdf:membership`, `frdf:degree` and `frdf:ineqType` as types of `rdf:Property` while properties are defined for each role assertion. In that way, Sesame is used

---

[1] FiRE can be found at `http://www.image.ece.ntua.gr/~nsimou/FiRE/`

as a back end for storing and querying RDF triples while FiRE is the front end by which the user can store and query a fuzzy knowledge base.

Since in our case we extend classical assertions to fuzzy assertions, new methods of querying such fuzzy information are possible. More precisely, in [9] the authors extend ordinary conjunctive queries to a family of significantly more expressive query languages, which are borrowed from the fields of fuzzy information retrieval. These languages exploit the membership degrees of fuzzy assertions by introducing weights or thresholds in query atoms. Similarly using FiRE and Sesame permits conjunctive fuzzy queries. Queries are converted from the FiRE syntax to the SeRQL query language supported by Sesame. Sesame engine evaluates the results which are then visualized by FiRE.

Queries consist of two parts: the first one specifies the individual(s) that will be evaluated while the second one states the condition that has to be fulfilled for the individuals. This query asks for individuals x and y, x has to participate in concept Beach to at least 0.7, it also has to be the subject of a contains assertion with participation greater than 1, having as a role-filler individual y which has to participate in concept Person to at least 0.8.

3.2   The Fuzzy Knowledge Base

In order to effectively categorize images and also improve the semantic segmentation process we have implemented an expressive terminology. The terminology defines new concepts that characterize an image and also refines concepts extracted by the classification modules considering regions' spatial configuration.

First, we present the input used as the assertional part of the fuzzy knowledge base provided by the analysis modules. After an initial segmentation, an image is divided into a number of segments. Their spatial relations extracted by the semantic RSST comprise the *RBox* of the fuzzy knowledge base. The classification algorithms evaluate a participation degree in a set of concepts for every segment. The obtained results are then fuzzed and used as positive assertions to represent the *ABox* of the fuzzy knowledge base. Hence, the alphabet of concepts **C** and roles **R** is: **C** = {*Sky Building Person Rock Tree Vegetation Sea Grass Ground Sand Trunk Dried-plant Pavement Boat Wave*} and **R** ={*above-of below-of left-of right-of contains*}. The set of individuals consist of the amount of segments obtained for each image together with the whole image. The *TBox* can be found in Table 1. As can be observed, concepts like Sky that are extracted by the classification modules have been re-defined using spatial relations.(Those concepts are shown in capitals.) Hence, SKY has been defined as a segment that was classified as Sky and has a above − of neighbor that is either Sea or Building or Vegetation. Additionally, higher concepts that refer to a segment have been defined like WavySea and SandyBeach also concepts like Beach that refer to the whole image and categorize it. Within our knowledge base Beach has been defined as an image that contains segments labeled as Sky and Sea. According to the defined terminology implicit knowledge is extracted. For every image *greatest lower bound* (glb) reasoning service is used for the defined concepts of the

Table 1. The terminology $TBox$

$\mathcal{T} = \{$SKY $\equiv$ Sky $\sqcap$ ($\exists$above $-$ of.Sea $\sqcup$ $\exists$above $-$ of.Building $\sqcup$ $\exists$above $-$ of.Vegetation)$,$
SAND $\equiv$ Sand $\sqcap$ $\exists$below $-$ of.Sea,
PAVEMENT $\equiv$ Pavement $\sqcap$ $\exists$below $-$ of.Building,
TRUNK $\equiv$ Trunk $\sqcap$ ($\exists$above $-$ of.Ground $\sqcup$ $\exists$above $-$ of.Grass),
VEGETATION $\equiv$ Grass $\sqcup$ Tree $\sqcup$ Vegetation,

WavySea $\equiv$ Sea $\sqcap$ Wave,
SandyBeach $\equiv$ Sea $\sqcap$ Sand,
PartOfComplexBuilding $\equiv$ Building $\sqcap$ ($\exists$left $-$ of.Building $\sqcup$ $\exists$right $-$ of.Building),

Beach $\equiv$ $\exists$contains.Sea $\sqcap$ $\exists$contains.SKY,
Landscape $\equiv$ $\exists$contains.VEGETATION,
City $\equiv$ $\exists$contains.Building $\sqcup$ $\exists$contains.Pavement$\}$

$\mathcal{R} = \{$contains, left $-$ of$^-$ = right $-$ of, above $-$ of$^-$ = below $-$ of$\}$

terminology. The obtained implicit results together with the explicit information provided by classifiers(i.e. *ABox*) are stored to a Sesame repository.

4 Experimental Results

In this section we present a series of experiments conducted to demonstrate the gain achieved using the proposed approach in comparison to other techniques. We have set up two datasets of images: One consisting of 500 images, which is accompanied by ground truth at the image level, i.e. we know that concepts either exist or not in the whole image, without any information to which region correspond. The second dataset consists of 350 images, for which we have a finer grained ground truth at a region level, i.e. annotation for every region (2185 regions in total).

In order to evaluate the performance of our integrated approach we compare the recognition rates to those of each individual classifier, as well as to a basic classification method. In the case of the first dataset we had to align the available image level ground truth to the region level classification results. We assumed that when a region has been classified to a concept with a certain degree of confidence, then the maximum degree (over all regions) can be propagated to the image itself. Following this procedure for every concept we end up with a list of concepts and confidence values detected *somewhere* in the image.

First Experiment: Evaluation at the image level. For this first experiment, we calculated the performance of a simple classification approach which is based on a simple color RSST segmentation, descriptor extraction and SVM classification. We examined the performance of the semantic segmentation, of the SVM classifier (2.2), of the bio-inspired classifier (2.2), as well as that of the fusion mechanism (2.3). Figure 2a illustrates the precision rate of the above four algorithms for all 15 concepts. Additionally we calculated the overall performance of the above four techniques, irrespectively to the concept, using a weighted average of precision and recall values of each concept. Each concept's weight depends

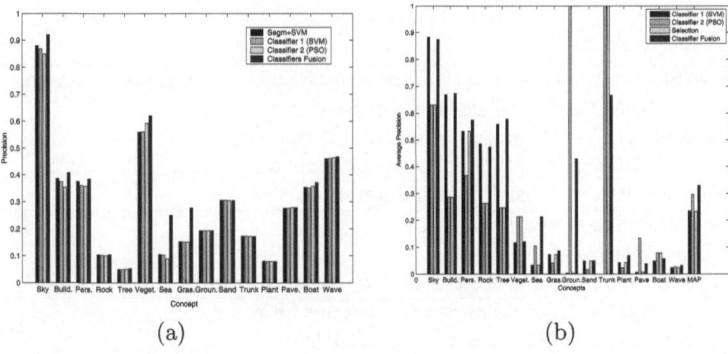

Fig. 2. Precision for the different classification results for every concept

on the frequency of appearance of that concept in the dataset according to the ground truth. Moreover, the weighted harmonic mean (F-measure) of precision and recall was calculated to measure the effectiveness of the classification. In the application of multimedia indexing, we consider precision more important measure than recall, since it is the user's preference to retrieve relevant content with little noise, rather than all the available relevant dataset (which is usually of immense size) and therefore in the computation of the harmonic mean the precision to recall rate is 2:1. The first three columns of Table 2 provide those figures. It is apparent that the NNET fusion provides the best precision for every single concept and also is the most effective (according to the F-measure), while the bio-inspired classifier tops in the recall figures.

Moreover, we calculated the precision and recall of a selected subset of concepts, the most frequent in the dataset. We observe (Table 2 last three columns) a significant increase of all figures, which can be explained by the fact that classifiers were better trained since more example samples were available. We have selected the 6 most frequent concepts, which correspond approximately to the two thirds of detected concepts in the whole dataset.

Second Experiment: Evaluation at the region level. In order to demonstrate the significance of our region-based approach to semantically index images, we set up another experiment, based on the second dataset, for which we have ground truth on the region level. The classification task consists of retrieving

Table 2. Average classification results for all concepts (image level granularity)

Technique	All Concepts			Frequent Concepts		
	Prec.	Rec.	F-meas.	Prec.	Rec.	F-meas.
Segm+SVM	0.45	0.58	0.48	0.57	0.63	0.58
Clasif.1 (SVM)	0.45	0.57	0.48	0.56	0.64	0.58
Clasif.2 (PSO)	0.44	0.82	0.52	0.56	0.85	0.63
NNET Fusion	0.48	0.71	0.54	0.60	0.72	0.64

regions expressing one of the considered semantic concepts. The performance has been measured using the standard precision and recall metrics. We are interested by the average precision to have the measure of the ability of a system to present only relevant regions.

Figure 2b shows the average precision for the four systems (PSO, SVM for classification, and our NNET in fusion, along with a simple selection approach based on the best classifier output over a validation set). We observe that our fusion model achieves respectable performance with respect to the number of concepts detected, in particular for certain semantic concepts (Building, Person, Tree, Sea, Grass, Sand and Dried plant). Here, NNET fusion combines the converging classifier outputs (PSO and SVM) to obtain an effective decision which improves upon the individual classifier outputs. In comparison to the classifier chosen by the selection, which due to low data representativity of the validation set has not allowed the best detection in the test set, the fusion mechanism is more robust. Interesting findings are obtained for the concepts (Vegetation, Pavement and Boat). The performance of fusion is lower than the result given by one of the two classifiers. This is due to both numerous conflicting classification and limited training data. This also explains the extreme cases obtained for concepts Ground and Trunk.

In order to measure the overall performance for the region-based image classification, we calculate the Mean Average Precision (MAP). The PSO classifier detects concepts with more precision than the SVM classifier, $MAP_{PSO} = 0.30$ and $MAP_{SVM} = 0.23$, while NNET fusion combines the two classifiers and allows an overall improvement $MAP_{NNET} = 0.33$. We observe that these figures are pretty lower than those of Table 2 $(0.48 - 0.54)$, but this should be expected since this evaluation metric has region level granularity. For instance, when searching for images of people in a beach (see also example in the following subsection) the evaluation metric for the image as a whole will consider the maximum degree of confidence for the concept Person, while the region-level approach will also detect the exact position of it in the image. This, we think, is a reasonable trade-off between spatial accuracy and global precision rate.

5   Conclusions

This paper contributes to the semantic indexing of images based on algorithms of varying granularity of semantic information, each one targeting to solve partially the problem of bridging the semantic gap. The integrated framework consists of a novel semantic image segmentation technique, a bottom-up image classification using two classifiers of different philosophy and a neural network to fuse the results of the classifiers. This intermediate outcome is further refined and enriched using fuzzy reasoning based on domain-specific knowledge in the formal representation of fuzzy description logics. Finally, the semantic description of the image is stored in a knowledge base which facilitates querying and retrieving of images. Future work of the authors includes implementation of more robust classifiers, integration of richer semantics and broader knowledge, as well as extension to video sequences.

References

1. Adamek, T., O'Connor, N., Murphy, N.: Region-based segmentation of images using syntactic visual features. In: Proc. Workshop on Image Analysis for Multimedia Interactive Services, WIAMIS 2005, Switzerland (April 2005)
2. Athanasiadis, T., Mylonas, P., Avrithis, Y., Kollias, S.: Semantic image segmentation and object labeling. IEEE Trans. on Circuits and Systems for Video Technology 17(3), 298–312 (2007)
3. Baader, F., McGuinness, D., Nardi, D., Patel-Schneider, P.F.: The Description Logic Handbook: Theory, implementation and applications. Cambridge University Press, Cambridge (2002)
4. Benmokhtar, R., Huet, B.: Neural network combining classifier based on dempster-shafer theory for semantic indexing in video content. In: International MultiMedia Modeling Conference, vol. 4351, pp. 196–205 (2007)
5. Chandramouli, K., Izquierdo, E.: Image classification using self organizing feature maps and particle swarm optimization. In: Proc. 7th International Workshop on Image Analysis for Multimedia Interactive Services, WIAMIS (2006)
6. Denoeux, T.: An evidence-theoretic neural network classifier. In: International Conference on Systems, Man and Cybernetics, vol. 3, pp. 712–717 (1995)
7. Klir, G.J., Yuan, B.: Fuzzy Sets and Fuzzy Logic: Theory and Applications. Prentice-Hall, Englewood Cliffs (1995)
8. Naphade, M., Huang, T.S.: A probabilistic framework for semantic video indexing, filtering and retrieval. IEEE Trans. on Multimedia 3(1), 144–151 (2001)
9. Pan, J.Z., Stamou, G., Stoilos, G., Thomas, E.: Expressive querying over fuzzy DL-Lite ontologies. In: Proceedings of the International Workshop on Description Logics (DL 2007) (2007)
10. Papadopoulos, G.T., Mezaris, V., Kompatsiaris, I., Strintzis, M.G.: Combining global and local information for knowledge-assisted image analysis and classification. EURASIP J. Adv. Signal Process 2007(2), 18 (2007)
11. Smeaton, A.F., Over, P., Kraaij, W.: Evaluation campaigns and trecvid. In: MIR 2006: Proceedings of the 8th ACM International Workshop on Multimedia Information Retrieval, pp. 321–330. ACM Press, New York (2006)
12. Snoek, C., Huurninkm, B., Hollink, L., de Rijke, M., Schreiber, G., Worring, M.: Adding semantics to detectors for video retrieval. IEEE Trans. on Multimedia 9(5), 144–151 (2007)
13. Stoilos, G., Stamou, G., Tzouvaras, V., Pan, J.Z., Horrocks, I.: Reasoning with very expressive fuzzy description logics. Journal of Artificial Intelligence Research 30(5), 273–320 (2007)
14. Straccia, U.: Reasoning within fuzzy description logics. Journal of Artificial Intelligence Research 14, 137–166 (2001)
15. Vapnik, V.: The Nature of Statistical Learning Theory. Springer, Heidelberg (2000)
16. Zhang, L., Lin, F., Zhang, B.: Support vector machine learning for image retrieval. In: International Conference on Image Processing, vol. 2 (2001)

Variability Tolerant Audio Motif Discovery

Armando Muscariello, Guillaume Gravier, and Frédéric Bimbot

IRISA (CNRS & INRIA), Rennes, France
METISS, 'Speech and Audio Processing' research group

Abstract. Mining of repeating patterns is useful in inferring structure in streams and in multimedia indexing, as it allows to summarize even large archives by small sets of recurrent items. Techniques for their discovery are required to handle large data sets and tolerate a certain amount of variability among instances of the same underlying pattern (like spectral variability and temporal distortion). In this paper, early approaches and experiments are described for the retrieval of such variable patterns in audio, a task that we call audio motif discovery, for analogy with its counterpart in biology. The algorithm is based on a combination of ARGOS [4] to segment the data and organize the search of the motifs, and a novel technique based on segmental dynamic time warping to detect similarities in the audio data. Moreover, precision-recall measures are defined for evaluation purposes and preliminary experiments on the word discovery case are discussed.

Keywords: audio pattern discovery, variable motif, dynamic time warping, normalized edit distance.

1 Introduction

1.1 Motivation

Discovery of repeating patterns for multimedia indexing is an emerging research field. The increasing possibility to capture and store large amounts of multimedia documents has led to the adoption of strategies to quickly access, process and browse through massive data sets. Identification of patterns that structurally characterize a multimedia archive aims at coherently organizing the collection by representing the archive through a set of specific, recurrent items. Recent work on audio thumbnailing of music catalogs point towards this direction [1][2]. Moreover, in many cases, learning the structure of a process by pattern discovery can be very useful in seeking a model that reflects the properties of the source that has generated the process itself. This is roughly what is done in computational biology, where the extraction of meaningful patterns (usually referred as motifs) in massive amounts of DNA and protein sequences plays a key role in the analysis and understanding of important biological functionalities [5].

Allowing only identical patterns to be recognized would dramatically limit the potential applications of motif discovery. For example in comparative genomics,

B. Huet et al. (Eds.): MMM 2009, LNCS 5371, pp. 275–286, 2009.

most of the time, patterns are allowed to present wild cards or indels, *e.g.* they are not necessarily identical, but present a certain degree of variability.

Our interest is focused on the retrieval of such recurring patterns in audio streams or data sets, a task that, for analogy with its counterpart in genomic, we call audio motif discovery. Typical examples in streams are repetition of jingles, advertisements, or even entire shows broadcasted multiple times in a day, whose identification allows for customization of the stream (by skipping commercial, for example). Identification of words and verbal expressions that inherently characterize a news, a lecture, a movie, is useful for summarization and enable the user to fastly browse trough the audio archive without relying on a transcribed version of the data. Techniques for retrieval of such motifs are required scalability to manage large data sets, flexibility to handle the large variety of motifs lenght, and robustness to sources of variability that make it difficult to detect multiple copies of the same motif (temporal distortions, spectral variability of the human voice). We propose in this paper one of such techniques that has been preliminary tested on the task of word discovery in speech and we plan to verify its performance in different audio motif discovery experiments.

1.2 Related Works

In the last few years, only few work have addressed and formalized the problem of unsupervised audio motif discovery.

In [3] an algorithm is proposed for motif discovery in time series, but the search is performed on a symbolic, intermediate level that is clearly a limitation for the application to the audio signal. In ARGOS [4], a scalable approach is used to detect repetition of multimedia objects in streams by only considering the audio portion, but variability is not taken into account as objects are supposed to be identical recordings broadcasted multiple times over the day.

In [6] fragments of speech are compared pairwise at the acoustic level by a segmental DTW (SDTW) and the output is used to build an adjacency graph (with times indexes as nodes and DTW scores as edges) followed by a clustering phase. However, this approach does not scale well for increasing large data sets as the number of comparisons grows quadratically with the number of segments. Moreover, SDTW shows higher complexity than conventional DTW.

1.3 Outline

The paper is organized as follows: a short introduction is done to specify the elementary subtasks that compose the problem, followed by the description of ARGOS, a procedure to segment the stream and organize the search. The main contribution of our work is in subsection 2.2, 2.3, 2.4, where three variants of a new segmental DTW algorithm are introduced for automatically discovering similarities in acoustic fragments. In section 3, a framework to evaluate the performance is proposed and preliminary results on a small data set are next presented. Finally, ideas for improvements and developments of the current work are discussed.

2   Description of the Algorithm

The audio motif discovery can be conceptually organized in four different subtasks:

1. the segmentation of the data into smaller segments to be compared for similarity detection.
2. the transformation of the raw data in an alternative, less redundant representation suitable for the comparisons.
3. the definition of a similarity measure and the inference of a proper threshold to discriminate (dis)similarity, that is to detect instances of the same motif.
4. the search procedure, that is the structural way to organize the comparison of the segments.

We tackle all these aspect in this section.

First, we remark the notable difference between the motif discovery and the search for previously known patterns (query by content) in stream or data sets, a problem well addressed in the scientific literature. In motif discovery, the searched objects (the queries of the search) are not known a priori, but must be inferred from the stream itself in an unsupervised way. As motifs endpoints or even presence in the stream is unknown, naive exhaustive strategies imply candidate motifs of every possible length in every part of the stream to be assumed as queries and searched along the entire stream. This approach is clearly unfeasible even for small data sets.

Alternatively we resort on ARGOS, a general purpose strategy that exploit the intrinsic repetitiveness in streams to efficiently segment the data and organize the search.

2.1   The ARGOS Approach

In ARGOS fixed length motif candidates (queries) are used, supposed to either coincide with the motif or include the motif as a portion of it. Moreover, the search for each query is not performed over the entire stream, but is rather restricted on its near future (or recent past) and a library is incrementally build where detected motifs are stored and used for retrieval of long term matches.

More specifically, at each step of the process, a portion of the incoming audio stream is broken into a pair query-buffer. The query is a segment of the portion of stream under processing, which is supposed to completely contain the motif. The buffer is the audio portion adjacent to the query and it represents the search-space where the query is seeked into.

The underlying assumption is that meaningful patterns repeat frequently, at least in a part of the stream, thus they are likely to repeat in their near future[1].

When a repetition of the current query in the buffer is detected, a reference model of the common pattern (the found motif) is stored in a library and used for future comparisons. As the process evolves, query and buffer shift along the

---

[1] Or in the recent past, as in the original work.

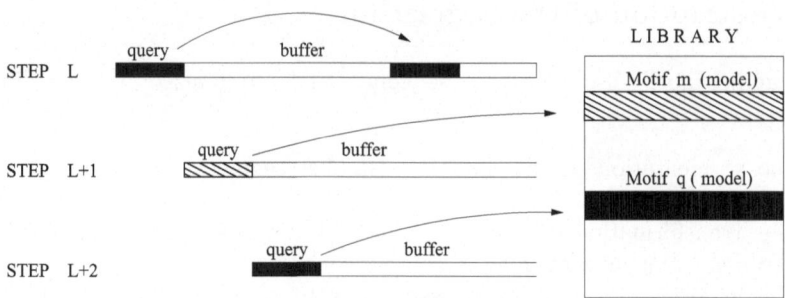

Fig. 1. ARGOS framework: at step L, the current query is not detected in the library but it is found in the buffer and the corresponding reference model is stored in the library as the q-th motif. At step L+1 query and buffer shift along the stream of a query length and the current query is retrieved in the library by comparison with the m-th motif. At step L+2 the new query, which happens to be another occurrence of the q-th motif, is retrieved by direct search in the library.

audio stream, and the new query is first seeked into the library (by comparison with the stored models) and, if not found in the library, in the search buffer (as illustrated in figure 1). It follows that each query is searched, at most, in the K motifs currently stored in the library plus the search buffer, unlike the exhaustive approach that implies a number of comparisons that quadratically grwos with the number of queries.

In the original work, the search is performed on the audio portion by time correlating distorted versions of the speech signal, obtained by only retaining a small part of the audio spectrum (about 200 Hz centered around the sixth Bark band). Such a reduction technique can decently perform only in a context where a very few samples are needed to discriminate (dis)similarity, that is, occurrences of the same motif are supposed to be practically identical and completely different from other motifs; it is therefore unsuitable in a word discovery task, and, in general, in a scenario where instances of the same motifs can exhibit a certain amount of variability. For this purpose, we propose to resort to a more accurate spectral representation of the audio signal (MFCC) and exploite the potential of dynamic programming for pattern identification. Several implementations of a new segmental DTW technique are carefully described in the following.

2.2 Segmental Locally Normalized DTW

DTW is a widely used technique for pattern recognition. In the classical version, it is used to detect similarity between two motif templates, a and b, by computing spectral frame vectors $\{u_i\}_{i=1}^M$ and $\{v_j\}_{j=1}^N$, and the frame-to-frame distance matrix $d(i,j), 1 \leq i \leq M, 1 \leq j \leq N$. Applying recursively dynamic programming (DP) relations, a path $P = [(1,1), \cdots, (M,N)]$ of length $L(P)$ is found and the corresponding average weight $W(P) = (d(1,1) + \cdots + d(M,N))/L(P)$ is compared against a spectal threshold ϕ to decide if a and b are similar.

As in our framework we can not rely on an *a priori* segmentation of the stream into exact motifs, this approach is not suitable since it only works when motifs endpoints are well defined. Indeed, motifs boundaries are not known in advance. Our goal is to be able to find a path P from (i_s, j_s) to (i_e, j_e), with $1 \leq i_s \leq i_e \leq M, 1 \leq j_s \leq j_e \leq N$, relaxing the boundary constraint of the classical approaches that force starting and ending point to be respectively at $(1, 1)$ and (M, N). We first consider the case $i_s = 1, i_e = M$, that is, we search a repetition of the whole vector u (query) into v (buffer).

The solution we propose relies on a heuristic that consists in locally minimizing the average weight of each path, both when selecting new starting points and when computing the paths itself, with same complexity as the conventional boundary-constrained approaches. We call it segmental locally normalized DTW (SLNDTW), as it allows for multiple paths with different starting points (Segmental) and it is based on a Local Normalization principle.

We define $L(i, j)$ as the length of the path starting from some $(1, j_s)$ up to (i, j), $D(i, j)$ the corresponding accumulated distance and $W(i, j) = D(i, j)/L(i, j)$ its average weight.

As a potential match can occur anywhere in v, we need a strategy to allow $j_s \neq 1, j_e \neq N$. We identify a starting point by comparing each cell $(1, j)$ with its left neighbour $(1, j - 1)$ (which has been evaluated previously, as computation proceeds from left to right, as in classical DTW): if $d(1, j)$ is less than $W(1, j)$ (the weight of the path obtained by adding $d(1, j)$ to $D(1, j - 1)$), then it is decided to start a new path from $(1, j)$ as a starting point of a potential matching sequence. Formally:
$\forall j, 1 \leq j \leq N$,

$$
\begin{cases}
\begin{aligned}
D(1, j) &= & d(1, j) \\
L(1, j) &= & 1
\end{aligned} \quad & \text{, if } d(1, j) < W(1, j) \\[2ex]
\begin{aligned}
D(1, j) &= D(1, j - 1) + d(1, j) \\
L(1, j) &= \quad L(1, j - 1) + 1
\end{aligned} \quad & \text{, otherwise}
\end{cases}
\tag{1}
$$

Except for $i = 1$, each path is computed by iteratively applying the DP relations following the local normalization paradigm, which consists in minimizing, at each point (i, j) of the computational grid $[1, \cdots, M] \times [1, \cdots, N]$, the weight $W(i, j)$, that is the quotient between the accumulated distance $D(i, j)$ and the path length $L(i, j)$. Formally:

$$
W(i, j) = \min \left[\frac{d(i, j) + D(i - 1, j)}{L(i - 1, j) + 1}, \frac{d(i, j) + D(i - 1, j - 1)}{L(i - 1, j - 1) + 1}, \frac{d(i, j) + D(i, j - 1)}{L(i, j - 1) + 1} \right]
\tag{2}
$$

The ending point (M, j_e) of a match is such that $W(M, j_e) < \phi, 1 \leq j_e \leq N$, where ϕ is a spectral threshold. If several such points exist, that is multiple occurrences of the query in the buffer occur, we just retain the first one and initialize a cluster in the library, modeling the motif as the average of the spectral frames put in correspondence by the DTW mapping. The other occurrences will be detected later when assumed as queries and searched in the library, and the reference model will be updated as well by averaging with the newly detected instances of the motif.

Like in conventional DTW we only need to scan the distance matrix d once to compute D and L (W is D/L), differently from SDTW, where after paths computation, each diagonal band needs to be re-evaluated for subpath identification.

Moreover, while in SDTW starting points are a priori selected by regularly sampling the first row of $[1, \cdots, M] \times [1, \cdots, N]$, in SLNDTW each cell $(1, j)$ is a starting point candidate.

It is worth noting that paths are not forced to be confined in diagonals of a pre-defined slope, and various local constraints can be applied, depending on the application, allowing for matches with different slopes.

2.3   Band Relaxed SLNDTW

SLNDTW aims at finding matches of the query in the search buffer. In our framework, this approach would be effective only if motifs were of fixed length and coincide exactly with the query. This is a strong assumption and far from realistic applicative contexts. If the length assumption restricts the number of retrievable motifs, the mismatch in time synchronization between motif and query dramatically decrease performance, as increasingly high path weights result from even sligth timeshiftings. We propose here a modification of SLNDTW, band relaxed SLNDTW, that relaxes the boundary constraints of SLNDTW selecting starting and ending points in a group of rows (band), instead of a single one, thus allowing to retrieve motif with different lengths, as illustrated in figure 2. This is achieved by dividing the grid $[1, \cdots, M] \times [1, \cdots, N]$ in three horizontal bands and selecting starting point in the first one and ending point in third, constraining all the paths to cross the second one. The starting band includes all $(i, j)|i \in [1, L_s]$, the central band includes points $(i, j)|i \in]L_s, L_s + L_c]$ and the ending band includes all points $(i, j)|i \in]L_s + L_c, M]$. Accordingly, motif lengths are allowed to vary from L_c to M.

More specifically:

1. $\forall(i, j)|i \in [1, L_s]$:

$$\text{if } d(i,j) < \left[\frac{d(i,j) + D(i-1,j)}{L(i-1,j)+1}, \frac{d(i,j) + D(i-1,j-1)}{L(i-1,j-1)+1}, \frac{d(i,j) + D(i,j-1)}{L(i,j-1)+1} \right]$$

   then (i, j) is the starting point of a new path, otherwise it is added to the path that minimizes $W(i, j)$. Note that this a generalization of eq. (1), as the same condition is expressed by considering the whole neighbourhood of (i, j) rather than the single cell at its left $(i, j - 1)$.
2. $\forall(i, j)|i \in]L_s, M]$ compute path as in eq. (2).
3. $\forall(i, j)|i \in [L_c + L_s, M]$ select the ending point of a match, if any, as in SLNDTW, and reconstruct the corresponding path.

In addition, we have applied an heuristic for the refinement of the boundaries that consists in extending the found match by adding new frames at the

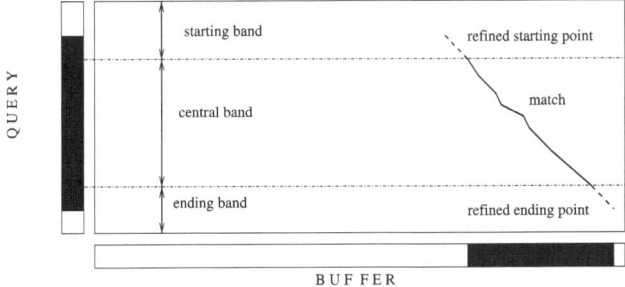

Fig. 2. Band relaexd SLNDTW: the motif completely includes the central band. After path reconstruction, boundaries are refined in the starting and ending band (dashed lines).

boundaries (following the local normalization paradigm), as long as the average weight of the extended path does not increase too much.

Formally:

1. Consider the path P with $W(P) = W_o$ ending in (i_e, j_e).
2. Select in the neighbourhood of (i_e, j_e) (composed of $(i_e + 1, j_e + 1), (i_e + 1, j_e), (i_e, j_e + 1))$ the point that, added to P, minimizes $W(P)$, and add it to P as its new ending point.
3. If $W(P) < W_o + 10\%W_o$, then repeat the procedure from 1, otherwise remove the new ending point from P and stop the procedure.

The same approach applies when extending the path backward from its starting point (i_s, j_s).

2.4   Fragmental SLNDTW

Band relaxed SNLDTW does not constrain motif and query to coincide, but it still assumes the motif to be located in the middle part of the query, such that it completely includes the central band. A simple generalization of the previous versions of the algorithm, that we call fragmental SLNDTW, allows to retrieve the sought motif regardless of its position in the query, by first retrieving a portion of it, *e.g.* a fragment. SLNDTW detects a match whenever a query coincide with a motif. By using queries small enough to be included in the motif, then there exists at least one fragment of the motif that coincide with one of the queries and that can be discovered by SLNDTW. Indeed, if $L_{min} \leq L_{motif} \leq L_{max}$, partitioning a L_{max} long query in $L_{min}/2$ long subqueries ensures that at least a $L_{min}/2$ long fragment of the motif coincide with one of the subqueries, and it is therefore retrievable by conventional SNLDTW. The entire match can be recovered afterwards, by extending the corresponding path as in the boundary refinement stage in Band relaxed SLNDTW.

For the sake of clarity we explicit the steps of the procedure and illustrate the scenario in figure 3:

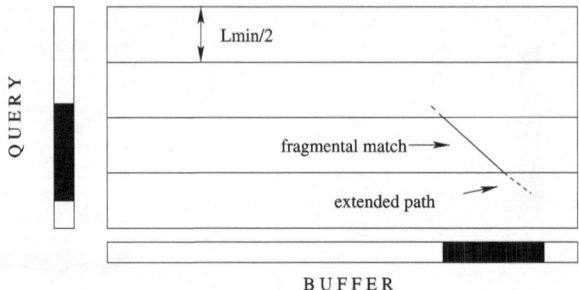

Fig. 3. Fragmental SLNDTW: partitiong the query in $L_{min}/2$ long subqueries ensures that a least a fragment of the motif coincide with a subquery. The entire match can be then recovered by extending the fragmental match.

1. divide the grid $[1, \cdots, M] \times [1, \cdots, N]$ in horizontal bands of length $L_{min}/2$, such as the i-th band includes all point $(i,j)|(i-1) \cdot L_{min}/2 + 1 \leq i \leq i \cdot L_{min}/2$.
2. perform a conventional SNLDTW in each band and reconstruct the found match, if any.
3. extend the path corresponding to the found match with the same heuristic used to refine boundaries in band SLNDTW.

This implementation of the technique has the advantage to enable the retrieval of a match whichever its position in the considered query, hence it shows higher flexibility than the two previous versions. It only constraints the motif minimum and maximum lenght, which is not a very limiting assumption in many applications.

Therefore, using an accurate spectral representation of the audio signal (MFCC) and combining the described method with ARGOS segmentation-search strategy, the motif discovery can be finally performed.

3   Evaluation

The evaluation of the performance relies on the analysis of the library of motifs constructed by the algorithm. We propose here a framework for the computation of a recall-precision curve. Precision aims at quantifying the level of purity of each cluster in the library, that is the ability of the algorithm to limit false hits as much as possible, while recall aims at measuring the ability to limit missed detection of motif's instances, or, equivalently, to retrieve, for each motif, as many exemplars as possible. In our framework, evaluation has been performed at the phonetic level relying on a transcribed version of speech data; accordingly we have resorted to *normalized edit distance* d [7] and a phonetic threshold θ to verify the (dis)similarity between motifs found by the algorithm at the spectral level.

We introduce the following notation:

- LB_i: i-th motif of the library LB.
- $LB_{i,j}$: j-th instance of the motif LB_i.
- m_i: cardinality of LB_i.
- $d(LB_{i,j}, LB_{i,k})$: distance between $LB_{i,j}$ and $LB_{i,k}$.
- c_i: centroid of LB_i

The centroid c_i of LB_i is defined as:

$$c_i = LB_{i,p} \text{ where } p = \arg \min_{1 \leq j \leq m_i} \sum_{k=1}^{m_i} d^2(LB_{i,j}, LB_{i,k}) \tag{3}$$

The precision of the i-th motif is thus computed as:

$$P_i(\theta) = \frac{\left(\sum_j \delta \left(d(LB_{i,j}, LB_{i,p} < \theta) \right) \right)}{m_i} = \frac{m_i'}{m_i} \tag{4}$$

where $\delta = 1$ if its argument is true, and 0 otherwise. It represents the fraction of instances $LB_{i,j}$ included in a sphere of center c_i and radius θ. The global precision $P(\theta)$ is the average of P_i over all motifs LB_i.

Let m_i'' be the number of entities M over the entire phonetic transcription such as $d(M, LB_{i,j}) < \theta$. The recall of the i-th cluster is the ratio:

$$R_i(\theta) = \frac{m_i'}{m_i''} \tag{5}$$

and the global recall $R(\theta)$ is computed by averaging over all motifs of the library.

4 Preliminary Experiments

The test data is composed of a 20 minute long French broadcast recording, sampled at 16 KHz. Words are uttered from different speakers (the conductor and the authors of the live reports) and no preliminary segmentation or pre-processing (like silence deletion) is performed. 13-dimensional MFCCs vector are extracted every 10 ms.

As the dimension of the processed file is quite small, even motifs occurring as few as 2 times are retained and considered for recall-precision evaluation: therefore the resulting numbers are not meant as statistically relevant measurements. Nonetheless, they are useful to evaluate and compare the performance of the different implementations of the algorithm.

In a 20 minutes bulletin, the time duration of each report is around 1 minute; as patterns inherently characterizing a 1 minute news have been supposed to repeat in a few seconds, we have arbitrarily set the buffer length to 13 seconds for all runs of the algorithm. As queries and motifs are supposed to coincide in conventional SLNDTW, the query length has been set to an average word length (0.6 second).

In Band relaxed SLNDTW, the motif is supposed to be located in the middle of the query. We have therefore used 1 second long queries. In the Fragmental SLNDTW, motifs are allowed to be located anywhere in the query. Given the flexibility of this last method, among all the possible choices, we have arbitrarily chosen 2 seconds long queries. Finally, in the Band relaxed version we have set $L_c = 0.3$ s and in the Fragmental SLNDTW we have set $L_{min}/2 = 0.3$ s.

The different versions of the algorithm have been tested for increasing values of the spectral thresholds ϕ, from $\phi = 8$ to $\phi = 12$. In some experiments we have noted that, even in the correct detection of two occurences of the same motif, certain phonemes at the boundaries of the two exemplars are not detected. In order to take into account the issue, we have empirically set the phonetic threshold θ to 0.35.

We have noted that, at least for $\phi \leq 10$, the resulting library of motifs exhibits a significative level of purity, as acoustically similar fragments are well grouped together. Motif length has mostly ranged from 0.45 s (set as minimum acceptable length)to 0.9 s. Example of retrieved motifs are: single words, usually including some phonemes from the preceding and following words (*les ambassadeurs du G*), or subwords shared in common by different words (*la position - la discussion*), or even small multi words locutions (*face a l'interdiction*), while the small breathings in between words have been notably the most frequently retrieved pattern. In some cases we have noted different clusters representing the same underlying motif that the algorithm has failed to merge together, in particular for words uttered by different speakers. In several occasions, repeating words have not been detected at all, either because the size of the buffer has revealed to be too short to detect them, or because different exemplars of the same word have shown higher spectral distances than expected.

From a quantitative point of view, the results of the experiments are summarized in figure 4 and 5. In figure 4 the number of found motifs for a certain value of ϕ is shown for the different versions of the algorithm. As expected, this number is always higher for Band relaxed and Fragmental SLNDTW with respect to conventional SNLDTW, since in this last case no variability in motif length is allowed and consequently, only 0.6 seconds repeating words (the query length used) can be detected; moreover only perfectly aligned exemplars are likely to be found, as slight misalignments, as already noted, infer significant distortions.

In figure 5 it can be observed that, for increasing values of ϕ, the precision P decreases, as false hits appear more frequently. Even if the the experiment was conducted on a small data set, it is noteworthy the high value of purity suggested by the computed precision, in particular for $\phi < 11$ and for the last two versions of SLNDTW.

The behaviour of the recall parameter R, for different values of ϕ is less straightforward to understand.

Indeed, in SLNDTW and Fragmental SLNDTW this value tends to increase from $\phi = 8$ to $\phi = 10$ and then to fall for larger values of ϕ. The same transition can be observed between $\phi = 9$ and $\phi = 10$ for Band relaxed SLNDTW.

We initially predicted that an increase of ϕ would be followed by a substantial improvement of R at the expense of P, as more instances of the same underlying

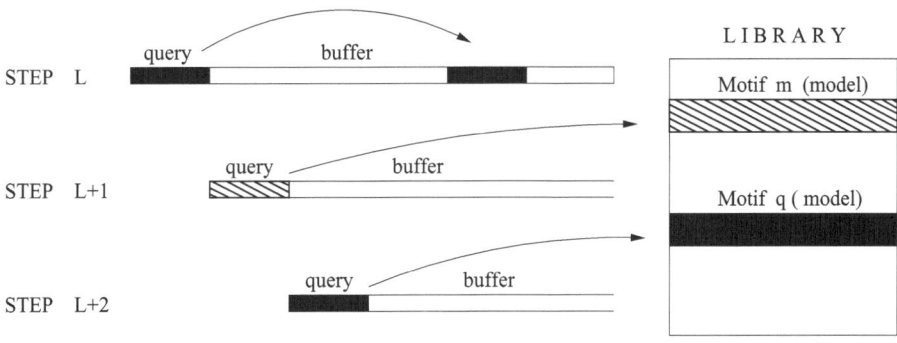

Fig. 4. Number of found motifs for the different algorithms and different values of θ

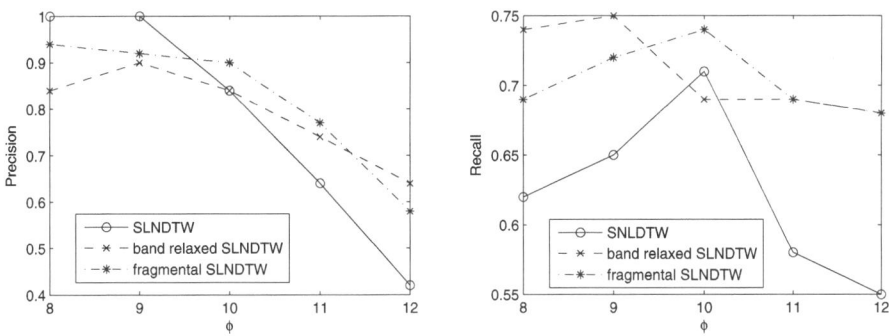

Fig. 5. Precision and recall curve for the different algorithms and different values of θ

motif -as well as more false hits- are likely to be detected for higher values of spectral threshold; instead, the way the reference model is built and updated in the library strictly relates recall and performance measures, as averaging false hits with the reference model tends to progressively reduce its representativeness, leading to missed detection of true instances of the same motif. In synthesis, updating the reference model is highly prone to error propagation, when increasing the spectral threshold. Moreover, as defined as in eq. (5), the recall is only computed over the found motifs, not taking into accounts those motifs that algorithm does not detect at all, that should contribute each with a single recall $R_i = 0$.

5 Conclusions and Future Works

In this work, we have addressed and formalized the task of audio motif discovery. We have proposed an algorithm that combines ARGOS and three different implementations of a novel DTW approach for audio similarities detection that seamlessly integrates into ARGOS. The algorithm has been tested on the word discovery case, and has shown promising results, at least in terms of precision. It exhibits a certain robustness to the typical spectral variability in speech when

detecting multiple realization of the same word. We plan to investigate its performance in different audio motif contexts.

Large scale experiments are needed to validate the preliminary results here presented and to test the sensitivity of the algorithm to variations of main parameters.
As far as the improvement of the current algorithm we note here that the most
remarkable limitation of the current method is that it limits the pattern discovery problem to the search and identification of low distortion regions in the local
distance matrix. However, we have noted that, for a variety of reasons (different
speakers, environmental conditions and so on), same words at different points in
the audio file present different values of (locally normalized) distance when compared against each other; that makes it difficult to set a fixed reliable spectral
threshold to discriminate between false and true matches. However, we have discovered visual similarities in their local distance matrices, which are consistent in
the majority of the compared instances, regardless of the distortion of the main
diagonal. We plan to investigate the nature of these patterns to improve the recognition task, by exploiting the large corpus of techniques in the image processing
literature. The ultimate goal is to build an adaptive model where different spectral
thresholds are set for each motif in the library and updated as new instances are
found. Moreover, in order to speed up the computation, technique for fast access
to the library can be applied (for example, by storing the motif in order of decreasing frequency of occurrence), together with techniques for fast approximation of
DTW.

References

1. Dannenberg, R.B., Hu, N.: Pattern Discovery Techniques in Music Audio. In: Third
   International Conference on Music Information Retrieval, pp. 63–70 (2002)
2. Peeters, G.: Deriving Musical Structures From Signal Analysis for Music Audio Summary Generation: Sequence and State Approach. Content Based Multimedia Indexing (2003)
3. Lin. J, Keogh, E., Lonardi, S., Pratel, P.: Finding Motifs in Time Series. In: ACM
   SIGKDD (2002)
4. Herley, C.: ARGOS: Automatically Extracting Repeating Objects from Multimedia
   Streams. IEEE Transactions on Multimedia 8 (2006)
5. Brazma, A., Jonassen, I., Eidhammer, I., Gilbert, I.: Approaches to Automatic Discovery of Patterns in Biosequences. J. Comp. Biology 5(2), 279–305 (1998)
6. Park, A., Glass, J.R.: Unsupervised pattern discovery in speech: IEEE Transaction
   on Acoustic. Speech and Language Processing 16 (2008)
7. Vidal, E., Marzal, A., Aibar, P.: Fast Computation of Normalized Edit Distances.
   IEEE Transaction on Pattern Analysis and Machine Intelligence 17(9) (1995)

Key Estimation Using Circle of Fifths

Takahito Inoshita and Jiro Katto

Graduate School of Fundamental Science and Engineering, Waseda University,
3-4-1 Ohkubo, Shinjuku-ku, Tokyo, 169-8555 Japan
{inoshita,katto}@katto.comm.waseda.ac.jp

Abstract. This paper presents a novel key estimation method of sound sources based on the music theory known as "circle of fifths". We firstly overview music theory and formulate the musical key analysis by vector operations. In detail, we separate music sources into small pieces and calculate FFT-based chroma vectors. They are converted to tonality vectors and COF (circle-of-fifth) vectors are calculated from the tonality vectors, which are mapped onto the circle of fifths coordinate. As a result, each music source can be represented by traces of COF vectors, which usually stay inside a single key region on the circle of fifths. Finally, HMM is applied to the traces of COF vectors in order to detect keys and their boundaries. Experiments using music databases are also carried out.

1 Introduction

Key Estimation is one of important methods in the field of automatic music transcription system. We can estimate the music key by applying macroscopic analysis of the harmony of a tune. On the other way, we can also estimate a chord progression and more microscopic features of a tune. These features may be also useful for music retrieval system.

Music keys are determined from the pitch set in a sufficient span of a tune. So far, many machine learning methods had been proposed [1][2][3]. Most of them apply HMM (Hidden Markov Model) to specific features of the sound such as MFCC (Mel-Frequency Cepstrum Coefficient) and chroma vectors for key estimation or chord estimation, in which EM algorithm is utilized to set up the HMM model by using labeled data. However, since the keys are independent of sorts of music instruments and melody lines, such supervised learning methods work well only for limited sorts of instruments. Furthermore, to make learning data is troublesome and the efficiency depends on the way to learn the data.

In this paper, we propose a new method for extracting features of tunes based on musical knowledge known as "Circle of Fifths" (COF), which projects a tune onto COF coordinate. We firstly separate music sources into small pieces and calculate FFT-based chroma vectors. They are converted to tonality vectors and COF vectors are calculated from the tonality vectors. Finally, they are mapped onto the circle of fifths coordinate (COF coordinate). As a result, each music source can be represented by traces of COF vectors. We then apply HMM to the traces of COF vectors to track music keys and detect their boundaries.

B. Huet et al. (Eds.): MMM 2009, LNCS 5371, pp. 287–297, 2009.
© Springer-Verlag Berlin Heidelberg 2009

In this research, we deal with only major keys. Minor keys have three scales (natural minor, harmonic minor and melodic minor) and a scale of the natural minor key consists of the same pitch set as its parallel key (A minor's parallel key is C major). Therefore, in this paper, when we talk about a key, we mean both of the key itself and its parallel key.

2 Proposal

Keys of a tune are determined by the pitch set in a sufficient span (usually several bars) of the tune. Generally, they are determined by which notes are used among twelve notes (C, C#, D, ..., B) in one octave. For instance, in a C major tune, seven notes [C, D, E, F, G, A, B] are mainly used. Our proposed method is to estimate their pitch sets efficiently. In Fig.1, the process overview of our proposal is shown.

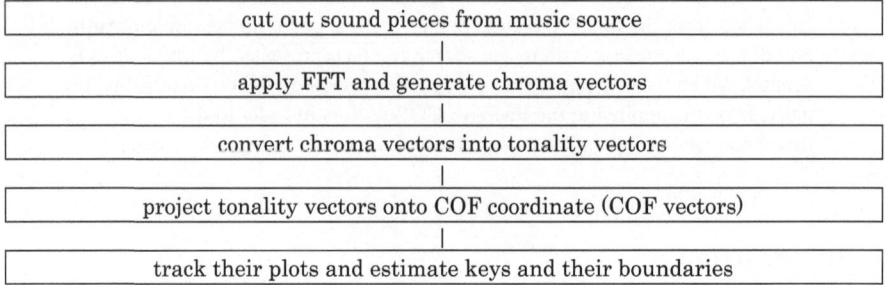

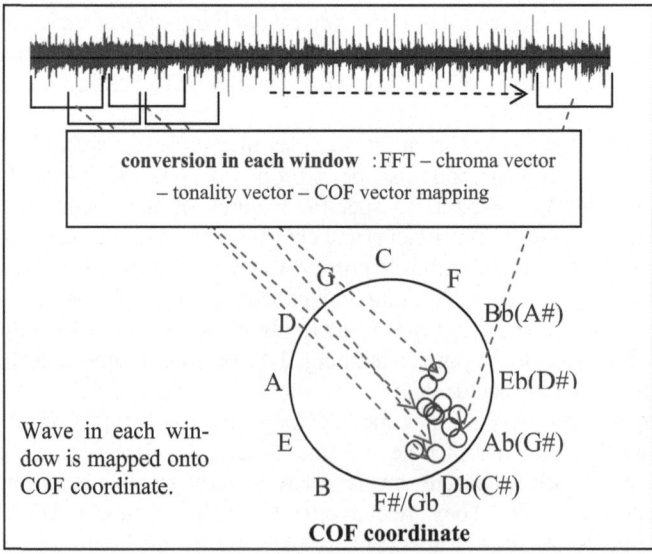

Fig. 1. Flow chart and mapping onto COF coordinate of the proposed method

2.1 Chroma Vector

A chroma vector is calculated from the frequency spectrum and represents how strong power each pitch has as defined in next equations.

$$\mathbf{C}(t) = \begin{bmatrix} c_C(t) \\ \vdots \\ c_B(t) \end{bmatrix}, \; |\mathbf{C}(t)| = 1, \tag{1}$$

$$c_K(t) = \int_{-\infty}^{\infty} BPF_K(\Psi(x))dx \tag{2}$$

where $\Psi(x)$ is the frequency spectrum of a tune and BPF_K is a filter which passes only frequency corresponding of the pitch $K(\in \{C, C\#, ..., B\})$ through. In the equation (1), we normalize a chroma vector because we want to prevent unfairness such that the vector in a span of large volume predominantly works in following processes. Therefore, a chroma vector shows the ratio of power in twelve notes in a span.

2.2 Tonality Vector

A tonality vector is calculated from a chroma vector and represents a probability of each key. So, it is a twelve dimension vector given by

$$\mathbf{K}(t) = \begin{bmatrix} k_C(t) \\ \vdots \\ k_B(t) \end{bmatrix}, \tag{3}$$

$$k_{P_n}(t) = \sum_{i=0}^{11} w_i f(c_{P_{i+n \, (\mathrm{mod}\,12)}}(t)) \quad (P_0 = C, \cdots, P_{11} = B) \tag{4}$$

where w_i is a weight to calculate a tonality vector from chroma and the tonality vector reflects weighted gravities of twelve notes in a certain key. In Spiral Array Model [4], the relation between keys and pitches is defined. In this research, we assign the weight according to the parameters of Spiral Array Model. Concretely speaking, the relation between key K and note n is measured through the primary triad T that connects them (A triad is musical harmony that consists of three notes. Primary triads are three important triads in a key. For instance, C triad, F triad and G triad are primary triads in C major.) As primary triad T corresponds to specific key K and note n does to specific primary triad T, the relation between n and T becomes higher. If there are more than one candidate of T for n and K, all the relation between n and T are summed up. For instance, the key G major and the note D have very high relation because D is the 5th note of the tonic and the root note of the dominant in the key. On the other hand, the key F# major and the note D have little relation because D is never the member note of any primary triad in the key. So, the weight of D in G major is bigger but, by contraries, the one in F# major is smaller.

In the equation (4), $f(\bullet)$ is a trimming function given by

$$f(x) = \frac{1}{6\left(1 + e^{24(1/12-x)}\right)}.$$
(5)

Its shape is shown in Fig.2.

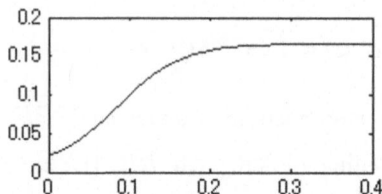

Fig. 2. Trimming function for tonality vector

By using this function, we can restrain unnecessary deviance of a tonality vector by a sudden peak of one note. For example, a case that only the note E appears in C major is supposed. E is an important member note in C major. However, if the chroma vector has a big value only on the element E, the tonality vector has a different feature from C major. In order to prevent this, a note whose power is over a threshold is restrained so that the power doesn't contribute to unexpected keys.

2.3 COF Vector

COF is one of music knowledge and expresses the relation of twelve keys. Twelve keys are put on circumference like Fig. 3, where the neighboring two keys have a similarity that six notes among seven notes of the pitch set is commonly used and only one note differs in semitone. For Example, C major is very similar to F major because C major has [C, D, E, F, G, A, B] as its member notes and F major has [C, D, E, F, G, A, Bb] as its member notes. On the other hand, C major is very dissimilar to F# major (whose member notes are [C#, D#, E#, F#, G#, A#, B]), therefore the two keys face each other.

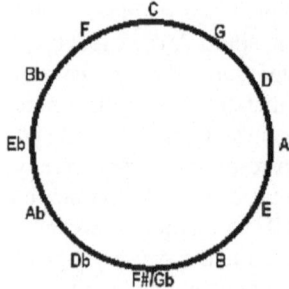

Fig. 3. Circle of Fifths

A COF vector is calculated from a tonality vector and mapped onto COF coordinate. A COF vector is a two-dimensional vector to express tonality in a certain span with similarity of keys. It is given by

$$COF(t) = \begin{bmatrix} x(t) \\ y(t) \end{bmatrix} = uK(t) \qquad (6)$$

where u is a set of twelve unit vectors that represent direction of all the keys. It is given by

$$u = \begin{bmatrix} \cos\left(0 \times \dfrac{\pi}{12} + \dfrac{\pi}{2}\right), & \cdots & ,\cos\left(11 \times \dfrac{\pi}{12} + \dfrac{\pi}{2}\right) \\ \sin\left(0 \times \dfrac{\pi}{12} + \dfrac{\pi}{2}\right), & \cdots & ,\sin\left(11 \times \dfrac{\pi}{12} + \dfrac{\pi}{2}\right) \end{bmatrix}. \qquad (7)$$

How to calculate COF vectors is visibly explained as follows. First, we assume that COF has a two-dimensional coordinate and define unit vectors for the direction of each key (Fig.4.(a)). Next, each unit vector is multiplied by the corresponding element in the tonality vector (Fig.4.(b)). Finally, a COF vector is given as a center of gravity vector of them (the bold arrow in Fig.4.(b)).

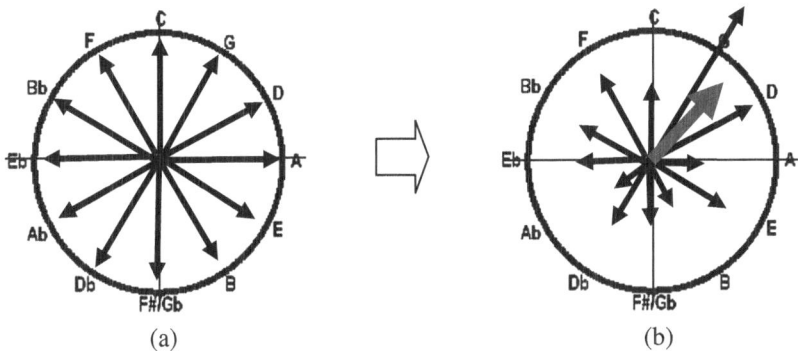

(a)   (b)

Fig. 4. (a) Unit vectors for the direction of each key. (b). COF vector which is the center of gravity vectors.

We can map one twelve-dimensional tonality vector to one vector on a plane. We call this two-dimensional vector "COF vector". This COF vector presents a key at a certain span by the direction of the vector. In the example of Fig.4.(b), the COF vector shows that the present key may be D major or G major. The COF vector also presents density of the key by the length of the vector. For example, if some long vectors pointing to similar direction exist, then the length of the COF vector becomes long. On the contrary, if elements of a tonality vector are scattered, the COF vector points to neighborhood of the origin. Harmony such as diminish chords or augmented chords corresponds to the latter case.

2.4 Judgment of Key Boundaries

We can get Fig.5 by projection of tonality vectors onto COF coordinate. Plots in the figure correspond to tips of COF vectors. We call these plots "COF plots".

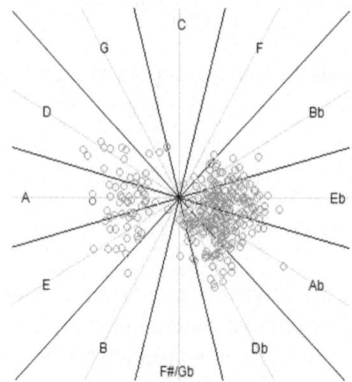

Fig. 5. Series of COF Plots (on COF Coordinate)

In Fig.6, COF plots along time axis are shown. The horizontal axis denotes time and the vertical one does angles of COF vectors on COF coordinate (standard (zero) angle is the direction of C major and positive direction of angle is counterclockwise).

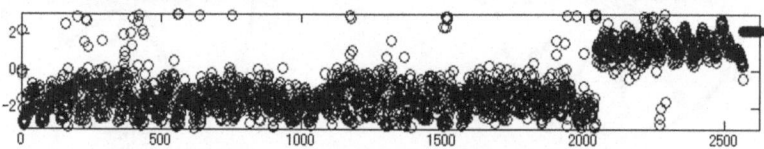

Fig. 6. Series of COF Plots (along Time Axis)

We aim to judge the key boundaries and to identify the keys for this series of COF plots. We want to identify stable regions of swinging plots and judge the translation promptly. For this purpose, we use Hidden Markov Model as a method to estimate keys and their boundaries. We expect that, different from MFCC or chroma vectors, COF plots are easy to handle, robust to track and independent of music instruments when we apply HMM.

2.4.1 HMM

HMM is one of probability models. It is a method to detect unknown (hidden) parameters from observable information. HMM is usually used in the field of speech recognition, genomics and also in music analysis [1][2][3]. HMM is suitable to detect patterns of sequential and flexible signals.

2.4.2 Parameter Settings for HMM

To estimate keys of a tune in our method, the following items are HMM model parameters.

(a) State Set

Each state corresponds to each key of C major, C# major, ..., or B major. There are twelve states, for which we don't define a particular initial state and a final state.

$$S_i = S(key_i) \qquad (i = 0,1,\cdots,11)$$
$$key_i \in \{Cmajor, C\#major, \cdots, Bmajor\}$$

(8)

(b) State Transition Probability

State transition is equal to key translation, namely modulation. We formulate this effect so that the close two keys on COF coordinate are easy to modulate to each other and the distant two are hard. This rule is defined by next equation (9),

$$a_{ij} = P(S_i S_j) = \frac{C}{e^{p\theta_{ij}} + e^{-p\theta_{ij}}}$$

(9)

where a_{ij} is a state transition probability from S_i to S_j, and θ_{ij} is an angle between key_i and key_j on COF coordinate. p is a penalty parameter about modulation, which means that the modulation hardly happens for larger p. C is a constant parameter to normalize the sum of a_{ij} for all possible transitions to 1. The graph of state transition function is shown in Fig.7. The horizontal axis means an angle difference between the current state (key) and the former state (key) and the vertical axis means the probability of the state transition.

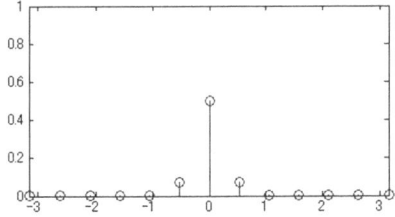

Fig. 7. State Transition Function   **Fig. 8.** Output Probability

(c) Output Probability

$f(o;S_i)$ is a probability that symbol o is output in state S_i. In our formulation, symbol o is a plot in COF plots. For all $S_i (i = 0,1,\cdots,11)$, it is necessary for $f(o;S_i)$ to be calculated. In this paper, $f(o;S_i)$ is defined according to how often COF plot o appears in state S_i,

$$f(o;S_i) = \frac{1}{2\pi}(1 + \cos(\theta_{diff}))$$ (10)

where θ_{diff} is given by

$$\theta_{diff} = \arg(S_i) - \arg(o) \cdot$$ (11)

In the equation (11), $\arg(\bullet)$ is an angle that represents direction and independent of its magnitude. The output probability is expressed as shown in Fig.8, where the horizontal axis is θ_{diff} and the vertical axis is corresponding $f(o;S_i)$. It is assumed that, when a plot is distant from the direction of a key, appearance probability of the plot is low.

(d) Output Signal Sequence
Defined by next equation. It corresponds to COF plot series.

$$\mathbf{O} = \{o(t)\} \qquad (0 \le t \le T)$$ (12)

(e)   State Sequence
Defined by next equation. It corresponds to the key series.

$$\mathbf{S} = \{S(t)\} \qquad (0 \le t \le T)$$ (13)

Estimating keys of a tune is equal to detecting the state sequence $\mathbf{S}$ from the output signal sequence $\mathbf{O}$. We use Viterbi algorithm to calculate the output signal sequence and to determine the most probable path.

Note that it is possible to learn the above parameters from training sets by using EM algorithm similar to conventional HMM approaches. However, we apply deterministic (and heuristic) equations as above because the purpose of this paper is to evaluate basic performance of our approach. Parameter learning by using actual data sets and performance comparison are further study.

3 Experiments

We implemented our proposed method by using C# and MATLAB, and executed experiments on a personal computer. We used thirty popular music pieces from the RWC Genre Database [5] and the RWC Popular Music Database [6], and ten classic music pieces from the RWC Classic Music Database [6]. In Fig.9, a result of projection onto COF coordinate is shown. We can see that there are clear clusters of COF plots in the directions of keys of the tune.

Furthermore, graphs of COF plot series along time axis are shown in Figs.10 and 11. We can see the harmony transition along time. Integers on the vertical axis represent the number of sharps of the key signature (flats are counted as negative numbers). For example, C major: 0, E major: 4, and Bb major: 2. Overlaid lines represent keys estimated by HMM.

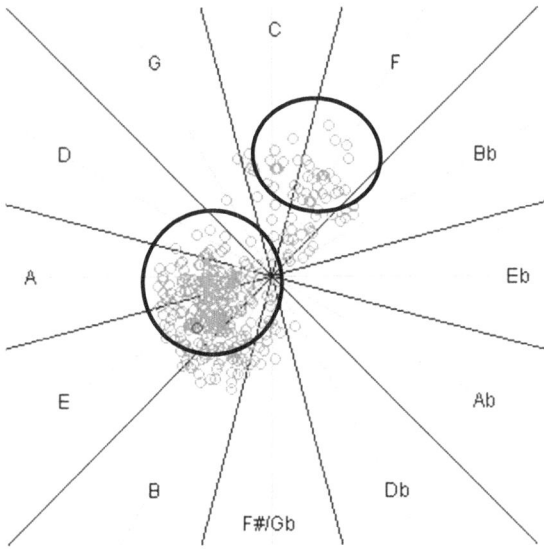

Fig. 9. Projection onto COF Coordinate in case of No.18 song from the RWC Popular Music Database that modulates from E major to F major

The ratio of correct answers is approximately 70%. Popular music pieces and Classic music pieces have similar results. The correct answers are given by trained people's listening to the tunes. In the following chart 1, correct keys of some music pieces we used and their ratio of correct answers are shown.

No. (in RWC Genre Database)	Genre	Correct Key(s)	Ratio of Correct Answers
1	Popular	G	87.40%
2	Popular	C	65.20%
4	Popular	[A-C-E]×2-Em-E	72.10%
6	Popular	Ab-A	97.60%
58-1	Classic	F#	62.60%
58-2	Classic	A	100.00%
59	Classic	D-A-G-D-Dm-D	60.30%
60	Classic	G	82.10%
61	Classic	Bb-Db-Bbm-Bb	52.30%
62	Classic	F#	100.00%
63	Classic	Db-Gb-Db-Db-E-Db	93.00%

Chart 1. Correct keys of some pieces and ratio of correct answers

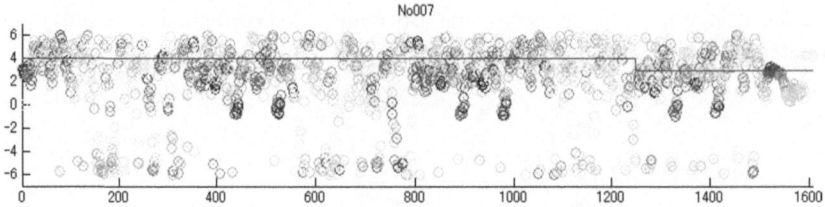

Fig. 10. Key Estimation by HMM (No.7 from the RWC Popular Music Database)

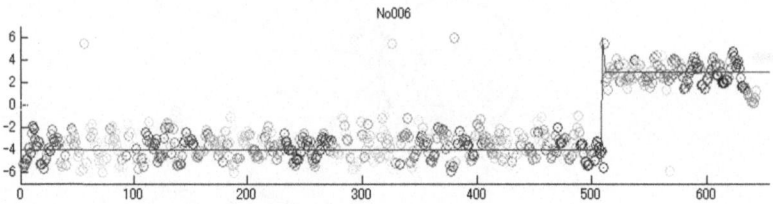

Fig. 11. Key Estimation by HMM (No.7 from the RWC Music Genre Database)

There is little difference of correct answer rate between popular music and classical music. The correct answer rate of music pieces that have frequent modulation or minor keys is lower. The reason No.2 has low correct answer rate is that the singer sometimes sings with blue note scale. Notes of blue note scale is different from notes of a diatonic (ordinary) scale, so it is thought that the result of No.2 is not good.

4 Conclusion

In this paper, we presented a new key estimation method which is independent of music genre and sorts of music instruments. The efficiency was shown by experiments for actual music sources. In our research, we didn't discriminate major keys and natural minor keys, but if we introduce minor keys of other two scales, more robust estimation will be expected. Furthermore, when we use more detailed COF vectors to estimate keys, we can regard them as microscopic features of a tune and apply them to music retrieval system.

References

[1] Lee, K., Slaney, M.: Automatic Chord Recognition from Audio Using an HMM with Su-pervisedLearning. In: ISMIR 2006 (2006)
[2] Noland, K., Sandler, M.: Key Estimation Using a Hidden Markov Model. In: ISMIR 2006
[3] Cabral, G., Pachet, F., Briot, J.-P.: Automatic X Traditional Descriptor Extraction: The Case of Chord Recognition. In: ISMIR 2005 (2005)

[4] Chew, E.: The Spiral Array: An Algorithm for Determining Key Boundaries. In: Anagnostopoulou, C., Ferrand, M., Smaill, A. (eds.) ICMAI 2002. LNCS, vol. 2445, p. 18. Springer, Heidelberg (2002)

[5] Goto, M., Hashiguchi, H., Ni-shimura, T., Oka, R.: RWC Music Database: Music Genre Database and Musical Instrument Sound Database. 2002-MUS-45-4 2002(40), 19–26 (2002)

[6] Goto, M., Hashiguchi, H., Ni-shimura, T., Oka, R.: RWC Music Database: Popular, Classical, and Jazz Music Databases. In: Pro-ceedings of the 3rd International Conference on Music Information Retrieval (ISMIR 2002), October 2002, pp. 287–288 (2002)

Feature Analysis and Normalization Approach for Robust Content-Based Music Retrieval to Encoded Audio with Different Bit Rates

Shuhei Hamawaki[1], Shintaro Funasawa[1], Jiro Katto[1], Hiromi Ishizaki[2], Keiichiro Hoashi[2], and Yasuhiro Takishima[2]

[1] Waseda University, 3-4-1 Okubo, Shinjuku-ku, Tokyo, 169-8555, Japan
{hamawaki,shint,katto}@katto.comm.waseda.ac.jp
[2] KDDI R&D Laboratories Inc, 2-1-15 Ohara, Fujimino-shi, Saitama 356-8502, Japan
{ishizaki,hoashi,takisima}@kddilabs.jp

Abstract. In order to achieve highly accurate content-based music information retrieval (MIR), it is necessary to compensate the various bit rates of encoded songs which are stored in the music collection, since the bit rate differences are expected to apply a negative effect to content-based MIR results. In this paper, we examine how the bit rate differences affect MIR results, propose methods to normalize MFCC features extracted from encoded files with various bit rates, and show their effects to stabilize MIR results.

Keywords: Mel-Frequency Cepstral Coefficient (MFCC), Content-based MIR Normalization.

1 Introduction

The recent development of various audio encoding formats such as MP3 (MPEG-1 Audio Layer-3), WMA (Windows Media Audio), and AAC (Advanced Audio Coding) have enabled efficient compression of music files with high sound quality. This technology has made possible the development of large-scaled online music distribution services. Furthermore, it has also become popular for customers of such services to share their personal "playlists," *i.e.*, lists of their favorite songs, on the Web. Such developments may lead to the realization of the "celestial jukebox," an application which accumulates all existing music in the world, and makes them accessible to application users.

Obviously, content-based music information retrieval (MIR) is an essential technology to make such an application usable. Therefore, many research efforts have been presented in this area. However, when considering a music collection accumulated for the celestial jukebox, it is clear that the collection consists of songs (audio files) encoded in various formats and/or bit rates. Therefore, content-based MIR must compensate the divergence of the features that are to be extracted from such songs. To the best of our knowledge, this problem has not been seriously considered in existing MIR research, since evaluations of such research are mainly conducted on data sets

B. Huet et al. (Eds.): MMM 2009, LNCS 5371, pp. 298–309, 2009.

individually constructed by the researchers, thus do not contain songs of various formats.

The objective of this research is two-fold. Mainly focusing on MFCC, a representative acoustic feature utilized in many existing work in the content-based MIR research area, we will examine influence of diverse audio file formats to MFCC feature extraction, and prove that the distortion of audio due to encoding cannot be ignored to develop an effective content-based MIR system. Secondly, we propose and evaluate MFCC normalization methods to compensate for the differences of MFCC features, which aim to reduce the effects of diverse bit rates to content-based MIR results.

2 Use of MFCCs in Music Retrieval

Mel-Frequency Cepstral Coefficients (MFCC) are acoustic features which are known to represent perceptually relevant parts of the auditory spectrum. Therefore, MFCC has been commonly used for speech recognition systems [7]. Furthermore, MFCCs have also been increasingly utilized in the field of content-based music analysis, such as genre classification, and audio similarity measures [8].

Spevak et al. [4] performs pattern matching on the sequences of MFCC to select a specific passage within an audio file. Deshpande et al. [5] convert MFCC features to a gray-scale picture, and use image classification methods to categorize audio files. MARSYAS [6] is a popular software framework for audio analysis, which uses MFCC as one of the features extracted from music for genre categorization, etc.

Furthermore, Sigurdsson et al. [1] have analyzed the robustness of MFCCs extracted from MP3 encoded files, and have concluded that MFCCs are sufficiently robust features, which can be utilized for content-based MIR. However, they have not provided any analysis about the effect of extracted MFCCs to content-based MIR results, which is the focus of this paper.

Generally, as the research efforts of the above conventional works indicate, MFCCs have generally been utilized as features, which express the timbral characteristics of music. While other aspects of music, e.g., rhythm, harmony, and melody, are also essential to develop effective MIR systems, MFCCs can be assumed as a representative feature for content-based MIR.

In the following sections, we first investigate the influence of MFCC features extracted from differently encoded audio files, and show that the influence is not neglectable for content-based MIR. We also propose methods to compensate this problem, and reduce influence to MIR results that are caused by encoding distortion.

3 Analysis of MFCCs of Variously Encoded Music

3.1 Influence on MFCC Values

First, we examine the variance of MFCCs extracted from MP3 files encoded in different bit rates, and compared them with MFCCs extracted from raw audio files. All MFCC values are calculated with window size 25ms, window interval 10 ms and 13-dimension (12-dimention+power). LAME 3.97 is used for encoding and decoding, and the Hidden Markov Model toolkit [9] is used for calculating MFCC. For each

MFCC dimension, we compared the MFCC values extracted from raw audio files (hereafter referred as *Raw_MFCC*) with MFCC values extracted from MP3-encoded files (hereafter referred as *MP3_MFCC*), with bit rates of 128kbps (44.1kHz) and 64 kbps (24kHz).

MFCC values of each dimension are extracted from the same portion of the raw and encoded files. Figure 1 illustrates the MFCC values of the 1st, 6th, and 12th dimensions, extracted from two Japanese pop songs (SONG_A: male artist, SONG_B: female artist). It is clear from this Figure that the values of MFCC extracted from raw audio and MP3 files are different from each other. For example, let us focus on the MFCC value differences of the 1st dimension (shown on the first two graphs of Figure 1). For SONG_A, the MFCC values extracted from the 128kbps MP3 file are generally higher than that of the raw audio file, while the MFCC values of the 96kbps MP3 file are lower. However, the general distribution of MFCC values is different for SONG_B. Namely, the MFCC values of the 96kbps MP3 file are closer to those of the raw audio file, which is clearly different from the above observations of the MFCC values extracted from SONG_A.

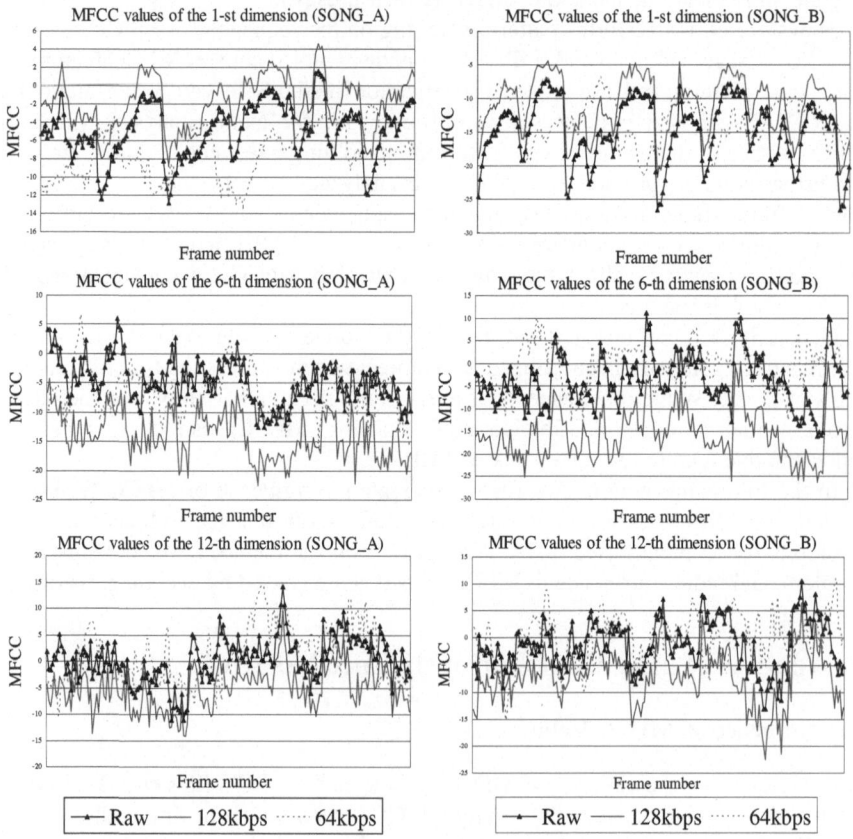

Fig. 1. Comparison of MFCC values extracted from MP3 files with various bit rates

Overall, the results of Figure 1 indicate that, even if the target song is the same, the MFCC values extracted from variously encoded files are different. Furthermore, it is also clear from the results of Figure 1, that the difference of MFCC values is dependent not only to the bit rate of MP3 encoding, but also to the acoustic features of the target song. These differences are expected to apply a significant impact to content-based MIR systems which utilize MFCC-based features, especially for music collections which consist of songs in various formats.

3.2 Influence on MIR

Next, we examine the effects of the difference of MFCC features to content-based MIR, based on an experimental content-based MIR system, and a music collection consisting of MP3 files with various bit rates.

For this experiment, we have developed a prototype MIR system, based on the MIR method proposed by Hoashi *et al.* [2], which utilizes the tree-based vector quantization (TreeQ) algorithm proposed by Foote [3]. TreeQ constructs the feature space to vectorize music, based on training data, *i.e.*, music with category labels. The training audio waveform is processed into MFCCs, and TreeQ recursively divides the vector space into bins each of which corresponds to a leaf of the tree. Once the quantization tree has been constructed, it can be used to vectorize input music data. We used the songs and sub-genre information of the RWC Genre Database [10] as the initial training data. Then, the method of Hoashi *et al.* is applied to automatically derive the training data set from the music collection for TreeQ, based on the results of clustering songs. This method enables the extraction of features that optimally express the characteristics of songs in any given music collection.

The music collection of our prototype MIR system consists of songs with various bit rates. Namely, the music collection consists of 2513 MP3 files of Japanese and Korean pop songs, whose bit rates range from 96kbps to 192kbps. Details of distribution of bit rate for that dataset are 96kbps (708files), 128kbps (589files), 160kbps (1195files), and 192kbps (21files).

First, we analyze the distribution of the vectors of songs with various bit rates, by plotting all song vectors on a two dimensional feature space. Namely, the dimensions of the song vectors are reduced to two, by selecting the first two elements of principal component analysis conducted on the vectors of the songs in the music collection.

Figure 2 shows the distribution of all vectors in our music collection on the two-dimensional feature space. From Figure 2, it is clear that, the vectors of 96 kbps songs are densely located in a small area of the feature space, whereas the song vectors of songs with higher bit rates are scattered evenly, regardless of the actual acoustic features of the songs.

This result indicates that song vectors used for content-based MIR are severely affected by the bit rates of the songs in the collection. An example of a problem which may occur as a result of this result, is a situation where a user submits a query song, which happens to be encoded with low bit rate. While songs which are perceptually similar to the query song may exist in the music collection, such songs may not be successfully retrieved by the MIR system, simply because the bit rates of the songs in the collection differ to that of the query song.

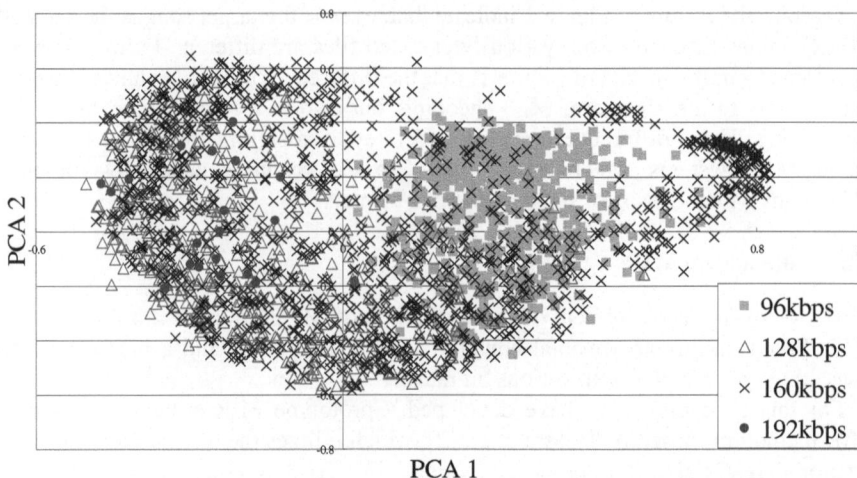

Fig. 2. Distribution of song vectors in 2D feature space

3.2.1 Experimental Data

Next, we examine how the divergence of song vectors extracted from songs with various bit rates will affect content-based MIR results. For the following experiment, we have prepared a music collection which consists of 96 Japanese pop songs. From this music collection, we generated four sets of music audio files: Raw (wav files with no compression), and MP3 files encoded in 192kbps (44.1kHz), 128kbps (44.1kHz), and 64kbps (24kHz).

3.2.2 Experiment Method

From the previous four sets of music audio files, we have constructed content-based MIR systems, following the method proposed in [2]. Namely, the feature space for each set (hereafter referred as: *Raw_hist*, *192_hist*, *128_hist*, and *64_hist*, respective to the format/bit rate of the music collection) is generated by the method of [2], and all songs in each data collection are vectorized based on the corresponding feature space. Furthermore, in order to simulate a music collection composed of songs in various formats, we have also generated a "mixed" data collection of MP3 files, by randomly selecting the bit rate of each song evenly in the experimental data set. Vectors of all songs in the mixed collection are also generated in the same way. We will refer to this feature space as "*mix_hist*."

3.2.3 Evaluation Measures

In order to analyze the difference between MIR results for song collections with various formats, we select a song as the MIR query, and calculate the similarity between the selected query and all other songs in each collection. The MIR results of *Raw_hist* are utilized as a reference, to which the results of the other MIR systems are compared. Query-to-song similarity is calculated based on the cosine distance between the query and song vectors.

The difference between the MIR results of the raw data set and the encoded data sets ({*192, 128, 64, mix*}_*hist*) is measured by calculating the correlation coefficient between the MIR results, *i.e.*, the list of songs and their similarity to the query. Correlation coefficient (*r*) between MIR results of *Raw_hist* (*R*) and other feature space (*H*), which consists of *N* (=95) cosine distance scores, are calculated by the following formula.

$$r = \frac{\sum_{K=1}^{N} \left(R_k - \overline{R} \right)\left(H_k - \overline{H} \right)}{\sqrt{\sum_{K=1}^{N} \left(R_k - \overline{R} \right)^2} \sqrt{\sum_{K=1}^{N} \left(H_k - \overline{H} \right)^2}} \tag{1}$$

where R_k denotes cosine distance between the query and the *k*-th song in *Raw_hist*, and $\overline{R}$ denotes the average cosine distance of all data from the query in *Raw_hist*. Similarly, H_k denotes the cosine distance between the query and the *k*-th song, and $\overline{H}$ denotes the average cosine distance for each system ({*192, 128, 64, mix*}_*hist*).

Moreover, as another criterion, we calculate the ratio of songs which appear in the top ten songs of the MIR results of both *Raw_hist*, and {*192, 128, 64, mix*}_*hist*. This ratio is hereafter referred to as *Coin* (which stands for "*coin*cidence"). In the following experiment, we calculate the correlation coefficient and *Coin* for each of the 96 songs, and use the average values for overall comparison of MIR results.

3.2.4 Result

Table 1 shows the average correlation coefficient, and *Coin* of the MIR results of *Raw_hist* and each MP3-based music collection. Furthermore, Figure 3 illustrates the differences between the MIR result of Raw_hist and the other MIR results. In Figure 3, all songs are sorted in descending order, based on their similarity to a specific query song in *Raw_hist*, and the query-to-song similarity of the other MIR systems are plotted according to the order of the sorted songs.

The results of Table 1 indicate that the difference of MIR results to *Raw_hist* increases along with the decrease of encoding bit rates. Another notable observation is the severe difference between the MIR results of *mix_hist* and *Raw_hist*, which can be

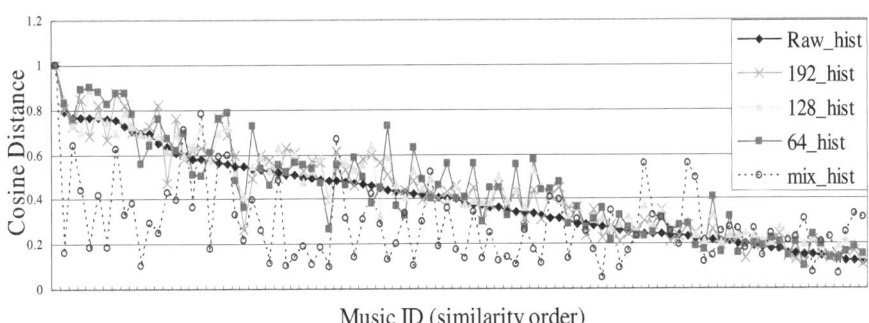

Fig. 3. Comparison of cosine distance of songs sorted by similarity in *Raw_hist*

Table 1. Average of correlation coefficient and *Coin* of MIR results

Feature space	Correlation	*Coin*
192_hist	0.900	6.28/10
128_hist	0.899	6.25/10
64_hist	0.850	5.25/10
mix_hist	0.219	2.23/10

observed from the low correlation coefficient and *Coin* of *mix_hist* in Table 1, and the scattered cosine distance of *mix_hist* results in Figure 3.

3.2.5 Discussions

As clear from the results of Table 1 and Figure 3, the difference of MFCC values extracted from audio files with different bit rates applies a significant impact to content-based MIR results. This is especially notable for music collections composed of a mixture of songs encoded with various bit rates, as can be observed from the results of *mix_hist*.

If the music database for a "*celestial jukebox*" is to be accumulated by collecting music data from various record companies and/or Web users, the resulting collection will consist of songs in various formats. The previous experimental results indicate that, existing content-based MIR methods, such as the method utilized in our previous experiments, must be able to handle the diversity of feature values that are expected to be extracted from songs with different formats.

The results in Table 1 show that, when the bit rate of songs in the music collection is fixed, the correlation to the original MIR results is high. Therefore, a naïve solution to resolve the difference of features extracted from mixed song collections is to unify the bit rate of all songs, prior to feature extraction. This bit rate unification can be conducted by adjusting the bit rate of all songs to the lowest bit rate of all songs in the music collection. By this method, the feature space is expected to be closer to the original feature space, than directly utilizing mixed features. However, if the minimum bit rate of songs in the music collection is extremely low, the amount of information to be lost in the bit rate adjustment process will be huge, especially for songs with high bit rates. Moreover, if a music file whose bit rate quality is lower than the minimum of the music files in the database is added to the collection, the feature space must be re-constructed.

In order to solve this problem, we propose methods to normalize MFCC values. Such methods are expected to resolve the variety of MFCCs, while avoiding the risky process to unify bit rate quality. Details of this method are described in the following chapter.

4   MFCC Normalization

We examine three normalization techniques, Cepstral Mean Normalization, Cepstral Variance Normalization, and Mean and Variance Normalization, in order to compensate the difference of MFCC values extracted from mixed song collections. All of the three methods aim to make MIR results close to the original feature space, where MFCC features are extracted from raw audio files. These normalization methods are used to reduce the influence of different environmental conditions in the field of speech recognition [11]. In the following methods, the mean and variance of MFCC values for each MFCC dimension are calculated for each song, based on all MFCCs extracted from the song in question. Details of the three methods are as follows.

4.1 Normalization Method

CMN: Cepstral Mean Normalization
CMN normalizes Cepstral vector by subtracting the average Cepstral vector from the original vector. This method can be expressed in the following formula.

$$\hat{C}(i) = C(i) - \mu(i) \tag{2}$$

where $\hat{C}(i)$ denotes the i-th dimensional Cepstram after normalization, $C(i)$ denotes the i-th dimensional Cepstram before normalization, and $\mu(i)$ denotes the average of i-th-dimensional Cepstral vector.

CVN: Cepstral Variance Normalization
CVN normalizes Cepstral vector by dividing the original Cepstral vector by the standard deviation.

$$\hat{C}(i) = \frac{C(i)}{\sigma(i)} \tag{3}$$

$\sigma(i)$ is the i-th dimensional Cepstral standard deviation .

MVN: Mean and Variance Normalization
MVN normalizes Cepstral vector by Cepstral average and standard deviation.

$$\hat{C}(i) = \frac{C(i) - \mu(i)}{\sigma(i)} \tag{4}$$

4.2 Result of Normalization

We first compare the *MP3_MFCC* (128kbps, 64kbps) and *Raw_MFCC* (Raw) values after normalization. Figure 4 shows the result of MVN normalization of the MFCC values of the same songs and MFCC dimensions presented in Figure 1.

From comparison of Figures 1 and 4, it is clear that the normalized MFCC values extracted from MP3 files (64kbps, 128kbps) have moved closer to the original MFCC (Raw) value, especially for MFCC values of 128kbps MP3 files are more overlapped with those of Raw in each graph. Similar results are also observed for other songs and normalization methods. This analysis proves that MFCC normalization is effective to reduce the difference of MFCC values extracted from variously encoded music files.

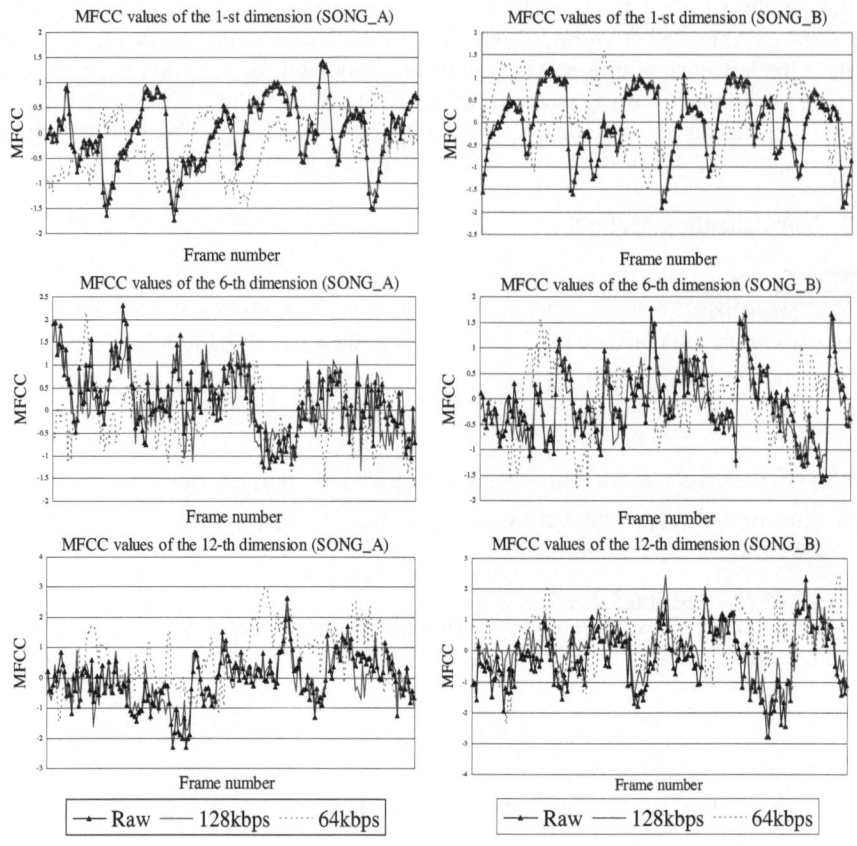

Fig. 4. Comparison of normalized MFCC values

Next, in order to examine the effects of MFCC normalization to the vectorization of music, we generated song vectors from MFCC values extracted from music files of the same database used in Figure 2 by MVN, and plotted all vectors on a two-dimensional graph generated by principal component analysis. This result is illustrated in Figure 5.

As obvious from the comparison of Figures 2 and 5, the biased distribution of vectors extracted from music files with different bit rates has been generally resolved by MVN normalization. Similar results are also observed for the other MFCC normalization methods. These results indicate that MFCC normalization is also effective to reduce the difference of MFCC-based song vectors extracted from audio files with variant bit rates.

Finally, in order to analyze how MFCC normalization affects content-based MIR results, we have conducted the same experiment as in Section 3.2.2, using the vectors generated from normalized MFCCs extracted from the mixed music collection. The results are compared with the results with those of *mix_hist* presented in Table 1 and Figure 3.

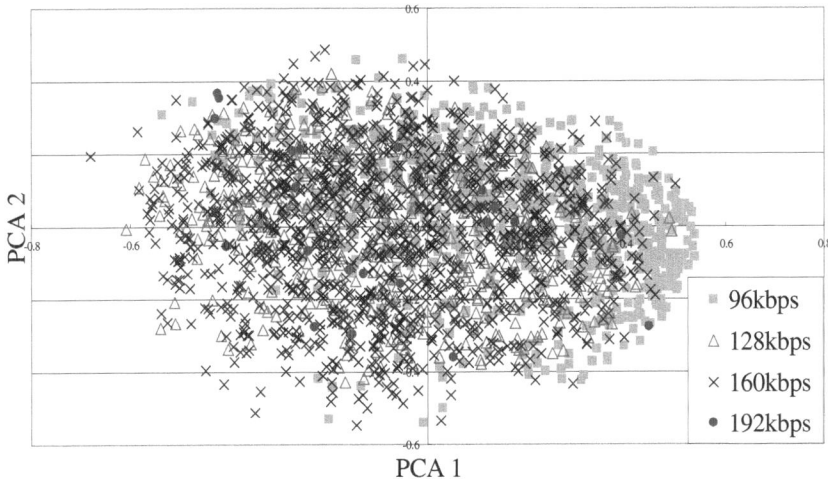

Fig. 5. Distribution of song vectors after normalization (MVN)

Table 2 shows the average correlation coefficient and *Coin* for each normalization method. Figure 6 shows cosine distance between a specific query and other songs, for *Raw_hist* and *mix_hist*, where MFCC values are normalized by MVN.

Table 2. Average correlation coefficient and Coin of MIR results of *mix_hist* with MFCC normalization

Normalization method	Correlation	*Coin*
CMN	0.714	4.04/10
CVN	0.439	2.77/10
MVN	0.859	4.52/10

It is clear from Table 2 that, all normalization methods have led to higher correlation coefficients and *Coin*, compared to the results of *mix_hist* in Table 1. This result indicates that MFCC normalization is effective to reduce the difference of MIR results for mixed music collections. Of the three proposed MFCC normalization methods, MVN has achieved the highest correlation coefficient and *Coin*. Similar conclusions can also be derived from Figure 6, where the difference between the raw and mixed MIR results has been significantly reduced, compared to the results of *mix_hist* presented in Figure 3.

Overall, the above experimental results indicate that, MFCC normalization is effective to resolve MIR result differences caused by MP3 files encoded with various bit rates, thus should be implemented for content-based MIR systems with music collections which consist of variously encoded music files.

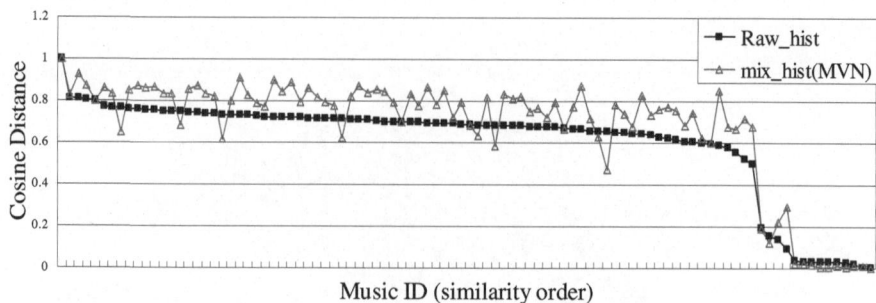

Fig. 6. Comparison of cosine distance of sorted songs after MFCC normalization

5 Conclusion and Future Work

In this paper, we have analyzed the difference of features extracted from music files with various bit rates, and their effect to content-based MIR results. Results of our analysis clearly show that, if the music collection consists of songs whose bit rates are mixed, the MIR results are significantly different from the results of music collections which consist of raw audio files. Furthermore, we confirmed that normalizing MFCC is effective to reduce the difference between MIR results for mixed music collections.

For the next step, we are investigating influences on other spectrum features like Flatness, Centroid, Rolloff and etc by encoding. We would also like to explore more optimal compensation methods, and conduct user-based evaluations of the MIR algorithms.

References

1. Sigurdsson, S., Petersen, K.B., Lehn-Schiøler, T.: Mel Frequency Cepstral Coefficients: An Evaluation of Robustness of MP3 Encoded Music. In: Proceedings of the International Conference on Music Information Retrieval (2006)
2. Hoashi, K., Matsumoto, K., Sugaya, F., Ishizaki, H., Katto, J.: Feature space modification for content-based music retrieval based on user preferences. In: Proceedings of ICASSP, pp. 517–520 (2006)
3. Foote, J.: Content-based retrieval of music and audio. In: Proceedings of SPIE, vol. 3229, pp. 138–147 (1997)
4. Spevak, C., Favreau, E.: SOUNDSPOTTER-A prototype system for content-based audio retrieval. In: Proceedings of the International Conference on Digital Audio Effects, pp. 27–32 (2002)
5. Deshpande, H., Singh, R., Nam, U.: Classification of musical signals in the visual domain. In: Proceedings of the International Conference on Digital Audio Effects (2001)
6. Tzanetakis, G., Cook, P.: MARSYAS: A framework for audio analysis. Organized Sound 4(3), 169–175 (2000)

7. Mermelstein, P.: Distance measures for speech recognition. Psychological and instrumental. Pattern Recognition and Artificial Intelligence, 374–388 (1976)
8. Logan, B.: Mel frequency cepstral coefficients for music modeling. In: Proceedings of the International Symposium on Music Information Retrieval (2000)
9. Slaney, M.: Auditory toolbox, version 2. Technical Report #1998-010, Interval Research Corporation (1998)
10. Goto, M., et al.: RWC Music Database: Music GenreDatabase and Musical Instrument Sound Database. In: Proceedings of the International Conference on Music Information Retrieval, pp. 229–230 (2003)
11. Viikki, O., Laurila, k.: Cepstral domain segmental feature vector normalization for noise robust speech recognition. Speech Communication 25, 133–147 (1998)

A Multimodal Constellation Model for Object Category Recognition

Yasunori Kamiya[1], Tomokazu Takahashi[2], Ichiro Ide[1], and Hiroshi Murase[1]

[1] Graduate School of Information Science, Nagoya University
Furo-cho, Chikusa-ku, Nagoya, 464-8601, Japan
kamiya@murase.m.is.nagoya-u.ac.jp,
{ide,murase}@is.nagoya-u.ac.jp
[2] Faculty of Economics and Information, Gifu Shotoku Gakuen University
1-38, Nakauzura, Gifu, 500-8288, Japan
ttakahashi@gifu.shotoku.ac.jp

Abstract. Object category recognition in various appearances is one of the most challenging task in the object recognition research fields. The major approach to solve the task is using the Bag of Features (BoF). The constellation model is another approach that has the following advantages: (a) Adding and changing the candidate categories is easy; (b) Its description accuracy is higher than BoF; (c) Position and scale information, which are ignored by BoF, can be used effectively. On the other hand, this model has two weak points: (1) It is essentially an unimodal model that is unsuitable for categories with many types of appearances. (2) The probability function that represents the constellation model takes a long time to calculate. In this paper we propose a "Multimodal Constellation Model" to solve the two weak points of the constellation model. Experimental results showed the effectivity of the proposed model by comparison to methods using BoF.

Keywords: Constellation model, Multimodalization, Speed-up, Object category recognition, EM algorithm.

1 Introduction

In this paper, we consider the problem of recognizing semantic categories with many types of appearances such as Car, Chair, and Dog under environment changes that include direction of objects, distance to objects, illumination, and backgrounds. This recognition task is challenging because object appearances widely varies by difference of objects in semantic categories and environment changes, which complicates feature selection, model construction, and training dataset construction. One of the application of this recognition task is image retrieval.

For these recognition tasks, a part-based approach, which uses many distinctive partial images as local features, is widely employed. By focusing on partial areas, this approach can handle a broad variety of object appearances. Typical

B. Huet et al. (Eds.): MMM 2009, LNCS 5371, pp. 310–321, 2009.

well-known methods include a scheme using Bag of Features (BoF) [3] and Fergus's constellation model [7]. BoF is an analogy to the "Bag of Words" model originally proposed in the natural language processing field. Approaches using BoF have been proposed: using classifiers such as SVM (e.g., [9][12][16]), and document analysis methods such as probabilistic Latent Semantic Analysis (pLSA), Latent Dirichlet Allocation (LDA), and Hierarchical Dirichlet Processes (HDP) (e.g., [2][6][13]).

The constellation model represents target categories by probability functions that represent local features that describe the common regions of objects in target categories and the spatial relationship between the local features. The number of regions is assumed to be five to seven. Details will be introduced in Section 2.1.

The constellation model has the following three advantages:

(a) *Adding and changing the target categories is easy.*
In this reseach field, recognition methods are often categorized as a "generative model" or a "discriminative model" [1]. This advantage is because the constellation model is a generative model. A generative model individually makes a model for each target category. Therefore the training process for adding target categories is only needed for the added target categories. For changing the already learnt target categories, it is only necessary to change the models used in the tasks; no other training process is necessary. On the other hand, discriminative models, which describe a decision boundary to classify all target categories, have to relearn the decision boundary each time adding or changing the target categories. For recognition performance, the discriminative model generally outperforms the generative model.

(b) *Description accuracy is higher than BoF due to continuous value expression.*
Category representation by BoF is a discrete expression by histogram formed by the numbers of local features corresponding to each codeword. On the other hand, since the constellation model is a continuous value expression by probability function, the description accuracy is higher than BoF.

(c) *Position and scale information can be used effectively.*
BoF ignores spatial information of local features to avoid complicated spatial relationship descriptions. On the other hand, the constellation model uses a probability function to represent rough spatial relationships as one piece of information to describe the target categories.

However the constellation model has the following weak points:

(1) Since it is essentially a unimodal model, it has low description accuracy when objects in the target categories have many types of appearances.

(2) The probability function that represents the constellation model takes a long time to calculate.

In this paper, we propose a model that improves the weak points of the constellation model. For weak point (1), we extend the constellation mode to a multimodal model. A unimodal model has to represent several types of appearances as one component. But by extension to a multimodal model, some appearances can be cooperatively described by components of the model, improving the accuracy category description. This improvement is the same as extending a representation by Gaussian distribution to that by Gaussian Mixture Model in local feature representation. In addition, we speed-up the calculation of the probability function to solve weak point (2).

Since advantages (b) and (c) are not often described in other papers, we quantitatively show their correctness in Section 4.4.

Another constellation model is proposed before Fergus's constellation model in [15]. Multimodalization of this model was done in [14], but the structure of these models considerably differs from Fergus's constellation model, and they have three weak points: they do not have the advantage (b) of Fergus's constellation model since the way to use local features is close to BoF, they do not use the information of common regions' scale, and they can not lean appearance and position simultaneously since the learning of appearance and position has a dependence. However, Fergus's constellation model takes a long time to calculate the probability function which represents the model, so it is unrealistic to multimodalize the model since the parameter estimation needs many time of probability function calculation. In this paper, we realize the multimodalization of Fergus's constellation model with the speeding-up the calculation of the probability function. Fergus's constellation model was also improved in [8], but the improvements are to become that the model can use many sorts of local features and to modify the positional relationship expression. For clarity, in this paper we focus on the basic Fergus's constellation model.

Image classification tasks can be classified into the following two types:

1. Classify images with target objects occupying most area of an image, and the object scales are similar (e.g. Caltech101/256).
2. Classify images with target objects occupy partial area of an image, and the object scales may differ (e.g. Graz, PASCAL).

The method proposed in this paper targets Type 1 images. It can, however, also handle Type 2 images using methods such as the sliding window method, and then handle them as Type 1 images.

The remainder of this paper is structured as follows. In Section 2, we describe the Multimodal Constellation Model, the speeding-up techniques, and the training algorithm. In Section 3, we explain the classification and describe our experiments in Section 4. Finally, we conclude the paper in Section 5.

2   Multimodal Constellation Model

In this section we describe Fergus's constellation model, then explain its multimodalization, and finally describe the speeding-up calculation.

2.1   Fergus's Constellation Model [7]

The constellation model describes categories by focusing on the common object regions in each category. The regions and the positional relationships are expressed by Gaussian distributions.

The model is described by the follow equation:

$$p(I|\Theta) = \sum_{\mathbf{h} \in H} p(A, X, S, \mathbf{h}|\Theta)$$

$$= \sum_{\mathbf{h} \in H} p(A|\mathbf{h}, \theta_A)p(X|\mathbf{h}, \theta_X)p(S|\mathbf{h}, \theta_S)p(\mathbf{h}|\theta_{other}), \qquad (1)$$

where I is an input image and Θ is the model parameters. Image I is expressed as a set of local features. Each local feature holds the feature vectors of appearance, position, and scale. A, X, and S is a set of feature vectors of appearance, position, and scale, respectively. In addition, as a hyperparameter, the model has the number of regions for description: R. $\mathbf{h}$ is a vector that expresses the combination of correspondences between local features extracted from image I and each region of the model. H is a set of all the combinations of correspondences. By $\sum_{\mathbf{h} \in H}$ all combinations are covered. $p(A|\mathbf{h}, \theta_A)$ is expressed as the multiplication of R Gaussian distributions. $p(X|\mathbf{h}, \theta_X)$ expresses a pair of x, y coordinates of each region as a $2R$ dimensional Gaussian distribution. $p(S|\mathbf{h}, \theta_S)$ is also expressed by one Gaussian distribution. For details refer to [7].

The part of the equation, which cyclopedically calculates all combinations between all local features and each region of the model, is in the form of summation. However, the part of the equation that describes a target category, $p(A, X, S, \mathbf{h}|\Theta)$, is substantively represented by multiplication of the Gaussian distributions. Therefore, Fergus's constellation model can be considered as a unimodal model.

2.2   Multimodalization

We define the proposed "Multimodal Constellation Model" as follows:

$$p_m(I|\Theta) = \sum_k^K \left\{ \prod_l^L G(\mathbf{x}_l|\theta_{k, \hat{r}_{k,l}}) \right\} \cdot p(k)$$

$$= \sum_k^K \left\{ \prod_l^L G(\mathbf{A}_l|\theta_{k, \hat{r}_{k,l}}^{(A)})G(\mathbf{X}_l|\theta_{k, \hat{r}_{k,l}}^{(X)})G(\mathbf{S}_l|\theta_{k, \hat{r}_{k,l}}^{(S)}) \right\} \cdot p(k) \qquad (2)$$

$$\hat{r}_{k,l} = \arg\max_r G(\mathbf{x}_l|\theta_{k,r})$$

where K is the number of components. If $K \geq 2$, then the model becomes multimodal. L is the number of local features extracted from image I, and $G(\ )$ is the Gaussian distribution. Also, $\Theta = \{\theta_{k,r}, p(k)\}$, $\theta = \{\boldsymbol{\mu}, \boldsymbol{\Sigma}\}$, $I = \{\mathbf{x}_l\}$, and $\mathbf{x} = (\mathbf{A}, \mathbf{X}, \mathbf{S})$. $\theta_{k,r}$ is a set of parameters of the Gaussian distribution of region r in component k. $\mathbf{x}_l$ is the feature vector of the l-th local feature. $\mathbf{A}, \mathbf{X}$, and $\mathbf{S}$, which are the feature vectors of appearance, position, and scale, respectively, are subvectors of $\mathbf{x}$. $p(k)$ is the existence probability of component k. $\hat{r}_{k,l}$ is the index of the most similar region to the local feature l of the image I, in component k. Moreover, R (number of regions) exists as a hyperparameter, though it does not appear explicitly in the equation.

2.3   Speeding-Up Techniques

Since the probability function that represents Fergus's constellation model takes a long time to calculate, estimating the model parameter is also time-consuming. In addition, this complicates multimodalization because multimodalization increases the number of parameters and thus completing the training in realistic time becomes impossible. Here we describe two speeding-up techniques.

[Simplifying matrix calculation]. For simplification, we assumed all covariance matrices to be diagonal as an approximation. This modification considerably decreases the calculation cost of $(\mathbf{x} - \boldsymbol{\mu})^t \boldsymbol{\Sigma}^{-1}(\mathbf{x} - \boldsymbol{\mu})$ and $|\boldsymbol{\Sigma}|$ needed for calculating the Gaussian distributions. The total calculation cost is reduced from $O(D^3)$ to $O(D)$ for $D \times D$ matrices. In particular, when assuming that $\boldsymbol{\Sigma}$ is a diagonal matrix whose diagonal components are σ_d^2,

$$(\mathbf{x} - \boldsymbol{\mu})^t \boldsymbol{\Sigma}^{-1}(\mathbf{x} - \boldsymbol{\mu}) = \sum_d^D \frac{1}{\sigma_d^2}(x_d - \mu_d)^2 \tag{3}$$

$$|\boldsymbol{\Sigma}| = \prod_d^D \sigma_d^2. \tag{4}$$

[Modifying $\Sigma_{h \in H}$ to $\prod_l^L$ and $\arg\max_r$]. The order of $\Sigma_{h \in H}$ in (1) is $O(L^R)$, where L is the number of local features and R is the number of regions. In actuality, even though A* search method is used for speeding-up in [7], the total calculation cost is still large. In the proposed method we changed $\Sigma_{h \in H}$ to $\prod_l^L$ and $\arg\max_r$. As a result, the cost is reduced to $O(LR)$.

This approach was inspired from [11] who targeted the classification of identical view angle car images captured by a static single camera, and modified the constellation model for this task. We referred to the part of calculation cost reduction.

Here we compare the expression of each model, and describe that Fergus's model and our model approximately have an equivalent description ability. First we describe each model with its calculation procedure. Fergus's model cyclopedically calculates probabilities of all combinations of correspondences between regions and local features. The final probability is calculated as a sum of these probabilities. The cyclopedic search of corresponding local features is done by $\Sigma_{h \in H}$. On the other hand, our model calculates the final probability using all the local features at once. This is expressed as $\prod_l^L$. After the region which is most similar to each local feature is selected ($\arg\max_r$), the probability to the region is calculated for each local feature. The final probability is calculated as a multiplication of these probabilities.

Next, we describe each model with its handling of occlusions (in particular, lack of necessary local features). Fergus's constellation model explicitly handles occlusion. When calculating probabilities for combinations of correspondences, some regions do not correspond to any local feature. This expresses the existence of occlusions. The probability of the occluded regions' combination is also modeled. For Fergus's constellation model, by such explicit handling, the probability considering occlusion is calculated. On the other hand, our model calculates the final probability using all the local features in an image at once. Therefore the final probability is calculated as a probability without the occluded local features. In addition, frequent occlusion patterns are learnt as one appearance of an object by multimodalization. This corresponds to the modeling the probability of occluded region's combination in Fergus's model. For our model, by these implicit handling, the probability considering occlusion is calculated.

At last, we consider images with unnecessary local features. For Fergus's constellation model, at the cyclopedic searches of corresponding local features, the probability for the combination of correspondences with unnecessary local features becomes small, therefore the final probability is almost not affected by unnecessary local features since it is calculated as a sum of probabilities of the combinations. On the other hand, for our model, since the final probability is calculated as a multiplication of each local feature's probability, unnecessary local features decrease the final probability. However, the probability decreases simultaneously for all candidate categories. Therefore the classification results is not affected by unnecessary local features.

According to [7], the actual computation time of Fergus's constellation model to estimate model parameters is 24–36 hours per model for R=6–7, L=20–30 per image, and using 400 training images. However, our model that applies the above two techniques takes around ten seconds to estimate the parameters in the same condition and K=1 (unimodal). In addition, even when $K \geq 2$ (multimodal), it only takes a few dozen seconds to estimate the parameters.

2.4 Parameter Estimation

Model parameter estimation is carried out using the EM algorithm [4]. Fig. 1 shows the model parameter estimation algorithm for the Multimodal Constellation Model. N denotes the number of training images, and n denotes the index of the training image. $\mathbf{x}_{n,l}$ denotes a feature vector of local feature l in training image n. $\hat{r}_{k,n,l}$ denotes $\hat{r}_{k,l}$ in training image n.

One difference with the general EM algorithm for the Gaussian Mixture Model is that the data that update $\boldsymbol{\mu}, \boldsymbol{\Sigma}$ are not per image but per local feature extracted from the images. Degree of belonging $q_{k,n}$ of training image n to component k is calculated in the E step, and then all local features extracted from training image n participate in the updating of $\boldsymbol{\mu}, \boldsymbol{\Sigma}$ based on the value of $q_{k,n}$. In addition, local feature l participates in the updating of $\boldsymbol{\mu}, \boldsymbol{\Sigma}$ of only region $\hat{r}_{k,n,l}$ to which local feature l corresponds.

3 Classification

The classification is performed by the following equation:

$$\hat{c} = \arg \max_{c} p_m(I|\Theta_c)p(c), \tag{5}$$

(1) Initialize model parameter $\theta_{k,r}$, and π_k.

(2) **E step** :

$$q_{k,n} = \frac{\pi_k p(I_n|\theta_k)}{\sum_k^K \pi_k p(I_n|\theta_k)} \quad , \qquad \text{where} \quad p(I_n|\theta_k) = \prod_l^L G(\mathbf{x}_{n,l}|\theta_{k,\hat{r}_{k,n,l}}).$$

(3) **M step** :

$$\boldsymbol{\mu}_{k,r}^{new} = \frac{1}{Q_{k,r}} \sum_n^N \sum_{l:(\hat{r}_{k,n,l}=r)} q_{k,n}\mathbf{x}_{n,l},$$

$$\boldsymbol{\Sigma}_{k,r}^{new} = \frac{1}{Q_{k,r}} \sum_n^N \sum_{l:(\hat{r}_{k,n,l}=r)} q_{k,n}\left(\mathbf{x}_{n,l} - \boldsymbol{\mu}_{k,r}^{new}\right)\left(\mathbf{x}_{n,l} - \boldsymbol{\mu}_{k,r}^{new}\right)^t,$$

$$\pi_k^{new} = \frac{N_k}{N},$$

$$\text{where} \quad Q_{k,r} = \sum_n^N \sum_{l:(\hat{r}_{k,n,l}=r)} q_{k,n} \quad , \quad N_k = \sum_n^N q_{k,n}.$$

(4) If parameter updating converges, the estimation process is finished, and $p(k) = \pi_k$, otherwise return to (2).

Fig. 1. Model parameter estimation algorithm for the Multimodal Constellation Model

where $\hat{c}$ is the resultant category, c is a candidate category for classification, and $p(c)$ is the prior probability of category c, which is calculated as the ratio of training image of category c to all candidate categories.

Since the constellation model is a generative model, it is easy to add categories or change candidate categories, and thus the training process is only independently needed first time a category is added. For changing already learnt candidate categories, it is only necessary to change the models used in the tasks. On the other hand, discriminative models makes one classifier (decision boundary) using all of the data for all candidate categories. Therefore it has the following two weak points: a training process is needed every time candidate categories are added and changed, and for relearning, all of the training data, needs to be keept.

4   Experiments

We evaluate the effectivity of multimodalization for constellation models by comparing two models, Multimodal Constellation Model ("Multi-CM") and Unimodal Constellation Model ("Uni-CM"). Uni-CM is equivalent to the proposed model when $K=1$ (unimodal).

We also compare the proposed model's performance to the two methods using BoF. "LDA+BoF" is a method using LDA, one document analysis method. "SVM+BoF" is a method using SVM. Multi-CM, Uni-CM, and LDA+BoF are generative models, SVM+BoF is a discriminative model, and LDA is a multimodal model.

Fig. 2. Target images in Caltech [7]   **Fig. 3.** Target images in Pascal [5]

Next, we discuss the influence of hyperparameters K and R on the classification rate and quantitatively show the two previously mentioned advantages of the constellation model.

As a preparation for the experiments, object areas were clipped from the images as target images using the object area information available in the dataset. We defined the task as classifying target images into correct categories. The classifying process was carried out for each dataset. Half of the target images were used for training and the rest for testing.

Two image datasets were used for the experiments. The first is the Caltech Database [7] ("Caltech"), and the other is the dataset used in the PASCAL Visual Object Classes Challenge 2006 [5] ("Pascal"). Caltech consists of four categories. Fig. 2 shows examples of the target images. The directions of the objects in these images are roughly aligned but their appearances widely varies. Pascal has ten categories. Fig. 3 shows examples of the target images. The direction and the appearance of objects in Pascal vary widely. Furthermore, the pose of objects in some categories (e.g., Cat, Dog, and Person) vary considerably. Therefore Pascal is considered more difficult than Caltech.

The identical data of local features are used for all methods compared here to exclude the influence of difference of local features on the classification rate. In addition, we experimented ten times by varying training and test images and used the average classification rate of ten times for comparison.

In this paper we empirically determined K (number of components) as five and R (number of regions) as 21. For the local features we used the KB detector [10] for detecting and the Discrete Cosine Transform (DCT) for describing. The KB detector outputs positions and scales of local features. Patch images are extracted using these information, and are described by the first 20 coefficients calculated by DCT excluding the DC. Therefore, the dimension of feature vector $\mathbf{x}$ is 23 ($\mathbf{A}$:20, $\mathbf{X}$:2, $\mathbf{S}$:1).

4.1   Effectivity of Multimodalization and Comparison to BoF

For validating the effectivity of multimodalization, we compared the classification rates of Multi-CM and Uni-CM. We also compared the proposed method to LDA+BoF and SVM+BoF, which are related methods. These related methods

Table 1. Effectivity of multimodalization and comparison to BoF, by average classification rates (%)

Dataset	LDA+BoF	SVM+BoF	Uni-CM	Multi-CM
Caltech	94.7	96.4	98.7	99.5
Pascal	29.6	27.9	37.0	38.8

have hyperparameters to represent the codebook size (k of k-means) for BoF. The number of assumed topics for LDA corresponds to the number of components K of Multi-CM. We show the best classification rates while changing these hyperparameters in the following results.

Table 1 shows that the classification rate of Multi-CM outperforms Uni-CM. This shows that multimodalization to a constellation model is effective to such datasets as Caltech and Pascal which contain many types of appearances in a category (e.g., Caltech-Face: differences of persons, Pascal-Bicycle: direction of bicycle).

Since the results also show that the proposed model obtains better classification rate than LDA+BoF (generative model) and SVM+BoF (discriminative model), we can obtain better classification performance with the constellation model than using methods based on BoF, for either generative or discriminative models.

4.2   Number of Components K

Here we discuss the influence of K, one of the hyperparameters of the proposed method, on the classification rate. K is changed in the range of 1 to 9 in increments of 2 to compare the classification rates at each K. When $K=1$, it is Uni-CM, and when $K \geq 2$ they are Multi-CM. The number of regions R is fixed to 21.

Figure 4 shows the results. Note that the scale of the vertical axis for each graph differs because the difficulty of each dataset differs greatly. The classification rates

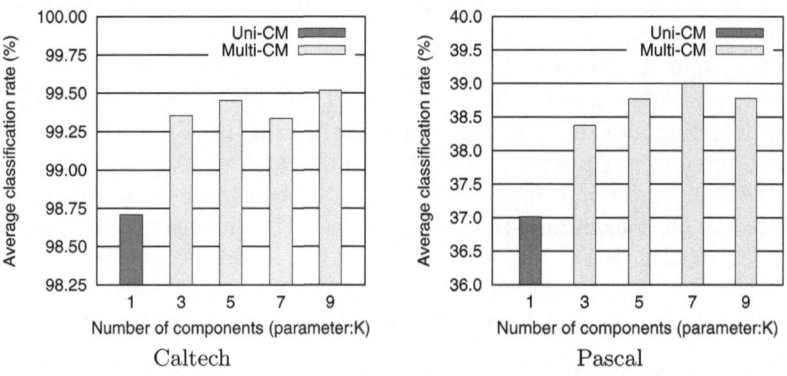

Fig. 4. Influence of K (number of components) on average classification rate

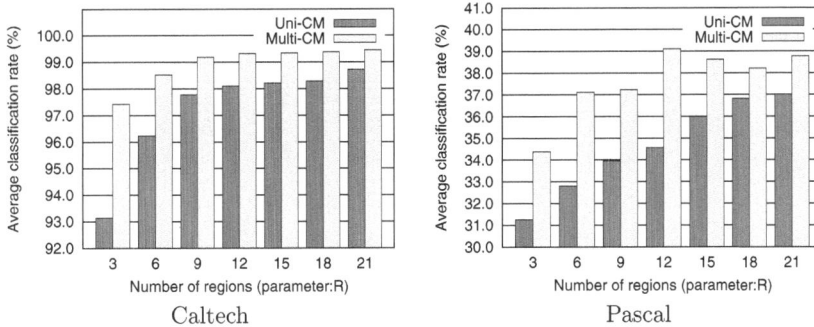

Fig. 5. Influence of R (number of regions) on average classification rate

saturate at K=5 for Caltech and at K=7 for Pascal because the appearance variation of objects for Pascal is bigger than Caltech. However, we can choose K=5 as a constant setting because these classification rates only differ slightly when $K \geq 2$.

In addition, the fact that the classification rates when $K \geq 2$ are better than K=1 shows the effectivity of multimodalization.

4.3   Number of Regions R

To discuss the influence of R, another hyperparameter of the proposed method, on the classification rate, we evaluated the classification rates by increasing R in the range of 3 to 21 in increments of 3, and the classification rate at each R is shown in Fig. 5. The number of components K is fixed to 5. The results contain the classification rates of Uni-CM and Multi-CM.

The improvement of classification rates saturate at R=9 for Caltech and at R=21 for Pascal. In addition, at all R, the classification rates of Multi-CM are better than Uni-CM, so the effectivity of multimodalization is also confirmed here.

For Fergus's constellation model, R=6–7 is the extent that the training process can be finished in realistic time. For the proposed method with the speed-up techniques, we increased R (number of regions) until the improvement of the classification rate saturated, in realistic time. Therefore the speeding-up techniques not only contributed to the realization of multimodalization but also to the improvement of the classification performance.

4.4   Continuous Value Expression and Position-Scale Information

Here, we quantitatively validate the advantages of the constellation model described in Section 1; (b) Description accuracy is higher than BoF due to continuous value expression and (c) Position and scale information ignored by BoF can be used effectively.

First, (b) is validated. The comparison of BoF and the constellation model should be performed on the condition only with the difference that a continuous value expression by a probability function and a discrete expression by a histogram, formed by the numbers of local features, correspond to each codeword.

Table 2. Validation of effectivity of continuous value expression and position-scale information, by average classification rate (%)

Dataset	LDA+BoF	Multi-CM no-X,S	Multi-CM
Caltech	94.7	96.5	99.5
Pascal	29.6	33.5	38.8

Therefore we compared LDA+BoF, which is a generative multimodal model identical to a constellation model, and Multi-CM without position and scale information that are not used in LDA+BoF ("Multi-CM no-X,S"). Next, to validate (c) we compared Multi-CM no-X,S and the normal Multimodal Constellation Model.

Table 2 shows the classification rates of these three methods. The classification rate of Multi-CM no-X,S is better than LDA+BoF, demonstrating the superiority of continuous value expression. The Multi-CM classification rate outperforms Multi-CM no-X,S. This shows that the constellation model can adequately use position and scale information.

5   Conclusion

We proposed a Multimodal Constellation Model for object category recognition. Our proposed method can train and classify faster than Fergus's constellation model and describe categories with a high degree of accuracy even when the objects in the target categories have many types of appearances.

The experimental results show the following effectivities of the proposed method:

- Performance improvement by multimodalization
- Performance improvement by speeding-up techniques, enabling use with more regions in realistic time.

We also compared Multi-CM to the methods using BoF, LDA+BoF, and SVM+BoF. Multi-CM showed higher performance than these methods. Furthermore we quantitatively showed the advantages of the constellation model; (b) Description accuracy is higher than BoF due to continuous value expression and (c) Position and scale information ignored by BoF can be used effectively. In Sections 1 and 3, by comparing generative and discriminative models, we also showed that the advantage (a) of the constellation model is that candidate categories can be easily added and changed.

References

1. Bishop, C.M.: Pattern Recognition and Machine Learning. Springer, Heidelberg (2006)
2. Bosch, A., Zisserman, A., Muñoz, X.: Scene classification via pLSA. In: Leonardis, A., Bischof, H., Pinz, A. (eds.) ECCV 2006. LNCS, vol. 3954, pp. 517–530. Springer, Heidelberg (2006)

3. Csurka, G., Dance, C.R., Fan, L., Willamowski, J., Bray, C.: Visual categorization with bags of keypoints. In: Proc. ECCV International Workshop on Statistical Learning in Computer Vision, pp. 1–22 (2004)
4. Dempster, A.P., Laird, N.M., Rubin, D.B.: Maximum likelihood from incomplete data via the EM algorithm. J. Royal Statistical Society, Series B 39(1), 1–38 (1977)
5. Everingham, M., Zisserman, A., Williams, C.K.I., Van Gool, L.: The PASCAL Visual Object Classes Challenge 2006 Results (VOC 2006) (2006), http://www.pascal-network.org/challenges/VOC/voc2006/results.pdf
6. Fei-Fei, L., Perona, A.P.: A bayesian hierarchical model for learning natural scene categories. In: Proc. IEEE Computer Society Conf. on Computer Vision and Pattern Recognition, vol. 2, pp. 524–531 (2005)
7. Fergus, R., Perona, P., Zisserman, A.: Object class recognition by unsupervised scale-invariant learning. In: Proc. IEEE Computer Society Conf. on Computer Vision and Pattern Recognition, vol. 2, pp. 264–271 (2003)
8. Fergus, R., Perona, P., Zisserman, A.: A sparse object category model for efficient learning and exhaustive recognition. In: Proc. IEEE Computer Society Conf. on Computer Vision and Pattern Recognition, vol. 1, pp. 380–387 (2005)
9. Grauman, K., Darrell, T.: The pyramid match kernel: discriminative classification with sets of image features. In: Proc. IEEE Int. Conf. on Computer Vision, vol. 2, pp. 1458–1465 (2005)
10. Kadir, T., Brady, M.: Saliency, scale and image description. Int. J. of Computer Vision 45(2), 83–105 (2001)
11. Ma, X., Grimson, W.E.L.: Edge-based rich representation for vehicle classification. In: Proc. IEEE Int. Conf. on Computer Vision, vol. 2, pp. 1185–1192 (2005)
12. Varma, M., Ray, D.: Learning the discriminative power-invariance trade-off. In: Proc. IEEE Int. Conf. on Computer Vision (2007)
13. Wang, G., Zhang, Y., Fei-Fei, L.: Using dependent regions for object categorization in a generative framework. In: Proc. IEEE Computer Society Conf. on Computer Vision and Pattern Recognition, vol. 2, pp. 1597–1604 (2006)
14. Weber, M., Welling, M., Perona, P.: Towards automatic discovery of object categories. In: Proc. IEEE Computer Society Conf. on Computer Vision and Pattern Recognition, vol. 2, pp. 101–108 (2000)
15. Weber, M., Welling, M., Perona, P.: Unsupervised learning of models for recognition. In: Vernon, D. (ed.) ECCV 2000. LNCS, vol. 1842, pp. 18–32. Springer, Heidelberg (2000)
16. Zhang, J., Marszalek, M., Lazebnik, S., Schmid, C.: Local features and kernels for classification of texture and object categories: A comprehensive study. Int. J. of Computer Vision (2), 213–238 (2007)

Robust Visual Content Representation Using Compression Modes Driven Low-level Visual Descriptors

Charith Abhayaratne and Farooq Muzammil

Department of Electronic and Electrical Engineering, University of Sheffield
Sheffield S1 3JD, United Kingdom
c.abhayaratne@sheffield.ac.uk
http://charith-abhayaratne.staff.shef.ac.uk

Abstract. In conventional visual content representation, low-level visual features are usually extracted from the highest quality and resolutions of visual contents. When visual content is scalable coded and utilised, their bit streams can be adapted at various nodes in multimedia usage chains to cater the variations in network bandwidths, display device resolutions and resources and usage preferences by just discarding insignificant resolution-quality layers. This can result in the existence of different version of the same content with dissimilar low-level visual features. Therefore, mapping of low level visual descriptors into content resolution-quality spaces is important in order to obtain low-level visual features that are robust to such content adaptations. A new scalable domain feature extraction using the compression modes and decisions is presented and its content based image retrieval performance is evaluated. The proposed scheme outperforms MPEG-7 visual descriptors in both the original image and scaled resolution-quality space domains.

Keywords: content representation, low-level descriptors, scalable coding, content adaptation, MPEG-7, CBIR, wavelets, EZW.

1 Introduction

Scalable coded visual content bit streams have to be adapted into bit streams with lower quality and spatio-temporal resolutions, when delivered within multimedia consumption chains from media content creators to the end user in order to address network, display device and usage requirements. In scalable coding, the source is decomposed into a hierarchical multi-resolution representation such as wavelets (as in JPEG2000 [1]) or spatio-temporal motion compensated pyramid decompositions (as in the scalable extension of MPEG-4/H.264 AVC [2]) and encoded to generate a bit stream corresponding to the highest visual quality and the largest spatio-temporal resolutions. Then the content adaptation is performed by extracting the relevant parts of these bit streams with the aid of bit stream description schemes. This can lead to having different versions, in terms of the visual quality and spatio-temporal resolution spaces, of the same

B. Huet et al. (Eds.): MMM 2009, LNCS 5371, pp. 322–332, 2009.

content at different nodes of the multimedia consumption chain. This type of content adaptation can affect the low-level visual features based descriptors, which are usually extracted on the uncompressed image domains using the original spatial-temporal resolutions. This type of mismatch of the features extracted from different versions of the same content can affect the content based image retrieval performance. Feature extraction using different versions after content adaptations can also lead to unnecessary effort.

A solution to these two problems is making the low-level visual descriptors extracted at the media production time to be content adaptation invariant. This kind of characteristic is vital in query image driven content based image retrieval (CBIR) applications where the image databases are distributed and the query image is of lower quality and lower resolution, due to content adaptation, than those of the images in the database. Current CBIR systems use the MPEG-7 visual descriptors [3,4], which are extracted in the pixel domain and thereby, are susceptible for the content adaptation processes. Moreover, modern multimedia applications employ a two layer data representation consisting of content and its metadata. The latter includes low-level visual features and semantic descriptors. When the content is scalable coded the two layers are not one to one mapped. Alternative to image-domain feature extractions, there have been some work on compressed and wavelet domain domain feature extraction for CBIR applications [5,6,7]. In either case, whenever the content is adapted new metadata needs to be created as there is no mechanism to adapt the metadata and re-map into the content.

As a solution we propose a new low level visual descriptor extracted in the scalable coded domain and mapped into scale-quality space of the content. This new description scheme utilises the compression modes and decisions involved in the scalable coding process. In all coding algorithms, such compression information is usually intrinsically spatially adaptive and based on the characteristics of the underlying content. Therefore, these compression modes and decision information carry information on the content that can be used as content descriptions. We explore this concept to extract a new set of features based on these compression modes and capable of describing the content accurately.

In this paper, we demonstrate our concept using the compression modes associated with the Embedded Zero tree wavelet (EZW) scalable image coding algorithm [8]. As the EZW symbols are available for each sub band and bit plane, it forms an intrinsic framework for mapping the description into different resolution-quality spaces of the content. Due to this one-to-one correspondence with the content resolution-quality spaces, we can arrange them hierarchically and use the highest components in the structure for content description in order to achieve content adaptation invariance. Moreover, this also facilitates integrating the description layer into the content layer itself and consequently minimising the efforts of feature extraction from different versions. The rest of the paper is organised as follows. In section 2, we present the effect of content adaptation on MPEG-7 visual descriptors. The new concept is presented in section 3, followed by evaluation of its performance in section 4. The concluding remarks and future work are presented in section 5.

2   Effects of Content Adaptation on MPEG-7 Descriptors

MPEG-7 defines a set of low-level visual descriptors based on the colour, texture, shape and motion properties of the content. The commonly used colour descriptors include dominant colour (DCD), colour structure (CSD) [9], Colour layout (CLD) [10], Scalable colour histogram (SCD) and the colour space. Texture descriptors include texture browsing, homogeneous texture and edge histogram (EHG), while shape descriptors include contour and region based shape models. Motion descriptors include camera motion, motion trajectory, parametric motion and motion activity descriptors. In CBIR systems these descriptors are either used alone or in combinations according to specific domains to compute similarity with the descriptors of a query image. These descriptors are usually defined using the features extracted on the original resolution at the highest visual quality.

We present the results of a small experiment carried out to explore the effect of content. We used the image database and its ground truth data available at the University of Washington object and concept recognition for CBIR web pages [11]. This ground truth database consists of 21 datasets of outdoor scene images and includes text file containing a list of visible objects for each image in the database. We used the object classifiers in the text file to device a scoring scheme to determine the most relevant images for a given query image. In this experiment, we considered three resolution levels of the same content, *i.e.*, full (0), half (1) and quarter (2), and three quality levels, *i.e.*, high quality (lossless compression (0)), average quality (moderate compression (5)) and low quality (high compression (8)). The combinations of different resolution-quality leads to nine content adaptation modes. The visual descriptors using all versions of the

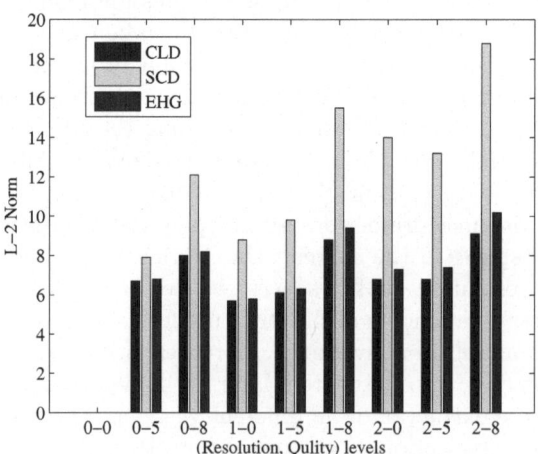

Fig. 1. L-2 Norm values for three descriptors (CLD, SCD and EHG) extracted on different resolution-quality spaces compared with those of the 0-0 space

content resulting from the nine content adaptation modes were extracted. The similarity of these descriptors extracted from the highest resolution and quality (0-0) version of the content were compared for similarity with those extracted from the other eight content adaptation modes versions (0-5, 0-8, 1-0, 1-5, 1-8, 2-0, 2-5, 2-8). The average similarity values in terms of the L-2 norm for three MPEG-7 descriptors, namely, scalable colour descriptor (SCD), the colour layout descriptor (CLD) and the Edge histogram descriptor (EHG) are shown in Fig. 1.

It is evident from the bar plots, that these descriptors result in increasing dissimilarity when the resolution and quality levels are reduced. They appear to be highly affected with the decreasing image quality compared to the resolution reductions. This is mainly due to, that most MPEG-7 have been designed to address the scaling invariance. Yet they do not demonstrate complete scale (resolution) invariance. In the rest of the paper we present a new methodology for extracting visual features based on compression decision modes to address these issues.

3 Methodology

The proposed low-level visual descriptor is based on the compression decision modes and arranged according to sub bands and bit plane significance in wavelet domain. We demonstrate this concept using the Embedded Zerotree Wavelet (EZW) [8] coding algorithm.

3.1 The Embedded Zerotree Wavelet (EZW) Algorithm Basics

Two main elements of current scalable image coding are wavelet transforms and embedded coding of wavelet coefficients. In embedded coding, bit streams for all other lower bit rates are embedded within any given bit rate of the coded image bit stream. This is achieved by grouping the bits in the coded bit stream according to their significance. The embedded coding algorithms use scalar quantisation in several passes, starting with a quantisation bin size corresponding to the largest quantisation step that gives at least one non-zero quantised coefficient and thereafter reducing the bin size progressively in successive passes up to the targeted bit rate. In lossless embedded coding, the above process is continued up to the unit quantisation bin size. Defining these quantisation bin sizes as 2^n with $n \in \{ msb, \ldots, 1, 0 \}$ (msb is the most significant bit plane number) corresponds to bit plane-wise embedded coding of the coefficients in the sign magnitude binary representation. In bit plane oriented embedded coding, each bit plane is coded from the most significant to the least significant bit plane by scanning from the lowest frequency sub band to the highest sub band across all decomposition levels. In embedded coding, each bit plane or output from each quantisation step in general terms is coded in two different coding passes, namely

1. Switching pass and
2. Refining pass.

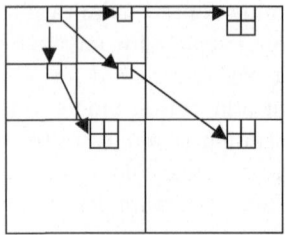

WT for a 2 scale wavelet transform

Fig. 2. Wavelet tree organisation

In the switching pass, coefficients which become significant in the current weighted bit plane are switched on followed by their signs. Refinement of already switched coefficients is done in the refinement pass.

An image, I, with $M \times N$ dimensions decomposed using a transform T produces the coefficient set $I_T(x, y)$, where $x = 0, \ldots, M - 1$ and $y = 0, \ldots, N - 1$. The rth bit plane BP_r represents a range $(2^r, 2^{r+1}]$ with a quantisation step 2^r. Therefore, as seen on the BP_r, the magnitude of any $I_T(x, y)$ can be categorised into three groups.

$$[I_T(x, y)]_{BP_r} = \begin{cases} S & if \quad 2^r \leq |I_T(x, y)| < 2^{r+1} \\ N & if \quad\quad |I_T(x, y)| < 2^r \\ X & if \quad\quad 2^{r+1} \leq |I_T(x, y)| \end{cases}$$

This type of classification results in a significance switching mask (SSM). In embedded coding terms, the coefficients identified as S type become significant in the current BP_r. The N type coefficients are the ones yet to become significant, whereas the X type coefficients are the ones which have already become significant in previously scanned bit planes. The encoder needs to code only the S and N type coefficients in the SSM, since the encoder and the decoder are synchronised according to the mask scanning order. The cost of embedded coding is the bits used to code N type coefficients in the SSM. Different strategies to address coding of N type coefficients has lead to new embedded coding algorithms. In

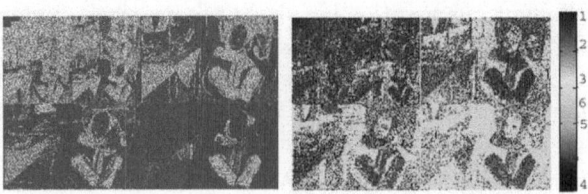

Fig. 3. Bit plane (left: dark=0 bright=0) and the corresponding classified bit map (right with Red=X, Orange=S+, Yellow=S-, Green=ZTN, Cyan=IZ, Blue=ZTR) for bit plane #3

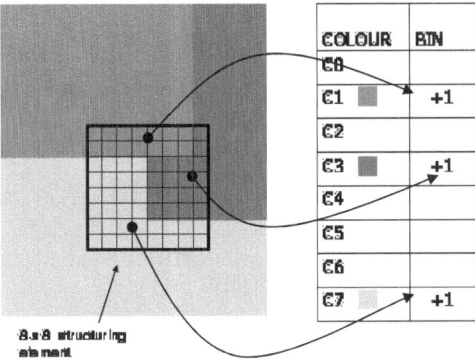

Fig. 4. The sliding window structural element based presence histogram computation

EZW [8], the quad tree relationship among the sub band coefficients (refer to Fig. 2) are exploited and categorised into coding symbols.

In the EZW technique, the S bits are coded with a single symbol irrespective of the sign followed by sign information. The N bits are categorised into two groups, hence represented by either of two symbols. If none of the descending coefficients in the wavelet tree which originated from an N bit is a type S, then that N bit is classified as a Zero Tree Root (ZTR) symbol and the descendants from that node need not be coded. Otherwise, it is classified as an Isolated Zero (IZ) symbol and coding along the tree is continued.

3.2 Reusing of EZW Decision Modes for Content Description

Since the encoder and decoder are synchronised by maintaining the current state of a coefficient (whether significant or not) and following the same scanning order, with the use of the SSM coding information one can classify the wavelet coefficients seen at a particular bit plane at both the encoder side and the decoder side into six classes. They are listed as follows:

1) X: A coefficient that has become significant in a previous bit plane.

2) S+: A coefficient that becomes significant in the current bit plane and contains a positive value.

3) S-: A coefficient that becomes significant in the current bit plane and contains a negative value.

4) ZTR: A Coefficient that is not yet significant and all its children nodes in the wavelet quad tree are also yet to become zero.

5) IZ: A Coefficient that is not yet significant, but has X, S+ or S wavelet quad tree nodes.

6) ZTN: A coefficient that is not yet significant and is a node of a wavelet quad tree whose root is a ZTR.

An example is shown in Fig. 3.

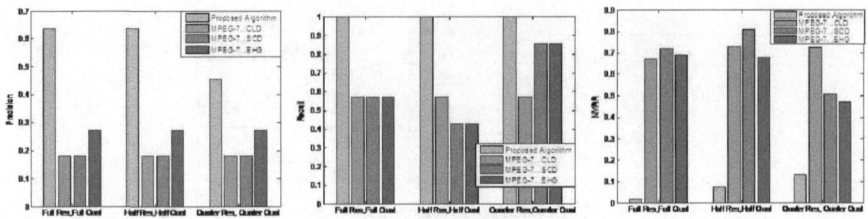

Fig. 5. Precision (top), Recall (middle) and NMRR (bottom) plots (Bar 1: The proposed method; Bars 2-4: CLD, CSD & EHG)

3.3   The Proposed Description Design

The proposed feature vector is generated by sub band by sub band scanning of each classified bit plane from the most significant bit plane to the lowest using a sliding window and generating a significance histogram which increments the count if the symbol class is present in the window.

The proposed feature vector is generated by scanning each of the classified bit planes from the most significant bit plane to the lowest and the lowest frequency sub band to the highest. A sliding window (structural element) is used to generate a histogram which captures the local structure defined by the classified SSM maps. The histogram increments the count of a bin pertaining to a particular SSM bit class if that symbol class is present within the window. The size of the window is adjusted when scanning sub bands from different decomposition levels to reflect the relationship of the scale seen by each of the sub bands. An example of the histogram computation is shown in Fig. 4.

Table 1. Retrieval performance comparison for the proposed method with those of MPEg-7 descriptors CLD, CSD & EHG for three different version of query images, 0-0, 1-5 and 2-8

	Query image type	Proposed Method	MPEG-7 CLD	MPEG-7 SCD	MPEG-7 EHG
Precision					
	0-0	0.63	0.2	0.2	0.28
	1-5	0.63	0.2	0.2	0.28
	2-8	0.48	0.2	0.2	0.28
Recall					
	0-0	1.00	0.55	0.55	0.55
	1-5	1.00	0.55	0.40	0.40
	2-8	1.00	0.55	0.82	0.82
ANMRR					
	0-0	0.02	0.65	0.72	0.68
	1-5	0.08	0.72	0.80	0.70
	2-8	0.12	0.74	0.50	0.48

This type of scanning results in a hierarchical feature descriptor which is directly mapped to the sub bands and bit planes of the wavelet transform of the content. Therefore when comparisons are made, only the sub bands and bit planes corresponding to the resulting content adaptation mode are considered. The new features (or feature adaptation) can be performed at the same time of the decoding of the content.

The size, structure and the usage of the proposed descriptor are presented in the following example. Assume the compression scheme uses a wavelet transform as a dyadic n-level decomposition resulting in $3n + 1$ subbands. For a typical 8 bit luminance component of an image, using an n-level wavelet transform results in $n + 8$ bit planes. Since the SSM histogram consists of 6 bins for 6 different pixel classes and we compute $(3n + 1)(n + 8)$ sub bands in all bit planes, the resulting size of the descriptor for the 8-bit luminance component of an image is

$$d_{original} = 6(3n + 1)(n + 8)$$

values. Let r be the resolution reduction factor, where the resolution is reduced by 2^r, and c is the quality reduction factor, where c least significant bits are discarded, due to a content adaptation process. Now the size of the descriptor is

$$d_{new} = 6(3(n - r) + 1)(n + 8 - c)$$

values, which are already embedded in the original descriptor as the top $3(n-r)+1$ subbands and $n + 8 - c$ bit palnes are retained unaffected in this process. The new descriptor can be derived at the time of decoding when the entropy decoded bit-planes and corresponding sub bands are becoming available. Then if this new version of the original image is used as query image to retrieve images from a database which consists of images with descriptors of size $d_{original}$, we only need to extract the relevant d_{new} values from the original descriptors for comparison.

4   Experimental Results

We used the image database and its ground truth data available at the University of Washington object and concept recognition for CBIR web pages [11] for the evaluation of the proposed descriptor. This ground truth database consists of 21 datasets of outdoor scene images and includes text file containing a list of visible objects for each image in the database. We used the object classifiers in the text file to device a scoring scheme to determine the most relevant images for a given query image in order to compute the precision, recall and normalised modified retrieval rank (NMRR).

The evaluations consisted of running 21 different query images (representing each of the data set) and considering a search space of total number of images in the database. Three different versions of query images (for each query) based aon three different resolution-quality level adaptations, namely 0-0, 1-5 and 2-8, were used. We compared the precision, recall and NMRR metrics, for content based image retrieval using the proposed method were with those of three MPEG-7 descriptors, Colour Layout Descriptor (CLD), Scalable Colour Descriptor (SCD)

Query (0-0) mode

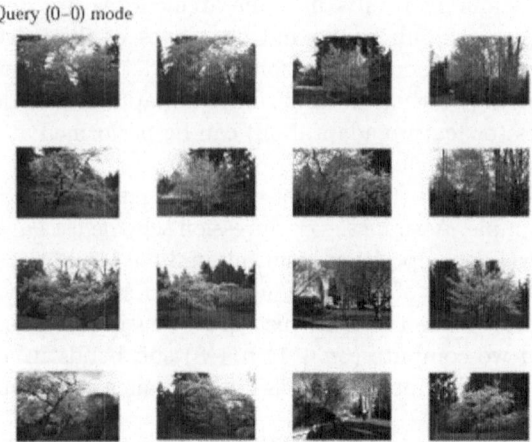

Fig. 6. Retrieval results for the 0-0 mode query image

and Edge Histogram Descriptor (EHG). The results in terms of average metric values for all 21 queries are shown in Table 1 and Fig. 5, where the three groups of bars in figures correspond to the performance when the above three test image categories were chosen, respectively.

For all three cases (the original version and two adapted versions), the proposed descriptor outperforms the featured MPEG-7 low level visual descriptors. The variation of retrieval performance to content adaptation is very low for the proposed descriptor compared to those for the MPEG-7 descriptors.

Fig. 6, Fig. 7 and Fig. 8 show the comparison of retrieval results using the proposed description scheme for the query image versions 0-0 (the original version),

Query (1-5) Mode

Fig. 7. Retrieval results for the 1-5 mode query image

Query (2-8) Mode

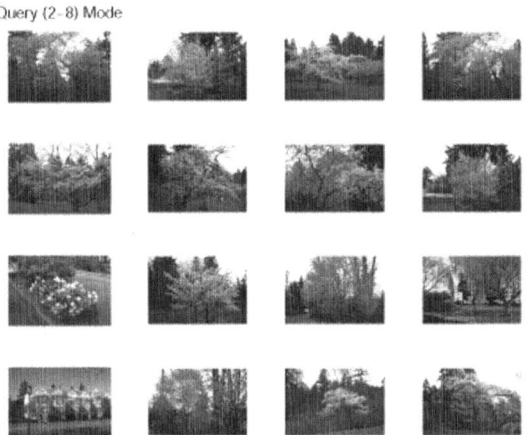

Fig. 8. Retrieval results for the 2-8 mode query image

1-5 (half resolution - medium quality) and 2-8 (quarter resolution - low quality), respectively. This shows example shows the consistency in retrieval performance for different resolution quality levels.

5   Conclusion

We have proposed a new low-level visual description scheme based on the compression decision modes in order to map the descriptor into the resolution-quality spaces of the content corresponding to content adaptation modes and to obtain the content adaptation invariance. We demonstrated this concept using the EZW scalable image coding algorithm. As the descriptor is structured according to the sub bands and bit planes it can easily be mapped to the hierarchical content representation. Since the compression decision modes are unaltered when content adaptation based on bit stream description schemes are performed, the proposed descriptor is minimally affected by the content adaptation. The proposed method outperforms the commonly used MPEG-7 low level visual descriptors based on single cues such as, colour, texture and edge, for all query image modes representing different resolution-quality levels corresponding to content adaptation modes. Further, it shows a low variation of retrieval performance when different content adapted versions of the query images as compared to the featured MPEG-7 descriptors.

References

1. Taubman, D.S., Marcellin, M.W.: JPEG2000 Image Compression Fundamentals, Standards and Practice. Springer, USA (2002)
2. ITU-T, JTC1, I.: Advanced video coding for generic audiovisual services. ITU-T Rec. ISO/IEC 14496-10 (2003)

3. Manjunath, B.S., Ohm, J.-R., Vasudevan, V.V., Yamada, A.: Color and texture descriptors. IEEE Trans. Circ. and Sys. for Video Tech. 11, 703–715 (2001)
4. Manjunath, B.S., Salembier, P.P., Sikora, T.: Introduction to MPEG-7: Multimedia Content Description Interface. John Wiley and Sons, Chichester (2002)
5. Lu, Z.-M., Li, S.-Z., Burkhardt, H.: A content-based image retrieval scheme in jpeg compressed domain. Int'l. Jnl. of Innovative Computing, Information and Contorl, 831–839 (2005)
6. Tian, Q., Sebe, N., Lew, M.S., Loupias, E., Huang, T.: Content-based image retrieval using wavelet-based salient points. Jnl. of Electronic Imaging 10(4), 835–849 (2001)
7. Liang, K.C., Kuo, C.C.J.: Waveguide: A joint wavelet-based image representation and description system. IEEE Trans. Image Processing 8(11), 1619–1629 (1999)
8. Shapiro, J.: Embedded image coding using zero trees of wavelet coeffiecients. IEEE Trans. Signal Processing 41(12), 3445–3462 (1993)
9. Messing, D.S., Van Beek, P., Errico, J.H.: The mpeg-7 colour structure descriptor: Image description using colour and local spatial information. In: Proc. IEEE ICIP, pp. 670–673 (2001)
10. Jasutani, E., Yamada, A.: The mpeg-7 colour layout descriptor: A compact feature description for high speed image/video segment retrieval. In: Proc. IEEE ICIP, pp. 674–677 (2001)
11. Li, Y., Shapiro, L.: Object and concept recognition for cbir image and ground truth database,
   http://www.cs.washington.edu/research/imagedatabase/groundtruth/

Spatial Hierarchy of Textons Distributions for Scene Classification

Sebatiano Battiato, Giovanni Maria Farinella, Giovanni Gallo, and Daniele Ravì

Image Processing Laboratory, University of Catania, IT
{battiato,gfarinella,gallo,ravi}@dmi.unict.it

Abstract. This paper proposes a method to recognize scene categories using bags of visual words obtained hierarchically partitioning into subregion the input images. Specifically, for each subregion the Textons distribution and the extension of the corresponding subregion are taken into account. The bags of visual words computed on the subregions are weighted and used to represent the whole scene. The classification of scenes is carried out by a Support Vector Machine. A k-nearest neighbor algorithm and a similarity measure based on Bhattacharyya coefficient are used to retrieve from the scene database those that contain similar visual content to a given a scene used as query. Experimental tests using fifteen different scene categories show that the proposed approach achieves good performances with respect to the state of the art methods.

Keywords: Scene Classification, Textons, Spatial Distributions.

1 Introduction

The automatic recognition of the context of a scene is a useful task for many relevant computer vision applications, such as object detection and recognition [1], content-based image retrieval (CBIR) [2] or bootstrap learning to select the advertising to be sent by Multimedia Messaging Service (MMS)[3]. Existing methods works extracting local concepts directly on spatial domain [4,5,6,2] or in frequency domain [7,8]. A global representation of the scene is obtained grouping together local information in different ways (e.g., histogram of visual concepts, spectra template, etc.). Recently, the spatial layout of local features [9] as well as metadata information collected during acquisition time [10] have been exploited to improve the classification task. Typically, memory-based recognition algorithms (e.g., k-nearest neighbor are employed, together with holistic representation of the scene, to assign the scene category skipping the recognition of the objects that are present in the scene [8].

In this paper we propose to recognize scene categories by means of bags of visual words [11] computed after hierarchically partitioning the images in subregions. Specifically, each subregion is represented as a distribution of Textons [12,6,13]. A weight inversely proportional to the extension of the related subregion is assigned to every distribution. The weighted Textons distributions are concatenated

B. Huet et al. (Eds.): MMM 2009, LNCS 5371, pp. 333–343, 2009.

to compose the final representation of the scene. Like in [9] we penalize distributions related to larger regions because they can involve increasingly dissimilar visual words. The scene classification is achieved by using a SVM [14].

The proposed approach has been experimentally tested on a database of about 4000 images belonging to fifteen different basic categories of scene. In spite of the simplicity of the proposal, the results are promising: the classification accuracy obtained closely matches the results of other state-of-the-art solutions [5,9,8]. To perform a visual assessment, the proposed representation of the scene is used in a simple content based retrieval system employing a k-nearest neighbor as engine and a similarity measure based on Bhattacharyya coefficient [15].

The rest of the paper is organized as follows: Section 2 describes the model we have used for representing the images. Section 3 illustrates the dataset, the setup involved in our experiments and the results obtained using the proposed approach. Finally, in Section 4 we conclude with avenues for further research.

2   Weighting Bags of Textons

Scene categorization is typically performed describing images through feature vectors encoding color, texture, and/or other visual cues such as corners, edges or local interest points. These information can be automatically extracted using several algorithms and represented by many different local descriptors. A holistic global representation of the scene is built grouping together such local information. This representation is then used during categorization (or retrieval) task.

Local features denote distinctive patterns encoding properties of the region from which have been generated. In Computer Vision these patterns are usually referred as "visual words" [4,16,17,9,11,13]: an image may hence be considered as a bag of "visual words".

To use the bag of "visual words" model, a visual vocabulary is built during the learning phase: all the local features extracted from the training images are clustered. The prototype of each cluster is treated as a "visual word" representing a "special" local pattern. This is the pattern sharing the main distinctive properties of the local features within the cluster. In this manner a visual-word vocabulary is built.

Through this process, all images from the training and the test sets may be considered as a "document" composed of "visual words" from a finite vocabulary. Indeed, each local feature within an image is associated to the closest visual word within the built vocabulary. This intermediate representation is then used to obtain a global descriptor. Typically, the global descriptor encodes the frequencies of each visual word within the image under consideration.

This type of approach leaves out the information about the spatial layout of the local features [9]. Differently than in text documents domain, the spatial layout of local features for images is crucial. The relative position of a local descriptor can help in disambiguate concepts that are similar in terms of local descriptor. For instance, the visual concepts "sky" and "sea" could be similar in terms of local descriptor, but are typically different in terms of position within the scene. The relative position can be thought as the context in which a visual word takes part respect to the other visual words within an image.

To overcome these difficulties we augment the basic bag of visual words representation combining it with a hierarchical partitioning of the image. More precisely, we partition an image using three different modalities: horizontal, vertical and regular grid. These schemes are recursively applied to obtain a hierarchy of subregions as shown in Figure 1.

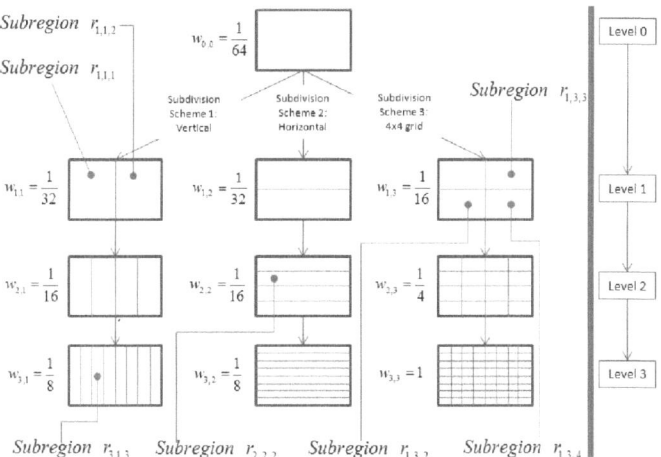

Fig. 1. Subdivision schemes up to the fourth hierarchical levels. The i_{th} subregion at level l in the subdivision scheme s is identified by $r_{l,s,i}$. The weights $w_{l,s}$ are defined by the Equation (1).

The bag of visual words representation is hence computed in the usual way, using a pre-built vocabulary, relatively to each subregion in the hierarchy. In this way we take into account the spatial layout information of local features. The proposed augmented representation hence, keeps record of the frequency of the visual words in each subregion (Figure 2).

A similarity measure between images may now be defined as follows. First, a similarity measure between histograms of visual words relative to corresponding regions is computed (the choice of such measure is discussed in Section 2.2). The connection of similarity values of each subregion are then combined into a final distance by means of a weighted sum. The choice of weight is justified by the following rationale: the probability to find a specific visual word in a subregion at fine resolution is sensibly lower than finding the same visual word in a subregion with higher resolution. We penalize similarity in larger subregion defining weights inversely proportional to the subregions size (Figure 1, Figure 2).

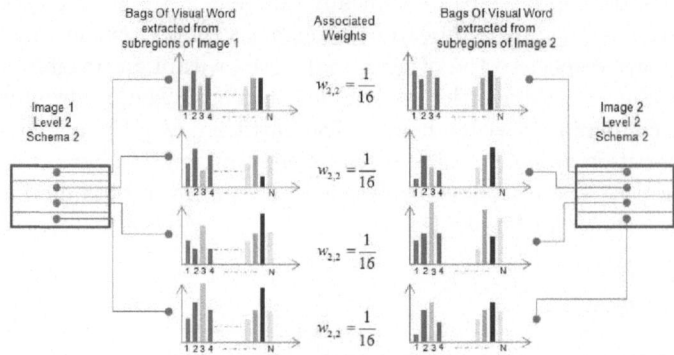

Fig. 2. A toy example of the similarity evaluation between two images I_1 and I_2 at level 2 of the subdivision schema 2. After representing each subregion $r^I_{2,2,i}$ as a distribution of Textons $B(r^I_{2,2,i})$, the distance $D_{2,2}(I_1, I_2)$ between the two images is computed taking into account the defined weight $w_{2,2}$.

Formally, denoting with $S_{l,s}$ the number of subregions at level l in the scheme s, the distances between corresponding subregions of two different images considered at level l in the scheme s, is weighted as follows:

$$w_{l,s} = \frac{S_{l,s}}{\max_{Level,Scheme}(S_{Level,Scheme})} \tag{1}$$

where *Level* and *Scheme* span on all the possible level and schemas involved in a predefined hierarchy.

The similarity measure on the weighted bags of Textons scheme is coupled with a k-nearest neighbor algorithm to retrieve, from the scene database, those that contain similar visual content to a given scene query. To recognize the category of a scene, the weighted bags of Textons of all subregions are concatenated to form a global feature vector. The classification is obtained using a Support Vector Machine [14].

In the following subsections we provide more details about the local features used to build the bag of visual words representation as well as more details on the the similarity between images.

2.1 Local Feature Extraction

Previous studies emphasize the fact that global representation of scenes based on extracted holistic cues can effectively help to solve the problem of rapid and automatic scene classification [8]. Because humans can process texture quickly and in parallel over the visual field, we considered texture as a good holistic cue candidate. Specifically, we choose to use Textons [12,6,13] as the visual words able to identify properties and structures of different textures present in the scene. To build the visual vocabulary each image in the training set is processed with a bank of filters. All responses are then clustered, pointing out the Textons vocabulary, by considering the cluster centroids. Each image pixel is then associated to the closest Texton taking into account its filter bank responses.

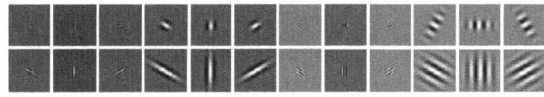

Fig. 3. Visual representation of the bank of 2D Gabor filters used in our experiments

More precisely good results have been achieved by considering a bank of 2D Gabor filters and the k-means clustering to build the Textons vocabulary. Each pixel has been associated with a 24-dimensional feature vector obtained processing each gray scaled image through 2D Gabor filters [18]:

$$G(x, y, f_0, \theta, \alpha, \beta) = e^{-(\alpha^2 x_2' + \beta^2 y_2')} \times e^{j2\pi f_0 x'} \qquad (2)$$

$$x' = x \cos \theta + y \sin \theta \qquad (3)$$

$$y' = -x \sin \theta + y \cos \theta \qquad (4)$$

The 24 Gabor filters (Figure 3) have size 49×49, obtained considering two different frequencies of the sinusoid ($f_0 = 0.33, 0.1$), three different orientations of the Gaussian and sinusoid (θ = -60°, 0, 60°), two different sharpness of the Gaussian major axis ($\alpha = 0.5, 1.5$) and two different sharpness of the Gaussian minor axis ($\beta = 0.5, 1.5$). Each filter is centered at the origin and no phase-shift is applied.

The experiments reported in Section 3 are performed by using a spatial hierarchy with three level ($l = 0,1,2$) and employing a visual vocabulary of 400 Textons.

2.2 Similarity between Images

The weigthed distance that we use is founded on similarity between two corresponding subregions when the bag of visual words have been computed on the same vocabulary.

Let $B(r_{l,s,i}^{I_1})$ and $B(r_{l,s,i}^{I_2})$ the bags of visual words representation of the i_{th} subregion at level l in the schema s of two different images I_1 and I_2. We use the metric based on Bhattacharyya coefficient to measure the distance between $B(r_{l,s,i}^{I_1})$ and $B(r_{l,s,i}^{I_2})$. Such distance measure has several desirable properties [15]: it imposes a metric structure, it has a clear geometric interpretation, it is valid for arbitrary distributions, it approximates the χ^2 statistic avoiding the singularity problem of the χ^2 test when comparing empty histogram bins.

The distance between two images I_1 and I_2 at level l of the schema s is computed as follows:

$$D_{l,s}(I_1, I_2) = w_{l,s} * \sum_i \sqrt{1 - \rho[B(r_{l,s,i}^{I_1}), B(r_{l,s,i}^{I_2})]} \qquad (5)$$

$$\rho[B(r_{l,s,i}^{I_1}), B(r_{l,s,i}^{I_2})] = \sum_T \sqrt{B(r_{l,s,i}^{I_1})_T * B(r_{l,s,i}^{I_2})_T} \qquad (6)$$

where $B(r_{l,s,i}^I)_T$ indicate the frequency of a specific Texton T in the subregion $r_{l,s,i}$ of the image I. The final distance between two images I_1 and I_2 is hence calculated as follows:

$$D(I_1, I_2) = D_{0,0} + \sum_l \sum_s D_{l,s} \qquad (7)$$

Observe that the level $l = 0$ of the hierarchy (Figure 1) corresponds to the classic bag of visual word model in which the metric based on Bhattacharyya coefficient is used to establish the distance between two images.

3 Experiments and Results

The dataset we have used contains more than 4000 images collected in [5,9,8]. Images are grouped in fifteen basic categories of scenes (Figure 4): coast, forest, bedroom, kitchen, living room, suburban, office, open countries, mountains, tall building, store, industrial, inside city, highway. These basic categories can be ensembled and described with a major level of abstraction (Figure 4): In vs. Out, Natural vs. Artificial. Moreover, some basic categories (e.g., bedroom, living room, kitchen) can be grouped and considered belonging to a single category (e.g. house).

In our experiments we splitted the database in ten different non overlapped subsets. Each subset was created in order to have approximatively the 10% of

Fig. 4. Some examples of images used in our experiments considering basic and superordinate level of description

Table 1. Confusion Matrix obtained considering the proposed approach on the fifteen basic classes of scenes. The average classification rates for individual classes are listed along the diagonal.

	Suburban	Cost	Forest	Highway	Inside City	Mountain	Open Country	Street	Tall Building	Office	Bedroom	Industrial	kitchen	Living Room	Store
Suburban	**97.72**	0.57	0.00	0.00	1.14	0.00	0.00	0.00	0.57	0.00	0.00	0.00	0.00	0.00	0.00
Coast	0.40	**81.76**	0.79	1.19	0.00	1.58	14.28	0.00	0.00	0.00	0.00	0.00	0.00	0.00	0.00
Forest	0.86	0.00	**92.23**	0.00	0.00	2.59	3.03	0.00	0.43	0.00	0.00	0.00	0.00	0.00	0.86
Highway	0.00	3.30	0.00	**89.00**	1.10	0.00	1.65	0.55	0.00	0.00	0.55	1.65	0.55	1.10	0.55
Inside City	0.46	0.00	0.00	0.00	**76.06**	0.00	0.00	4.14	1.38	0.00	0.92	8.75	0.92	1.84	5.53
Mountain	0.00	1.12	1.50	0.37	0.00	**89.15**	5.26	0.37	0.37	0.00	0.00	1.12	0.00	0.37	0.37
Open Country	0.00	15.67	2.09	2.09	0.34	3.83	**74.27**	0.34	0.34	0.00	0.34	0.69	0.00	0.00	0.00
Street	0.00	0.00	0.00	0.47	2.85	0.00	0.00	**90.04**	0.47	0.00	0.47	3.33	0.00	0.95	1.42
Tall Building	0.00	0.00	0.79	0.00	4.36	1.58	0.79	0.00	**82.19**	0.00	1.58	4.36	1.98	0.79	1.58
Office	0.00	0.00	0.00	0.00	0.00	0.00	0.00	0.00	0.00	**92.86**	1.30	0.00	1.30	4.54	0.00
Bedroom	0.00	0.65	0.00	0.65	0.00	2.59	0.65	0.65	0.65	6.49	**62.62**	3.24	8.44	11.42	1.95
Industrial	0.44	2.67	0.89	1.33	9.82	2.23	2.67	0.89	3.12	0.00	3.12	**61.23**	2.23	2.67	6.69
Kitchen	0.00	0.69	0.00	0.00	2.72	0.68	0.00	0.00	0.68	6.12	9.52	3.40	**61.23**	11.56	3.40
Living Room	0.00	0.00	0.49	0.49	0.98	0.00	0.49	0.00	0.49	5.91	12.80	2.95	7.38	**63.59**	4.43
Store	0.00	0.00	0.00	0.00	6.92	1.73	0.00	0.00	0.86	0.00	1.29	4.76	1.73	5.19	**77.52**

Table 2. Natural vs. Artificial results

	Natural	Artificial
Natural	**97.26**	2.74
Artificial	2.28	**97.71**

Table 3. In vs. Out results

	In	Out
In	**96.41**	3.59
Out	7.41	**92.59**

images of a specific class. The classification experiments have been repeated ten times considering the i_{th} subset as training and the remaining subsets as test. A ν-SVC [19] was trained at each run and the per-class classification rates were recorded in a confusion matrix in order to evaluate the classification performance at each run.

The averages from the individual runs are reported through confusion matrices in Tables 1, 2, 3 (the x-axis represents the inferred classes while the y-axis represents the ground-truth category).

The overall classification rate is 79.43% considering the fifteen basic classes, 97.48% considering the superordinate level of description Natural vs. Artificial, 94.5% considering the superordinate level of description In vs. Out. These results are comparable and in some cases better than the state of art approaches working on basic and superordinate level description of scenes [5,7,9,8,20]. For example,

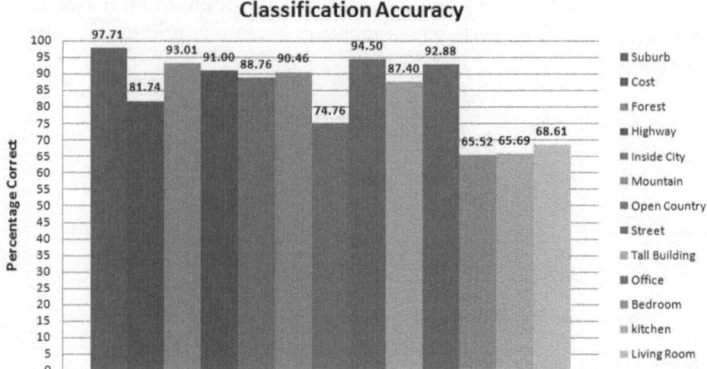

Fig. 5. Classification accuracy considering the thirteen basic categories used in [5]

in [5] the authors considered thirteen basic classes obtaining 65.2% classification rate. We applied the proposed technique to the same dataset used in [5] achieving a classification rate of 84% (Figure 5).

Obviously, the classification accuracy increases ($\cong$89%) if the images belonging to the categories bedroom, kitchen and living room are grouped and described as house scene. Moreover, the method proposed in this paper achieves better results with respect to our previous work [20], were the overall classification rate was 75% considering the only ten basic classes, 90.06% considering the superordinate level of description In vs. Out, 93.4% considering the superordinate level of description Natural vs. Artificial.

Another way to measure the performances of the proposed approach is to use the rank statistics [5,2] of the confusion matrix results. Rank statistics shows

Fig. 6. Examples of images retrieved employing the proposed approach. The query images are on the left, and top three closest images are shown on the right.

Table 4. Rank statistics of the two best choices on the fifteen basic classes

	Suburban	Coast	Forest	Highway	Inside City	Mountain	Open Country	Street	Tall Building	Office	Bedroom	Industrial	Kitchen	Living Room	Store	Overall
1	97.72	81.76	92.23	89.00	76.06	89.15	74.27	90.04	82.19	92.86	62.62	61.23	61.23	63.59	77.52	**79.43**
2	98.29	96.04	95.26	92.30	84.81	94.41	89.94	93.37	86.55	97.40	74.04	71.05	72.79	76.39	82.28	**86.99**

the probability of a test scene correctly belongs to one of the most probable categories (Table 4). Using the two best choices on the fifteen basic classes, the mean categorization result increases to 86.99% (Table 4). Taking into account the rank statistics, it is straightforward to show that most of the images which are incorrectly categorized as first match are on the borderline between two similar categories and therefore most often correctly categorized with the second best match (e.g., Coast is classified as Open Country).

Finally we compared the performances of the classic bag of visual words model (corresponding to the level 0 in the hierarchy of Figure 1) with respect to the proposed hierarchical representation. Experiments have shown that the proposed model achieves better results (8% on average).

To perform a visual assessment, Figure 6 shows some examples of images retrieved employing a k-nearest neighbor and the similarity measure described in Section 2. The query images are depicted in the first column, whereas the first three closest images are reported in the other columns. The closest images are semantically consistent in terms of visual content to the related query images.

4 Conclusion

This paper has presented an approach for scene categorization based on bag of visual words representation. The classic approach is augmented by computing it on subregions defined by three different hierarchically subdivision schemes and properly weighting the Textons distributions with respect to the involved subregions. The weighted bags of visual words representation is coupled with a Support Vector Machine to perform classification. A similarity distance based on Bhattacharyya coefficient is used together with a k-nearest neighbor to retrieve scenes. Despite its simplicity, the proposed method has shown promising results with respect to state of the art methods. The proposed hierarchy of features produces a description of the image only slightly heavier than the classical bag of words representation, both in terms of storage as well as in terms of time retrieval allowing at the same time to obtain effective results. Future works should be devoted to perform a depth comparison between different kind of features used to build the visual vocabulary (e.g., Textons vs. SIFT) for scene classification. Moreover, the proposed method should be compared with respect to other approaches working on spatial (e.g., Spatial Pyramid Matching [9], pLSA [4], etc.) as well as on frequency domains [21,22].

References

1. Torralba, A.: Contextual priming for object detection. International Journal of Computer Vision 53(2), 169–191 (2003)
2. Vogel, J., Schiele, B.: Semantic modeling of natural scenes for content-based image retrieval. International Journal of Computer Vision 72(2), 133–157 (2007)
3. Battiato, S., Farinella, G.M., Giuffrida, G., Sismeiro, C., Tribulato, G.: Using visual and text features for direct marketing on multimedia messaging services domain. Multimedia Tools and Applications Journal(in press, 2008)
4. Bosch, A., Zisserman, A., Munoz, X.: Scene classification via pLSA. In: Leonardis, A., Bischof, H., Pinz, A. (eds.) ECCV 2006. LNCS, vol. 3954, pp. 517–530. Springer, Heidelberg (2006)
5. Fei-Fei, L., Perona, P.: A hierarchical bayesian model for learning natural scene categories. In: IEEE Computer Science Society International Conference of Computer Vision and Pattern Recognition (CVPR), San Diego, CA, USA (June 2005)
6. Renninger, L.W., Malik, J.: When is scene recognition just texture recognition? Vision Research 44, 2301–2311 (2004)
7. Ladret, P., Guérin-Dugué, A.: Categorisation and retrieval of scene photographs from jpeg compressed database. Pattern Analysis & Application 4, 185–199 (2001)
8. Oliva, A., Torralba, A.: Modeling the shape of the scene: a holistic representation of the spatial envelope. International Journal of Computer Vision 42, 145–175 (2001)
9. Lazebnik, S., Schmid, C., Ponce, J.: Beyond bags of features: Spatial pyramid matching for recognizing natural scene categories. In: IEEE Conference on Computer Vision and Pattern Recognition, vol. II, pp. 2169–2178 (2006)
10. Matthew, R.B., Jiebo, L.: Beyond pixels: Exploiting camera metadata for photo classification. Pattern Recognition 38(6), 935–946 (2005)
11. Sivic, J., Zisserman, A.: Video Google: A text retrieval approach to object matching in videos. In: Proceedings of the International Conference on Computer Vision, October 2003, vol. 2, pp. 1470–1477 (2003)
12. Julesz, B.: Textons, the elements of texture perception, and their interactions. Nature 290, 91–97 (1981)
13. Varma, M., Zisserman, A.: A statistical approach to texture classification from single images. International Journal of Computer Vision 62(1–2), 61–81 (2005)
14. Shawe-Taylor, J., Cristianini, N.: Support Vector Machines and other kernel-based learning methods. Cambridge University Press, Cambridge (2000)
15. Comaniciu, D., Ramesh, V., Meer, P.: Kernel-based object tracking. IEEE Trans. Pattern Anal. Mach. Intell. 25(5), 564–575 (2003)
16. Dance, C., Willamowski, J., Fan, L., Bray, C., Csurka, G.: Visual categorization with bags of keypoints. In: ECCV International Workshop on Statistical Learning in Computer Vision (2004)
17. Shotton, J., Johnson, J., Cipolla, M.,, R.: Semantic texton forests for image categorization and segmentation. In: IEEE Computer Science Society International Conference of Computer Vision and Pattern Recognition, CVPR (2008)
18. Gonzalez, R.C., Woods, R.E.: Digital Image Processing, 3rd edn. Prentice-Hall, Inc, Upper Saddle River (2006)
19. Chang, C.C., Lin, C.J.: LIBSVM: a library for support vector machines (2001)

20. Battiato, S., Farinella, G.M., Gallo, G., Ravì, D.: Scene categorization using bag of textons on spatial hierarchy. In: IEEE International Conference on Image Processing - ICIP 2008 (2008)

21. Farinella, G.M., Battiato, S., Gallo, G., Cipolla, R.: Natural Versus Artificial Scene Classification by Ordering Discrete Fourier Power Spectra. In: Proceedings of 12th International Workshop on Structural and Syntactic Pattern Recognition (SSPR)-Satellite event of the 19th International Conference of Pattern Recognition (ICPR). LNCS. Springer, Heidelberg (2008)

22. Battiato, S., Farinella, G.M., Gallo, G., Messina, E.: Classification of compressed images in constrained application domains. In: SPIE-IS&T 21th Annual Symposium Electronic Imaging Science and Technology 2009 - Digital Photography V (2009)

Approximate Retrieval with HiPeR: Application to VA-Hierarchies

Nouha Bouteldja, Valerie Gouet-Brunet, and Michel Scholl

CEDRIC/CNAM-Wisdom, 292, rue Saint-Martin - F75141 Paris Cedex 03
{nouha.bouteldja,valerie.gouet,scholl}@cnam.fr

Abstract. In this article, we present an approximate technique that allows accelerating similarity search in high dimensional vector spaces. The presented approach, called HiPeR, is based on *a hierarchy* of subspaces and indices: it performs nearest neighbors search across spaces of different dimensions, starting with the lowest dimensions up to the highest ones, aiming at minimizing the effects of the curse of dimensionality. In this work, HiPeR has been implemented on the classical index structure VA-File, providing VA-Hierarchies. The model of precision loss defined is probabilistic and non parametric and quality of answers can be selected by user at query time. HiPeR is evaluated for range queries on 3 real data-sets of image descriptors varying from 500,000 vectors to 4 millions. The experiments show that this approximate technique improves retrieval by saving I/O access significantly.

Keywords: Approximate Retrieval, Multidimensional Indexing, Range Queries, VA-File.

1 Introduction

During the last years, similarity search has drawn considerable attention in multimedia systems, decision support and data mining. In these systems, there is the need for finding a small set of objects which are similar to a given query object. Content-based image retrieval (CBIR) is one example where the objects to be retrieved are images, videos or parts of them. Usually, similarity search is implemented as *nearest neighbor search* (k-NN) or *range query*. This article focuses on range queries i.e. retrieving all the multidimensional points at a distance lower than a threshold ϵ from the query.

To accelerate the retrieval process, a large number of multidimensional access methods (MAM) have been proposed in the literature [12]. If the dimension of the space is high, MAM's performance suffers from the well-known curse of dimensionality phenomenon (CoD) and sequential scan outperforms hierarchical index traversal [16]. The VA-file [16] was first proposed as an amelioration of sequential scan. Other methods perform retrieval on one-dimensional vectors obtained from multidimensional vectors mappings, e.g. the Pyramid technique [2]. Last but not least, some hybrid techniques were proposed such as the GC-Tree [6] or the KpyrRec [14].

In [3], we proposed HiPeR, for Hierarchical and Progressive Retrieval, a new approach based on a hierarchy of index structures and designed for speeding up exact

B. Huet et al. (Eds.): MMM 2009, LNCS 5371, pp. 344–355, 2009.

retrieval of nearest neighbors. HiPeR proposes to speed up search in a multidimensional space by mapping the objects in the space into objects in a hierarchy of spaces with increasing dimensions. First steps referred to as filtering steps, provide a fast answer by using low-dimensional vectors. Then the answer is refined by using higher dimensional vectors. In contrast to classical feature selection techniques [8], HiPeR can perform *exact* retrieval and manage *dynamic* databases without recomputing the features: specific dimension reduction methods *which are data-independent* are involved to build the hierarchy of vectors. As HiPeR, some MAM accelerate retrieval by first using lower dimensions and then refine the answer by using more dimensions [9], [1], [7]. However, these indices differ from HiPeR mainly in the two following points: first they are not designed for progressive retrieval i.e. they do not present intermediate results to the user (except [7]). Second, they are *simple* indices. In contrast, HiPeR utilizes a *hierarchy of indices*: one of these indices may be used in one or more levels of HiPeR. As several progressive techniques [4], HiPeR uses a hierarchy of finer and finer features of the same entities for retrieval. But, HiPeR is more general: it proposes a generic and consistent model for the design of a *description and index independent* hierarchy.

Built upon on a first description and assessment of HiPeR for exact retrieval [3], this paper generalizes the approach to approximate retrieval [11]. The main contributions of this paper are : (1) a probabilistic and non parametric model for precision control is defined where the precision can be chosen at query time, (2) a performance evaluation which shows the effectiveness of HiPeR.

The paper is organized as follows: section 2 presents the general concepts of HiPeR, followed by section 3 where the scheme for approximate retrieval is described. HiPeR is evaluated in section 4 on various data-sets. Finally, section 5 concludes.

2   Exact Retrieval with HiPeR

HiPeR is a hierarchical and progressive method. It is based on a hierarchy of multidimensional indices, that allows to accelerate retrieval by minimizing the curse of dimensionality effects. It is progressive since the hierarchy allows to quickly return a first result to the user, before refining it progressively until satisfaction. In the following the concept and general properties of HiPeR are presented.

Let E be an entity described by v^E, a d-dimensional point in space V. Defining a hierarchy for v^E consists in building an ordered set of n ($n \geq 2$) vectors:

$$H_n(v^E) = \{v_1^E, v_2^E, ..., v_{n-1}^E, v_n^E = v^E\} \tag{1}$$

where $v_i^E = m_i(v_{i+1}^E), \forall i \in 1..n-1$. Each $v_i \in V_i$ is obtained from $v_{i+1} \in V_{i+1}$ by a mapping m_i, with $d_i < d_{i+1}$ and $d_n = d$. According to this definition, entities are now described into several feature spaces $\{V_1, V_2, ..., V_n = V\}$.

Let $\mathcal{N}_V(E)$ be the set of the nearest neighbors (NN) of entity E in space V, retrieved by similarity search (range query or k-nn query). In order to accelerate the retrieval of $\mathcal{N}_V(E)$, we exploit the hierarchy defined above by performing search successively in subsets of the different feature spaces: NN search is done in space V_i, prior to space V_{i+1}, $i < n$. The initial NN search takes as an entry the whole set of features V_1. The subset of neighbors $\mathcal{N}_{V_i}(E)$ resulting from the search in V_i is used as *an entry* for the

NN search in space V_{i+1}. The lower the dimension, the more efficient the filter; the higher the dimension the closer the result to the $\mathcal{N}_V(E)$ answer set.

According to the NN retrieval strategy, some constraints have to be satisfied. In the following, we detail these constraints for range queries. When an exact search is needed, the intermediate queries, involving spaces V_i, should bring a super set $\mathcal{N}_{V_i}(E)$ of the answers of the final space V_n ($\mathcal{N}_{V_n}(E)$). Relation 2 then has to be satisfied:

$$\mathcal{N}_{V_i}(E) \supseteq \mathcal{N}_{V_{i+1}}(E) \quad \forall i \in 1..n-1 \tag{2}$$

Intermediate feature spaces V_i ($i < n$) may describe less precisely the entities and then needlessly provide larger sets of NN that contain non relevant entities. But on the other hand, it is well-known that NN retrieval is much faster at low dimension: indeed CoD effects are not yet significant.

Let $dist$ be the distance measure, and E' another entity characterized by the hierarchy $H_n(v^{E'}) = \{v_1^{E'}, ..., v_n^{E'}\}$ involving the same mappings $m_i, i \in 1..n-1$ defined for E. We suppose that $dist$ is sufficiently generic to apply or to be adapted to all the spaces of the hierarchy. In [3], we proposed two families of mapping that apply for any distance L_p. In the case of range queries, we further assume that the sphere radius ϵ is the same at all levels in the hierarchy. Then, if the following implication 3 is satisfied, it guarantees that, relation 2 is satisfied too.

$$dist(v_i^E, v_i^{E'}) \geq \epsilon \Rightarrow dist(v_{i+1}^E, v_{i+1}^{E'}) \geq \epsilon \quad \forall i \in 1..n-1 \tag{3}$$

Condition 3 expresses that vectors that are not neighbors in V_i cannot be neighbors in V_{i+1}. On the other hand, two neighbors in V_i are not necessary neighbors in V_{i+1}.

Scanning the hierarchy can be performed until the last level n is reached so as to perform an *exact* retrieval or may stop, according to some criteria such as the user satisfaction, at iteration $i < n$ bringing back to the user a subset of the exact answer set.

3   Approximate Retrieval with HiPeR

In this section, we present a algorithm for *approximate search* with VA-Hierarchies. The proposed model is inspired from an existing approximate VA-File algorithm called "VA-BND", revisited in section 3.1. Because we are interested in ϵ-sphere queries, in section 3.2 we propose a new approximate model called "ϵ-VA-BND". Finally, adaptation to VA-hierarchies is specified in section 3.3.

3.1   Approximate VA-File for k-NN

VA-BND [15] is based on the following observation: reducing the size of the vector approximation cells saves retrieval time while modifying the exact answers set only slightly. In the VA-BND strategy, the only difference with exact k-NN retrieval concerns altering the size of the approximations: for each approximation cell, the lower and upper bounds are modified with a shift parameter α allowing to reduce the cell's size.

Let $\delta_l(p, q) = dist(q, p) - lBnd(q, p)$ be the difference between the distance and the lower bound between a query q and a point p. To quantify the precision loss in NN retrieval when using the shifted lower bound, VA-BND assumes the knowledge of function f^{δ_l} which gives the frequency of each value of δ_l. The probability of loosing NN with VA-BND when searching the k-NN of a query, under the assumption of uniformity and independence of the database points distribution, is then bounded by $k.P(\alpha)$ where $P(\alpha) = \int_0^\alpha f^{\delta_l}(\rho)d\rho$. The approach is similar for upper bounds. In the following section, we introduce another precision loss model, suited for ϵ-sphere queries.

3.2 ϵ-VA-BND Algorithm

VA-BND was designed for k-NN queries, Algorithm ϵ-VA-BND (see algorithm 1) is the variant for ϵ-queries, adapted to approximate search by adding function $Alter$ $(lBnd, uBnd, \alpha)$ that alters the exact bounds as following:

$$lBnd' = lBnd + \alpha \quad \text{and} \quad uBnd' = uBnd - \alpha \tag{4}$$

Algorithm 1. ϵ-VA-BND(F,Q)

Input : F a Vector Approximation File of size N, Q a sphere query with center q and
              radius ϵ, α the shift parameter of Equation 4
Output: V the set of NN vectors
```
//  Retrieves the set V of vectors inside Q
```
$V :=$ empty;
for $i = 1, N$ **do**
    $a := F$.GetApproximation(i);
    GetBounds($a, q, lBnd, uBnd$);
    Alter($lBnd, uBnd, \alpha$);
    ```// Filtering rule #1```
    if $lBnd < \epsilon$ **then**
        $v :=$ GetVector(a);
        ```// Filtering rule #2```
        if $uBnd < \epsilon$ **then** $V+=\{v\}$;
        else
            $d :=$ GetDistance(v, q);
            if $d < \epsilon$ **then** $V+=\{v\}$;
        end if;
    end if;
end for;
return V;

Here filtering rule #1 allows to load only the vectors associated with the cells which intersect Q. The vectors are read from the vector file (VF) using function $GetVector()$ which loads the page including the vector only if not already loaded. Filtering rule #2 avoids distance computation when the approximation cell is inside the query.

Model for Precision Loss Estimation. The estimation of the precision loss in NN retrieval using ϵ-VA-BND differs from the one of VA-BND, mainly in the following point: for a fixed shift α, the precision loss also depends on ϵ. Indeed, if the query range is small then the probability of a wrong answer when changing the bounds is small; see

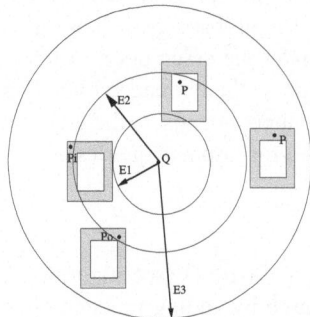

Fig. 1. ϵ-VA-BND: illustration of precision loss with different values of ϵ (E_1, E_2 and E_3)

Fig. 2. Example of cumulated histograms of f^d (distances), f^lBnd (lBnd) and $f^{lBnd'}$ with two values of α that give $lBnd'_1$ and $lBnd'_2$. Histograms are computed for 100 queries using 1M points among a 128-dimensional uniform data-set.

Fig 1, when $\epsilon = E_1$ precision loss is null. This probability increases with ϵ ($\epsilon = E_2$) until reaching a maximum value. Then it decreases with ϵ until reaching zero where the range query includes all the approximations even with altered bounds ($\epsilon = E_3$). This is confirmed by Fig. 3(a) which plots effective precision loss using ϵ-VA-BND versus ϵ and for different values of α and for a uniform data-set.

Let first study the probability P_l of the effective precision loss PL_l due to replacing $lBnd$ by $lBnd'$. When $lBnd$ is shifted for a given cell we may *loose correct answers*. Suppose that, for a fixed value of ϵ, we know in advance: n_d the number of points inside the query and n_{lBnd} (resp. $n_{lBnd'}$) the number of approximation cells that intersect the same query when using $lBnd$ (resp. $lBnd'$), then it is easy to estimate PL_l. Indeed, if $n_{lBnd'}$ is lower than n_d (see Fig. 2 with $lbnd'_1$), the number of missed points is *at least* equal to $n_d - n_{lBnd'}$; so the probability of missing nearest neighbors is $\frac{n_d-n_{lBnd'}}{n_d}$ at least. Otherwise, when $n_{lBnd'}$ is higher than n_d (see Fig. 2 with $lbnd'_2$), the probability to eliminate a correct neighbor is $\frac{n_{lBnd}-n_{lBnd'}}{n_{lBnd}}$. As a matter of fact, in the general case, the probability P_l of missing points with $lBnd'$ is defined as:

$$P_l = R_l + (1 - R_l) \times \frac{n_{lBnd} - n_{lBnd'}}{n_{lBnd}} \tag{5}$$

with $R_l = \frac{n_d-n_{lBnd'}}{n_d}$ if $n_d > n_{lBnd'}$ and 0 otherwise. Since values of n_d, n_{lBnd} and $n_{lBnd'}$ are not known in advance, we estimate n_d, n_{lBnd} by sampling the database and then to approximate $n_{lBnd'}$ using n_{lBnd}, as follows: after database indexing and before retrieval, a sample set of queries S_q is chosen among the whole database. For each query q_0 of S_q, the distance and the $lBnd$ bound between q_0 and each data-set vector are computed. Then, the cumulated histogram CH^d (CH^{lBnd}resp.) of the frequency function f^d (f^{lBnd} resp.) is computed. CH^d gives for each ϵ value, the ratio n_d of the number of neighbors inside a query, while CH^{lBnd} provides an approximation of the ratio of n_{lBnd}, for each ϵ value. Finally, given a shift α, an approximation of $n_{lBnd'}$ is deduced by shifting histogram CH^{lBnd} with α.

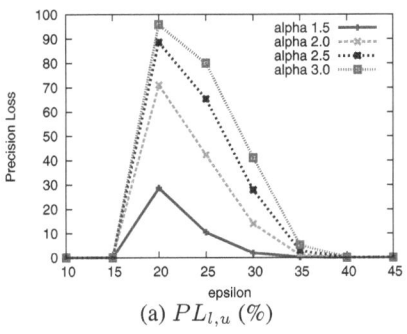 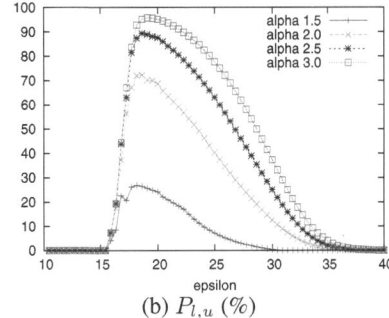

(a) $PL_{l,u}$ (%)   (b) $P_{l,u}$ (%)

Fig. 3. Average precision loss vs. ϵ with ϵ-VA-BND using a uniform data-set of 1M 64-dimensional vectors: (a) Effective precision loss $PL_{l,u}$, (b) Estimation of the precision loss $P_{l,u}$

It is important to note that the computation of $f^{lBnd'}$ is not performed. Estimation of $n_{lBnd'}$ from CH^{lBnd} allows to compute P_l quickly, given CH^d and CH^{lBnd}. Consequently, the computation of the precision loss is done on-line for a given α, when retrieving the neighbors of a query.

A similar study can be conducted for upper bounds when using $uBnd'$ to define P_u, the probability of precision loss PL_u. But note that taking $uBnd'$ into account instead of $uBnd$ implies a possible *add of false answers*. Altering upper bounds saves *CPU computation*, whereas modifying lower bounds saves *both I/O access and CPU time*. Actually, replacing $uBnd$ by $uBnd'$ allows avoiding distance computation using rule #2 in algorithm 1, because cells become smaller. Altering $lBnd$ eliminates more cells by using rule #1 in algorithm 1, so their related points are not loaded from disk and the distance computations between the query and these points are avoided.

With the definitions of P_l and P_u, many expressions of the total precision loss can be defined. In our experiments, the effective precision is defined as the intersection between the exact answer set E and the approximate answer set A over their union, and the corresponding precision loss as its complement, i.e: $PL_{l,u} = 1 - \frac{|A \cap E|}{|A \cup E|}$. The estimation of the precision loss is then defined as follows:

$$P_{l,u} = \frac{P_l + P_u}{1 + P_u} \tag{6}$$

since (i) $PL_{l,u}$ can be rewritten as $PL_{l,u} = 1 - \frac{|E| - |A^-|}{|E| + |A^+|}$ where A^- (resp. A^+) is the set of points missed in (resp. added to) the answer set, due to bounds altering and (ii) since A^- (resp. A^+) is estimated as $P_l * |E|$ (resp. $P_u * |E|$).

In order to assess this estimator, the estimated precision loss $P_{l,u}$ is compared to the effective precision loss $PL_{l,u}$ in Fig. 3. Both are plotted versus ϵ, for various values of α. One can observe that $P_{l,u}$ fits $PL_{l,u}$ quite well.

3.3 Approximate VA-Hierarchies

In the HiPeR hierarchy, each d_i-dimensional feature space ($1 \leq i \leq n$) is potentially indexed by an index Idx_i. A n-level hierarchy based on VA-Files, in all the levels, is called a VA-Hierarchy and denoted by VA-H_n in the following.

To exploit the hierarchy of index structures, any two descriptors v_j^E and v_i^E ($1 \leq j < i \leq n$) associated with the same entity E must have the same identifier in the hierarchy. In order to avoid I/O increase with a VA-hierarchy and since a VA-File is based on approximations [16], we create hierarchies that only utilize approximations in the first levels which reside in main memory: I/O are necessary only at the last level to fetch the features; this ensures that I/O access with exact retrieval using HiPeR is at worst equal to the one given by the simple indices (without using HiPeR). In a VA-hierarchy, each entity E is defined by an approximation a_i^E (resp. a_j^E) in VA-File VA_i (resp. VA_j) defined at level i (resp. j). Approximations as well as data vectors are identified by their rank in the VA-File. Therefore, VA_i and VA_j are built so that two approximations a_i^E and a_j^E are inserted in the same order in the respective approximations files; see [3] for more details and for an implementation of HiPeR with another index.

In the following, we first generalize the ϵ-VA-BND scheme to a VA-hierarchy, then we detail the model proposed for estimating the associated global precision loss.

Algorithm for Approximate Retrieval. As already stated, the retrieval process in the low-dimensional spaces only exploits the approximation files. As a matter of fact, filtering using upper bounds (rule #2 of Algorithm 1) becomes useless here since it was designed for diminishing vector distance computations and distances are not computed at these levels. The filtering algorithm designed for each VAF_i of feature space $V_i, i < d$ is defined in Algorithm 2: for each approximation the cell with ID c_{id} returned by a previous retrieval in space V_{i-1} (the lower bound $lBnd$ between cell of same ID in VAF_i and query Q_i is first computed via function $GetBound()$). Then $lBnd$ is shifted by α_i using function $Alter()$. Obviously, when $i = 1$, the query is compared to all the approximations of VAF_1. Retrieval at the last level n is a little bit different, since both upper and lower bounds are shifted to compute the final answer set and the vectors are read.

Model for Global Precision Loss Estimation. Let $P_{l,u}^i$ be the probability that an error occurs if the retrieval is performed the first time with level i using all the approximations of VAF_i as if there were no prior filtering of approximations by steps 1 to $i - 1$. $P_{l,u}^i$ is the probability of precision loss when bounds (lower bounds if $i < n$; lower and

---

Algorithm 2. ϵ-VAH-BND$_i(F_i, Q_i, A_k)$

Input : F_i a Vector Approximation File of size N, Q_i a sphere query with center q_i and
radius ϵ, α_i the shift parameter at level i, A_k the vector of approximation IDs
found at a previous level (k < i)

Output: A_i the vector of approximation IDs at level i

```
//  Computes A_i set of approximation IDs that intersect Q_i
A_i := empty;
for c_id in A_k do
    a := F_i.GetApproximation(c_id);
    GetBound(a, q_i, lBnd);
    Alter(lBnd, α_i);
    //  Filtering rule #1
    if lBnd < ε then  A_i+={c_id};
end for;
return A_i;
```

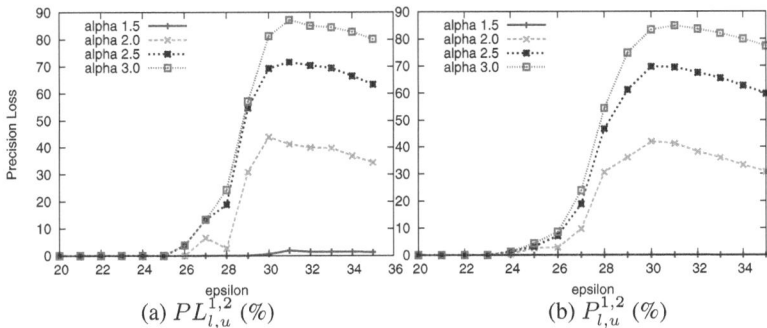

Fig. 4. Average precision loss vs. ϵ with approximate VA-Hierarchy composed of 2 levels: (a) Effective precision loss $PL_{l,u}^{1,2}$, (b) Estimation of the precision loss $P_{l,u}^{1,2}$

upper bounds if $i = n$) are shifted by α_i. Such a probability has been already defined in section 3.2. To define the global precision loss when all the levels of the hierarchy are used together, it is necessary to specify probabilities $P_l^{1,n}$ and $P_u^{1,n}$ that estimate proportions of respectively correct NN eliminated and false NN added to the answer set: since upper bounds are shifted only at the last level, $P_u^{1,n}$ is defined as $P_u^{1,n} = P_u^n$, whereas probability of loosing correct answers $P_l^{1,n}$ is defined as follows:

$$P_l^{1,n} = P_l^{1,n-1} + (1 - P_l^{1,n-1}).P_l^n \text{ with } P_l^{1,1} = P_l^1 \qquad (7)$$

Having $P_l^{1,n}$ and $P_u^{1,n}$, the global precision loss estimation $P_{l,u}^{1,n}$ can be deduced from Equation 6.

The effective loss in precision $PL_{l,u}^{1,n}$ and its estimation $P_{l,u}^{1,n}$ are displayed in Figure 4 versus ϵ and for various values of α. The hierarchy is composed of $n = 2$ levels (dim. 64-128). Vectors with dimension 64 are computed using partial p-norms mappings, from a distribution of 1 Million uniform points in dimension 128. We observe that $P_{l,u}^{1,n}$ fits $PL_{l,u}^{1,n}$ well.

To sum up, we sketch the approximate retrieval process at query time, with an n-depth VA-Hierarchy and a given query size ϵ: the user has to provide the query and the precision loss $P_{l,u}^{1,n}$ that he/she tolerates. For simplicity, we suppose that $P_l^{1,n} = P_u^{1,n}$ (probabilities of loosing correct answers and adding wrong ones are identical) and that precision losses P_l^i are identical $\forall i \in 1..n$. Under these assumptions, the P_l^i can be deduced from equations 6 and 7 and P_u^n computation is direct. At each level i, having the precision loss P_l^i (and P_u^n at $i = n$), the corresponding shift α_i is then deduced from the cumulated histograms CH^d, CH^{lBnd} (and CH^{uBnd} at last level).

4 Experiments

To demonstrate the relevance of HiPeR for nearest neighbor retrieval, we performed an extensive experimental evaluation up to 4 million images of heterogeneous contents downloaded from user-generated-content web sites. From these images three data-sets were generated using the following CBIR descriptors: (1) Discrete Fourier Transform

[5] of the image signal, generating the DFT database; (2) SIFT local descriptors [10], producing the $LOWE$ data-set (here only a sub-set of the image collection is used); (3) RGB histogram [13] of each image, generating the RGB database. These descriptions are computed at the same dimension (128, imposed by descriptor SIFT) in order to perform comparisons in the same conditions; they are traditionally associated with distance L_1. The databases generated provide very distinct distributions, as illustrated by the mean and standard deviation values of L_1 distance distributions obtained (normalized into $[0, 1]$): $5.8e^{-3} \pm 7.13e^{-3}$ with DFT, $0.65 \pm 9.82e^{-2}$ with $LOWE$ and 0.77 ± 0.17 with RGB.

In the following experiments, all results correspond to an average over 100 queries chosen randomly among each database. First, algorithm ϵ-VA-BND is evaluated in terms of precision of the answers, CPU time and I/O access. Then, the gain achieved by integrating it into VA-Hierarchies is evaluated. In the following the proposed techniques are compared to the VA-File since it does not face the curse of dimensionality with the tested databases (see experiments of [3]).

4.1 Evaluation of Algorithm ϵ-VA-BND

Algorithm ϵ-VA-BND, presented in section 3.2 for approximate retrieval with sphere queries, is evaluated on the three data-sets at dimension 128. Here, the impact of shift α of equation 4 is studied in terms of precision of answers as well as of I/O access and CPU time compared to that obtained with exact retrieval. The impact of shifting lower and upper bounds $lBnd$ and $uBnd$ is experimented separately. We vary α until achieving a loss in precision $P_{l,u}$ of 30%, where roughly a third of the nearest neighbors retrieved may be incorrect. Note that in the current experiment, the query size ϵ is fixed to the value corresponding to a query returning on the average 1000 neighbors for data-sets DFT and RGB, and 4000 neighbors in the case of $LOWE$.

Varying α has a very small impact on CPU time. In fact, CPU time mostly covers time spent for computing lower and upper bounds; after the filtering step, the number of remaining distances to compute (here real L_1 distances to feature vectors) is very small compared to the whole database size. For example with the $LOWE$ data-set remaining distances represent 0.18% of the database size. While shifting lower bounds allows filtering out approximation cells and thus reducing CPU computation and I/O access, shifting upper bounds allows only saving distance computation by increasing the use of filtering rule #2 (see section 3.2). Since the improvement in CPU time when modifying

Table 1. ϵ-VA-BND algorithm evaluation: I/O gain and precision loss P_l (%) when scaling the database

	Database size (in Millions)					
	0.5	1	1.5	2	3	4
I/O Gain	94.80	91.76	90.03	90.11	88.74	85.42
P_l	63.42	28.74	16.04	15.42	4.93	0.40
DFT ($\alpha = 1200 = 0.1\epsilon$)						
I/O Gain	39.25	39.22	39.48	39.39	39.46	39.22
P_l	3.14	3.10	3.11	3.15	3.09	3.14
$LOWE$ ($\alpha = 150 = 0.1\epsilon$)						
I/O Gain	38.32	39.16	38.85	28.26	39.23	38.71
P_l	3.64	3.84	5.22	5.12	4.72	4.47
RGB ($\alpha = 3000 = 0.2\epsilon$)						

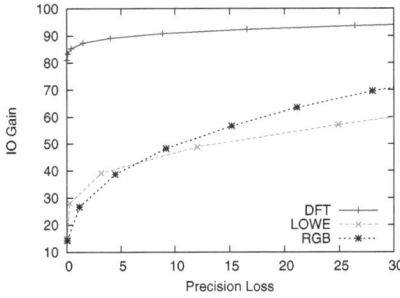
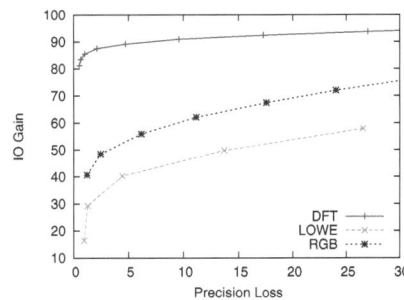

Fig. 5. ϵ-VA-BND: I/O gain vs. precision loss P_l ($P_l = 0$ does not imply $\alpha = 0$)

Fig. 6. AVA-H: I/O gain versus precision loss $P_{l,u}^{1,3}$

upper bounds is negligible for these data-sets, in the remaining experiments we focus on lower bounds only and then on precision loss P_l.

Fig. 5 illustrates the impact of shifting lower bounds on I/O access. For the three distributions, we observe a significant I/O gain : it is about 40% with the $LOWE$ and RGB sets for a precision loss lower than 5%. Gains with the DFT set are very important ($> 80\%$), even with a very small amount of lost correct answers ($P_l < 1\%$). This last result reveals that the cells of the VA-File probably do not approximate this distribution very well : the exact retrieval algorithm leads to I/O access for outlier vectors.

In table 1, the databases size is scaled. For each data-set, the same values of ϵ and α are used for the different sizes.

For both $LOWE$ and RGB data-sets, one can observe that I/O gain is almost constant when the database size is scaled. The precision loss is as well almost constant when increasing the database size. Here, P_l could probably be estimated from one of these samples, and then be used for larger data-sets. The behavior of DFT is different, the precision loss is sensitive to changes in the database size. Obviously, this does not mean that we can not achieve small precision loss with important I/O gains when the data-set size is small, but that the estimation of the precision loss cannot be made on a sample of DFT, because data is skewed.

4.2 Approximate VA-Hierarchies (AVA-H)

In this section, we study the performance of HiPeR with the approximate scenario, according to the model described for VA-Hierarchies VA-H$_n$ in section 3.3. Here a three-level hierarchy VA-H$_3$ is used in the experiments (dim. 32-64-128). Shift α_i is the same for all three levels; precision loss $P_{l,u}^{1,3}$ can be estimated from equation 7. Recall that the approximate version of hierarchies of VA-Files saves I/O access (at last level n), while the hierarchy itself (in an exact or approximate context) allows to save CPU time significantly [3]. Note that set α_i to 0 whatever $i < n$ and α_n to α would *at worst* allow to achieve the I/O gain observed by using one level with the ϵ-VA-BND algorithm.

Fig. 6 displays I/O gain versus precision loss for the different distributions. Again, we observe that I/O gain is significant, while keeping reasonable precision loss. Integrating approximate retrieval in the VA-Hierarchies improves the gain even for the ϵ-VA-BND algorithm used alone at dimension 128 (for instance the reader can compare results for the RGB data-set in figures 5 and 6).

Table 2 illustrates the scalability of AVA-H performance, for fixed values of α_i and ϵ. As in the previous section, we observe that RGB and $LOWE$ data-sets are robust when scaling the database size while DFT is not. The best improvement is obtained with RGB.

Table 2. AVA-H evaluation: I/O gain and precision loss $P_{l,u}^{1,3}$ (%) when scaling the database

	Database size (in Millions)					
	0.5	1	1.5	2	3	4
I/O Gain	94.85	91.83	90.12	90.19	88.82	85.50
$P_{l,u}^{1,3}$	63.81	29.43	16.80	16.18	5.69	1.04
DFT ($\alpha_1 = \alpha_2 = \alpha_3 = 1200 = 0.1\epsilon$)						
I/O Gain	39.36	39.30	39.57	39.49	39.52	39.31
$P_{l,u}^{1,3}$	3.52	3.52	3.51	3.57	3.50	3.56
$LOWE$ ($\alpha_1 = \alpha_2 = \alpha_3 = 150 = 0.1\epsilon$)						
I/O Gain	49.94	50.66	53.04	53.03	52.44	51.88
$P_{l,u}^{1,3}$	3.50	3.65	4.83	4.87	4.44	4.11
RGB ($\alpha_1 = \alpha_2 = \alpha_3 = 2500 = 0.17\epsilon$)						

5   Conclusion and Future Work

This paper was devoted to the study of similarity search in collections of high-dimensional points. HiPeR is a new framework for nearest neighbors retrieval based on a *hierarchy* of features spaces. With HiPeR, retrieval can be performed under an exact retrieval scenario, see [3], as well as under an *approximate* scenario where quality is guaranteed according to a probabilistic model. In this paper, the approximate scenario for HiPeR was developed and experimented on VA-Files as a basic index structure, leading to VA-Hierarchies. The experiments, performed on several real data-sets with different distributions up to 4 million (M) of points, demonstrated that the HiPeR strategy proposed for approximate retrieval improves retrieval by *significantly* saving I/O access (see figures 5 and 6, and table 2). HiPeR also proved to be robust wrt scalability when varying the database size from 500,000 points to 4M (see tables 1 and 2).

To sum up, according to the classification of algorithms for approximate retrieval proposed in [11], HiPeR has the followings characteristics: it was designed for vector spaces (**VS**). In the current implementation, it is $\mathbf{VS}_{L_p}$ because the families of mapping used are proposed for L_p distances. Accelerating retrieval is done by changing the original space (**CS**). The current application to VA-File with algorithm VA-BND also puts HiPeR in category $\mathbf{RC}_{AP}$ where the approaches reduce the number of compared objects by pruning some parts of the space. The model of precision loss defined for HiPeR is probabilistic and non parametric ($\mathbf{PG}_{npar}$) because very little assumptions are made on the data distribution. Finally, HiPeR is an interactive approach (**IA**) in the sense that quality of answers is selected by user at query time.

In this work, we experimented only homogeneous hierarchies, where each level is indexed by the same structure. As a future work, we intend to use the most adapted index for each level of a given hierarchy.

Acknowledgement. The authors thank the reviewers for their constructive comments.

References

1. Andoni, A., Indyk, P.: Near-optimal hashing algorithms for approximate nearest neighbor in high dimensions. In: FOCS, pp. 459–468 (2006)
2. Berchtold, S., Böhm, C., Kriegel, H.: The pyramid-technique: towards breaking the curse of dimensionality. In: SIGMOD, pp. 142–153 (1998)
3. Bouteldja, N., Gouet-Brunet, V., Scholl, M.: HiPeR: Hierarchical progressive exact retrieval in multi-dimensional spaces. In: SISAP, pp. 25–34 (2008)
4. Bouteldja, N., Gouet-Brunet, V., Scholl, M.: The many facets of progressive retrieval for CBIR. In: PCM (2008)
5. Bracewell, R.N.: The Fourier Transformation and its Applications, 2nd edn. McGraw-Hill, New York (1978)
6. Cha, G., Chung, C.: The GC-tree: a high-dimensional index structure for similarity search in image databases. IEEE Transactions on Multimedia, 235–247 (2002)
7. Ferhatosmanoglu, H., Tuncel, E., Agrawal, D., Abbadi, A.E.: Approximate nearest neighbor searching in multimedia databases. In: ICDE, USA, pp. 503–521 (2001)
8. Guyon, I., Elisseeff, A.: An introduction to variable and feature selection. In: JMLS, pp. 1157–1182 (2003)
9. Lin, K., Jagadish, H.V., Faloutsos, C.: The tv-tree: An index structure for high-dimensional data. VLDB, 517–542 (1994)
10. Lowe, D.G.: Distinctive image features from scale-invariant keypoints. IJCV, 91–110 (2004)
11. Patella, M., Ciaccia, P.: The many facets of approximate similarity search. In: SISAP, pp. 10–21 (2008)
12. Samet, H.: Foundations of Multidimensional and Metric Data Structures. The Morgan Kaufmann Series in Computer Graphics (2006)
13. Swain, M.J., Ballard, D.H.: Color indexing. In: IJCV, pp. 11–32 (November 1991)
14. Urruty, T.: KpyrRec: a recursive multidimensional indexing structure. In: IJPEDS (2007)
15. Weber, R., Böhm, K.: Trading quality for time with nearest neighbor search. In: EDBT, pp. 21–35 (2000)
16. Weber, R., Schek, H., Blott, S.: A quantitative analysis and performance study for similarity-search methods in high-dimensional spaces. In: VLDB, pp. 194–205 (1998)

A Novel Multi-reference Points Fingerprint Matching Method

Keming Mao, Guoren Wang, Changyong Yu, and Yan Jin

Institute of Computer System, Northeastern University, Shenyang, China
wanggr@mail.neu.edu.cn

Abstract. Fingerprint matching is a challenging problem due to complex distortion in fingerprint image. In this paper, a multi-reference points matching method is proposed to solve the problem. First, a new feature description $Minutiae$-$Cell$, which is constructed by the minutiae and its neighbor ridges, is used to represent the local structure of the fingerprint. The proposed matching method consists of three stages, including the original matching stage ,the purifying stage and the fingal matching stage. In the original matching stage, minutiae pairs that potentially matched are found based on the $Minutiae$-$Cell$ and the. Then the purifying stage is carried out to obtain the true matched minutiae pairs. Instead of using only one reference pair, the final matching stage deals with the remaining minutiae from template and query fingerprints by comparing their distance to the true matched minutiae pair set. The matching score is composed of the results of purifying stage and final matching stage. The proposed method overcomes the problems of distortion and noises existing in the fingerprint image. Experimental results show that the performance of the proposed algorithm is satisfying.

Keywords: fingerprint matching, multi-reference, minutiae-cell, multi-stage.

1 Introduction

For its uniqueness and immutability [1,2,13], fingerprint is currently one of the most widely used biometric features in automatic identification systems. The key issue of the fingerprint recognition is the matching algorithm. Given two fingerprint images, the matching task is to judge whether they are identical or not. Although there already exists many fingerprint matching methods, it is still a hard problem as fingerprint data may involves image elastic distortion, and the fingerprint preprocessing stage may also bring noises.

Fingerprint matching has been widely investigated and many matching methods have been proposed. These methods can be mainly classified into two categories: texture-based[3,4] and minutiae-based[5,7,8,9,10]. In [3], fingerprint image is filtered in a number of directions and a fixed-length feature vector $FingerCode$ is extracted. The Euclidean distance between $FingerCode$s of template and query fingerprints is calculated for matching. The method in [4] uses eight orientation Gabor filters to extract the ridge feature maps to represent, align and match fingerprint image. In [13], when extracting minutiae, the shape and location of its associated ridge is also recorded. After alignment of the reference minutiae, a string representation of both minutiae set is

B. Huet et al. (Eds.): MMM 2009, LNCS 5371, pp. 356–366, 2009.

constructed and a dynamic-programming string matching algorithm is implemented. In [8], minutiae is first organized by delanuay triangulation, then RBF is used to estimated the translation and rotation parameters. After regulate the minutiae of query fingerprint, the matched minutiae pairs constitute the matching result. As a whole, texture-based method utilizes the while feature of fingerprint and the distribution of gray level of the images is used for matching. While minutiae-based method makes use of local feature of fingerprint, hence point matching method is adopted and the number of matched minutiae pairs counts for the matching result.

This paper proposes a novel multi-reference points fingerprint matching method. First, a novel structure named $Minutiae\text{-}Cell$ is devised to represent the local feature of the fingerprint. In [5,6,7], they mainly use a center minutia in connection with its neighbor minutiae to construct a topology to express the local structure of the fingerprint. However, the fingerprint may not have enough minutiae or the structure may incorporate spurious one, which can heavily affect the performantce of fingerprint local matching. Using $Minutiae\text{-}Cell$ cannot only avoid the problems brought by missing or spurious minutiae, but also combines the useful neighbor ridge information. The original matching stage is carried out on the basis of matching the $Minutiae\text{-}Cell$s of template and query fingerprints. Using the results obtained above, a minutiae pair set called potentially matched minutiae pair set(PMS for short) is obtained. The PMS is processed in the purifying stage and the true matched minutiae pair set(TMS for short) is gained. The TMS is considered as an union. In the final matching stage, the remaining minutiae of template and query fingerprints are compared according to their distance to TMS. Methods proposed in [5,9,10] use one pair of minutiae as the reference and compare other minutiae in accordance with the reference pair. Due to the elastic distortion and intrinsic noise in the fingerprint image, using only one reference point may bring errors. The proposed method uses multi-reference points as the basis to compare the residuary minutiae, which can overcome the defect of using one reference pair. The results of purifying stage and final matching stage form the matching score together.

The remainder of this paper is organized as follows. We give an overview on problem statement of fingerprint matching in Section 2. Section 3 introduces the structure of $Minutiae\text{-}Cell$. Section 4 describes the proposed fingerprint matching method in detail. Performance evaluation is exhibited in Section 5. Finally, Section 6 concludes this paper.

2   Problem Statement

Fingerprint is composed of ridges and valleys and there are also local ridge discontinuities, known as minutiae [1]. Minutiae is the symbol of a fingerprint. The location and type of minutiae that exist in a fingerprint make the fingerprint unique. There are two basic types of minutiae: ridge ending and ridge bifurcation. As shown in Fig.2, ridge ending is the location where ridge terminates and ridge bifurcation is the location where a ridge splits into two separate ridges. The direction of corresponding minutiae is marked with dashed line.

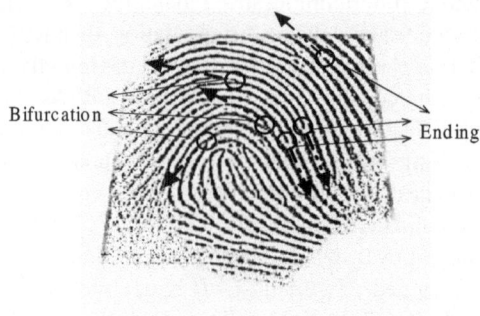

Fig. 1. Fingerprint minutiae

The combination of minutiae in a fingerprint make the fingerprint unique. So most fingerprint identification systems are based on minutiae matching. A minutia m_i can be represented as $\{x_i, y_i, \theta_i, t_i\}$, where x_i and y_i are the coordinate of m_i, θ_i is the direction of m_i, t_i is the type of m_i(ending or bifurcation). Therefore a fingerprint can be expressed as a minutiae set:

$$F = \{m_1, m_2, ..., m_N\} \tag{1}$$

where N is the number of minutiae in a fingerprint. So given a template and a query fingerprint, the matching issue can be regarded as the problem of point matching and whether they are identical can be judged by comparing two minutiae sets. However, due to the presence of noise and elastic distortion, fingerprint matching is still far beyond solved.

3   Construction of Minutiae-Cell

Methods in [5,6,11], they select a center minutia as well as its neighbor minutiae to construct a topology to represent the local feature of a fingerprint. And the corresponding relative distance and angle between minutiae, which are invariant to translation and rotation, are used for local matching and local alignment. However, these structures may not be very robust and precise because of the noises and elastic distortion exist in fingerprint image, especially in the existence of missing or spurious minutiae. This paper devises a novel structure named *Minutiae-Cell*, which is constructed using a center minutia and its useful neighbor ridges information, to describes the local feature of a fingerprint.

As shown in Fig.3 (a), the curves denote the ridges of a fingerprint, let minutiae A be a ridge ending, and the dashed line indicates its direction. Fig.3 (b) demonstrates the corresponding *Minutiae-Cell* constructed by minutiae A. Here some notations are given in Table 1. In the table, BAD_i and BI_i are defined by Formulas (2) and (3) as follows:

$$BAD_i = BA_i - \theta_A \tag{2}$$

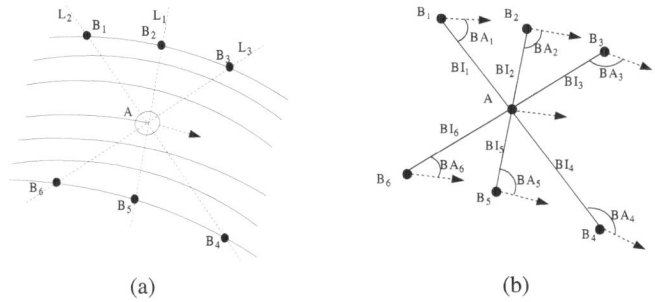

(a)   (b)

Fig. 2. The structure of $Minutiae\text{-}Cell$

Table 1. Notation Description 1

Notation	Description
BaseLine	As shown in Fig 3 (a), making a line L_1 perpendicular to the direction of A. Another two lines L_2 and L_3 can be obtained by circumvolving L_1 anti-clockwise and clockwise $45°$ respectively. L_1, L_2 and L_3 are called **BaseLine**.
BasePoint	As shown in Fig 3 (a), $\{B_1, ..., B_6\}$ are in a clockwise order the intersection points of **BaseLine** L_1, L_2 and L_3 with the ridges which are the third neighbor ridge of the ridge minutiae A resides in. $\{B_1, ..., B_6\}$ are called **BasePoint**.
BaseAngle	As shown in Fig 3 (b), $\{BA_1, ..., BA_6\}$ are called **BaseAngle**, which are the angle differences between the orientation of line segment B_iA and the corresponding orientation of tangent by pass the **BasePoint** B_i on its associate ridges.
BaseAngleDiff	As shown in Fig 3 (b), $\{BAD_1, ..., BAD_6\}$ are called **BaseAngleDiff**, which are the angle differences between **BaseAngle** $\{BA_1, ..., BA_6\}$ and the orientation of minutia A. Which can be obtained by Formula (2) :
BaseInterval	As shown in Fig 3 (b), **BaseInterval** $\{BI_1, ..., BI_6\}$ are the lengths of line segment of **BasePoint** $\{B_1, ..., B_6\}$ with minutia A, which can be obtained using Formula (3):

$$BI_i = |L(B_i, A)| \tag{3}$$

Then $Minutiae\text{-}Cell$ can be defined as below:

Definition 1 (Minutiae-Cell). *A **Minutiae-Cell** is an aggregation, which is composed of* $\{A_T, BAD_1, ..., BAD_6, BI_1, ..., BI_6\}$. *Where A_T is the type of minutia A, BAD_i and BI_i are the corresponding **BaseAngleDiff** and **BaseInterval** of minutia A.*

4 Fingerprint Matching

This paper proposes a multi-reference points fingerprint matching method. First, the potentially matched minutiae pair set (PMS for short) is calculated by matching the $Minutiae$-$Cell$s of template and query fingerprints. Then the true matched minutiae pair set (TMS for short) is obtained by purifying PMS. Finally, the remaining minutiae are tested in order to gain the final matched minutiae pairs by comparing their distance from the corresponding minutiae to TMS.

4.1 Original Matching Stage

It can be seen from the topology of $Minutiae$-$Cell$ that BAD_i and BI_i are features that are invariant to rotation and translation. So elements in the $Minutiae$-$Cell$ can be used to describe the local feature in a fingerprint correctly. In this way, a fingerprint can be described as a set of $Minutiae$-$Cell$s. Comparing local features of template and query fingerprints can be transformed into the problem of comparing the corresponding $Minutiae$-$Cell$s of theirs. Here function S_{Mc}, which is used for measuring the similarity of two $Minutiae$-$Cell$ is defined as Formula (4):

$$S_{Mc}(M, N) = \sum_{k=1}^{6} \left(w_k \times |M_{BAD_k} - N_{BAD_k}| \right)$$
$$+ \quad \sum_{k=1}^{6} \left(v_k \times |M_{BI_k} - N_{BI_k}| \right)$$
$$+ \quad u_1 \times \left(D_{BAD} + D_{BI} \right)$$
$$+ \quad u_2 \times \left(M_{A_T} - N_{A_T} \right) \tag{4}$$

where $(w_k, v_k)(1 \leq k \leq 6)$ and u_i are the weight parameters. D_{BAD} and D_{BI} are the variance of $|M_{BAD_k} - N_{BAD_k}|(1 \leq k \leq 6)$ and $|M_{BI_k} - N_{BI_k}|(1 \leq k \leq 6)$ respectively. While the smaller S_{Mc} two $Minutiae$-$Cell$s get, the more similar two minutiae are and so is the corresponding local feature of two fingerprints. In this way a set of minutiae pairs with lower S_{Mc} are obtained. These minutiae pairs comprise a set which is regarded as potentially matched minutiae pair set and we use PMS for short. Here the definition of PMS is given below:

Definition 2 (Potentially matched minutiae pair set(PMS)). $PMS = \{(M_i^T, M_i^Q) \mid S_{Mc}(M_i^T, M_i^Q) < T_{pms} .\}$

where M_i^T and M_i^Q are minutiae from template and query fingerprint respectively and T_{pms} is a certain threshold.

4.2 Purifying Stage

Due to the image quality and intrinsic noise, there may exists some fake matched minutiae pairs in PMS. These fake elements must be removed so as to perform the following steps of matching. The true matched minutiae pair set is the result of purifying the PMS.

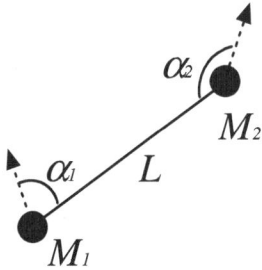

Fig. 3. Demonstration of element in E_T

Here, two graphs G_T and G_Q are used to represent PMS. $G_T = \{V_T, E_T\}$ denotes the minutiae in template fingerprint, where set V_T is composed of the minutiae of template fingerprint in PMS. As shown in Fig.4.2, M_1 and M_2 are two minutiae in V_T, α_1 and α_2 are the inclination angles between the direction of minutiae and the line connecting M_1 to M_2. L is the distance between M_1 and M_2. Then a triplet $\{\alpha_1, \alpha_2, L_{12}\}$ is used to indicate the edge between M_1 and M_2. E_T is composed of all the edges between every two minutiae in V_T. $G_Q = \{V_Q, E_Q\}$, which denotes the graph of query fingerprint, can be gained in the same way as G_T.

In this way, by comparing the relationship between corresponding edges in E_T and E_Q, elements in V_T and V_Q can be purified and the fake matched minutiae pair can be deleted. The procedure can be described as follows:

1. Constructing G_T and G_Q from PMS;
2. For one pair (M_i^T, M_i^Q) in PMS, comparing the distance between the corresponding edges containing M_i^T and M_i^Q in E_T and E_Q as Formulas (5), (6) and (7):

$$fs(E_T(i,j), E_Q(i,j)) = \begin{cases} 1 & \text{if } |\alpha_i^T - \alpha_i^Q| \leq \delta_\alpha, \\ & |\alpha_j^T - \alpha_j^Q| \leq \delta_\alpha, and \\ & |L_{i,j}^T - L_{i,j}^Q| \leq \delta_L \\ 0 & \text{else} \end{cases} \tag{5}$$

$$tc(i) = \sum_{\forall j, \ E_T(i,j) \in E_T \ and \ E_Q(i,j) \in E_Q} fs(E_T(i,j), E_Q(i,j)) \tag{6}$$

$$fc(i) = \frac{1}{Nu_i} \times tc(i) \tag{7}$$

where $E_T(i,j)$ is the edge between m_i and m_j in E_T, $fs(E_T(i,j), E_Q(i,j))$ denotes the similarity between two edges, $tc(i)$ is the **template confidence** of ith element in PMS, $fc(i)$ is the final confidence of ith element in PMS, Nu_i is the total number of the edges containing minutia M_i^T in E_T;

3. If $fc(i)$ is less than a threshold, then (M_i^T, M_i^Q) is considered as fake and is removed from PMS, M_i^T and M_i^Q are deleted from V_T and V_Q respectively. Those edges containing M_i^T and M_i^Q are also removed from E_T and E_Q;
4. Iterate all minutiae pairs in PMS, and repeat step 2 and 3 until all elements are checked.

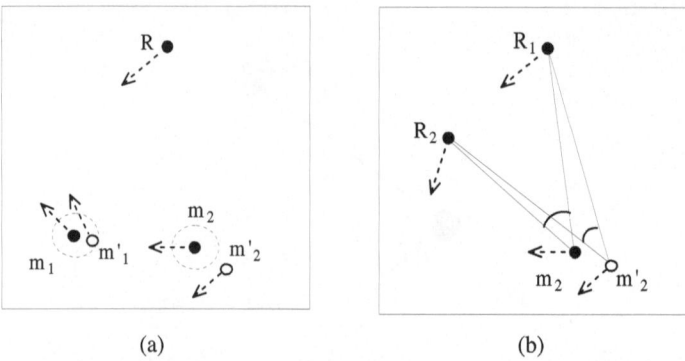

(a)   (b)

Fig. 4. Single-reference and multi-reference

After getting rid of all fake matched minutiae pairs, the PMS is purified and the remaining minutiae pairs constitute the TMS.

4.3 Final Matching Stage

In [7,9,10,12,13], they select one minutiae pair as reference, and translate other minutiae according to the reference minutia. However, using only one reference pair may not be very precise due to the elastic distortion.

As shown in Fig.4.3 (a), R is the single reference point, (m_1, m_1') and (m_2, m_2') are two true matched minutiae pairs from template and query fingerprints. The circles around m_1 and m_2 are bounding boxes. It can be seen that the minutiae pair (m_2, m_2') is not considered matched, since m_2' is beyond the matching scope of m_2. In order to avoid this condition, a novel multi-reference points matching mechanism is devised. As shown in Fig.4.3 (b), R_1 and R_2 are two reference points, which are elements from TMS. Whether m_2 and m_2' are matched or not can be judged according to their relative distance and angle to two reference points together. Here TMS is used as the multi-reference points set. For two minutiae M_t and M_q from the template and query fingerprints, $Dif(M_t, M_q, TMS)$ is used to measure their similarity, as shown in equation (8):

$$
\begin{aligned}
Dif(M_t, M_q, TMS) = \sum_{i=1}^{N-1} & \big((|L(M_i^T, M_t)| - |L(M_i^Q, M_q)|)j \\
& + (|L(M_{i+1}^T, M_t)| - |L(M_{i+1}^Q, M_q)|)j \\
& + (|R(M_i^T, M_{i+1}^T, M_t) - R(M_i^Q, M_{i+1}^Q, M_q)|)k \\
& + (|\angle(M_i^T, M_{i+1}^T, M_t) - \angle(M_i^Q, M_{i+1}^Q, M_q)|)l \\
& + (|\theta_{M_i^T} - \theta_{M_t}| - |\theta_{M_i^Q} - \theta_{M_q}|)m \\
& + (|\theta_{M_{i+1}^T} - \theta_{M_t}| - |\theta_{M_{i+1}^Q} - \theta_{M_q}|)m\big)
\end{aligned}
\qquad (8)
$$

where $L(R_1m_2, R_2m_2)$ and $L(R_1m_2', R_2m_2')$ are distances from m_2 and m_2' to two reference points respectively. $\angle R_1m_2R_2$ and $\angle R_1m_2'R_2$ are inclination angles between (m_2, m_2') and two reference points. The $LengthRatio$ $R(M_i, M_j, M_k)$ is defined as the ratio of the Euclidean distance between points M_i, M_k and M_j, M_k, as shown in Formula (9):

$$R(M_i, M_j, M_k) = \frac{|L(M_i, M_k)|}{|L(M_j, M_k)|} \tag{9}$$

Moreover, element (M_i^T, M_i^Q) in TMS is arranged in a descendent order according to S_{MC}, N is the capacity of TMS, θ_x is the direction of minutiae x. The result of function Dif is a polynomial, whose form likes $A_1i + A_2j + A_3k + A_4l + A_5m$. So the similarity of two minutiae can be defined as Formula (10):

$$Sim(M_i, M_j) = sqrt\left(\sum_{i=1}^{5}\left(p_i * A_i^2\right)\right) \tag{10}$$

where p_i are weight parameters.

If the similarity between two minutiae belows a threshold, they are regarded as matched. After comparing all the minutiae in template and query fingerprints, final matching score $FMSCore(F_t, F_q)$ can be obtained as Formula (11):

$$FMSCore(F_t, F_q) = \sqrt{\frac{(N_1 + N_2)^2}{N^T N^Q}} * 100 \tag{11}$$

where F_t and F_q are template fingerprint and query fingerprint, N_1 and N_2 are the number of matched minutiae pairs in the purifying stage and the final matching stage respectively. N^T and N^Q are the number of minutiae in template and query fingerprints respectively.

5   Performance Evaluation

In this paper, method in [14] is used to preprocess the fingerprint image. In order to evaluate the performance, the algorithm is evaluated on databases provided by FVC 2004 [15] which is widely used for public testing. Its DB_1A and DB_2A sets are all contain 800 images(100 samples, 8 instance for each). Our algorithm is implemented using Java programming language and executed on a PC with Celeron-M 1500MHZ CPU and 512 RAM.

5.1   Test for Purifying PMS

The experiment in this section is performed to analyze the purifying ability to PMS. Due to the image quality, the PMS obtained in the original matching stage contains some fake elements. Here we randomly choose 60 fingerprint samples from databases, and every two fingerprint images in one sample are used for testing. As shown in Table 2, the column represents the size of PMS and corresponding TMS. It can be seen that after purifying, the size of corresponding TMS is reduced to dominate values of 2 and 3.

Table 2. Purifying ability

(a) DB1A				(b) DB2A		
SIZE	PMS	TMS		SIZE	PMS	TMS
1	∅	4%		1	∅	5%
2	4%	29%		2	3%	33%
3	7%	40%		3	5%	42%
4	15%	27%		4	12%	20%
5	35%	∅		5	38%	∅
6	30%	∅		6	34%	∅
7	8%	∅		7	8%	∅
≥8	1%	∅		≥8	∅	∅

5.2 Distribution of Matching Score

This experiment is used to evaluate the matching score distribution of homo-fingerprints and hetero-fingerprints. Fig.5.2 illustrates that matching score are distributed mainly in two regions. The horizontal coordinate is the matching score between two fingerprints, while the vertical coordinate denotes distribution of corresponding matching score. The values for hetero-fingerprints and homo-fingerprints are around 17 and 55, which means that with the proposed multi-reference points method, more true matched minutiae pairs can be enclosed. Therefore a higher matching score is gained and the distinguishing ability is upgraded.

5.3 Test for ROC Curve

In order to estimate the capability of the proposed method, we implement methods in [11] and [16] and comparing them with our proposed method. ROC curve, which is used to represent the same responses under different criterions, is usually used to measure the performance of a recognition method. In this section ROC curve is used to test for

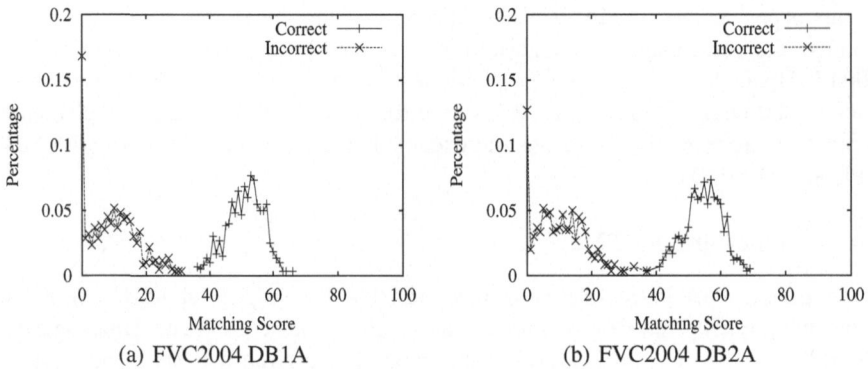

(a) FVC2004 DB1A   (b) FVC2004 DB2A

Fig. 5. Distribution of matching score

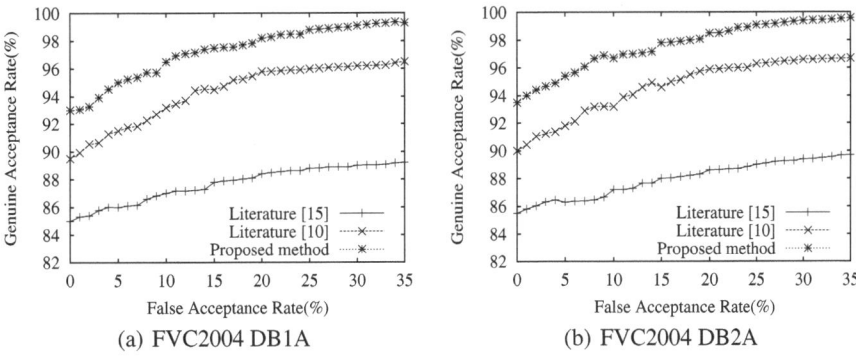

Fig. 6. ROC curve

matching ability of the proposed method. As shown in Fig.5.3, the ROC curves demonstrate that the proposed multi-reference points matching method can greatly enhance the matching accuracy.

6 Conclusion and Future Work

This paper proposes an efficient multi-reference points fingerprint matching method. By comparing the $Minutiae\text{-}Cell$s of the template and query fingerprints, the PMS is obtained in original matching stage. Then TMS is gained by purifying PMS according to the corresponding relationship between minutiae. The final matching stage is carried out by comparing the distance from the remaining minutiae to TMS. Comparing to previous methods, the proposed method overcomes the shortcomings of matching with only one reference pair, whose effectiveness and efficiency are shown in the experiments over the open databases.

Due to the fact that accurate feature detection is very important to fingerprint matching stage, our future work will emphasize on the preprocessing of fingerprint image and fingerprint minutiae extraction.

Acknowledgments. This research was partially supported by the National Natural Science Foundation of China (Grant No. 60773221, 60773219 and 60803026), National 863 Program of China (Grant No. 2007AA01Z192 and 2006AA09Z139), National Basic Research Program of China (Grant No. 2006CB303103), and the Cultivation Fund of the Key Scientific and Technical Innovation ProjectMinistry of Education of China(Grant No. 706016).

References

1. Anil, K.J., Lin, H., Ruud, M.B.: On the individuality of fingerprint. Jounal of IEEE Trans. on PAMI 19(6), 302–314 (1997)
2. Yager, N., Amin, A.: Fingerprint verfication based on minutiae features: a review. Journal of Pattern Anal. Appl. 7(1), 94–113 (2004)

3. Jain, A.K., Prabhakar, S., Hong, L., Pankanti, S.: Filterbank-based fingerprint matching. Journal of IEEE Transactions on Image Processing 9(5), 846–859 (2000)
4. Ross, A., Reisman, J., Jain, A.K.: Fingerprint matching using feature space correlation. In: Tistarelli, M., Bigun, J., Jain, A.K. (eds.) ECCV 2002. LNCS, vol. 2359, pp. 48–57. Springer, Heidelberg (2002)
5. Ratha, N.K., Bolle, R.M., Pandit, V.D., et al.: Robust fingerprint authentication using local structural similarity. In: Proc. of Fifth IEEE Workshop on App. of Computer Vision, pp. 29–34 (2000)
6. Yu, K.D., Na, S., Choi, T.-Y.: A Fingerprint Matching Algorithm Based on Radial Structure and a Structure-Rewarding Scoring Strategy. In: Kanade, T., Jain, A., Ratha, N.K. (eds.) AVBPA 2005. LNCS, vol. 3546, pp. 656–664. Springer, Heidelberg (2005)
7. Mao, K., Wang, G., Yu, G.: A Novel Fingerprint Matching Method by Excluding Elastic Distortion. In: Haritsa, J.R., Kotagiri, R., Pudi, V. (eds.) DASFAA 2008. LNCS, vol. 4947, pp. 348–363. Springer, Heidelberg (2008)
8. Wang, C., Gavrilova, M., Luo, Y., et al.: An efficient algorithm for fingerprint matching. In: Proc. of ICPR 2006, pp. 1034–1037 (2000)
9. Luo, X., Tian, J., Wu, Y.: A minutiae matching algorithm in fingerprint verification. In: Proc. of ICPR 2000, pp. 833–836 (2000)
10. Jiang, X., Yau, W.: Fingerprint Minutiae Matching Based on the Local and Global Structures. In: Proc. of ICPR 2000, pp. 6038–6041 (2000)
11. Wang, C., Gavrilova, M.L.: A Novel Topology-Based Matching Algorithm for Fingerprint Recognition in the Presence of Elastic Distortions. In: Gervasi, O., Gavrilova, M.L., Kumar, V., Laganá, A., Lee, H.P., Mun, Y., Taniar, D., Tan, C.J.K. (eds.) ICCSA 2005. LNCS, vol. 3480, pp. 748–757. Springer, Heidelberg (2005)
12. Lee, D., Choi, K., KIm, J.: A robust fingerprint matching algorithm using local alignment. In: Proc. of ICPR 2002, vol. 3, pp. 803–806 (2002)
13. Jain, A., Hong, L., Bolle, R.: On-Line Fingerprint Verification. Journal. of IEEE Trans. on PAMI 19(4), 302–314 (1997)
14. Hong, L., Wan, Y., Jain, A.: Fingerprint image enhancement: Algorithm and performance evaluation. Journal of IEEE Trans. on PAMI 20(8), 777–789 (1998)
15. Maio, D., Maltoni, D., Cappelli, R., et al.: FVC2004: Third fingerprint verification competition. In: Zhang, D., Jain, A.K. (eds.) ICBA 2004. LNCS, vol. 3072, pp. 1–7. Springer, Heidelberg (2004)
16. Jain, A., Hong, L., Pankanti, S., et al.: An identity-authentication system using fingerprints. Proc. of the IEEE 85(9), 1365–1388 (1997)

HVPN: The Combination of Horizontal and Vertical Pose Normalization for Face Recognition

Hui-Zhen Gu[1], Yung-Wei Kao[1], Suh-Yin Lee[1], and Shyan-Ming Yuan[1,2]

[1] Department of Computer Science and Engineering
National Chiao Tung University, 1001 Ta Hsueh Rd., Hsinchu 300, Taiwan
[2] Department of Computer Science and Engineering
Asia University, Lioufeng Rd., Wufeng , Taichung County, Taiwan
{hcku,ywkao}@cs.nctu.edu.tw, sylee@csie.nctu.edu.tw,
smyuan@cis.nctu.edu.tw

Abstract. Face recognition has received much attention with numerous applications in various fields. Although many face recognition algorithms have been proposed, usually they are not highly accurate enough when the poses of faces vary considerably. In order to solve this problem, some researches have proposed pose normalization algorithm to eliminate the negative effect cause by poses. However, only horizontal normalization has been considered in these researches. In this paper, the HVPN (Horizontal and Vertical Pose Normalization) system is proposed to accommodate the pose problem effectively. A pose invariant reference model is re-rendered after the horizontal and vertical pose normalization sequentially. The proposed face recognition system is evaluated based on the face database constructed by our self. The experimental results demonstrate that pose normalization can improve the recognition performance using conventional principal component analysis (PCA) and linear discriminant analysis (LDA) approaches under varying pose. Moreover, we show that the combination of horizontal and vertical pose normalization can be evaluated with higher performance than mere the horizontal pose normalization.

Keywords: pose normalization, face recognition.

1 Introduction

Face recognition has recently received much attention with numerous applications in various fields such as commercial and surveillance systems [1]. Although there have been a large number of approaches designed for face recognition including appearance-based feature methods [2], it is still very challenging to get accurate recognition under varying pose and illumination [1]. Hence, the pose and illumination problems are two significant issues for face recognition.

For pose problem, we further divide it into two sub-problems: feature-complete pose problem and non-feature-complete pose problem. In feature-complete pose problem, all the human face features (such as eyes, mouth, nose, etc.) are presented in the training/testing images. On the other hand, the non-feature-complete problem contains

B. Huet et al. (Eds.): MMM 2009, LNCS 5371, pp. 367–378, 2009.

training/testing images with incomplete human face features. For instance, if the face is rotated too much, the mouth may not be shown in the captured image. In this case, it is too difficult to be recognized, even by human. Hence, in this paper, we focus on proposing a method to eliminate the effect of feature-complete pose problem of face recognition.

Fig. 1. shows an example of varying pose of a face image. The performance of face recognition system drops significantly when pose variations present. Many researches are presented for the pose problem, such as view-based eigenspace [3], active appearance model (AAM) [4], and elastic graph matching (EGM) [5]. A view-based eigenspace method defines numerous face classes, called the characteristic views for each person. The person with the closest characteristic view is the recognized identification. AAM utilizes a statistical model to capture the appearance of a face. This model can be used to synthesize faces from unseen viewpoints. However, these two approaches acquire multiple training images under varying pose conditions to handle various poses of testing images. In reality, it may not so easy to prepare the face images with all the poses for each training identification in many applications. EGM proposes a facial graph structure based on fiducial points and uses a cost function to compute the distortion between the test face and the trained reference faces. Then EGM tries to compensate the distortion caused by different poses. However, the EGM acquire settling the corresponding relation between test face and its reference. The EGM practically find the optimal test graph that minimizes the cost function. Usually, these corresponding relations need to be manually extracted.

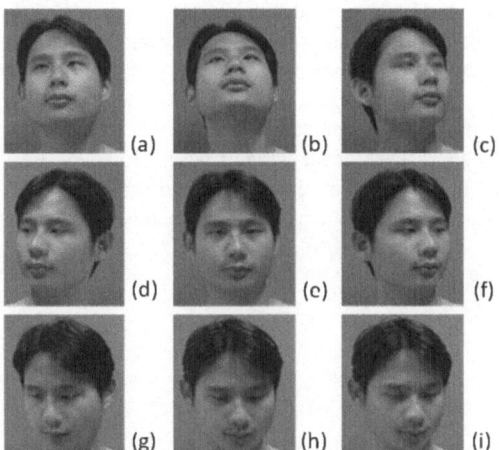

Fig. 1. A pose variation example

In order to solve these problems, [6] proposed a two-step automatic morphing algorithm under few training images. This algorithm generates pose-normalized faces for both training and testing images automatically based on single training images. The pose normalization is conducted by mirroring, morphing technique [7], and the proposed automatic corresponding-relation extraction algorithm. However, this algorithm only normalizes face images horizontally. Vertical pose normalization is needed for generating a more frontal face image. For example, in Fig. 1., the horizontal normalization result of pose (a) and pose (c) is approximated to pose (b), which is not as frontal as pose (e). Also, the normalization result of pose (g) and pose (i), approximated to pose (h), is not frontal enough compared with pose (e). However, vertical pose normalization can not be conducted followed by the same process.

In this paper, we propose the HVPN (Horizontal and Vertical Pose Normalization) system to combine both horizontal and vertical normalization. HVPN extends the concept of horizontal pose normalization and propose a pose detection algorithm based on a face model to further normalizes the face images vertically. Since the structure of human face is symmetric horizontally, not vertically, we can not acquire two different poses from single pose simply by mirroring the image as in horizontal pose normalization. Hence, we assume that there are two cameras taking two testing images simultaneously as a pair, with two different viewpoints: top and bottom. After the horizontal and vertical pose normalization, we calculate an approximated fontal face for recognition. Finally, we show that the combination of horizontal and vertical pose normalization can be evaluated with higher performance than mere the horizontal pose normalization.

This paper is organized as follows: section 2 describes the related backgrounds of this paper. Section 3 presents the combination of horizontal and vertical pose normalization. Section 4 illustrates the evaluation of HVPN and the comparison with its subsystems. Finally, the conclusion is drawn.

2 Backgrounds

In this chapter, we introduce the backgrounds of morphing technique [7], horizontal pose normalization algorithm [6], principal component analysis (PCA) [8], and linear discriminant analysis (LDA) [9] respectively as followings.

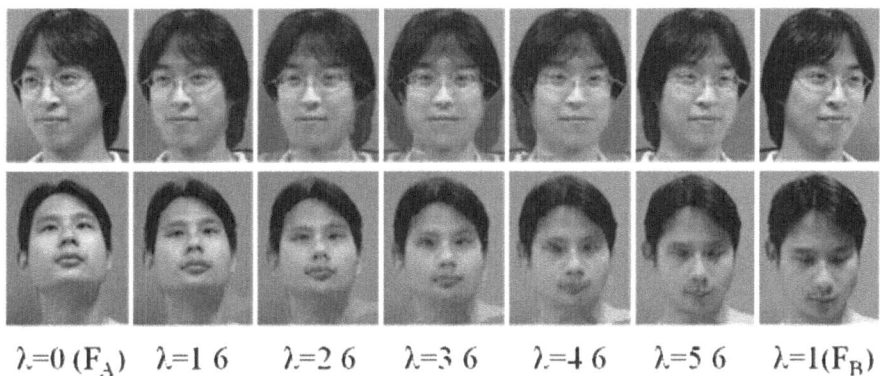

$\lambda=0\,(F_A)$ $\lambda=1\,6$ $\lambda=2\,6$ $\lambda=3\,6$ $\lambda=4\,6$ $\lambda=5\,6$ $\lambda=1(F_B)$

Fig. 2. A series of morphing results with different parameter λ

2.1 Morphing

Morphing [7] is the process of continuously transforming a source image F_A into at target image F_B in terms of different interpolation parameter λ, as illustrated in Fig. 2. As the morphing proceeds, it changes one digital image into another by cross-dissolve. Cross-dissolve is a weighted combination of two images controlled by λ as:

$$F = \lambda \times F_A + (1-\lambda) \times F_B \qquad (1)$$

In order to cross-dissolve the corresponding positions accurately, we need to acquire corresponding feature lines. Each corresponding line is used to interpolate the new position by Beier-Neely's Field Morphing Technique.

2.2 Horizontal Pose Normalization Algorithm

The horizontal pose normalization algorithm [6] utilizes morphing algorithm to accommodate the pose problem and propose an automatic corresponding algorithm to enhance the efficiency of the pose normalization process. There are three phases of the algorithm: global feature matching, local feature matching and morphing operation.

Global feature matching finds out the corresponding contour and facial features between two faces F_A and the mirror image of F_A: F_B. In the beginning, images E_A and E_B are detected by Canny filter [10] from F_A and F_B, and all the connected components are extracted from E_A and E_B as as $\boldsymbol{Com_A} = \{com_{A,1}, com_{A,2},..., com_{A,m}\}$, and $\boldsymbol{Com_B} = \{com_{B,1}, com_{B,2},...,com_{B,n}\}$. By defining $S_{A,X}{}^{-1}(com_{A,i})=k$, which implies the ith component of E_A is located in the kth element after sorting, the optimal correspondence $\boldsymbol{Corr} = \{corr_1, corr_2,..., corr_n\}$ (where $corr_k = \{(com_{A,i}, com_{B,j}) \mid com_{A,i} \in \boldsymbol{Com_A}, com_{B,j} \in \boldsymbol{Com_B}\}$) can be defined as:

$$\{corr_k\}_{k=1}^{k=n} = \underset{(com_{A,i},\, com_{B,j})}{\arg\min} \; ((S_{A,X}^{-1}(com_{A,i}) - S_{B,X}^{-1}(com_{B,j}))^2 +$$

$$(S_{A,Y}^{-1}(com_{A,i}) - S_{B,Y}^{-1}(com_{B,j}))^2) \qquad (2)$$

In local feature matching, the control points $CP_A=\{cp_{A,1}, ..., cp_{A,m}\}$ and $CP_B=\{cp_{B,1}, ..., cp_{B,n}\}$ for E_A and E_B are first extracted by the corner response (CR) function. After that, the vector difference method is defined to determine the corresponding relationship between $cp_{A,i}$ and $cp_{B,j}$. $cp_{Ai}=\{cp^1_{A,i}, ..., cp^s_{A,i}\}$, $cp_{Bj}=\{cp^1_{B,j}, ..., cp^r_{B,j}\}$. If $(com_{A,i}, com_{B,i}) \in corr_k$, the standard point of $com_{A,i}$, $cp^s_{A,i}$, and the standard point of $com_{B,j}$, $cp^r_{B,j}$, are selected as the standard points pair of the $corr_k$. The vector length difference $VD(cp^s_{A,i}, cp^r_{B,j})$ is defined as:

$$VD(cp^s_{A,i}, cp^r_{B,j}) = \left\| cp^s_{A,i} - cp^1_{A,i} \right\| + \left\| cp^r_{B,j} - cp^1_{B,j} \right\| \qquad (3)$$

Finally, the corresponding control points are extracted and are defined as $\boldsymbol{CorrCP}=\{corrCP_1,..., corrCP_n\}$, where $corrCP_k = \{(cp^s_{A,i}, cp^r_{B,j}) \mid cp^s_{A,i} \in com_{A,i}, cp^r_{B,j} \in com_{B,j}, VD(cp^s_{A,i}, cp^r_{B,j}) < \delta \}$.

In the last phase: morphing operation, the pose normalization module synthesizes two different perspective view images. For F_A and the mirror image of F_A: F_B, the parameter $\lambda = 0.5$ is selected for interpolation in Eq. (1). The new synthesized image by automatic morphing algorithm will be an approximated horizontal frontal face with pose normalization.

3   Combination of Horizontal and Vertical Pose Normalization

The system overview of HVPN is shown in Fig. 3. Generally, in the surveillance system, the camera is deployed higher than the subject. In this case, the captured face images are almost non-frontal, except that the user looks up toward the camera. In order to calculate the approximated frontal face image, only one image with viewpoint from top is not enough. The other image with viewpoint from bottom is also needed. In horizontal pose normalization, the other viewpoint from left/right can be easily calculated by mirroring the image based on the horizontal symmetric characteristic of human face. However, the mirroring image of image with viewpoint from top doesn't result in the image with viewpoint from bottom, since human face has no vertical symmetric characteristic. Hence, in HVPN, we assume that there are two cameras taking pictures simultaneously as a pair with different viewpoints: top and bottom.

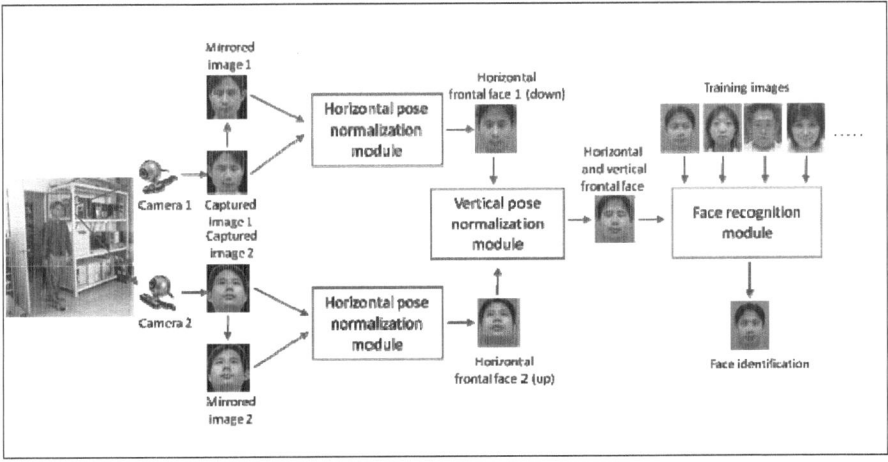

Fig. 3. System overview of HVPN

After the face images are captured by the two cameras, they are used to generate the mirrored image, and horizontally normalized by horizontal pose normalization module with their mirrored images respectively. The two horizontal pose normalization results are further sent to the vertical pose normalization to generate horizontal and vertical frontal face, which is approximated to the real frontal face. Finally, the horizontal and vertical frontal face will be treated as testing image of face recognition module for face identification.

The algorithm for horizontal pose normalization is introduced in section 2.2. Similar to horizontal pose normalization, the vertical pose normalization follows four steps: global feature matching, local feature matching, pose estimation, and morphing operation. However, the parameter λ in Eq. (1) should be caculated by pose estimation, not the fixed value 0.5 in the horizontal pose normalization. Moreover, Based on the original horizontal pose normalization algorithm, we design a voting mechanism for better vector difference results. The voting mechanism can be adopted for both horizontal and vertical pose normalization modules.

3.1 Pose Estimation

In the horizontal pose normalization, the parameter λ in Eq. (1) for morphing operation can be easily set as 0.5. However, the parameter λ will not be 0.5 all the time. For example, in Figure. 1, the value of λ for pair (a), (b), and (c) will be close to 0.5, 0, and 1 respectively. The situation of pair (b) occurs when the person faces to the upper camera, or his hight is close to the height of upper camera. Similarly, the situation of pair (c) occurs when the person faces to the lower camera, or his height is close to the height of lower camera. In order to calculate the accurate λ for generating the most frontal face image, we develop the pose estimation mechanism.

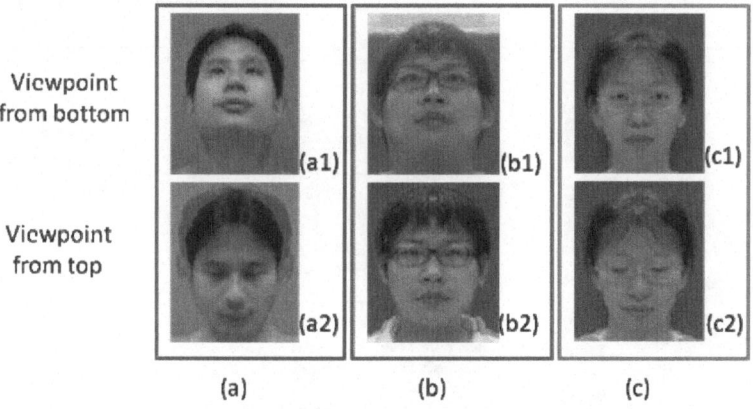

Fig. 4. Examples of captured images

The vertical pose normalization requires two face images, which are the results processed by the horizontal pose normalization module. Before conducting the morphing operation, two central points of the two input images will be extracted first by pose estimation. We design two feature models for central point extraction: the positive feature model, and the negative feature model, as shown in Fig. 5.

The positive model $P = \{(p_{x1}, p_{y1}), (p_{x2}, p_{y2}), ..., (p_{xp}, p_{yp})\}$ defines the region where we expect the color (gray level) is dark. On the contrary, the negative model $N = \{(n_{x1}, n_{y1}), (n_{x2}, n_{y2}), ..., (n_{xq}, n_{yq})\}$ defines the region where we expect the color is light. The positive feature model and negative feature model will be placed on the images together. Since the results of horizontal pose normalization is normalized to the central line, we only have to move the models up and down to find the central point. Fig. 6. illustrates the process of model adaptation. In Fig. 6. models in process (c) are located most closely to the actual face features.

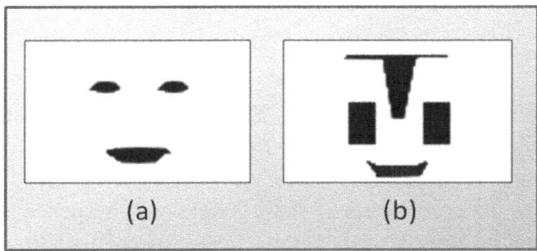

Fig. 5. Feature models. (a) positive feature model (b) negative feature model.

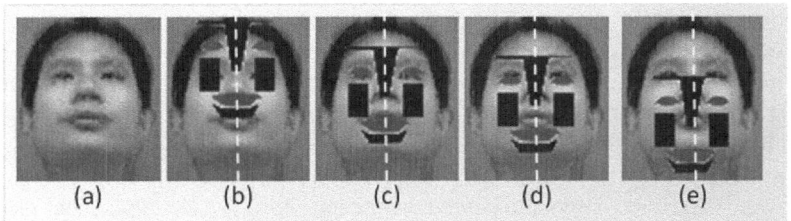

Fig. 6. Process of model adaptation

During the model adaptation, the score is calculated by the models in each position. The models located most closely to the actual face features will result in the smallest score. The smallest score selection function is defined as:

$$MinScore = \min_{1 \le j \le h} \sum_{i=1}^{p} Color\ (\ p_{xi}, p_{yi}\ ) - \sum_{i=1}^{q} Color\ (\ n_{xi}, n_{yi}\ ) \tag{7}$$

The position offset of models, j, varies from 1 to h, where $h = image\ height - model\ height$. Moreover, the function $Color(x,y)$ represents the gray level value of pixel located at (x,y). After the $MinScore$ is calculated, the offset j is determined. Hence, the central point position, $CentralPos$, of face image will be:

$$CentralPos = (\ \frac{Image\ Width}{2}, j + \frac{Model\ Height}{2}\ ) \tag{8}$$

The two input images of the vertical pose normalization, up and down, will be processed by the model adaptation, and the two $CentralPoses$, $CentralPos_1$ and $CentralPos_2$, will be extracted respectively. Moreover, the expected central point, ECP, will be trained by averaging the central points of each subject's frontal face images. Finally, the parameter λ can be calculated in E.q. (9), where function $Y(P)$ represents the y-axis value of point P.

$$\lambda = \frac{Y(ECP) - Y(CentralPos_1)}{Y(CentralPos_2) - Y(CentralPos_1)} \tag{9}$$

3.2 Voting Mechanism

In the vector length difference method as Eq. (3), the standard points $cp^l_{A,i}$ and $cp^l_{B,j}$ are required for judging the correctness of each $cp^s_{A,i}$ and $cp^r_{B,j}$ pairs. The judging mechanism requires judges for correctness decisions of corresponding control points. In this mechanism, the correctness of these judges will influence the quality of their decisions significantly. Hence, we develop a voting mechanism to improve the quality of these judges.

Heuristically speaking, the smaller corresponding components are, the higher accuracy of their left-most points correspondence. In general, the large component (e.g. the component of face contour) may break into several sub-components. The larger corresponding components are, the larger displacement of the two left-most points may occur. Hence, we select the first k minimum corresponding components $mCorr=\{mcorr_1, mcorr_2, ... mcorr_k\}$ (where $mCorr \subset Corr$) and the left-most point of each component to be the *top-level-judges* $TLJ=\{(j_{A,1}, j_{B,1}), (j_{A,2}, j_{B,2}), ..., (j_{A,k}, j_{B,k})\}$, where $\{ TLJ_i = (j_{A,i}, j_{B,i}) \mid (com_{A,m}, com_{B,n}) \in mcorr_i, cp^l_{A,m} = j_{A,i}, cp^l_{B,n} = j_{B,i} \}$. In other words, each $mcorr_i$ contains two components, $com_{A,m}$ and $com_{B,n}$, and their left-most control points, $cp^l_{A,m}$ and $cp^l_{A,n}$, form the *top-level-judge* $(j_{A,i}, j_{B,i})$.

After defining the top-level-judges, their opinions are expressed by the vector length difference $OP=\{op_1, op_2, ..., op_k\}$, and $op_i= TVD_i (cp^l_{A,m}, cp^l_{B,n})$ is defined as:

$$TVD_i(cp^l_{A,m}, cp^l_{B,n}) = \begin{cases} 1, & \text{if } \left\| cp^l_{A,m} - j_{A,i} \right\| + \left\| cp^l_{B,n} - j_{B,j} \right\| \leq \delta \\ 0, & \text{otherwise} \end{cases} \tag{10}$$

In Eq. (7), if the vector difference of $(cp^l_{A,m}, cp^l_{B,n})$ and $(j_{A,i}, j_{B,i})$ is smaller than a pre-defined threshold δ, then the top-level-judge approves the quality of judge $(cp^l_{A,m}, cp^l_{B,n})$, and set op_i as 1. Otherwise, the judge is disapproved, and the op_i is set as 0. For each judge, if over half of the k judges vote for it, that is:

$$\sum_{i=1}^{k} op_i \geq \frac{k}{2} \tag{11}$$

Then this judge is used to be the standard points as in Eq. (3). Otherwise, Eq. (3) will be replaced by:

$$VD(cp^s_{A,i}, cp^r_{B,j}) = \left\| cp^s_{A,i} - j_{A,1} \right\| + \left\| cp^r_{B,j} - j_{B,1} \right\| \tag{12}$$

In this case, the original judge $(cp^l_{A,m}, cp^l_{B,n})$ is not qualified. The standard points will be replaced by $(j_{A,1}, j_{B,1})$, the left-most points of the smallest corresponding components.

4 Experiments

We evaluate the HVPN system based on the face database constructed by our self. The database contains 40 distinct persons with twelve images (six pairs) per person. The images were taken by varying the pose. The examples of database images are listed in Table 1.

Table 1. Examples of database images

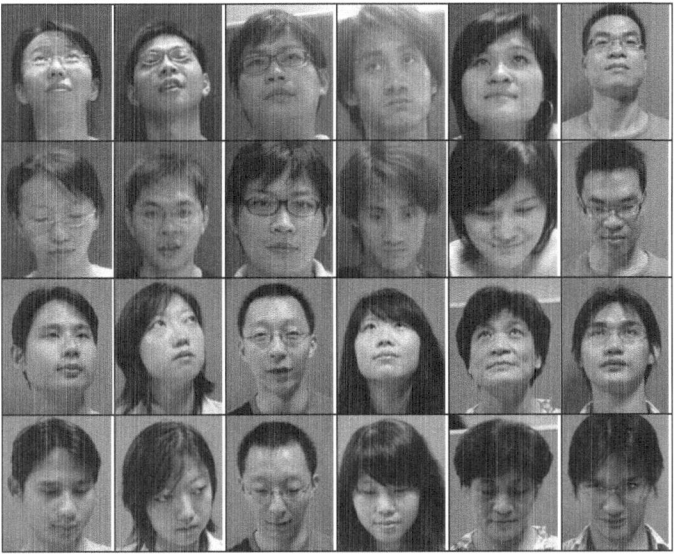

In order to reveal the improvement of *HVPN*, we define three more subsystems for comparison: *ORIGINAL*, *UP*, and *DOWN*. The subsystem *ORIGINAL* processes all the captured images without any kind of pose normalization. The subsystem *UP* selects a subset of images which are captured by the lower camera to be the testing dataset for recognition. Similarly, the subsystem *DOWN* selects a subset of images which are captured by the upper camera. Both *UP* and *DOWN* subsystems perform only the horizontal pose normalization for their testing datasets. In *HVPN*, all the captured images are horizontally and vertically normalized sequentially. Finally, these systems share the same training dataset which contains three frontal face images per person. Moreover, these training images are also pose-normalized horizontally and vertically for further frontal correction.

The PCA and LDA recognition algorithms are implemented for these four systems respectively. The experiment results of PCA are shown in Table 2 and Fig. 7, and the experiment results of LDA are shown in Table 3 and Fig. 8.

In Table 2 and Fig. 7, the recognition rate of *ORIGINAL* is very low based on our database. More training data will make it better, but it is only little improvement. For horizontal pose normalization, *UP* and *DOWN* performs better than *ORIGINAL*. Moreover, in general, the recognition rates of *DOWN* is slightly higher than the rates of *UP*. However, their recognition rates are still not high enough. Finally, for *HVPN*, which adopts both horizontal and vertical pose normalization, significantly outperforms than the previous three systems.

Table 2. Experiment results of PCA (1)

	# of training data		
	1	2	3
ORIGINAL	0.458	0.517	0.52
UP	0.467	0.525	0.533
DOWN	0.517	0.542	0.629
HVPN	0.886	0.945	0.967

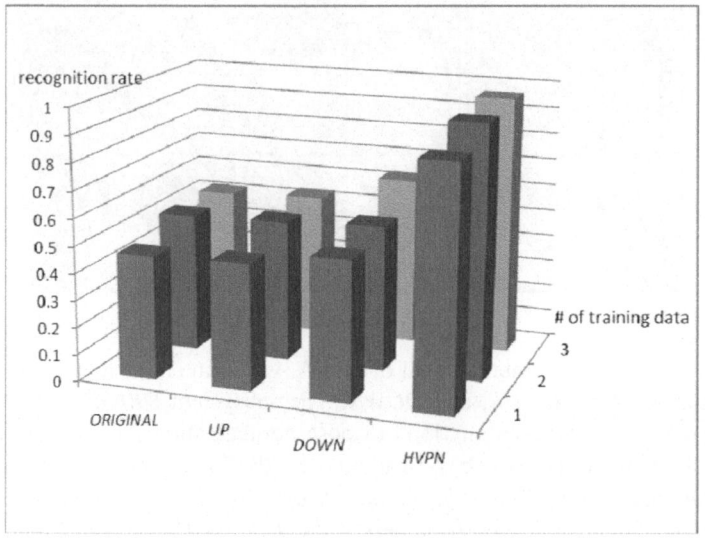

Fig. 7. Experiment results of PCA (2)

In LDA, there is a difficulty confronted that S_W may be singular. In order to overcome the complication of a singular S_W, the method Fisherface [12] is proposed to solve this problem. The relative recognition rates of LDA are basically the same as the rates of PCA, as shown in Table 3 and Fig. 8. In addition, in general, LDA has slightly better improvement than PCA. This experiment shows that the concept of horizontal and vertical pose normalization can be applied to different kind of face recognition algorithms.

Table 3. Experiment results of LDA (1)

	# of training data		
	1	2	3
ORIGINAL	0.458	0.533	0.542
UP	0.467	0.575	0.558
DOWN	0.517	0.667	0.713
HVPN	0.886	0.958	0.975

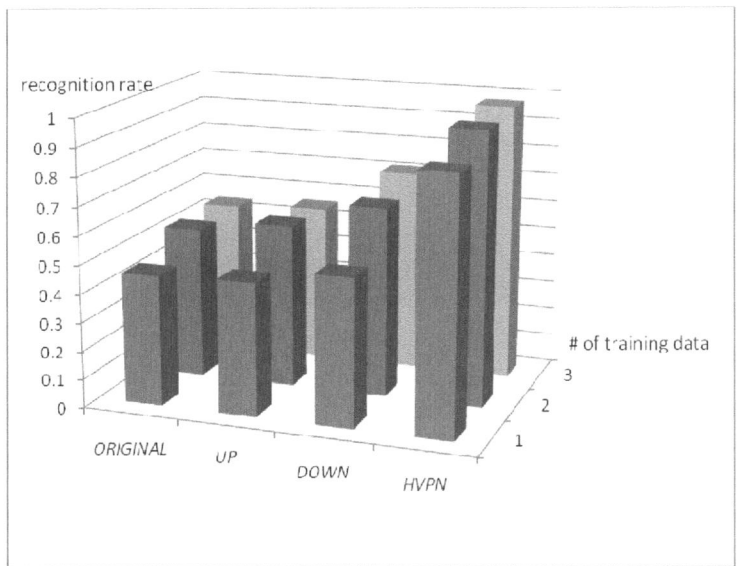

Fig. 8. Experiment results of LAD (2)

5   Conclusion

In conclusion, we propose the HVPN (Horizontal and Vertical Pose Normalization) system to solve the feature-complete pose problem of face recognition. In our previous work, the horizontal pose normalization method has been proposed. In HVPN, the vertical issue is included to generate a more approximated frontal face for the more accurate recognition, especially when there exists considerable face-up or face-down poses within the captured images. Such technique can be applied to the applications of surveillance, which usually deploys the cameras above the subjects. Beyond the original horizontal pose normalization algorithm, we further improve it by the vertical pose normalization concept, pose estimation, and voting mechanism. HVPN is evaluated based on the face database constructed by our self. The experimental results demonstrate that pose normalization can improve the recognition performance using

PCA and LDA approaches under varying pose. Moreover, we show that the combination of horizontal and vertical pose normalization can be evaluated with higher performance than mere the horizontal pose normalization.

References

1. Zhao, W., Chellappa, R.A., Phillips, P.J., Rosenfeld: Face recognition: a literature survey. ACM Computing Surveys, 399–458 (2003)
2. Turk, M.A., Pentland, A.: Face recognition using eigenfaces. In: Proc. IEEE Conf. CVPR, pp. 586–591 (1991)
3. Pentland, A., Moghaddam, B., Starner, T.: View-based and modular eigenspaces for face recognition. In: Proc. Of IEEE Conf. CVPR, pp. 84–91 (1994)
4. Cootes, T., Walker, K., Taylor, C.: View-based active appearance models. In: Proc. Of Intl. Conf. on FG, pp. 227–238 (2000)
5. Wiskott, L., Fellous, J.M., Kruger, N., Vonder Malsburg, C.: Face recognition by elastic bunch graph matching. IEEE Trans. Pattern Analysis and Machine Intelligence 19(7), 775–779 (1997)
6. Gu, H.-Z., Lee, S.-Y.: Automatic Morphing for Face Recognition. The Tenth World Conference on Integrated Design & Process Technology, IDPT (2007)
7. Beier, T., Neely, S.: Feature-based image metamorphosis. SIGGRAPH 26, 35–42 (1992)
8. Belhumeur, P.N., Hespanha, J.P., Kriegman, D.J.: Eigenfaces vs. Fisherfaces: Recognition using class specific linear projection. IEEE Trans. Pattern Analysis and Machine Intelligence 19(7), 711–720 (1997)
9. Martinez, A.M., Kak, A.C.: PCA versus LDA. IEEE Trans. Pattern Analysis and Machine Intelligence 23(2), 228–233 (2001)
10. Canny, J.F.: A computational approach to edge detection. IEEE Trans. Pattern Analysis and Machine Intelligence 8(6), 679–698 (1986)
11. Chien, J.-T., Wu, C.-C.: Discriminant waveletfaces and nearest feature classifiers for face recognition. IEEE Trans. Circuits System Video Technology 14(1), 42–49 (2004)
12. Belhumeur, P.N., Hespanha, J.P., Kriegman, D.J.: Eigenfaces vs. Fisherfaces: Recognition using class specific linear projection. IEEE Trans. Pattern Analysis and Machine Intelligence 19(7), 711–720 (1997)

3D Multimedia Data Search System Based on Stochastic ARG Matching Method

Naoto Nakamura, Shigeru Takano, and Yoshihiro Okada

Graduate School of Information Science and Electrical Engineering, Kyushu University
744, Motooka, Nishi-ku, Fukuoka-shi, Fukuoka, 819-0395, Japan
{n-naka,takano,okada}@i.kyushu-u.ac.jp

Abstract. This paper treats a 3D multimedia data retrieval system based on a stochastic Attributed Relational Graph (ARG) matching method. ARG can be used to represent the structural feature of data, so using ARG as feature representation of 3D multimedia data, it is possible to accurately retrieve the user required data similar to his/her query in terms of its component structure. In this paper, the authors propose a 3D multimedia data search system consisting of an image/video-scene search system, a 3D model search system and a motion data search system. Each search system works commonly with a stochastic ARG matching engine. Experimental results show that the proposed system can effectively retrieve 3D multimedia data similar to the user's query in terms of component structure of the data. Especially, its 3D model search system and motion search system have better experimental results than that of other search systems.

Keywords: Stochastic ARG matching, Video scene search, 3D model search, Motion search.

1 Introduction

Recently, most PC users can enjoy 3D multimedia contents without difficulty because of high performance of PC. Many video contents and 3D Computer Graphics (CG) contents have been created and stored for various application fields including movie and game industries, Web services, and so on. The management of 3D multimedia data has become important because when a content creator wants to use some already existing data, he/she must find them in the database of huge number of data. In such a case, we need any 3D multimedia data search system that allows us to efficiently retrieve our required data.

Contents-based multimedia data retrieval has become popular recently because contents of data are very effective and intuitive for us to specify our required data. For contents-based data retrieval, a component structure of the data is important factor. Attributed Relational Graph (ARG) can be used to represent structural feature of data besides its individual component information. ARG consists of vertices, edges and attributes. If feature vectors are assigned to vertices or edges of a general graph, the graph becomes an ARG. Using ARG as feature representation of multimedia data, a user can retrieve his / her required data similar to the entered query data by calculating the similarity between their two ARGs. There are some search systems using

B. Huet et al. (Eds.): MMM 2009, LNCS 5371, pp. 379–389, 2009.

ARG matching methods, but few using stochastic ARG matching method [1]. Stochastic ARG matching method indicates good accuracy of data search.

In this paper, we propose a 3D multimedia data search system based on a stochastic ARG matching method. This system can retrieve images/video-scenes, 3D models and motion data. We establish ARG construction methods for image/video-scene frame, 3D model and motion data, respectively. In this system, it is possible to specify combination of 3D models and motion data as a query when searching 3D scene data for 3D graphics applications. 3D model and motion data are usually stored in a different type of a file, but recently, various kinds of data can be written in one file like a COLLADA file [2]. When a user searches this kind of data, combined query of 3D model and motion data must be entered. To achieve good results, efficient combinations of features used as attributes of ARGs should be selected, so we describe what kind of features are used in each search system. For video scene search, our system can retrieve scenes similar to the query in terms of the component structure. For 3D model search system and motion search system, our method has good experimental results in comparison with other search methods.

The rest of this paper is organized as follows: In Sec. 2, we show related works. Sec. 3 introduces stochastic ARG matching method. In Sec. 4, we explain each component of proposed 3D multimedia data search system, i.e., the video scene search system, the 3D model data search system and the motion data search system. We also show experimental results of searches using each system in Sec. 5. Sec. 6 describes prospective 3D multimedia contents search system using three main search systems combined. Finally, we conclude this paper in Sec. 7.

2 Related Works

There are many methods for multimedia data search. Sivic and Zisserman proposed a video scene search method using local region descriptor to represent objects in a frame [3][4]. A local region descriptor is invariant for the viewpoint. They adapted text retrieval technique for video scene search system using the concept of visual words. Anjulan and Canagarajah proposed different approach using similar method [5]. They extracted local descriptor from all frames, not only keyframes. Consequently, their method obtains robustness for changing of the camera position. Though, in these methods, structural information is not considered.

For 3D model search, Osada et al. used a histogram of distances between any two random points on a 3D model surface as a feature of the model [6]. This method called D2 has good evaluation results in their paper. Our 3D model search system indicates better evaluation results than those of D2 method in our experiments. ARG matching is strongly related to the topology information of 3D models. Hiraga, et al. proposed topology matching technique using Multi-resolutional Reeb Graphs (MRGs) [7]. Kaku, et al. proposed a similarity measure between 3D models using their OBBTrees [8]. MTGs and OBBTrees have a graph structure, but these are not enough to represent a structural feature of content. A node of ARG can be attached a feature vector, so using ARG, the user can represent structural features for content retrieval, intuitively.

There are not many researches on motion data search systems, we can say that it is not enough, yet. Müller et al. proposed an efficient motion search method [9]. They use a geometric feature which represents geometric relations between specified points of kinematic chain. They also separate motion data into several segments using the geometric feature. Lin uses a geometric feature which is modification of feature proposed in [9], and she also uses the concept of motion curve matching to reduce the computational cost [10].

Using ARG as a feature of multimedia data, efficient search system is realized in terms of structural similarity of components. Park et al. construct ARGs using line features of a face image, and proposed person authentication system using them [11]. Papic et al. express an alphabet by an ARG, and proposed a character recognition system which has robustness for changing camera angle [12]. Qureshi established a new method of ARG construction from an image, and defined similarity [13]. In this method, extracted primitives are considered as vertices of ARG. This method has robustness for changing lightness. Zhang also proposed video scene search system based on stochastic ARG matching method [1] used in our method. Generally, extracting regions with accuracy is very difficult. In our method, all images decomposed into layers to extract regions which have accurate shapes. In this paper, we propose 3D multimedia data search system consisting of image/video-scene, 3D model, and motion data search systems. There has not been such a system so far.

3 Stochastic ARG Matching Method

Our system employs a stochastic ARG matching method [1] to measure the similarity between two 3D multimedia data. In this section, we start with the definition of the ARG.

Definition. An ARG is a triple $G = (V, E, A)$, where V is the vertex set, E is the edge set, and A is the attribute set that contains a unary attribute a_i assigned to each vertex $n_i \in V$ and a binary attribute a_{ij} assigned to each edge $e_{ij} = (n_i, n_j) \in E$.

To define the similarity measure between two graphs G^s and G^t, we introduce some notations. Let H_p denote a binary random variable according to two hypotheses: The hypothesis $H_p = 1$ means that G^t is similar to G^s, and the hypothesis $H_p = 0$ implies that G^t is not similar to G^s. The unary features of G^s and G^t are denoted by Y_i^s, $1 < i < N$, and Y_k^t, $1 < k < M$, respectively, and the binary ones of G^s and G^t are denoted by Y_{ij}^s, $1 < i, j < N$ and Y_{kl}^t, $1 < k, l < M$ respectively. We define two vectors: $Y^s = (Y_1^s, ... Y_N^s, Y_{11}^s, Y_{12}^s, ... Y_{NN}^s)$ and $Y^t = (Y_1^t, ... Y_M^t, Y_{11}^t, Y_{12}^t, ... Y_{MM}^t)$. Let $p(Y^t | Y^s, H_p = h)$ be the probability of transforming G^s into G^t. The similarity measure of G^s and G^t is defined by

$$S(G^s, G^t) = \frac{p(Y^t | Y^s, H_p = 1)}{p(Y^t | Y^s, H_p = 0)}. \tag{1}$$

For details on calculation of (1), refer the paper [1] or [14].

4 Components of 3D Multimedia Data Search System

3D multimedia data include images, movies, 3D models, motion data and so on. In our 3D multimedia data search system, any data is represented as an ARG. So, it is important to determine how to construct an ARG from its data. In this section, we explain the construction of ARGs from an image/video-scene frame, 3D model and motion data, respectively.

4.1 Image/Video-Scene Search System

The construction method of ARG from an image consists of three steps, segmentation step, layerization step and construction step. In this system, we employ a segmentation method based on color information. We use HSV components of each pixel. After the segmentation process, using the layerization method described in [14], we decompose the segmented image into some layers. One layerization example is shown in Fig. 1.

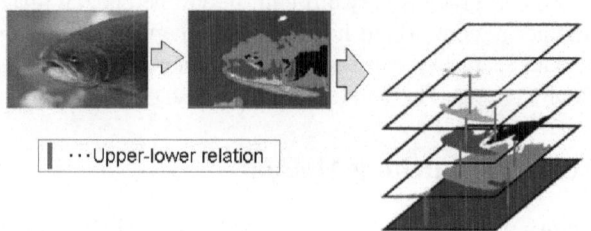

Fig. 1. Layerized regions have upper-lower relationship between them

A layerized image consists of some layers which include some regions and upper-lower relationships. If the user considers the regions as vertices and the upper-lower relationships as edges, he / she can construct a graph from the layerized image, and if feature values of a region are assigned to the corresponding vertex, the graph becomes a kind of ARG.

4.2 3D Model Search System

We construct a graph from each 3D model by considering components of the 3D model (e.g. head, body in a human model) as its vertices and parent-child relationships between two components as its edges. All components of a 3D model have features. Using these features as vertex attributes of the graph of a 3D model, we can obtain ARG of the 3D model. Fig.2 shows one composite 3D model and its ARG.

4.3 Motion Search System

Generally, one motion data consists of skeleton data and time series data which include translation and rotation data of each joint. A skeleton data is a tree structure of joints and bones. So, a skeleton can be considered as a graph, and if the user assigns some feature values to each joint and bone, he / she can construct an ARG from a motion data. Of course, feature values are extracted from time series data.

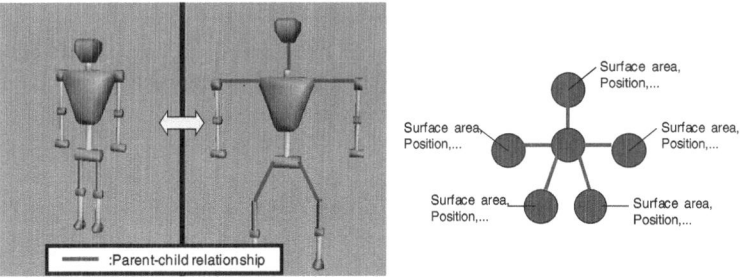

Fig. 2. ARG example of a 3D model

One feature value of a joint we employ is spatial occupancy probability of the joint. This probability is calculated by analyzing the existence ratio of the joint in each of 32 separated spaces for whole motion. Fig. 3 shows explanatory images.

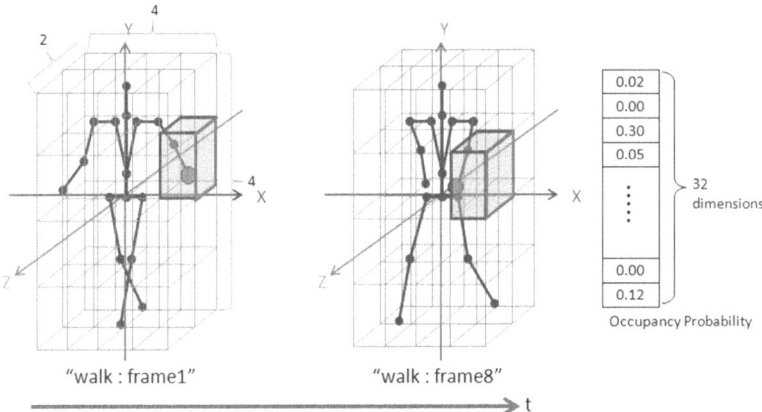

Fig. 3. Spatial occupancy probability

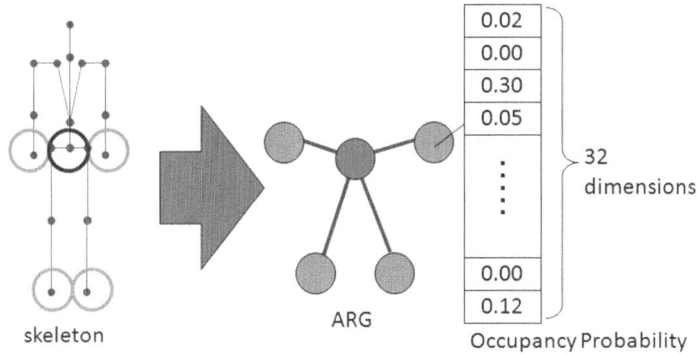

Fig. 4. Every node has 32 dimensional feature vector

To specify semantics of human motion, end-effectors, which are leaf nodes of a tree structure represented as a skeleton, are significant joints, i.e., left and right hand and foot joints except a head. So, we construct a graph using root node and leaf nodes of the skeleton tree and this can reduce the computational cost of similarity calculation. We construct an ARG from a motion data as shown in Fig. 4.

5   Experiments

The Sec. 4 explained main three data search systems. In this section, we show some experimental results of each system.

5.1   Experiments of Video Scene Search System

Using the technique mentioned Sec. 4.1, we have already developed a video scene search system [14]. However, the system [14] needs huge calculation time. To reduce this computational cost, the proposed system in this paper uses scene-change (cut-change) extraction method. For efficient query input, we also added sketch query input interface to the system. The system extracts significant key-frames from a video that mean scene-change (cut-change) frames based on chi-square test [16] and construct ARGs of them as preprocessing, and when the user searches some scenes, he / she draws a query image by a paint tool. The similarities between ARG of the query image and ARGs of the extracted key-frames are calculated using stochastic ARG matching method

In order to achieve good results, it is important to select important feature values for attributes. We did some experiments to find a good combination of feature empirically. We employ H components, area size, circumference length and DoC of a region as unary attribute, and pair of H components as binary attribute.

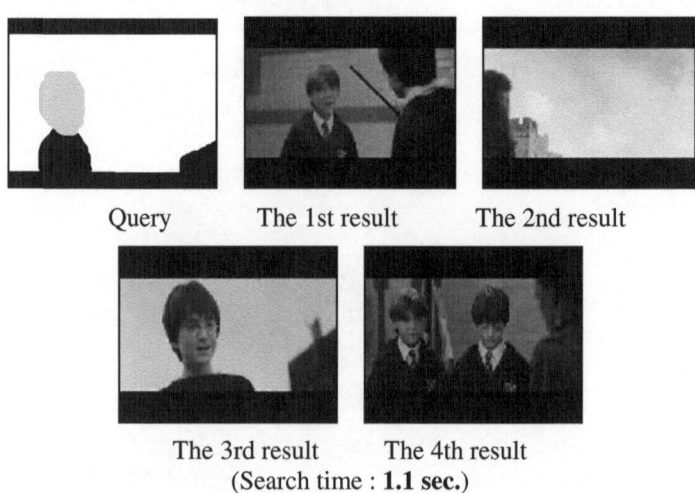

Query   The 1st result   The 2nd result

The 3rd result   The 4th result
(Search time : **1.1 sec.**)

Fig. 5. Example result of video scene search

When the user wants to searches any video scenes, he / she can specify a query scene as a hand sketch image using the painting interface of the system. Fig. 5 shows results of scene search trial. Using this system, we can retrieve scene-frame images which are similar to the query in terms of the content structure of the images. Its search time is not fast but acceptable level for practical use.

5.2 Experiments of 3D Model Search System

For 3D model search, we employ four features as unary attributes, and two features as binary attributes. Unary features include surface area, position, flatness and sphericity. Position means the distance between the center of the 3D model and the center of its component corresponding to the vertex. Flatness F is defined as follows:

$$F = \frac{a+b}{2c},$$

where a and b are the lengths of the first and second longest edges of the bounding box of the component respectively, and c is that of the shortest edge. F is 1 when the shape of a component is like a cube. F becomes bigger when the shape becomes flatter like a board or longer like a pen. Sphericity S is defined as follows:

$$S = 36\pi \frac{V^2}{A^3}, \qquad 0 \le S \le 1,$$

where V and A are the volume and the surface area of the component respectively. S is 1 when the shape of a component is perfect sphere. S is regarded as complexity of a component shape. A simpler shape like a sphere has a greater value and a more complex shape has a smaller value. Binary features are the pairs of flatness of two components which have a parent-child relationship between them.

Using this technique described above we developed a 3D model search system using stochastic ARG matching method [15]. When the user searches some 3D models, he / she specifies a query 3D model.

We performed experiments of 3D model search. In advance, we made a 3D model database that contains 149 models classified into 21 classes. Parent-child relationships of these 3D models are defined manually. We compared our method with D2 method which is a popular search method for 3D models. For evaluation, we used three criteria called "First tier", "Second tier" and "Top match". They are defined as follows.

First tier: This criteria represents the percentage of top $(k-1)$ matches (excluding the query) from the query's class, where k is the number of 3D models of the class.

$$\text{First tier} = \frac{\text{Top}(k-1)\text{matches}}{k-1}$$

Second tier: This criterion is the same type of "First tier", but for the top $2(k-1)$ matches.

$$\text{Second tier} = \frac{\text{Top2}(k-1)\text{matches}}{k-1}$$

Top match: This criterion means the percentage of test in which the top match was from the query's class.

The results are shown in Table 1. As for both "First tier" and "Second tier", the averages of our system's results are better than those of D2. Although its average search time is not better than that of D2, this is not a serious problem because we can use parallel processing techniques to reduce this calculation cost.

Table 1. Results of 3D model search

Method	Our proposed method			D2		
Class (No. of contents)	First tier	Second tier	Top match	First tier	Second tier	Top match
airplane (10)	0.59	0.99	0.20	0.42	0.59	0.70
ball (7)	1.00	1.00	1.00	1.00	1.00	1.00
bed (6)	0.23	0.37	0.17	0.23	0.23	0.50
car (10)	0.80	0.81	0.91	0.84	0.96	1.00
chair (7)	0.48	0.62	0.43	0.45	0.57	0.86
chess (11)	0.78	1.00	0.00	0.42	0.49	1.00
cupboard (6)	0.43	0.63	0.83	0.63	0.87	0.83
helicopter (6)	0.40	0.57	0.17	0.13	0.37	0.50
lamp (7)	0.10	0.12	0.14	0.07	0.10	0.29
light (7)	0.21	0.24	0.00	0.17	0.19	0.29
missile (6)	0.17	0.30	0.17	0.13	0.30	0.00
monitor (5)	0.10	0.27	0.17	0.40	0.40	0.60
PC (6)	0.47	0.80	0.67	0.33	0.47	0.67
robot (8)	0.54	0.73	0.75	0.27	0.39	0.50
shelf (5)	0.35	0.35	0.80	0.10	0.10	0.40
ship (6)	0.13	0.17	0.50	0.33	0.47	0.50
sign (10)	0.70	0.84	0.00	0.60	0.72	0.70
sofa (7)	0.24	0.43	0.29	0.29	0.55	0.86
sword (6)	0.37	0.67	0.33	0.60	0.67	0.83
table (7)	0.33	0.38	0.57	0.21	0.29	0.29
toilet (6)	0.25	0.40	0.60	0.30	0.50	0.60
Average	**0.41**	**0.56**	**0.41**	**0.38**	**0.49**	**0.61**
Search time	1176.2 sec.			30.3 sec.		

5.3 Experiments of Motion Search System

Using the method described Sec. 4.3, we developed a motion search system based on stochastic ARG matching method. For evaluation of the system, we made a motion database which includes 66 motion data, and they are clustered into 7 classes. For the evaluation, we employed three criteria described above, i.e., "First tier", "Second tier" and "Top match". Then we compared performance of our motion search system with that of our previous motion search system [17] whose similarity feature is basically the same as that of our system proposed in this paper. In [17], when calculating similarity of two motions, an error (Euclid distance) is calculated for each of spatial occupancy probabilities of four end-effecter joints and their average is used as dissimilarity between the two motions. On the other hand, the system proposed in this paper calculates similarity using stochastic ARG matching method. Table 2 shows experimental results. As for both "Second tier" and "Top match", the averages of our proposed system's results are better than those of the previous system.

Table 2. Motion search results

Method	Our proposed method			Our previous method		
Class (No. of contents)	First tier	Second tier	Top match	First tier	Second tier	Top match
arise (7)	0.07	0.27	0.13	0.48	0.69	0.57
jump (12)	0.24	0.48	0.25	0.26	0.41	0.50
kick (6)	0.86	1.00	1.00	0.25	0.54	0.50
sit (7)	0.23	0.77	0.50	0.50	0.67	0.50
throw (6)	0.14	0.71	1.00	0.13	0.18	0.13
tumble (10)	0.18	0.27	0.40	0.38	0.48	0.86
walk (18)	0.82	0.94	1.00	0.81	0.93	1.00
average	0.45	0.70	0.68	0.45	0.60	0.64
Search time	5.7 sec.			2.0 sec.		

6 3D Multimedia Contents Search System

The previous sections explained main three data search systems, i.e., the image/video-scene search system, the 3D model data search system and the motion data search system. Since all of the three systems use stochastic ARG matching method commonly for their similarity calculation, it is easy to combine them and possible to develop a 3D multimedia contents search system. Currently, we have been developing such a system. Our prospective 3D multimedia contents search system works as described below.

As shown in Fig. 6, for searching image/video scene, the user draws a sketch image as the query. Also for searching 3D models and motion data, the user specifies a multimedia content itself as the query. In addition, the user can specify the combination of a 3D model and a motion data as the query. Recently, 3D multimedia contents and their feature attributes have become treated as one file, e.g., a COLLADA file and MPEG7. In such a case, query composition is very effective for 3D multimedia contents search as shown in Fig. 7.

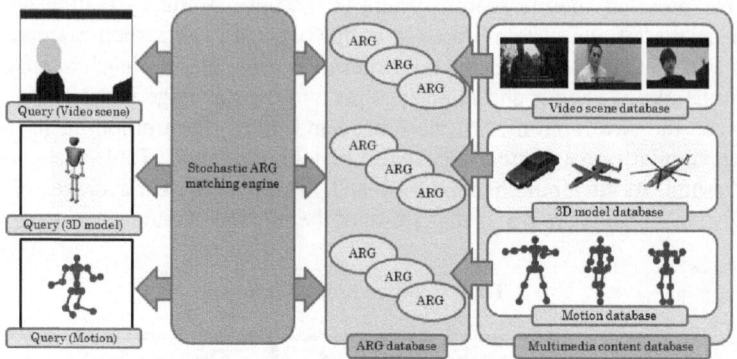

Fig. 6. Overview of 3D multimedia contents search system.

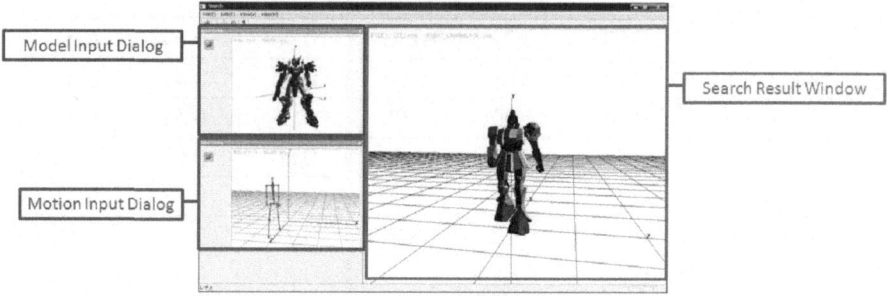

Fig. 7. Snapshot of 3D multimedia contents search from a database consisting of COLLADA files each including one or more kinds of 3D multimedia data

7 Conclusion

In this paper, we evaluated stochastic ARG matching method for image/video-scene frame data search, 3D model data search and motion data search, and proposed 3D multimedia contents search system based on stochastic ARG matching method. We described how to extract feature attributes and how to construct an ARG for each of image/video-scene frame data, 3D model data and motion data, respectively. From the experimental results of each search system for each type of data, it is said that we could retrieve our required 3D multimedia data similar to their queries in terms of their component structures. In particular, we obtained good results in the evaluations of search methods for 3D model and motion data as compared with other search methods.

As future works, we will complete to develop a 3D multimedia contents search system like the prospective system introduced in this paper especially to support various file formats, MPEG7, a COLLADA file. We will also improve our stochastic ARG matching engine to reduce its calculation cost by using parallel processing techniques.

References

1. Zhang, D., Chang, S.: Stochastic Attributed Relational Graph Matching for Image Near-Duplicate. Columbia University ADVENT Technical Report 206-2004-6 Columbia University (2004)
2. KHRONOS Group, http://www.khronos.org/collada/
3. Sivic, J., Zisserman, A.: Video Google: A Text Retrieval Approach to Object Matching in Videos. In: Proceedings of the 9th IEEE ICCV 2003 international conference on computer vision, pp. 1470–1477 (2003)
4. Sivic, J., Zisserman, A.: Efficient Object Retrieval from Videos. In: Proceedings of EUSIPCO 2004 the 12th European Signal Processing Conference, pp. 1737–1740 (2004)
5. Anjulan, A., Canagarajah, N.: Video Scene Retrieval Based on Local Region Features. In: Proceedings of ICIP 2006 International Conference on Image Processings, pp. 3177–3180 (2006)
6. Osada, R., et al.: Matching 3D Models with Shape Distributions. In: Proceedings of International Conference on Shape Modeling and Applications, pp. 154–165 (2001)
7. Hiraga, M., et al.: Topology Matching for Fully Automatic Similarity Estimation of 3D Shapes. In: Proceedings of ACM SIGGRAPH 2001, pp. 203–212 (2001)
8. Kaku, K., Okada, Y., Niijima, K.: Similarity Measure Based on OBBTree for 3D Model Search. In: Proceedings of CGIV 2004 International Conference on Computer Graphics, Imaging and Visualization, pp. 46–51. IEEE CS Press, Los Alamitos (2004)
9. Müller, M., Röder, T., Clausen, M.: Efficient Content-Based Retrieval of Motion Capture Data. In: Proceedings of ACM SIGGRAPH 2005, pp. 677–685 (2005)
10. Lin, Y.: Efficient Motion Search in Large Motion Capture Databases. In: Bebis, G., Boyle, R., Parvin, B., Koracin, D., Remagnino, P., Nefian, A., Meenakshisundaram, G., Pascucci, V., Zara, J., Molineros, J., Theisel, H., Malzbender, T. (eds.) ISVC 2006. LNCS, vol. 4291, pp. 151–160. Springer, Heidelberg (2006)
11. Park, B., et al.: Face Recognition Using Face-ARG Matching. IEEE Transactions on Pattern Analysis and Machine Intelligence 27(12), 1982–1988 (2005)
12. Papic, V., Djurovic, Z., Kovacevic, B.: OCR Based on ARG Matching Algorithm. In: Proceedings of The Sixth World Congress on Intelligent Control and Automation 2006, vol. 2, pp. 10445–10449 (2006)
13. Qureshi, R., Ramel, J., Cardot, H.: Graphic Symbol Recognition Using Flexible Matching of Attributed Relational Graphs. In: Proceedings of 6th IASTED International Conference on Visualization, Imaging, and Image Processing (VIIP), pp. 383–388 (2006)
14. Nakamura, N., Takano, S., Niijima, K.: Video Scene Retrieval Based on The Layerization of Images and The Matching of Layer-Trees. In: Proceedings of IVCNZ 2005 Image and Vision Computing New Zealand 2005, pp. 449–454 (2005)
15. Nakamura, N., Okada, Y., Niijima, K.: 3D Model Search Based on Stochastic ARG Matching. In: Proceedings of IEEE ICME 2006 International Conference on Multimedia and Expo, pp. 197–200. IEEE CS Press, Los Alamitos (2006)
16. Nagasaka, A., Tanaka, Y.: Automatic Video Indexing and Full Video Search for Object Appearances. Visual Database System II, 113–127 (1992)
17. Okada, Y., Etou, H., Niijima, K.: Intuitive Interfaces for Motion Generation and Search. In: Grieser, G., Tanaka, Y. (eds.) Dagstuhl Seminar 2004. LNCS (LNAI), vol. 3359, pp. 49–67. Springer, Heidelberg (2005)

3D Face Recognition Using R-ICP and Geodesic Coupled Approach

Karima Ouji[1], Boulbaba Ben Amor[2], Mohsen Ardabilian[1], Liming Chen[1], and Faouzi Ghorbel[3]

[1] LIRIS, Lyon Research Center for Images and Intelligent Information Systems, Ecole Centrale de Lyon. 36, av. Guy de Collongue, 69134 Ecully, France
[2] LIFL, Computer Science Laboratory of Lille, Telecom Lille1, Cité scientifique - Rue Guglielmo Marconi 59653 Villeneuve d'Ascq Cedex BP 20145
[3] GRIFT, Groupe de Recherche en Images et Formes de Tunisie, Ecole Nationale des Sciences de l'Informatique, Tunisie

Abstract. While most of existing methods use facial intensity images, a newest ones focus on introducing depth information to surmount some of classical face recognition problems such as pose, illumination, and facial expression variations. This abstract summarizes a new face recognition approach invariant to facial expressions based on dimensional surface matching. The core of our recognition/authentication scheme consists of aligning then comparing a probe face surface and gallery facial surfaces. In the off-line phase, we build the 3D face database with neutral expressions. The models inside include both shape and texture channels. In the on-line phase, a partial probe model is captured and compared either to all 3D faces in the gallery for identification scenario or compared to the genuine model for authentication scenario. The first step aligns probe and gallery models based only on static regions of faces within a new variant of the well known Iterative Closest Point called on R-ICP (Region-based Iterative Closest Point) which approximates the rigid transformations between the presented probe face and gallery one. R-ICP result is two matched sets of vertices in the both static and mimic regions of the face surfaces. For the second step, two geodesic maps are computed for the pair of vertices in the matched face regions. The recognition and authentication similarity score is based on the distance between these maps. Our evaluation experiments are done on 3D face dataset of IV2 french project.

Keywords: 3D Face Recognition, ICP, R-ICP, Geodesics Computation, Segmentation, Mimics, Biometric Evaluation.

1 Introduction

Over the past few years, biometrics and particularly face recognition and authentication have been applied widely in several applications such as recognition inside video surveillance systems, and authentication within access control devices. However, as described in the *Face Recognition Vendor Test* report published in [1], as in other reports, most commercial face recognition technologies

B. Huet et al. (Eds.): MMM 2009, LNCS 5371, pp. 390–400, 2009.

suffer from two kinds of problems. The first one concerns inter-class similarity such as twins'classes, and fathers and sons'classes. Here, people have similar appearances which make their discrimination difficult. The second, and the more important complexity, is due to intra-class variations caused by changes in lighting conditions, pose variations (i.e. three-dimensional head orientation), and facial expressions. Lighting conditions change dramatically the 2D face appearance. Consequently approaches only based on intensity images are insufficient to employ. Pose variations present also a considerable handicap for recognition by performing comparisons between frontal face images and changed viewpoint images. In addition, compensation of facial expressions is a difficult task in 2D-based approaches, because it significantly changes the appearance of the face in the texture image.

In this paper we introduce a new face recognition/authentication method based on new face modality: *3D shape of face*. The remainder of the paper is organized as follows: Section (2) reviews the recent progress in 3D face recognition research field. Section (3) describes an overview of the proposed 3D face recognition approach. In Section (4), we focus on developed works for 3D vs. 3D face matching via a region based variant of *ICP* called *R-ICP*. The section (5) describes the geodesic computation technique for facial expression compensation. In section (6), we emphasize the evaluations of the developed method on 3D face database.

2 Recent Progress on 3D Face Recognition

Current state-of-the-art in face recognition is interesting since it contains works which aim at resolving problems regarding this challenge. The majority of these works use intensity facial images for recognition or authentication, called 2D model-based techniques. A second family of recent works, known as 3D model-based, exploits three-dimensional face shape in order to mitigate some of these variations. Where some of them propose to apply subspace-based methods, others perform shape matching algorithm. Figure 1 presents our vision and taxonomy for the face recognition techniques which can be categorized in four classes: 2D vs. 2D, 3D vs. 3D, multimodal 2D+3D, and 2D vs. 2D via 3D.

As described in [2,3], classical linear and non-linear dimensional reduction techniques such as *PCA* and *LDA* are applied to range images from data collection in order to build a projection sub-space. Further, the comparison metric computes distances between the obtained projections. Shape matching-based approaches rather use classical 3D surface alignment algorithms that compute the residual error between the surface of probe and the 3D images from the gallery as already proposed in our works [4,5] and others as [6] and [7].

In [8], authors present a new proposal which considers the facial surface (frontal view) as an isometric surface (i.e. length preserving). Using a global transformation based on geodesics, the obtained forms are invariant to facial expressions. After the transformation, they perform a classical rigid surface matching and *PCA* for sub-space building and face matching. Authors in [9] propose

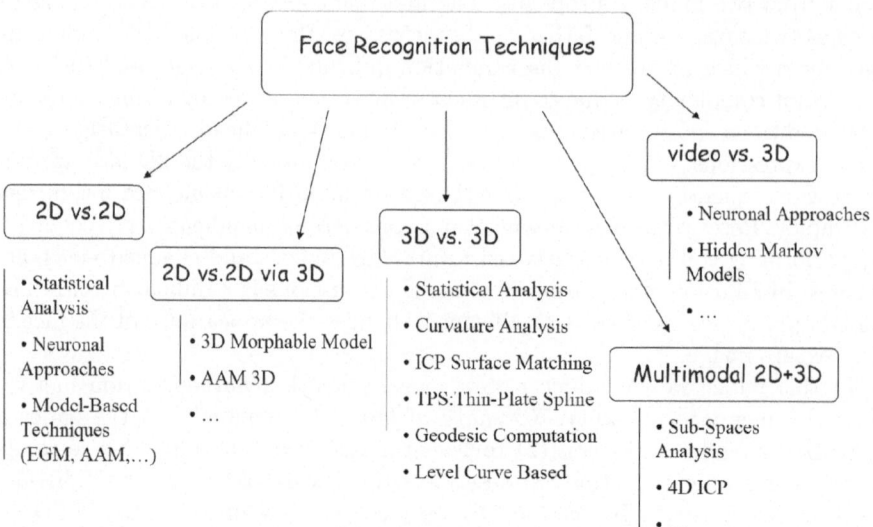

Fig. 1. A taxonomy of face recognition techniques

to approximate facial surface by indexed sets of level curves of a continuous function, such as the depth function, defined on these surfaces. In [10,11], we propose a new similarity metric based on corresponding list provided by ICP surface matching and geodesic maps computed on 3D Gallery and probe faces.

A good reviews and comparison studies of some of these techniques (both 2D and 3D) are given in [12] and [13]. Another interesting study which compares *ICP* and *PCA* 3D-based approaches is presented in [14]. Here, the authors show a baseline performance between these approaches and conclude that *ICP*-based method performs better than a *PCA*-based method. Their challenge is expression changes, particularly "eye lip open/closed" and "mouth open/closed".

In the present paper, we discuss accuracy of a new 3D face recognition method using the *R-ICP*-based algorithm with a particular similarity metric based on geodesic maps computation. A new multi-view and registered 3D face database which includes 3D gallery and probe models is collected in order to perform significant experiments.

3   Overview of the Proposed Approach

Our identification/authentication approach is based on dimensional surfaces of faces. As illustrated by figure 2, we build the face gallery with neutral expressions. The models inside include both shape and texture channels: *the off-line phase*. Second, a probe model is captured and compared to all gallery faces (if identification scenario) or compared to the genuine model (if authentication scenario): *the on-line phase*.

The core of our recognition/authentication scheme consists of aligning then comparing the probe and gallery facial surfaces. The first step, approximates

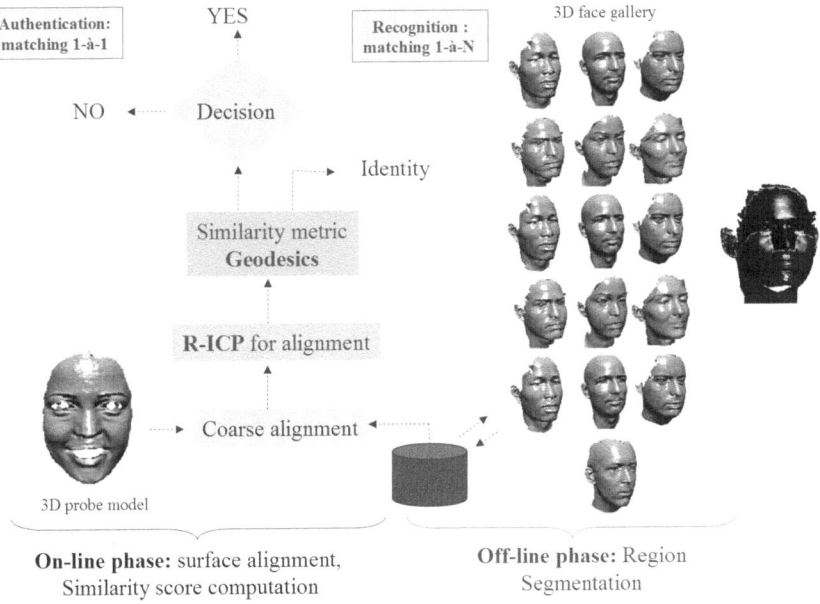

Fig. 2. Overview of the proposed 3D face matching method

the rigid transformations between the presented probe face and gallery one, a coarse alignment step and then a fine alignment step via *R-ICP* (Region Based Iterative Closest Point) are applied. This algorithm is a region based iterative procedure minimizing the *MSE (Mean Square Error)* between points in probe model and the closest points in the gallery model[15,16]. One of the outputs of the algorithm result is two matched sets of points in the both surfaces.

For the second step, two geodesic maps are computed for the pair of vertices in the matched surfaces. The recognition and authentication similarity score is based on the distance between these maps.

4   R-ICP for 3D Face Alignment

One of interesting ways for performing verification/identification is the 3D shape matching process. Many solutions are developed to resolve this task especially for range image registration and 3D object recognition. The basic algorithm is the Iterative Closest Point developed by *Besl et al.*, in [17].

In our approach we consider first a coarse alignment step, which approximates the rigid transformation between models and bring them closer. Then we perform a fine alignment algorithm which computes the minimal distance and converges to a minima starting from the initial solution. The fine alignment is based on a new variant of the Iterative Closet Point algorithm [17].

ICP is an iterative procedure minimizing the *Mean Square Error (MSE)* between points in one view and the closest vertices, respectively, in the other. At

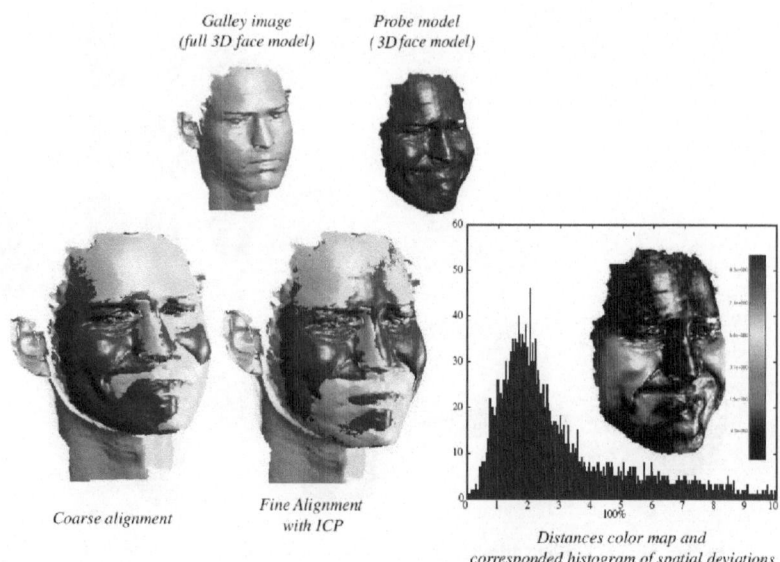

Fig. 3. ICP-based 3D surface alignement

each iteration of the algorithm, the geometric transformation that best aligns the probe model and the 3D model from the gallery is computed. Intuitively, starting from the two sets of vertices $P = \{p_i\}$, as a reference data, and $X = \{y_i\}$, as a test data, the goal is to find the rigid transformation (R, t) which minimizes the distance between these two sets. The target of *ICP* consists in determining for each vertex p_i of the reference set P the nearest vertex in the second set X within the meaning of the Euclidean distance. The rigid transformation, minimizing a least square criterion (1), is calculated and applied to each point of P:

$$E(R, t) = \frac{1}{N} \sum_{i=0}^{N} \|(Rp_i + t) - y_i\|^2 \tag{1}$$

This procedure is alternated and iterated until convergence (i.e. stability of the minimal error). Indeed, total transformation (R, t) is updated in an incremental way as follows: for each iteration k of the algorithm: $R = R_k R$ and $t = t + t_k$. The criterion to be minimized in the iteration k becomes (2):

$$E(R_k, t_k) = \frac{1}{N} \sum_{i=0}^{N} \|(R_k(Rp_i + t) + t_k) - y_i\|^2 \tag{2}$$

The *ICP* algorithm presented above always converges monotonically to a local minimum [17]. However, convergence to a global minimum needs a good initialization. For this reason, coarse alignment procedure is necessary before the fine one (cf. Figure 3).

ICP algorithm extracts only rotation and translation which characterize rigid deformations between probe model and gallery one. However, facial expressions lead to non rigid deformations unable to be modelled just by rotation and translation. Thus, it is necessary to identify and distinguish mimic region which is sensible to expressions variations from static one. In this paper, we propose to align only static regions of probe and gallery surfaces within a new variant of ICP called on R-ICP (Region-based Iterative Closest Point). R-ICP approximates the rigid transformations between the static regions of either probe face and gallery one and use the following convergence criteria:

$$E_{R-ICP}(R_k, t_k) = E_{staticPts}(R_k, t_k) \tag{3}$$

Static and Mimic regions are fixed by mimics segmentation method already presented in [15,16]. R-ICP provides two matched sets of vertices belonging to static regions of the matched face surfaces (see figure 4).

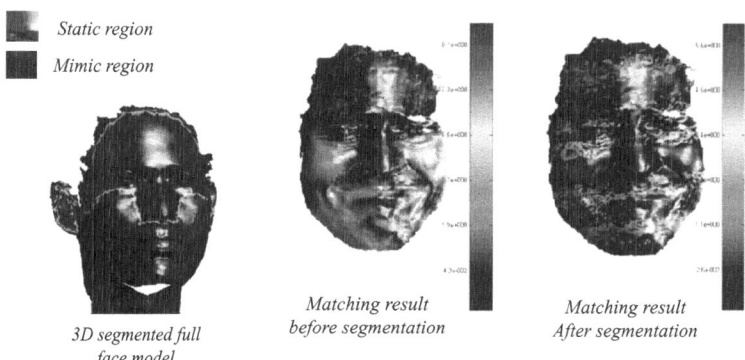

Static region

Mimic region

3D segmented full
face model

Matching result
before segmentation

Matching result
After segmentation

Fig. 4. Region-based ICP for more significant 3D face alignment and matching

5   Geodesics for 3D Face Comparison

In a second stage, we propose to compute geodesic distances between pairs of points on both probe and gallery facial surfaces since this type of distances is invariant to both rigid and nonrigid transformations, as concluded in [8]. Therefore, an efficient numerical approach called the *fast marching method* [18] is applied for geodesic computations. A geodesic is the shortest path between two points on the considered surface as shown by figure 5[19].

5.1   Fast Marching on Triangulated Domains

The *fast marching method*, introduced by *Sethian* [19] is a numerically consistent distance computation approach that works on rectangular grids. It was extended to triangulated domains by *Kimmel & Sethian* in [18]. The basic idea is an efficient numerical approach that solves the *Eikonal* equation $|\nabla u| = 1$, where

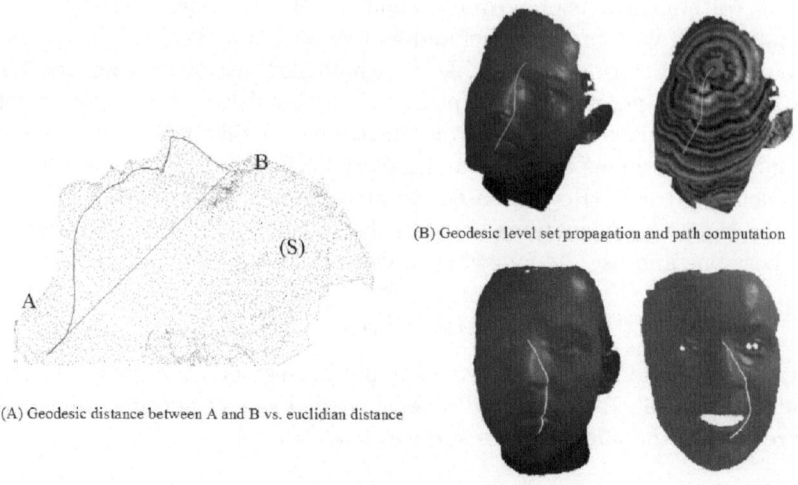

(B) Geodesic level set propagation and path computation

(A) Geodesic distance between A and B vs. euclidian distance

(C) Influence of mimic region on geodesic distance evaluation

Fig. 5. Geodesic path computation for 3D face recognition

at the source point s the distance is zero $u(s) = 0$, namely. The solution u is a distance function and its numerical approximation is computed by a monotone update scheme that is proven to converge to the *'viscosity'* smooth solution.

The idea is to iteratively construct the distance function by patching together small plans supported by neighboring grid points with gradient magnitude that equals one. The distance function is constructed by starting from the sources point, S, and propagating outwards. Applying the method to triangulated domains requires a careful analysis of the update of one vertex in a triangle, while the u values at the other vertices are given. For further details in this theory, we refer to [18].

5.2   Application to 3D Face Recognition

After *R-ICP* alignment step, we propose to compute geodesic maps on overlapped surfaces in both probe and gallery facial surfaces. We dispose of a list of the corresponding vertices already provided by *R-ICP*. As shown by figure 6, the source vertex in probe model is noted S_1 and its correspondant in gallery face model: the source vertex S_2.

We propose to calculate a geodesic distance map on the probe model via the extension of *fast marching method* to triangulated domains proposed by *Sethian & Kimmel* [18]. In fact, the algorithm starts on the source vertex S_1 and propagates along all the facial surface saving on every met vertex the geodesic distance which separate him to the source vertex S_1. All these distances make up the vector V_1 (the first geodesic map). Each line of V_1 contains the geodesic distance separating S_1 and the vertex having the index i of the probe mesh. Then, we compute geodesic distance map on the gallery mesh with the same principle. In this case, the source vertex is a vertex S_2 and geodesic distance map is a vector V_2 . Each line of V_2 contains the geodesic distance separating S_2

from the vertex of the gallery mesh corresponding to the vertex having the index i of the gallery mesh. Finally, we compute the vector V as $V[i] = |V_2[i] - V_1[i]|$. The similarity metric used for the recognition test is the standard deviation of the built vector V.

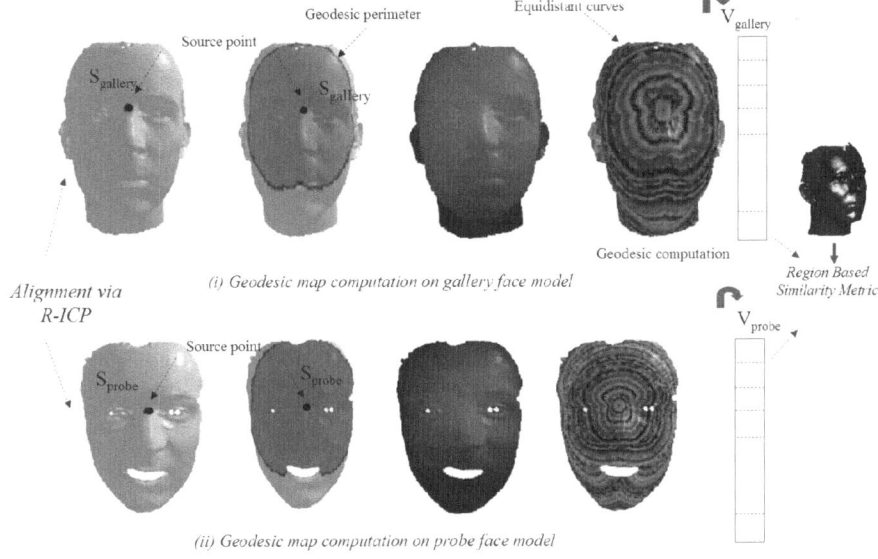

Fig. 6. Geodesic maps computation

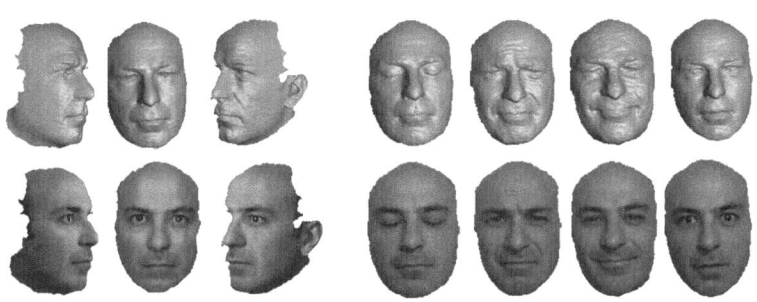

(A) 3D face models and associated textures with pose and facial expression variations

(B) 3D face model with Illumination variations   (C) Shape and texture channels of a full 3D face model

Fig. 7. $ECL - IV^2$: new multi-view registred 3D face database

Geodesic distances are sensitive to the elasticity of the face surface especially in the presence of a severe expression variation. Thus, in our approach, we ignore completely mimic region and consider only vertices which are situated on the static one. In other words, V_1 and V_2 contain only geodesic distance from source point to points belonging to the static region of the face surface.

6   Experiments and Future Works

In this section we present our first experimental results of the presented approach performed on $ECL - IV^2$ 3D face database. Figure 7 illustrates $ECL - IV^2$ database which contains about 50 subjects with 50 multiview 3D models, and 400 3D probe models including variations in facial expressions, poses and illumination [4]. Proposed approach is invariant to illumination variations since the

Experiments	(f)	(e)	(h)	(d)	(s)	(all)
rank-one rate (%)	96	84	86	86	84	87.2

Legend: (f) frontal with neutral expressions, (e) closed eyes, (h) happy, (d) disgusting, (s) surprise, and (all) all probe images.

Fig. 8. Rank-one recognition rates

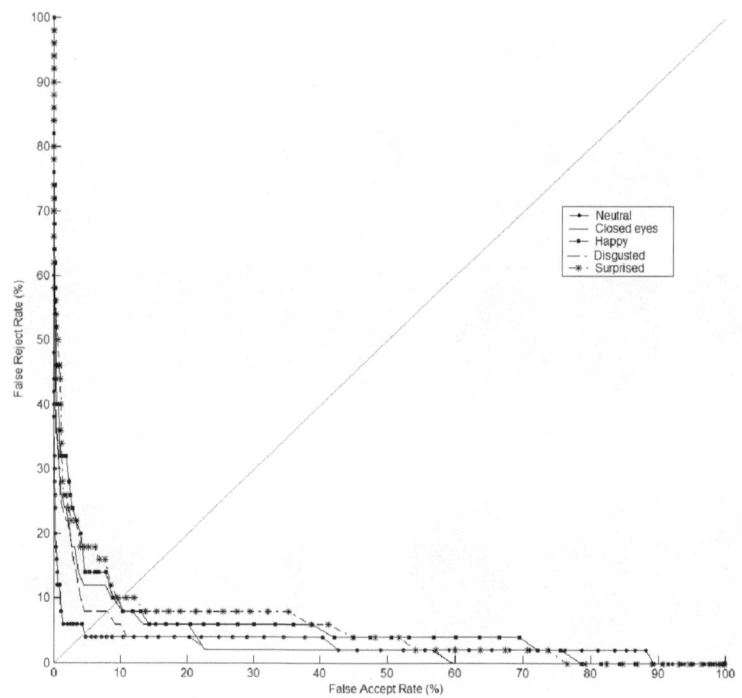

Fig. 9. DET (Error trade-off) curves

texture information is not employed. In the evaluation step, we try to study the invariance of the proposed approach to non rigid deformations caused by expressions.

For our experiments, the gallery contains 50 frontal 3D model with neutral expressions. Probe database has 250 frontal 3D models with 5 type of expressions variations : neutral, closed eyes, disgusting, happy and surprise. We produce for each experiment, labelled by the considered variation, both the error trade-off curve for authentication scenario and the rank-one recognition rates for identification scenario. Figure 8 presents the recognition rates for the elementary experiments and the global one. The *global Recognition Rate (RR)* is equal to 87.2%. We present in figure 9 Error trade-off curves for each expression variation.

First results show the efficiency of the geodesic descriptor for dealing with expression variations. However, $ECL - IV^2$ database contains severe expression variations, as shown by figure 7. In this case, elasticity can intervene even for static region of the face and the geodesic hypothesis is no more valid. In our future work, we plan to get also profit from the rich 3D information situated on mimic region especially that mimic region constitute more than a half of the totality of the facial surface.

References

1. Phillips, P.J., Grother, P., Micheals, R.J., Blackburn, D.M., Tabassi, E., Bone, J.M.: Technical report NIST. FRVT 2002: Evaluation Report (Mars 2003)
2. Pan, G., Wu, Z., Pan, Y.: Automatic 3D Face Verification From Range Data. In: Proc. IEEE International Conference on Acoustics, Speech, and Signal Processing, pp. 193–196 (2003)
3. Malassiotis, S., Strintzis, M.G.: Pose and Illumination Compensation for 3D Face Recognition. In: Proc. IEEE International Conference on Image Processing, pp. 91–94 (2004)
4. Ben Amor, B., Ardabilian, M., Chen, L.: New Experiments on ICP-based 3D face recognition and authentication. In: Proceeding of International Conference on Pattern Recognition (ICPR 2006), pp. 1195–1199 (2006)
5. Ben Amor, B., Ouji, K., Ardabilian, M., Chen, L.: 3D Face recognition by ICP-based shape matching. In: Proceeding of IEEE International Conference on Machine Intelligence (ICMI 2005) (2005)
6. Beumier, C., Acheroy, M.: Automatic 3D Face Authentication. Image and Vision Computing 18, 315–321 (2000)
7. Xiaoguang, L., Jain, A.K.: Integrating Range and Texture Information for 3D Face Recognition. In: Proc. 7th IEEE Workshop on Applications of Computer Vision, pp. 156–163 (2005)
8. Bronstein, A.M., Bronstein, M.M., Kimmel, R.: Three-dimensional face recognition. International Journal of Computer Vision (IJCV), 5–30 (August 2005)
9. Samir, C., Srivastava, A., Daoudi, M.: Three-Dimensional Face Recognition Using Shapes of Facial Curves. IEEE Transactions on Pattern Analysis and Machine Intelligence 28(11), 1858–1863 (2006)
10. Ouji, K., Ben Amor, B., Ardabilian, M., Ghorbel, F., Chen, L.: 3D Face Recognition using ICP and Geodesic Computation Coupled Approach. In: IEEE/ACM SITIS, Hammamet, Tunisie (Décembre 2006)

11. Ben Amor, B., Ouji, K., Ardabilian, M., Ghorbel, F., Chen, L.: 3D Face Recognition using ICP and Geodesic Computation Coupled Approach. In: Signal Processing for image enhancement and multimedia processing. Springer, Heidelberg (2007)

12. Chang, K.I., Bowyer, K.W., Flynn, P.J.: An Evaluation of Multi-modal 2D+3D Face Biometrics. IEEE Transactions on PAMI 27, 619–624 (2005)

13. Xu, C., Wang, Y., Tan, T., Quan, L.: Depth vs. Intensity: Which is More Important for Face Recognition? In: Proc. 17th International Conference on Pattern Recognition (2004)

14. Chang, K.J., Bowyer, K.W., Flynn, P.J.: Effects on facial expression in 3D face recognition. In: Proceedings of the SPIE, vol. 5779, pp. 132–143 (2005)

15. Ben Amor, B., Ardabilian, M., Chen, L.: Enhancing 3D Face Recognition By Mimics Segmentation. In: Intelligent Systems Design and Applications (ISDA 2006), pp. 150–155 (2006)

16. Ben Amor, B., Ouji, K., Ardabilian, M., Chen, L.: Une nouvelle approche d'appariement 3D oriente regions pour la reconnaissance faciale. In: Taima 2007, Hammamet, Tunisie (2007)

17. Besl, P.J., McKay, N.D.: A Method for Registration of 3-D Shapes. Proc. IEEE Trans. Pattern Anal. Mach. Intell 14, 239–256 (1992)

18. Sethian, J.A., Kimmel, R., et al.: Computing Geodesic Paths on Manifolds. Proc. Natl. Acad. Sci. 95(15), 8431–8435 (1998)

19. Sethian, J.A.: A Fast Marching Level Set Method for Monotonically Advancing Fronts. Proc. Nat. Acad. Sci 93, 4 (1996)

Mining Association Patterns between Music and Video Clips in Professional MTV

Chao Liao[1], Patricia P. Wang[2], and Yimin Zhang[2]

[1] Tsinghua University, Beijing, China, 100084
liaoc02@mails.tsinghua.edu.cn
[2] Intel China Research Center, Beijing, China, 100080
{patricia.p.wang,yimin.zhang}@intel.com

Abstract. Video and music clips in MTV match together in particular ways to produce attractive effect. In this paper, we use a dual-wing harmonium model to learn and represent the underlying association patterns between music and video clips in professional MTV. We also use the discovered patterns to facilitate automatic MTV generation. Provided with a raw video and certain professional MTV as template, we generate a new MTV by efficiently inferring the most related video clip for every music clip based on the trained model. Our method shows encouraging result compared with other automatic MTV generation approach.

Keywords: music video generation, harmonium model, association pattern.

1 Introduction

More and more digital camcorders come into people's life. It is very common to record important scenes and events for personal remembrance. However, since the quality of video captured from handheld devices is very low, it makes good sense to cut out the exciting parts from the video and decorate them with proper music. There are several existing systems for video editing, such as Adobe Premiere, Ulead Video Studio, Microsoft Movie Maker and Muvee autoProducer. But still video editing is not an easy job, which requires significant editing skill, aesthetic sense and a lot of time. In this paper, we propose a new approach to automatically generate MTV-style video from raw materials by mining the association patterns between music and video clips in professional MTVs.

There has been some empirical knowledge on how to make media exciting and popular. According to the study in Visual Story [1], the film industry makes their products more intense and interesting by contrasting video components like color, movement and rhythm, etc [2]. This guideline encourages us compositing different types of visual elements together to make MTV better. Another study in [3] further concerns the repetitive sections as prelude, interlude and coda in MTV, which can help to make the results more reasonable on semantic aspects. These two guidelines each focus on one major issue in automatic MTV generation: content selection and composition.

B. Huet et al. (Eds.): MMM 2009, LNCS 5371, pp. 401–412, 2009.
© Springer-Verlag Berlin Heidelberg 2009

Most previous works have put their emphasis on the content selection problem. They first extract visual highlights from raw video, weakly coupled with music, or even worse, absolutely independent from music. Then they align the visual highlights with music based on assumption or empirical knowledge. In our method, video and music are strongly coupled (actually treated as pairs in the training phase). We match video with music based on how good they fit discovered association patterns, which are learned from a large dataset of professional MTV. And the visual highlights are implicitly chosen since they match better with certain music clips.

The contribution of this paper can be summarized into 3 points: i) we associate video and music data together to discover association patterns using a dual-wing harmonium [5] which is previously studied in image retrieval; ii) the training method for the harmonium is extended to adapt to new assumption made on the distribution of audio feature; iii) we give out intuitive representations for discovered association patterns with their most representative clips, and use the patterns to measure the similarity between arbitrary MTV. These patterns partially reflect professional MTV editor's skills and are quite valuable information both in the content selection and composition problem in automatic MTV generation.

2   Related Work

Many groups have reported their work on automatic MTV generation. In Foote et al's work [6], video clips are measured by "unsuitability score", which is based on camera motion and exposure. Those video clips with excessive camera motion or overexposure are more likely to be discarded. Significant changes in sound track are detected as boundaries for audio clips. By calculating self-similarity matrix and matching it with check-board kernel, the peak response will locate the significant change. The composition mainly focuses on fixing the video clip length with the audio clip.

In Wang et al's work [7], they use multi-modal feature analysis and alignment to detect the semantic of events in sports video. They also proposed video-centric and music-centric schemes to match video and audio clips. Although their method introduced semantic information, they require the original data to be pre-edited broadcast video, and the semantic editing rules are pre-defined by users.

HUA et al [3] segment out highlight clips from video and audio by analyzing their temporal structures and repetitive patterns. The composition is based on matching the tempos of the music repetitive patterns with the motions intensities. Attention model and transformation effects are also discussed in their work in [8].

The rest of the paper is organized as follows. The association model used in our method known as dual-wing harmonium is introduced in section 3. The details of implementation and experiment results are presented in section 4. Section 5 gives conclusion and our future work.

3   Approach

We have illustrated the framework of our approach in Fig. 1. We first divide the sample MTVs into small clips, and extract video and audio features from them. In order to

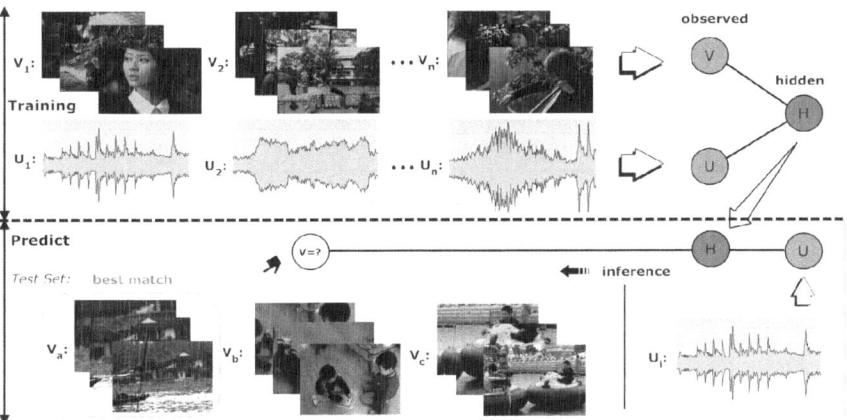

Fig. 1. Framework of our approach. MTVs in the training set are divided into clips to train our model. The rules following which video and music clips are associated together are represented by the hidden node in the **H** space.

obtain association patterns, we use a dual-wing harmonium model to combine these features and produce low-dimensional representations in **H** space. In this way, each clip will correspond to a point in the **H** space. By clustering these points, we can figure out several groups of similar clips. These groups are considered as association patterns, and utilized to guide automatic MTV generation. In the phase of predicting, the model will infer the most related video clip in raw video for a given music clip.

3.1 Notation

- The vector $V = (v_1, v_2, \cdots, v_M)$ denotes the features of video clip. M is the length of **V**. Each $v_i \in (-\infty, +\infty)$ is a component from the color and structure tensor histogram [9] of the video clip.
- The vector $U = (u_1, u_2, \cdots, u_N)$ denotes the features of music clip. N is the size of **U**. Each $u_j \in (-\infty, +\infty)$ is a feature extracted from time domain or spectral domain (detail in section 4).
- The vector $H = (h_1, h_2, \cdots, h_K)$ denotes the position of the input music video clip in the **H** space. K is the length of **H**. The hidden node **H** can be thought of as "latent semantic aspects" which define how the inputs are generated or as the predictors resulted from a discriminative model taking the inputs [5]. Here, we simply view **H** as a combined low-dimensional representation for the input data.

3.2 Harmonium Model

We use Dual-Wing Harmonium Model (DWH) [5, 13] to combine video and audio data, as well as capture the latent rules under which they are associated together.

DWH has two significant advantages over other models that are also capable of representing semantic aspects, for example, Latent Semantic Indexing (LSI) and Latent Dirichlet Allocation (LDA). First, DWH can model multi-modal data like video and music, while other models are designed for single-model data like text. The other important difference is the inference cost. These models can be treated as two-layer graphical models, and inference with these models can be very expensive when hidden nodes are conditionally dependent on each other, according to Welling et al. in [4]. But inference in DWH can be very efficient because the hidden nodes in this model are not connected to each other.

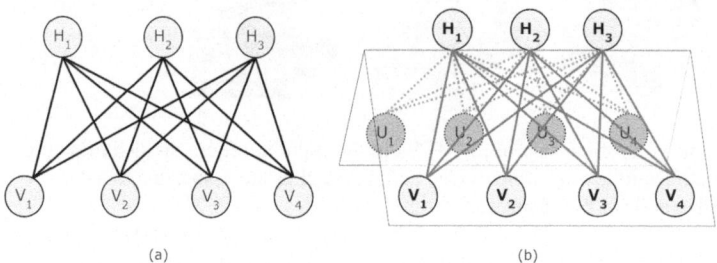

(a)   (b)

Fig. 2. (a)Basic Harmonium Model and (b)Dual-Wing Harmonium

3.2.1 The Basic Harmonium Model

Harmonium model is first studied in [10], it is also known as "combination machine" or "restricted Boltzmann machine". Welling [4] has extended the harmoniums into the exponential family to make them widely applicable. However, harmonium model still suffer from a global normalization factor which presents both in the evaluation of input data probability and model parameters.

A typical harmonium model, illustrated in Fig.2 (a), contains one layer of latent nodes, **H**, and one layer of input nodes, **V**. As we can see, **H** and **V** are fully connected while the latent nodes **H** themselves are not connected. Hence the conditional distribution between two layers can be factorized over individual nodes:

$$p(v \mid h) = \prod_i p(v_i \mid h), \, p(h \mid v) = \prod_k p(h_k \mid v) \qquad (1)$$

This property is the basis for efficient inference with harmonium model. The random field induced in this harmonium has the exponential family form as follows:

$$p(v,h) \propto \exp\left\{ \sum_{ia} \theta_{ia} f_{ia}(v_i) + \sum_{kb} \lambda_{kb} g_{kb}(h_k) + \sum_{ikab} W_{ia}^{kb} f_{ia}(v_i) g_{kb}(h_k) \right\} \qquad (2)$$

Where $\left\{ f_{ia}(\cdot), g_{kb}(\cdot) \right\}$ denote the features of the variable v_i and h_k, $\left\{ \theta_{ia}, \lambda_{kb}, W_{ia}^{kb} \right\}$ denote the set of parameters associated with their corresponding potential functions. These parameters must be resolved to get a tractable form for $p(v,h)$.

In the following, we represent the conditional distributions between model variables with these parameters. So when the model for conditional distribution is determined, we can resolve the parameters, and have them replaced here to get a specific form of $p(v,h)$.

First we define the log-normalization factors $\{A_i, B_k\}$ as:

$$\int_{v_i} \exp\left\{\sum_a \theta_{ia} f_{ia}(v_i)\right\} dv_i = \exp A_i\left(\{\theta_{ia}\}\right) \tag{3}$$

$$\int_{h_k} \exp\left\{\sum_b \lambda_{kb} g_{kb}(h_k)\right\} dh_k = \exp B_k\left(\{\lambda_{kb}\}\right) \tag{4}$$

The marginal distribution can be obtained by integrating out the other variable:

$$p(v) = \int_h p(v,h)\,dh$$

$$\propto \exp\sum_{ia}\theta_{ia}f_{ia}(v_i)\prod_k \int_{h_k}\exp\left\{\sum_b\left(\lambda_{kb}+\sum_{ia}W_{ia}^{kb}f_{ia}(v_i)\right)g_{kb}(h_k)\right\}dh_k \tag{5}$$

$$= \exp\left\{\sum_{ia}\theta_{ia}f_{ia}(v_i)+\sum_k B_k\left(\{\hat{\lambda}_{kb}\}\right)\right\}$$

And similarly, we can get

$$p(h) \propto \exp\left\{\lambda_{kb}g_{kb}(h_k)+\sum_i A_i\left(\{\hat{\theta}_{ia}\}\right)\right\} \tag{6}$$

Where the shifted parameters are defined as:

$$\hat{\lambda}_{kb} = \lambda_{kb}+\sum_{ia}W_{ia}^{kb}f_{ia}(v_i) \tag{7}$$

$$\hat{\theta}_{ia} = \theta_{ia}+\sum_{kb}W_{ia}^{kb}g_{kb}(h_k) \tag{8}$$

Now we can derive the conditional distribution from marginal distribution:

$$p(v\mid h) = \frac{p(v,h)}{p(h)} \propto \prod_i \exp\left\{\sum_a \hat{\theta}_{ia}f_{ia}(v_i)-A_i\left(\{\hat{\theta}_{ia}\}\right)\right\} \tag{9}$$

$$p(h\mid v) = \frac{p(v,h)}{p(v)} \propto \prod_k \exp\left\{\sum_b \hat{\lambda}_{kb}g_{kb}(h_k)-B_k\left(\{\hat{\lambda}_{kb}\}\right)\right\} \tag{10}$$

These conditional distributions are also in exponential family form. When these conditional distributions are determined, we can resolve the parameters and have them replaced in equation (2) to get the specific form of joint probability $p(v,h)$.

3.2.2 Dual-Wing Harmonium Model

The dual-wing harmonium model studied by Xing et al. in [5] is an extension from basic harmonium model. In this model, each wing represents a special type of input source. Specifically speaking, we have extended his model to represent both audio and video data, i.e. one wing for video features extracted from the video clip and another wing for audio features from the music clip, illustrated in Fig.2 (b). Different from Xing's original work, the observed nodes on the audio wing are continuous random variables rather than discrete ones like text features. According to Ellis's study on audio feature statistics in [12], MFCC features are almost perfectly uncorrelated to each other, but their distribution doesn't look exactly Gaussian. However, since we have audio features beside MFCC, such as ZCR, spectral centroid and spread, power and flux, etc., Gaussian distribution is still good approximation for them all. The formula for parameter estimation is also changed based on this assumption.

We assume the components in **U** and **V** follows Gaussian distribution:

$$p\left(v_i \mid h\right) = N\left(v_i \mid \sigma_{1i}^2\left(\alpha_i + \sum_k h_k W_{ik}\right), \sigma_{1i}^2\right) \tag{11}$$

$$p\left(u_j \mid h\right) = N\left(u_j \mid \sigma_{2j}^2\left(\beta_j + \sum_k h_k U_{jk}\right), \sigma_{2j}^2\right) \tag{12}$$

Where $\left(\alpha_i, \beta_j\right)$ denote the shift parameters, and $\left(W_{ik}, U_{jk}\right)$ capture the coupling between hidden nodes and inputs. The mean values are both determined from weighted combinations of **H**. This is motivated by thinking hidden units **H** as latent topic which define how the inputs are generated. And the scale coefficients σ^2 before the mean values are to ensure the consistency between the probabilities of observed nodes and hidden nodes. As a matter of fact, the scale coefficient cancels in the first parameter in the exponential family form of Equation (11-12), and reduces the overall complexity.

Come to the hidden nodes, we model them with a unit-variance Gaussian distribution. In this distribution, the mean value is determined by a weighted combination from the observed nodes on both wings.

$$p\left(h_k \mid v, u\right) = N\left(h_k \mid \sum_i v_i W_{ik} + \sum_j u_j U_{jk}, 1\right) \tag{13}$$

With equation (11-13), we can resolve their exponential family form parameters, and replace them in the general form of $p(v,u,h)$, as shown in last section 3.2.1. Or we can simply use the following method to get a tractable form for joint probability. Both methods yield the same result:

$$\begin{aligned} p\left(u,v\right) &\propto \frac{p\left(u,v\right)}{p\left(h\right)} = \frac{p\left(u,v \mid h\right)}{p\left(h \mid u,v\right)} = \frac{p\left(u \mid h,v\right) p\left(v \mid h\right)}{p\left(h \mid u,v\right)} \\ &= \frac{p\left(u \mid h\right) p\left(v \mid h\right)}{p\left(h \mid u,v\right)} = \frac{\prod_i p\left(v_i \mid h\right) \prod_j p\left(u_j \mid h\right)}{\prod_k p\left(h_k \mid v,u\right)} \end{aligned} \tag{14}$$

Putting equation (12-14) together, we can get the following result:

$$p\left(v,u\right) \propto \exp\left\{\begin{array}{c}\sum_i \alpha_i v_i + \sum_j \beta_j u_j - \dfrac{1}{2}\sum_i \dfrac{v_i^2}{\sigma_{1i}^2} - \dfrac{1}{2}\sum_j \dfrac{u_j^2}{\sigma_{2j}^2} \\[2mm] + \dfrac{1}{2}\sum_k \left(\sum_i v_i W_{ik} + \sum_j u_j U_{jk}\right)^2\end{array}\right\} \tag{15}$$

3.2.3 Learning from Associated Clips

The parameters for the model can be learned by minimizing the Kullback-Leibler divergence between the data distribution $\hat{p}$ and the equilibrium distribution p over the harmonium random field [11], which is equivalent to maximizing the log-likelihood of the data. By taking derivatives of the log-likelihood of the data with respect to the model parameters $\left(\alpha_i, \beta_j, W_{ik}, U_{jk}\right)$, we can obtain the learning rules which change the parameters attempting to match the expectation values under the data distribution and the model distribution [4]:

$$\delta\alpha_i = \langle v_i\rangle_{\hat{p}} - \langle v_i\rangle_p, \delta\beta_j = \langle u_j\rangle_{\hat{p}} - \langle u_j\rangle_p$$
$$\delta\left(W_{ik}\right) = \langle v_i h_k'\rangle_{\hat{p}} - \langle v_i h_k'\rangle_p, \delta\left(U_{jk}\right) = \langle u_j h_k'\rangle_{\hat{p}} - \langle u_j h_k'\rangle_p \tag{16}$$

Where h_k' stands for $\sum_i v_i W_{ik} + \sum_j u_j U_{jk}$ and $\langle\cdot\rangle_q$ denotes the expectation value under distribution q.

Direct computing of the equilibrium distribution P is intractable, and an approximate inference method is needed to estimate these model expectations. Since a quite large number of iterations need to be performed before Gibbs sampling can reach the equilibrium distribution, we use "Contrastive Divergence" [11] to reduce the complexity. In CD, we just run one full step Gibbs Sampling from the observed data and then we update the parameters. Since Gibbs sampling is always started from the observed data, the result won't wander away from the data distribution. Hinton also shows in [11] that the equilibrium should already be reached when the distribution is not changed at all on first step sampling.

To generate a similar style MTV according to the input sample, we utilize the inference function of the model. For each music clip, we match it with a top-ranking video clip in the raw video by sorting all video clips in a descending order of $p\left(v\,|\,u\right)$ [5, 13].

4 Experiments

The association pattern for music and video clips in a MTV depends on many factors, such as its editor's taste or the music style. To explore these association patterns, we have collected over 100 MTVs in different categories, from both male and female singers, both Chinese and English, both single and band group. We try to collect MTVs in albums so they would have been edited by the same editor. These MTVs are segmented into video and music clips with the same time length t. Since the video data usually has integer frame rate of 25 or 30 fps, t should tolerate this ambiguity, so MTVs with different fps can be segmented into same number of clips. Further more, t should provide easy mapping to media time, since we also need to locate music and video clips in media file. In practice, we set t to 1 second.

Although it is common to divide video by shots, we eventually choose to divide by time lengths. The advantage is that we can avoid the length balance problem when video and music clips with different time length need to match together. And the shot change patterns are also important. They won't be discovered once the video is divided by shots. The shortcoming is that the shot consistency is not guaranteed when connecting neighbor clips in the generated MTV.

From each video clip, we extract 512 dimensional color histogram in the RGB space and 17 dimensional structure tensor histogram. The color histogram represents the color distribution as well as color richness in the video clip. The structure tensor histogram represents the motion intensity and direction in the video clip. Both of them are important measure for visual highlights. For each music clip, we extract its zero crossing rates in time domain, and its centroid, spread and the first 10 MFCC coefficients in spectral domain. We also extract the power, flux and low energy ratio in spectral window as its features. All these features are normalized to guarantee they have unit-variance.

The hidden nodes number K is set to 30. Better performance can usually be achieved with larger K [13], but the improvement will be smaller when K is bigger than some threshold, and the computational complexity is growing with K. The model is trained using contrastive divergence with 2000 steps of iteration. And the parameters W and U are also initialized by SVD on the feature data to alleviate the problem which allows multiple parameter configurations to share the same marginal likelihood [4, 5].

4.1 Association Pattern

The music video clips are mapped to **H** space after harmonium training. Since the dimension of **H** (30) is much smaller than that of video features (529), the model has provided us with a low-dimensional representation for the input data. We subsequently apply a k-means clustering procedure. Every cluster in the **H** space is considered to be an association pattern. We perform the experiment both on single album and on whole dataset. We actually find more interesting association patterns in single album than whole dataset, which proves products from same editor tell the editing rules better. But generally speaking, the semantic level for the discovered pattern depends on features we choose. The audio features chosen in our experiments have the power to discriminate different people's voice, because they are also widely used in speech recognition.

We illustrate 5 association patterns out of 20 patterns learned by the model from an album of 10 MTVs in Fig 3. The album is from a band group of three girls, known as S.H.E. In AP18, three girls' faces are shown when all of them are singing. In AP17, only two girls are singing, and only two faces are shown. AP20 and AP16 both capture the solo scenes where only one girl is singing. AP16 could be confusing in first glance, unless we notice that in the first picture still only one girl is singing, and in the third picture the cartoon girl also refers to the same singer. Since the color and tensor

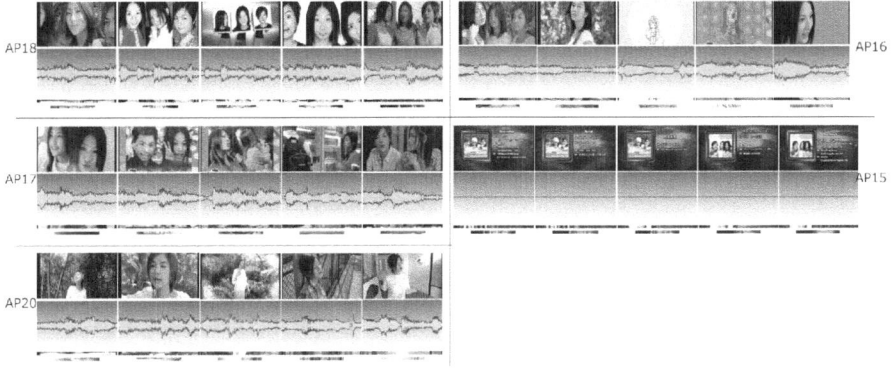

Fig. 3. Several association patterns found in an album of 10 MTVs. Different association patterns are separated by dark lines. In each pattern, we list 5 most representative music video clips. For each of them, we show its intuitive representations in a column. From top to bottom, these representations are: the first picture in video clip, the waveform for music clip, the horizontal slice and the vertical slice which crosses the center of the video clip. The waveform in AP15 means silence.

directions are quite diverse in these patterns, the audio features play a dominant role to distinguish clips by singer's voice. Video features can also be dominant in other circumstances. For example, AP15 shows a special pattern where MTV headers match with silence. The color and tensor directions in MTV headers are quite similar, so video features are more dominant than audio ones in these patterns.

More complicated association patterns can also be discovered by training the model on the entire dataset. Some of the discovered patterns are illustrated in Fig 4. Since these MTVs are produced by various editors, the data points in the **H** space can be even harder to group together, and the discovered patterns should be considered as common rules followed by all editors. In this sense, AP19 represents the pattern where music highlight match with small motion of singers' heads. AP9 also captures music highlight but with richer motion. In AP18, the camera is barely moved and the music is not intense. In AP13, loud voice well matches with dark decorating scenes. And AP12 is one pattern representing shot change. Since neither video nor audio features are dominant in these patterns, the underlying rules are somehow difficult to understand. However, these patterns still show up frequently in sample MTV, not depending on whether we can decode them from representative clips or not.

4.2 Comparison

We compare our result with MUVEE the auto Producer in two aspects. The style option for MUVEE is set to *Classic Style*. However, the algorithm used in MUVEE is unknown. For objective evaluation, we would like to compare their similarity to input MTV sample. For subjective evaluation, we compare the results by user study.

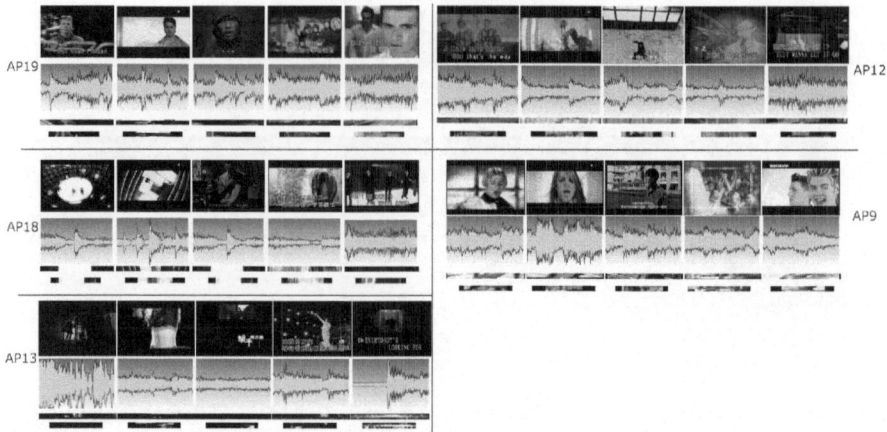

Fig. 4. Association patterns from 102 MTVs. Clips from same category are in one column. From left to right, the categories are: Backstreet boys, Britney Spears, Jay Zhou, Yanzi Sun, West life.

4.2.1 Similarity

Using the method in [14], we represent MTV with a sequence of signatures extracted from music video clips, except the signature here is simply the association pattern label. We train our model on Jay's album-fantasy, and choose 2 songs from it to generate MTV. We measure the similarity between auto-generated result and original MTV in two aspects: *Exact match* and *Histogram divergence*. *Exact match* is the total count that two sequences have same pattern labels in all positions. *Histogram divergence* is the K-L divergence between the histograms of two sequences. Since some histogram bins could be zero, contribution from these bins are ignored in the divergence. The smaller the *Histogram divergence* is, the more similar two sequences are. The comparison result is listed in Table 1.

Table 1. Similarity Measure

MTV	Exact match		Histogram divergence	
Music	MUVEE	Ours	MUVEE	Ours
Song 1	68/233	90/233	32.02/233	10.12/233
Song 2	59/238	87/238	76.17/238	43.24/238
Average	26.99%	37.59%	-	-

The scores show that our results are more similar to original MTV than MUVEE in both *Exact match* and *Histogram divergence*. Recall the second guide line in MTV generation, the sequence of the original MTV contains the information for repetitive sections such as prelude, interlude and coda. In this sense, our method complies with the second guide line better than MUVEE.

4.2.2 Subjective Evaluation

We choose 4 songs from different categories, and match them with the same raw video. 5 graduate students are required to give a score from 0 to 1 to each of the 8 MTVs on both video content and music video matching. The average result is listed in Table 2.

Table 2. Subjective Evaluation

Music Type	MUVEE		Ours	
	Content	Match	Content	Match
Chinese Fast	0.70	0.64	0.62	0.75
Chinese Slow	0.72	0.71	0.61	0.72
English Fast	0.78	0.65	0.65	0.75
English Slow	0.76	0.70	0.62	0.70
Average	0.74	0.68	0.63	0.73

The *Match* score tells how well users think the video change matches with music beats. The result indicates that our method shows perceptible improvement in *Match* compared with MUVEE, especially when the music style is fast. The *Content* score tells how excited users feel about the video scenes. The result shows our method is less attractive on this aspect. According to the users, the number of scenes in our result seems not as many as in MUVEE's. This actually reflects our method's limitation that we cannot guarantee shot consistency or scene loss in the result. We can further improve the final quality by collaborating with video highlight selection algorithms.

5   Conclusion

In this paper, we use a dual-wing harmonium model to discover association patterns from professional MTV. The sample MTV are divided into music video clips from which video and audio features are extracted. The model combines these features and discovers association patterns by clustering the sample data in hidden semantic space. We further generate similar-style MTV by inference most related video clip from raw video with respect to each music clip in a given song. The association patterns can be used to measure the similarity between the generated result and the original MTV.

While previous MTV generation systems mainly depend on empirical knowledge to match video with audio, our method gives a useful insight into the association pattern between video and music data. However, depending on which features we choose, the discovered pattern can sometimes be hard to understand, when no feature in the pattern is dominant. And because we divide video clips with fixed time length, we cannot guarantee the shot consistency in generated MTV. Our future work will be introducing the third modal data: lyrics into our framework, and combining our method with other highlight selection algorithms to further improve the result quality.

References

1. Block, B.A.: The visual story: seeing the structure of film, TV, and new media. Focal Press, Boston (2001)
2. Sam, Y., Eugenia, L., et al.: The automatic video editor. In: Proceedings of the eleventh ACM international conference on Multimedia, Berkeley, CA, USA. ACM, New York (2003)
3. Xian-Sheng, H.U.A., Lie, L.U., et al.: Automatic music video generation based on temporal pattern analysis. In: Proceedings of the 12th annual ACM international conference on Multimedia. ACM, New York (2004)
4. Welling, M., Rosen-Zvi, M., et al.: Exponential family harmoniums with an application to information retrieval. In: Advances in Neural Information Processing Systems, vol. 17, pp. 1481–1488 (2005)
5. Xing, E., Yan, R., et al.: Mining associated text and images with dual-wing harmoniums. In: Proceedings of the 21th Annual Conf. on Uncertainty in Artificial Intelligence (UAI 2005). AUAI press (2005)
6. Foote, J., Cooper, M., et al.: Creating music videos using automatic media analysis. In: Proceedings of the tenth ACM international conference on Multimedia, pp. 553–560 (2002)
7. Wang, J., Xu, C., et al.: Automatic generation of personalized music sports video. In: Proceedings of the 13th annual ACM international conference on Multimedia, pp. 735–744 (2005)
8. Xian-Sheng, H.U.A., Lie, L.U., et al.: P-Karaoke: personalized karaoke system. In: Proceedings of the 12th annual ACM international conference on Multimedia. ACM, New York (2004)
9. Ngo, C.W., Pong, T.C., et al.: Motion analysis and segmentation through spatio-temporal slices processing. IEEE Transactions on Image Processing 12(3), 341–355 (2003)
10. Smolensky, P.: Information processing in dynamical systems: foundations of harmony theory. Mit Press Computational Models Of Cognition And Perception Series, pp. 194–281 (1986)
11. Hinton, G.E.: Training Products of Experts by Minimizing Contrastive Divergence. Neural Computation 14(8), 1771–1800 (2002)
12. DAn Ellis. Comparing features statistics: MFCCs, MSGs, etc (1999),
    http://www.icsi.berkeley.edu/~dpwe/respite/multistream/
    msgmfcc.html
13. Yang, J., Liu, Y., et al.: Harmonium Models for Semantic Video Representation and Classification. In: SIAM Conf. Data Mining (2007)
14. Arun, H., Kiho, H., et al.: Comparison of sequence matching techniques for video copy detection. In: Minerva, M.Y., Chung-Sheng, L., Rainer, W.L. (eds.) SPIE, vol. 4676, pp. 194–201 (2001)

Semi-supervised Learning of Caricature Pattern from Manifold Regularization

Junfa Liu[1,2], Yiqiang Chen[1], Jinjing Xie[1,2], Xingyu Gao[1], and Wen Gao[1,3]

[1] Institute of Computing Technology, Chinese Academy of Sciences,
Beijing, China, 100190
[2] Graduate School of Chinese Academy of Sciences, Beijing, China, 100190
[3] Institute of Digital Media, Peking University, Beijing, China, 100871
{liujunfa,yqchen,xiejinjing,gaoxingyu,wgao}@ict.ac.cn

Abstract. Automatic caricature synthesis is to transform the input face to an exaggerated one. It is becoming an interesting research topic, but it remains an open issue to specify the caricature's pattern for the input face. This paper proposed a novel pattern prediction method based on MR (manifold regularization), which comprises three steps. Firstly, we learn the caricature pattern by manifold dimension reduction, and select some low dimensional caricature pattern as the labels for corresponsive true faces. Secondly, manifold regularization is performed to build a semi-supervised regression between true faces and the pattern labels. In the third step of offline phase, the input face is mapped to a pattern label by the learnt regressive model, and the pattern label is further transformed to caricature parameters by a locally linear reconstruction algorithm. This approach takes advantage of manifold structure lying in both true faces and caricatures. Experiments show that, low dimensional manifold represents the caricature pattern well and the semi-supervised regressive model from manifold regularization can predict the target caricature pattern successfully.

1 Introduction

Caricature brings more non-verbal information than pure face in HCI (Human Computer Interactive) field. Especially in digital life nowadays, there are wide applications. For example, when chatting on MSN, or in some online games, one can use his or her own caricature as the avatar. In this case, people can communicate freely while hiding their true faces for private consideration. In another case, the children would stay longer in an educational virtual environment if they can contact other friends with the interface of caricatures.

Traditional caricatures are mainly created by the artists manually. Since the artists make it according to the people's facial features, what about the computer to do that? Recently, there are increasing works on caricature generation [1~8]. Some of the works can be concluded as "regularity-based" class, which discover the facial characteristics by interactive observation or statistical comparison. Brennan [1] is an earlier author who invents an interactive system to create cartoon face. The user perceives the face's key characteristics by observation and exaggerates it in the next step. PICASSO [2] is a famous system to generate cartoon face. The main idea is to calculate

B. Huet et al. (Eds.): MMM 2009, LNCS 5371, pp. 413–424, 2009.

an average face first, then compare its features with the input face. The difference will be enlarged. Ergun Akleman [3] proposed feature-based warping algorithm. In this approach, users only need to arrange the source and target line according to the facial features. The warped face is very smooth and nature. Pei-Ying Chiang [4] works out the average face and exaggerates the prominent features of the input face after comparison with the average face. Bruce Gooch et al [5] present a method for creating two-tone illustrations and warping the face to a caricature according to the artificial grid regularity. This way needs professional skills.

Some other works are in "learning-based" class. Lin Liang et al [6] learn some prototypes by PLS(partial least-squares) and combine several prototypes to reflect the personal facial characteristics. H. Chen et al [7] build statistical model from a sample sets that are created by an artist with unified style, and then generate the target feature by a nonparametric sampling module. Junfa Liu et al [8] learn regressive model in eigenspace to map true face to caricature. This approach transforms harmoniously the face based on multi-features.

In this paper, we proposed an approach for mapping learning from true face to caricature. We learn the mapping model based on a 2D true face database and a 2D caricature database. Before learning, we perform dimension reduction for all the caricatures by manifold algorithm to get a caricature pattern map, so all the caricatures can be represented by the low dimensional features, the pattern coordinates on the pattern map. The mapping model is further learnt between the 2D true faces and the pattern map by manifold regularization algorithm.

The rest of the paper is arranged as follows: In section 2, we describe the problem and motivation of the paper. Section 3 introduces LLE (Locally Linear embedding) for generating caricature pattern map. In section 4, based on the pattern map, MR is interpolated as the regressive learning method. Section 5 demonstrates how to apply this model for caricature generation. The experiment and its result are introduced in section 6. In the last section, we draw a conclusion for this paper and make a schedule for our future work.

2   Problem Statement and Our Motivation

The artist creates caricature mainly by facial shape exaggerating and texture rendering. The mentioned works above just concentrate on the shape aspect. This paper also focuses on shape exaggeration. The principle is like this: First, from a input image (Figure 1(a)), the facial feature in terms of the facial mesh X is extracted (Figure 1(b)), and then the facial mesh is warped to a new one X^* (Figure 1(c)) by a regularity or learnt regressive model $X^* = f(X)$. According to the vertexes of the new mesh, the face texture is warped to produce the caricature (Figure 1(d)). So the problem is how we can get a good mesh transformation function f.

From the related works above, we find that regularity-based approach is difficult to use, for the user need some art background to discover the facial feature and specify the transformation degree. On the other hand, learning-based approach can generate the result with less interaction while discovering multi-features and transforming the face harmoniously.

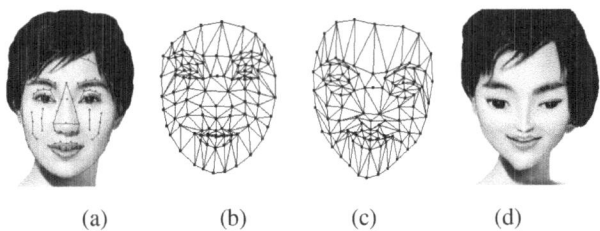

(a)   (b)   (c)   (d)

Fig. 1. The principle of caricature generation

However, there are also improving space for the learning approaches in [6,7,8]. In [6] and [7], the learning is supervised, and there are limited samples in the training set, so the result model needs to be generalized for importing more samples. In [8], the model is learnt in linear space built by PCA (Principal Component Analysis), and the number of eigenvectors is up to 17. It inspirits us to build the learning space with nonlinear models. The experiments in this paper and [9] indeed show the nonlinear model, the manifold, is suitable to describe the face distribution with potential advantages. So our goal is to develop nonlinear learning program, while importing large mount of training samples. We select MR [10] as the learning algorithm, and the reasons are as follows.

Firstly, our learning problem is semi-supervised. In our data configure of 2D true faces and caricatures, there are some pairs. Each pair means a true face and a caricature referring to the same person. Those pairs can be regarded as the supervised samples, while the other samples are unsupervised. So on the whole, it is a semi-supervised problem. MR is just a such kind of algorithm.

Secondly, faces are proved to be distributed in manifold. Some previous works have similar conclusions [9]. MR just supposes the manifold as the geometry of the marginal distribution. So it is reasonable for us to build regressive model f between true faces and caricatures under the MR framework.

3   Build Caricature Pattern Map with LLE

In order to generate the caricature, we need to predict the target mesh parameters for the input face. Due to the mesh parameters are high dimensional features, it is nature for us to change the mesh parameters to low dimensional caricature pattern. However, even in the sight of the artists, it's hard to classify the caricature pattern into numbers of limited classes, so it is better to discover the distribution of the pattern, and build continuous pattern map. Manifold is such an analysis tool to discover the underlying structure of the data. Further more, faces is already proved by many research such as [9] lying on low dimensional manifold in high dimensional space. In this paper, we also provide some evidences for that supposition in the following section. Another reason for us to adopt LLE is that, by LLE, it is easy to perform inverse transformation from low dimensional pattern to high dimensional mesh. That is to say, once we get the pattern parameters of the caricatures by LLE learning, it is convenient to convert the pattern parameters to high dimensional mesh parameters. It is further explained in section 5.1.

3.1 Data Preparing

As we know, the general method for an artist to create the caricature is to exaggerate the shape of the original face, so in this paper, we represent both faces and caricatures with shape parameters. We extract all the shape parameters from the true face and caricatures. In fact, those caricatures are created by the artists from all over the world, and are collected from the Internet, and magazines. Some true faces and caricatures are showed in Figure 4. For copyright consideration, just the shapes are given, and all the texture is omitted.

To detect the faces in the photograph automatically, and extract the shape parameters of the faces accurately, we adopt ASM (Active Shape Model) algorithm. ASM is an efficient method to extract shape feature from images through training [13]. However, at present, ASM is not effective for caricatures. So we only use ASM to process the true face photograph, and process the caricatures by manual way.

We collect 1027 caricatures. All these shapes $X_i = (x_{i0}, y_{i0}, ...x_{i(n-1)}, y_{i(n-1)})$ construct the pattern training set $\{X_i\}$. Since the data come from different sources, we need align all the shapes to a same scale before next operation. We choose the average face $\overline{X}$ as the standard scale. All faces are transformed to the average face's scale. The procedure needs to construct two matrixes first:

$$
A_i = \begin{bmatrix} x_{i0} & -y_{i0} & 1 & 0 \\ y_{i0} & x_{i0} & 0 & 1 \\ \vdots & \vdots & \vdots & \vdots \\ x_{i(n-1)} & -y_{i(n-1)} & 1 & 0 \\ y_{i(n-1)} & x_{i(n-1)} & 0 & 1 \end{bmatrix}_{2n\times4} \qquad Z = \begin{bmatrix} s\cos\theta \\ s\sin\theta \\ t_x \\ t_y \end{bmatrix}
$$

Where, n is the sum number of the samples. t_x and t_y are the translations, s is the scaling coefficient, and θ is the rotation angle of the original faces. They construct the transforming matrix Z.

We calculate Z according to A_i and $\overline{X}$:

$$
\overline{X} = A_i Z \Rightarrow Z = (A_i'A_i)^{-1}A_i'\overline{X} \tag{1}
$$

Finally, apply Z to the target shape X_i':

$$
X_i' = A_iZ = A_i(A_i'A_i)^{-1}A_i'\overline{X} \tag{2}
$$

3.2 Dimension Reduction with LLE

There are some kinds of manifolds, such as LLE, ISOMap, Eigenmap and so on. We choose LLE as the preprocessing approach in this research. We first briefly describe the principle of LLE, and then give the reason why we use it.

LLE is one of the earliest reported manifold dimension reduction method [9]. According to LLE algorithm, each face, including caricature, can be expressed as the linear combination of k nearest neighbors. It means the faces can be reconstructed by a weight matrix, which describes the distances between that face and its neighbors. The reconstruction errors is measured as Equation (3).

$$\varepsilon(W) = \sum_i | X_i - \sum_j W_{ij} X_j |^2 \qquad (3)$$

The weight matrix W_{ij} is what we unknown. To compute it, we need to minimize the reconstruction errors. There are two constrains: $\sum_j W_{ij} = 1$ and $W_{ij} = 0$, if X_j is not one of the k nearest neighbors of X_i. Once the weights are worked out, we can begin the procedure of dimension reduction while fixing the weights. We suppose a face X in high dimension maps to a low dimension embedding Y representing the global internal coordinates on the manifold. The Y can be computed by minimizing the cost function:

$$\Phi(Y) = \sum_i | Y - \sum_j W_{ij} Y_j |^2 \qquad (4)$$

Here, we fix the weight W_{ij}, and specify the dimension to d for the vector Y. The minimizing problem can be transformed into an eigenvector problem, which is well posed to solve in linear algebra.

According to the principle, LLE supposes the data lies on a low dimensional geometric structure. So we make a test to see if 2D caricatures meet this supposition. We obtained positive result that the faces come from latent manifold structure. Figure 2 shows a map of analogous triangle while all the caricatures are reduced into 2-dimensional space.

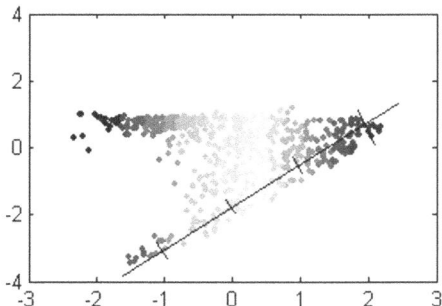

Fig. 2. Manifold map of caricatures

We take the coordinates on the triangle map as the training labels. We also reconstruct the caricatures according to the coordinates, which is interpreted in details in section 3.3 and 5.2.

3.3 Sampling Test in the Pattern Map

To further test that the 2-dimensional map of the manifold can represent the caricature pattern, we sample some points on the map and observe what is gong on.

To reflect some regularities, we select all points along the same line, which is drawn in Figure 2. Total 31 points are selected. The horizontal value changes from -1 to 2 with step 0.1 and the vertical value changes from -3 to 0.51 with step 0.117. After recovering the caricature for each point through locally linear reconstruction algorithm, as expected, the points which are neighbors appear with similar expression and pose. Four key frames are listed in the following Figure 3. These frames map respectively to the four points with cross line on Figure 2. How to recover the caricature from the points is detailed in section 5.2.

Fig. 3. Sampling in caricature pattern map

4   Manifold Regularization for Faces

Regularization is a well built mathematical approach for solving ill-posed inverse problems. It is widely used in machine learning problem [11], and many popular algorithms such as SVM, splines and radial basis function can be broadly interpreted as the instance of regularization with different empirical cost functions and complexity measures. In this paper, we take manifold regularization [10] as semi-supervised pattern learning approach to predict the target face's caricature pattern.

4.1   The Framework of Manifold Regularization

Here we give a brief introduction to manifold regularization, whose detail can be referred in [10]. Given a set of data with labels $\{x_i, y_i\}_{i=1,2,...,l}$, the standard regularization in *RKHS* (Reproducing Kernel Hillbort Space) is to estimate the function f^* by a minimizing:

$$f^* = \arg\min_{f \in H_K} \frac{1}{l} \sum_{i=1}^{l} V(x_i, y_i, f) + \gamma \|f\|_K^2 \tag{5}$$

Where V is some a loss function, and $\|f\|_K^2$ is the penalizing on the *RKHS* norm reflecting smoothness conditions on possible solutions. The classical Representer Theorem states that the solution to this minimization problem exists in *RKHS* and can be written as:

$$f^*(x) = \sum_{i=1}^{l} \alpha_i K(x_i, x) \tag{6}$$

Substituting this form in the problem above, it is transformed to optimize α^*. In the case of the squared loss function of $V(x_i, y_i, f) = (y_i - f(x_i))^2$. We can get final RSL (Regularized Least Squares) solution :

$$\alpha^* = (K + \gamma I)^{-1} Y \tag{7}$$

M. Belkin, et al [10] extended the standard framework to manifold regularization, which is described as the following form:

$$f^* = \arg\min_{f \in H_K} \frac{1}{l} \sum_{i=1}^{l} V(x_i, y_i, f) + \gamma_A \|f\|_K^2 + \gamma_I \|f\|_I^2 \tag{8}$$

The differences between manifold regularization and standard framework lie in two aspects. The first is the former incorporate geometric structure of the marginal distribution P_X in the minimizing, which is reflected by the third item $\|f\|_I^2$. While minimizing, the coefficient γ_I controls the complexity of the function in the intrinsic geometry of P_X and γ_A controls the complexity of the function in ambient space. M. Belkin, et al [10] employ Laplacian manifold to represent the geometric structure embedded in high dimensional data. The second difference is the importing of unlabeled data $\{X_i\}_{i=l+1}^{i=u}$ by manifold regularization. While the lost function is calculated only by the labeled samples as before, when calculating the third penalizing item $\|f\|_I^2$, manifold regularization imports large mount of unlabeled samples that reflect the manifold structure. So the solution changed into a new form as Equation (9). The difference between Equation (9) and (6) is that the former imports u samples, which are unlabeled.

$$f^*(x) = \sum_{i=1}^{l+u} \alpha_i^* K(x, x_i) \tag{9}$$

And the corresponsive solution of α^* is in Equation (10). $J = diag(1,1,...,0,0)$ with the first l diagonal entries as 1 and the rest 0. $\mathbf{L}$ is the Laplacian graph. We can notice that if $\gamma_I = 0$, which means we ignore the unlabeled samples, the Equation (10) will be identical with Equation (7).

$$\alpha^* = \left(JK + \gamma_A lI + \frac{\gamma_I l}{(u+l)^2} LK \right)^{-1} Y \tag{10}$$

4.2 Training Data Labeling

We prepared total 1841 true face photographs and 1027 caricatures. Then, we need prepare training pairs from those pictures. Obviously, to get corresponsive caricature for all the true faces or get corresponsive true faces for all the caricatures is labor-consuming and time-consuming work. Fortunately, semi-supervised learning by manifold regularization makes it easy. We just need to choose partial samples of them to buildup the training pairs. Total 198 pairs are prepared well. Five pairs are listed in Figure 4. The top row is true faces and the bottom row is corresponsive caricatures.

So for our manifold regularization problem, the true face set is $\{X_i\}_{i=1}^{i=l+u}$, and the former l samples are labeled as $\{P_i\}_{i=1}^{l}$. Here, P_i is the sample's coordinates in the pattern map obtained in section 3. It is based on this semi-supervised dataset that we learn the mapping function $f(x)$ between the true face and its caricature's pattern by manifold regularization.

Fig. 4. Some pairs of true faces and caricatures

4.3 Mapping Function Learning Based on MR

Manifold regularization performs semi-supervised learning based on the supposition that the data is embedded in a low dimensional manifold. We make a test of the true faces.

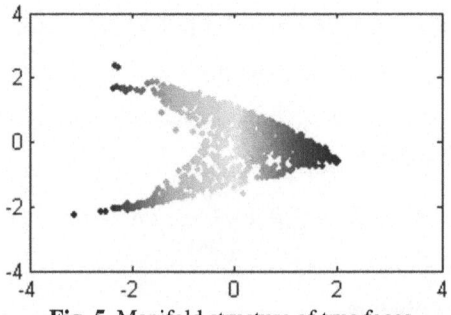

Fig. 5. Manifold structure of true faces

Figure 5 shows a regular analogous triangle when the dimension of the samples are reduced to 2. The triangle can be regarded as the latent structure. Lying on this structure, we employ the framework of manifold regularization to learn the regressive model between true faces and caricatures.

In our case, the element $\{y_i\}$ is a two dimensional vector $\{y_{i1}, y_{i2}\}$ that is the ordinate on the caricature manifold map, so we need to train a function with multi-dimensional output:

$$f(x) = \{f_1(x), f_2(x)\} = \sum_{i=1}^{l+u} \alpha_i^* K(x, x_i) \tag{11}$$

Where, the result α^* and $\mathbf{Y}$ will be a Matrix instead of a vector as before.

$$\alpha^* = \left(JK + \gamma_A lI + \frac{\gamma_I l}{(u+l)^2} LK \right)^{-1} \mathbf{Y} \tag{12}$$

5 Caricature Synthesis Based on Pattern Prediction

The process of caricature synthesis is automatic. True face photograph is inputted first, and then facial feature in terms of the facial mesh X is extracted. We also use the ASM module to detect the face and extract the facial shape. So the mesh is obtained without interaction. Once the mesh data X is obtained, its label, the pattern coordinates, $P^* = \{f_1(X), f_2(X)\}$ can be derived by the learnt function in Equation (11). Next, we use locally linear reconstruction algorithm to reconstruct the caricature for P^* taking advantage of LLE.

5.1 Locally Linear Reconstruction

P^* is just a pattern label of the input face, so we need to reconstruct the caricature mesh in high dimensional feature space. Since the low dimensional manifold map is generated by LLE, we can take advantage of LLE's property to handle this task. It is just an inverse transformation of LLE and it is just why we choose LLE as the algorithm to reduce feature's dimension.

In LLE, the dimension reduction defines a mapping function from high dimensional face to low dimensional manifold feature, which is $f : X \rightarrow Y$. In the procedure of dimension reduction, the weights for sample's neighbors keep fixed. Similarly, we can define a reverse mapping $f^{-1} : Y \rightarrow X$, which increases the dimension while keeping the weights unchanged. This reverse mapping transforms the manifold feature to the target caricature.

The process is: Given Y', searching within the 2D manifold map, we can get k nearest neighbors Y_j' for Y', and then compute the weights W_{ij}' by minimizing the reconstruction errors as Equation (3). We know that each coordinates Y_j' maps to an original 2D caricature X_j' in the sample space, so the final result X' can be constructed by:

$$X' = \sum_{j=1}^{k} W_{ij}' X_j' . \tag{13}$$

5.2   Caricature Generation

Once we get X', the locally linear combination of X_j', we can perform image warping to generate the final caricature.

Image warping is to generate a target image from the source face image [12]. The vertexes of mesh X are regarded as the controlling points on the source image and the vertexes of mesh X' are regarded as the controlling points on the target image. We called the target image caricature after warping.

6   Experiments

In this paper, manifold regularization is performed based on a true face data X. The size of the set is 1841, with 198 samples labeled. Those labels come from low dimensional caricature pattern map obtained by LLE algorithm, and the training set for LLE is made up of total 1027 caricatures.

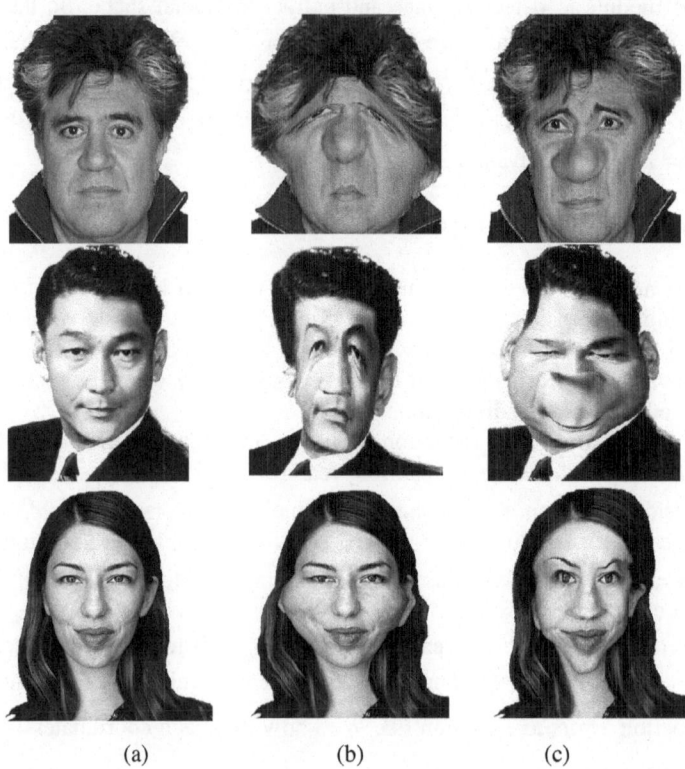

(a)   (b)   (c)

Fig. 6. The experiment result.(a) is the original face. (b) is generated by PCA-base algorithm. (c) is generated by MR-based algorithm.

We show some results in Figure 6 and compare them with the results from the algorithm in paper [8]. The approach in paper [8] also performs regressive learning in subspace for caricature generation. However, there are two main differences with this paper. One is the subspace in that paper is linear, which is constructed by PCA. The other is that we take advantage of plenty of unlabeled data to recover the geometric structure, which can promise more robust mapping learning. Through subjective comparison, we can notice that the algorithm in this paper provides more harmonious transformation for the final caricatures.

Objective evaluation is also given. We compared the results between PCA-based approach in [8] and MR-based approach in this paper, and take 'Similarity' and 'Exaggeration' as two metrics. Twelve people evaluate all the results and give scores to them. Table 1 shows the average score of each item. We can draw the conclusion that MR-based approach performs well than PCA-based approach.

Table 1. Scores of the results generated by two approaches

Results / Metrics	Result 1		Result 2		Result 3		Average	
	MR	PCA	MR	PCA	MR	PCA	MR	PCA
Similarity	3.78	3.30	3.69	3.54	3.36	3.42	3.61	3.42
Exaggeration	3.90	3.92	4.11	3.97	3.88	3.48	3.96	3.79

7 Conclusion and Future Works

In this paper, manifold learning by LLE shows that the low dimensional geometric structure exists in both caricatures and true faces. So we take full advantage of manifold regularization, which considers intrinsic geometric structure reflected by importing unlabeled samples. We proposed a semi-supervised regression for caricature pattern predicting based on manifold regularization framework, and generate labels from the low dimensional pattern map. Comparison with linear regression by PCA shows that manifold can represent nonlinear feature of faces and caricatures. The regressive learning is more effective to discover the relationship between true faces and caricatures , and the caricature label is obtained by LLE dimension reducing.

As stated at the beginning of section 2, caricature creation also involves texture rendering. Based on the result in this paper, some rendering algorithm can be added to make the caricature more attractive, which is just our future work.

Acknowledgements

We would like to thank Dr. Dong Wang and Mr. Wang Hu for their work to collect and process the caricature data. This work was supported by National Natural Science Foundation of China (60775027) and (60575032).

References

1. Brennan, S.: Caricature generator. Massachusettes Institute of Technology, Cambridge (1982)
2. Koshimizu, H., Tominaga, M., Fujiwara, T., et al.: On Kansei facial processing for computerized facial caricaturing system Picasso. In: Proceedings of IEEE International Conference on Systems, Man, and Cybernetics, Tokyo, pp. 294–299 (1999)
3. Akleman, E.: Making caricature with morphing. In: Visual Proceedings of ACM SIGGRAPH 1997, p. 145 (1997)
4. Chiang, P.-Y., Liao, W.-H., Li, T.-Y.: Automatic Caricature Generation by Analyzing Facial Features. In: 2004 Asian Conference on Computer Vision, Jeju Island, Korea, January 27-30 (2004)
5. Gooch, B., Reinhard, E., Gooch, A.: Human facial illustrations: Creation and psychophysical evaluation. ACM Trans. Graph. 23(1), 27–44 (2004)
6. Chen, H., Xu, Y., Shum, H., Zhu, S., Zheng, N.: Example based facial sketch generation with non-parametric sampling. In: ICCV 2001, pp. II: 433–II: 438 (2001)
7. Liang, L., Chen, H., Xu, Y.-Q., Shum, H.-Y.: Example-based Caricature Generation with Exaggeration. In: IEEE Proceedings of the 10th Pacific Conference on Computer Graphics and Applications (2002)
8. Liu, J., Chen, Y., Gao, W.: Mapping Learning in Eigenspace for Harmonious Caricature Generation. In: 14th ACM International Conference on Multimedia, Santa Barbara, USA, October 22-27, 2006, pp. 683–686 (2006)
9. Roweis, S.T., Saul, L.K.: Nonlinear dimensionality reduction by locally linear embedding. Science 290, 2323–2326 (2000)
10. Belkin, M., Niyogi, P., Sindhwani, V.: Manifold Regularization: a Geometric Framework for Learning from Labeled and Unlabeled Examples. Journal of Machine Learning Research 7, 2399–2434 (2006)
11. Evgeniou, T., Pontil, M., Poggio, T.: Regularization Networks and Support Vector Machines. In: Advances in Computational Mathematics, vol. 13, pp. 1–50 (2000)
12. Wolberg, G.: Digital Image Warping. IEEE Computer Society Press, Los Alamitos (1990)
13. Cootes, T.F., Taylor, C.J., Cooper, D., Graham, J.: Active shape models–their training and application. Computer vision and image understanding 61(1), 38–59 (1995)
14. Blanz, V., Vetter, T.: A morphable model for the synthesis of 3D-faces. In: Proc. SIGGRAPH 1999, pp. 187–194 (1999)
15. Shet, R.N., Lai, K.H., Edirisinghe, E.A., Chung, P.W.H.: Use of Neural Networks in Automatic Caricature Generation: An Approach Based on Drawing Style Capture. In: Marques, J.S., Pérez de la Blanca, N., Pina, P. (eds.) IbPRIA 2005. LNCS, vol. 3523, pp. 343–351. Springer, Heidelberg (2005)
16. Sousa, M.C., Samavati, F., Brunn, M.: Depicting Shape Features with Directional Strokes and Spotlighting. In: IEEE Proceedings of the Computer Graphics International (2004)

An Image Inpainting Algorithm Based on Local Geometric Similarity[*]

Pan Qi[1,2], Xiaonan Luo[1,2], and Jiwu Zhu[3]

[1] Computer Application Institute, Sun Yat-Sen University, Guangzhou, China
[2] Key Laboratory of Digital Life(Sun Yat-Sen University), Ministry of Education
lnslxn@sysu.edu.cn
[3] Dept. Marketing, Guangdong Pharmaceutical University, Guangzhou, China
angelflying66@yahoo.com.cn

Abstract. This paper proposes a novel noniterative orientation adaptive image inpainting algorithm. Assuming the image can be locally modeled, the filling process is formulated as a linear optimization problem, which the optimal coefficients can be adapted to match an arbitrary-oriented edge based on *local geometric similarity*. We provided A Weighted Least Square (WLS) method is provided to offer a convenient way of finding the optimal solution, which the weight function is selected based on the non local means. We also present Group Marching method (GMM) as the propagation scheme such that sharp edges are well propagated into the missing region layer by layer while maintaining the local geometric similarity. A number of examples on real and synthetic images demonstrate the effectiveness of our algorithm.

Keywords: Edge-directed, Fast Marching Method (FMM), Inpainting, Interpolation, Least Square Method.

1 Introduction

Along with the progress of multimedia techniques, digital inpainting has found wide applications in image or video processing, ranging from automatic scratch removal, logo erasing to special effects such as object disappearance. Inpainting is the filling in of unknown regions of an image with the use of information from surrounding areas.

Researchers have proposed numerous methods for inpainting images. There are two major research directions: one is based on texture synthesis [1], often suffering from huge computational loads. Another direction is focus on linear structure images. In this paper, we mainly discuss the latter.

The human visual systems are highly sensitive to edge structure, which convey much of the image semantics, so a key requirement for image inpainting algorithms is to faithfully propagate the sharp edges into the missing region. A number of inpainting

---

[*] This work is supported by the National Science Fund for Distinguished Young Scholars (No.60525213) and the Key Project (Project No. 60533030) of NSFC, and 973 Program of China (Project No.2006CB303106).

B. Huet et al. (Eds.): MMM 2009, LNCS 5371, pp. 425–434, 2009.

algorithms [2]-[5] inspired by the partial differential equations (PDE) of physical heat flow, fill in the target region by propagating image information continuously in iso-phote directions (An isophote is defined as a curve of constant intensity on image. Isophote direction is orthogonal to edge direction). There are variation-based methods, e.g. , the total variation (TV) inpainting model [4], based on the Euler–Lagrange equa-tion, employs anisotropic diffusion based on the contrast of the isophotes inside the inpainting domain. The inpainting model cannot connect contours across very large distances and does not connect broken edges (single lines embedded in a uniform background). The Curvature-Driven Diffusion (CDD) model [5], takes into account geometric information of isophotes when defining the 'strength' of the diffusion proc-ess, allowing both for isophotes to be connected across large distances, and their direc-tions to be kept continuous across the edge of the inpainting region. But the resulting interpolated segments appear blurry. All above methods essentially solve a Partial Differential Equation (PDE) that propagating along the isophotes subject to various assumptions. Since there are no local criteria for stopping the inpainting, the process is constantly applied to all masked pixels, regardless of the local smoothness of the region. As a result, computationally expensive operations might be unnecessarily performed.

To avoid nontrivial iterative and reduce computation complexity, there are ap-proaches different from the PDEs. Alexndru Telea[6] estimate the image smoothness as a weighted average over a known image neighborhoods of the pixel to inpaint and use the fast marching method (FMM) to propagate the isophotes. Zhaozhong wang etc. [7] search for an isophote at an unfilled point and perform a 1D smoothing along the isophote to avoid the smoothness across it. These approaches speed up the inpaint-ing. But they explicitly estimate edge direction, which the penalty to image quality is high if the estimated edge direction is wrong.

In this paper, we propose a noniterative algorithm without explicit estimate iso-phote orientation. Features at the observed sample are corresponding to those at the pixel to be estimated along the same orientation, which we called the *local geometric similarity*. Therefore, assuming the unknown pixel and its neighboring pixels (re-ferred to as *training window*) are roughly from a single model, the unknown pixel can be estimated from its nearest neighbors (a subset of the training window, referred to as *neighborhood window*) to match an arbitrarily-oriented edge.

The assumption of the training window and the neighborhood window are from a single model is largely dependent on a proper choice of the training window, all pix-els in training window should be directional corresponding to those in neighborhood window strictly. Therefore we provide Weighted Least Square(WLS) method, which increases the contribution of the most similar training window.

The quality of the output image can be influenced by the order in which the filling process proceeds. Li's related work [11] to solve error-concealment problem employs sequential filling mode, inevitably resulting in error-propagating, uses the linear merge strategy at the price of increase computational complexity to alleviate it. Similar to [6] and [7], our work employs layer-filling mode, always inpaints first the unknown points just touching the known boundary. All such points form a layer of unknowns, and the inpainting is propagated layer by layer. However, our propagating mode is different from those in [6] and [7]. We use Group marching method (GMM) [7], which can avoid error-propagating in the same layer.

This paper is organized as follows. In section 2 we introduce our proposed methods. The experimental results are presented in section 3. Section 4 provides the conclusion.

2   Mathematical Model and the Least Square Optimization

2.1   Mathematical Model

Consider Fig. 1, in which one must inpaint the point situated on the boundary of the region to inpaint. Assuming y is the interesting unknown pixel, our problem is to estimate y with minimum uncertainty from its local *neighborhood window* and we call it $B(\varepsilon, n)$. ($B(\varepsilon, n) = \{x \in \Omega, \|y - x\|_2 \leq \varepsilon\}$, where ε is a searching radius, n is the number of pixels in the window).

$$y = \beta^T x \tag{1}$$

Where coefficients $\beta = [\beta_1, \beta_2, \cdots, \beta_n]^T$ is a $n \times 1$ column vector. $x = [x_1, x_2, \cdots, x_n]$ is a $n \times 1$ column vector containing pixels in $B(\varepsilon, n)$.

We take a training window of $B(\varepsilon, m)$, which also includes pixels in $B(\varepsilon, n)$, assuming every training pixel and its n neighbors satisfy Eq.(1), the MSE over set $B(\varepsilon, m)$ in the optimization can be written as,

$$MSE = \|W(x - C\beta)\|_2^2 \tag{2}$$

Where

$$C = \begin{bmatrix} C_1 \\ C_2 \\ \vdots \\ C_m \end{bmatrix} = \begin{bmatrix} x_1(1) & x_1(2) & \cdots & x_1(n) \\ x_2(1) & x_2(2) & \cdots & x_2(n) \\ & & \vdots & \\ x_m(1) & x_m(2) & \cdots & x_m(n) \end{bmatrix}$$

C is a $m*n$ matrix with its rows consisting of the n neighbors of the m training pixels, W = diag $[w_1, w_2, \ldots, w_m]$ is a diagonal matrix, are assigning a confidence that patches C_i and x are to be close to each other.

It should be noted that since some neighbors of y might not be available; we have to pick out the valid neighbors to form a proper training window. The concept is proposed in [11] but not emphasized the directional correspondence, which is a kernel of the *local geometric similarity*.

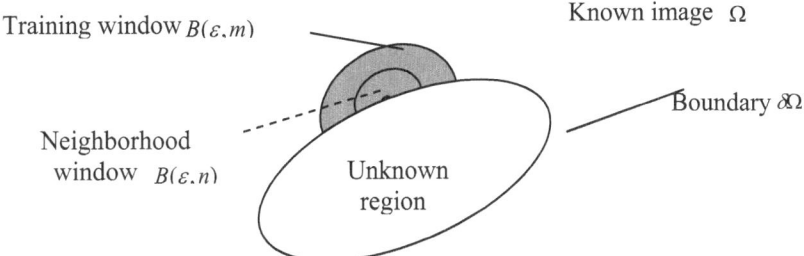

Training window $B(\varepsilon, m)$ Known image Ω

Boundary $\partial\Omega$

Neighborhood
window $B(\varepsilon, n)$ Unknown
region

Fig. 1. The inpainting model

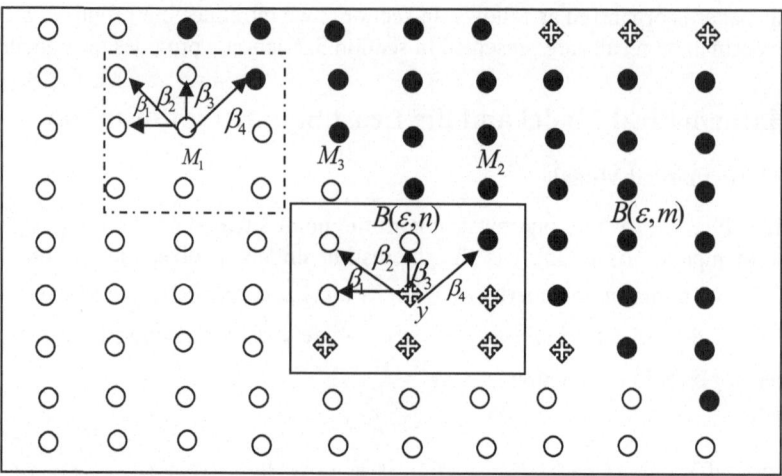

Fig. 2. The choice of training window. The train window is an example of a 45° sharp edge. The black dots and white dots all represent the known pixel with different pixel value. The crosses represent the unknown pixel.

There are two explanations about valid neighbors (Fig. 2). One explanation referred to as the validity of pixels in $B(\varepsilon, m)$. Only if neighbors in $B(\varepsilon, m)$ satisfy two conditions: known and directional corresponding to the neighbors of the current pixel y, would they be treated valid. The reason is that each element of x denotes the directional contribution of those to the current pixel. The contribution β is learned from valid neighbors in $B(\varepsilon, m)$ along the same direction. Since pixels in $B(\varepsilon, m)$ live along the same isophote as those in $B(\varepsilon, n)$, it is very likely that their derived optimal would also work for $B(\varepsilon, n)$.

Another is the validity of pixels of in $B(\varepsilon, n)$. A pixel is valid if it is known, which the same as [11] is. x is the valid set in $B(\varepsilon, n)$. c_i is the valid set in $B(\varepsilon, m)$. It is easy to see that both x and c_i are varying inside the image region, depending on specific location of estimated pixel and missing information.

2.2 Weighted Least Squared Optimization

The aim of using training window is based on the assumption that all pixels are roughly from a single model. It means that the current pixel has the same characteristics as those in the training window. In fact, it is not the real case. As shown in Fig.2, the current pixel and its valid neighbors are defined as a *pattern*. All valid pixels in the training window are divided into three groups: *non-edge pattern, desired edge pattern,* and *undesired edge pattern.* For example, M_2 belongs to non-edge pattern, M_1 belongs to desired edge pattern, and M_3 belongs to undesired one. It can be easily seen that the desired edge pattern will provide the most plentiful information to estimate the current pixel, non-edge pattern much less. But the undesired edge pattern has negative contribution.

Our goal is to make a good estimation from the current pixel, not for the whole training window. Even when the solution of β fits the training window well, it is still possible that it is not good for our goal at all. WLS method is proposed to attempt to alleviate the problem by giving different weights to the contributions of different pixels, especially decreasing the negative contribution of the undesired edge pattern. Thus a weighted sum of squared errors is minimized:

$$MSE_{weighted} = \left\| W(x - C\beta) \right\|_2^2 \tag{3}$$

A natural way to determine the weight depends on how close the pixel in the training windows is to the current pixel. The weight decreases the contribution of the pixels geometrically farther from y. But it often fails to satisfy our desire. For example, M_1 is desired to given more weight than M_2, the result is on the contrary.

The key in overcoming the above difficulty remains to recognize local geometric similarity. Features along the same direction contained in local geometric similarity not only include geometric distance but also include pixel similarity. Therefore the weight can be defined as,

$$w_i = \frac{1}{\left\| (C_i - x) \right\|_2) + \Delta} \tag{4}$$

Where Δ is a quantity introduced to avoid division-by-zero error. (Experimentally we set $\Delta = 1$.)

Eq.(4) calculates the pixel differences of neighbors between observed pixel in the training window and the current pixel. This is a direct method to select the most similar desired edge pattern (e.g., M_1) in training window. In order to alleviate the negative effect of undesired edge pattern as small as possible, the current pixel is considered not to belong to the desired edge pattern, we use Eq. (5) instead of Eq. (4),

$$w_i = \frac{1}{\left\| (C_i - x) \right\|_2 \cdot \sigma(C_i) + \Delta} \tag{5}$$

Where $\sigma(\cdot)$ is local variance of input vector.

The second term of Eq. (5) is mainly aim to decrease the contribution of undesired edge pattern. Although the weight of the non-edge pattern is possibly increased because of the second term, its contribution to the current pixel is trivial and neutral.

Next, our objective is to solve (3) to find an optimal solution. For the case that C has full rank, we can get a unique solution easily. But one possible situation is that the data set C is often not full-ranked, so the problem is ill-posed. In such case the regularization approach, regarded the problem as the constrained minimization of the following cost function:

$$MSE_{regularization} = W \left\| y - C\beta \right\|_2 + \lambda \left\| L\beta \right\|_2 \tag{6}$$

Where L is the regularization operator, is often chosen to be a smoothing function such as the identity matrix. λ ($\lambda > 0$) is the regularization parameter, λ controls the tradeoff between these terms and represents the amounts of regularization. It can be easily shown from regularization theory [12] that the resultant coefficient vector β will be

$$\hat{\beta} = (C^T W C + \lambda L^T L)^{-1} C^T W C \tag{7}$$

The above strategy is clearly visible in Fig. 3, the inpainting is better visually when the weights are added (Fig. 3(c)).

Optimal coefficients of each pixel must be calculated from its local window by Eq. (7), resulting in huge computational loads. In order to manage the computational complexity, the adaptation method is only applied to edge pixel. (A pixel is declared to be edge pixel if the local variance in its neighborhoods is above a preselected threshold.) For non-edge pixel we estimate its value by averaging pixels in the neighboring window.

2.3 Propagation Scheme

The above scheme is inpainting for a single point. Inpainting the entire image needs to handle the unfilled points one by one. We propose layer propagating mode. Along with information recovery using the mode, the error will be also propagated because previously recovered pixels are also used to resolve the uncertainty of unknown pixels in addition to the original known pixels, especially when the inpainted area are thick.

Since the current pixel relies on the information of previous layer, the layer propagating pattern can not avoid layer-propagated error. But the error brought by the previous recovered pixel in the same layer can be alleviated by using Group Marching method (GMM)[8]. In brief, the FMM is an algorithm that solves the Eikonal equation:

$$|\nabla T| = 1 \text{ on } \Omega, \text{ with } T = 0 \text{ on } \partial\Omega . \tag{8}$$

The solution T of Eq.(8) is the distance map of the Ω pixels to the boundary $\partial\Omega$. The level sets, or isolines, of T are exactly the successive boundaries $\partial\Omega$ of the shrinking Ω that we need for inpainting. The FMM guarantees that pixels of $\partial\Omega$ are always processed in increasing order of their distance to boundary T, i.e., that we always inpaint the closest pixels to the known image area first. GMM is a modified version of the FMM [6] that advances a group of grid points simultaneously rather than sorting the solution in a layer. A group of points in the same layer are estimated independently such that their travel times do not alter each other in the update procedure. And the neighbor points of join the current layer after computing their travel times. GMM can avoid error-propagating in the same layer and reduce the computational complexity of the FMM while maintaining the same accuracy. Experimental result (Fig. 3) shows that our strategy is effective.

3   Experimental Results

In this section, we show some typical applications of our inpainting scheme, which include simple disocclusions, restoration of a photo with scratches, text removal from an image, and the special effect of removing an object from a scene. We also compare our algorithm with existing ones. Since most existing objective metrics of image quality cannot consider the visual masking effect around an arbitrarily-oriented edge [9]. We shall only rely on measure the performance of different algorithms by a subjective view to the results. Fortunately, the improvements brought by our inpainting algorithm over existing ones can often be easily observed when the inpainted images are viewed at a normal distance.

Our first experiment show the performance of the proposed model in the inpainting of a synthetic image. Fig. 4 gives the comparative results on the "cross" image in Fig. 4(a). From Fig. 4(f) we can see that the fine vertical and horizontal edge structures are well preserved by our algorithm.

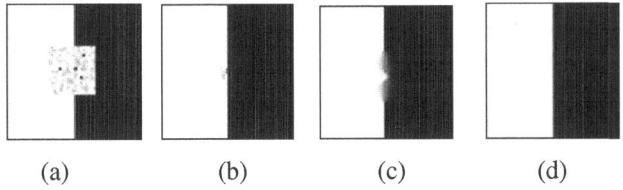

Fig. 3. The inpainting results are better visually when using WLS method. (a) Original image, the noise region denotes the inpainting region, (b) Result image using LMMSE and GMM, (c) Result image using WLS and FMM, (d) Result image using WLS and GMM.

The second experiments show the performance of the proposed algorithm in restoration of real scene images with inpainting regions of different forms and sizes.

Fig.5 is an example of inpainting color photograph. The missed portion of eyebrow restored by our method is slightly inferior to result by Tschumperle-Deriche [3], but marked eye is reconstructed the best. Fig.6 shows the portions of two girls of the example taken from [2]. Although details in the nose and two eyes of the middle girl could not be completely restored, our method can reconstruct the eyes at higher level of its visual quality.

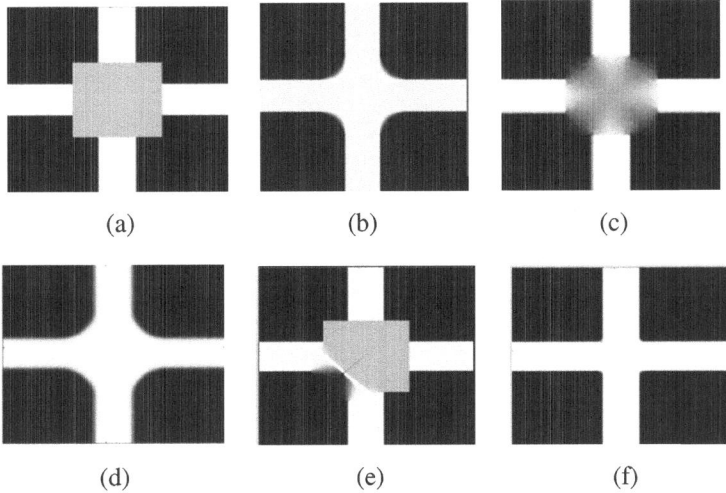

Fig. 4. Impainting a cross (The stripe width is 20 pixels; initial gap distance is 50 pixels). (a) Initial data of cross (inpainting region in gray), (b) Tschumperle-Deriche [3], (c) CDD [5], (d) modified Cahn-Hilliard equation [13] (*cf.* Fig. 2(c) in [13]), (e) isophote propagating [7], (f) our algorithm.

Fig.7 provides additional result to remove real objects in images using the proposed algorithm. Fig.8 provide two examples of inpainting the video frame. The first row is an example of inpainting thick regions. The second row is an example where overimposed text is removed from the image. It is clear that our algorithm can achieve good visual effects: sharp, no color artifacts.

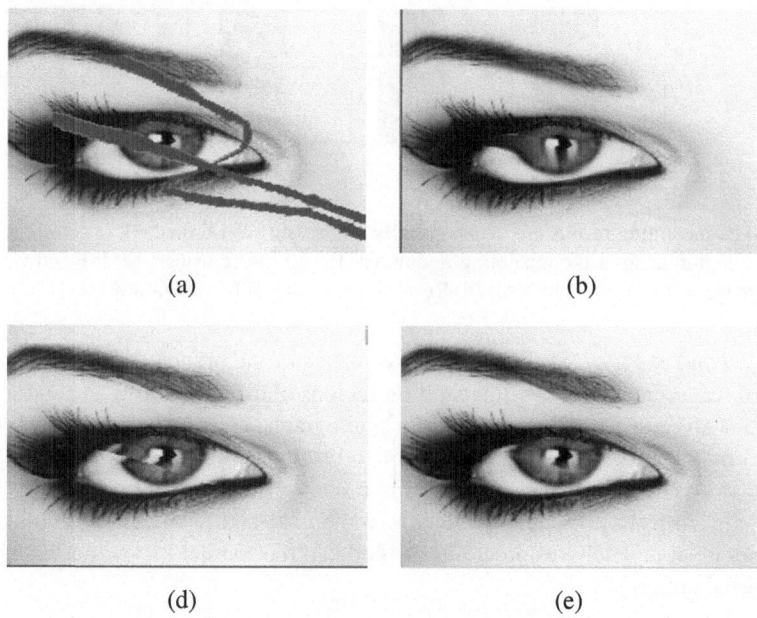

Fig. 5. Color photograph with lines obscuring parts of the image. (a) original image, (b) Tschumperle-Deriche [3], (c) FMM [6], (d) our algorithm.

In our implementation, the neighboring window size and the threshold to declare an edge pixel threshold are set to 8, the neighboring window size set to 4. The threshold *th* to decide whether the pixel is belong to the desired edge pattern is set to 10^{-2}. The global regularization parameter λ is set 0.01. Experimentally the effect of the choice of λ is small in the range of 10^{-5} to 10^{-2} for these tested images.

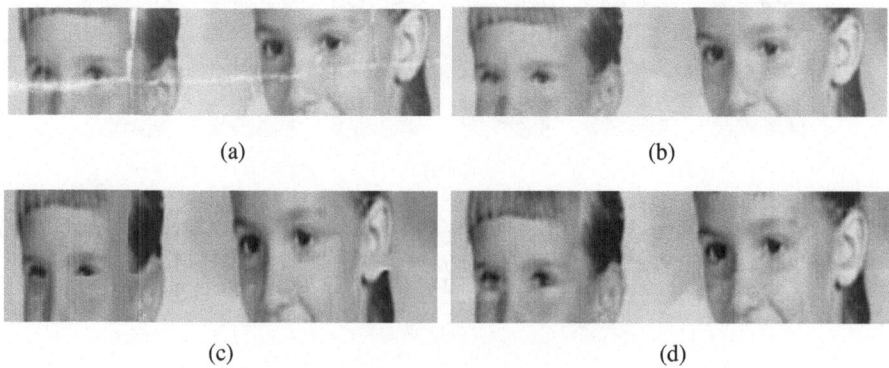

Fig. 6. Removing scratches in a damaged old photograph taken from [2]. (a) original image; (b) Bertalmio [2]; (c) Tschumperle-Deriche [3]; (d) our algorithm.

Fig. 7. Inpainting to remove objects. (a) original image, (b) the target region has been selected and marked with a red boundary, (c) result image.

Our algorithm can achieve better results than existing methods and run more quickly than PDE-based methods [2]-[5]. Since the computation of solving linear equation is typically negligible when compared to the fast algorithm [6] and [7]. (For Fig.8, it spends almost 3s to implement the inpainting using visual C++ 6.0). Dramatic reduction of complexity can be achieved for image containing a small fraction of edge pixels. Here we do not provide comparisons between our algorithm and the methods based on texture synthesis, since we mainly aim to inpaint structure images.

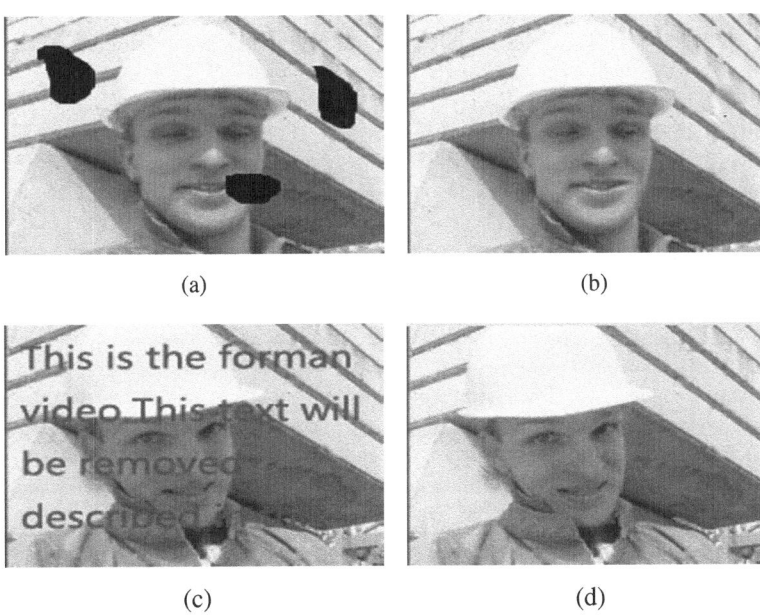

(a)   (b)

(c)   (d)

Fig. 8. Inpainting the Foreman video. (a) the damaged frame, (b) result image, (c) the damaged frame in which the letter has been removed, (d) result image.

4 Conclusion

In this paper, we present a novel inpainting algorithm. Each unknown pixel estimate is adapted by the local geometric similarity between the neighboring window and the training window, the isophote direction is built into the algorithm itself. We provide WLS method which offers a convenient way of finding the optimal solution to fully exploit the geometric similarity. It is superior to existing methods in preserving sharp edges and isophote direction continuity. Therefore ,it has the capability of inpainting thick areas without over-smoothing effects.

Finally, we want to note that a natural extension of the proposed method is it can be employed to improve error concealment results [11].

References

1. Ashikhmin, M.: Synthesizing natural textures. In: 2001 ACM Symposium on Interactive 3D Graphics, pp. 217–226. ACM Press, Los Angeles (2001)
2. Bertalmio, M., Sapiro, G., Caselles, V., Ballester, C.: Image Inpainting. In: Proceedings of SIGGRAPH 2000, pp. 417–424. ACM Press, New Orleans (2000)
3. Tschumperle, D., Deriche, R.: Vector-valued image regularization with PDES's: A common framework for different application. IEEE Trans. pattern Anal. Mach. Intell. 27, 506–517 (2005)
4. Chan, T., Shen, J.: Mathematical models for local non-texture inpainting. SIAM J. Appl. Math. 62, 1019–1043 (2001)
5. Chan, T., Shen, J.: Non-texture inpainting by curvature-driven diffusions. J. Visual Comm. Image Rep. 12, 436–449 (2001)
6. Telea, A.: An image inpainting technique based on the fast marching method. J. Graphics Tools 9, 23–34 (2004)
7. Wang, Z., Zhou, F., Qi, F.: Inpainting thick image regions using isophote propagation. In: Proc. IEEE Int. Conf. Image Processing, vol. 3, pp. 689–692. IEEE Press, Altanta (2006)
8. Kim, S.: An O(N) level set method for Eikonal equation. SIAM J. Scientific Computing 22, 2178–2193 (2001)
9. Li, X., Orchard, M.: Edge directed prediction for lossless compression of natural images. IEEE Trans. Image Processing 10, 813–817 (2001)
10. Li, X., Orchard, M.: New edge directed interpolation. IEEE Trans. Image Processing 10, 1521–1526 (2000)
11. Li, X., Orchard, M.: Novel sequential error concealment techniques using orientation adaptive interpolation. IEEE Trans. on Circuits and Systems for video technology 12, 30–40 (2000)
12. Kang, M.G., Katsagelos, A.K.: Simultaneous iterative image restoration and evaluation of the regularization parameter. IEEE Trans. Signal Process 40, 2329–2334 (1992)
13. Bertozzi, A.L., Esedoglu, S., Gillette, A.: Inpainting of Binary Images Using the Cahn–Hilliard Equation. IEEE Trans. Image Processing 16, 285–291 (2007)

Evidence Theory-Based Multimodal Emotion Recognition

Marco Paleari, Rachid Benmokhtar, and Benoit Huet

EURECOM
2229, route des Cretes,
Sophia Antipolis, France
{paleari,benmokhtar,huet}@eurecom.fr

Abstract. Automatic recognition of human affective states is still a largely unexplored and challenging topic. Even more issues arise when dealing with variable quality of the inputs or aiming for real-time, unconstrained, and person independent scenarios. In this paper, we explore audio-visual multimodal emotion recognition. We present SAMMI, a framework designed to extract real-time emotion appraisals from non-prototypical, person independent, facial expressions and vocal prosody. Different probabilistic method for fusion are compared and evaluated with a novel fusion technique called NNET. Results shows that NNET can improve the recognition score (CR$^+$) of about 19% and the mean average precision of about 30% with respect to the best unimodal system.

1 Introduction

It is commonly accepted that in most media, human communications forms, and notably in art expressions, emotions represent a valuable source of information. Changes in people's affective state play a significant role in perception and decision making during human to human interaction. Several studies have, therefore, been investigating how to automatically extract and use the affective information in everyday Human Computer Interactions (HCI) scenarios [1].

The ability to recognize and track the user affective state has the potential to enable a computing system to initiate interactions with the user based on changes in the perceived affective state rather than to simply respond to commands. Furthermore emotions can be used as valuable characteristics to dynamically tag media for future retrieval or summarization which may help to bridge the semantic gap.

In this paper, we explore audio-visual multimodal emotion recognition of acted emotions and a novel fusion technique [2] called NNET which bases on Evidence Theory.

Related works usually focus on three main modalities for the automatic recognition of the affective states; these are:

1. **Physiology:** The affective state is appraised through the modulations emotions exert to the Autonomous Nervous System (ANS). Signals such as heath

B. Huet et al. (Eds.): MMM 2009, LNCS 5371, pp. 435–446, 2009.

beat or skin conductivity are detected through ad hoc input devices. The estimation can be very reliable [3,4] and it is less sensitive to the acting of emotions than the one extracted from the auditory and visual modalities. The main limitation is related to the intrusiveness of the sensing devices which make this modality impracticable for most HCI scenarios.

2. **Visual:** The affective state is evaluated as a function of the modulations of emotions on facial expressions, gestures, postures, and generally body language. The data are captured through a camera, allowing for non-intrusive system configurations. The systems are generally very sensitive to the video quality both in term of Signal to Noise Ratio (SNR) and in term of illumination, pose, and size of the face on the video and is the most sensitive to false, acted facial expressions. Most of the works use facial expressions [5,6,7,8]; only few use gesture, posture, or combinations of gestures with facial expressions [9].

3. **Auditory:** The affective state can finally be estimated as a modulation of the vocal signal. In this case data are captured through a microphone, once again, allowing for non intrusive system configurations [10]. The estimation can be very accurate. The processing needs clean voice data; SNR inferior to 10 dB can severely reduce the quality of the estimation [11]. Furthermore the processing still cannot handle the presence of more than one voice in the audio stream.

Only few works have investigated the possibility to fuse together visual and auditory affective estimation [12,13,11]. Most of them only did person dependent affect recognition. Some of them took into account non realistic scenarios with people having dots on their faces to enhance the tracking of the facial movements and none of them, to our knowledge, took into account low or variable quality videos. Furthermore we could not retrieve information about the computational cost of the algorithms involved and in particular we were not able to discern the systems working in real time from the others.

In our scenario a person should be able to sit in front of her computer and have her affective status appraised in real time starting from the video with audio retrieved from a standard web-cam. The video quality is therefore much lower than the one currently used for research, as well as the audio. Furthermore, even though, person dependent evolution of the training set will be available we would like the system to work with any person sitting in front of the computer requiring therefore person in-dependency. In this kind of scenario we also have to foresee issues with the input signals, for example in the case more people are speaking at once or no ambient light is present to enlighten the user face.

In this paper we present SAMMI [14,15], a system which uses multimodality to overcome modality dependent signal issues and to improve the accuracy of the recognition while in presence of both signals together with different classifier fusion techniques. We, then, present NNET, a tool presented in [2], which uses the Evidence Theory to extract reliable classifications. We used such a system for fusing together the results from the unimodal classifiers; we detail and comment the results of these experiments.

2   eNTERFACE'05

One characteristic which seriously affect the performance of an emotion recognition system is related to the quality of the data used for training and testing. In realistic scenarios a system cannot deal with all the kind of data. Having a training database including samples as similar as possible to the true scenario is therefore crucial.

A part from the quality of the samples (both in term of SNR, compression, illumination, etc. and in term of the quality of the acting/spontaneous emotions expressions) a factor which obviously influences the results is the number of considered emotions. Indeed, some databases which were used in literature only consists of 2-3 emotions, some arrive at 16.

Unfortunately, the researching community still lack of available good quality multimodal audio-visual databases. We based our research on the eNTERFACE'05 database. The eNTERFACE database [16] is a publicly available multimodal audio-visual emotion database containing videos of subjects coming from 14 different nationalities.

The base contains 44 subjects presenting the 6 "universal" human emotions (anger, disgust, fear, happiness, sadness, and surprise), through 5 different sentences. The average video length is about 3 seconds summing up to 1320 shots and more than one hour of video. Videos are recorded in a Lab environment: Subjects are in frontal view with studio lightening condition and gray uniform background (see Fig. 1). Audio is recorded with a high quality microphone placed at around 30 cm from the subject mouth. All experiments were driven in English although only about 14% of the subjects were native English speaker. Subjects were not professional actors.

We have previously [15] evaluated the quality of this database pointing out some weaknesses of the base mainly related to compression issues (See Fig. 2) and to the quality of the emotional expression acted by the 44 subjects. In particular, one characteristic influencing our results is the fact that the database has one single tag per shot. Our scenarios often need a real-time, frame-to-frame, evaluation of the performed emotion; we are, therefore, trying to extract information that the one that it is given to us. Furthermore, the lack of neutral

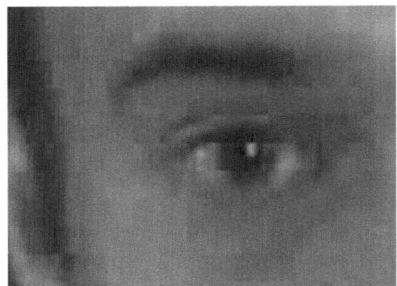

Fig. 1. Example frame   **Fig. 2.** Zoom on the eye

samples in the database cause a not irrelevant number of "transitional"/neutral frames to be tagged as emotionally relevant and used for training. An ad-hoc system built up to extract one single evaluation per shot would easily improve the recognition score of our system.

In [15] we also point out how some of these peculiarities motivate us to develop algorithms which should be robust in realistic scenarios.

3   SAMMI

We have overviewed the eNTERFACE bimodal database. In this section, we detail SAMMI: Semantic Affect-enhanced MultiMedia Indexing, a framework explicitly designed for extracting reliable real-time emotional information through multimodal fusion of affective cues.

The main objective of SAMMI is to emotionally tag video. In this contest, emotions can play an important role, but we claim that they cannot play a sole role and should be coupled with other semantic tag to build effective HCIs. SAMMI (see Fig. 3) does this by coupling affective information with other content information extracted with state of the art techniques [17,18].

A module called "Dynamic Control" in Fig. 3 is committed to adapt the various fusion algorithms and content based concept extractors to the quality of the signals in input. For example, if the sound quality is detected to be low then, the relevance of the vocal emotional estimation with respect to the one of the video emotional estimation will be reduced. This is very important in order to make the system more reliable and to loose some constraints.

For the purpose of this paper, we will concentrate on the modules committed to extract the emotional appraisal. These modules work on two inputs: The video for the facial expressions and the audio for the prosodic vocal expressions.

3.1   Feature Extraction

Facial Expressions: For our system we have chosen to base our system on facial feature points (FP) (see Fig. 5) and tested two approaches: The first based on

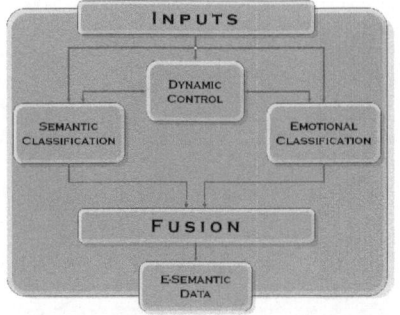

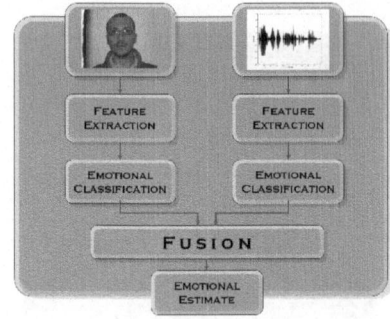

Fig. 3. SAMMI's architecture   **Fig. 4.** Multimodal emotion recognition

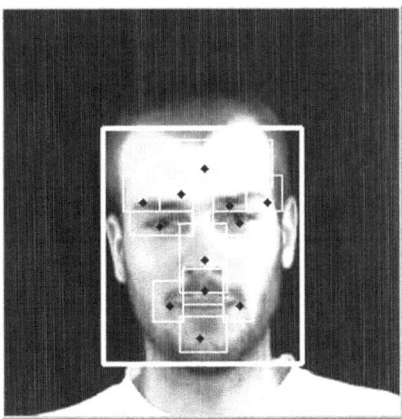

Fig. 5. Facial Feature Points

the facial FP absolute movements and the second based on relative movements of couples of facial FP[1].

We want SAMMI to run in real-time, setting a constraint in term of complexity of the algorithms we could use. We are therefore using the Tomasi implementation of the Lukas Kanade (LK) algorithm which is embedded in the Intel OpenCV library [19].

We have built a computationally cheap feature point detector for the first frame. This module works as follows: It analyzes the first frame and detect the position of the face, of the eyes and of the mouth with three classifiers based on Haar-features; it detects 12 FP regions by applying a 2D face template to the found face; for each found region we search points[2] which will be tracked with the Lukas Kanade algorithm; finally for each region it computes the center of mass of the points belonging to that particular region finally obtaining the coordinates of 12 points which will be used for the emotional estimation.

This algorithm presents some limitations. Firstly, because the Haar-based classifier demonstrates not to be precise enough. In particular, even though the face is very often correctly recognized, the surrounding bounding box can sensibly change between two consecutive frames. We tried to partially overcome this issue by computing multiple positions in subsequent frames and by intelligently choosing the most probable bounding box; this approach does nevertheless make us lose some information about the first frames.

Secondly, our 2D model works with scaling/zooming of the face (the Haar-based classifiers deal with this transformation), and, thanks to the fact that

---

[1] For example, we take into account the openness of the mouth or the shape of the eyebrows simply by computing the distance between the top and bottom point of the mouth, or by looking at the relative vertical position of two points on the eyebrows.

[2] The number of these points may vary according to lightening conditions, on the particular region, and on the subject. We imposed a maximum at 50 points per region.

the LK points tend to attach to the position with big intensity changes in the luminance of the image, it also deals with small rotations around the z axis (i.e. the axis perpendicular to the screen plane) and x axis (i.e. the horizontal axis) but does not work properly for the rotation around the y axis (i.e. the vertical one). A 3D model will be more appropriate but it will also need some more computational power to be computed. Further works will investigate the possibility to apply such a model.

Thirdly, although in average the founded points should follow the movements inside the feature point regions, the estimation of the movement may not be precise enough. A different scheme for FP extraction is being currently tested in our laboratory which directly computes the position of the relevant FPs by analyzing the vertical and horizontal histograms of the mouth and eyes regions [20] and by applying some simple morphological operations [21].

Vocal Expressions: Our approach to the extraction of affective appraisals from the voice is similar to the one described by Noble in [10]. The approach bases on the PRAAT open source software [22]. Through PRAAT we extract the fundamental frequency f_0, the first 5 formants f_1, f_2, f_3, f_4, f_5, the signal intensity, the harmonicity (i.e. the degree of acoustic periodicity, also called Harmonics-to-Noise Ratio), ten Mel-Frequency Cepstral Coefficients (MFCC) and ten Linear Predictive Coefficients (LPC).

This approach has one main limitation; indeed the same information about the spectral envelope of the vocal tract is represented three different times with three different methods. The quantity of overlapping information is therefore significant. Although SVM should be able to handle big feature vectors, it is often better to reduce the size of the training vector to reduce the complexity of the model.

3.2   Emotional Classification

Two different classifiers are currently used for testing which are Support Vector Machines (SVM) and Neural Networks (NN).

We want to take into account the temporal information brought by the evolution of the video and audio signals to the emotions. For this purpose, we temporally window the signals (the FP positions or the audio features). One second windows are currently being used for every signal. For each windowed signal we compute two models: One statistical evaluation based on mean value, standard deviation, variance, 5 quantiles, minimum, and maximum (with the relative positions inside the 1 second window); and one polynomial evaluation based on a first grade polynomial regression coupled with the number of the zero crossings.

3.3   Classifier Fusion

Classifier fusion is an important step of the classification task. It improves recognition reliability by taking into account the complementarity between classifiers.

Several schemes have been proposed in the literature according to the type of information provided by each classifier as well as their training and adaptation abilities. A state of the art is proposed in [23].

SAMMI performs fusion between estimations resulting from different classifiers or modalities. The output of such a module boosts the performances of the system. Since with NN and SVM the classification step is computationally cheap, we are allowed to use multiple classifiers at the same time without impacting too much on the performances. From the other side classification boosting, with too many classifiers, it is not an available option.

Multiple classifier fusion strategies have been tested and evaluated including Max, Vote, Mean, Bayesian combination and the new NNET which will be discussed in the following section.

4   Evidence Theory

Probabilistic methods have an inherent limitation: Most treat imprecision but ignore the uncertainty and ambiguity of the system (information to be fused). Evidence theory allows dealing with the uncertain data.

4.1   Applications to Fusion

The objective is to associate for each object x (frame), one class from the set of classes $\Omega = \{w_1, .., w_M\}$. This association is given via a set of training of N samples. Each sample can be considered as a part of belief for one class of Ω. This belief degree can be assimilated to evidence function m^i, with 2 focal elements: The class of x^i noted w_q, and Ω. So, if we consider that the object x^i is near to x, then a part of belief can be affected to w_q and the rest to Ω. The mass function is obtained by decreasing function of distance as follow:

$$\begin{cases} m^i(\{w_q\}) = \alpha^i \phi_q(d^i) \\ m^i(\Omega) = 1 - \alpha^i \phi_q(d^i) \end{cases} \tag{1}$$

Where $\phi(.)$ is a monotonically decreasing function such as an exponential function $\phi_q(d^i) = \exp\left(-\gamma_q(d^i)^2\right)$, and d^i is an Euclidean distance between the vector x and the ith vector of training base. $0 < \alpha < 1$ is a constant which prevents a total affectation of mass to the class w_q when x and i^{th} samples are equal. γ_q is a positive parameter defining the decreasing speed of mass function. A method for optimizing parameters (α, γ_q) has been described in [24].

We obtain N mass functions, which can be combined into a single one using the equation (Eq. 2).

$$m(A) = (m^1 \oplus ... \oplus m^N) = \sum_{(B_1 \cap ... \cap B_N) = A} \prod_{i=1}^{N} m^i(B_i) \tag{2}$$

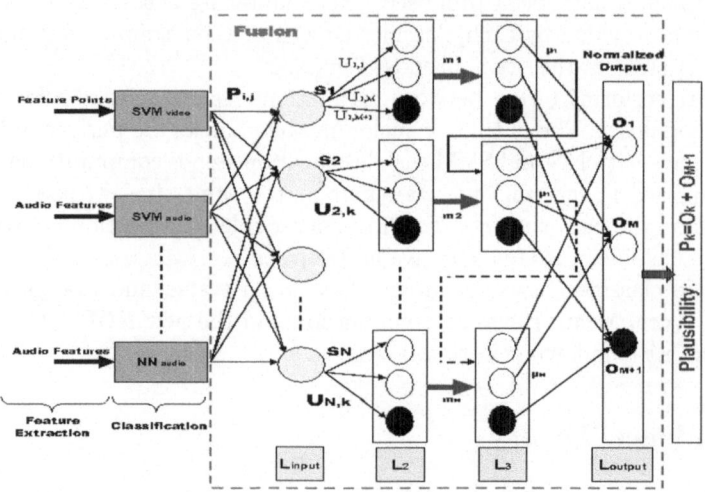

Fig. 6. NNET classifier fusion structure

4.2 Neural Network Based on Evidence Theory

We propose to resume work already made with the evidence theory in the connectionist implementation [2,24], and to adapt it to classifier fusion. For this aim, an improved version of Radial Basis Function neural network based on evidence theory [2] which we call NNET, with one input layer L_{input}, two hidden layers L_2 and L_3 and one output layer L_{output} (Fig. 6) has been devised. Each layer corresponds to one step of the procedure as briefly described below:

Layer L_{input}: Contains N units (prototypes). It is identical to an RBF network input layer with an exponential activation function ϕ. d is a distance computed using training data and dictionary created (clustering method). K-means is applied on the training data in order to create a "visual" dictionary of the frames.

$$s^i = \alpha^i \phi(d^i) \tag{3}$$

Layer L_2: Computes the belief masses m^i (Equ. 4) associated to each prototype. It is composed of N modules of $M+1$ units each (Equ. 5). The units of module i are connected to neuron i of the previous layer. Note that each frame can belong to only one class.

$$\begin{cases} m^i(\{w_q\}) = \alpha^i u_q^i \phi(d^i) \\ m^i(\Omega) = 1 - \alpha^i \phi(d^i) \end{cases} \tag{4}$$

$$\begin{aligned} m^i &= (m^i(\{w_1\}), ..., m^i(\{w_{M+1}\})) \\ &= (u_1^i s^i, ..., u_M^i s^i, 1 - s^i) \end{aligned} \tag{5}$$

where u_q^i is the membership degree to each class w_q, q class index $q = \{1, ..., M\}$.

Layer L_3: The Dempster-Shafer combination rule combines N different mass functions in one single mass. It's given by the conjunctive combination (Eq. 2). For this aim, the activation vector $\vec{\mu^i}$ can be recursively computed using the following formula:

$$\begin{cases} \mu^1 = m^1 \\ \mu_j^i = \mu_j^{i-1} m_j^i + \mu_j^{i-1} m_{M+1}^i + \mu_{M+1}^{i-1} m_j^i \\ \mu_{M+1}^i = \mu_{M+1}^{i-1} m_{M+1}^i \end{cases} \tag{6}$$

Layer L_{output}: In [24], the output is directly obtained by $O_j = \mu_j^N$. The experiments show that this output is very sensitive to the number of prototype, where for each iteration, the output is purely an addition of ignorance. Also, we notice that a small change in the number of prototype can change the classifier fusion behavior. To resolve this problem, we use normalized output (Eq. 7). Here, the output is computed taking into account the activation vectors of all prototypes to decrease the effect of an eventual bad behavior of prototype in the mass computation.

$$O_j = \frac{\sum_{i=1}^{N} \mu_j^i}{\sum_{i=1}^{N} \sum_{j=1}^{M+1} \mu_j^i} \tag{7}$$

The different parameters $(\Delta u, \Delta \gamma, \Delta \alpha, \Delta P, \Delta s)$ can be determined by gradient descent of output error for an input pattern x. Finally, the maximum of plausibility P_q of each class w_q is computed.

$$P_q = O_q + O_{M+1} \tag{8}$$

5 Results

In this section, we will see how this novel approach performs on our database and we explain the results. We used roughly 60% of the data (i.e. 912 shots) for training the classifiers and the NNET and the remaining (i.e. 378 shots) for the evaluation. The results are obtained by testing the system on the remaining 5 subjects (the train base is rather unbalanced presenting 20% samples for the emotion anger, 18% for disgust, 14% for fear, 14% for happiness, 19% for sadness, and finally 13% for surprise).

The performance has been measured using the standard precision and recall metrics, in particular the Mean Average Precision (MAP) for the first 33% of the responses and the Positive Classification Rate (CR$^+$).

In the Table 1, we compare the results obtained from the NNET classifier fusion with the NN and SVM classifier outputs as well as with the Max, Vote, Mean, Beyesian combination fusion systems.

Firstly, we notice that Bayesian combination and NNET approaches outperform other systems in term of CR$^+$ and MAP. Both systems improve the CR$^+$ of

Table 1. Classification accuracy for all emotions

	Anger	Disgust	Fear	Happiness	Sadness	Surprise	CR$^+$	MAP
Video NN	0.420	0.366	0.131	0.549	0.482	0.204	0.321	0.205
Audio NN	0.547	0.320	0.151	0.496	0.576	0.169	0.354	0.234
Video SVM	0.342	0.342	0.193	0.592	0.426	0.244	0.320	0.211
Audio SVM	0.627	0.220	0.131	0.576	0.522	0.162	0.361	0.253
Max	0.612	0.378	0.120	0.619	0.586	0.185	0.384	0.260
Vote	**0.666**	0.422	0.142	0.622	0.495	0.161	0.391	0.296
Mean	0.635	0.406	0.150	0.721	0.600	0.206	0.415	0.331
Bayesian	0.655	**0.440**	0.159	**0.743**	0.576	0.235	**0.430**	0.335
NNET	0.542	0.388	**0.224**	0.633	**0.619**	**0.340**	0.428	**0.337**

a relative 19% and the MAP of a relative 32% with respect to the best unimodal system.

Secondly, some interesting points can be discussed regarding the performances per concept:

- NNET improves the CR$^+$ of the emotions which are usually classified with the worst scores (i.e. fear and surprise). This phenomenon can be explained by the positive impact of the evidence theory in the conflicting situations, where the incertitude is taken into account.
- A less positive impact can be observed for the NNET on some other emotions due to the limitation of our trains set when classification rates of the unimodal systems are already good (e.g. anger or happiness).
- The Bayesian combination fusion system achieves better improvements on the emotions which are usually better recognized by the unimodal systems (e.g. anger or happiness). This is normal because the product between the evaluations, intrinsic in the Bayesian combination returns much higher results for the emotions which are consistently recognized by the unimodal systems.

These results give us the impression that the NNET tool could be used in some scenarios when the objective is to maintain the average classification score while reducing the margin between the best recognized and the worst recognized emotions.

Indeed, NNET demonstrates to be a valuable tool, when dealing with incertitude and specifically when wanting to discern positive samples from negative samples; if for example we had in our testing base neutral samples, then NNET will probably do a good job in cutting these samples out. In our particular case, we observe that the Evidence Theory characteristics, boosting up results when multiple concepts are concurrently present in one scene, cannot be exploited.

NNET presents, nevertheless, some drawbacks: Firstly, it needs a training step which is not demanded by the other classifier fusion techniques discussed in this paper; Secondly, NNET are more computationally expensive than the other fusion techniques.

6   Concluding Remarks

In this paper, we have presented SAMMI, a framework for semantic affect-enhanced multimodal indexing of multimedia excerpts, and NNET, a classifier fusion technique based on the evidence theory. We have therefore seen how these two systems works together and we have commented the results.

NNET improves the CR^+ of about the 19% and the MAP of about the 32% with respect to the best unimodal classification system. Average results are similar to the one obtained by a classifier fusion system based on the Bayesian combination, but we have discussed how the evidence theory allows to improve the score of the worst recognized emotions thus reducing the gap between the best and the worst recognized emotions.

Future works will investigate new classification method such as Gaussian Mixture Models (GMM) and Hidden Markov Model (HMM). HMMs are very promising in the case of emotions since it allows us to better take into account the temporal information of the affective expressions [25].

A dimensionality reduction techniques such as Linear Discriminant Analysis (LDA), Principal Component Analysis (PCA), or Non-negative Matrix Factorization (NMF) will be tested, to reduce the size of the feature vectors used as input of the classifiers [26].

References

1. Picard, R.: Affective Computing. MIT Press, Cambridge (1997)
2. Benmokhtar, R., Huet, B.: Neural network combining classifier based on Dempster-Shafer theory for semantic indexing in video content. In: Cham, T.-J., Cai, J., Dorai, C., Rajan, D., Chua, T.-S., Chia, L.-T. (eds.) MMM 2007. LNCS, vol. 4351, pp. 196–205. Springer, Heidelberg (2006)
3. Lisetti, C., Nasoz, F.: Using noninvasive wearable computers to recognize human emotions from physiological signals. EURASIP Journal on ASP 11, 1672–1687 (2004)
4. Villon, O., Lisetti, C.L.: Toward Building Adaptive User's Psycho-Physiological Maps of Emotions using Bio-Sensors. In: Proceedings of KI (2006)
5. Mase, K.: Recognition of facial expression from optical flow. Proceedings of IEICE Transactions E74, 3474–3483 (1991)
6. Essa, I.A., Pentland, A.P.: Coding, Analysis, Interpretation, and Recognition of Facial Expressions. IEEE Transactions PAMI 19(7), 757–763 (1997)
7. Cohen, I., Sebe, N., Garg, A., Lew, S., Huang, T.: Facial expression recognition from video sequences. In: Proceedings of ICME, pp. 121–124 (2002)
8. Pantic, M., Rothkrantz, L.: Toward an Affect-Sensitive Multimodal Human-Computer Interaction. Proceedings of IEEE 91, 1370–1390 (2003)
9. Gunes, H., Piccardi, M.: Bi-modal emotion recognition from expressive face and body gestures. Journal NCA 30(4), 1334–1345 (2007)
10. Noble, J.: Spoken Emotion Recognition with Support Vector Machines. PhD Thesis (2003)
11. Zeng, Z., Hu, Y., Liu, M., Fu, Y., Huang, T.S.: Training combination strategy of multi-stream fused hidden Markov model for audio-visual affect recognition. In: ACM MM, pp. 65–68 (2006)

12. Busso, C., Deng, Z., Yildirim, S., Bulut, M., Lee., C., Kazemzadeh, A., Lee, S., Neumann, U., Narayanan, S.: Analysis of emotion recognition using facial expressions, speech and multimodal information. In: Proceedings of ICMI, pp. 205–211 (2004)
13. Audio-Visual Affect Recognition through Multi-Stream Fused HMM for HCI. In: CVPR. vol. 2 (2005)
14. Paleari, M., Huet, B., Duffy, B.: SAMMI, Semantic Affect-enhanced MultiMedia Indexing. In: SAMT (2007)
15. Paleari, M., Huet, B.: Toward Emotion Indexing of Multimedia Excerpts. In: CBMI (2008)
16. Martin, O., Kotsia, I., Macq, B., Pitas, I.: The eNTERFACE05 Audio-Visual Emotion Database. In: Proceedings of ICDEW (2006)
17. Galmar, E., Huet, B.: Analysis of Vector Space Model and Spatiotemporal Segmentation for Video Indexing and Retrieval. In: ACM CIVR (2007)
18. Benmokhtar, R., Huet, B.: Multi-level Fusion for Semantic Video Content Indexing and Retrieval. In: Proceedings of AMR (2007)
19. IntelCorporation: Open Source Computer Vision Library: Reference Manual (November 2006), http://opencvlibrary.sourceforge.net
20. Vukadinovic, D., Pantic, M.: Fully automatic facial feature point detection using Gabor feature based boosted classifiers. In: Proceedings of IEEE ICSMC, pp. 1692–1698 (2005)
21. Sohail, A.S.M., Bhattacharya, P.: Detection of Facial Feature Points Using Anthropometric Face Model. In: Proceedings of SPIEMP, vol. 31, pp. 189–200 (2006)
22. Boersmal, P., Weenink, D.: Praat: doing phonetics by computer (January 2008), http://www.praat.org/
23. Benmokhtar, R., Huet, B.: Classifier fusion: Combination methods for semantic indexing in video content. In: Kollias, S.D., Stafylopatis, A., Duch, W., Oja, E. (eds.) ICANN 2006. LNCS, vol. 4132, pp. 65–74. Springer, Heidelberg (2006)
24. Denoeux, T.: An evidence-theoretic neural network classifer. In: Proceedings of IEEE SMC, vol. 31, pp. 712–717 (1995)
25. Cohen, I., Garg, A., Huang, T.S.: Emotion recognition from facial expressions using multilevel HMM. In: NIPS (2000)
26. Benmokhtar, R., Huet, B.: Low-level feature fusion models for soccer scene classification. In: 2008 IEEE ICME (2008)

Sketch-on-Map: Spatial Queries for Retrieving Human Locomotion Patterns from Continuously Archived GPS Data

Gamhewage C. de Silva, Toshihiko Yamasaki, and Kiyoharu Aizawa

Department of Information and Communication Engineering
The University of Tokyo, 102B2, 7-3-1 Hongo, Bunkyo-ku, Tokyo 113-8656, Japan
{chamds,yamasaki,aizawa}@hal.t.u-tokyo.ac.jp

Abstract. We propose a system for retrieving human locomotion patterns from tracking data captured within a large geographical area, over a long period of time. A GPS receiver continuously captures data regarding the location of the person carrying it. A constrained agglomerative hierarchical clustering algorithm segments these data according to the person's navigational behavior. Sketches made on a map displayed on a computer screen are used for specifying queries regarding locomotion patterns. Two basic sketch primitives, selected based on a user study, are combined to form five different types of queries. We implement algorithms to analyze a sketch made by a user, identify the query, and retrieve results from the collection of data. A graphical user interface combines the user interaction strategy and algorithms, and allows hierarchical querying and visualization of intermediate results. The sketch-based user interaction strategy facilitates querying for locomotion patterns in an intuitive and unambiguous manner.

Keywords: Sketch-based querying, Locomotion patterns, Spatial queries, GPS data, Multimedia retrieval.

1   Introduction

Continuously archived location data, obtained by tracking persons or objects, are useful in several application areas such as surveillance, navigational assistance, and behavioral studies. While different types of sensors are used for tracking indoors or in medium-sized outdoor areas, the Global Positioning System (GPS) provides a means of tracking over a very wide geographical area with reasonable accuracy. The tracking data can be indexed by date, time and location, in order to speed up retrieval.

In some applications such as traffic parameter estimation, it is often necessary to search the archived data for a particular pattern of locomotion. Such queries can be categorized as *spatial queries* [8]. This is usually performed by reducing the search space using other criteria and viewing the tracking results manually to retrieve the desired locomotion pattern. Ability to query a collection of tracking

B. Huet et al. (Eds.): MMM 2009, LNCS 5371, pp. 447–458, 2009.

data directly by a particular locomotion pattern will greatly enhance the efficiency of retrieval, and allow identification and analysis of long term behavioral patterns. Therefore, developing spatial queries to retrieve locomotion patterns in large collections of tracking data solves an important research problem.

However, facilitating spatial queries on a collection of tracking data from a large geographical area is a challenging task. This task is further complicated when the data are captured over a long period of time. There should be an intuitive and non-restrictive way to input queries on locomotion patterns into a computer. Such queries can entail very different levels of complexity. For example, possible queries might include the following:

- "Which route did I take when I went from Tokyo to Yokohama last month?"
- "How many times have I travelled to places outside Tokyo since January?"

Sketching is a common method used by people to specify or describe patterns of movement. With several common factors such as area, distance and direction, sketching and locomotion has an intuitive mapping between them. Despite different sketching habits and techniques, people are able to interpret sketches made by others. Therefore, sketching is a highly prospective candidate for synthesizing queries on locomotion patterns.

In this research, we propose a system for spatial querying of locomotion patterns in a large collection of continuously archived GPS data. The queries are specified by making sketches with a pointing device on a map displayed on a computer screen. We design a user interaction strategy that facilitates searching for different types of locomotion patterns with sketches that are simple, intuitive and unambiguous. We also design and implement algorithms for searching for segments of GPS data that match the patterns specified by the queries. The system consists of a graphical user interface that combines the user interaction strategy and the algorithms with interactive visualization for efficient retrieval.

The rest of this paper is organized as follows: Section 2 is a brief review of related work; Section 3 outlines the aquisition of GPS data; Section 4 describes the user interaction strategy, and the algorithms for retrieval; Section 5 presents the user interface and describes how the systems is used for retrieval; Section 6 contains a brief discussion regarding the design and implementation issues; Section 7 concludes the paper with suggestions for future directions.

2   Related Work

A number of researches use continuously archived GPS data to associate photos and video with locations and create visualizations on maps [5][9][15]. Morris et al. [12] propose a framework for automatic modeling of recreation travel using GPS data collected at recreation sites. The *Cabspotting Project* [1] analyses a collection of GPS data from a large number of taxi cabs in an urban area in order to discover the invisible dynamics contained within the data. Liao et al. [11] propose a hierarchical Markov model that can learn and infer a person's daily movements using GPS data.

There has been some research towards a framework for spatial querying of locomotion patterns. Egenhofer [4] demonstrated how imprecise spatial queries can be dealt with in a comprehensible manner, using topological relations. A relational algebra is proposed there, for verifying the consistency of the resulting topological representations. Gottfried [7] uses a locomotion base and a set of relations to represent locomotion patterns, with emphasis on healthcare applications. However, an effective user interaction strategy for submitting queries is essential to utilize the above framework to retrieve locomotion patterns.

So far, there has been little research on user interfaces for spatial querying. Ivanov and Wren [8] use simple spatial queries to specify the direction of movement along a corridor for video retrieval from surveillance cameras. Kimber et al. [10] propose a method of object based video playback, that can be used as a means of querying for locomotion patterns. Recently, we proposed three basic types of sketch-based queries for retrieval of human locomotion patterns from a home-like smart environment [2]. However, having been designed for a small area with bounded regions, this system is not scalable to an outdoor environment.

3   Data Acquisition

This research is based on a collection of continuously archived GPS data from a handheld GPS receiver. One of the authors has been continuously carrying a *Garmin*® *GPSmap 60CSx* GPS receiver for data acquisition, since November 2007. Data are collected at all times other than when signals are not received. The author also carried a *SenseCam*® device [16] on certain days, for verification purposes. The following is a summary of the data considered in this work:

- Duration: November 21, 2007 to April 20, 2008
- Area: Covers an approximate land area of 200,000km^2
- Altitudes: 0 to 950 m above mean sea level
- Speeds: Up to 294 km/h
- Total distance travelled: 13500 km (approx.)
- Signal reception: 8-24 hours per day (approx.)

The sampling interval of the GPS receiver is 1 second. Contiguous samples corresponding to the same GPS coordinates are combined to form a *location record* in the format shown in Table 1. The average speed is calculated by dividing the

Table 1. Format of GPS Location Records

Date and Time	Altitude	Distance	Duration	Speed	Direction	Lattitude	Longitude
2007/11/22 9:22:02	29 m	24 m	0:00:13	7 km/h	199°	N35°44.713'	E139°44.755'
2007/11/22 9:22:15	29 m	39 m	0:00:21	7 km/h	200°	N35°44.700'	E139°44.749'
2007/11/22 9:22:36	29 m	31 m	0:00:17	7 km/h	198°	N35°44.681'	E139°44.741'

distance between current and previous samples by the difference between the starting timestamps of the two entries. The direction recorded is the angle of the vector from previous location to current, measured clockwise from north. The number of entries during a day varies between approximately 2000 and 20,000, according to the movement of the person and the availability of signals. The average number of location records is approximately 3000 per day.

A few problems arise when extracting location and motion information using GPS data. Due to poor or no reception of signals, the receiver might fail to record data at certain locations. Hence, the collected data form a discrete time sequence that is 'undefined' for certain time intervals. Several factors contribute to the amount of noise present in GPS data [13], making it difficult to model and eliminate noise. Therefore, the proposed system has to be designed to perform well with incomplete and noisy data.

4   System Description

We take the following approach to facilitate querying the continuously archived location records for locomotion patterns by sketching on a geographical map. First, the GPS data are grouped to form segments according to two basic types of locomotion. The user interaction strategy is designed by identifying basic sketch primitives required for defining locomotion patterns and combining them to form queries. Algorithms are designed for querying the collection of segments using parameters extracted from the sketched queries. A grapical user interface is designed and implemented to integrate the segments, queries and algorithms. The following subsections decribe each of these in detail.

4.1   Segmentation of GPS Data

The result of data acquisition, as described in Section 3, is a large number of location records ordered by time. We intend to combine these records to form a set of non-overlapping *locomotion segments*, representing the nature of the person's movement. The user queries can now be made on the collection of the segments instead of the entire data set, allowing more efficient retrieval. We select the following two classes of locomotion, for segmentation of location records:

1. **Navigating:** instances of locomotion where the person makes a regular change of location with time. Examples are walking, driving or riding in a vehicle.
2. **Non-navigating:** instances of locomotion where a person stays within a small neighborhood. Examples are a room, a bus stop etc.

We employ a constrained hierarchical clustering algorithm [3] to cluster the location records into locomotion segments. This algorithm is capable of classifying location records at an average accuracy of 94.4%. The average accuracy of the timestamps at segment boundaries is approximately 2 minutes and 45 seconds.

Table 2. Attributes of *Navigating* Segments

Starting Time	Ending Time	Starting Location	Ending Location
2007/11/27 10:32:41	2007/11/27 13:21:20	N35°37.866', E139°16.032'	N35°37.820', E139°16.039'
2007/11/27 13:27:40	2007/11/27 16:29:11	N35°37.864', E139°16.024'	N35°39.894', E139°45.695'

Table 3. Attributes of *Non-nagivating* Segments

From	To	Mean Location	Maximum deviation
2007/11/27 10:16:23	2007/11/27 10:32:41	N35°37.938' ,E139°16.188'	0.001161
2007/11/27 13:21:20	2007/11/27 13:27:40	N35°37.844' ,E139°16.036'	0.000276

The location records are indexed by the results of classification, for efficient querying. Tables 2 and 3 show example entries of indices for navigating and non-navigating segments respectively. The standard deviations of the lattitudes and longitudes of locations in non-navigating segments are calculated and compared, and the larger value is recorded as *maximum deviation* in Table 3. This is intended to be used in visualization of results.

4.2 User Interaction Strategy

Our objective here is to design a user interaction strategy that allows the user to query for locomotion patterns by making a sketch pattern on a map. This should allow the user to submit different types of queries in a simple and intuitive manner. There should be no ambiguity between different types of queries. The relative complexity of queries is also important. Less specific queries, resulting in a large amount of results, should take less effort to sketch. On the other hand, it is fine for specific and more detailed queries to require more time and effort to sketch them. The algorithms should be sufficiently robust to interpret the sketches correctly, despite different sketching habits and speeds. We take a user-centered approach based on that of a previous system we developed for querying locomotion patterns in an indoor environment [2], for designing a strategy that fulfills the above objectives.

In real-life descriptions of locomotion patterns, a person is usually referred to as being within a *region*, or moving along a given *path* within or between such regions. Therefore we identify the entities "region" and "path" as the *query primitives* for locomotion patterns. The size and boundaries of regions are sometimes approximate or even ambiguous, while they can be precisely specified at other times. When describing a path, sometimes only the starting and ending locations are important. On other occasions, the path traversed is important. This diversity of detail is inherent to sketching, making it a strong candidate for specifying locomotion patterns.

We select *sketch primitives* for the query primitives mentioned above, based on the results of a user study on sketching locomotion patterns. During one section of this study, we asked the subjects to sketch multiple locomotion patterns and studied the common notations among sketches. We observed that a region was specified with a closed or near-closed curve in approximately 85% of the sketches. In 75% of the sketches, paths were specified with arrows with arrowheads drawn in different styles. It was also observed that some of the subjects implied the direction of a path by the direction the line was drawn, instead of drawing an arrowhead. Based on these observations, we select the following two sketch primitives for a region and a path. The user draws a closed curve on the map to specify the enclosing region. A path is specified by sketching a line, to which an arrowhead is automatically added. These two sketch primitives form the basis of the following detailed spatial queries:

- **Type 1: staying within a region:** The user specifies the region by sketching a closed curve around it. Figure 1a corresponds to the query "in Ireland."
- **Type 2: entering a region:** The user specifies the region, and draws a path into the region from outside of it. Figure 1b corresponds to the query "entering Stanford University premises"
- **Type 3: leaving a region:** The user specifies the region, and draws a path from inside of the region to the outside. Figure 1c corresponds to the query "leaving Stanford University premises."
- **Type 4: moving from one region to another, irrespective of the actual path taken:** The user specifies the two regions (in any order), and

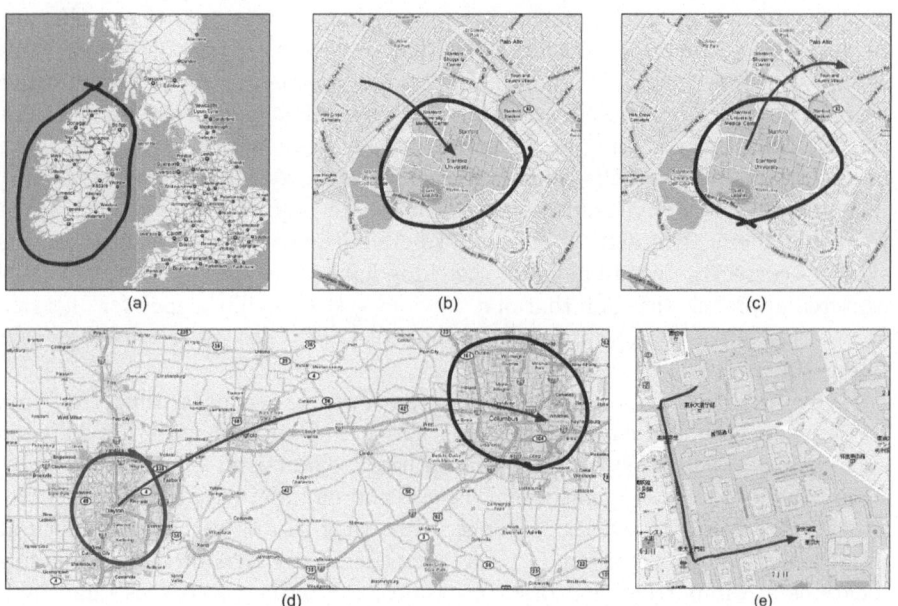

(a)   (b)   (c)

(d)   (e)

Fig. 1. Different types of spatial queries

then draws a path from the originating region to the destination. Figure 1d corresponds to the query "From Dayton to Columbus."

– **Type 5: specific path:** The user draws the path that he/she wishes to retrieve, on the map. The path has to be drawn as an open curve, to prevent misdetection as a region. Figure 1e corresponds to a query for a specific path within the premises of the University of Tokyo.

The queries are sketched on images created by extracting map segments from the *Google Maps* Database [6]. A query results in one or more ordered set of points in the form of $P = \{p_1, p_2, ...p_N\}$ where $p_i = (X_i, Y_i)$ are specified in image coordinates. After preprocessing and coordinate conversion (from screen coordinates to latitudes and longitudes), the system analyzes the sketch and determines the type of query. Search algorithms are selected accordingly to extract and display the results. The following section describes these stages in detail.

4.3   Search Algorithms

First, the sets of points are processed to identify the type of sketch primitive they belong to. If a set of points forms a closed curve, it is identified as a region primitive and trimmed to remove the parts that do not enclose the region. If a set of points does not form a closed curve, it is identified as a path primitive.

The type of the query is determined after preprocessing using a hierarchical decision making process, following the columns in Table 4 from left to right. This method prevents ambiguities in interpretation of query types. The possibilities that are not listed in the table are not recognized as valid queries. However, the decision making process can be expanded to cover such possibilities, where necessary. For example, a query with multiple regions and no path can be used to query for segments within only those regions.

In the next stage, the points are converted from image coordinates to geographical coordinates (latitudes and longitudes). Since Google Maps use Mercator's projection with an adjustment, we calculate these points using the inverse Mercator projection [14]. After conversion, a path is represented as an ordered set of points $P = \{p_1, p_2, ..., p_N\}$ on the path. A region is represented by a set of points $R = \{r_1, r_2, ..., r_K\}$ along its perimeter. The detected region(s) and path are submitted as input to the search algorithm for the appropriate query type. The following is a description of the search algorithms we propose:

Table 4. Identifying the Type of Query

No. of Primitives	No. of Regions	Relationship between the path and region/s	Query Type
1	1	N/A	1
1	0	N/A	5
2	1	Path starts inside the region	2
2	1	Path finishes inside the region	3
3	2	Path starts inside one region and finishes inside the other	4

– **Query type 1**
To perform this query type, we retrieve all segments (both navigating and non-navigating) that are contained within the region specified by the sketch. The results are ordered by the starting time of the segments.

– **Query type 2**
We retrieve all navigating segments with their starting points contained in the sketched region. The results are ordered by the starting time of the segments.

– **Query type 3**
We retrieve all navigating segments with their end points contained in the sketched region. The results are ordered by the starting time of the segments.

– **Query type 4**
Let R_1 be the region where the path starts from, and R_2 be the region where the path ends. First, we extract navigating segments that have starting points in R_1. From this set of segments, the set of segments with end points in R_2 are extracted. The results are ordered by the starting time of the segments.

– **Query type 5**
We define a *search area* by expanding the dimensions of the bounding box of the sketched path by 10% in each direction. We extract a set of *candidate paths* by selecting all navigating segments contained within this search area. For each candidate path $C = \{c_1, c_2, ..., c_M\}$ selected as above, we apply the following directional matching algorithm.

1. Set overall mean distance $D = 0$
2. for the first point c_1 in the selected candidate path C, find the closest point p_a in P
3. Add the geographical distance between c_1 and p_a to D
4. Repeat steps 2 and 3 for the next point in C and $P' = \{p_a, p_{a+1}, ..., p_N\}$ until all points in C are used in the calulation
5. Divide D by M and record the overall mean distance

This algorithm looks for navigating segments that are similar to the sketched path, while preserving direction. The results are presented to the user in ascending order of the overall mean distance. The common approach is to set a threshold value and remove the results that have higher distances than the threshold value. However, given that sketches can be imprecise, we believe that it is desirable to display all the results after ordering them accordng to the similarity.

5   User Interface Design

We design a graphical user interface based on the above strategy for retrieval of locomotion patterns. The interface is designed in such a way that only a pointing device is necessary to use it. The interface facilitates hierarchical segmentation of the data collection interactively using spatial queries, temporal queries or a combination of them to retrieve the desired results. The following sections describe how the user interface allows these types of queries.

5.1   Temporal Querying

The temporal queries also can be specified using sketches, making the interaction consistent with the query-by-sketch user interaction strategy for spatial queries. The users can sketch on a calendar-like interface to select a duration to retrieve data from. Figure 2a shows how a user queries for the duration "from the 2nd to the 5th of January, 2008". Where only one item is selected, clicking can be used in place of sketching, facilitating faster interaction.

Figure 2b shows the results retrieved from a temporal query. Once a selection is made, the map is scaled and scrolled to show only the regions where data have been captured. The non-navigating segments are shown as circles with the mean location as the center and scaled maximum deviation as the radius. The radius

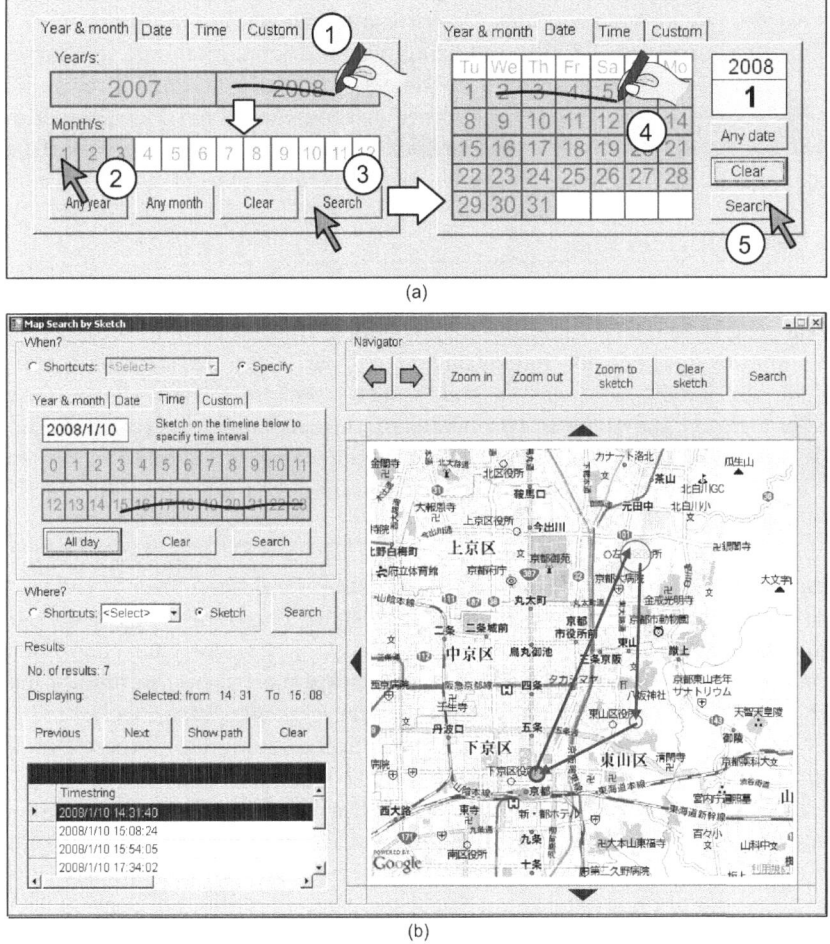

(a)

(b)

Fig. 2. Submitting temporal queries by sketching

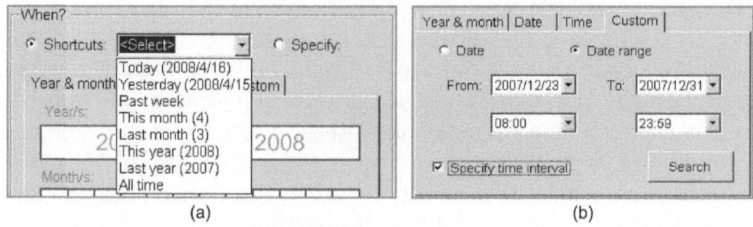

Fig. 3. Additional methods for submitting temporal queries

of the circle visualizes the confidence of the location estimation. This helps the user to identify the exact location with his memory and knowledge, where the accuracy of the data is less. The navigating segments are visualized with arrows. The detailed results for the segments are shown to the left of the map, and can be selected one at a time. The selected result is shown in red on the map.

Temporal querying is facilitated using two additional methods, to allow easier input. The user can choose some frequently-used time intervals directly from a combo box (Figure 3a). While the above methods are easy to use, sometimes it might be necessary to query the data for more precise time intervals. To allow this, controls for custom querying are provided in a separate tab (Figure 3b).

5.2   Spatial Querying

The user can start a spatial query by navigating the map to the region that he/she wishes to query. In addition to zooming, unzooming and scrolling, which are common methods for navigating to a location on an electronic map, we include the facility to *zoom to sketch*. The user can draw a closed curve to specify a region and zoom in to that region directly, as illustrated by Figure 4a. This is much faster and more efficient than the conventional method of zooming and scrolling, as both the location and the amount of zoom required can now be specified using a single interaction.

We implemented the user interaction strategy described in Section 4.3, to facilitate spatial querying. After the user reaches the desired area of the map, he can sketch spatial queries and retrieve the results. The results for non-navigating segments are shown in the same format as that of temporal querying. For navigating segments, the actual GPS data points are plotted on the map, joined by lines. The color of the data points and the line segments change from blue to red with time, to indicate direction. Figures 4b and c show spatial queries of Types 4 and 5 respectly, together with the retrieved results.

The user can perform more detailed searches, by combining temporal and spatial searches. A temporal query reduces the search space on the map by scrolling and zooming in to the area where GPS data were recorded for the specified interval. Instead of browsing the retrieved segments (described in Section 5.1), the user can submit a sketch and filter the results.

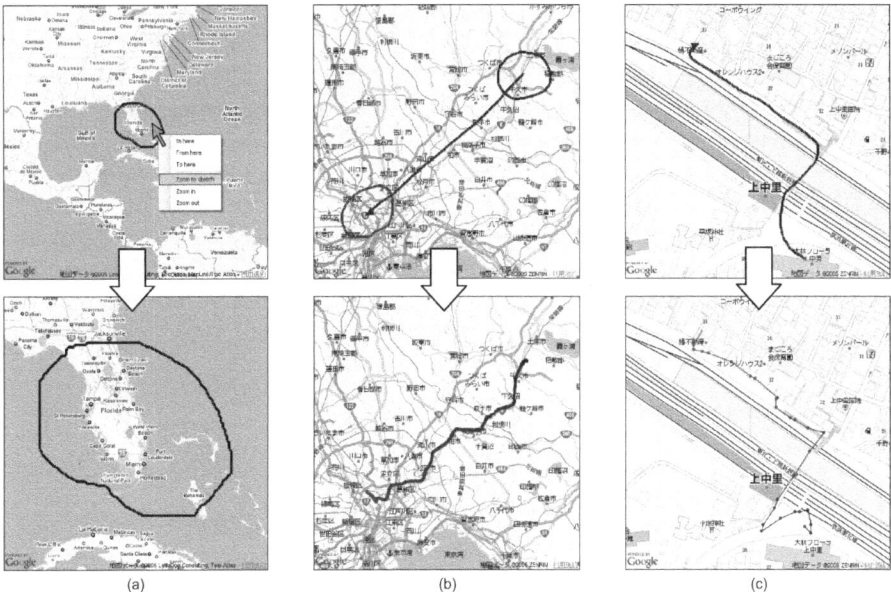

Fig. 4. Example queries and results

6   Discussion

While there exist other researches that classify GPS data into activities at higher semantic levels, we decided to segment the data into only two basic classes of locomotion. The main reason for this decision is the logical mapping of simple sketches to such classes. The sketch primitive "path" maps naturally to *navigating* segments. Both *navigating* and *non-navigating* segments can be referred to as contained within a "region".

Speed is one of the important aspects in locomotion patterns. While regions and paths map naturally from sketches to locomotion patterns, specifying the speed seems not so straightforward. The system will be much more versatile if speed can be incorporated to the queries in a way that is easy to specify.

There were several programming issues in implementing the proposed user interaction strategy on publicly available application programming interfaces for mapping. For example, Google Maps API does not allow sketching in the same way as a typical drawing application (that is, by holding the mouse button down and moving the pointer to make the sketch). We use several programming workarounds to enable free hand sketching on the map.

7   Conclusion

We have developed a system for retrieving human locomotion patterns from continuously archived GPS data. The proposed sketch-based interaction strategy provides an intuitive way of querying the large collection of data. Five types of queries have been designed by combining two simple sketch primitives, making effective and unambiguous querying possible. The clustering algorithm and the user interaction strategy are integrated using an interface that supports both spatial and temporal querying, facilitating fast retreival of results. The clustering algorithm and the user interaction strategy can be applied to other applications based on GPS data, such as vehicle fleet monitoring and interfaces for navigational support systems.

The user interaction strategy can be enhanced by both designing new types of queries using the current primitives, and adding new primitives. Creating a formal model for the queries including time and speed will increase the versatility of spatial queries. We are working on designing user studies for evaluating the usability of the proposed system and obtaining feedback.

References

1. Cabspotting. Exploratorium: Museum of science, art and human perception (2006), http://cabspotting.org
2. de Silva, G.C., Yamasaki, T., Aizawa, K.: Spatial querying for retrieval of locomotion patterns in smart environments. In: Proc. ACM Multimedia 2007, pp. 803–806. ACM SIGMM (September 2007)
3. de Silva, G.C., Yamasaki, T., Aizawa, K.: Human Locomotion Segmentation by Constrained Hierarchical Clustering of GPS Data. In: Proc. ITE 2008 (August 2008) (to appear)
4. Egenhofer, M.: Spatial query by sketch. Journal of Visual Languages and Computing 8(4), 403–424 (1997)
5. Gemmell, J., Aris, A., Roger, R.L.: Telling stories with mylifebits. In: IEEE ICME (July 2005)
6. Google. Google maps api - google code (2008), http://code.google.com/apis/maps/
7. Gottfried, B.: Spatial health systems. In: Pervasive Health Conference and Workshops, pp. 81–87. ACM SIGMM (2006)
8. Ivanov, Y.A., Wren, C.R.: Toward spatial queries for spatial surveillance tasks. In: Proc. Pervasive PTA 2006, pp. 803–806. ACM SIGMM (September 2006)
9. Kim, I.-J., Ahn, S.C., Ko, H., Kim, H.-G.: Persone: Personalized experience recording and searching on networked environment. In: ACM CARPE (October 2006)
10. Kimber, D., Dunnigan, T., Girgensohn, A., Shipman, F., Turner, T., Yang, T.: Trailblazing: Video playback control by direct object manipulation. In: IEEE ICME 2007, July 2007, pp. 1015–1018 (2007)
11. Liao, L., Patterson, D.J., Fox, D., Kautz, H.: Learning and Inferring Transportation Routines. Artificial Intelligence 171(5-6), 311–331 (2007)
12. Morris, S., Gimblett, R., Barnard, K.: Probabilistic travel modeling using GPS data. In: Int'l Congress on Simulation and Modeling, pp. 61–66 (December 2005)
13. Parkinson, B.W., Gilbert, S.W.: Navstar: Global positioning system - ten years later. Proceedings of the IEEE 71(10), 1177–1186 (1983)
14. Snyder, J.P.: Map Projections - A Working Manual, U.S. Geological Survey Professional Paper. United States Government Printing Office, Washington, D.C. (1987)
15. Tancharoen, D., Yamasaki, T., Aizawa, K.: Practical experience recording and indexing of life long video. In: ACM CARPE 2005, pp. 61–66 (November 2005)
16. Wood, K., Fleck, R., Williams, L.: Playing with SenseCam. In: UbiComp (2004)

Personalized News Video Recommendation

Hangzai Luo[1], Jianping Fan[1], Daniel A. Keim[2], and Shin'ichi Satoh[3]

[1] CS Department, UNC-Charlotte, USA
{hluo,jfan}@uncc.edu
[2] University of Konstanz
keim@uni-konstanz.de
[3] NII, Tokyo, Japan
satoh@nii.ac.jp

Abstract. In this paper, a novel framework is developed to support personalized news video recommendation. First, multi-modal information sources for news videos are seamlessly integrated and synchronized to achieve more reliable news topic detection, and the contexts between different news topics are extracted automatically. Second, topic network and hyperbolic visualization are seamlessly integrated to support interactive navigation and exploration of large-scale collections of news videos at the topic level, so that users can gain deep insights of large-scale collections of news videos at the first glance. In such interactive topic network navigation and exploration process, users' personal background knowledge can be exploited for selecting *news topics of interest* interactively, building up their mental models of news needs precisely and formulating their queries easily by selecting the visible news topics on the topic network directly. Our system can further recommend the relevant web news, the new search directions, and the most relevant news videos according to their importance and representativeness scores. Our experiments on large-scale collections of news videos have provided very positive results.

Keywords: Topic network, personalized news video recommendation.

1 Introduction

There are more than 30,000 television stations in the world, these television stations broadcast large amounts of TV news programs (news videos) every day. Due to the large number of broadcast channels and TV news programs, finding news videos of interest is not a trivial task: (a) Most existing content-based video retrieval (CBVR) systems assume that users can formulate their information needs precisely either in terms of keywords or example videos. Unfortunately, users may not be able to know what is happening now (i.e., if they know it, it is not a news), thus it is very hard for them to find the suitable keywords or example videos to formulate their news needs precisely without obtaining sufficient knowledge of the available news topics of interest. Thus there is an urgent need to develop new techniques for detecting news topics of interest from large-scale collections of news videos to assist users on finding news videos of interest more effectively. (b) Because the same news topic can be discussed in many TV channels and news programs, topic-based news search may return large

B. Huet et al. (Eds.): MMM 2009, LNCS 5371, pp. 459–471, 2009.

amount of news videos and thus simple news search via topics may bring the serious problem of information overload to the users. (c) Most existing CBVR systems treat all users equally while completely ignoring the diversity and rapid change of their search interests. Besides the rapid growth of broadcast TV channels and news programs, we have also observed different scenarios of news needs from different users, thus it is very difficult to come up with a *one size fits all* approach for accessing large-scale collections of news videos. (d) The keywords for news topic interpretation may not be expressive enough for describing the rich details of video contents precisely and using only the keywords may not be able to capture users' search intentions effectively. Thus visualization is becoming a critical component of personalized news video recommendation system [3-8]. (e) The objectives for personalized video recommendation and content-based video retrieval are very different, which make it unsuitable to directly apply the existing CBVR techniques for supporting personalized video recommendation. Thus supporting personalized news video recommendation is becoming one important feature of news services [1].

In this paper, we have developed a novel framework to support personalized news video recommendation, and our framework is significantly different from other existing works: (a) Rather than performing semantic video classification and automatic video content understanding on the single-modal channel of news videos, we have seamlessly integrated multi-modal information channels (audio, video and closed captions) to achieve more reliable news topic detection. (b) The associations among the news topics (i.e., inter-topic contexts) are determined automatically and an interestingness score is automatically assigned to each news topic via statistical analysis. Such interestingness scores are further used to select the news topics of interest and filter out the less interesting news topics automatically. (c) A hyperbolic visualization tool is incorporated to enable interactive topic network exploration and allow users to gain deep insights of large-scale collections of news topics at the first glance, so that they can make better search decisions and find the news topics of interest interactively according to their personal preferences. The user's personal knowledge, search intentions and contexts, which are disclosed and captured in the interactive topic network navigation and exploration process, can be taken into consideration for personalizing the topic network and the search results. (d) A novel video ranking algorithm is developed for recommending the relevant web news, the new search directions and the most relevant news videos according to their importance and representativeness scores for a given news topic.

2 Related Work

The Informedia Digital Video Library project at CMU has achieved significant progresses on analyzing, indexing and searching of large-scale collections of news videos [11-12], and several applications have been reported, such as semantic video understanding, multi-modal decision fusion, keyword-based video retrieval and query result visualization. Unfortunately, automatic video understanding is still an open problem for computer vision [7-8].

Visualization is widely used to help the users explore large amount of data collections and find interesting parts interactively [3-8]. In-spire [3] has been developed for visualizing and exploring large-scale text document collections, where statistics of news reports is put on a world map to inform the audiences of the "hotness" of regions and the relations among the regions. One major problem for such geographical location-based visualization approach is that some hot regions (such as middle-east) may be too busy but other places may be empty. TimeMine [4] is proposed to detect the most important reports and organize them through the timeline with the statistical models of the word usage. Another system, called newsmap [5], can organize news topics from Google news on a rectangle, where each news story covers a visualization space that is proportional to the number of related news pages reported by Google. News titles are drawn in the visualization space allocated to the relevant news topic.

It is very attractive to visualize the news topics according to their importance scores, but another aspect of news topics (i.e., inter-topic contexts) are missed by all these existing techniques (e.g., this could be a serious problem for all these existing techniques because the news topics of inetrest may never happen individually). Context between the news topics is also very important for users to make better search decisions, especially when the users are not familiar with the available news topics and their search goals or ideas are still fuzzy. The inter-topic context can give a good approximation of the interestingness of the news topics (i.e., like PageRank for characterizing the importance of web pages). Thus it is very attractive to integrate topic network (i.e., news topics and their inter-topic contexts) for characterizing the interestingness of the news topics, assisting users on making better search decisions and suggesting the future search directions.

ThemeRiver [6] can visualize large-scale collections of news documents with the keywords or the themes. ThemeRiver can intuitively represent the distribution structure of the themes and the keywords in the collections. Such distribution structures of the themes and the keywords may be useful for disclosing statistical knowledge of large-scale collections of news documents, but they may not make any sense to the users according to their goals of news search because there is an interest gap between the distribution structures and the users' real news needs (e.g., news analysts may care such statistical knowledge, but general users as the news seekers may just care the news topics of interest and their inter-topic contexts).

When large-scale news collections come into view, the number of the available news topics could be very large and displaying all of them to the users may mislead them. To visualize the news topics of interest in a size-limited screen, most existing algorithms have to select the most significant news topics of interest according to their definitions of importance. Unfortunately, the importance score of a news topic may depend on two issues: (a) the relative importance of the given news topic in the pool of large-scale news video collections; (b) the personal preferences for each particular user which may not be known at the beginning. Thus selecting and disclosing only the most important news topics of interest according to the pre-defined criteria may hinder users to access some news topics, which are strongly related with their personal preferences but may not be significant in the large-scale news video collections. For example, the news topics for NBA playoff may be very interesting for basketball fans, but the news topics for president candidate ellection may always dominate the pool of news topics and have higher interestingness scores in general. Thus there is an urgent need to develop new algorithms which are able to take the user's personal preferences into consideration for defining the personalized interestingness scores of the news topics.

There are two well-accepted approaches for supporting personalized information retrieval [9-10]: *content-based filtering* and *collaborative filtering*. Unfortunately, all these existing personalized information recommendation techniques largely depend on the collections of users' profiles and the available text context descriptions, thus they cannot support new users effectively because their profiles may not be available. Because of the shortage of the available text descriptions of news videos, all these existing techniques cannot directly be extended for enabling personalized news video recommendation and there is an urgent need to develop news frameworks.

3   Personalized News Topic Recommendation

In this paper, an interactive approach is developed by incorporating *topic network* and hyperbolic visualization to recommend the *news topics of interest* for assisting users on accessing large-scale collections of news videos more effectively. To do this, an automatic scheme is first developed to construct the topic network for representing and interpreting large-scale collections of news videos at the topic level. In addition, a hyperbolic visualization technique is integrated to enable interactive navigation and exploration of large-scale topic network and recommend the news topics of interest according to the users' personal preferences.

Topic detection is important because many people often want to identify some specific news stories or topics that are relevant to their personal interests. For the TV news programs, there are three multi-modal information channels (audio, video and closed captions) that can be integrated and be synchronized to enable more reliable news topic detection. Because the inherent property of speech is purely semantic, lexical search from automatic speech recognition (ASR) transcripts has been treated as the most successful strategy for content-based video retrieval. The problem with the ASR transcripts is that the spoken words may not completely cover the abundant semantic contents available in the news video.

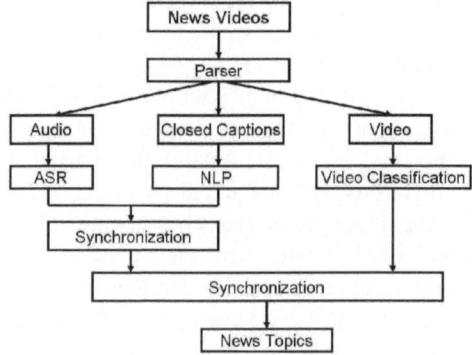

Fig. 1. The flowchart for synchronizing multiple sources for news topic detection

As shown in Fig. 1, we have developed a new scheme for automatic news topic detection by taking the advantage of multi-modal information channels (cross-media). First, automatic speech recognition (ASR), natural language processing (NLP), and semantic video classification are performed parallelly on these three multi-modal information channels to determime the keywords for news topic description from both the audio channel and the closed captions and detect the video concepts from the video channel. Second, the audio channel is synchronized with the closed captions, and the video channel is further synchronized with the audio channel and the closed captions. Finally, the news topic detection results from these three multi-modal information channels are integrated to boost the performance of our news topic detection algorithm. After the closed captions are synchronized with the news videos, we can assign the video shots to the most relevant news topics that are accurately detected from the closed captions. Thus all the video shots, which locate between the start time and the end time of a given new topic (that has been detected from the closed captions), are assigned to the given news topic automatically. Integrating multi-modal information channels for news topic detection can significantly enhance the detection accuracy.

The inter-topic contextual relationships are obtained automatically, where both the cosine similarity and the mutual similarity for the relevant news topics are used to define a new measurement for determining their inter-topic associations more precisely. The inter-topic context $\Upsilon(C_i, C_j)$ between two news topics C_j and C_i is determined by:

$$\Upsilon(C_i, C_j) = \alpha \cdot \Phi(C_i, C_j) + \beta \cdot \Psi(C_i, C_j), \qquad \alpha + \beta = 1 \qquad (1)$$

where the first part $\Phi(C_i, C_j)$ denotes the cosine similarity between the term weights for the text terms to interpret the news topics C_j and C_i, the second part $\Psi(C_i, C_j)$ indicates the mutual similarity between the text terms for interpreting the news topics C_j and C_i according to their co-occurrence probability, α and β are their relative importances.

The cosine similarity $\Phi(C_i, C_j)$ between the text terms for interpreting the news topics C_j and C_i can be defined as:

$$\Phi(C_i, C_j) = \frac{\sum_{l=1}^{N} w_l(C_i) \cdot w_l(C_j)}{\sqrt{\sum_{l=1}^{N} w_l(C_i)^2} \sqrt{\sum_{l=1}^{N} w_l(C_j)^2}} \qquad (2)$$

where N is the number of news documents (closed caption documents) in our collections, $w_l(C_i)$ and $w_l(C_j)$ are the weights for the text terms for interpreting the news topics C_j and C_i.

$$\begin{cases} w_l(C_i) = \log(f_l(C_i) + 1.0) \cdot \log \frac{N+1}{f_l + 0.5} \\ \\ w_l(C_j) = \log(f_l(C_j) + 1.0) \cdot \log \frac{N+1}{f_l + 0.5} \end{cases} \qquad (3)$$

where $f_l(C_i)$ and $f_l(C_j)$ are the frequencies of the text terms for interpreting the news topics C_j and C_i in the lth news document (closed caption document), f_l is the frequency of the lth news document which the news topics C_j and C_i occur in. The higher value of the cosine similarity $\Phi(C_i, C_j)$ implies the stronger association $\Upsilon(C_i, C_j)$ between the relevant news topics C_j and C_i.

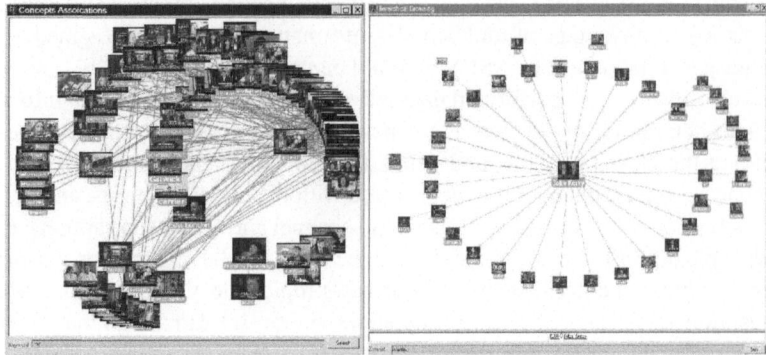

Fig. 2. Our large-scale topic network for organizing large-scale news videos

The mutual similarity $\Psi(C_i, C_j)$ between the news topics C_j and C_i can be defined as:

$$\Psi(C_i, C_j) = \log \frac{p(C_i, C_j)}{p(C_i) \cdot p(C_j)} \tag{4}$$

where $p(C_i, C_j)$ is the co-ocurrence probability of the relevant news topics C_j and C_i in the corpus, $p(C_i)$ and $p(C_j)$ are the individual ocurrence probability of the news topics C_j and C_i in the corpus. The underlying assumption behind the mutual similarity measurement $\Psi(C_i, C_j)$ is that two news topics co-occur frequently if they are strongly relevant. The higher value of the mutual similarity $\Psi(C_i, C_j)$ implies the stronger contexts $\Upsilon(C_i, C_j)$ between the relevant news topics C_j and C_i.

Thus each news topic is automatically linked with multiple relevant news topics with the higher values of the inter-topic contexts $\Upsilon(\cdot, \cdot)$. A portion of our large-scale topic network is given in Fig. 2, where the news topics are connected and organized according to the strength of their associations, $\Upsilon(\cdot, \cdot)$. One can observe that such topic network can provide a good global overview of large-scale collections of news videos at the topic level and can precisely characterize the interestingness of the relevant news topics, thus it can be used to assist users on making better search decisions.

To integrate the topic network for supporting personalized topic recommendation, it is very attractive to achieve graphical representation and visualization of the topic network, so that the users can obtain a good global overview of large-scale collections of news videos at the first glance and make better search decisions in the interactive topic network exploration and navigation process. Thus the underlying topic network visualization techniques should be able to provide a good balance between the local detail and the global context. The local detail is used to help users focus on the news topics of interest in their current focus. The global context is needed to tell the users where the other relevant news topics are (i.e., which news topics they can search for next step) and their contextual relationships with the news topic in the current focus, such global context can suggest the new search directions effectively. Thus supporting visualization and interactive navigation of the topic network is becoming a complementary and necessary component for personalized news video recommendation system and it may lead to the discovery of unexpected news videos and guide the future search directions effectively.

Unfortunately, visualizing large-scale topic network in a 2D system interface with a limited screen size is not a trivial task. To achieve more effective visualization of large-scale topic network, we have developed multiple innovative techniques: (a) highlighting the news topics according to their interestingness scores for allowing users to obtain the most important insights at the first glance; (b) integrating hyperbolic geometry to create more space for large-scale topic network visualization and reduce the potential overlappings via interactive exploration.

We have integrated both the popularity of the news topics and the importance of the news topics to determine their interestingness scores. The popularity of a given news topic is related to both the number of TV news programs which have discussed the given news topic and the time length for the same TV news program to report the given news topic. If one news topic is discussed by more TV news programs simultaneously or reported by the same TV news program repeatedly for a long time, it tends to be more interesting in general. The importance of a given news topic is related to its linkage structure with other news topics on the topic network. If one news topic is related to more news topics on the topic network, it tends to be more interesting. For example, the news topic for "roadside bond in Iraq" may strongly relate to the news topics of "gas price increase" and "stock price decrease". Thus the interestingness score $\rho(C_i)$ for a given news topic C_i is defined as:

$$\rho(C_i) = \lambda \cdot \frac{e^{m(c_i)} - e^{-m(c_i)}}{e^{m(c_i)} + e^{-m(c_i)}} + \eta \cdot \frac{e^{t(c_i)} - e^{-t(c_i)}}{e^{t(c_i)} + e^{-t(c_i)}} + \gamma \cdot \frac{e^{k(c_i)} - e^{-k(c_i)}}{e^{k(c_i)} + e^{-k(c_i)}} \qquad (5)$$

where $\lambda + \eta + \gamma = 1$, $m(c_i)$ is the number of TV news programs which have discussed or reported the given news topic C_i simultaneously, $t(c_i)$ is the time length (days) for the same TV news program to report the given news topic C_i repeatedly, $k(c_i)$ is the number of news topics linked with the given news topic C_i on the topic network. Such interestingness scores can be used to highlight the most interesting news topics and eliminate the less interesting news topics for reducing the visual complexity for large-scale topic network visualization and exploration.

Supporting graphical representation and visualization of the topic network can provide an effective solution for exploring large-scale collections of news videos at the topic level and recommending the *news topics of interest* to the users interactively for assisting them to make better search decisions. However, visualizing large-scale topic network in a 2D system interface with a limited screen size is a challenging task. We have investigated multiple solutions to tackle this challenge task: (a) A string-based approach is incorporated to visualize the topic network with a nested view, where each news topic node is displayed closely with the most relevant news topic nodes according to the values of their associations. The underlying inter-topic contexts are represented as the linkage strings. (b) The geometric closeness of the news topic nodes is related to the strength of their inter-topic contexts, so that such graphical representation of the topic network can reveal a great deal about how these news topics are connected. (c) Both geometric zooming and semantic zooming are integrated to adjust the levels of visible details automatically according to the discerning constraint on the number of news topic nodes that can be displayed per view.

Our approach for topic network visualization has exploited hyperbolic geometry [8]. The hyperbolic geometry is particularly well suited for achieving graph-based layout of the topic network, and it has "more space" than Euclidean geometry. The essence of our approach is to project the topic network onto a hyperbolic plane according to the inter-topic contexts, and layout the topic network by mapping the relevant news topic nodes onto a circular display region. Thus our topic network visualization scheme takes the following steps: (a) The news topic nodes on the topic network are projected onto a hyperbolic plane according to their inter-topic contexts by performing curvilinear component analysis (CCA), and such CCA process can be obtained automatically by preserving the local inter-topic contexts between the neighboring news topic nodes on the topic network, e.g., through minimizing the following error function:

$$E(\{C_i\}) = \frac{1}{2} \sum_{i=1}^{n} \sum_{j>i}^{n} \sigma_{ij} |\delta(C_i, C_j) - \Upsilon(C_i, C_j)|^2 \tag{6}$$

where $\Upsilon(C_i, C_j)$ is the strength of the inter-topic context between the news topics C_i and C_j, the weight factors σ_{ij} are chosen as a bounded and monotically descreasing function to allow the CCA projection algorithm to preserve the strong inter-topic contexts than of weak inter-topic contexts (i.e., preserving the contexts between neighboring news topic nodes on the topic network), and $\delta(C_i, C_j)$ is the location distance between the news topics C_i and C_j on the hyperbolic plane.

$$\delta(C_i, C_j) = 2 \cdot arctanh \left(\frac{|X_{c_i} - X_{c_j}|}{|1 - X_{c_i} \bar{X}_{c_j}|} \right) \tag{7}$$

where X_{c_i} and X_{c_j} are the physical locations of the news topics on the hyperbolic plane. In our current experiments, the weigh factors σ_{ij} are characterized by using a sigmoid function:

$$\sigma_{ij} = \frac{e^{\Upsilon(C_i, C_j)}}{e^{\Upsilon(C_i, C_j)} + 1} \tag{8}$$

Through CCA projection, our algorithm can precisely preserve the local inter-topic contexts, and the global geometry is also preserved effectively because the nearest neighborhoods for the neighboring news topics are overlapped. (b) After such context-preserving projection of the news topic nodes is obtained, Poincaré disk model [8] is used to map the news topic nodes on the hyperbolic plane onto a 2D display coordinate. Poincaré disk model maps the entire hyperbolic space onto an open unit circle, and produces a non-uniform mapping of the news topic nodes to the 2D display coordinate.

4   Personalized News Video Recommendation

Because the same news topic may be reported many times in the same TV news program or be discussed simultaneously by many TV news programs for different broadcast stations, the amount of the news videos under the same news topic could be very large. Thus topic-based news search via simply keyword matching may return large amount of news videos which are relevant to the same news topic. To reduce user's information overload, it is very important to develop new algorithms for ranking the news videos under the same news topic and recommending the most relevant news videos according to their importance and representiveness scores.

The news videos, which are relevant to the given news topic C_j, are ranked according to their importance and representiveness scores. For the given news topic C_j, the importance and representativeness score $\varrho(x|C_j)$ for one particular news video x is defined as:

$$\varrho(x|C_j) = \epsilon e^{-\Delta t} + (1-\epsilon)\frac{e^{\sigma(x|C_j)} - e^{-\sigma(x|C_j)}}{e^{\sigma(x|C_j)} + e^{-\sigma(x|C_j)}} \tag{9}$$

$$\sigma(x|C_j) = \zeta \cdot v(x|C_j) + \nu \cdot r(x|C_j) + \varsigma \cdot q(x|C_j)$$

where $\zeta + \nu + \varsigma = 1$, Δt is the time difference between the broadcast time for the given news video x for the particular TV news program and the time for the user to submit their requests, $v(x|C_j)$ is the visiting times for the given news video x from all the users, $r(x|C_j)$ is the rating score of the given news video x from all the users, $q(x|C_j)$ is the quality of the given news video.

We separate the time factor from other factors for news video ranking because the time factor is more critical than other factors for news video ranking (i.e., one topic can be treated as the news because it is new and tell people what is happening recently or what is discussing recently) and most people may just want to know the most recently reports for the given news topic. The quality $q(x|C_j)$ is simply defined as the frame resolution and the length of the given news video x. If a news video has higher frame resolution and longer length (be discussed for longer time), it should be more important and representative for the given news topic.

After the users' search goals (i.e., which are represented by the accessed news topics) are captured interactively, our personalized news video recommendation system can: (a) recommend top 5 news videos according to their importance and representativeness scores; (b) recommend other news topics of interest on the topic network which are most relevant to the accessed news topic and suggest them as the future search directions according to the user's current preferences, where the accessed news topic is set as the current focus (i.e., the center of the topic network); (c) recommend the most relevant online web news which are relevant with the accessed news topic, so that the user can also read the most relevant online web news; (d) record the user's search history and preferences for generating more reliable personalized topic network to make better recommendation in the future. Some experimental results are given in Fig. 3, and one can

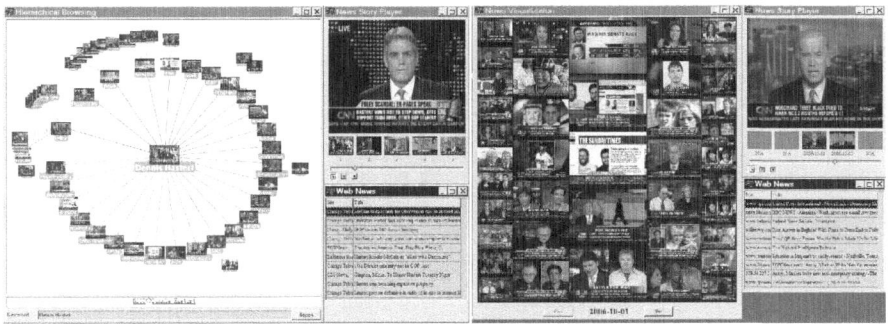

Fig. 3. Two examples for supporting personalized multi-modal news recommendation

conclude that our personalized news video recommendation system can effectively support multi-modal news recommendation from large-scale collections of news videos.

5   Algorithm Evaluation

We carry out our experimental studies by using large-scale collections of news videos (3 TV news channels captured 24 × 7 for more than 3 months). The topic network which consists of 4000 most popular news topics is learned automatically from large-scale collections of news videos. Our work on algorithm evaluation focus on: (1) evaluating the performance of our news topic detection algorithm and assessing the advantages for integrating multi-modal information channels for news topic detection; (2) evaluating the response time for supporting change of focus in our system, which is critical for supporting interactive navigation and exploration of large-scale topic network to enable user-adaptive topic recommendation; (3) evaluating the performance (efficiency and accuracy) of our system for allowing users to look for some particular news videos of interest (i.e., personalized news video recommendation);

Automatic news topic detection plays an important role in our personalized news video recommendation system. Based on this observation, our algorithm evaluation for our automatic news topic detection algorithm focuses on comparing its performance difference by combining different information channels for automatic news topic detection. We have compared three combination scenarios for news topic detection: (a) only the closed captions are used for news topic detection; (b) the closed captions and the audio channel are integrated and synchronized for news topic detection; (c) the closed captions, the audio channel and the video channel are seamlessly integrated and synchronized for news topic detection. As shown in Fig. 4, integrating multi-modal information channels (cross-media) for news topic detection can enhance the performance of our algorithm significantly.

One critical issue for evaluating our personalized news video recommendation system is the response time for supporting change of focus to enable interactive topic

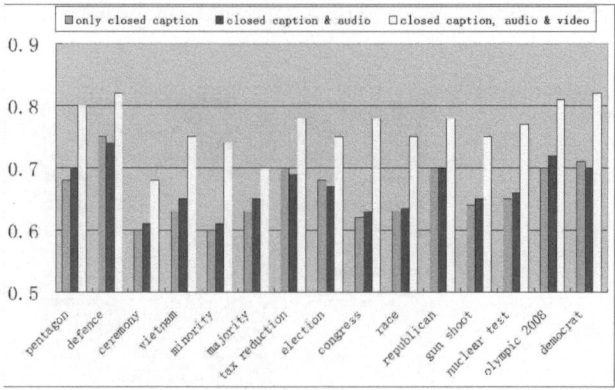

Fig. 4. The comparision results of our automatic news topic detection algorithm by integrating different information channels

network navigation and exploration, which is critical for supporting user-adaptive topic recommendation. In our system, the change of focus is used for achieving interactive exploration and navigation of large-scale topic network. The *change of focus* is implemented by changing the Poincaré mapping of the news topic nodes from the hyperbolic plane to the display unit disk, and the positions of the news topic nodes in the hyerbolic plane need not to be altered during the focus manipulation. Thus the response time for supporting change of focus depends on two components: (a) The computational time T_1 for re-calculating the new Poincaré mapping of large-scale topic network from a hyperbolic plane to a 2D display unit disk, i.e., re-calculating the Poincaré position for each news topic node; (b) The visualization time T_2 for re-layouting and re-visualizing the new Poincaré mapping of large-scale topic network on the display disk unit.

Because the computational time T_1 may depend on the number of news topic nodes, we have tested the performance differences for our system to re-calculate the Poincaré mappings for different numbers of news topic nodes. Thus our topic network with 4000 news topic nodes is partitioned into 5 different scales: 500 nodes, 1000 nodes, 2000 nodes, 3000 nodes, 3500 nodes and 4000 nodes. We have tested the computational time T_1 for re-calculating the Poincaré mappings of different numbers of news topic nodes when the focus is changed. From our experiments, we find that the computational time T_1 and the visualization time T_2 are not sensitive to the number of news topics, and thus re-calculating the Poincaré mapping and re-visualization for large-scale topic network can almost be achieved in real time. Thus our system can support change of focus in real time and achieve interactive navigation and exploration of large-scale topic network effectively.

Table 1. The precision and recall for supporting personalized news video recommendation

news topics	policy	pentagon	change	dennis hastert	matter
P/R	95.6% /97.3%	98.5% /98.9%	100% /99.2%	95.3% /88.3%	85.2% /85.3%
news topics	implant	wedding	haggard	scandal	ethic
P/R	90.2% /93.5%	96.3% /94.5%	96.5% /92.8%	96.6% /97.3%	93.3% /95.6%
news topics	gate	steny hoyer	democrat	safety	investigation
P/R	95.9% /96.8%	96.5% /96.2%	96.3% /97.1%	94.5% /94.8%	93.3% /96.5%
news topics	majority	leader	confirmation	child	tax reduction
P/R	99.2% /98.6%	93.8% /99.3%	94.5% /93.8%	91.3% /91.5%	98.5% /96.9%
news topics	secretary	veterm	ceremony	beijing 2008	program
P/R	100% /98.8%	99.8% /99.2%	99.3% /96.6%	99.2% /97.3%	83.5% /90.2%
news topics	honor	vietnam	lesson	teacher	conduct
P/R	91.2% /93.5%	98.8% /96.7%	90.3% /91.6%	93.8% /94.5%	87.92% /88.3%
news topics	minority	indonesia	president	republican	amish
P/R	100% /99.6%	96.8% /97.7%	100% /96.8%	91.6% /92.8%	99.5% /91.6%
news topics	o.j. sinpson	trial	money	nuclear test	china
P/R	95.6% /99.4%	90.5% /90.3%	100% /90.6%	100% /97.6%	97.3% /95.2%
news topics	john kerry	military	race	north korea	japan
P/R	100% /96.5%	100% /93.2%	100% /97.8%	100% /99.3%	98.5% /95.6%
news topics	election	leadship	school gun shoot	sex	message
P/R	100% /95.5%	92.8% /90.3%	100% /96.7%	97.5% /98.2%	88.3% /87.6%

For a given news topic of interest (news topic that is accessed by the particular user interactively), our system can further allow users to look for the most relevant news videos for the given news topic according to their importance and representative scores. To evaluate the effeciency and the accuracy of our personalized news video recommendation system, the *benchmark metric* includes *precision P* and *recall R*. The precision P is used to characterize the accuracy of our system for finding the most relevant news videos according to their importance and representativeness scores for the given news topic, and the recall R is used to characterize the efficiency of our system for finding the most relevant news videos according to their importance and representativeness scores for the given news topic.

Table 1 gives the precision and recall of our personalized news video recommendation system. From these experimental results, one can observe that our system can support personalized news video recommendation effectively, thus users are allowed to obtain the most relevant news videos according to their importance and representativeness scores for the requested news topic.

6   Conclusions

A novel framework is developed to support personalized news video recommendation. To allow users to obtain a good global overview of large-scale collections of news videos at the topic level, topic network and hyperbolic visualization are seamlessly integrated to achieve user-adaptive topic recommendation. Thus users can obtain the *news topics of interest* interactively, build up their mental models of news needs easily and make better search decisions by selecting the visible news topics directly. Our system can further recommend the relevant web news, the new search directions, and the most relevant news videos according to their importance and representativeness scores. Our experiments on large-scale collections of news videos have provided positive results.

Acknowledgment

This work is supported by National Science Foundation under 0601542-IIS and 0208539-IIS. Hangzai Luo is recently supported by Shanghai Pujiang Program under 08PJ1404600, NSFC 60496325 and 60803077, CSM 07dz5997, 863 R & D 2006AA010111.

References

1. Marchionini, G.: Information seeking in electronic environments. Cambridge University Press, Cambridge (1997)
2. Yang, B., Mei, T., Hua, X.-S., Yang, L., Yang, S.-Q., Li, M.: Online video recommendation based on multimodal fusion and relevance feedback. In: ACM CIVR 2007, pp. 73–80 (2007)
3. Wise, J.A., Thomas, J., Pennock, K., Lantrip, D., Pottier, M., Schur, A., Crow, V.: Visualizing the non-visual: Spatial analysis and interaction with information from text documents. In: IEEE InfoVis 1995, pp. 51–58 (1995)

4. Swan, R.C., Allan, J.: TimeMine: visualizing automatically constructed timelines. In: ACM SIGIR (2000)
5. Weskamp, M.: "Newsmap", `http://www.marumushi.com/newsmap/index.cfm`
6. Havre, S., Hetzler, B., Whitney, P., Nowell, L.: ThemeRiver: Visualizing thematic changes in large document collections. IEEE Trans. on Visualization and Computer Graphics 8(1), 9–20 (2002)
7. Luo, H., Fan, J., Yang, J., Ribarsky, W., Satoh, S.: Large-scale new video classification and hyperbolic visualization. In: IEEE VAST 2007, pp. 107–114 (2007)
8. Luo, H., Fan, J., Yang, J., Ribarsky, W., Satoh, S.: Exploring large-scale video news via interactive visualization. In: IEEE VAST 2006, pp. 75–82 (2006)
9. Lai, W., Hua, X.-S., Ma, W.-Y.: Towards content-based relevance ranking for video search. In: ACM Multimedia, pp. 627–630 (2006)
10. Teevan, J., Dumais, S., Horvitz, E.: Personalized search via automated analysis of interests and activities. In: ACM SIGIR (2005)
11. Wactlar, H., Hauptmann, A., Gong, Y., Christel, M.: Lessons learned from the creation and deployment of a terabyte digital video library. IEEE Computer 32(2), 66–73 (1999)
12. Christel, M.G., Yang, R.: Merging stryboard strategies and automatic retrieval for improving interactive video search. In: ACM CIVR 2007(2007)

Facet-Based Browsing in Video Retrieval: A Simulation-Based Evaluation

Frank Hopfgartner, Thierry Urruty, Robert Villa, and Joemon M. Jose

Department of Computing Science
University of Glasgow
Glasgow, United Kingdom
{hopfgarf,thierry,villar,jj}@dcs.gla.ac.uk

Abstract. In this paper we introduce a novel interactive video retrieval approach which uses sub-needs of an information need for querying and organising the search process. The underlying assumption of this approach is that the search effectiveness will be enhanced when employed for interactive video retrieval. We explore the performance bounds of a faceted system by using the simulated user evaluation methodology on TRECVID data sets and also on the logs of a prior user experiment with the system. We discuss the simulated evaluation strategies employed in our evaluation and the effect on the use of both textual and visual features. The facets are simulated by the use of clustering the video shots using textual and visual features. The experimental results of our study demonstrate that the faceted browser can potentially improve the search effectiveness.

Keywords: aspect based browsing, video retrieval, user simulation, log file analysis.

1 Introduction

With the rapid increase of online video services, such as YouTube, the need for novel methods of searching video databases has become more pressing. Much recent work, such as that represented by the TRECVID [6] research effort, aims to tackle the more difficult problems of content based video retrieval. However, overall performance of video retrieval systems to date are unsatisfactory. A number of interactive retrieval systems are proposed to address the many limitations of the state-of-the-art systems (e.g. [1,3]).

Most of these systems follow a "one result list only" approach, that is, the user query is focused on only one particular issue. In this approach, a user is not able to follow similar ideas he or she might think of during a retrieval session. Users can have a multi-faceted interest, which might evolve over time. Instead of being interested in only one topic at one time, users can search for various independent topics such as politics or sports, followed by entertainment or business.

In this paper, we study the concept of facet-based retrieval. We base our study on an improved version of an interactive video retrieval system which has

B. Huet et al. (Eds.): MMM 2009, LNCS 5371, pp. 472–483, 2009.

been introduced in [7] and propose a novel simulation methodology to evaluate the effectiveness of faceted browsing in which we simulate users creating new facets in an interface. We then discuss different strategies used in our simulation. Furthermore, we support our results by exploiting logfiles of a user study.

The rest of the paper is organised as follows. In Section 2 we introduce the research area of interactive video retrieval. Furthermore, we argue for the use of a facet-based graphical interface and present our system. Then, we propose a simulated user evaluation methodology. In Section 3, we first propose to iteratively cluster retrieval results based on their visual features. The results of the iterative clustering approach indicate that faceted browsing can be used to improve retrieval effectiveness. Subsequently, we analyse user logs from a previous user evaluation study [7] to verify our results in Section 4. In Section 5, we discuss the results of our experiment.

2   Interactive Video Retrieval

In this section, we discuss prior approaches in interactive video retrieval. Then, in Section 2.1, we introduce the concept of facet-based browsing and present our facet-based graphical interface in Section 2.2. Finally, in Section 2.3, we argue for the use of simulation to evaluate a video retrieval engine.

2.1   Background

Current interactive retrieval systems mainly addresses issues of query specification and result browsing. They all follow the same retrieval methodology: even though results will be presented in various different manners, the interfaces present the user only *one* single result list.

However, a user can have a multi-faceted interest, which might evolve over time. For example, a user interested in different aspects of football games wants to collect video shots showing (a) offside situations and (b) penalty kicks. Both situations are related, as they are both common situations in a football game; even though, within the game, there is no obvious relation between a player being offside and a penalty kick. While the state-of-the-art video retrieval interfaces provide only *one* search facility at one time, a user interested in the mentioned football aspects would have to perform his search tasks sequentially session by session, i.e. in searching for (a) and then starting a new session for (b). This means that if a user first wants to focus on finding video clips showing offside situations (a) and, during this search session, finds clips showing free kick situations (b), he has to decide whether he wants to continue searching for the offside situations (a) or to change his focus and continue searching for free kicks (b). Either way, at least one search trail will get lost, as the user has to ignore it. A facet-based retrieval interface, however, provides the user facilities to start additional retrieval sessions (facets) simultaneously and to reorganise materials between these parallel searches.

In order to address many of the problems identified here, we have developed a faceted retrieval system.

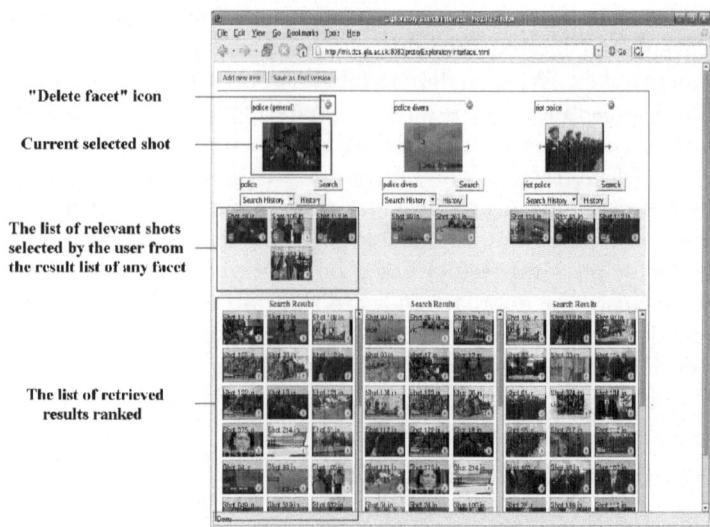

Fig. 1. Screenshot of the facet browsing interface

2.2   A Facet-Based Video Retrieval System

In this section, we introduce the implementation of a facet-based video retrieval system (see Figure 1). Further details can be found in [7]. As in most retrieval systems, it is divided into a frontend and a backend system.

It is split into one or more vertical panels, each panel representing a step or facet. When the system is initially started up, a single empty panel is displayed on the left of the screen, ready for the user. New panels can be created using the "Add new item" button on the top left of the screen, and will appear at the end of the storyboard, at the far right.

The interface makes extensive use of drag and drop. Shots on the search result list can be dragged and dropped onto the relevant shots area, which will add the shot to the facet's list of relevant shots. There is no restriction on what facet a result can be dragged onto, therefore it is possible to drag a result from one facet directly onto the relevant list of a different facet. Relevant shots can also be dragged and dropped between the different facets list of relevant shots, allowing the reorganisation of material across the different facets. Relevant shots can be removed from the relevance lists using a delete button given on the bottom left of each shot's keyframe.

2.3   Evaluation Methodology

Most interactive video retrieval systems are evaluated in laboratory based user experiments. This methodology, based on the Cranfield evaluation methodology, is inadequate to evaluate interactive systems [4]. The user-centred evaluation schemes are very helpful in getting valuable data on the behaviour of interactive search systems. However, they are expensive in terms of time and repeatability of such experiments is questionable. It is almost impossible to test all the variables involved in an interaction and hence compromises are needed on many aspects of testing. Furthermore, such methodology is inadequate in benchmarking various underlying adaptive retrieval algorithms. An alternative way of evaluating such systems is the use of simulations.

Finin [2] introduced one of the first user simulation modelling approaches. The "General User Modelling System" (GUMS) allowed software developers to test their systems by feeding them with simple stereotype user behaviour. Hopfgartner and Jose [4] employed a simulated evaluation methodology which simulated users interacting with state-of-the-art video retrieval systems. They argue that a simulation can be seen as a pre-implementation method which will give further opportunity to develop appropriate systems and subsequent user-centred evaluations. However, this approach to evaluate is not mature enough and we need to develop techniques to simulate user behaviour appropriate for the system under consideration.

Our objective is to study the bounds of the proposed faceted browser. We therefore employ the simulated evaluation methodology which assumes a user is acting on the system. If such a user is available, he or she will do a set of actions that, in their opinion, will increase the chance of retrieving more relevant documents. One way of doing this is to select relevant videos. By using a test collection like TRECVID, we will be able to use relevant documents available for our simulation.

In this paper, we adapt the simulation approach in simulating users interacting with a facet-based video retrieval interface. We discuss different strategies used in our evaluation. Starting from a text query, we first propose to iteratively cluster retrieval results based on their visual features in Section 3. The results of the iterative clustering approach indicate that faceted browsing can be used to improve retrieval effectiveness. In Section 4, we subsequently analyse user logs from a previous user study to verify our results.

3   Iterative Clustering

In this section, we present our method to simulate users creating new facets. The idea is to make use of clustering to create groups of similar objects. The clusters are assumed to be the facets of a user's search need and are hence used in the simulation. First, we explain the mechanisms of our algorithm using an iterative clustering technique, then we detail our experimental setup and the various simulations we made before finally discussing the experiment results.

3.1   Iterative Clustering Methodology

The main goal of our facet-based interface is to help the user to create a complex query with separated and structured views of different queries. Our iterative clustering approach mainly aims to simulate the user in his or her search task. Clusters of our algorithm are assumed to be the facets a real user may create in a search process. A user's first query has a high probability of being general, with the retrieved set of results containing different semantic topics. Our iterative clustering algorithm starts at this step. First, we cluster the retrieved results using textual and visual features. We assume that the top k clusters form the k facets of a user's need and use them to create more specific queries. These queries will then be used to automatically propose new sets of results in new facets. Finally, the iterative clustering process is used to find new facets and refine the queries and consequently the retrieved results.

As we have a small set of retrieved results, we choose to use agglomerative hierarchical clustering and the single link method [5]. Let C, D be two clusters, So_C, So_D the respective set of objects of clusters C and D, the single linkage equation between C and D is given by the following formulas:

– for visual features of images representing video shots we use:

$$D_{visual\ SL}(C, D) = \text{Min}\{d(i, j), \forall i \in So_C \text{ and } \forall j \in So_D\}$$

where $d(i, j)$ is the Euclidean distance;
– for text queries, we use:

$$D_{text\ SL}(C, D) = \text{Max}\{d(i, j), \forall i \in So_C \text{ and } \forall j \in So_D\}$$

where $d(i, j)$ is the number of common annotation keywords between two documents.

The output of a hierarchical clustering algorithm is a dendogram. The number of clusters wanted is a parameter of our algorithm, which is used to create the k clusters. We then create a new query for each cluster. For visual features, we choose the medoid of the cluster to create the new visual query. The new text query is based on the most common keywords annotating the cluster. A new search is launched to retrieve k new sets of results corresponding to the k new queries.

We apply clustering on the initial results of the query above. The resulting clusters are used for identifying new facets and subsequently new queries are generated, as explained above. The process is repeated iteratively to identify new facets and hence new queries as well. This iteration can be done in two ways. The first method is completely automatic: results from the first clustering call are directly clustered again to add more precision to the queries. This requires a *number of iterative calls* parameter, denoted N_{ic}. The number of facets N_f that are proposed to the user at the end of the iterative phase is equal to $N_f = k^{N_{ic}}$, so both parameters k and N_{ic} should be low. A "facet waiting queue" may be required if these parameters are too high. The second method requires interactions with the user. At the end of the first clustering phase, new results are displayed in the facet-based interface. Then, for each facet, we simulate the user's actions, e.g., he may choose to delete it, to keep it, or to launch a new clustering call. Such actions are simulated based on the number of relevant documents in each cluster. For example, clusters with more relevant documents are used as a facet. This "user-simulated interactive" method has some advantages: first it is better adapted to the free space of the interface as the user may delete non relevant facets before each new call; and finally, it does not require the N_{ic} parameter.

In the following sections, we present the experiment setup and our various experiments which lead to the main conclusion that faceted browsing can improve the effectiveness of the retrieval.

3.2   Experiment Setup

Our different experiments are based on the TRECVID 2006 dataset. Each of the 24 topics provided in the data collection contains a query of several keywords and a judgement list of 60 to 775 relevant documents. We compute iteratively the precision values of the clusters and automatically select the k best sets of results for the next iterative call. These are the sets of results that have the highest precision, as our goal is to simulate the actions of a user creating new facets. For our experiments, we set $k = 3$, because our list containing 100 results is too small to perform a clustering for higher k values.

3.3   Simulation with Single Features

In our experiments, we simulate users creating new facets in the faceted browser. A visual query is based on visual features of one or several images. For this set of experiments, we separately used five different low-level features: dominant colour, texture, colour layout, contour shape and edge histogram. For text features, we test two different methodology: (1) query expansion with one, two and three keywords and (2) new text query using two to five new keywords. We record the evolving precision values for various steps of our iterative clustering approach based on visual feature query only.

Table 1 presents the results of our iterative clustering algorithm. For each topic and each feature, we compare the precision of our results with respect to the initial text query, and split the topics in three different categories:

- the precision value of the best results decreases more than 2%, denoted "−";
- the precision value of the best results is almost stable, denoted "=";
- the precision value of the best results increases more than 2%, denoted "+";

Table 2 presents the results for our text experiments. A "positive" effect means that our iterative clustering methodolgy within three facets improve the overall precision of the retrieved results after the initial text query.

As an example, the iterative clustering results based on the texture features increase the precision of results for six topics (out of 24). However, for half of the topics the precision decreases. The conclusion we can draw from both tables is that visual and text features are not reliable for every query. However, for some of the topics, they are useful and improve the precision of the retrieved results. This corroborates with the findings presented at the TRECVID workshop [6].

Table 1. Results using only visual features queries compare to initial text query

Visual features	−	=	+
dominant colour	14	10	0
colour layout	14	6	4
texture	12	6	6
edge histogram	11	5	8
contour shape	17	3	4
Average	13.6	6	4.4

Table 2. Results using text query expansion and k new keywords as text queries

Text queries	no effect	positive effect	number of new relevant documents
add 1	17	7	40
add 2	15	9	63
add 3	16	8	51
new 2	14	10	40
new 3	14	10	51
new 4	13	11	57
new 5	15	9	49
new 6	14	10	45

3.4 Combined Simulation with All Features

In this section, we consider the best facets obtained by individual features. The idea here is not to combine all features in one query but to present every feature in different facets, so the user can choose the relevant features and have a faceted browser showing a lot more relevant documents than the initial retrieved results.

Figure 2 shows the evolution of the number of relevant documents displayed in the faceted browser with respect to the number of facets/features used. We observe that the more facets/features we combine, the more relevant documents are retrieved. So combining facets improves the recall value of relevant results but decreases the precision. A higher recall will help the user to select the relevant

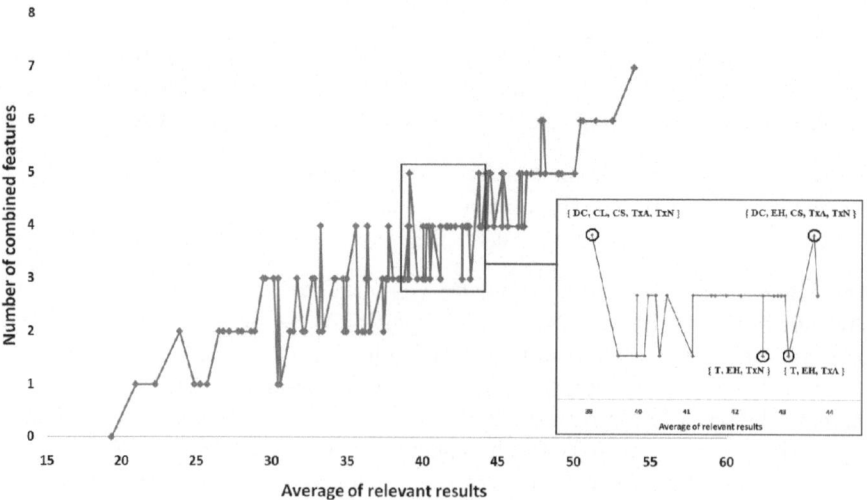

Fig. 2. Average number of relevant documents displayed in the interface with respect to the number of combined features used

Table 3. Best combinations of features

DC	×	×	-	-	×	×	-	-	-	×	-	-	-	×	-	-
CL	×	-	×	-	-	-	-	-	-	-	-	-	-	-	-	-
T	×	×	-	-	-	×	-	×	-	-	-	-	×	-	-	-
EH	×	-	-	×	-	-	-	-	-	-	-	-	-	-	-	-
CS	×	×	-	-	-	-	×	×	×	×	-	-	-	-	×	-
TxA	×	-	-	-	-	-	×	-	-	-	×	-	-	-	-	-
TxN	×	×	-	-	×	-	-	-	×	-	-	×	-	-	-	-
ARD	19.3	43.1	47.8	47.9	48.1	48.1	48.9	49.0	49.1	50.0	50.4	50.5	50.5	51.4	52.5	53.8

results for next query faster. The right part of the figure focuses on the most relevant combinations of three facets which are texture, edge histogram and one of the text feature, query expansion or new 4 keywords, and the less relevant combinations of five facets which contains both dominant colour, contour shape and both text features. These results show that the texture and edge histogram seems to be the best visual features to combine and also that using only one of the two text query models is enough.

Finally, we present in Table 3 the best combination of features to obtain the best relevance for the faceted browser. A "×" means that we do not use the feature in the combination and a "-" means that the feature is part of the combination. Each column represents a feature. We denote "DC", "CL", "T", "EH", "CS", "TxA" and "TxN" for dominant colour, colour layout, texture, edge histogram, contour shape, text query expansion adding 2 keywords and text query with 4 new keywords, respectively. The last column shows the average number of relevant documents per topic denoted "ARD". The first row shows the baseline run with no combination of facets, the second row presents the best combination of three feature, the next rows show the top combination of features. Thus, the last row shows the results of all features combination.

Observing these results, we conclude that colour layout and texture are the best visual features as they are almost always used in the top combination of features. It can also be observed that the feature contour shape is almost useless as we improve the average number of new relevant documents per topic by only one in the combination (see the difference between the two last rows of the table). Another interesting conclusion can be drawn when comparing the initial text query that has only an average of 19.3 relevant documents per topic with the best three combination of features ($ARD = 43.1$) or with all combined features ($ARD = 53.8$). We can double the effectiveness of the faceted browser using one of the best combination of up to three facets/features and almost triple its effectiveness with a combination of all features.

3.5   Discussion

In this section, we have presented various experiments which aim at showing the potential benefits of the faceted browser. Our results highlight the fact that new facets provided by iterative calls of the clustering algorithm might increase the precision of the retrieved results and have a higher probability of displaying new relevant documents in new facets of the interface.

We have evaluated all possible combinations of the best simulated facets representing one feature each which shows the real potential of the faceted browser. The number of relevant documents displayed doubles for a combination of three facets and almost triples with all facets.

Our fundamental premise in our simulated study is that users do actions that maximise the retrieval of relevant documents. For example, in a interactive user scenario, we assume that the users choose better relevant clusters or keywords to add to a new facet. He or she may also easily delete a facet that does not correspond to their search task, which we presume will result in much better results with real user interactions than with our simulated clustering methodology.

4   Exploiting User Experiments

In order to verify the above results, we conducted another set of simulated experiments based on logged data of a user experiment on the system described in Section 2.2. The user study was aimed at sudying the user perception, satisfaction and performance using the faceted browser. A brief overview is provided in Section 4.1. Exploiting the logfiles of this user study, we introduce and evaluate a new retrieval model which updates search queries by incorporating the content of other facets. The approach will be introduced in Section 4.2.

4.1   User Experiment

In the user experiment [7], two tasks were defined, aiming to reflect two separate broad user needs. Task A is the more open of the two tasks, and asks the user to discover material reflecting international politics at the end of 2005 (the period of time covered by the TRECVID 2006 data). Task B asked for a summary of the trial of Saddam Hussein to be constructed, including the different events which took place and the different people involved (such as the judge). This later task, which is still multi-faceted, was less open ended than the former task. Fifteen subjects took part in the study. Six users performed search Task A and nine participants performed search Task B for 30 minutes and filled in a questionnaire.

4.2   Methodology

Identifying Usage Patterns. After performing the initial user study, we analysed the resulting logfiles and extracted user behaviour information. The following data was captured in the logs: *Creating* and *Deleting* a new facet, triggering a new *Search* in a facet, *Moving from facet* a shot from the relevance list of facet F_1 to a different facet F_2, *Dragging from player* a shot directly onto a relevant results list of a facet, and finally, *Dragging from results* a shot onto a relevance list.

The log entries provide us with information about the users' interaction behaviour such as: when a user created a new facet, which search query he/she triggered or which results he/she judged to be relevant for this particular facet. We exploited these information in our simulation process. In the following section, we use these patterns to study how facet based browsing can influence the retrieval performance in repeating users' interaction steps and updating the retrieval results.

Relevance Judgements. Since Tasks A and B are not from TRECVID, ground truth data for our simulation was based on pooling all sets R_i of shots d moved to the relevance list by user i. Let d_K = be a vector representing shot K, defined as

$$d_K = \{d_{K1}...d_{KN}\}, \text{where } N \text{ is the number of users } and \ d_{Ki} = \begin{cases} 1, & d_K \in R_i \\ 0, & \text{otherwise} \end{cases}$$

Using:

$$F_1(d_K) = \begin{cases} 1, & (\sum_{i=1}^{N} d_{Ki}) = 1 \\ 0, & \text{otherwise} \end{cases} \quad F_2(d_K) = \begin{cases} 1, & (\sum_{i=1}^{N} d_{Ki}) \geq 2 \\ 0, & \text{otherwise} \end{cases}$$

we created two relevance judgement lists:

$$L_1 = \{d_K : F_1(d_K) = 1\} \ and \ L_2 = \{d_K : F_2(d_K) = 1\} \tag{1}$$

(Assuming that a keyframe is relevant within the given topic when is was selected by any user for L_1 and by at least two users for L_2.)

Simulation Strategies. The retrieval model of our user study was simple: the users enter textual search queries in each facet and the backend system returns a list of shots which are represented by a keyframe in the result list of the facet. Users interacted with the result list by selecting relevant shots, playing a shot, creating facets, etc. However, user feedback such as selecting a shot as relevant for this facet or the content and status of other facets are not used in retrieving or suggesting new facets. Hence, we use the user study as a baseline run B and try to improve its retrieval performance by introducing a new retrieval model which incorporates the content of other facets.

Our simulation procedure uses the following steps. First of all, we analysed the user queries in the log files and confirmed that users took advantage of the facets and used them to search for variations of the same concept. For instance in Task A (international politics), participants used the facets to search for different politicians, i.e. "George Bush" in facet F_1 and "Tony Blair" in facet F_2. We concluded that facets were used to focus more on specific sub concepts of each topic. Following the identified pattern, we performed a simulation run S.

In this run, we took advantage of the explicit relevance feedback given by each user in marking shots as relevant for a facet. We used these shots as a query expansion source and determined query candidate terms for each iteration in each facet by expanding queries from the relevant rated keyframes at step x. If

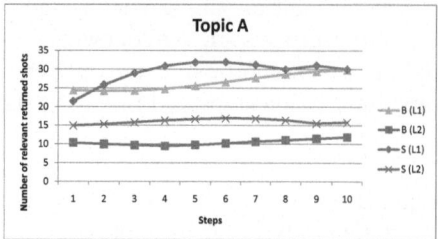
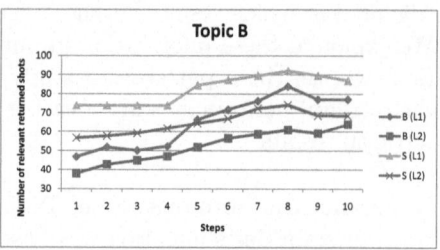

Fig. 3. Number of relevant returned results over all steps in Topic A

Fig. 4. Number of relevant returned results over all steps in Topic B

a term appears in more than one facet within this step x, we removed it from the facet which contained more candidate terms and used these candidate terms as a new search query. In other words, we reduce the number of query terms in a facet, when the query term is used in another facet with less query terms at the same time. This results in a more focused retrieval for the facets, as double entries will be avoided.

4.3 Results

For evaluating the performance of our baseline system and the simulation runs, we firstly divided the users's search sessions into separate steps, being the beginning of a new iteration in any facet. For each step, we then combined the result lists of each facet in its current iteration.

In a next step, we evaluated our runs using the two created relevance judgement lists L_1 and L_2 as introduced in Section 4.2. Figures 3 and 4 show the mean number of relevant retrieved results over all steps in Topic A and B, respectively. As expected, using the relevance judgements list L_1 returns a higher retrieval performance in all cases than using L_2. This matches with common sense, a larger list of relevant documents used for evaluation results in a higher number of relevant retrieved documents. The decreasing number of retrieved shots in some cases is the direct consequence of users closing facets in later steps of their retrieval session. The results within these facets hence get lost, resulting in a decrease of retrieved results.

It can be seen for both search tasks, that the simulation run S outperformed the baseline run B, which indicates that considering the content of other facets to re-define a user's search query can improve the retrieval performance. Hence, a retrieval model which takes the content of other facets into account can outpferm a classical "one-resultlist only" model.

5   Conclusion

In this paper, we have introduced a facet-based approach to interactive video retrieval. We employed clustering techniques to identify potential facets and used in our simulation. The results of our study demonstrate the potential benefits of a faceted search and browsing system. In addition to the results of our simulated evaluation on the TRECVID collection, we have explored the logs of a real user-centred evaluation and the results corroborate that of the simulation methodology.

The experiments were conducted on a large data set given by the TRECVID and hence support the validity of our experiments. However, it is well known that the TRECVID search topics are so diverse and the issue of performance variation from topic to topic. This explains some of the performance problems we encountered in some of the topics. In addition to this, simulated methodologies are one end of spectrum of a series of evaluations needed before multimedia systems are deployed. It allows us to benchmark various retrieval approaches and also search strategies like the faceted browsing. This results need to be verified by the use of a real user-centred evaluation which we are exploring now.

Acknowledgments

This research was supported by the European Commission under the contracts FP6-027026-K-SPACE and FP6-027122-SALERO.

References

1. Christel, M., Concescu, R.: Addressing the challenge of visual information access from digital image and video libraries. In: JCDL (Denver, CO), pp. 69–78 (2005)
2. Finin, T.W.: GUMS: A General User Modeling Shell. In: User Models in Dialog Systems, pp. 411–430 (1989)
3. Heesch, D., Howarth, P., Magalhães, J., May, A., Pickering, M., Yavlinski, A., Rüger, S.: Video retrieval using search and browsing. In: TREC 2004 (2004)
4. Hopfgartner, F., Jose, J.: Evaluating the Implicit Feedback Models for Adaptive Video Retrieval. In: ACM MIR 2007, vol. 09, pp. 323–332 (2007)
5. Jain, A.K., Dubes, R.C.: Algorithms for Clustering Data. Prentice-Hall, Englewood Cliffs (1988)
6. Smeaton, A.F., Over, P., Kraaij, W.: Evaluation campaigns and trecvid. In: MIR 2006, pp. 321–330. ACM Press, New York (2006)
7. Villa, R., Gildea, N., Jose, J.M.: A Faceted Search Interface for Multimedia Retrieval. In: SIGIR 2008, pp. 775–776. ACM Press, New York (2008)

A User Experience Model for
Home Video Summarization

Wei-Ting Peng[1], Wei-Jia Huang[2], Wei-Ta Chu[3],
Chien-Nan Chou[2], Wen-Yan Chang[2], Chia-Han Chang[2], and Yi-Ping Hung[1,2]

[1] Graduate Institute of Networking and Multimedia,
National Taiwan University, Taipei, Taiwan
[2] Department of Computer Science & Information Engineering,
National Taiwan University, Taipei, Taiwan
[3] Department of Computer Science & Information Engineering,
National Chung Cheng University, Chiayi, Taiwan

Abstract. In this paper, we propose a novel system for automatically summarizing home videos based on a user experience model. The user experience model takes account of user's spontaneous behaviors when viewing videos. Based on users' reaction when viewing videos, we can construct a systematic framework to automate video summarization. In this work, we analyze the variations of viewer's eye movement and facial expression when he or she watching the raw home video. We transform these behaviors into the clues of determining the important part of each video shot. With the aids of music analysis, the developed system automatically generates a music video (MV) style summarized home videos. Experiments show that this new type of editing mechanism can effectively generate home video summaries and can largely reduce the efforts of manual summarization.

Keywords: User experience model, video summarization, facial expression, eye movement.

1 Introduction

With the growing availability and portability of digital video cameras, making home videos has become much more popular. Although there is a number of commercial editing software that helps users to edit videos, not all of them can process a lengthy video easily; even friendly graphical interface and powerful editing functions are provided. Moreover, users need to have much domain knowledge of video editing and should be skilled in using the complicated tools.

Shooting video is fun but editing is proven frustrating. Hence, users incline to put the video footage on the shelf without further intention to elaborately editing. To ease video editing, video summarization has been studied for years. Ma et al. [2] proposed a framework of user attention models to extract essential video content automatically. Hanjalic [3] modeled the influence of three low-level features based on user excitement. Kleban et al. [4] describes contributions in the high level feature and search tasks. Mei et al. [5] further integrated the knowledge of psychology to classify the capture-intents into seven categories.

B. Huet et al. (Eds.): MMM 2009, LNCS 5371, pp. 484–495, 2009.

We also proposed an automatic home video skimming system [1]. In this work, a system was developed to automatically analyze video and a user-selected music clip. For video shots, the system eliminates shots with blurred content or drastic motion. For music, the system detects onset information and estimates tempo of the entire melody. With the aids of the editing theory[6][7] and the concepts of media aesthetics[8][9][10], the system matches selected video shots with music tempo, and therefore facilitates users to make an MV-style video summary that conforms to editing aesthetics without difficulties.

Although the systems described above can achieve satisfactory performance, we found that most of them are based on content-based audiovisual features. Video clips are often unreasonably selected because there is high motion or high color/intensity contrast in them. What human want to see or like to see is not properly considered. To this end, we propose a new approach to conduct video editing in this paper. A novel system based on the human viewing behaviors is developed to generate a home video summary. To our knowledge, the proposed approach is one of the first works to exploit human behavior and analyze users' intention for video editing.

Some studies [11][12]indicate that most people look at the same place all the time while watching movies, because movies consist of a series of shots and are well organized by editors to make a coherent story. Robert et al. [13] recorded the eye movements of twenty normally-sighted subjects as each watched six movie clips. More than half of the time the distribution of subjects' gaze fell within a region which area is less than 12% of the movie scene.

In our case, raw home videos are often not well organized or have clear targets. Therefore, in viewing a home video, humans are forced to move their eyes to search for targets of interest. On the contrary, if humans concentrate their gaze to a fixed region, it indicates that the corresponding video clips have clear targets/topics or have nice shooting conditions. This idea drives us to exploit the behaviors of eye movement in video editing.

In addition to eye movement, we also have to consider user's preference in selecting video clips of interest. Emotion analysis is a practical research issue in many fields. Much attention has been drawn to this topic in computer vision applications such as human-computer interaction, robot cognition, and behavior analysis. In this work, we perform facial expression analysis [14][15][16] to detect where the viewer likes or dislikes the displaying video clip, and use it as the foundation of video summarization.

By integrating eye movement and facial expression analysis, we introduce a user experience model and index the important part of each shot in raw home video automatically. Based on our approach, users can conduct video editing by "viewing videos". This approach makes home video editing more humanistic.

The remainder of this paper is organized as follows. The complete system framework is described in Section 2. Section 3 shows eye movement detection processes, and Section 4 describes the method of facial expression recognition. The development of the user experience model is presented Section 5. Experimental results are reported in Section 6, and conclusions are given in Section 7.

2   System Framework

In our previous work [1], to elaborately incorporate video clips with music, we respectively perform analysis from video and music perspectives. In video analysis, we first drop bad video frames that are ill-lit or blurred, then we segment the video into shots. For background music, we estimate the tempo information based on the occurrence frequency of onsets. We integrated them on the basis of the guidelines of media aesthetics.

In this work, we further integrate the content-based approach with the proposed user experience model. Figure 1 demonstrates the system framework. In addition to content-based importance measure, how humans behave in viewing the raw videos provides the clues about whether the user likes or dislikes the corresponding video clips. From the perspective of video editing, whether users like the video clips indicates the corresponding importance to form the video summary. Therefore, Figure 1 shows that the left part captures humans' behaviors and transforms them into importance measures to facilitate automatic video editing.

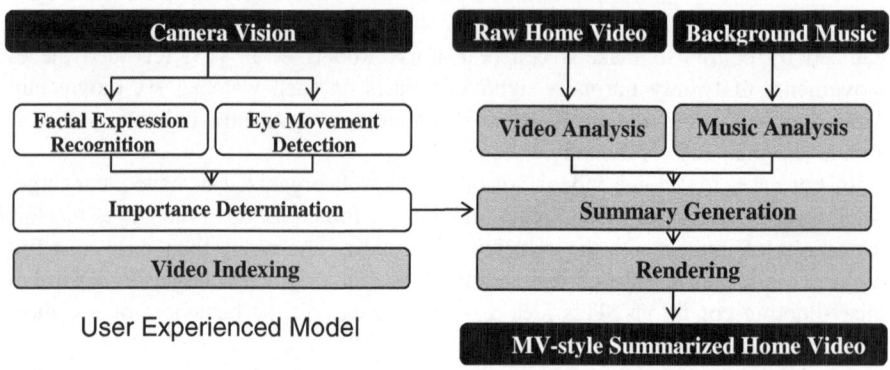

Fig. 1. Structure of the proposed system

Note that the major difference between this work and conventional ones is that we incorporate psychometric model into video summarization, which was not well acquainted by computer science researchers before.

3   Eye Movement Detection

In eye movement detection, we adopt two visual features: the centers of the eyeballs and the corners of the eyes. To extract these features, face recognition is detected in advance and the position of eyes are then located based on the face region.

● **Face detection:** To extract eye movement features, we need to identify where the eyes are. Although we can directly apply an eye detection process to video frames, the search region is too large. Therefore, we perform face detection first to locate the position of the face, and then we can detect eyes more efficiently. In this system, we exploit the Viola-Jones face detection algorithm [17].

- **Eye detection:** Based on the facial geometry [18], we simplify the procedure of eye detection only on the possible regions. As the face detection, the cascaded Adaboost is also used for eye detection.
- **Feature extraction:** Once the locations of eyes are obtained, we can extract the centers and corners of eyes. For finding the centers of the eyeballs, we apply the Gaussian filter to the image to detect the dark circles of the iris. The center of an eyeball is detected from the location with the minimum value. To detect the corners of the eyes, we use the method proposed in [19], which utilizes Gabor wavelets to localize possible corners. The positions of centers of eyeballs and corners of a video frame represent the characteristics of eyes. The variation of this characteristic along time is the eye movement information. Figure 2 shows the results of eye movement detection in a frame.

Fig. 2. Results of eye movement detection. The red rectangle represents the location of face. The center of an eyeball and the corners of an eye are presented inside the green rectangle.

4   Facial Expression Recognition

In addition to detecting eye movement, we also incorporate facial expression recognition in our system. Instead of analyzing the six-class expression [20], we only consider two types of emotion, positive and negative, in our work. By recognizing the positive and negative emotions, our system can understand users' intention and recognize video frames that users are interested in.

Recent advances in facial expression recognition have shown that a satisfied performance can be achieved by using hybrid representation [16][21] . Based on these studies, both local facial components and global face are adopted in our work. Besides the components of eyes, nose, and mouth, we also use the areas of middle of eyebrows and cheek to address the wrinkle variations. As the method in [16], we adopt manifold learning and fusion classifier to integrate the multi-component information for facial expression recognition.

Given a face image I , a mapping $M : R^d \times c \to R^t$ is constructed by

$$M(I) = [m_1(I_1), m_2(I_2), \ldots, m_c(I_c)], \tag{1}$$

where c is the number of components, $m_i(\cdot)$ is an embedding function learned from the manifold of component i, and I_i is a d-dimensional sub-image of the i-th component. Then, the multi-component information is encoded to a t-dimensional feature vector $M(I)$, where $t \geq c$. To characterize the significance of components from the embedded features, a fusion classifier $F : R^t \rightarrow \{Positive, Negative\}$ is used based on a binary classifier SVM. By applying this method, users' emotion can be recognized in our system. Figure 3 depicts the results of facial expression recognition.

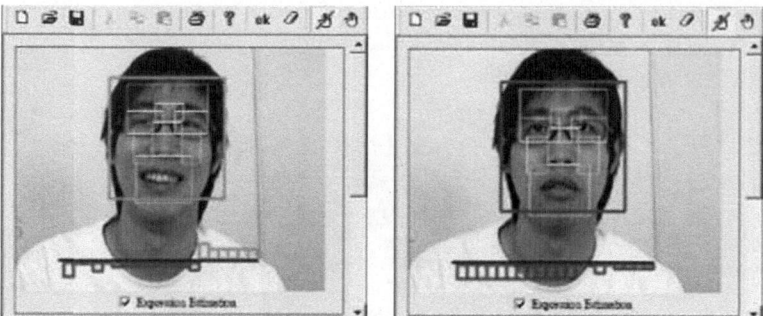

Fig. 3. Results of facial expression recognition. Left: positive expression. Right: Negative expression.

5   User Experience Model

After analyzing facial expression and eye movement, we can define a user experience model to determine important frames of each shot. The details are described in the following sections.

5.1   Importance Determination by Eye Movement

Goldstein et al. [22] classified eye movement into three categories, fixations, smooth pursuits or saccades. They reported that if the moving velocity is larger than 200 degree/second, this period of eye movement is viewed as a saccade. In this work, we take saccades into account because they indicate attention shifting by the viewers. The more saccades occur in a shot, the lower interesting in this shot for the viewer. According to psychology researches [23][24][25], we can define the importance measure of each shot as follows.

Let $\delta(i)$ represents whether a saccade occurs at the ith video frame.

$$\delta(i) = \begin{cases} 1 & \text{if } v_e(i) > \epsilon, \\ 0 & \text{otherwise,} \end{cases} \tag{2}$$

where $v_e(i)$ is the estimated eye moving velocity, and ϵ is the threshold for saccade detection. Note that due to the limitation of the accuracy in eye tracking and the variant sampling rate of cameras, the threshold ϵ can be adjusted in different situations.

The moving velocity is estimated by the difference between two neighboring detected eyeball locations divided by the time duration.

To measure the importance value of each frame, we apply a sliding window W with size $(2w + 1)$ to the results of eye tracking. The importance value of the ith frame is

$$I_e(i) = (2w + 1) - \sum_{k=i-\frac{w}{2}}^{i+\frac{w}{2}} \delta(k). \tag{3}$$

According to this measurement, the importance of the ith frame is reduced if more adjacent frames are detected with saccades. In other words, in video summarization, we prefer to skip video frames that the viewer doesn't fix his gaze.

5.2 Importance Determination by Facial Expression

As described in Section 4, we defined the results of facial expression as two types of emotion, positive or negative. Let $\phi(i)$ represent the recognition result of facial expression at the ith video frame. We set $\phi(i)$ is 1 if the result is positive. Otherwise, $\phi(i)$ is set to zero.

Because human facial expression doesn't change drastically in a short duration, we apply a sliding window with size $(2w + 1)$ to the results of facial expression analysis. By using this strategy, we are able to filter out some noises caused by loss of face tracking and obtain more reasonable results.

The importance value of the ith frame is then calculated by

$$I_a(i) = \sum_{k=i-\frac{w}{2}}^{i+\frac{w}{2}} \phi(k). \tag{4}$$

By using this formulation, the frames that the viewer has high positive expression in viewing them will be selected in the video summary.

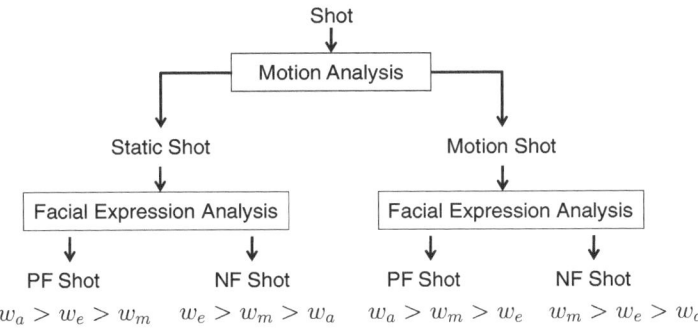

PF : Positive Facial Expression
NF: Negative Facial Expression

Fig. 4. Illustration of weighting coefficients conditions

5.3 Importance Fusion

In the above, we have defined the importance for each frame based on human viewing behaviors. Then, we further integrate a content-based feature that substantially describes the importance of frames.

In our previous work [1], we consider camera motion as an important factor. If motion acceleration varies frequently and significantly, the video segment is usually annoying and is less likely to be selected in the video summary. Because the variation of viewer's eye movement and facial expression hardly represent this characteristic, we also take camera motion into account in this work.

Let f_{ij} denote the jth frame of the ith shot. We estimate the frame's importance values by combining the motion-based importance $I_m(f_{ij})$, the eye-based importance $I_e(f_{ij})$, and the expression-based importance $I_a(f_{ij})$:

$$I(f_{ij}) = w_m \times I_m(f_{ij}) + w_a \times I_a(f_{ij}) + w_e \times I_e(f_{ij}) \qquad (5)$$

where w_m, w_a and w_e are weighting coefficients controlling the relative importance of camera motion, facial expression and eye movement. According to our studies, these weighting coefficients can be varied in different situations. For examples, after motion analysis we can label each shot as static or motion (including pan, tilt, and zoom). In motion shots, w_m can be larger than w_e, because eye movement research [12] states that eyes tend to concentrate on the center of screen when humans see videos with rapid moving content. In this situation, w_e doesn't provide useful information. In static shots, w_e can be larger than w_m conversely. Viewers try to search important objects in static shots. If the viewer can't find any attractive targets, then his eyes will move back and forth and produce events of saccades.

Furthermore, we can emphasize w_a when the corresponding shot is detected with positive facial expression. This indicates there is something important in that shot. The priority of these weighting coefficients can be illustrated in Fig. 4.

5.4 Summary Generation

We define the weighting coefficients and calculate the importance values of the frames in each shot after the processes described above. In this section, we will briefly describe the method of summarization generation. Basically, this method is similar to our previous work except we propose a new way to consider human's behaviors in video editing. Details of the summarization method please refer to [1].

According to the tempo of the user-selected music [1], the length of the targeted summarized shot has been determined. Assume that there would be N targeted shots in the summary videos, on the basis of music tempo information. In addition, we perform shot change detection for the raw home videos and accordingly obtain M video shots, $N < M$, which are called raw shots in the following. Now the problem is to select parts of these M raw shots to construct N target shots. Before the selection process, the shots with blur or over-exposure/under-exposure are first eliminated. Thus there would be fewer than M raw shots to be examined in the selection process.

For each raw shot, we define a sliding window which length is the same as the corresponding targeted shot. Based on this sliding window, the importance value $I(f_{ij})$ is calculated accordingly, and the optimal subshot with the maximum importance value is selected to be the representative part of this raw shot. The process is illustrated in Fig. 5.

Through the processes described above, the selected subshots are concatenated as the final video summary. In this work, human's behaviors play the role of determining

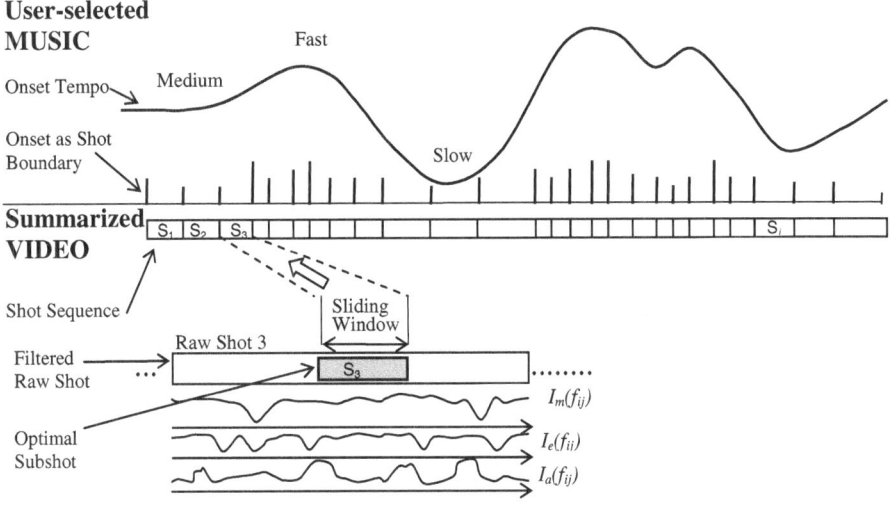

Fig. 5. Illustration of subshot selection

the importance of each shot (or each frame further). Using human's behavior as the clues for selection rather than content-based characteristic is the most important contribution of this work.

6 Experimental Results

We describe the implementation framework and experiment settings as follows.

● Implementation Framework
In order to speed up the processes of facial expression analysis and eye tracking, we separate these tasks and respectively handle each of them on one computer. All these computers are connected with Network Time Protocol (NTP) to ensure synchronization. The signal captured from the user's face is forwarded to two computers, as shown in Figure 6.

Test clips were shown on a monitor with a screen that is 40-cm wide. Participants were seated at a distance of about 40-cm from the screen, and the viewing angle subtended by the screen is approximately 52 degrees.

● Participants
We invited 10 subjects (7 males and 3 females) who are students majoring in computer science and volunteered to be in the experiment. Participants are from 20 to 35-year old. All participants were unaware of and were uninformed about the specific purpose of the experiment.

● Evaluation Data
We evaluate the proposed method based on two video sequences, each with the length of about 5 minutes. These two sequences were captured by amateurs and are typical home videos that have worse video quality. The content in the first video is about traveling, and all subjects are not familiar with the people who appear in the video.

On the contrary, all subjects are familiar with the people who appear in the second video. The specification of the test videos is listed in Table 1.

Table 1. Evaluation data

Title	Category	Shot	Time
Video1	Travel	26	5min 41sec
Video2	Mountain Climbing	11	5min 39sec

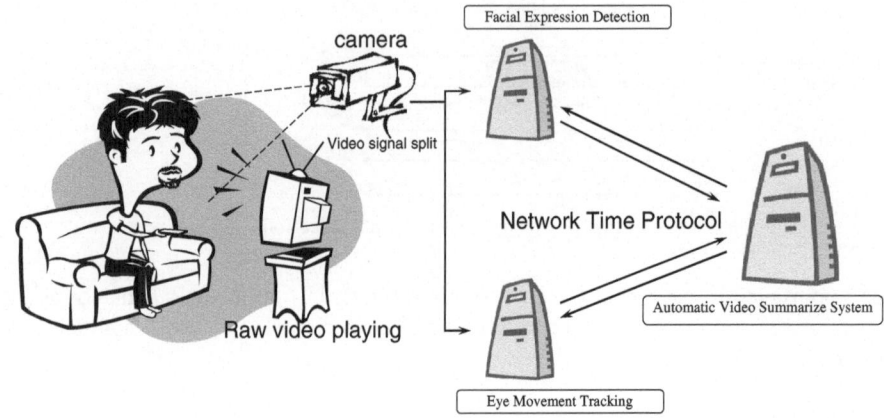

Fig. 6. The distributed scenario in the real-time implementation

● Evaluation Method

All subjects viewed the videos twice. At the first time, the developed system records their eye movement and facial expression data. At the second time, subjects are requested to manually tag the important part of each shot that would be the ground truth and can be used to judge the goodness of the automatic summary.

In order to understand the influence of eye movement and facial expression, we use three different kinds of summarization methods. The first one is using only the data of eye movement; the second one is using only the data of facial expression; and the last one exploits both eye movement and facial expression. The experiment last about an hour for one subject.

● Results and discussion

Since subjects had manually tagged the important parts of each shot, we can compare these clips with the generated summaries. Unlike other works that evaluate summary system by subjective scoring, we use a quantitative measurement called *"match rate"* to evaluate our system. Assume that the set of user-selected clips (ground truth) is G, and the set of automatically-selected clips is A, the match rate is defined as:

$$Match\ rate = \frac{|A \cap G|}{S}, \tag{6}$$

where the $|G|$ denotes the time duration (in seconds) of the set of ground truth and the length of summary time is S.

We set the length of summary as 20% of the original videos. Table 2 shows the mean performance of summarization judged by ten subjects, in terms of match rate. We can see that both using eye movement and facial expression are feasible methods to summarize videos. Fusing both factors according to the guidelines describe in Sec. 5.3 would introduce better performance.

To further demonstrate that a user experience model is practicable, we manually label the results of facial expression and combine them to produce summaries. It's not un-expectable that the match rates of the summaries based on true facial expression results are increasing. Although facial expression recognition is still a hard topic, we can see that the performances between UEM and FE in Table 2 are reasonably close. These results lead to the conclusion that the user experience model is quite useful in video summarization.

We also study the usability of video summaries in terms of match rate. According to our study, when match rate of the summarized videos is higher than 50%, the subjects usually feel that it's a good summary. Therefore, we can see that results in Table 2 are not far from appreciation.

Table 2. Experimental results

Title	Type	Eye Match (%)	Face Match (%)	Eye & Face Match (%)
Video1	UEM	33.7	29	34.3
	FE Ground Truth	---	29.9	40.8
Video2	UEM	39.2	44.4	49.9
	FE Ground Truth	---	47.2	61.8

UEM: User experience model. FE: Facial expression

7 Conclusions

A novel system based on a user experience model is proposed in this paper for automatic home video summarization. In this work, we address the variations of viewer's eye movement and facial expression when he or she watches the raw home videos. By analyzing user's intention, our system can automatically select the important parts of video shots that they are interested. In our experiments, it shows that this new type of editing method can effectively generate home video summaries. A satisfied match rate of viewer's preference in shots also can be obtained. Currently, this work can be treated as the foundation of video summarization based on physiological studies. In the future, we will pay attention to this topic by incorporating other human perceptions.

Acknowledgments

This work was supported in part by the National Science Council, Taiwan, under grant NSC 95-2221-E-002-209-MY3, and by the Excellent Research Projects of National Taiwan University, under grant 95R0062-AE00-02.

References

[1] Peng, W.T., Chiang, Y.H., Chu, W.T., Huang, W.J., Chang, W.L., Huang, P.C., Hung, Y.P.: Aesthetics-based Automatic Home Video Skimming System. In: Satoh, S., Nack, F., Etoh, M. (eds.) MMM 2008. LNCS, vol. 4903, pp. 186–197. Springer, Heidelberg (2008)

[2] Ma, Y.F., Hua, X.S., Lu, L., Zhang, H.J.: A generic framework of user attention model and its application in video summarization. IEEE Trans. on Multimedia 7(5), 907–919 (2005)

[3] Hanjalic, A.: Multimodal approach to measuring excitement in video. In: Proceedings of IEEE International Conference Multimedia and Expo. (2003)

[4] Kleban, J., Sarkar, A., Moxley, E., Mangiat, S., Joshi, S., Kuo, T., Manjunath, B.S.: Feature fusion and redundancy pruning for rush video summarization. In: Proceedings of the international workshop on TRECVID video summarization (2007)

[5] Mei, T., Hua, X.S., Zhou, H.Q., Li, S.: Modeling and mining of users' capture intention for home videos. IEEE TMM 9(1), 66–77 (2007)

[6] Goodman, R.M., McGrath, P.: Editing Digital Video: The Complete Creative and Technical Guide. McGraw-Hill/TAB Electronics (2002)

[7] Chandler, G.: CUT BY CUT: Editing Your Film or Video, Michael Wiese (2006)

[8] Zettl, H.: Sight, sound, motion: Applied media aesthetics, Wadsworth (1998)

[9] Dorai, C., Venkatesh, S.: Computational media aesthetics: Finding meaning beautiful. IEEE Multimedia 8, 10–12 (2001)

[10] Mulhem, P., Kankanhalli, M.S., Hassan, H., Yi, J.: Pivot vector space approach for audio-video mixing. IEEE Multimedia IO(2), 28–40 (2003)

[11] Stelmach, L., Tam, W.J.: Processing image sequences based on eye movements. In: Proceedings of SPIE Human Vision, Visual Processing and Digital Display V, vol. 2179 (1994)

[12] Tosi, V., Mecacci, L., Pasquali, E.: Scanning eye movements made when viewing film: preliminary observations. International Journal Neuroscience (1997)

[13] Goldstein, R.B., Woods, R.L., Peli, E.: Where people look when watching movies: Do all viewers look at the same place? Computers in Biology and Medicine (2006)

[14] Essa, I.A., Pentland, A.P.: Coding, Analysis, Interpretation, and Recognition of Facial Expressions. IEEE Trans. on PAMI 19(7), 757–763 (1997)

[15] Bartlett, M.S., Littlewort, G., Frank, M., Lainscsek, C.: Recognizing Facial Expression: Machine Learning and Application to Spontaneous Behavior. In: Proceedings of IEEE Conference on Computer Vision and Pattern Recognition, vol. 2, pp. 568–573 (2005)

[16] Chang, W.Y., Chen, C.S., Hung, Y.P.: Analyzing Facial Expression by Fusing Manifolds. In: Proceedings of Asian Conference on Computer Vision Conference (2007)

[17] Viola, P., Jones, M.J.: Robust real-time face detection. International Journal of Computer Vision 57(2), 137–154 (2004)

[18] Al-Oayedi, A., Clark, A.F.: An algorithm for face and facial-feature location based on gray-scale information and facial geometry. In: Proceedings of International Conference on Image Processing and Its Applications, vol. 2, pp. 625–629 (1999)

[19] Sirohey, S., Rosenfeld, A.: Eye detection in a face image using linear and nonlinear filters. Pattern Recognition 34, 1367–1391 (2001)

[20] Ekman, P., Friesen, W.V.: Unmasking the face. Prentice-Hall, Englewood Cliffs (1975)

[21] Schwaninger, A., Wallraven, C., Cunningham, D.W., Chiller-Glaus, S.D.: Processing of identity and emotion in faces: a psychophysical, physiological and computational perspective. Progress in Brain Research 156, 321–343 (2006)

[22] Goldstein, R.B., Peli, E., Lerner, S., Luo, G.: Eye Movements While Watching a Video: Comparisons Across Viewer Groups. Vision Science Society (2004)

[23] Klein, R.M., Pontefract, A.: Does oculomotor readiness mediate cognitive control of visual attention: Revisited! Attention and performance 15, 333–350 (1994)

[24] Germeys, F., d'Ydewalle, G.: The psychology of film: perceiving beyond the cut. Psychological Research 71, 458–466 (2007)

[25] Liversedge, S.P., Findlay, J.M.: Saccadic eye movements and cognition. Trends in Cognition Sciences 4, 6–14 (2000)

Author Index